Tim Conners

Duchesne East   RM 328

527-9168

William Mendenhall
University of Florida

James E. Reinmuth
University of Oregon

STATISTICS

for

Management and Economics

SECOND EDITION

Duxbury Press

North Scituate, Massachusetts

Duxbury Press
A DIVISION OF WADSWORTH PUBLISHING COMPANY, INC.

Statistics for Management and Economics, Second Edition, was edited and prepared for composition by Service to Publishers, Inc. Interior design was provided by Mr. David Earle and the cover was designed by Mr. Oliver Kline. The text was set by J. W. Arrowsmith Ltd.

L.C. Cat. Card No.: 73-89883
ISBN 0-87872-058-8

PRINTED IN THE UNITED STATES OF AMERICA

4 5 6 7 8 9 10—78 77 76

Contents

Preface   xi

ONE   What Is Statistics?   1

    1.1   Illustrative Statistical Problems   1
    1.2   The Population and the Sample   2
    1.3   The Role of Statistics in Research   3
    1.4   The Statistician and Business Decision Making   4
    1.5   Summary   5
    1.6   A Note to the Reader   6

TWO   Useful Mathematical Notation   9

    2.1   Introduction   9
    2.2   Functional Notation   9
    2.3   Numerical Sequences   13
    2.4   Summation Notation   15
    2.5   Useful Theorems Relating to Sums   18
    2.6   Summary   21

THREE   Describing Sets of Measurements   25

    3.1   Introduction   25
    3.2   Frequency Distributions   26
    3.3   Other Graphical Methods   31
    3.4   Numerical Descriptive Methods   35
    3.5   Measures of Central Tendency   36
    3.6   Measures of Variability   39
    3.7   On the Practical Significance of the Standard
          Deviation   46

3.8	A Short Method for Calculating the Variance	50
3.9	Estimating the Mean and Variance for Grouped Data	53
3.10	Linear Transformations of Data	56
3.11	Summary	58

FOUR Probability   65

4.1	Introduction	65
4.2	The Sample Space	66
4.3	Compound Events	72
4.4	Event Relations	75
4.5	Two Probability Laws and Their Use	80
4.6	Bayes' Law	83
4.7	Subjective Probability	85
4.8	Random Variables	86
4.9	Summary	87

FIVE Random Variables and Probability Distributions   93

5.1	Random Variables	93
5.2	A Classification of Random Variables	94
5.3	Probability Distributions for Discrete Random Variables	95
5.4	Continuous Random Variables and Their Probability Distributions	98
5.5	Mathematical Expectation	100
5.6	Summary	104

SIX The Binomial and Poisson Probability Distributions   109

6.1	Introduction	109
6.2	The Binomial Experiment	109
6.3	The Binomial Probability Distribution	111
6.4	The Mean and Variance for the Binomial Variable	115
6.5	Lot Acceptance Sampling	118
6.6	A Test of an Hypothesis	120
6.7	The Poisson Distribution	122
6.8	Summary	127

SEVEN The Normal Probability Distribution   135

7.1	Introduction	135
7.2	The Central Limit Theorem	136

7.3	Random Samples	142
7.4	Tabulated Areas of the Normal Probability Distribution	144
7.5	The Normal Approximation to the Binomial Distribution	147
7.6	Summary	157

EIGHT Statistical Inference   163

8.1	Introduction	163
8.2	Types of Estimators	165
8.3	Point Estimation of a Population Mean	172
8.4	Interval Estimation of a Population Mean	175
8.5	Estimation from Large Samples	180
8.6	Estimating the Difference Between Two Means	180
8.7	Estimating the Parameter of a Binomial Population	183
8.8	Estimating the Difference Between Two Binomial Parameters	185
8.9	Choosing the Sample Size	187
8.10	A Statistical Test of an Hypothesis	191
8.11	A Large-Sample Statistical Test	193
8.12	Some Comments on the Theory of Tests of Hypotheses	204
8.13	Summary	205

NINE Inference from Small Samples   213

9.1	Introduction	213
9.2	Student's t Distribution	213
9.3	Small-Sample Inferences Concerning a Population Mean	217
9.4	Small-Sample Inferences Concerning the Difference Between Two Means	220
9.5	A Paired-Difference Test	225
9.6	Inference Concerning a Population Variance	229
9.7	Comparing Two Population Variances	234
9.8	Summary	238

TEN Decision Making Under Uncertainty   247

10.1	Introduction	247
10.2	Certainty Versus Uncertainty	248
10.3	Analysis of the Decision Problem	250
10.4	Expected Monetary Value Decisions	256

10.5	Justification of Expected Monetary Value Decisions	259
10.6	The Economic Impact of Uncertainty	261
10.7	Decision Making That Involves Sample Information	263
10.8	Other Topics in Modern Decision Making	270
10.9	Summary	275

ELEVEN   Quality Control   285

11.1	Introduction	285
11.2	Control Charts	286
11.3	Control Charts for Variables	290
11.4	The Proportion Defective Chart for Attribute Data	298
11.5	The c Chart	302
11.6	Lot Acceptance Sampling for Defectives	305
11.7	Lot Acceptance Sampling for Continuous Random Variables	313
11.8	Other Quality-Control Techniques	315
11.9	Summary	317

TWELVE   Linear Regression and Correlation   323

12.1	Introduction	323
12.2	A Simple Linear Probabilistic Model	325
12.3	The Method of Least Squares	328
12.4	Calculating s^2, an Estimator of σ^2	331
12.5	Inferences Concerning the Slope of Line β_1	333
12.6	Estimating the Expected Value of y for a Given Value of x	336
12.7	Predicting a Particular Value of y for a Given Value of x	339
12.8	A Coefficient of Correlation	341
12.9	The Additivity of Sums of Squares	346
12.10	A Multivariate Prediction Model	348
12.11	Solving the Least-Squares Equations	350
12.12	Further Comments on Multiple Regression	358
12.13	Summary	360

THIRTEEN   The Analysis of Variance   369

13.1	Introduction	369
13.2	The Analysis of Variance	370
13.3	A Comparison of More Than Two Means	379

13.4	An Analysis of Variance Table for a Completely Randomized Design	**384**
13.5	Estimation for the Completely Randomized Design	**384**
13.6	A Randomized Block Design	**386**
13.7	The Analysis of Variance for a Randomized Block Design	**388**
13.8	Estimation for the Randomized Block Design	**393**
13.9	Summary	**394**

FOURTEEN Elements of Time Series Analysis **401**

14.1	Introduction	**401**
14.2	Components of Time Series	**403**
14.3	Smoothing Methods	**408**
14.4	Adjustment of Seasonal Data	**414**
14.5	Index Numbers	**417**
14.6	Summary	**424**

FIFTEEN Forecasting Models **431**

15.1	Introduction	**431**
15.2	Probabilistic Forecasting Models	**432**
15.3	A Least-Squares, Sinusoidal Model	**434**
15.4	The Autoregressive Forecasting Model	**438**
15.5	An Exponential Smoothing Forecasting Model	**445**
15.6	The Exponentially Weighted Moving Average Forecasting Model	**451**
15.7	A Growth Model	**458**
15.8	Summary	**462**

SIXTEEN Analysis of Enumerative Data **471**

16.1	A Description of the Experiment	**471**
16.2	The Chi-Square Test	**473**
16.3	A Test of an Hypothesis Concerning Specified Cell Probabilities	**474**
16.4	Contingency Tables	**476**
16.5	$r \times c$ Tables with Fixed Row or Column Totals	**481**
16.6	Other Applications	**483**
16.7	Summary	**484**

SEVENTEEN   Nonparametric Statistics   **491**

        17.1   Introduction   **491**
        17.2   A Comparison of Statistical Tests   **493**
        17.3   The Sign Test for Comparing Two Population
              Distributions   **494**
        17.4   The Mann–Whitney *U* Test for Comparing
              Two Population Distributions   **498**
        17.5   The Wilcoxon Rank-Sum Test for a Paired
              Experiment   **504**
        17.6   The Runs Test: A Test for Randomness   **507**
        17.7   Rank Correlation Coefficient   **511**
        17.8   Some General Comments on Nonparametric
              Statistical Tests   **514**

Appendix :   Tables   **523**

Glossary   **563**

Answers   **571**

Index   **593**

Preface

New facets of our technology—the impact of the computer in the analysis and sorting of data, the development of sophisticated production and econometric models, and the increased complexity of business decision making—demand that today's businessman understand at least the basic concepts of probability and statistics. The introductory statistics courses of past years, which simply explored methods of data collection, measurement, and description while minimizing the contributions of inferential analysis, no longer suffice. Business students need a clear understanding of the scientific method and the use of statistics in making inferences based on observed data.

We believe that it is important for the student to see inference as the objective of statistics and to understand why statistical inference-making procedures function better than those based on intuition. An awareness of the role probability plays in making inferences is essential. Consequently, we have welded the theories of probability and inference together throughout the book.

Although this text is designed to be used for a two-term introductory course in business statistics, the end of the ninth chapter would provide a logical breaking point for a one-term course. The first nine chapters provide comprehensive coverage of the elements of statistical inference. The remaining chapters discuss analytical methods used in specific experimental situations. The mathematical prerequisite for this book is at most a course in college algebra. Some sections, specifically Sections 3.10, 4.6, and 4.7, may be excluded without loss of continuity. Exercises are graduated in difficulty; all students can solve some and a substantial number can solve most.

Inference is explained in the first chapter as the objective of statistics, and the introduction to every subsequent chapter discusses the role the new material will play in making inferences and measuring their reliabilities. Probability, the vehicle for using sample information to make inferences, is discussed through the concept of the sample space. Chapters on decision making under uncertainty, quality control, time series, and forecasting have been included to provide a complete coverage of the available statistical tools for the business statistician. Many examples and exercises with practical applications in the various areas of business have been included to indicate the broad applicability of statistical methodology to business and economics.

Those familiar with other statistics texts will note that this text coins some terms not found elsewhere. Terms such as "the empirical rule" and "bound on the error of estimate" are offered in this text as rules of thumb, to summarize and simplify sometimes complicated underlying theoretical notions.

Highlighting is another feature of this text. Definitions, theorems, rules, and important formulas are set off in boxes. Significant words, phrases, and comments are included within the text in color. The purpose of the boxes and contrasting color is to focus the attention of the student to material of primary relevance and importance in each chapter. This should save the student the task of identifying and setting off the material himself.

The following diagram helps to explain the logical dependence of the chapters:

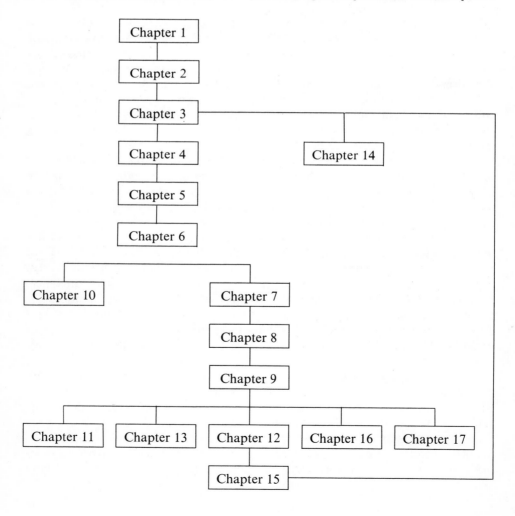

A semiprogrammed study guide is available that can assist students who have individual difficulties with the subject matter.

The authors are grateful to the editorial staff of Duxbury Press, especially to Alexander Kugushev, for assistance and cooperation in the preparation of this book. Thanks are due to a number of colleagues and friends of both authors for their helpful comments. Special thanks are due M. James Dunn for assistance in reading rough drafts of the original manuscript and to Jack Butler for his assistance in the preparation of Chapter 15. Thanks are also due P. L. Claypool, Oklahoma State University; D. James Croft, University of Utah; George Heitmann and Roger Pfaffenberger, Pennsylvania State University; and William Whiston, University of Massachusetts, for their helpful reviews of the manuscript, and to D. R. Cox, A. Hald, S. M. Selby, D. L. Burkholder, R. A. Wilcox, and C. W. Dunnett for their kind permission to use tables reprinted in the Appendix. Finally, we acknowledge the constant encouragement and assistance of our wives and children and their partnership in this writing endeavor.

William Mendenhall
James E. Reinmuth

Chapter One

What Is Statistics?

1.1   Illustrative Statistical Problems

What is statistics? How does it function? How does it help to solve certain business problems? Rather than attempt a definition at this point, let us examine several problems that might come to the attention of the business statistician. From these business problems we can select the essential elements of a statistical problem.

The investment managers of a $200 million mutual fund portfolio must decide whether to enter new stocks into the portfolio, sell some of the stocks currently in the portfolio, or both. Current trends of the market, price–earnings ratios, prevailing governmental taxation policies, and many other factors are observed as they relate to each security under consideration. On the basis of this information forecasts are constructed and the appropriate decision is made.

The production of a manufacturing plant is dependent upon many factors unique to the type of manufacturing plant under consideration. By observing these factors and the production over a period of time, we can construct a prediction equation relating production to the observed factors. Then prediction of the plant's future production for a given set of factor conditions can be made by substituting values of the factors into the prediction equation. Methods of identifying the important factors needed for the prediction equation as well as a method for assessing the error of prediction will be discussed in subsequent chapters.

Marketing research offers another example of a prediction problem. From the data obtained in an opinion survey, the market analyst must decide whether there exists sufficient demand for his product; and if this demand exists, he must select the package design, the best selling price, and the market area. All these questions could be answered from predictions and inferences based on his sample survey data.

Associated with and sometimes apart from the problem of prediction, the statistician is concerned with decision making based upon observed data. In capital budgeting problems, the objective is to accept the alternative that maximizes cash flow, expected return, or some other criteria. A measure of the value of each alternative may be obtained from a variety of sources, depending upon the type of problem. The business statistician must then make the decision, in the face of uncertainty, which maximizes his objectives.

A small business must decide each morning how many units of a perishable commodity should be stocked. The expected demand level, the costs for a shortage or an overstock, and the relative frequencies with which each possible demand level might occur are considered by the manager before deciding on a particular inventory level.

Consider the inspection of purchased items in a manufacturing plant. On the basis of an inspection, each lot of incoming goods must be either accepted, or rejected and returned to the supplier. The inspection might involve drawing a sample of 10 items from each lot and recording the number of defectives. The decision to accept or reject the lot could then be based on the number of defective items observed.

A company manufacturing complex electronic equipment produces some systems which function properly but also some which, for unknown reasons, do not. In attempting to find out what makes good systems good and bad systems bad, we might make certain internal measurements on a system in order to find important factors that differentiate between an acceptable and an unacceptable product. From a sample of good and bad systems, data could then be collected that might shed light on the fundamental design or on production variables affecting system quality.

These problems illustrate that business statistics involves much more than data gathering and graphical presentations. Modern statistics offers a variety of analytical procedures to aid the business statistician in making decisions under uncertainty. It is not to be assumed by the reader that uncertainties exist only within a business context or that modern statistics applies only to business. The emphasis of this text, though, will be to show the applications of statistical techniques to business problems. Other areas of application will be suggested through the exercises at the end of each chapter.

1.2   The Population and the Sample

The above examples are varied in nature and complexity, but each involves prediction or decision making or both. In addition, each involves sampling. A specified number of items (objects or bits of information)—a sample—is drawn from a much larger body of data, which we shall call the population. Note that the word "population" refers to data and not to people. The market researcher draws a sample of opinions from the statistical population which represents the entire potential market for his product. Recording the historical frequencies of demand for a perishable commodity gives a sample of all possible daily levels of demand that have occurred in the past or may occur in the future. In the sampling inspection problem, we assume that each sample of 10 items is a representative sample of the process from which it was selected.

Definition

A *population* is the set representing all measurements of interest to the sample collector.

In all the examples given above, we are primarily interested in the population. However, in most instances it is impractical or far too costly to observe or measure every element in the entire population. We select a sample that is hopefully a small-scale representation of the underlying population. The sample may be of immediate interest, but we are primarily interested in describing the population from which the sample is drawn.

Definition

A *sample* is a subset of measurements selected from the population of interest.

1.3   The Role of Statistics in Research

The objective of statistics is to make inferences about certain characteristics of a population based upon information contained in a sample. Consistent with this objective we should begin with a precise definition of our problem. Once we have identified our objective and the characteristics of the population associated with this objective, we can gather relevant sample data, analyze the data, and make inferences about the population based on the sample data. We must then state our conclusions in a form that would be understandable to the manager or business executive responsible for implementing our experimental findings. This is often the most difficult task of the entire research problem, but if we do not adequately communicate with the manager to allow for implementation and follow up, our research will be meaningless. Often, a business research group contains an individual whose only job is to effectively explain the results of experimental findings in a nontechnical language the audience can readily understand. The importance of effective communication of our results cannot be overestimated.

One of the most important steps in a statistical investigation is planning the method of selecting the sample. Thus when we select a sample from the population, we suppose the observed data contains a given quantity of information. This information is purchased with time and money expended in controlled experimentation or data collection. Furthermore, we might suspect that a given expenditure would yield varying amounts of information for various methods of experimentation. Such is, in fact, the case. Essential to statistical problems is the design of the experiment, or sampling procedure, which will enable the businessman to purchase a specified amount of information at minimum cost. This aspect of a statistical problem is less important when data collection is inexpensive. On the other hand, in market research surveys, in the testing of complex electronic systems, in the inspection of new products in an assembly line, and in many other data-collecting situations that are very costly, the design of the experiment of sampling procedure assumes a very important role.

To summarize, a statistical problem involves

1. *A precise definition of the problem and its objectives.*
2. *Design of the experiment or sampling procedure.*
3. *Collection and analysis of data.*
4. *The making of inferences about the population based upon sample information.*
5. *Effective communication of the experimental findings to management.*

1.4   The Statistician and Business Decision Making

Statistics is an area of science concerned with the extraction of information from numerical data and its use in making inferences about a population from which the data are obtained. In some respects the statistician quantifies information and studies various designs and sampling procedures, searching for the procedure that yields the most information in a given situation for a fixed expenditure. We might liken data to a lemon and say that the statistician is concerned with squeezing or extracting as much information from the data as possible. Finally, we consider the matter of inference. Everyone has made many predictions and decisions, and it is clear that some people are better predictors and decision makers than others. The statistician studies various inferential procedures, looking for the best predictor or decision-making process for a given situation. Even more important, he provides information concerning the goodness of an inferential procedure. When we predict, we would like to know something about the error in our prediction. If we make a decision, what is the chance that our decision is incorrect? Our built-in individual prediction and decision-making systems do not provide immediate answers to these important questions and can be evaluated only by observation over a long period. In contrast, statistical procedures do provide answers to these questions.

The business statistician is concerned with problems which require statistical analysis and which arise in many areas of business. These occur in production, studies of industrial dynamics of the firm, long-range planning for plant structure, inventory management, and quality control. The problems that may be encountered are varied in nature but similar in the respect that their solutions must all be consistent with the goals of the firm.

In finance and business economics most of the problems encountered require a statistical forecast or an economic projection. Sales forecasting, capital budgeting, long-range financial planning, and portfolio management provide examples of the overall financial requirements of the firm which must be studied and developed through forecasting methods. The marketing and general management areas of business use statistical forecasts to project sales into future periods, project expected advertising expenditures, estimate future personnel and equipment needs, and solve any other problem having to do with the long-range goals of the firm.

The illustrative business problems of Section 1.1 showed how statistical techniques may be applied to some of the areas mentioned within this section. Whether the business is large or small and regardless of the area of the firm we are considering, statistics can be used as an aid in answering some of the questions that may arise. The actual application of statistical methods to all types of business problems will be shown through the examples and exercises within the text.

1.5   Summary

Statistics is an area of science concerned with the design of experiments or sampling procedures, the analysis of data, and the making of inferences about a population of measurements from information contained in a sample. The statistician is concerned with developing and using procedures for design analysis, and inference making which will provide the best inferences for a given expenditure. In addition to making the best inference, he is concerned with providing a quantitative measure of the goodness of the inference-making procedure. Also, it is essential that the business statistician provide a means of effectively communicating his experimental conclusions to management.

1.6   A Note to the Reader

We have stated the objective of statistics and, it is hoped, have answered the question: What is statistics? The remainder of this text is devoted to the development of the basic concepts involved in statistical methodology. In other words, we wish to explain how statistical techniques actually work and why they work.

Statistics is a theory of information in which applied mathematics plays a major role. Most of the fundamental rules (called *theorems* in mathematics) are developed and based upon a knowledge of the calculus or higher mathematics. Inasmuch as this is meant to be an introductory text, we omit proofs except where they can be easily derived. Where concepts or theorems can be shown to be intuitively reasonable, we shall attempt to give a logical explanation. Hence we shall attempt to convince the reader with the aid of examples and intuitive arguments rather than with rigorous mathematical derivations.

Like any other business technique, common sense must be employed when applying statistical methods to the solution of a real problem. Since inferences are made about a population from sample data, the inferences are meaningful only if the sample is selected from the population of interest. For example, if we proposed a study to find the average height of all students at a particular university, we would not select our entire sample from the members of the basketball team. The basketball players should be represented within a sample in approximately the same proportion that they exist within the entire university. Another common misuse of statistics is in making comparisons. The National Safety Council claims that on a holiday weekend there are about twice as many highway deaths as on an ordinary weekend. One might conclude that driving on a holiday weekend is much less safe than driving on an ordinary weekend. This is true only if the traffic volume is about the same for all weekends, an unreal assumption. It is important that we view all statistics and sets of data with a critical eye and apply common sense and intuition about the problem to our decision format before arriving at a conclusion. The conclusions which apply to a particular problem are unique to that problem and seldom apply to other or related problems.

The reader should refer occasionally to this chapter and review the objective of statistics, its role in business research, and the elements of a statistical problem. Each of the following chapters should, in some way, be directed toward answering the questions posed here. Each is essential to completing the overall picture of the role of statistics in business and public administration.

References

Careers in Statistics. American Statistical Association and the Institute of Mathematical Statistics, 1962.

Huff, D., and Irvina Geis, *How to Lie with Statistics.* New York: W. W. Norton & Company, Inc., 1954.

Reichmann, W. J., *Use and Abuse of Statistics.* London: Methuen & Company Ltd., 1961.

Chapter Two

Useful Mathematical Notation

2.1   Introduction

Presuming that the reader is familiar with elementary algebra, we shall omit a general review of that subject. However, two topics of elementary algebra—functional notation and summation notation—are used extensively in the following chapters and are worthy of discussion at this point.

2.2   Functional Notation

Let us consider two sets* of elements (objects, numbers, or anything we want to use) and their relation to one another. Let the symbol x represent an element of the first set and y an element of the second. One could specify a number of different rules defining relationships between x and y. For instance, if our elements are people, we have rules for determining whether x and y, two persons, are first cousins. Or, suppose that x and y are integers taking values 1, 2, 3, 4, ... For some reason, we might wish to say that x and y are "related" if $x = y$.

Now let us direct our attention to a specific relationship useful in mathematics called a functional relation between x and y.

---

* A set is a collection of specific things.

Definition

A *function* consists of two sets of elements and a defined correspondence between an element of the first set, x, and an element of the second set, y, such that for each element x there corresponds one, and only one, element y.

A function may be exhibited as a collection of ordered pairs of elements, written (x, y). In fact, a function is often defined as a collection of ordered pairs of elements with the property stated in the definition.

Most often, x and y will be variables taking numerical values. The two sets of elements would represent all the possible numerical values that x and y might take, and the rule defining the correspondence between them would be an equation. For example, if we state that x and y are real numbers and that

$$y = x + 2,$$

then y is a function of x. Assigning a value to x (that is, choosing an element of the set of all real numbers), there corresponds one, and only one, value of y. When $x = 1$, $y = 3$. When $x = -4$, $y = -2$, and so on.

The area A of a circle is related to the radius r by the formula

$$A = \pi r^2.$$

Note that if we assign a value to r, the value of A can be determined from the formula. Hence A is a function of r. Likewise, the circumference of a circle, C, is a function of the radius.

As a third example of a functional relation, consider a classroom containing 20 students. Let x represent a specific body in the classroom and y represent a name. Is y a function of x? To answer the question, we examine x and y in light of the definition. We note that each body has a name y attached to it. When x is specified, y will be uniquely determined. According to our definition, y is a function of x. Note that the defining rule for functional relations does not require that x and y take numerical values. We shall encounter an important functional relation of this type in Chapter 4.

Having defined a functional relation, we may now turn to functional notation Mathematical writing frequently uses the same phrase or refers to a specific object many times in the course of a discussion. Unnecessary repetition wastes the reader's time, takes up valuable space, and is cumbersome to the writer. Hence the mathematician resorts to mathematical symbolism, which is, in some respects, a type of mathematical shorthand. Rather than state "The area of a circle A is a function of the radius *r*," the mathematician would write $A(r)$. The expression

$$y = f(x)$$

tells us that *y* is a function of the variable appearing in parentheses, namely *x*. Note that this expression does not tell us the specific functional relation existing between *y* and *x*.

Consider the function of *x*,

$$y = 3x + 2.$$

In functional notation, this would be written as

$$f(x) = 3x + 2.$$

It is understood that $y = f(x)$.

Functional notation is especially advantageous when we wish to indicate the value of the function *y* when *x* takes a specific value, say $x = 2$. For the above example, we see that when $x = 2$,

$$y = 3x + 2$$
$$= 3(2) + 2$$
$$= 8.$$

Rather than write this, we use the simpler notation

$$f(2) = 8.$$

Similarly, $f(5)$ would be the value of the function when $x = 5$:

$$f(5) = 3(5) + 2$$
$$= 15 + 2$$
$$= 17.$$

Definition

To find the *value of the function* when x equals any value, say $x = c$, we substitute the value of c for x in the equation and obtain

$$f(c) = 3c + 2.$$

Example 2.1   *Given a function of x,*

$$g(x) = \frac{1}{x} + 3x.$$

(a) *Find g(4).*

$$g(4) = \frac{1}{4} + 3(4)$$

$$= .25 + 12$$

$$= 12.25.$$

(b) *Find g(0).*

$$g(0) = \frac{1}{0} + 3(0).$$

Division by zero is mathematically undefined, so g(0) does not exist.
(c) *Find g(1/a).*

$$g\left(\frac{1}{a}\right) = \left(\frac{1}{1/a}\right) + 3\left(\frac{1}{a}\right)$$

$$= a + \frac{3}{a}$$

$$= \frac{a^2 + 3}{a}.$$

Example 2.2   *Let $p(y) = (1 - a)a^y$. Find $p(2)$ and $p(3)$.*

$$p(2) = (1 - a)a^2,$$
$$p(3) = (1 - a)a^3.$$

Example 2.3   *Let $f(y) = 4$. Find $f(2)$ and $f(3)$.*

$$f(2) = 4,$$
$$f(3) = 4.$$

Note that $f(y)$ always equals 4, regardless of the value of y. Hence when a value of y is assigned, the value of the function is determined and will equal 4.

Example 2.4   *Let $f(x) = x^2 + 1$ and $g(x) = x + 2$. Find $f[g(x)]$. We find $f[g(x)]$ by substituting $g(x)$ for x in the function $f(x)$. Thus*

$$f[g(x)] = [g(x)]^2 + 1$$
$$= (x + 2)^2 + 1$$
$$= x^2 + 4x + 4 + 1$$
$$= x^2 + 4x + 5.$$

2.3   Numerical Sequences

In statistics we shall be concerned with samples consisting of sets of measurements. There will be a first measurement, a second, and so on. Introducing the notation of a mathematical sequence at this point will provide us with a simple notation for discussion of data and will, at the same time, supply our first practical application of functional notation. This will, in turn, be used in the summation notation introduced in Section 2.4.

A set of objects, $a_1, a_2, a_3, a_4, \ldots$, ordered in the sense that we can identify the first member of the set a_1, the second a_2, and so on, is called a sequence. Most often, $a_1, a_2, a_3, \ldots$, called elements of the sequence, are numbers but this is not a requirement. For example, the numbers

$$1, 5, 4, 8, 7, 11, 10, \ldots$$

form a sequence moving from left to right. Note that the elements are ordered only in their position in the sequence and need not be ordered in magnitude. Likewise, in some card games, we are interested in a sequence of cards; for example,

10, jack, queen, king, ace.

Although nonnumerical sequences are of interest, we shall be concerned solely with numerical sequences. Specifically, data obtained in a sample from a population will be regarded as a sequence of measurements.

Since sequences will form an important part of subsequent discussions, let us turn to a shortcut method of writing sequences utilizing functional notation. Inasmuch as the elements of a sequence are ordered in position in the sequence, it would seem natural to attempt to write a formula for a typical element of the sequence as a function of its position. For example, consider the sequence

$$3, 4, 5, 6, 7, \ldots,$$

where each element in the sequence is one greater than the preceding element. Let y be a position variable for the sequence so that y can take values $1, 2, 3, 4, \ldots$. Then we might write a formula for the element in position y as

$$f(y) = y + 2.$$

Thus the first element in the sequence would be in position $y = 1$, and $f(1)$ would equal

$$f(1) = 1 + 2 = 3.$$

Likewise, the second element would be in position $y = 2$, and the second element of the sequence would be

$$f(2) = 2 + 2 = 4.$$

A brief check convinces us that this formula works for all elements of the sequence. Note that finding a proper formula (function) is a matter of trial and error and requires a bit of practice.

Example 2.5   *Given the sequence*

$$1, 4, 9, 16, 25, \ldots,$$

find a formula expressing a typical element in terms of a position variable y.

We note that each element is the square of the position variable; hence

$$f(y) = y^2.$$

Example 2.6   *The formula for the typical element of the following sequence is not so obvious:*

$$0, 3, 8, 15, 24, 35, \ldots.$$

The typical element would be

$$f(y) = y^2 - 1.$$

Readers of mathematical writings (and this includes the authors) prefer consistency in the use of mathematical notation. Unfortunately, this is not always practical. Writers are limited by the number of symbols available and also by the desire to make their notation consistent with some other texts on the subject. Hence x and y are very often used in referring to a variable but we could just as well use i, j, k, or z. For instance, suppose that we wish to refer to a set of measurements and denote the measurements as a variable y. We might write this sequence of measurements as

$$y_1, y_2, y_3, y_4, y_5, \ldots,$$

using a subscript to denote a particular element in the sequence. We are now forced to choose a new position variable (since y has been used). Suppose that we use the letter i. Then we could write a typical element as

$$f(i) = y_i.$$

Note that, as previously, $f(1) = y_1, f(2) = y_2$, and so on.

2.4   Summation Notation

As we shall observe in Chapter 3, in analyzing statistical data we shall often be working with sums of numbers and need a simple notation for indicating a sum.

For instance, consider the sequence of numbers

$$1, 2, 3, 4, 5, \ldots$$

and suppose that we wish to discuss the sum of the squares of the first four numbers of the sequence. Using summation notation this would be written as

$$\sum_{y=1}^{4} y^2.$$

Interpretation of the summation notation is relatively easy. The Greek letter $\sum$ (capital sigma), corresponding to "S" in the English alphabet (the first letter in the word "sum"), tells us to sum elements of a sequence. A typical element of the sequence is given to the right of the summation symbol, and the position variable, called the variable of summation, is shown beneath. For our example, y^2 is a typical element, y is the variable of summation, and the implied sequence is

$$1, 4, 9, 16, 25, 36, \ldots.$$

Which element of the sequence should appear in the sum? The position of the first element in the sum is indicated below the summation sign, the last above. The sum would include all elements proceeding in order from the first to last. Thus, in our example, the sum would include the sum of the elements commencing with the first and ending with the fourth:

$$\sum_{y=1}^{4} y^2 = 1 + 4 + 9 + 16$$

$$= 30.$$

Example 2.7

$$\sum_{y=2}^{4} (y - 1) = (2 - 1) + (3 - 1) + (4 - 1)$$

$$= 6.$$

Example 2.8

$$\sum_{x=2}^{5} 3x = 3(2) + 3(3) + 3(4) + 3(5)$$

$$= 42.$$

We emphasize that the typical element is a function only of the variable of summation. All other symbols are regarded as constants.

Example 2.9

$$\sum_{i=1}^{3} (y_i - a) = (y_1 - a) + (y_2 - a) + (y_3 - a).$$

In this example note that i is the variable of summation and that it appears as a subscript in the typical element.

Example 2.10

$$\sum_{i=1}^{2} (x - i + 1) = (x - 1 + 1) + (x - 2 + 1)$$

$$= 2x - 1.$$

Example 2.11

$$\sum_{y=2}^{4} y - 1 = (2 + 3 + 4) - 1$$

$$= 8.$$

Note the difference between Example 2.7 and Example 2.11. The quantity $(y - 1)$ is the typical element in Example 2.7, whereas y is the typical element in Example 2.11.

2.5   Useful Theorems Relating to Sums

Consider the summation

$$\sum_{y=1}^{3} 5.$$

The typical element is 5 and it does not change. The sequence is, therefore,

$$5, 5, 5, 5, \ldots$$

and

$$\sum_{y=1}^{3} 5 = 5 + 5 + 5$$

$$= 15.$$

Theorem 2.1

Let c be a constant (an element that does not involve the variable of summation) and y be the variable of summation. Then

$$\sum_{y=1}^{n} c = nc.$$

Proof

$$\sum_{y=1}^{n} c = c + c + c + c + \cdots + c,$$

where the sum involves n elements. Then

$$\sum_{y=1}^{n} c = nc.$$

Example 2.12

$$\sum_{y=1}^{4} 3a = 4(3a) = 12a.$$

Example 2.13

$$\sum_{i=1}^{3} (3x - 5) = 3(3x - 5).$$

(Note that i is the variable of summation.)

A second theorem is illustrated using Example 2.8. We note that 3 is a common factor in each term. Therefore,

$$\sum_{y=2}^{5} 3y = 3(2) + 3(3) + 3(4) + 3(5)$$

$$= 3(2 + 3 + 4 + 5)$$

$$= 3 \sum_{y=2}^{5} y.$$

It would appear that the summation of a constant times a variable is equal to the constant times the summation of the variable.

Theorem 2.2

Let c be a constant. Then

$$\sum_{i=1}^{n} cy_i = c \sum_{i=1}^{n} y_i.$$

Proof

$$\sum_{i=1}^{n} cy_i = cy_1 + cy_2 + cy_3 + \cdots + cy_n$$

$$= c(y_1 + y_2 + \cdots + y_n)$$

$$= c \sum_{i=1}^{n} y_i.$$

The constant *c* need only be a term whose value does not depend on the variable of summation. For instance, in the expression

$$\sum_{y=1}^{4} x^2 y$$

the term x^2 is not a function of *y*, the variable of summation. Therefore, it can be considered a constant. Thus

$$\sum_{y=1}^{4} x^2 y = x^2 \sum_{y=1}^{4} y$$

$$= x^2(1 + 2 + 3 + 4)$$

$$= 10x^2.$$

Theorem 2.3

$$\sum_{i=1}^{n} (x_i + y_i + z_i) = \sum_{i=1}^{n} x_i + \sum_{i=1}^{n} y_i + \sum_{i=1}^{n} z_i.$$

Proof

$$\sum_{i=1}^{n} (x_i + y_i + z_i) = x_1 + y_1 + z_1 + x_2 + y_2 + z_2 + x_3 + y_3$$

$$+ z_3 + \cdots + x_n + y_n + z_n.$$

Regrouping, we have

$$\sum_{i=1}^{n} (x_i + y_i + z_i)$$

$$= (x_1 + x_2 + \cdots + x_n) + (y_1 + y_2 + \cdots + y_n) + (z_1 + z_2 + \cdots + z_n)$$

$$= \sum_{i=1}^{n} x_i + \sum_{i=1}^{n} y_i + \sum_{i=1}^{n} z_i.$$

In words, we would say that the summation of a typical element which is itself a sum of a number of terms is equal to the sum of the summations of the terms.

Theorems 2.1, 2.2, and 2.3 can be used jointly to simplify summations. Consider the following examples:

Example 2.14

$$\sum_{x=1}^{3} (x^2 + ax + 5) = \sum_{x=1}^{3} x^2 + \sum_{x=1}^{3} ax + \sum_{x=1}^{3} 5$$

$$= \sum_{x=1}^{3} x^2 + a \sum_{x=1}^{3} x + 3(5)$$

$$= (1 + 4 + 9) + a(1 + 2 + 3) + 15$$

$$= 6a + 29.$$

Example 2.15

$$\sum_{i=1}^{4} (x^2 + 3i) = \sum_{i=1}^{4} x^2 + \sum_{i=1}^{4} 3i$$

$$= 4x^2 + 3 \sum_{i=1}^{4} i$$

$$= 4x^2 + 3(1 + 2 + 3 + 4)$$

$$= 4x^2 + 30.$$

2.6   Summary

Two types of mathematical notations have been presented, functional notation and summation notation. The former is used in summation notation to express the typical element as a function of the variable of summation. Other uses for functional notation will be discussed in Chapter 4. Summation notation will be employed in Chapter 3 and succeeding chapters.

Exercises

1. Given $f(y) = 4y + 3$, find
    (a) $f(0)$ (b) $f(1)$ (c) $f(2)$
    (d) $f(-1)$ (e) $f(-2)$ (f) $f(a^2)$
    (g) $f(-a)$ (h) $f(1 - y)$

2. Given $f(y) = \dfrac{y^2 - 1}{y}$, find

   (a) $f(2)$ (b) $f(-3)$ (c) $f(-1)$
   (d) $f(x)$ (e) $f(a - 1)$

3. Given $f(x) = x^2 - x + 1$, find

   (a) $f(-2)$ (b) $f(a + b)$

4. If $g(y) = \dfrac{y^2 - 1}{y + 1}$, find

   (a) $g(1)$ (b) $g(-1)$ (c) $g(4)$
   (d) $g(-a^2)$

5. If $p(x) = (1 - a)^x$, find $p(0)$ and $p(1)$.

6. If $f(x) = 3x^2 - 3x + 1$ and $g(x) = x - 3$, find

   (a) $f(1/2)$ (b) $g(-3)$ (c) $f(1/x)$
   (d) $f[g(x)]$

7. If $h(x) = 2$, find

   (a) $h(0)$ (b) $h(1)$ (c) $h(2)$

Utilize Theorems 2.1, 2.2, and 2.3 to simplify and evaluate the following summations.

8. $\displaystyle\sum_{y=1}^{3} y^3$ 9. $\displaystyle\sum_{y=1}^{3} 6$

10. $\displaystyle\sum_{x=2}^{3} (1 + 3x + x^2)$ 11. $\displaystyle\sum_{i=1}^{5} (x^2 + 2i)$

12. $\displaystyle\sum_{y=0}^{5} (x^2 + y^2)$ 13. $\displaystyle\sum_{x=0}^{2} (x^3 + 2ix)$

14. $\displaystyle\sum_{x=1}^{4} (x + xy^2)$ 15. $\displaystyle\sum_{i=1}^{2} (y_i - i)$

16. $\displaystyle\sum_{i=1}^{n} (y_i - a)$ 17. $\displaystyle\sum_{i=1}^{n} (y_i - a)^2$

Using the following set of measurements, answer Exercises 18 through 23.

i	1	2	3	4	5	6	7	8	9	10	11	12	13
y_i	3	12	10	-6	0	11	2	-9	-5	8	-7	4	-5

18. $\displaystyle\sum_{i=1}^{13} 2y_i$ 19. $\displaystyle\sum_{i=1}^{13} (2y_i - 5)$

20. $\displaystyle\sum_{i=3}^{10} y_i^2$ 21. $\displaystyle\sum_{i=1}^{10} (y_i^2 + y_i)$

22. $\displaystyle\sum_{i=1}^{13} (y_i - 2)^2$ 23. $\displaystyle\sum_{i=1}^{13} y_i^2 - \frac{1}{13}\left(\sum_{i=1}^{13} y_i\right)^2$

Supplementary Exercises

Verify the following identities. Each of them is a shortcut formula that will be used in later chapters. The symbols $\bar{x}$ and $\bar{y}$ appearing in these identities have the following definitions:

$$\bar{x} = \frac{\sum_{i=1}^{n} x_i}{n}, \qquad \bar{y} = \frac{\sum_{i=1}^{n} y_i}{n}.$$

1. $$\sum_{i=1}^{n} (x_i - \bar{x})^2 = \sum_{i=1}^{n} x_i^2 - \frac{\left(\sum_{i=1}^{n} x_i\right)^2}{n}$$

2. $$\sum_{i=1}^{n} (x_i - \bar{x})(y_i - \bar{y}) = \sum_{i=1}^{n} x_i y_i - \frac{\left(\sum_{i=1}^{n} x_i\right)\left(\sum_{i=1}^{n} y_i\right)}{n}$$

3. $$\frac{\sum_{i=1}^{n} (y_i - \bar{y})^2}{n-1} = \frac{1}{n-1}\left[\sum_{i=1}^{n} y_i^2 - \frac{1}{n}\left(\sum_{i=1}^{n} y_i\right)^2\right]$$

4. $$\frac{\sum_{i=1}^{n} (x_i - \bar{x})(y_i - \bar{y})}{\sum_{i=1}^{n} (x_i - \bar{x})^2} = \frac{n\sum_{i=1}^{n} x_i y_i - \left(\sum_{i=1}^{n} x_i\right)\left(\sum_{i=1}^{n} y_i\right)}{n\sum_{i=1}^{n} x_i^2 - \left(\sum_{i=1}^{n} x_i\right)^2}$$

Chapter Three

Describing Sets of Measurements

3.1   Introduction

After a brief detour in Chapter 2, we return to the main objective of our study—making inferences about a large body of data, the population, based upon information contained in a sample. A most peculiar difficulty arises: how will the inferences be phrased? How do we describe a set of measurements, whether they be the sample or the population? If the population were before us, how could we describe this large set of measurements?

Numerous texts have been devoted to the methods of descriptive statistics—that is, the methods of describing sets of numerical data. Essentially, these methods can be categorized as graphical methods and numerical methods. In this text we shall restrict our discussion to a few graphical and numerical methods which are useful not only for descriptive purposes but also for statistical inference. Some common numerical methods have been eliminated from our discussion so as not to disrupt continuity. Such methods are redundant in the presence of high-speed electric desk calculators and electronic computers and would contribute little, if any, to the main objective of our study. The reader interested in descriptive statistics not contained within this chapter should refer to the references listed at the end of the chapter.

A remark is necessary at this point. The graphical methods that follow can be applied to either a set of population measurements or sample measurements without making a specific distinction as to which case is in effect. Numerical descriptive measures also apply to both population and sample measurements but use different symbols to indicate whether the measure was obtained from the set of population measurements or from a sample set.

3.2   Frequency Distribution

It would seem natural to introduce appropriate graphical and numerical methods of describing sets of data through consideration of a set of real data. The data presented in Table 3.1 represent the price–earnings ratios for the common stocks of 25 companies for the year 1969.

Table 3.1   *Price–Earnings Ratios for 25 Common Stocks*

20.5	19.5	15.6	24.1	9.9
15.4	12.7	5.4	17.0	28.6
16.9	7.8	23.3	11.8	18.4
13.4	14.3	19.2	9.2	16.8
8.8	22.1	20.8	12.6	15.9

A cursory examination reveals that the largest price–earnings ratio in the sample is 28.6 and the smallest, 5.4. One might ask how the other 23 price–earnings ratios are distributed over the interval from 5.4 to 28.6. To answer this question we divide the interval into an arbitrary number of equal subintervals, the number being determined by the amount of data available. (As a rule of thumb, the number of subintervals chosen would range from 5 to 20; the larger the amount of data available, the more subintervals employed.) For the preceding data we might use the subintervals 5.00 to 8.99, 9.00 to 12.99, 13.00 to 16.99, ... Note that the points dividing the subintervals have been chosen so that it is impossible for a measurement to fall on the point of division, thus eliminating any ambiguity regarding the disposition of a particular measurement. The subintervals, called classes in statistical language, form cells or pockets. We wish to determine the manner in which the measurements are distributed in the pockets, or classes. A tally of the data from Table 3.1 is presented in Table 3.2.

The 25 measurements fall in one of six classes, which, for purposes of identification, we shall number from 1 to 6. The identification number appears in the first column of Table 3.2 and the corresponding class boundaries are given in the second column. The third column of the table is used for the tally, a mark entered opposite the appropriate class for each measurement falling in the class. For example, 3 of the 25 measurements fall in class 1, 5 in class 2, and so on. The number of measurements falling in a particular class, say class i, is called the *class frequency* and is designated by the symbol f_i. The class frequency is given in the fourth column of Table 3.2. The last column of the table presents the fraction of the total number of measurements falling in each class. We call this the relative frequency. If we let n represent the total number of measurements, for instance, in our example $n = 25$, then the relative frequency for the ith class would equal f_i divided by n:

$$\text{relative frequency} = \frac{f_i}{n}.$$

Table 3.2 *Tabulation of Relative Frequencies for the 25 Price–Earnings Ratios*

CLASS i	CLASS BOUNDARIES	TALLY	CLASS FREQUENCY f_i	RELATIVE FREQUENCY
1	5.00–8.99	|||	3	3/25
2	9.00–12.99		5	5/25
3	13.00–16.99		7	7/25
4	17.00–20.99		6	6/25
5	21.00–24.99	|||	3	3/25
6	25.00–28.99			1	1/25

Total   25

The resulting tabulation can be presented graphically in the form of a frequency histogram, Figure 3.1. Rectangles are constructed over each interval, their height being proportional to the number of measurements (class frequency)

Figure 3.1 *Frequency Histogram*

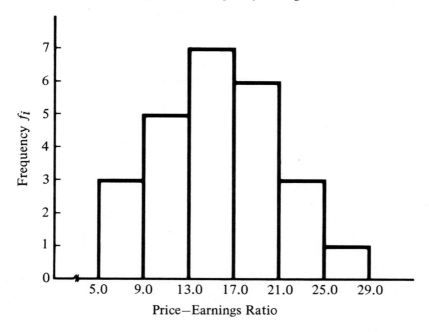

falling in each class interval. Viewing the frequency histogram, we see at a glance the manner in which the price–earnings ratios are distributed over the interval.

It is often more convenient to modify the frequency histogram by plotting class relative frequency rather than class frequency. A relative frequency histogram is presented in Figure 3.2. Statisticians rarely make a distinction between the frequency histogram and the relative frequency histogram and refer to either as a frequency histogram or simply a histogram. The two diagrams, when drawn to the same scale, are identical, the only difference being the dimensions of the vertical axis.

Although we are interested in describing the set of $n = 25$ measurements, we are much more interested in the population from which the sample was drawn. We might view the 25 price–earnings ratios as a representative sample drawn from a population consisting of all the firms whose stock was listed by the New York Stock Exchange in 1969. If we had the price–earnings ratios for all the firms in our population, we could construct a population relative frequency histogram. However, gathering the data from the entire population may be very costly and time consuming. Thus, a representative sample may be the best and only information we have to describe the population.

Let us consider the relative frequency histogram for the sample in greater detail. What fraction of the firms had price–earnings ratios equal to 17.0 or greater?

Figure 3.2   *Relative Frequency Histogram*

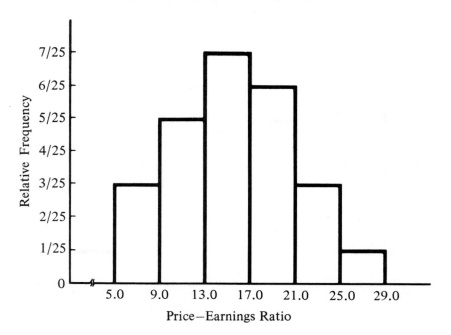

Checking the relative frequency histogram, we see that the fraction would involve all classes to the right of 17.0. Using Table 3.2, we see that 10 companies had price–earnings ratios greater than or equal to 17.0. Hence the fraction is 10/25, or 40 percent. We note that this is also the percentage of the total area of the histogram in Figures 3.1 and 3.2 that is lying to the right of 17.0. Suppose that we were to write each one of the 25 price–earnings ratios on a piece of paper, place them in a hat, and then draw one piece of paper from the hat. What is the chance that this paper would contain a price–earnings value greater than or equal to 17.0? Since 10 of the 25 pieces of paper are marked with numbers greater than or equal to 17.0, we would say that we have 10 chances out of 25. Or, we might say that the probability is 10/25. The reader has undoubtedly encountered the word "probability" in ordinary conversation, and we are content to defer definition and discussion of its significance until Chapter 4.

Let us now direct attention to the population from which the sample was drawn. What fraction of the firms in the population of all New York Stock Exchange firms for 1969 had price–earnings ratios greater than or equal to 17.0? If we possessed the relative frequency histogram for the population, we could give the exact answer to this question. Unfortunately, we are forced to make an inference from our sample information. Our estimate for the true population fraction or proportion, based upon the sample information, would likely be 10/25, or 40 percent. Without knowledge of the population relative frequency histogram we would infer that the population histogram is similar to the sample histogram and that approximately 40 percent of the price–earnings ratios in the population are greater than or equal to 17.0. Most likely, this estimate would be in error. We shall examine the magnitude of this error in Chapter 8.

The relative frequency histogram is often called a frequency distribution because it shows the manner in which the data are distributed along the abscissa of the graph. We note that the rectangles constructed above each class are subject to two interpretations. They represent the fraction of observations falling in a given class. Also, if a measurement is drawn from the data, a particular class relative frequency is also the chance or probability that the measurement will fall in that class. The most significant feature of the sample frequency histogram is that it provides information on the population frequency histogram which describes the population. We would expect the two frequency histograms, sample and population, to be similar. Such is the case. The degree of resemblance will increase as more and more data are added to the sample. If the sample were enlarged to include the entire population, the sample and population would be synonymous and the histograms would be identical.

> *In summary, the purpose of a graphical representation is to provide a meaningful, concise, and easy-to-interpret summary of a set of numerical data.*

If the data can be categorized, an easy way to present the results graphically is to construct a frequency distribution. As a general rule, the construction of a frequency distribution should satisfy the following principles:

1.   All classes, with the possible exception of the smallest and largest class, should be of equal width. This allows us to make uniform comparisons of the class frequencies.

2.   Class boundaries should never overlap. In other words, each measurement should belong to only one class.

3.   All the measurements should be contained within the classes. If possible the smallest class should contain the smallest measurement, and the largest class should contain the largest measurement.

It is usually best to have from 5 to 20 classes. If the number of classes is too small, we might be concealing important characteristics of the data by grouping. If we have too many classes, empty classes may result and the distribution be meaningless. The number of classes should be determined from the amount of data present and the uniformity of the data. A small sample and/or a uniform distribution of measurements would suggest that fewer classes are needed.

As a general rule for finding the width of each class to use in the construction of our class boundaries, divide the difference between the largest and smallest measurement by the number of classes desired and add enough to the quotient to arrive at a convenient figure for class width.

For example, suppose that we wish to group the 36 incomes of the employees of a small firm into five classes, where the smallest income is \$5,500 and the largest is \$29,500. Applying our rule,

$$\text{class width} = \frac{\$29{,}500 - \$5{,}500}{5} = \$4{,}800.$$

More conveniently, we could use \$5,000 as our class width. The class boundaries would then be

$$\$5{,}000\text{--}\$9{,}999$$
$$\$10{,}000\text{--}\$14{,}999$$
$$\$15{,}000\text{--}\$19{,}999$$
$$\$20{,}000\text{--}\$24{,}999$$
$$\$25{,}000\text{--}\$29{,}999$$

Here, none of our principles for the construction of frequency distribution is violated. However, if our data were widely dispersed, we might wish to make the lower or upper class open ended. For instance, if the president's \$100,000 salary is included as the 37th income value, our largest class would be $25,000 and over. If we were to apply the class width rule, empty classes would occur and would confuse the interpretation of our results.

3.3   Other Graphical Methods

Often data collected from different time periods or geographical areas are best presented by use of statistical tables, charts, or pictograms. The principles behind the construction and use of each are quite simple and need little discussion.

A statistical table is a classified or subdivided frequency distribution comparing the relative frequencies for several different samples. The samples may be from different time periods, different geographical areas, different but related firms, different areas within a firm, and so on. Within each sample the classifications must be the same so that we can perform a meaningful cross analysis of the data.

Bar charts line charts, and ratio charts are designed to serve as visual summaries of our data. Usually line and ratio charts are a plot of points tracing a firm's profits, sales, or productivity, or their change over time. Bar charts and pictograms are pictorial frequency histograms. Many other types of graphical and pictorial methods are useful for the business statistician, but time limits our discussion within this chapter.

Table 3.3 shows the breakdown of the employees of a small, Midwestern manufacturing firm for the years 1966 through 1969. The classifications for each of the four years are the same, so we can make meaningful comparisons among the years. They are, however, not unique and are constructed at the discretion of the statistician. The entries within Table 3.3 are subdivisions of the total and are not necessarily percentages of the total. Percentages can sometimes be misleading unless the subgroup or sample totals are nearly equal.

Table 3.3   *Employee Analysis for the Nebraska Company*

	1966	1967	1968	1969
Total	100	115	110	150
College graduates	40	44	42	58
Male	37	40	39	48
Female	3	4	3	10
High school graduates	60	71	68	92
Male	50	58	56	69
Female	10	13	12	23

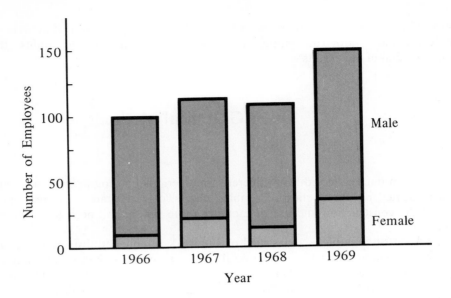

Figure 3.3   *Bar Graph*

Figure 3.3 shows how a bar chart could be used to display pictorially some of the employee data for the Nebraska Company. The bar chart is easy to read and provides a quick analysis of the data. Bar charts are not ordinarily as finely subdivided as a classification table, since the extra partitions would tend to clutter the appearance of the bar chart and lose simplicity, its main objective. The bar chart could have been constructed in other ways had we chosen to do so. We could have illustrated the same information by drawing three separate rectangles (bars) for each year, showing separately the number of male employees, the number of female employees, and the total number of employees. The type of bar chart employed is not important as long as the chart is factual and easy to interpret.

Figure 3.4 illustrates the use of a bar chart and a line chart together. The bars indicate the number of rental units built each year, and the line, the number of houses built each year. Many readers, such as loan companies, commercial banks, and real estate agencies, would be interested not so much in the exact number of rental units and homes built, but in the relation of the total of one to the total of the other. Contrasting representations like those shown in Figure 3.4 clearly depict this relation.

Although bar charts are the most common pictorial representations of data, pie charts are usually employed to show percentage breakdowns at a given point in time. One could construct a pie chart for each year for the Nebraska Company showing the ratio of male versus female employees. However, this would tend to clutter the appearance of the presentation and destroy its simplicity.

The primary usefulness of a pie chart is that it allows the reader to see quickly how much of the total is represented by each subdivision of the total. If we

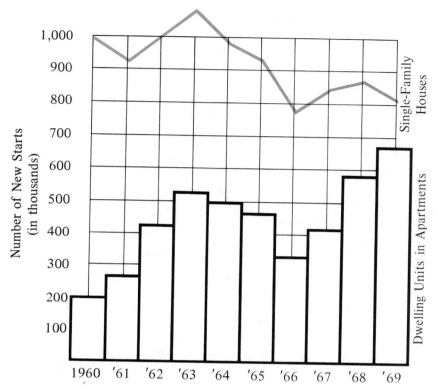

Figure 3.4   *New Housing Starts and New Available Rental Units in the United States from 1960 through 1969 (Source: U.S. Department of Commerce, Census Bureau)*

wish as well to indicate the magnitude in dollars or units of each subdivision, we can list these values on the chart. As long as simplicity is maintained, we should include as much information as possible in our pictorial presentation to best convey our intended message.

In Figure 3.5, two separate pie charts illustrate the income and expenditures for the U.S. budget dollar for the fiscal year 1970. Each pie chart is partitioned according to the amount of the total contributed by each of its components. The circular pie chart, whose central angles sum to 360 degrees, is assumed to contain 100 percent of the total. For the income pie chart of Figure 3.5, excise taxes, since they comprise 8 percent of the total, would be represented within a sector with a central angle of

$$\frac{360 \text{ degrees}}{100 \text{ percent}}(8 \text{ percent}) = 28.8 \text{ degrees}.$$

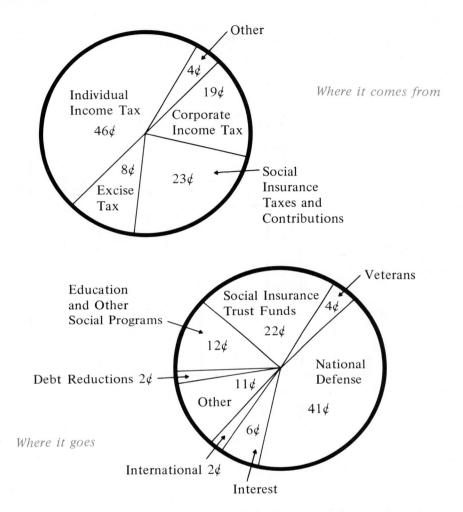

Figure 3.5   *U.S. Budget Dollar, Fiscal Year* 1970
(Source: Bureau of the Budget)

Each of the other components of income is represented within the circular pie chart for income in a similar manner such that the sectors representing all the components of income together cover the entire chart.

The main purpose of any chart is to give a quick, easy-to-read-and-interpret pictorial representation of data which is more difficult to obtain from a table or a complete listing of the data.

The type of chart or graphical presentation used and the format of its construction is incidental to its main purpose. A well-designed graphical presentation can effectively communicate the data's message in a language readily understood by almost everyone.

3.4   Numerical Descriptive Methods

Graphical methods are extremely useful in conveying a rapid general description of collected data and in presenting data. This statement supports, in many respects, the saying that a picture is worth a thousand words. There are, however, limitations to the use of graphical techniques for describing and analyzing data. For instance, suppose that we wish to discuss our data before a group of people and have no method of describing the data other than verbally. Unable to present the histogram visually, we would be forced to use other descriptive measures which would convey to the listeners a mental picture of the histogram. A second and not so obvious limitation of the histogram and other graphical techniques is that they are difficult to use for purposes of statistical inference. Presumably we use the sample histogram to make inferences about the shape and position of the population histogram which describes the population and is unknown to us. Our inference is based upon the correct assumption that some degree of similarity will exist between the two histograms, but we are then faced with the problem of measuring the degree of similarity. We know when two figures are identical, but this situation will not likely occur in practice. If the sample and population histograms differ, how can we measure the degree of difference or, expressing it positively, the degree of similarity? To be more specific, we might wonder about the degree of similarity between the histogram, Figure 3.2, and the frequency histogram for the population of price–earnings ratios from which the sample was drawn. Although these difficulties are not insurmountable, we prefer to seek other descriptive measures which readily lend themselves for use as predictors of the shape of the population frequency distribution.

The limitations of the graphical method of describing data can be overcome by the use of numerical descriptive measures. Thus we would like to use the sample data to calculate a set of numbers that will convey to the statistician a good mental picture of the frequency distribution and will be useful in making inferences concerning the population.

Definition

Numerical descriptive measures computed from the entire set of measurements within a population are called parameters; *those computed from sample measurements are called* statistics

---

3.5 Measures of Central Tendency

In constructing a mental picture of the frequency distribution for a set of measurements, we would likely envision a histogram similar to that shown in Figure 3.2 for the data on price–earnings ratios. One of the first descriptive measures of interest would be a measure of central tendency, that is, a measure of the center of the distribution. We note that the price–earnings data ranged from a low of 5.4 to a high of 28.6, the center of the histogram being located in the vicinity of 16.0. Let us now consider some definite rules for locating the center of a distribution of data.

One of the most common and useful measures of central tendency is the arithmetic average of a set of measurements. This is also often referred to as the arithmetic mean or, simply, the mean of a set of measurements.

Definition

The arithmetic mean of a set of n measurements $y_1, y_2, y_3, \ldots, y_n$ is equal to the sum of the measurements divided by n.

Recall that we are always concerned with both the sample and the population, each of which possesses a mean. In order to distinguish between the two, we shall use the symbol $\bar{y}$ for the mean of the sample and μ (the Greek letter mu) for the mean of the population. The mean of the sample data can be calculated using our definition,

---

$$\bar{y} = \frac{\sum\limits_{i=1}^{n} y_i}{n},$$

---

and can be used as a measure of central tendency for the sample.

Example 3.1 *Find the mean of the set of measurements 2, 9, 11, 5, 6:*

$$\bar{y} = \frac{\sum\limits_{i=1}^{n} y_i}{n} = \frac{2 + 9 + 11 + 5 + 6}{5} = 6.6.$$

Even more important, $\bar{y}$ will be employed as an estimator (predictor) of μ, the mean of the population which is unknown.

For example, the mean of the data, Table 3.1, is equal to

$$\bar{y} = \frac{\sum\limits_{i=1}^{n} y_i}{n} = \frac{400}{25} = 16.0.$$

Note that this falls approximately in the center of the set of measurements. The mean of the entire population of price–earnings ratios is unknown to us, but if we were to estimate its value, our estimate of μ would be 16.0.

A second measure of central tendency is the median.

Definition

The *median* of a set of n measurements $y_1, y_2, y_3, \ldots, y_n$ is defined to be the value of y that falls in the middle when the measurements are arranged in order of magnitude. If the number of measurements is even, we choose the median as the value of y halfway between the two middle measurements.

Example 3.2   *Consider the set of measurements*

$$9, 2, 7, 11, 14.$$

Arranging the measurements in order of magnitude, 2, 7, 9, 11, 14, we would choose 9 as the median.

Example 3.3   *Consider the set of measurements*

$$9, 2, 7, 11, 14, 6.$$

Arranged in order of magnitude, 2, 6, 7, 9, 11, 14, we would choose the median halfway between 7 and 9, which is 8.

Our rule for locating the median may seem a bit arbitrary for the case where we have an even number of measurements, but recall that we calculate the sample median either for descriptive purposes or as an estimator of the population median. If it is used for descriptive purposes, we may be as arbitrary as we please. If it is used as an estimator of the population median, "the proof of the pudding is in the eating." A rule for locating the sample median is poor or good depending upon whether it tends to give a poor or good estimate of the population median.

A third measure sometimes used as a measure of central tendency is the mode.

Definition

The mode of a set of n measurements $y_1, y_2, y_3, \ldots, y_n$ is defined to be the value of y occurring with the greatest frequency.

Example 3.4   *Consider the set of measurements*

$$9, 2, 7, 11, 14, 7, 2, 7.$$

The value 7 occurs three times, 2 occurs twice, and the others, once each. Thus 7 is the mode of our set of measurements.

The mode is generally not a good measure of central tendency, since our data may be grouped such that the greatest frequencies occur nowhere near the central area of the distribution. Also, it is possible that the mode is not unique if the greatest frequency occurs at more than one value. If the distribution is multimodal, knowing the modes tells us little about the central tendency of the distribution. However, in many instances the mode of a distribution is an important statistic. The purchasing manager for a clothing store is concerned about the modal sizes and modal styles before placing his orders while the median size or the arithmetic mean of sizes may be meaningless to him. Other areas of business where the mode is important, particularly in the study of consumer demands, should be evident to the reader. In summary, the mode should be considered only a descriptive statistic indicating the most likely outcome, often an important characteristic, but not, in general, an accurate measure of central location for a distribution of data.

Definition

A frequency distribution, for which values of the measured variable equidistant from the mean occur with equal frequency, is said to be symmetric.

We might mention that when the frequency distribution is unimodal and symmetric the mean, median, and mode are equal. When the distribution is not symmetric, we say it is skewed, and we have at least two different values for the mean, median, and mode.

The reader will note that we have not specified a symbol for the population median or mode. This is because most common methods of statistical inference suitable for an elementary course in statistics are based upon the sample mean rather than the median or mode. We say this, being wholly aware of the popularity of the median in the social sciences and the mode in demand analysis, but point out that they are used more often for descriptive purposes than for statistical inference. We also note that other measures of central tendency exist which have practical application in certain situations, but limitations of time and space forbid their discussion here. As we proceed in this text we shall use the sample mean, exclusively, as a measure of central tendency.

3.6   Measures of Variability

Having located the center of a distribution of data, our next step is to provide a measure of the variability or dispersion of the data. Consider the two distributions shown in Figure 3.6. Both distributions are located with a center at $y = 4$, but there is a vast difference in the variability of the measurements about the mean for the two distributions. The measurements in Figure 3.6(a) vary from 3 to 5; in Figure 3.6(b) they vary from 0 to 8. Variation is a very important characteristic of data. For

Figure 3.6   *Variability or Dispersion of Data*

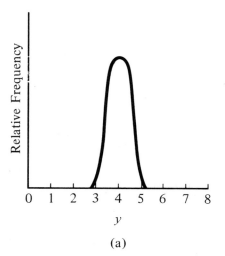

(a)

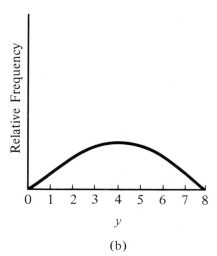

(b)

example, if we are manufacturing bolts, excessive variation in the bolt diameter would imply a high percentage of defective product. On the other hand, if we are using an examination to discriminate between good and poor accountants, we would be most unhappy if the examination always produced test grades with little variation, as this would make discrimination very difficult indeed. In addition to the practical importance of variation in data, it is obvious that a measure of this characteristic is necessary to the construction of the mental image of the frequency distribution. Numerous measures of variability exist, and we shall discuss a few of the most important.

The simplest measure of variation is the range.

Definition

The range of a set of n measurements $y_1, y_2, y_3, \ldots, y_n$ is defined to be the difference between the largest and smallest measurement.

For our price–earnings ratios, Table 3.1, we note that the measurements varied from 5.4 to 28.6. Hence the range is equal to $(28.6 - 5.4) = 23.2$.

Unfortunately, the range is not completely satisfactory as a measure of variation. Consider the two distributions of Figure 3.7. Both distributions have the same range, but the data of Figure 3.7(b) are more variable than the data of Figure

Figure 3.7   *Distribution with Equal Ranges and Unequal Variability*

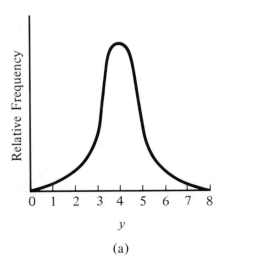

(a)

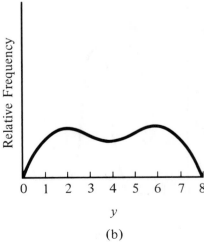

(b)

3.7(a). To overcome this limitation of the range, we introduce quartiles and per-centiles Remember that if we specify an interval along the *y*-axis of our histogram, the percentage of area under the histogram lying above the interval is equal to the percentage of the total number of measurements falling in that interval. Since the median is the middle measurement when the data are arranged in order of magnitude, the median would be the value of *y* such that half the area of the histogram would lie to its left, half to the right. Similarly, we might define quartiles as values of *y* that divide the area of the histogram into quarters.

Definition

Let $y_1, y_2, \ldots, y_n$ be a set of n measurements arranged in order of magnitude. The lower quartile is a value of y that exceeds 1/4 of the measurements and is less than the remaining 3/4. The second quartile is the median. The upper quartile (third quartile) is a value of y that exceeds 3/4 of the measurements and is less than 1/4.

Locating the lower quartile on a histogram, Figure 3.8, we note that 1/4 of the area lies to the left of the lower quartile, 3/4 to the right. The upper quartile is the value of *y* such that 3/4 of the area lies to the left, 1/4 to the right.

For some applications, it is preferable to use percentiles.

Figure 3.8   *Location of Quartiles*

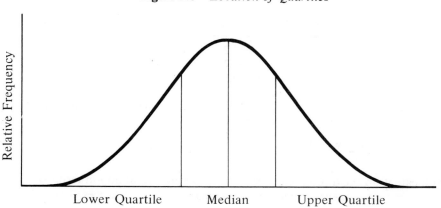

Definition

Let $y_1, y_2, \ldots, y_n$ be a set of n measurements arranged in order of magnitude. The pth *percentile* is a value of y such that at most p percent of the measurements are less than the value y and at most $(100 - p)$ percent are greater.

For example, the 90th percentile for a set of data would be a value of y that exceeds 90 percent of the measurements and is less than 10 percent. Just as in the case of quartiles, 90 percent of the area of the histogram would lie to the left of the 90th percentile.

The range possesses simplicity in that it can be expressed as a single number. Quartiles and percentiles, on the other hand, are more sensitive measures of variability, but several numbers must be given to provide an adequate description. Can we find a measure of variability expressible as a single number but more sensitive than the range?

Consider, as an example, the set of measurements 5, 7, 1, 2, 4. We can depict these data graphically, as in Figure 3.9, by showing the measurements as dots falling along the y-axis. Figure 3.9 is called a dot diagram.

Calculating the mean as the measure of central tendency, we obtain

$$\bar{y} = \frac{\sum\limits_{i=1}^{n} y_i}{n} = \frac{19}{5} = 3.8$$

Table 3.4   *Computation of* $\sum\limits_{i=1}^{n} (y_i - \bar{y})^2$

y_i	$y_i - \bar{y}$	$(y_i - \bar{y})^2$	y^2
5	1.2	1.44	25
7	3.2	10.24	49
1	−2.8	7.84	1
2	−1.8	3.24	4
4	.2	.04	16
$\sum\limits_{i=1}^{5} y_i = 19$	0	22.80	95

and locate it on the dot diagram. We can now view variability in terms of distance between each dot (measurement) and the mean, $\bar{y}$. If the distances are large, we can say that the data are more variable than if the distances are small. Being more explicit, we shall define the deviation of a measurement from its mean to be the

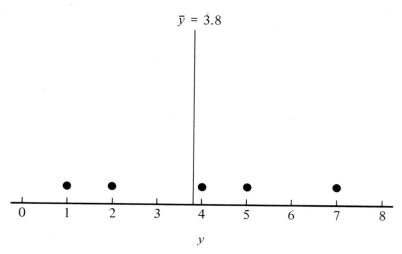

Figure 3.9 *Dot Diagram*

quantity $(y_i - \bar{y})$. Note that measurements to the right of the mean represent positive deviations, and those to the left, negative deviations. The values of y and the deviations for our example are shown in the first and second columns of Table 3.4.

If we now agree that deviations contain information on variation, our next step is to construct a formula based upon the deviations which will provide a good measure of variation. As a first possibility we might choose the average of the deviations. Unfortunately, this will not work because some of the deviations are positive, some are negative, and the sum is actually equal to zero. This can easily be shown using our summation theorems (see Chapter 2).

Given n measurements $y_1, y_2, \ldots, y_n$,

$$\sum_{i=1}^{n} (y_i - \bar{y}) = \sum_{i=1}^{n} y_i - \sum_{i=1}^{n} \bar{y}$$

$$= \sum_{i=1}^{n} y_i - n\bar{y}$$

$$= \sum_{i=1}^{n} y_i - n\frac{\sum_{i=1}^{n} y_i}{n}$$

$$= \sum_{i=1}^{n} y_i - \sum_{i=1}^{n} y_i = 0.$$

Note that the deviations, the second column of Table 3.4, sum to zero.

The reader will readily observe an easy solution to this problem. Why not calculate the average of the absolute values of the deviations? This method has, in fact, been employed as a measure of variability, but it tends to be unsatisfactory for purposes of statistical inference. We prefer overcoming the difficulty caused by the sign of the deviations by working with the sum of their squares,

$$\sum_{i=1}^{n} (y_i - \bar{y})^2.$$

For a fixed number of measurements, when this quantity is large, the data will be more variable than when it is small.

Definition

The *variance* of a *population* of N measurements $y_1, y_2, \ldots, y_N$ is defined to be the average of the square of the deviations of the measurements about their mean, μ. The population variance is denoted by σ^2 (σ is the lowercase Greek letter sigma), where

$$\sigma^2 = \sum_{i=1}^{N} \frac{(y_i - \mu)^2}{N}.$$

Typically, we do not have all the population measurements available and must be satisfied with a set of sample measurements selected from the population.

Definition

The *variance* of a set of n *sample* measurements $y_1, y_2, \ldots, y_n$ is defined to be the sum of the squared deviations of the measurements about their mean, $\bar{y}$, divided by $(n-1)$. The sample variance is denoted by s^2, where

$$s^2 = \sum_{i=1}^{n} \frac{(y_i - \bar{y})^2}{n-1}.$$

For example, we may calculate the variance for the set of $n = 5$ sample measurements presented in Table 3.4. The square of the deviation of each measurement is recorded in the third column of Table 3.4. Adding, we obtain

$$\sum_{i=1}^{5} (y_i - \bar{y})^2 = 22.80.$$

The sample variance would equal

$$s^2 = \sum_{i=1}^{n} \frac{(y_i - \bar{y})^2}{n-1} = \frac{22.80}{4} = 5.70.$$

The reader may wonder about the apparent inconsistency in definition of the population and sample variances. Recall that we use the sample mean, $\bar{y}$, as an estimator of the population mean, μ. Although it was not specifically stated, we wished to convey the impression that the sample mean provides good estimates of μ. In the same vein, it might seem reasonable to assume that

$$s'^2 = \sum_{i=1}^{n} \frac{(y - \bar{y})^2}{n}$$

would provide a good estimate of the population variance, σ^2, based upon a set of sample measurements. However. it can be shown that. for small samples (n small), s'^2 tends to underestimate σ^2, and the sample variance s^2 provides better estimates of σ^2 than does s'^2. Note that s^2 and s'^2 differ only in the denominator where n is replaced by $(n - 1)$ and that when n is large, s'^2 and s^2 will be approximately equal. In later chapters we shall have numerous occasions for use of an estimator of the population variance, σ^2. In all our calculations, we shall use s^2 rather than s'^2.

At this point the reader will be understandably disappointed with the practical significance attached to variance as a measure of variability. Large variances imply a large amount of variation, but this statement only permits comparison of several sets of data. When we attempt to say something specific concerning a single set of data, we are at a loss. For example, what can be said about the variability of a set of data with a variance equal to 100? The question cannot be answered with the facts at hand. We shall remedy this situation by introducing a new definition, and, in Section 3.7, a theorem and a rule.

Definition

The *standard deviation* of a set of n sample measurements $y_1, y_2, y_3, \ldots, y_n$ is equal to the positive square root of the variance.

Analogous to the above definition, the population standard deviation, σ, is equal to the positive square root of the population variance, σ^2.

The variance is measured in terms of the square of the original units of measurement. If the original measurements were in inches, the variance would be expressed in square inches. Taking the square root of the variance, we obtain the standard deviation, which, most happily, returns our measure of variability to the original units of measurement. The sample standard deviation is

$$s = \sqrt{s^2} = \sqrt{\frac{\sum\limits_{i=1}^{n} (y_i - \bar{y})^2}{n - 1}},$$

and the population standard deviation is σ. As an aid for remembering, note that the symbol s is the first letter in the word "standard."

Having defined the standard deviation, we might wonder why we bothered to define the variance in the first place. Actually, both the variance and the standard deviation play an important role in statistics, a fact that the reader must accept on faith at this stage of our discussion.

3.7   On the Practical Significance of the Standard Deviation

We now introduce an interesting and useful theorem developed by the Russian mathematician, Tchebysheff. Proof of the theorem is not difficult, but we omit it from our discussion.

Tchebysheff's Theorem

Given a number k greater than or equal to 1 and a set of n measurements $y_1, y_2, \ldots, y_n$, at least $(1 - 1/k^2)$ of the measurements will lie within k standard deviations of their mean.

Tchebysheff's theorem applies to any set of measurements, and for purposes of illustration we could refer to either the sample or the population. We shall use the notation appropriate for populations, but the reader should realize that we could just as easily use the mean and standard deviation for the sample.

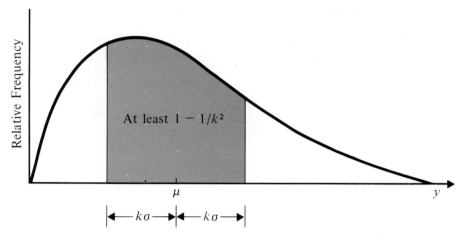

Figure 3.10   *Illustrating Tchebysheff's Theorem*

The idea involved in Tchebysheff's theorem is illustrated in Figure 3.10. An interval is constructed by measuring a distance of $k\sigma$ on either side of the mean, μ. Note that the theorem is true for any number we wish to choose for k as long as it is greater than or equal to 1. Then, computing the fraction $1 - 1/k^2$, we see that Tchebysheff's theorem states that at least that fraction of the total number, n, of measurements will lie in the constructed interval.

Let us choose a few numerical values for k and compute $1 - 1/k^2$ (see Table 3.5). When $k = 1$, the theorem states that at least $1 - 1/(1)^2 = 0$ of the measurements

Table 3.5   *Illustrative Values of $1 - 1/k^2$*

k	$1 - 1/k^2$
1	0
2	3/4
3	8/9

lie in the interval $\mu - \sigma$ to $\mu + \sigma$, a most unhelpful and uninformative result. However, when $k = 2$, we observe that at least $1 - 1/(2)^2 = 3/4$ of the measurements will lie in the interval $\mu - 2\sigma$ to $\mu + 2\sigma$. At least 8/9 of the measurements will lie within three standard deviations of the mean.

To apply Tchebysheff's theorem to describe sample data, it is proper to use s' rather than s (s', defined in Section 3.6, is a quantity slightly smaller than s) for use in constructing intervals about the mean. We shall ignore this minute point because it is of no practical importance. The theorem always holds true when s is used instead of s'. Second, s and s' will be nearly equal when n is large (and satisfactory for descriptive purposes when n is as small as 10). Finally, note that we are interested primarily in describing populations, not samples. Examples describing small sets of simple measurements are presented solely to demonstrate the use of Tchebysheff's theorem.

Example 3.5   *The mean and variance of a sample of $n = 25$ measurements are 75 and 100, respectively. Use Tchebysheff's theorem to describe the distribution of measurements.*

Solution   *We are given $\bar{y} = 75$ and $s^2 = 100$. The standard deviation is $s = \sqrt{100} = 10$. The distribution of measurements is centered about $\bar{y} = 75$, and Tchebysheff's theorem states:*

1. *At least 3/4 of the 25 measurements lie in the interval $\bar{y} \pm 2s = 75 \pm 2(10)$, that is, 55 to 95.*

2. *At least 8/9 of the measurements lie in the interval $\bar{y} \pm 3s = 75 \pm 3(10)$, that is, 45 to 105.*

We emphasize the "at least" in Tchebysheff's theorem because the theorem is very conservative, applying to *any* distribution of measurements. In most situations, the fraction of measurements falling in the specified interval will exceed $1 - 1/k^2$.

We now state a rule that describes accurately the variability of a bell-shaped distribution and describes reasonably well the variability of other mound-shaped distributions of data. The frequent occurrence of mound-shaped and bell-shaped distributions of data in nature and hence the applicability of our rule leads us to call it the empirical rule

The Empirical Rule

Given a distribution of measurements that is approximately bell-shaped (see Figure 3.11), the interval

1. *$\mu \pm \sigma$ will contain approximately 68 percent of the measurements.*
2. *$\mu \pm 2\sigma$ will contain approximately 95 percent of the measurements.*
3. *$\mu \pm 3\sigma$ will contain approximately 99.7 percent of the measurements.*

The bell-shaped distribution, Figure 3.11, is commonly known as the normal distribution and will be discussed in detail in Chapter 7. The point we wish to make here is that the empirical rule is extremely useful and provides an excellent description of variation for many types of data.

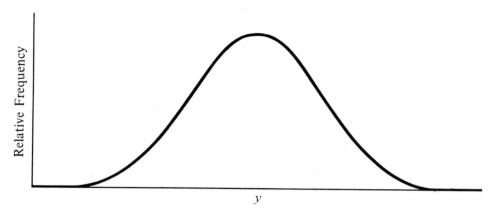

Figure 3.11   *Normal Distribution*

Example 3.6   *A time study was conducted to determine the length of time necessary to perform a specified operation in a manufacturing plant. The length of time necessary to complete the operation was measured for each of n = 40 workmen. The mean and standard deviation were found to equal 12.8 and 1.7, respectively. To describe the data, we calculate the intervals*

$$\bar{y} \pm s = 12.8 \pm 1.7, \text{ or } 11.1 \text{ to } 14.5,$$

$$\bar{y} \pm 2s = 12.8 \pm 2(1.7), \text{ or } 9.4 \text{ to } 16.2,$$

$$\bar{y} \pm 3s = 12.8 \pm 3(1.7), \text{ or } 7.7 \text{ to } 17.9$$

According to the empirical rule, we would expect approximately 68 percent of the measurements to fall in the interval 11.1 to 14.5, 95 percent in the interval 9.4 to 16.2, and 99.7 percent in the interval 7.7 to 17.9.

If we doubt that the distribution of measurements is mound-shaped or wish, for some other reasons, to be conservative, we can apply Tchebysheff's theorem and be absolutely certain of our statements. Tchebysheff's theorem would tell us that at least 3/4 of the measurements fell in the interval 9.4 to 16.2 and at least 8/9 in the interval 7.7 to 17.9.

Before leaving this topic we might wonder how well the empirical rule applies to the price–earnings ratios of Table 3.1. We will show, in Section 3.8, that the mean and standard deviation for the $n = 25$ measurements is $\bar{y} = 16.0$ and $s = 5.6$. The appropriate intervals were calculated and the number of measurements falling in each interval recorded. The results are shown in Table 3.6 with k in the first column and the interval, $\bar{y} \pm ks$, in the second column, using $\bar{y} = 16.0$ and

$s = 5.6$. The frequency or number of measurements falling in each interval is given in the third column and the relative frequency in the fourth column.

Table 3.6   *Frequency of Measurements Lying Within k Standard Deviations; Data of Table 3.1*

k	INTERVAL, $\bar{y} \pm ks$	FREQUENCY IN INTERVAL	RELATIVE FREQUENCY
1	10.4–21.6	16	.64
2	4.8–27.2	24	.96
3	0–32.8	25	1.0

3.8   A Short Method for Calculating the Variance

The calculation of the variance and standard deviation of a set of measurements is no small task regardless of the method employed, but it is particularly tedious if one proceeds, according to the definition, by calculating each deviation individually as shown in Table 3.4. We shall use the data of Table 3.4 to illustrate a

Table 3.7   *Table for Simplified Calculations of $\sum\limits_{i=1}^{n} (y_i - \bar{y})^2$*

	y_i	y_i^2
	5	25
	7	49
	1	1
	2	4
	4	16
Total	19	95

shorter method of calculation. The tabulations are presented in Table 3.7 in two columns, the first containing the individual measurements and the second containing the squares of the measurements. We now calculate

$$\sum_{i=1}^{n} y_i^2 - \frac{\left(\sum_{i=1}^{n} y_i\right)^2}{n} = 95 - \frac{(19)^2}{5}$$

$$= 95 - \frac{361}{5} = 95 - 72.2$$

$$= 22.8;$$

notice that it is exactly equal to the sum of squares of the deviations, $\sum_{i=1}^{n} (y_i - \bar{y})^2$, given in the third column of Table 3.4.

This is no accident. We will show that the sum of squares of the deviations is always equal to

$$\sum_{i=1}^{n} (y_i - \bar{y})^2 = \sum_{i=1}^{n} y_i^2 - \frac{\left(\sum_{i=1}^{n} y_i\right)^2}{n}.$$

The proof is obtained by using the summation theorems, Chapter 2:

$$\sum_{i=1}^{n} (y_i - \bar{y})^2 = \sum_{i=1}^{n} (y_i^2 - 2\bar{y}y_i + \bar{y}^2)$$

$$= \sum_{i=1}^{n} y_i^2 - 2\bar{y} \sum_{i=1}^{n} y_i + \sum_{i=1}^{n} \bar{y}^2$$

$$= \sum_{i=1}^{n} y_i^2 - \frac{2\sum y_i}{n} \sum y_i + n\bar{y}^2$$

$$= \sum_{i=1}^{n} y_i^2 - \frac{2}{n}(\sum y_i)^2 + n\left(\frac{\sum_{i=1}^{n} y_i}{n}\right)^2$$

or

$$\sum_{i=1}^{n} (y_i - \bar{y})^2 = \sum_{i=1}^{n} y_i^2 - \frac{\left(\sum_{i=1}^{n} y_i\right)^2}{n}.$$

We call this formula the shortcut method of calculating the sums of squares of deviations needed in the formulas for the variance and standard deviation. Comparatively speaking, it is short because it eliminates all the subtractions required for calculating the individual deviations. A second and not so obvious advantage is that it tends to give better computational accuracy than the method utilizing the deviations. The beginning statistics student frequently finds the variance that he has calculated at odds with the answer in the text. This is usually caused by rounding off decimal numbers in the computations. We suggest that rounding off be held at a minimum, since it may seriously affect the result of computation of the variance. A third advantage is that the shortcut method is especially suitable for use on electric desk calculators, some of which accumulate

$$\sum_{i=1}^{n} y_i \quad \text{and} \quad \sum_{i=1}^{n} y_i^2$$

simultaneously.

Before leaving this topic, we shall calculate the standard deviation for the $n = 25$ price–earnings ratios, Table 3.1. The student may verify the following:

$$\sum_{i=1}^{n} y_i = 400,$$

$$\sum_{i=1}^{n} y_i^2 = 7,154.02.$$

Using the shortcut formula,

$$\sum_{i=1}^{n} (y - \bar{y})^2 = \sum_{i=1}^{n} y_i^2 - \frac{\left(\sum_{i=1}^{n} y_i \right)^2}{n}$$

$$= 7,154.02 - \frac{(400)^2}{25} = 7,154.02 - 6,400$$

$$= 754.02.$$

It follows that the standard deviation is

$$s = \sqrt{\frac{\sum_{i=1}^{n} (y_i - \bar{y})^2}{n-1}} = \sqrt{\frac{754.02}{24}} = 5.6.$$

Example 3.7   *Calculate $\bar{y}$ and s for the measurements 85, 70, 60, 90, and 81.*

Solution

y_i	y_i^2
85	7,225
70	4,900
60	3,600
90	8,100
81	6,561
386	30,386

$$\bar{y} = \frac{386}{5} = 77.2 .$$

$$\sum_{i=1}^{n} (y_i - \bar{y})^2 = \sum_{i=1}^{n} y_i^2 - \frac{\left(\sum_{i=1}^{n} y_i\right)^2}{n}$$

$$= 30,386 - \frac{(386)^2}{5}$$

$$= 30,386 - 29,799.2$$

$$= 586.8.$$

Thus

$$s = \sqrt{\frac{\sum_{i=1}^{n} (y_i - \bar{y})^2}{n-1}} = \sqrt{\frac{586.8}{4}} = \sqrt{146.7}$$

$$= 12.1.$$

3.9   Estimating the Mean and Variance for Grouped Data

Often the only data available for analysis are listed in the form of a frequency histogram. Company reports often list data only in terms of class frequencies; governmental and news media sources usually use some type of a bar chart to display pertinent data. In such cases we may not know the exact values of the measurements falling within the class intervals. When this situation occurs, there is no way to compute the exact values of the sample mean and variance.

    There is, however, a method for approximating the mean, $\bar{y}$, and the variance, s^2, when only grouped data are available. This method is based upon the assumption that the midpoint of each class in the grouped frequency classification is approximately equal to the arithmetic mean of the measurements contained within that class. The midpoint of a particular class i will be denoted by the symbol m_i. Now, suppose that the midpoints do actually equal the mean of the measurements within their respective classes. Then, for a particular class i, if we multiply m_i by f_i, the frequency within class i, we obtain the total of the measurements within class i. Summing the class totals then gives us the sum total of all measurements contained within the frequency distribution and $\bar{y}$ can be found by taking this sum total over the total number of measurements, n, in the usual manner. Naturally, the accuracy of the approximated mean obtained by using class midpoints depends heavily on the degree to which the midpoints accurately reflect the arithmetic mean of the measurements contained within each respective class. Usually, such approximations are quite reliable, especially when the class frequencies, f_i, are of sufficient size to guarantee a rather even "coverage" of measurements over each class. For approximating the variance s^2 when only grouped data are available, one follows a procedure that generalizes the shortcut formula for computation of s^2 introduced in Section 3.8.

    If data are grouped according to frequency of occurrence in each of k nonoverlapping classes, then the mean $\bar{y}$ and variance s^2 of the measurements contained within the grouping are approximated by, respectively,

$$\bar{y} \approx \frac{\sum\limits_{i=1}^{k} f_i m_i}{n}$$

and

$$s^2 \approx \frac{\sum\limits_{i=1}^{k} f_i m_i^2 - \left(\sum\limits_{i=1}^{k} f_i m_i\right)^2 \Big/ n}{n-1},$$

where m_i is the midpoint and f_i is the frequency of measurements within class i.

(*Note:* The symbol $\approx$ means "is approximately equal to.")

    Table 3.8 summarizes the computations necessary to $\bar{y}$ and s^2 from the frequency distribution of $n = 25$ price–earnings ratios for 25 common stocks shown

Table 3.8 *Class Frequencies and Class Midpoints for the*
25 Price–Earnings Ratios Listed in Table 3.2

CLASS i	CLASS BOUNDARIES	f_i	m_i	$f_i m_i$	$f_i m_i^2$
1	5.00–8.99	3	7	21	147
2	9.00–12.99	5	11	55	605
3	13.00–16.99	7	15	105	1,575
4	17.00–20.99	6	19	114	2,166
5	21.00–24.99	3	23	69	1,587
6	25.00–28.99	1	27	27	729
	Totals	25		391	6,809

in Table 3.2. The computations required by the grouped data formulas given above are greatly simplified when the data are organized as in Table 3.8. Using these formulas, the mean can be approximated from the grouped data as

$$\bar{y} \approx \frac{\sum_{i=1}^{6} f_i m_i}{25} = \frac{391}{25} = 15.64,$$

while the approximation to the variance of the measurements is found by computing

$$s^2 \approx \frac{\sum_{i=1}^{6} f_i m_i^2 - \left(\sum_{i=1}^{6} f_i m_i\right)^2 \Big/ 25}{24}$$

$$= \frac{6,809 - (391)^2/25}{24}$$

$$= \frac{693.76}{24}$$

$$= 28.91.$$

Since the approximation to the variance of the $n = 25$ price–earnings ratios is 28.91, the approximate standard deviation is

$$s \approx \sqrt{28.91} = 5.377.$$

In Section 3.8 we found the actual mean and standard deviation of the ungrouped sample of the $n = 25$ price–earnings ratios to be

$$\bar{y} = 16 \qquad \text{and} \qquad s = 5.6,$$

respectively. Thus the approximations obtained from the grouped frequency distribution of the price–earnings ratios (Table 3.2) appear to be satisfactory approximations to the assumed obtainable values, $\bar{y}$ and s.

Although it was mentioned within Section 3.2 that the classes should be of equal width, the classes do not need be of equal width to apply the grouped data mean and variance formulas. All that need be assumed is that the class midpoints are, respectively, approximately equal to the arithmetic mean of the measurements within the classes. The grouped data procedures are not applicable, however, in the case where one or more of the classes is open-ended. This is clearly evident as, in such cases, it becomes impossible to find class midpoints for the open-ended classes.

3.10   Linear Transformations of Data

Often when we wish to make comparisons between two or more sets of data, some of the data sets are listed in a measuring system different from the others. A union official may wish to compare the retirement incomes of the employees of two automobile manufacturing plants, one in Detroit and one in Paris. A buyer is interested in comparing the gasoline economy of a British car, rated in kilometers per imperial gallon, to the economy of an American car, rated in miles per gallon. In each case comparisons cannot be made unless we transform all the sets of data to a common scale of measure. What we must do is find the mathematical relationship between a reference set of data and all the other sets of data. Then, applying the known mathematical relationship between the various data sets, we transform all the other sets of data to the scale of measure of the reference set.

If we are then interested in computing the mean and variance or standard deviation in a common scale of measurement as numerical descriptive measures for each set of data, it is not necessary that we first transform each measurement to the common scale. For instance, if the union official mentioned above samples the retirement incomes of 50 Parisian automobile manufacturing employees, it is not necessary that he convert each of the 50 incomes from units of francs to dollar units before computing the numerical descriptive measures in dollar units. Knowing the mean, variance, and standard deviation in francs, he can convert them to their equivalent values in units of dollars by applying the following theorem, which we shall call the coding theorem. Its proof will be omitted but can easily be constructed from the definitions given earlier for the mean and variance.

Theorem 3.1 The Coding Theorem

Suppose that $\bar{y}$ and s_y^2 are the mean and variance of a set of n measurements $y_1, y_2, \ldots, y_n$. If we transform each measurement y_i by the linear transformation $x_i = a + by_i$, where a and b are any real numbers, then the mean of the transformed data is

$$\bar{x} = a + b\bar{y},$$

and the transformed variance is

$$s_x^2 = b^2 s_y^2.$$

Similarly, the transformed standard deviation would be

$$s_x = |b| s_y.$$

We have phrased the coding theorem in terms of the sample mean and variance. However, the theorem applies as well for the transformed population mean and variance.

Example 3.8 *In* 1973 *the employees of the Volkswagen assembly plant in Munich earned an average salary of* 15,200 *marks with a standard deviation of* 1,000 *marks. To compare these West German wages to those of American automobile factory workers, we would have to transform the mean and standard deviation from marks to dollars. At the current rate of exchange,* 1 *mark =* .39 *dollar. Thus*

$$\bar{x}(dollars) = .39\bar{y}(marks)$$
$$= .39(15,200)$$
$$= 5,928$$

and

$$s_x(dollars) = .39 s_y(marks)$$
$$= .39(1,000)$$
$$= 390.$$

Since the rate of exchange relating West German marks to American dollars involves only a multiplicative constant, the addition constant from our theorem is assumed to be zero. Likewise, if our data are coded only by adding a constant to each measurement, the multiplicative constant becomes 1. In the latter case, the variance of the transformed data remains unchanged.

Example 3.9   *The daily high temperatures from Stockholm, Sweden, for the month of April had a mean of 10 degrees centigrade and a variance of 50 degrees squared centigrade. For comparative purposes we must convert to Fahrenheit degrees by the following transformation: Fahrenheit degrees = 32 + (9/5)centigrade degrees. Applying the coding theorem,*

$$\bar{x}(Fahrenheit) = 32 + (9/5) \cdot 10$$
$$= 50 \; degrees \; Fahrenheit$$

and

$$s_x^2(Fahrenheit) = (9/5)^2 \cdot 50$$
$$= 162 \; degrees \; Fahrenheit \; squared.$$

3.11   Summary

The objective of a statistical study is to make inferences about a characteristic of a population based upon information contained in a sample. Since populations are sets of data, we first need to consider ways to phrase an inference about a set of measurements. This latter point constituted the objective of our study in Chapter 3.

Methods for describing sets of measurements fall into one of two categories, graphical methods and numerical methods. The relative frequency histogram is an extremely useful graphical method for characterizing a set of measurements. Other methods are useful as long as they provide a complete, easy-to-read-and-interpret summary of the data. Numerical descriptive measures are numbers that attempt to create a mental image of the frequency distribution. We have restricted the discussion to measures of central tendency and variation, the most useful of which are the mean and standard deviation. Although the mode is not generally a measure of central tendency, its importance in characterizing demand levels should not be ignored by the business statistician. While the mean possesses intuitive significance, the standard deviation is significant only when used in conjunction with Tchebysheff's theorem and the empirical rule. The objective of sampling is the description of the population from which the sample was obtained. This is accomplished by using the sample mean, $\bar{y}$, and the statistic, s^2, as estimators of the population mean μ and the variance σ^2.

Many descriptive methods and numerical measures have been presented in this chapter, but these constitute only a small percentage of those which might have been discussed. In addition, many special computational techniques usually found in elementary texts have been omitted. This choice was necessitated by the limited time available in an elementary course and because the advent and common use of electronic computers have minimized the importance of special computational formulas. But, more important, the inclusion of such techniques would tend to detract from and obscure the main objective of modern statistics and this text— statistical inference.

Exercises

1. Conduct the following experiment: Toss a coin 10 times and record y, the number of heads observed. Repeat this process $n = 50$ times, thus providing 50 values of y. Construct a relative frequency histogram for these measurements.

2. The following table shows the sales of a small manufacturing plant over the years 1960 to 1973.

YEAR	DOMESTIC SALES	FOREIGN SALES	TOTAL SALES
1960	$46,000	$14,000	$60,000
1961	52,500	13,500	66,000
1962	67,000	18,000	85,000
1963	88,500	21,500	110,000
1964	107,000	33,000	140,000
1965	140,000	35,000	175,000
1966	142,000	28,000	170,000
1967	156,000	34,000	190,000
1968	178,500	36,500	215,000
1969	186,000	39,000	225,000
1970	190,000	41,000	231,000
1971	189,000	40,000	229,000
1972	192,000	39,000	231,000
1973	195,000	43,000	238,000

    Construct a bar chart like the one in Figure 3.3 to depict the above sales distribution.

3. The following distribution shows the number of families in a small town according to their annual family incomes:

ANNUAL FAMILY INCOME	NUMBER
Under $5,000	2,400
5,000–9,999	5,900
10,000–19,999	1,000
20,000 or over	700

Construct a pie chart showing the percentage of the town's families belonging to each annual family income class.

4. A manufacturer of automatic washers has obtained data on 1,000 of their 1973 automatic washers relating to the time of ownership until the first necessary major repair. The data range from 0 weeks to 113 weeks. Give the class boundaries if these data are to be grouped into 10 classes.

5. The following measurements represent the number of defective transistors found in 25 lots of 1,000 transistors shipped by an overseas supplier:

42	28	51	26	33
43	32	34	35	32
34	35	35	31	27
45	31	29	37	46
34	37	39	54	38

Construct a relative frequency histogram for these data.

6. The following distribution shows the number of shareholders in the Python Corporation according to the number of shares owned.

NO. SHARES	NO. SHAREHOLDERS
Under 1,000	486
1,000–1,999	372
2,000–2,999	210
3,000–3,999	117
4,000–4,999	43
5,000–5,999	27
6,000 and over	13

(a) Construct a relative frequency histogram for these data.
(b) Construct a bar chart to depict these data.

7. Before deciding whether or not to hire another checkout clerk, the manager of a department store gathered data on the amount of waiting time before service of 250 customers. The waiting times ranged from 0 minutes to 19.75 minutes. If the manager wants to use a five-class table for representation of the data, give appropriate class boundaries.

8. The following $n = 6$ measurements represent the number of workdays missed due to illness during the past year by six employees of the Mallon Company:

$$9, 3, 2, 7, 4, 5.$$

Calculate $\bar{y}, s^2$, and s.

9. The following $n = 7$ measurements represent the gain or loss in the daily closing price of a security for seven consecutive market days:

$$-4, -5, -1, 0, 3, 2, -2.$$

Calculate $\bar{y}, s^2$, and s.

10. Calculate $\bar{y}, s^2$, and s for the data in Exercise 1.

11. Calculate $\bar{y}, s^2$, and s for the data in Exercise 5.

12. Refer to the histogram constructed in Exercise 1 and find the fraction of measurements lying in the interval $\bar{y} \pm 2s$. (Use the results of Exercise 10.) Are the results consistent with Tchebysheff's theorem? Is the frequency histogram of Exercise 1 relatively mound-shaped? Does the empirical rule adequately describe the variability of the data in Exercise 1?

13. Repeat the instructions of Exercise 12 using the interval $\bar{y} \pm s$.

14. Refer to the data in Exercise 5. Find the fraction of measurements falling in the intervals $\bar{y} \pm s$ and $\bar{y} \pm 2s$. Do these results agree with Tchebysheff's theorem and the empirical rule?

15. The following five measurements represent the amount of milk, in ounces, discharged by an automatic milk dispenser: 7.1, 7.2, 7.0, 7.3, 7.0. Calculate $\bar{y}, s^2$, and s.

16. Refer to Exercise 15. Calculate the fraction of measurements in the intervals $\bar{y} \pm s$ and $\bar{y} \pm 2s$. Do these results agree with Tchebysheff's theorem? Why is the empirical rule inappropriate for describing the variability of these data?

17. Why do statisticians prefer the use of s^2 rather than s'^2 in estimating a population variance σ^2?

18. The gross monthly incomes for 400 employees from the Assembly Company were found to have a mean and variance equal to $600 and $4,900, respectively. Use Tchebysheff's theorem to describe the variability of the incomes. If the distribution of incomes were mound-shaped, approximately how many of the incomes would fall in the interval $530 to $670? Approximately how many incomes would be expected to exceed $740?

19. Television commercials on a certain television station average 35 seconds in length of air time with a standard deviation of 5 seconds. If the distribution of air time for commercials on the television station is mound-shaped, approximately what fraction of total commercials would last from 30 to 40 seconds?

20. A study has shown that television commercials lasting longer than 40 seconds are excessively long and ineffective in communicating the intended message. What fraction (approximately) of the television commercials of the television station described in Exercise 19 could be considered to be excessively long?

21. A florist has recorded the following number of customers for each of 30 consecutive workdays:

72	89	78	87	86
40	73	83	77	82
70	60	63	56	59
72	44	28	68	69
98	52	68	74	53
84	81	77	73	71

Construct a relative frequency histogram for the number of customers per day.

22. (a) Compute $\bar{y}, s^2$, and s for the data in Exercise 21.
(b) Find the lower quartile, the upper quartile, and the 90th percentile of the distribution formed by the data in Exercise 21.

23. Refer to Exercise 22. Find the number of scores in the intervals $\bar{y} \pm s$ and $\bar{y} \pm 2s$ and compare with Tchebysheff's theorem and the empirical rule.

24. Find the range for the data in Exercise 21. Find the ratio of the range to s. If one possessed a large amount of data having a bell-shaped distribution, the range would be expected to equal how many standard deviations? (Note that this provides a rough check for the computation of s.)

25. Find the ratio of the range to s for the data in Exercise 5.

26. The rule of thumb found in Exercise 24 for a large amount of data (more than 25 measurements) can be extended to smaller amounts of data obtained in sampling from a bell-shaped distribution. Thus the calculated s should not be far different from range divided by the appropriate ratio found in the following table:

No. measurements	5	10	25
Expected ratio of range to s	2.5	3	4

(a) For the data in Exercise 5, estimate s as suggested. Compare this estimate with the calculated s.
(b) For the data in Exercise 21, estimate s as suggested. Compare this estimate with the calculated s.

27. A machining operation produces bolts with an average diameter of .51 inch and a standard deviation of .01 inch. If the distribution of bolt diameters is bell-shaped (approximately normal), what fraction of total production would possess diameters falling in the interval .49 to .53 inch?

28. Refer to Exercise 27. Suppose that the bolt specifications required a diameter equal to $.5 \pm .02$ inch. Bolts not satisfying this requirement are considered to be defective. If the machining operation functioned as described in Exercise 27, what fraction of total production would result in defective bolts?

29. From the following data, a student calculated s to be .263. On what grounds might we doubt his accuracy? What is the correct value (nearest hundredths)?

17.2	17.1	17.0	17.1	16.9
17.0	17.1	17.0	17.3	17.2
17.1	17.0	17.1	16.9	17.0
17.1	17.3	17.2	17.4	17.1

30. Refer to Exercise 6 and suppose that greatest number of shares held by any of the 1,268 shareholders is 6,999. Estimate the mean and variance of the number of shares held by each shareholder.

31. In January the Parkville City Commission published the following frequency distribution classifying the amount of property taxes paid during the previous year by each of the city's 442 residential property owners.

AMOUNT PAID (DOLLARS)	FREQUENCY
Under 100	27
100–199	85
200–299	217
300–399	81
400–499	32

(a) Use the computing formulas for grouped data to approximate the mean and standard deviation of the amount of property taxes paid by each of the town's residential property owners.

(b) Use the empirical rule to approximate the proportion of Parkville property owners who paid from $156 to $347 in property taxes during the past year.

32.   The Parkville City Commission has decided to offer property tax relief to those residential property owners whose past year property taxes were above the 84th percentile. Use the empirical rule to approximate the minimum amount of property taxes necessary to qualify for tax relief in Parkville.

Supplementary Exercises

1.   The British Automobile Company advertises the fact that an economy test involving 50 of their standard model automobiles showed the average kilometers per U.S. gallon to be 31.0, with a variance of 21. Find the mean and variance of the gasoline economy of the cars that were tested in terms of miles per U.S. gallon. (*Hint:* 1 kilometer = .622 mile.)

2.   Carpeting is commonly priced in the United States in terms of the cost per square yard. A carpet manufacturer wishes to market a carpet in Great Britain which sells for $8.50 per square yard in the United States. What should be the manufacturer's selling price in dollars per square meter if he expects to have an equivalent selling price for the carpet in both the United States and Britain? (*Hint:* 1 square meter = 10.76 square feet.)

3.   The three major U.S. automobile manufacturers have each enjoyed enormous success by equipping many of their cars with a proven and efficient V–8 engine with approximately 290 cubic inches of displacement. If the United States converts to the metric standard, what would be the advertised displacement of this engine in cubic centimeters? (*Hint:* 1 inch = 2.54 centimeters.)

4.   The daily low temperatures during the month of May in Yakima, Washington, average 50 degrees Fahrenheit with a standard deviation of 18 degrees Fahrenheit. What is the average daily low temperature during the month of May in Yakima in degrees centigrade?

5.   Yakima, Washington, is located in the center of a very rich valley known for its production of apples, pears, and cherries. May is a very critical month in the development of these fruits on the trees and if, during this critical development period, the temperature drops below zero degrees centigrade, the young fruit can be damaged and an entire year's crop wiped out. Using the empirical rule, find the approximate percentage of the days in May which are likely to be cold enough to place the Yakima Valley fruit crops in danger.

References

Freund, J. E., *Modern Elementary Statistics.* 4th ed. Englewood Cliffs, N.J.: Prentice-Hall, Inc., 1973.

Mode, E. B., *Elements of Statistics.* 3rd ed. Englewood Cliffs, N.J.: Prentice-Hall, Inc., 1961.

Neiswanger, W. A., *Elementary Statistical Methods as Applied to Business and Economic Data.* New York: Macmillan Publishing Co., Inc., 1956.

Chapter 4

Probability

4.1   Introduction

As stated in Chapter 1, the objective of statistics is to make inferences about a population based on information contained in a sample. Since the sample provides only partial information about the population, we require a mechanism that will accomplish this objective. Probability is such a mechanism; it enables us to use the partial information contained in a set of sample data to infer the nature of the larger set of data, the population. How we use probability to make inferences is best illustrated by considering an example.

A manufacturer wishes to compare consumer preference for two packages (call them A and B) designed for his product. Suppose it is thought that design A is preferred. To test this assumption, 20 consumers are randomly selected, presented with both packages, and asked to select the design they prefer. Suppose that all 20 consumers indicate a preference for design B. What would you conclude about your assumption?

The answer to this question requires that we make an inference from a sample of 20 responses to the population associated with all possible purchasers of the manufacturer's product. Let a 1 denote a consumer response favoring design A and 0 a consumer favoring design B. Then we wish to infer whether the fraction of "ones" in the population of "ones" and "zeros" is greater than .5. If it is, the original assumption that design A is preferred may be taken as true. Noting that none of the consumers preferred design A, we would conclude that the assumption is false. To see how we are actually using probability to reach this conclusion, let us examine our reasoning.

If, in fact, the assumption is true that consumers prefer design A, the fraction of all potential purchasers of the product must be greater than $\frac{1}{2}$, and we would expect that something near the same fraction would be observed in the sample of 20 responses. Instead, none of the 20 consumers preferred design *A*, a result that is highly improbable if the assumption is correct. Since the result is so improbable, we conclude that the assumption is not correct. Thus, implicit in the reasoning process is a reliance on the notion of probability.

It may be noted that, in the foregoing, the sample results were so extremely contrary to the original assumption that a decision to reject the assumption could be made quite readily. Suppose, however, that the sample of 20 consumer responses indicated that 3 favored design *A* and 17 favored *B*. Would we still conclude that the sample is so improbable that we would reject the original assumption? Or, suppose that 8 favored *A* and 12 favored *B*? What would we then conclude about the original assumption? To answer these questions we would want to know "how improbable" a particular sample is. In other words, we would need to find the probability of a sample as extreme as that observed, given that the original assumption were true. Having determined this probability, we are in a position to decide whether the assumption is reasonable or should be rejected as untrue. Thus probability provides the necessary mechanism for making inferences about the population on the basis of sample evidence.

4.2   The Sample Space

Data are obtained either by observation of uncontrolled events in nature or by controlled experimentation in the laboratory. To simplify our terminology we seek a word that will apply to either method of data collection and hence define an experiment to be the process by which an observation (or measurement) is obtained. Note that the observation need not be numerical. Typical examples of experiments are

1. Recording the income of a factory worker.
2. Interviewing a buyer to determine his brand preference for a particular product.
3. Recording the price of a security at a particular time.
4. Inspecting an assembly line to determine if more than the allowable number of defectives is being produced.
5. Recording the type and size of policy sold by an insurance salesman.

A population of measurements results when the experiment is repeated many times. For instance, we might be interested in the length of life of television tubes produced in a plant during the month of June. Testing a single tube to failure and measuring the length of life would represent a single experiment, while repetition of the experiment for all tubes produced during this period would generate the entire population. A sample would represent the results of a small group of experiments selected from the population.

Let us now direct our attention to a careful analysis of some experiments and the construction of a mathematical model for the population. A by-product of our development will be a systematic and direct approach to the solution of probability problems.

We commence by noting that each experiment may result in one or more outcomes, which we shall call events and denote by capital letters. Consider the following experiment.

Example 4.1   *Toss a die and observe the number appearing on the upper face. Some events would be*

> *event A: observe an odd number.*
> *event B: observe a number less than* 4.
> *event E_1: observe a* 1.
> *event E_2: observe a* 2.
> *event E_3: observe a* 3.
> *event E_4: observe a* 4.
> *event E_5: observe a* 5.
> *event E_6: observe a* 6.

These events do not represent a complete listing of all possible events associated with the experiment but suffice to illustrate a point. You will readily note a difference between events A and B and events E_1, E_2, E_3, E_4, E_5, and E_6. Event A will occur if event E_1, E_3, or E_5 occurs, that is, if we observe a 1, 3, or 5. Thus A could be decomposed into a collection of simpler events, namely, E_1, E_3, and E_5. Likewise, event B will occur if E_1, E_2, or E_3 occurs and could be viewed as a collection of smaller or simpler events. In contrast, we note that it is impossible to decompose events E_1, E_2, E_3, ..., E_6. Events E_1, E_2, ..., E_6 are called simple events and A and B are compound events.

Definition

An event that cannot be decomposed is called a simple event. *Simple events will be denoted by the symbol E with a subscript.*

Events $E_1, E_2, ..., E_6$ represent a complete listing of all simple events associated with Example 4.1. An interesting property of simple events is readily apparent. An experiment will result in one and only one of the simple events. For instance, if a die is tossed, we will observe a 1, 2, 3, 4, 5, or 6, but we cannot possibly observe more than one of the simple events at the same time. Hence a list of simple events provides a breakdown of all possible outcomes of the experiment. For purposes of illustration, consider the following examples:

Example 4.2   *Toss a coin. Simple events:*

> *event E_1: observe a head.*
> *event E_2: observe a tail.*

Example 4.3   *Toss two coins. Simple events:*

EVENT	COIN 1	COIN 2
E_1	Head	Head
E_2	Head	Tail
E_3	Tail	Head
E_4	Tail	Tail

It would be extremely convenient if we were able to construct a model for an experiment which could be portrayed graphically. We do this in terms of point sets. To each simple event we assign a point, called a sample point. Thus the symbol E_1 will now be associated with either simple event E_1 or its corresponding sample point. The resulting diagram is called a Venn diagram.

Example 4.1 may be viewed symbolically in terms of the Venn diagram shown in Figure 4.1. Six sample points are shown, corresponding to the six possible simple events enumerated in Example 4.1. Likewise, the tossing of two coins, Example 4.3, is an experiment that possesses four sample points.

Definition

The set of all sample points for the experiment is called the sample space and is represented by the symbol S. We say that S is the totality of all sample points.

What is an event in terms of the sample points? We recall that event A, Example 4.1, occurred if any one of the simple events E_1, E_3, or E_5 occurred. That

Figure. 4.1   *Venn Diagram for Die Tossing*

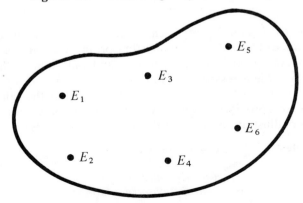

is, we observe A, an odd number, if we observe a 1, 3, or 5. Event B, a number less than 4, occurs if E_1, E_2, or E_3 occurs. Thus, if we designate the sample points associated with an event, the event is as clearly defined as if we had presented a verbal description of it. The event "observe E_1, E_3, or E_5" is obviously the same as the event "observe an odd number."

Definition

   An event is a collection of sample points.

    Keep in mind that the foregoing discussion refers to the outcome of a single experiment and that the performance of the experiment will result in the occurrence of one and only one sample point. Obviously, an event will occur if any sample point in the event occurs.

    An event could be represented on the Venn diagram by encircling the sample points in that event. Events A and B for the die-tossing problem are shown in Figure 4.2. Note that points E_1 and E_3 are in both events A and B and that both A and B occur if either E_1 or E_3 occurs.

    Populations of observations are obtained by repeating an experiment a very large number of times. Some fraction of this very large number of experiments will result in E_1, another fraction in E_2, and so on. From a practical point of view, we think of the fraction of the population resulting in an event A as the probability of A. Putting it another way, if an experiment is repeated a large number of times, N, and A is observed n times, the probability of A is

$$P(A) = \frac{n}{N}.$$

Figure 4.2   *Events A and B for Die Tossing*

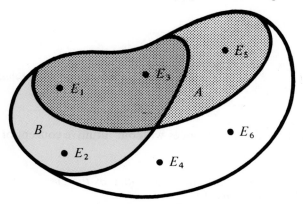

In practice, the composition of the population is rarely known and hence the desired probabilities for various events are unknown. Mathematically speaking, we ignore this aspect of the problem and take the probabilities as given, hence providing a model for a real population. For instance, we would assume that a large population of die tosses, Example 4.1, would yield

$$P(E_1) = P(E_2) = \cdots = P(E_6) = 1/6.$$

That is, we assume that the die is perfectly balanced. Is there such a thing as a perfectly balanced die? Probably not, but we would be inclined to think that the probability of the sample points would be so near 1/6 that our assumption is quite valid for practical purposes and provides a good model for die tossing.

We complete our model for the population by adding the following:

> *To each point in the sample space we assign a number called the probability of E_i, denoted by the symbol $P(E_i)$, such that*
>
> 1. $0 \le P(E_i) \le 1$, *for all i.*
> 2. $\sum_{S} P(E_i) = 1$.

The two requirements placed upon the probabilities of the sample points are necessary in order that the model conform to our relative frequency concept of probability. Thus we require that a probability be greater than or equal to 0 and less than or equal to 1 and that the sum of the probabilities over the entire sample space, S, be equal to 1. Furthermore, from a practical point of view we would choose the $P(E_i)$ in a realistic way so that they agree with the observed relative frequency of occurrence of the sample points.

We are now in a position to state a simple rule for the probability of any event, say event A.

Definition

The probability of an event A is equal to the sum of the probabilities of the sample points in A.

Note that the definition agrees with our intuitive concept of probability.

Example 4.4   *Calculate the probability of the event A for the die-tossing experiment of Example 4.1.*

Solution   *Event A is "observe an odd number" and includes points E_1, E_3, and E_5. Hence*

$$P(A) = P(E_1) + P(E_3) + P(E_5)$$
$$= 1/6 + 1/6 + 1/6$$
$$= 1/2.$$

Example 4.5   *Calculate the probability of observing exactly one head in a toss of two coins.*

Solution   *Construct the sample space, letting H represent a head, T a tail.*

EVENT	FIRST COIN	SECOND COIN	$P(E_i)$
E_1	H	H	1/4
E_2	H	T	1/4
E_3	T	H	1/4
E_4	T	T	1/4

It would seem reasonable to assign a probability of 1/4 to each of the sample points. We are interested in

Event A: observe exactly one head.

Sample points E_2 and E_3 are in A. Hence

$$P(A) = P(E_2) + P(E_3)$$
$$= 1/4 + 1/4$$
$$= 1/2.$$

Example 4.6   *The personnel director of a company plans to hire two salesmen from a total of four applicants. If he is completely incapable of correctly ranking the applicants according to their ability and, in effect, selects them at random, what is the probability that he accidentally selects the two "best" candidates?*

Solution   *The experiment consists of selecting two applicants from the four available. Suppose that applicants vary in ability and let (1), (2), (3), and (4) denote the applicants, with (1) and (2) representing the best and second best.*

Then the sample points in S are

SAMPLE POINT	PAIR SELECTED	PROBABILITY
E_1	(1), (2)	1/6
E_2	(1), (3)	1/6
E_3	(1), (4)	1/6
E_4	(2), (3)	1/6
E_5	(2), (4)	1/6
E_6	(3), (4)	1/6

Since each selection would be equiprobable, the probability assigned to each sample point is 1/6.

Define event A: The personnel director selects the two best applicants. Since A will occur only if E_1 occurs,

$$P(A) = P(E_1) = 1/6.$$

Note that we have constructed a probabilistic model for a population that possesses, in addition to elegance, a great deal of utility. It provides us with a simple, logical, and direct method for calculating the probability of an event or, if you like, the probability of a sample drawn from a theoretical population. The student having prior experience with probability problems will recognize the advantage of a systematic procedure for their solution. The disadvantages soon become apparent. Listing the sample points can be quite tedious, and one must be certain that none has been omitted. The total number of points in the sample space S may run into the millions.

We do not wish to pursue this point but simply mention that mathematical methods are available to simplify the counting procedure. A few useful theorems for counting sample points may be found in textbooks on combinatorial mathematics. In addition, we will study a second method for calculating the probability of an event in the following sections.

4.3   Compound Events

Most events of interest in practical situations are compound events that require enumeration of a large number of sample points. Actually, we find a second approach available for calculating the probability of events which obviates the listing of sample points and is therefore much less tedious and time consuming. It is based upon the classification of events, event relations, and two probability laws that will be discussed in Sections 4.4 and 4.5, respectively.

Compound events, as the name suggests, are formed by a composition of two or more events. Composition takes place in one of two ways, or in a combination of the two, a union or an intersection

---

Definition

Let A and B be two events in a sample space S. The union of A and B is defined to be the event containing all sample points in A or B or both. We denote the union of A and B by the symbol (A ∪ B).

Defined in ordinary terms, a union is the event that *either* event A or event B or both A and B occur. For instance, in Example 4.1,

$$\text{event } A: E_1, E_3, E_5.$$
$$\text{event } B: E_1, E_2, E_3.$$

The union $(A \cup B)$ would be the collection of points E_1, E_2, E_3, and E_5. This is shown diagrammatically in Figure 4.3.

Figure 4.3   *Event $(A \cup B)$ in Example* 4.1

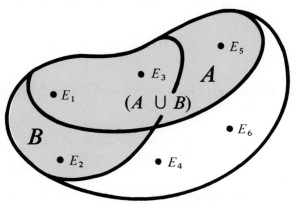

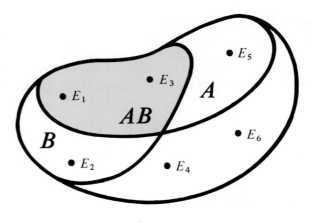

Figure 4.4   *Intersectiòn AB*

Definition

   Let A and B be two events in a sample space S. The intersection of A and B *is the event composed of all sample points that are in both A and B. An intersection of events A and B is represented by the symbol AB. (Some authors use A ∩ B.)*

   The intersection AB is the event that *both* A and B occur. It would appear in a Venn diagram as the overlapping area between A and B. The intersection AB for Example 4.1 would be the event consisting of points E_1 and E_3. If either E_1 or E_3 occurs both A and B occur. This is shown diagrammatically in Figure 4.4.

Example 4.7   *Refer to the experiment, Example 4.3, where two coins are tossed and define*

   event A: at least one head.
   event B: at least one tail.

Define event A, B, AB, and (A ∪ B) as collections of sample points.

Solution   *Recall that the sample points for this experiment were*

E_1: HH (*head on first coin, head on second*).
E_2: HT.
E_3: TH.
E_4: TT.

The occurrence of sample points E_1, E_2, and E_3 implies and hence defines event A. The other events could similarly be defined:

event B: E_2, E_3, E_4.
event AB: E_2, E_3.
event $(A \cup B)$: E_1, E_2, E_3, E_4.

Note that $(A \cup B) = S$, the sample space, and is thus certain to occur.

4.4   Event Relations

We shall define three relations between events: complementary, independent, and mutually exclusive events. You will have many occasions to inquire whether two or more events bear a particular relationship to one another. The test for each relationship is inherent in the definition, as we will illustrate, and their use in the calculation of the probability of an event will become apparent in Section 4.5.

Definition

The *complement* of an event A is the collection of all sample points in S and not in A. The complement of A is denoted by the symbol $\bar{A}$.

Since

$$\sum_S P(E_i) = 1,$$

$$P(A) + P(\bar{A}) = 1,$$

and

$$P(A) = 1 - P(\bar{A}),$$

---

which is a useful relation for obtaining $P(A)$ when $P(\bar{A})$ is known or easily calculated.

Two events are often related in such a way that the probability of occurrence of one depends upon whether the second has or has not occurred. For instance, suppose that one experiment consists in observing the weather on a specific day. Let A be the event "observe rain" and B be the event "observe an overcast sky." Events A and B are obviously related. The probability of rain, $P(A)$, is not the same as the probability of rain given prior information that the day is cloudy. The probability of A, $P(A)$, would be the fraction of the entire population of observations that result in rain. Now let us look only at the subpopulation of observations resulting in B, a cloudy day, and the fraction of these which result in A. This fraction, called the conditional probability of A given B, may equal $P(A)$ but we would expect the chance of rain, given that the day is cloudy, to be larger. The conditional probability of A, given that B has occurred, is denoted as

$$P(A|B),$$

where the vertical bar in the parentheses is read "given" and events appearing to the right of the bar are the events that have occurred.

We shall define the conditional probabilities of B given A and A given B as follows:

Definition

$$P(B|A) = \frac{P(AB)}{P(A)}$$

and

$$P(A|B) = \frac{P(AB)}{P(B)}.$$

Table 4.1   *Two-Way Table for Events A and B*

	A	$\bar{A}$
B	n_{11}	n_{12}
$\bar{B}$	n_{21}	n_{22}

The fact that this definition is consistent with our relative frequency concept of probability is obvious after a bit of thought but is perhaps more easily seen by viewing the following construction. Suppose that an experiment is repeated a large number of times, N, resulting in both A and B, AB, n_{11} times; A and not B, $A\bar{B}$, n_{21} times; B and not A, $\bar{A}B$, n_{12} times; and neither A nor B, $\bar{A}\bar{B}$, n_{22} times. We present these results in a two-way table, Table 4.1. Note that $n_{11} + n_{12} + n_{21} + n_{22} = N$. It follows that

$$P(A) = \frac{n_{11} + n_{21}}{N},$$

$$P(B) = \frac{n_{11} + n_{12}}{N},$$

$$P(A|B) = \frac{n_{11}}{n_{11} + n_{12}},$$

$$P(B|A) = \frac{n_{11}}{n_{11} + n_{21}},$$

$$P(AB) = \frac{n_{11}}{N}.$$

Using these probabilities, it is easy to see that

$$P(B|A) = \frac{P(AB)}{P(A)}$$

and

$$P(A|B) = \frac{P(AB)}{P(B)}.$$

Example 4.8   *Calculate $P(A|B)$ for the die-tossing experiment, Example 4.1.*

Solution   *Events A and B are defined as follows:*

   event A: observe an odd number (E_1, E_3, E_5).
   event B: observe a number less than 4 (E_1, E_2, E_3).

Given that B has occurred, we are concerned only with sample points E_1, E_2, and E_3, which occur with equal frequency. Of these, E_1 and E_3 imply event A. Hence

$$P(A|B) = 2/3.$$

Or we could obtain $P(A|B)$ by substituting into the equation

$$P(A|B) = \frac{P(AB)}{P(B)} = \frac{1/3}{1/2} = 2/3.$$

Note that $P(A|B) = 2/3$ while $P(A) = 1/2$, indicating that A and B are dependent upon each other.

Definition

Two events, *A and B, are said to be* independent *if either*

$$P(A|B) = P(A)$$

or

$$P(B|A) = P(B).$$

Otherwise, the events are said to be dependent.

We will note that if $P(A|B) = P(A)$, then $P(B|A)$ will also equal $P(B)$. Similarly, if $P(A|B)$ and $P(A)$ are unequal, then $P(B|A)$ and $P(B)$ will be unequal.

A third useful event relation was observed but not specifically defined in our discussion of simple events. Recall that an experiment could result in one and only one simple event. No two could occur at exactly the same time. Two events, *A* and *B*, are said to be mutually exclusive if, when one occurs, it excludes the possibility of occurrence of the other. Another way to say this is to state that the intersection, *AB*, will contain no sample points. It would then follow that $P(AB) = 0$.

Definition

Two events, *A and B, are said to be* mutually exclusive *if the event AB contains no sample points.*

Figure 4.5   *Mutually Exclusive Events*

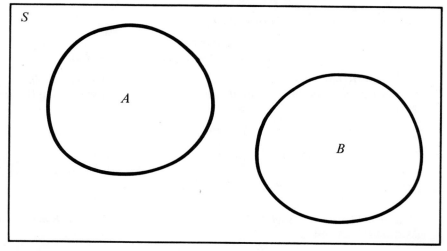

Mutually exclusive events have no overlapping area in a Venn diagram (see Figure 4.5).

Example 4.9   *Are events A and B, Example 4.1, mutually exclusive? Are they complementary? Independent?*

Solution

$$\text{event } A: E_1, E_3, E_5.$$
$$\text{event } B: E_1, E_2, E_3.$$

It is obvious that event AB includes points E_1 and E_3 and that $P(AB)$ is not equal to zero. Therefore, A and B are not mutually exclusive. They are not complementary because B does not contain all points in S that are not in A.

The test for independence lies in the definition. That is, we shall check to see if $P(A|B) = P(A)$
From Example 4.8, $P(A|B) = 2/3$. *Then since* $P(A) = 1/2$,

$$P(A|B) \neq P(A),$$

and events A and B are, by definition, dependent.

Example 4.10   *Experience has shown that a particular union–management contract negotiation has led to a contract settlement within a 2-week period 50 percent of the time, the union strike fund has been adequate to support a strike 60 percent of the time, and both of these conditions have been satisfied 30 percent of the time. What is the probability of a contract settlement given you know that the union strike fund is adequate to support a strike? Is settlement of a contract within a 2-week period dependent on whether the union strike fund is adequate to support a strike?*

Solution   *Define the following events:*

event A: a contract settlement is reached within a 2-week period.

event B: the union strike fund is adequate to support a strike.

Thus we wish to find $P(A|B)$.
   We are given that $P(A) = .50$, $P(B) = .60$, and $P(AB) = .30$. Then

$$P(A|B) = \frac{P(AB)}{P(B)} = \frac{.30}{.60} = .50.$$

To determine whether events A and B are dependent, we compare $P(A|B)$ and $P(A)$. Since

$$P(A|B) = P(A) = .50,$$

by definition events A and B are independent.

4.5   Two Probability Laws and Their Use

As previously stated, a second approach to the solution of probability problems is based upon the composition of events, event relations, and two probability laws, which we now state. The "laws" can be simply stated and taken as fact as long as they are consistent with our model and with reality. The first, called the multiplicative law of probability follows directly from the definition of conditional probability. It provides a formula for calculating the probability of an intersection.

The Multiplicative Law of Probability

Given two events, A and B, the probability of the intersection, AB, is

$$P(AB) = P(A)P(B|A)$$

$$= P(B)P(A|B).$$

If A and B are independent, $P(AB) = P(A)P(B)$.

We shall illustrate use of the multiplicative law by an example.

Example 4.11   *Ten contaminated cartons of serum were accidentally mixed and shipped to a customer. If the lot received contained 100 cartons and if two are selected at random, what is the probability that both will be defective?*

Solution   *Define the events*

$$A: the\ first\ is\ defective.$$
$$B: the\ second\ is\ defective.$$

Then AB will be the event that both are defective and

$$P(AB) = P(A)P(B|A).$$

$P(A) = .10$ *since there are 10 defectives in the lot of 100, but $P(B|A) = 9/99$ since, after the first is selected and found to be defective, there are 99 cartons remaining, of which 9 are defective. Thus*

$$P(AB) = P(A)P(B|A)$$

$$= \left(\frac{10}{100}\right)\left(\frac{9}{99}\right) = \frac{1}{110}.$$

The second law of probability, called the additive law, applies to unions:

The Additive Law of Probability

The probability of a union $(A \cup B)$ is equal to

$$P(A \cup B) = P(A) + P(B) - P(AB).$$

If A and B are mutually exclusive,

$$P(AB) = 0 \qquad and \qquad P(A \cup B) = P(A) + P(B).$$

The additive law conforms to reality and our model. The sum, $P(A) + P(B)$, contains the sum of the probabilities of all sample points in $(A \cup B)$ but includes a double counting of the probabilities of all points in the intersection, AB. Subtracting $P(AB)$ gives the correct result.

Example 4.12   *The residents of a retirement community on the West Coast were surveyed to determine readership of available newspapers within the city. It was found that 50 percent of the residents read the Atlas, 25 percent read the Bugle, and 5 percent read both newspapers. Suppose that a single resident is selected at random and questioned concerning his or her newspaper readership. Define*

> *event A : a resident reads the Atlas.*
> *event B : a resident reads the Bugle.*

Find the probability of the events A, B, AB, and $A \cup B$.

Solution   *The experiment involves the selection of a single resident of the retirement community and noting the newspapers which he or she reads. One sample point will correspond to the selection of each resident in the community, and the sample points will be equiprobable. Then since 50 percent of the residents read the Atlas, half of the sample points in S will be in event A and*

$$P(A) = .5.$$

Similarly,

$$P(B) = .25.$$

Since 5 percent read both newspapers,

$$P(AB) = .05.$$

Then

$$P(A \cup B) = P(A) + P(B) - P(AB)$$
$$= .5 + .25 - .05 = .7.$$

The use of the probability laws for calculating the probability of a compound event is less direct than the listing of sample points and it requires a bit of experience and ingenuity. The approach involves the expression of the event of interest as a union or intersection (or combination of both) of two or more events whose probabilities are known or easily calculated. This can often be done in many ways. The trick is to find the right combination, a task that requires no little amount of creativity in some cases. The usefulness of event relations is now apparent. If the event of interest is expressed as a union of mutually exclusive events, the probabilities of the intersection need not be known. If they are independent, we need not know the conditional probabilities to calculate the probability of an intersection. Example 4.13 illustrates the use of the probability laws and the technique described above.

Example 4.13   *An oil prospector will drill a succession of holes in a given area to find a productive well and will stop drilling with his first success. The probability that he is successful on any given trial is .2. If his total resources allow the drilling of no more than two holes, what is the probability that he locates a productive well?*

Solution   *Let us list the events which, when occurring, accomplish the objective of the problem. If we define*

> A: *a productive well is found within two trials,*
> S_1: *a productive well is found on the first trial,*
> S_2: *a productive well is found on the second trial,*
> F_1: *a dry well is found on the first trial,*
> F_2: *a dry well is found on the second trial,*

then we see the event A will occur if

>   1. *He strikes oil on the first trial, S_1, or*
>   2. *He hits a dry well on the first trial and strikes oil on the second, $F_1 S_2$.*

Thus

$$A = S_1 \cup F_1 S_2.$$

Note that these events are mutually exclusive. Then

$$P(A) = P(S_1 \cup F_1 S_2)$$
$$= P(S_1) + P(F_1 S_2)$$

since the events S_1 and $(F_1 S_2)$ are mutually exclusive.

Since

$$P(S_1) = P(S_2) = .2$$

and

$$P(F_1) = P(F_2) = .8,$$

the outcome "success" or "dry" at any trial is independent of the outcome at any other trial. Applying the multiplicative law,

$$P(F_1 S_2) = P(F_1)P(S_2)$$

$$= (.8)(.2)$$

$$= .16.$$

Substituting,

$$P(A) = P(S_1) + P(F_1 S_2)$$

$$= .2 + .16$$

$$= .36.$$

4.6   Bayes' Law

In the usual sense of conditional probability, we seek the probability of some event A given that an event B has occurred. Usually, we say that event A is an end effect for which event B is a possible cause and that B and A are sequenced, in that order, over time. For instance, we might be interested in the conditional probability, $P(A|B)$, where A is the event "an insurance salesman sells 15 policies" and B is the event "the salesman contacts 40 clients." Suppose we know after the fact that the salesman sold 15 policies last week but do not know how many clients were contacted. That is, how might we find the probability that some particular event B is the "cause" among many possible causes of a known end effect, A? Such probabilities are given by Bayes' law, which we state below without proof.

Bayes' Law

Let B be an event and $\bar{B}$ be its complement. If A is another event that occurs if and only if B or $\bar{B}$ occurs, then the probability

$$P(B|A) = \frac{P(A|B)P(B)}{P(A|B)P(B) + P(A|\bar{B})P(\bar{B})}.$$

Our computed probability $P(B|A)$ is called the posterior probability of the event B given the information contained in event A. The simple probabilities $P(B)$ and $P(\bar{B})$ are called the prior probabilities of the events B and $\bar{B}$, respectively. In a sense, Bayes' law is updating or revising the prior probability $P(B)$ by incorporating the observed information contained within event A into the model. For instance, if we want to find the probability, after the fact, that our salesman contacted 40 clients last week, $P(B)$, the proportion of work weeks he has contacted 40 clients ignores the information that is contained in the known event A, the event that he sold 15 policies last week. However, the posterior probability $P(B|A)$ reflects both the prior and current information and provides a more efficient model for our problem.

Sometimes the conditional probabilities $P(A|B)$ and $P(A|\bar{B})$ or the simple probabilities $P(B)$ and $P(\bar{B})$ are not known exactly. When they are not known, empirical or subjective estimates are often used in their stead with varying degrees of accuracy. This problem is explored in some detail in Chapter 10.

Example 4.14 *A department store is considering adopting a new credit management policy in an attempt to reduce the number of credit customers defaulting on their payments. The credit manager has suggested that in the future credit should be discontinued to any customer who has twice been a week or more late with his monthly instalment payment. He supports his claim by noting that past credit records show that 90 percent of all those defaulting on their payments were late with at least two monthly payments. Suppose from our own investigation we have found that 2 percent of all credit customers actually default on their payments and that 45 percent of those who have not defaulted have had at least two "late" monthly payments. Find the probability that a customer with two or more late payments will actually default on his payments and, in light of this probability, criticize the credit manager's credit plan.*

Solution *Let the events L and D be defined as follows:*

L: a credit customer is 2 or more weeks late with at least two monthly payments,

D: a credit customer defaults on his payments,

and let $\bar{D}$ denote the complement of event D. We seek the conditional probability

$$P(D|L) = \frac{P(L|D)P(D)}{P(L|D)P(D) + P(L|\bar{D})P(\bar{D})}.$$

From the information given within the problem description, we find that

$$P(D|L) = \frac{(.90)(.02)}{(.90)(.02) + (.45)(.98)}$$

$$= \frac{.0180}{.0180 + .4410}$$

$$= .0392.$$

Therefore, if the credit manager's plan is adopted, the probability is only about .04, or the chances are only about 1 in 25, that a customer who loses his credit privileges would actually have defaulted on his payments. Unless management would consider it worthwhile to detect one prospective "defaulter" at the expense of losing 24 good credit customers, the credit manager's plan would be a poor business policy.

4.7 Subjective Probability

Probability is a measure of one's belief in a particular outcome of an experiment. Thus a number is assigned to each sample point in such a way that

$$0 \le P(E_i) \le 1$$

and

$$\sum_S P(E_i) = 1.$$

Supposedly, the number assigned to sample point E_i, $i = 1, 2, \ldots$, is a measure of the experimenter's belief that this sample point will occur when the experiment is conducted one time.

For many experiments we may view the probability of an event, the measure of our belief in its outcome, as the fraction of times the event will occur in a long series of repetitions of the experiment. This we referred to as the relative frequency concept of probability. Other experiments are not so easy to interpret. In particular, how do you view the probability of an event for an experiment that can be conducted only once because of the cost or the nature of the event? For example, the event that profit will rise next year after a corporate merger is associated with an experiment that can never, under identical circumstances, be repeated. The raising or lowering of the prime interest rate at a particular point in time is also an experiment that can only be conducted once.

To answer the preceding question, we return to our opening statement. Probability is a measure of one's belief in the outcome of a particular event. If we confine our attention to experiments that can be repeated, we may wish to interpret the measure in terms of the relative frequency concept of probability. Then the sample point probabilities can be compared (as a check) with observed frequencies of occurrence of the sample points for a small number of trials. Experiments that cannot be repeated require a subjective evaluation of the probabilities of the sample points or, equivalently, the probability of an event. No opportunity will be available for an empirical check. These probabilities are usually specified by a person who is familiar with the experiment and who relies on his experience to acquire a reasonably accurate probability for the event. For example, a government economist is familiar with administration policies and current trends in the financial market. Thus he should be able to assign a reasonably accurate probability to the event that the prime interest rate will be raised (or lowered) at a particular point in time. (That they are frequently unable to accomplish this task is indicated by the conflicting statements by experts regarding the probability or occurrence of various economic events.) Probabilities assigned to events that are acquired subjectively and based on "experience" are called subjective probabilities or, sometimes, personal probabilities.

How one acquires the probabilities of the sample points or the probability of any event is irrelevant as long as the quantities so acquired give reasonably accurate measures of the likelihood of the outcome of the events. Specifically, the accuracy of the results obtained by applying the laws of probability for calculating the probability of an event will depend on the accuracies of the probabilities assigned to the sample points or to events appearing in the stated event composition. Incorrect assumptions will lead to incorrect conclusions.

4.8   Random Variables

In Section 4.2 we defined an experiment as the process by which an observation (or measurement) is obtained. Although the observations resulting from an experiment are not always numerically valued, most experiments produce data that are either quantitative or can be quantified by assigning numbers to represent categories. Thus we have particular interest in those experiments that result in numerically valued outcomes.

Suppose that the variable measured in an experiment is denoted by the symbol y. The variable y is called a random variable if the value that y assumes is a chance or random event. Stated more precisely,

---

Definition

A random variable y is a numerically valued function whose values correspond to the various outcomes of an experiment.

For example, consider the sampling of 20 consumers who are asked whether they prefer package design A or B. The number of consumers who indicate that they prefer design A may be regarded as a variable y that assumes any of the values $0, 1, 2, \ldots, 20$. Each of these values corresponds to a particular experimental outcome, where the experiment consists of drawing a sample of 20 consumers' responses and noting how many indicate a preference for package design A. The variable y is a random variable since the value that y assumes is an outcome that cannot be predicted with absolute certainty in advance of the experiment; that is, the particular value that y takes is a chance or random event.

You may recall from our earlier discussion of this sampling problem (Section 4.1) that the probabilities assumed by the random variable y are needed to make an inference concerning the preferences of all possible purchasers of the manufacturer's product. These probabilities, one associated with each value of y, are called the probability distribution for y.

4.9   Summary

The theories of both probability and statistics are concerned with samples drawn from a population. Probability assumes the population known and calculates the probability of observing a particular sample. Statistics assumes the sample to be known and, with the aid of probability, attempts to describe the frequency distribution of the population, which is unknown. Chapter 4 is directed toward the construction of a model, the sample space, for the frequency distribution of a population of observations. The theoretical frequencies, representing probabilities of events, can be obtained by one of two methods:

1. The summation of the probabilities of the sample points in the event of interest.

2. The joint use of event composition (compound events) and the laws of probability.

Exercises

The following exercises are appropriate for Section 4.2.

1. A committee is composed of 2 men and 1 woman. One member is to be selected as committee chairman, another as secretary. Specify the sample points in the following events:
    (a) S: the sample space.
    (b) A: the older man is selected as chairman.
    (c) B: a man is selected as chairman.
    (d) C: the woman is selected as secretary.
    (e) D: events A and C occur.
    (f) E: event B or event C or both occur.

2. Refer to Exercise 1 and suppose that each individual committee member has an equal chance of being selected as either chairman or secretary. Compute the probabilities of the events A, B, C, D, and E by summing the probabilities of the appropriate sample points.

3. Patients arriving at a hospital outpatient clinic can select one of two stations for service. Suppose that physicians are randomly assigned to the stations and that the patients have no station preference. Three patients arrive at the clinic and their selection of stations is observed.
   (a) List the sample points for the experiment.
   (b) Let A be the event that each station receives at least one patient. List the sample points in A.
   (c) Make a reasonable assignment of probabilities to the sample points and find $P(A)$.

4. An airline company at present has four flights per day from New York to London. The first two flights are in the morning, the last two are in the afternoon. To conserve fuel, the airline is going to cancel two flights. If the flights to be canceled are randomly chosen, what is the probability that a morning and an afternoon flight will still be available?

5. Corporate bonds are rated A^+, A, B^+, B, or C, depending on the stability of the issuing firm. A novice bond buyer is unaware of the difference in corporate ratings and thus selects two firms at random from five. If each of the five firms has a different rating, what is the probability that he does not buy any bonds rated C? What is the probability that he buys only bonds rated A^+ or A?

6. A small advertising firm consists of two men and one woman. The firm has two clients who are particularly difficult to deal with. To decide who sees the first client, one person is randomly selected from the three. The same procedure is followed for the second client.
   (a) Find the probability that both clients are served by the same person from the advertising firm.
   (b) Find the probability that both clients are served by men.
   (c) Find the probability that both the events described in (a) and (b) occur simultaneously.

7. A company has vacancies for two positions of vice president. The vacancies are to be filled by randomly selecting two people from a list of four. The following people are on the list: the company president's son and daughter, and a man and woman who have worked for the company for a long period of time.
   (a) What is the probability that at least one of the president's children will be selected?
   (b) What is the probability that neither woman will be selected?

8. At the beginning of each month, a company decides whether to spend $100 or $200 on advertising for that month. Each decision has the same probability of occurring every month.
   (a) What is the probability that in three consecutive months a total of more than $400 is spent on advertising?
   (b) What is the probability that $100 is spent all three months?

The following exercises are appropriate for Sections 4.3, 4.4, and 4.5.

9. The 50 employees of the Johnson Accounting Agency are categorized below according to the number of years they have been employed by Johnson and their highest educational degree attained. One person is selected at random from the agency as a candidate for further education in a specialized area. Let events A, B, C, D, E, F, and G be defined as labeled below. Find $P(A)$, $P(B)$, $P(E)$, $P(F)$, $P(AF)$, $P(DG)$, $P(AB)$, $P(A \cup F)$, $P(C \cup F)$, $P(F \cup G)$, $P(A \cup B \cup C)$, $P(A \cup B \cup F)$.

	YEARS SENIORITY			
	(A) 0–5	(B) 6–10	(C) 11–15	(D) Over 15
High school (E)	1	0	2	3
Bachelor's degree (F)	8	14	6	4
Master's degree (G)	5	5	1	1

10. The table shows the location of all 200 stores in a trade association by city type and geographic region.

CITY TYPE	GEOGRAPHIC REGION			
	EAST B_1	SOUTH B_2	MIDWEST B_3	FAR WEST B_4
Large A_1	35	10	25	25
Small A_2	15	10	15	15
Suburb A_3	25	5	10	10

One store is to be selected at random from the trade association to be used in testing the sales appeal of a new product. Calculate the following probabilities and then describe each probability specifically in terms of the above problem: $P(A_1)$, $P(B_3)$, $P(A_1B_4)$, $P(B_1|A_3)$, $P(A_2 \cup B_3)$, $P(B_1 \cup B_4)$, and $P(B_2B_4)$.

11. Each week, George Davis invests $50 in the securities market, a bank savings account, a corporate bond account, or a savings bond. He invests in each with probability .5, .2, .2, and .1, respectively. For a given week, find
(a) The probability that he will not invest in the securities market.
(b) The probability that he will invest in either the securities market or a savings bond.
(c) The probability that he will invest in the securities market, a bank savings account, or a savings bond.

12. Refer to Exercise 1. Find $P(A|B)$, $P(A|C)$, and $P(B|C)$. Calculate the probabilities of the events AB, AC, BC, and $(A \cup B)$ using the additive and multiplicative laws of probability. Are A and B independent? Mutually exclusive? Are B and C independent? Mutually exclusive?

13. A certain company encourages its employees to participate in some type of physical exercise. A survey indicates that 40 percent play golf, 50 percent bowl, and 25 percent play golf and bowl. Suppose that a single employee is chosen at random and questioned concerning his physical activities. Define the following events:
    event A: the employee plays golf.
    event B: the employee bowls.
Find $P(A)$, $P(B)$, $P(AB)$, $P(A \cup B)$, and $P(A|B)$.

14.   A company is going to temporarily hire two secretaries from a secretarial pool. One hundred secretaries are available. Twenty type under 40 words per minute, fifty type from 40 to 60 words per minute, and the rest type over 60 words per minute.
(a) Find the probability that both secretaries type over 60 words per minute.
(b) Find the probability that the first types under 40 words per minute, the second from 40 to 60.
(c) Find the probability that the first types from 40 to 60 words per minute, the second under 40.
(d) Find the probability that one types under 40 words per minute, the other from 40 to 60.

15.   The 500 credit customers of the Mallon Company are categorized according to the number of years they have held a credit account with Mallon and their average monthly account balance. One credit account has been selected at random to see if it is delinquent.

	UNDER 5 YEARS	5 YEARS OR OVER
Under $100	40	160
$100 or over	160	140

Let the following events be defined:
   A: the average monthly balance is under $100 for the account selected.
   B: the selected credit account is under 5 years in age.
Find the following:
(a) $P(A)$
(b) $P(\bar{B})$
(c) $P(AB)$
(d) $P(\bar{A} \cup B)$
(e) Are A and B independent?

16.   Through a certain broker, 100 stocks are available. Sixty are on the New York Exchange; 30 are preferred stocks, and 20 are preferred stocks on the New York Exchange. A man goes to the broker and buys a stock from the New York Exchange. (He is unaware that some stocks are preferred.) Given that he bought a stock from the New York Exchange, what is the probability that it is preferred?

17.   Suppose it is known that at a particular company, the probability of remaining with the company 10 years or more is 1/6. A man and a woman start work at the company on the same day.
(a) What is the probability that the man will work there less than 10 years?
(b) What is the probability that both the man and woman will work there less than 10 years? Assume that they are unrelated and hence that their lengths of service are independent of each other.
(c) What is the probability that one or the other, or both, will work longer than 10 years?

18.   A shipping firm keeps two vehicles in readiness for local deliveries. Owing to the demand on their time and the chance of mechanical failure, the probability that a specific vehicle will be available when needed is 9/10. The availability of one vehicle is independent of the other.
(a) In the event of two large orders, what is the probability that both vehicles will be available?
(b) What is the probability that neither will be available?
(c) If one service call is placed, what is the probability that the delivery will be made (i.e., what is the probability that a vehicle will be available)?

The following exercises are appropriate for Section 4.6.

19. As items come to the end of a production line, an inspector chooses which items are to go through a complete inspection. Ten percent of all items produced are defective. Sixty percent of all defective items go through a complete inspection, and 20 percent of all good items go through a complete inspection. Given that an item is completely inspected, what is the probability that it is defective?

20. Each of two appliance stores (stores I and II) sell each of two brands of washing machines (brands A and B). These are the only stores selling these machines. The probability that someone shops at store I is 3/4. The probability that someone shopping at store I buys brand A is 1/3. The probability that someone shopping at store II buys brand A is 1/4. Given that someone bought a brand A washing machine, what is the probability that it was purchased at store I?

Supplementary Exercises

21. Over a long period of time, three-fourths of all applicants have passed a company's managerial trainee examination. If three employees sit for the examination, based on past experience what is the probability that two will pass? At least two will pass?

22. A salesman figures that the probability of his consummating a sale during the first contact with a client is .4 but improves to .55 on the second contact if the client did not buy during the first contact. Suppose that the salesman will make one and only one return call to any client. If the salesman contacts a client, calculate
    (a) The probability that the client will buy,
    (b) The probability that the client will not buy.

23. A certain article is visually inspected successively by two inspectors. When a defective article comes through, the probability that it gets by the first inspector is .1. Of those that do get past the first inspector, the second inspector will "miss" 5 out of 10. What fraction of the defectives will get by both inspectors?

24. The Ace Trucking Company is considering bidding on a shipping contract. They feel they will win the contract with probability 1/2 if Speedy Trucking Service does not submit a bid, but the probability they will win the contract if Speedy does bid is 1/4. If the probability is 3/4 that Speedy Trucking Service will submit a bid, what is the probability that the Ace Trucking Company will win the shipping contract?

25. A man takes either a bus or the subway to work, with probabilities .3 and .7, respectively. When he takes the bus, he is late on 30 percent of the days. When he takes the subway, he is late on 20 percent of the days. If the man is late for work on a particular day, what is the probability that he took the bus?

26. A company is going to buy two new desks for its office. The purchaser of the desks randomly chooses 2 from a total of 5 available. Although the purchaser does not know it, one desk has a major defect, two have minor defects, and two are in perfect condition.
    (a) What is the probability that both desks that are purchased are in perfect condition?
    (b) What is the probability that the desk with the major defect is purchased?

27. The manager of a store is going to hire two people. The first position requires the handling of money, the second does not. Four people apply for the jobs, and all seem equally qualified to the manager. Thus he selects two people at random from the four available and decides to assign the first person chosen to the position that requires the

handling of money. If two of the applicants are actually not suited for the first position, what is the probability that exactly one of these applicants will be hired and not have to handle money?

28. The probability that a business executive is in a good mood on any particular day is .7. If four days are independently chosen, what is the probability that the executive is not in a good mood on at least one of these days?

29. A department store is going to run a sale on a particular item for one, two, or three days. The probability that the store chooses to run the sale for one day is .2, two days is .3, and three days is .5. The probability of selling all the items in stock if the sale is held one, two, or three days is .1, .7, or .9, respectively. What is the probability that all items in stock are sold by the store during the sale?

30. A manufacturer has two machines that produce a certain product. Machine I produces 45 percent of the product, and machine II produces 55 percent. Machine I produces 10 percent defective items; and machine II produces 8 percent defective items. If a defective item is observed, what is the probability that it was produced by machine II?

References

Cramer, H., *The Elements of Probability Theory and Some of Its Applications.* New York: John Wiley & Sons, Inc., 1955 (Stockholm: Almqvist and Wiksell, 1954).

Feller, W., *An Introduction to Probability Theory and Its Applications*, Vol. 1, 3rd ed. New York: John Wiley & Sons, Inc., 1968.

Hymans, S. H., *Probability Theory with Applications to Econometrics and Decision-Making.* Englewood Cliffs, N.J.: Prentice-Hall, Inc., 1967.

King, W. R., *Probability for Management Decisions.* New York: John Wiley & Sons, Inc., 1968.

Chapter 5

Random Variables and Probability Distributions

5.1   Random Variables

Recall that an experiment is the process of collecting a measurement or observation. Most experiments of interest yield a numerical measurement that varies from sample point to sample point and hence is called a random variable Restating the definition presented in Section 4.8, a random variable is a numerical-valued function whose values correspond to the various outcomes of an experiment. The daily closing price of an industrial stock is a numerical event Observing the number of defects on a piece of new furniture or recording the grade-point average of a particular student are other examples of experiments yielding numerical events. The population associated with the experiment results when the experiment is repeated a number of times and a relatively large body of data is obtained. As previously noted, we never actually measure each member of the population, but we can certainly conceive of doing so. In lieu of this, we wish to obtain a small set of these measurements, called the sample, and use the information in the sample to describe or, equivalently, make inferences about the population.

We have stated that a measurement obtained from an experiment results in a specific value of the random variable of interest and represents a measurement drawn from a population. How can a single measurement or a larger sample of, say, n measurements be used to make inferences about the population of interest? With the consumer preference study of Section 4.1 firmly in mind, you might calculate the probability of the observed numerical event—the sample—for a large set of possible populations and choose the one that gives the highest probability of observing the sample. We like to think that the method of inference described above appears reasonable and intuitively appealing, but note that it is not claimed to be the best, however "best" might be defined. (This procedure is the basis for one of the important methods for the statistical estimation of the parameters of a population and can be shown to provide "good" inferences in many situations.) We defer further discussion of inference until Chapter 6. At this point it is sufficient to note that the procedure requires a knowledge of the probability associated with each value of the random variable. In other words, we require the probability distribution for the random variable that represents the theoretical frequency histogram for the population of numerical measurements. The theory of probability presented in Chapter 4 provides the mechanism for calculating these probabilities for some random variables.

5.2   A Classification of Random Variables

Random variables are classified as one of two types: discrete or continuous.

Definition

A *discrete random variable* is one that can assume a countable number of values.

Typical examples of discrete random variables are

1. The number of automobiles sold per month.

2. The number of accidents in a particular manufacturing plant for a given week.

3. The number of customers waiting at a supermarket checkout counter.

4. The number of television tubes produced in a given hour.

A discrete random variable may be identified by noting the number of values that it can assume. If a random variable can assume only a finite number or a countable infinity of values, it is discrete. For example, if y represents the number of errors a mechanic can make in an assembly operation, y can assume a finite number of values, $0, 1, 2, 3, \ldots, n$, where n is the total number of steps in the assembly operation. The number of years, y, until a corporation achieves \$1 billion in assets could conceivably be infinite, but y is still a discrete random variable. The number of values that y can assume is countably infinite, since we can imagine a count that could be continued indefinitely.

A continuous random variable is defined as follows.

Definition

A continuous random variable is one that can assume the infinitely large number of values corresponding to the points on a line interval.

For example, suppose that we measured the distance between a supplier and a buyer and represented this distance as the random variable, y. If an exact measuring instrument could be used, each value of y could be viewed theoretically as a point on the line interval between the supplier and buyer. Thus we could associate each value of y with one of an infinitely large number of points lying on a line interval. Other examples of continuous random variables are weight, time, temperature, humidity, and pressure.

The distinction between discrete and continuous random variables is an important one in that different probability models are required for each. The probabilities associated with each value of a discrete random variable can be assigned in such a way that the probabilities sum to 1. This is not possible with continuous random variables, since they can assume an infinitely large number of values. Accordingly, we shall consider the probability distributions for discrete and continuous random variables separately in the following two sections.

5.3 Probability Distributions for Discrete Random Variables

The probability distribution for a discrete random variable is a formula, table, or graph providing the probability associated with each value of the random variable. Since each value of the variable y is a numerical event, we may apply the methods of Chapter 4 to obtain the appropriate probabilities.

Example 5.1 *Consider an experiment that consists of tossing two coins and let y equal the number of heads observed. The sample points for this experiment with their respective probabilities are as given. Find the probability distribution for y.*

SAMPLE POINT	COIN 1	COIN 2	$P(E_i)$	y
E_1	H	H	1/4	2
E_2	H	T	1/4	1
E_3	T	H	1/4	1
E_4	T	T	1/4	0

Solution   *We would assign the value $y = 2$ to point E_1, $y = 1$ to point E_2, and so on. The probability of each value of y may be calculated by adding the probabilities of the sample points in that numerical event. The numerical event $y = 0$ contains one sample point, E_4; $y = 1$ contains two sample points, E_2 and E_3; and $y = 2$ contains one point, E_1. The values of y with respective probabilities are given in Table 5.1. Observe that*

$$\sum_{y=0}^{2} p(y) = 1.$$

Table 5.1   *Probability Distribution for y (y = Number of Heads)*

	SAMPLE POINTS	
y	IN y	$p(y)$
0	E_4	1/4
1	E_2, E_3	1/2
2	E_1	1/4

$$\sum_{y=0}^{2} p(y) = 1$$

The probability distribution for y is shown graphically in Figure 5.1.

To illustrate how we use the probability distribution for a discrete random variable to make inferences, let us consider again the problem (introduced in Section 4.1) of deciding whether package design A is preferred to design B. The experiment

Figure 5.1 *Probability Histogram for p(y) in Example 5.1*

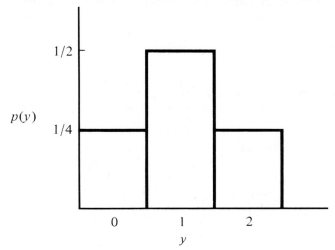

that was designed to answer this question consists of randomly selecting 20 consumers and asking each which package design he prefers. Then, noting the number,
y, of consumers in the sample favoring package design A, the question immediately
arises: How small should this number be before we conclude that package design B
is preferred to design A? To answer this question, we need to find the probability
of an observed sample result.

The easiest way to approach this problem is by way of analogy to a coin-
tossing experiment. If the fraction of all consumers favoring package design A
is at least $\frac{1}{2}$ (let us assume that it is exactly $\frac{1}{2}$), then observing the response of a
randomly selected consumer is analogous to tossing a fair coin. Likewise, the ran-
dom sampling of 20 consumers' responses is analogous to the tossing of 20 fair
coins (a simple extension of the two-coin-tossing experiment considered earlier).
Thus the random variable y, the number of consumers favoring package design A,
corresponds to the number of heads in a toss of 20 coins. For both experiments,
y can assume any of the values $0, 1, 2, \ldots, 20$, with associated probabilities $p(0)$,
$p(1), p(2), \ldots, p(20)$ given by the same probability distribution. Although the exact
probability distribution for this experiment will be discussed in Chapter 6, we
present its graph in Figure 5.2.

From this graph of the probability distribution for y, we observe that the
largest probability is that associated with the value $y = 10$, which is to be expected
if $\frac{1}{2}$ of all consumers favor package design A. Moreover, we note that it is highly
improbable that as few as $y = 3$ or even $y = 5$ consumers favor design A in the sample
if the fraction in the population of all consumers is $\frac{1}{2}$. If $y = 0$, the result is so extremely improbable that we would conclude that the assumption is false. Thus

Figure 5.2   *Probability Distribution for y, the Number of Consumers
Favoring Package Design A; $n = 20$, $p = \frac{1}{2}$*

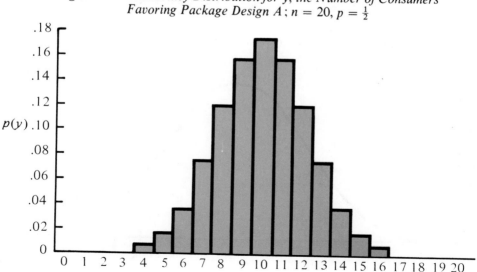

if $y = 0$ or some very small value, we would infer that the population of responses from consumers purchasing the manufacturer's product indicates that less than $\frac{1}{2}$ favor package design A.

5.4   Continuous Random Variables and Their Probability Distributions

As indicated in Section 5.2, continuous random variables can assume the infinitely large number of values corresponding to points on a line interval. Since it is not possible to assign a probability to each of an infinitely large number of points and have these probabilities sum to 1 (as for discrete random variables), a different approach is used to generate the probability distribution for a continuous random variable. The approach that we adopt uses the concept of a relative frequency histogram such as that for the 25 price–earnings ratios, Figure 3.2. Recall that the width of the class interval in Figure 3.2 was determined in accordance with the number of measurements involved. If more and more measurements are obtained, we might reduce the width of the class interval. The outline of the histogram would change slightly, for the most part becoming less and less irregular. When the number of measurements becomes very large and the intervals very small, the relative frequency histogram would appear, for all practical purposes, as a smooth curve, Figure 5.3.

The relative frequency associated with a particular class in the population is the fraction of measurements in the population falling in that interval and also is the probability of drawing a measurement in that class. If the total area under the

Figure 5.3   *Relative Frequency Histogram for a Population*

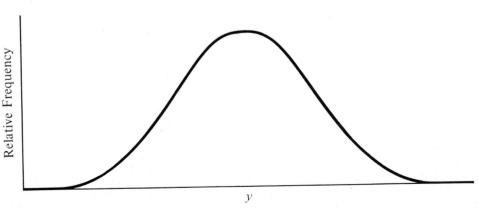

Price—Earnings Ratio

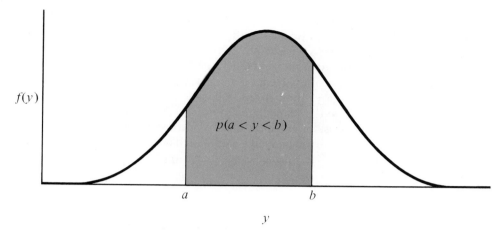

Figure 5.4   *Probability Distributions f(y)*

relative frequency histogram were adjusted to equal 1, areas under the frequency curve would correspond to probabilities. Indeed, this was the basis for the application of the empirical rule in Chapter 2.

Let us construct a model for the probability distribution for a continuous random variable. Assume that the random variable, y, may take values on a real line as in Figure 5.3. We will then distribute 1 unit of probability along the line much as a person might distribute a handful of sand, each measurement in the population corresponding to a single grain. The probability, grains of sand or measurements, will pile up in certain places, and the result will be the probability distribution as in Figure 5.4. The depth or density of probability, which varies with y, may be represented by a mathematical equation $f(y)$, called the probability distribution (or the probability density function) for the random variable y. The function $f(y)$, represented graphically in Figure 5.4, provides a mathematical model for the population relative frequency histogram that exists in reality. The total area under the curve, $f(y)$, is equal to 1, and the area lying above a given interval will equal the probability that y will fall in that interval. Thus the probability that $a < y < b$ (a is less than y and y is less than b) is equal to the shaded area under the density function between the two points a and b.

A question remains. How do we choose the model—that is, the probability distribution, $f(y)$, appropriate for a given physical situation? Fortunately, we will find that most data collected on continuous random variables have mound-shaped frequency distributions, often very nearly bell-shaped. A probability model that provides a good approximation to such population distributions is the normal probability distribution, which we shall study in detail in Chapter 7.

The practice of adopting a model $f(y)$ that can only be expected to approximate the population relative frequency curve requires some comment. It is, of course, a practice that could lead to an invalid conclusion—if an inappropriate model is chosen out of poor judgment or insufficient knowledge of the phenomenon under study. On the other hand, it represents a strategy which, when appropriately applied, has been found highly successful in scientific research. The equations, formulas, and various numerical expressions used in all the sciences are simply mathematical models that provide approximations to reality, the goodness of which are evaluated through experimental application. Hence a model is evaluated in terms of the results of its application: decisions or predictions in business situations. Necessarily, such evaluation is made outside the immediate application of the model, through comparison with the other lines of evidence and by further experimentation. Do the resulting inferences fit in with the body of accumulated evidence? Are the deductions that follow from these inferences verified experimentally? If so, the model has proved its worth.

5.5   Mathematical Expectation

The probability distributions, described in Sections 5.3 and 5.4, provides a model for the theoretical frequency distribution of a random variable and hence must possess a mean, variance, standard deviation, and other descriptive measures associated with the theoretical population that it represents. Recalling that both the mean and variance are averages (Sections 3.5 and 3.6), we shall confine our attention to the problem of calculating the average value of a random variable defined over a theoretical population. This average is called the expected value the random variable.

The method for calculating the population or expected value of a random variable can be more easily understood by considering an example. Let y equal the number of heads observed in the toss of two coins. For convenience, we give $p(y)$:

y	$p(y)$
0	1/4
1	1/2
2	1/4

Let us suppose that the experiment is repeated a large number of times, say $n = 4{,}000{,}000$ times. Intuitively, we would expect to observe approximately 1 million zeros, 2 million ones, and 1 million twos. Then the average value of y would equal

$$\frac{\text{sum of measurements}}{n} = \frac{1{,}000{,}000(0) + 2{,}000{,}000(1) + 1{,}000{,}000(2)}{4{,}000{,}000}$$

$$= \frac{1{,}000{,}000(0)}{4{,}000{,}000} + \frac{2{,}000{,}000(1)}{4{,}000{,}000} + \frac{1{,}000{,}000(2)}{4{,}000{,}000}$$

$$= (1/4)(0) + (1/2)(1) + (1/4)(2).$$

Note that the first term in this sum is equal to $(0)p(0)$, the second is equal to $(1)p(1)$, and the third is equal to $(2)p(2)$. The average value of y is then equal to

$$\sum_{y=0}^{2} yp(y) = 1.$$

You will observe that this result was not an accident and that it would be intuitively reasonable to define the expected value of y for a discrete random variable as follows.

Definition

   Let y be a discrete random variable with probability distribution $p(y)$ and let $E(y)$ represent the expected value of y. Then

$$E(y) = \sum_{y} yp(y),$$

where the elements are summed over all values of the random variable y.

Note that if $p(y)$ is an accurate description of the relative frequencies for a real population of data, then $E(y) = \mu$, the mean of the population. We shall assume this to be true and let $E(y)$ be synonymous with μ.

The method for calculating the expected value of y for a continuous random variable is rather similar from an intuitive point of view, but, in practice, it involves the use of the calculus and is therefore beyond the scope of this text.

Example 5.2   *A grocer stocks enough of a perishable commodity each morning to cover the expected daily demand. Having recorded the daily demand over a long period of time, the grocer found the following probability distribution for y, the daily demand.*

y	1	2	3	4	5
$p(y)$	1/10	2/10	4/10	2/10	1/10

Then the expected value of y would be

$$E(y) = \sum_{y=1}^{5} yp(y) = (1)p(1) + (2)p(2) + \cdots + (5)p(5)$$

$$= (1)(1/10) + (2)(2/10) + (3)(4/10)$$
$$+ (4)(2/10) + (5)(1/10)$$

$$= \frac{30}{10} = 3.$$

Example 5.3   *Eight thousand tickets are to be sold at $1 each in a lottery conducted to benefit the local fire company. The prize is a $3,000.00 automobile. If Ed Smith has purchased two tickets, what is his expected gain?*

Solution   *Smith's gain, y, may take one of two values. Either he will lose $2 (that is, his gain will be $-\$2$) or he will win $2,998.00 with probabilities 7,998/8,000 and 2/8,000, respectively. The probability distribution for the gain, y, is*

y	p(y)
-2.00	$\dfrac{7,998}{8,000}$
$\$2,998.00$	$\dfrac{2}{8,000}$

The expected gain will be

$$E(y) = \sum_y yp(y)$$

$$= (-2.00)\frac{7,998}{8,000} + (\$2,998.00)\frac{2}{8,000}$$

$$= -\$1.25.$$

Recall that the expected value of y is the average of the theoretical population that would result if the lottery were repeated an infinitely large number of times. If this were done, Smith's average or expected gain per lottery would be a loss of $1.25.

Example 5.4   *Consider the problem of determining the yearly premium for a $1,000.00 insurance policy covering an event which, over a long period of time, has occurred at the rate of 2 times in 100. Let y equal the yearly financial gain to the insurance company resulting from the sale of the policy and let C equal the unknown yearly premium. We shall calculate the value of C such that the expected gain, E(y), will equal zero. Then C is the premium required to break even. To this the company would add administrative costs and profit.*

Solution   *We would suppose that the expected gain, E(y), would depend upon C. Using the requirement that the expected gain must equal zero, we have*

$$E(y) = \sum_y yp(y) = 0.$$

Since the expression on the left side of this equation depends upon C, we can solve the equation to find the value of C for which $E(y) = 0$.

The first step in the solution is to determine the values that the gain, y, may take and then to determine p(y). If the event does not occur during the year, the insurance company will gain the premium or y = C dollars. If the event does occur, the gain will be negative—will be a loss—amounting to y = −(1,000 − C) dollars. This will be the amount the insurance company must pay, less the amount of the premium already collected. The probabilities associated with these two values of y are 98/100 and 2/100, respectively. The probability distribution for the gain would be

y = gain	p(y)
C	$\dfrac{98}{100}$
−(1,000 − C)	$\dfrac{2}{100}$

Setting the expected value of y equal to zero and solving for C, we have

$$E(y) = \sum_y yp(y)$$

$$= C\left(\frac{98}{100}\right) + [-(1,000 - C)](2/100) = 0$$

or

$$\frac{98}{100}C + \frac{2}{100}C - 20 = 0$$

and

$$C = \$20.$$

Concluding, if the insurance company were to charge a yearly premium of $20, the average gain calculated for a large number of similar policies would equal zero. The actual premium would equal $20 plus administrative costs and profit.

The insurance premium problem can be extended to include any number of gains to the insurance company by solving for the premium, C, in the expression

$$E(y) = \sum_y yp(y) = 0,$$

where y is the random variable representing the insurance company's gains. The difficulty in a practical problem of this type is to identify each gain and associate with that gain a meaningful probability that it will occur. An actuary, a mathematical statistician employed by the insurance company, is an individual who attempts to compute the gains, risks, and premiums associated with an insurance policy.

We have learned how to find the mathematical expectation for a random variable. Let us now consider the problem of finding the mathematical average or expectation for some function of y, for instance, the quantity $(y - \mu)^2$. The average value of $(y - \mu)^2$ is, by definition, the population variance, σ^2. The rule for finding the expected value of a function of y, say $g(y)$, is as follows:

Definition

   Let y be a discrete random variable with probability distribution $p(y)$, and let $g(y)$ be a numerical-valued function of y. Then the expected value of $g(y)$ is

$$E[g(y)] = \sum_y g(y)p(y).$$

where the elements are summed over all values of the random variable y.

The function $g(y)$ may be any numerical-valued function of y, but we consider only the function y itself, whose expected value is the population mean μ, and $(y - \mu)^2$, whose expectation is the population variance σ^2. The reader may obtain the expected value for other functions of y and other random variables, the results of which will agree with our preceding definition.

   Example 5.5   *Find the variance, σ^2, for the population associated with Example 5.1, the coin-tossing problem. The expected value of y was shown to equal 1.*

   Solution   *The variance is equal to the expected value of $(y - \mu)^2$ or*

$$= E[(y - \mu)^2] = \sum_y (y - \mu)^2 p(y)$$

$$= (0 - 1)^2 p(0) + (1 - 1)^2 p(1) + (2 - 1)^2 p(2)$$

$$= (1)(1/4) + 0(1/2) + (1)(1/4)$$

$$= 1/2.$$

Then $\sigma = \sqrt{\tfrac{1}{2}} = .707$. Note how $\mu = 1$ and $\sigma = .707$ describe the probability distribution, Figure 5.1.

5.6   Summary

   Random variables, representing numerical events defined over a sample space, may be classified as discrete or continuous random variables, depending upon whether the number of sample points in the sample space is or is not countable. The theoretical population frequency distribution for the discrete random variable is called a probability distribution and may be derived using the technique of Chapter 4. The model for the frequency distribution for a continuous random variable is a mathematical function, $f(y)$, called a probability distribution or probability density function. This function, usually a smooth curve, is defined over a line interval and is chosen such that the total area under the curve is equal to 1. The probabilities associated with a continuous random variable are given as areas under the probability distribution, $f(y)$.

A mathematical expectation is the average of a random variable calculated for the theoretical population defined by its probability distribution.

Exercises

1. A salesman figures that each contact results in a sale with probability .2. During a given day he contacts two prospective clients. Calculate the probability distribution for y, the number of clients who sign a sales contract. [*Hint*: Let F indicate the event that a single contact fails to buy. Then $P(0) = P(FF) = P(F)P(F) = (.8)^2 = .64$.] Construct a probability histogram for y.

2. An investor has decided to invest his money in two different stocks. He has his choice narrowed down to two common stocks and two preferred stocks. Unable to choose between these, he randomly chooses two stocks from the four. Find the probability distribution for y, the number of preferred stocks he chooses. Construct a graph of the probability distribution.

3. A manufacturer knows that 10 percent of all lots of bearings purchased for his production contain at least one defective bearing. He purchases two lots of bearings each week. Find the probability distribution for y, the number of lots received each week that contain at least one defective bearing. Construct a probability histogram for y.

4. Refer to Example 5.1. Simulate the experiment by tossing two coins 100 times. After each toss record y, the number of heads appearing. Construct a relative frequency histogram for this sample and compare it with the population probability distribution. If the sampling process were repeated $n = 100,000$ times (instead of $n = 100$) and you constructed a relative frequency histogram for the data, how would your histogram compare with the probability distribution for the population?

5. Simulate the experiment described in Exercise 2 by marking four pieces of cardboard, or coins, so that two represent common stocks and two represent preferred stocks. Place these in a hat, mix, draw two, and record y, the numer of "preferreds" observed. Replace the two drawn in the hat and repeat the process until a total of $n = 100$ observations on y have been recorded. Construct a relative frequency histogram for this sample and compare it with the population probability distribution, Exercise 2. If the sampling process were repeated $n = 100,000$ times (instead of $n = 100$) and you constructed a relative frequency histogram for the data, how would your histogram compare with the population probability distribution, Exercise 2?

6. Let y represent the number of times a housewife visits a grocery store in a 1-week period. Assume that the following is the probability distribution of y.

y	$P(y)$
0	.1
1	.5
2	.3
3	.1

Find the expected value of y. This is the average number of times a housewife visits the store.

7. A salesman contacts four people during a normal working day. Let the following be the probability distribution for y, the number of clients who buy his product.

y	$P(y)$
0	.1
1	.3
2	.4
3	.1
4	.1

Find the average number of sales he makes per day.

8. A new product is shown to three customers. The following is the probability distribution for y, the number of customers buying the product.

y	$P(y)$
0	1/12
1	3/12
2	4/12
3	4/12

Find the expected value and variance of y.

9. Refer to Exercise 8. Construct a probability histogram for y. Calculate σ and find the probability that y will lie within 2σ of μ. Does this agree with Tchebysheff's theorem? Do μ and σ characterize $P(y)$?

10. Refer to Exercise 2. Find the expected value and variance of y. If you performed the simulation in Exercise 5, calculate $\bar{y}$ and s^2 for the 100 measurements. Compare these values with the expected value and variance of y.

11. Refer to Exercise 10. Calculate σ and find the probability that y will lie within 2σ and μ. Does this agree with Tchebysheff's theorem? Do μ and σ characterize $P(y)$?

12. A personnel director wishes to select three of five candidates interviewed. Although all five candidates appear to be equally desirable, there likely exists a "best" candidate, a second best, and so on. Refer to the three, and unknown, best candidates as "successes" and let y equal the number of "successes" appearing in the personnel director's selection; that is, $y = 1, 2,$ or 3. Find the probability distribution for y. Construct a probability histogram for y. What is the probability that he selects at least two of the three best?

13. A mail-order magazine-subscription service receives orders for one, two, and three-year subscriptions with probability 1/2, 1/4, and 1/4, respectively. For each subscription year, they receive a \$1 commission. What is the subscription service's expected commission for each order received?

14. A potential customer for a \$20,000 fire insurance policy possesses a home in an area, which, according to experience, may sustain a total loss in a given year with probability of .001 and a 50 percent loss with probability .01. Ignoring all other partial losses, what premium should the insurance company charge for a yearly policy in order to break even?

15. In a county containing a large number of rural homes 60 percent are thought to be insured against fire. Three rural home owners are chosen at random from the entire population and y are found to be insured against a fire. Find the probability distribution for y. What is the probability that at least two of the three will be insured?

16. A person owns a car valued at $4,000. He desires to buy insurance to protect himself against loss due to accidental damage. From past experience it is known that in a given year a car of this type may be totally destroyed with probability .005. The car may also suffer damages of $1,000 or $2,000 with probabilities .1 and .01, respectively. Ignoring all other partial losses, what premium should the insurance company charge for a yearly policy in order to break even?

17. A manufacturing representative is considering the option of taking out an insurance policy to cover possible losses incurred by marketing a new product. If the product is a complete failure, the representative feels that a loss of $80,000 would be incurred; if it is only moderately successful, a loss of $25,000 would be incurred. Insurance actuaries have determined from market surveys and other available information that the probabilities the product will be a failure or only moderately successful are .01 and .05, respectively. Assuming that the manufacturing representative would be willing to ignore all other possible losses, what premium should the insurance company charge for the policy in order to break even?

References

Fraser, D. A. S., *Statistics: An Introduction.* New York: John Wiley & Sons, Inc., 1958. Chapters 3 and 4.

Freund, J. E., *Mathematical Statistics.* Englewood Cliffs, N.J.: Prentice-Hall, Inc., 1962. Chapters 3 and 4.

Hadley, G., *Introduction to Business Statistics.* San Francisco: Holden-Day, Inc., 1968. Chapter 2.

Mosteller. F.. R. E. K. Rourke, and G. B. Thomas, Jr., *Probability with Statistical Applications.* 2nd ed. Reading, Mass.: Addison-Wesley Publishing Company, Inc., 1970. Chapter 5.

Spurr, W. A., and C. P. Bonini, *Statistical Analysis for Business Decisions.* Rev. ed. Homewood, Ill.: Richard D. Irwin, Inc., 1973. Chapters 7 and 8.

Chapter 6

The Binomial and Poisson Probability Distributions

6.1 Introduction

In Chapter 5 we found that random variables defined over a finite or count-ably infinite number of points are called discrete random variables. Examples of discrete random variables abound in business and economics, but two discrete probability distributions model a large number of these applications.

In this chapter we will study the binomial probability distribution and the Poisson probability distribution, noting their development as logical models for discrete processes observed in different business settings. Throughout the study of Chapter 6, it will be necessary to refer back to Chapter 5 and the definition of a probability distribution, a formula or model that assigns a probability to each possible numerical outcome of an experiment. Thus the nature of the experiment itself and the numerical outcomes of the experiment must be considered before selecting the appropriate probability distribution to model the process.

6.2 The Binomial Experiment

One of the most elementary, useful, and interesting discrete random variables is associated with the coin-tossing experiment. In this experiment either one coin is tossed n times or n coins are each tossed once. The observation "head" or "tail" is then recorded for each toss. In an abstract sense, numerous coin-tossing experiments of practical importance are conducted daily in the social sciences, physical sciences, and industry.

To illustrate, we might consider a sample survey conducted to predict voter preference in a political election. Interviewing a single voter bears a similarity, in many respects, to tossing a single coin, because the voter's response may be in favor of our candidate—a "head"—or it may be opposition (or indicate indecision)— a "tail." In most cases, the fraction of voters favoring a particular candidate will not equal one-half, but even this similarity to the coin-tossing experiment is satisfied in national presidential elections. History demonstrates that the fraction of the total vote favoring the winning presidential candidate in most national elections is very near one-half.

Similar polls are conducted in the social sciences, in industry, in education. The sociologist is interested in the fraction of rural homes that have been electrified ; the cigarette manufacturer desires knowledge concerning the fraction of smokers who prefer his brand ; the teacher is interested in the fraction of students who pass his course. Each person sampled is analogous to the toss of an unbalanced coin (since the probability of a "head" is usually not 1/2).

Firing a projectile at a target is similar to a coin-tossing experiment if a "hit the target" and a "miss the target" are regarded as a head and a tail, respectively. A single missile will result in either a successful or an unsuccessful launching. A new drug will prove either effective or ineffective when administered to a single patient, and a manufactured item selected from a production line will be either defective or nondefective. With each contact, either a salesman will consummate a sale or no sale will result. Although dissimilar in some respects the experiments described above will often exhibit, to a reasonable degree of approximation, the characteristics of a binomial experiment.

Definition

A *binomial experiment* is one that possesses the following properties:

1. *The experiment consists of n identical trials.*

2. *Each trial results in one of two outcomes. For a lack of better nomenclature, we shall call the one outcome a success, S, and the other a failure, F.*

3. *The probability of success on a single trial is equal to p and remains the same from trial to trial. The probability of a failure is equal to* $(1 - p) = q$.

4. *The trials are independent.*

5. *We are interested in y, the number of successes observed during the n trials.*

Very few real-life situations will perfectly satisfy the requirements stated above, but this is of little consequence as long as the lack of agreement is moderate and does not affect the end result. For instance, the probability of drawing a buyer favoring a particular product in a marketing research survey remains approximately constant from trial to trial as long as the population of buyers is relatively large in comparison with the sample. If 50 percent of a population of 1,000 buyers prefer product A, then the probability of drawing an A on the first interview will be $1/2$. The probability of an A on the second draw will equal 499/999 or 500/999, depending on whether the first draw was favorable or unfavorable to A. Both are near $1/2$ and would continue to be for the third, fourth, and nth trial as long as n is not too large. Hence $P(A)$ remains approximately $1/2$ from trial to trial and, for all practical purposes, we could regard the trials as independent. On the other hand, if the number of buyers in the population is 10, and 5 favor product A, then the probability of A on the first trial is $1/2$; the probability of A on the second trial is 4/9 or 5/9, depending on whether A was or was not drawn on the first trial. For small populations, the probability of A will vary appreciably from trial to trial, independence will not exist, and the resulting experiment will not be a binomial experiment.

6.3   The Binomial Probability Distribution

Having defined the binomial experiment and suggested several practical applications we now turn to a derivation of the probability distribution for the random variable, y, the number of successes observed in n trials. Rather than attempt a direct derivation, we will obtain $p(y)$ for experiments containing $n = 1, 2$, and 3 trials and leave the general formula to the reader's intuition.

For $n = 1$ trial, we have two sample points, E_1 representing a success, S, and E_2 representing a failure, F, with probabilities p and $q = (1 - p)$, respectively. The values $y = 1$ would be associated with E_1 and $y = 0$ with E_2. The resulting probability distribution for y is given in Table 6.1.

The probability distribution for an experiment consisting of $n = 2$ trials is derived in a similar manner and is presented in Table 6.2. The four sample points associated with the experiment are presented in the first column with the notation SF implying a success in the first trial and a failure on the second.

Table 6.1   *p(y) for a Binomial Experiment, n = 1*

SAMPLE POINTS	$P(E_i)$	y
E_1 S	p	1
E_2 F	q	0

y	$p(y)$
0	q
1	p

$$\sum_{y=0}^{1} p(y) = q + p = 1$$

Table 6.2   *p(y) for a Binomial Experiment, n = 2*

SAMPLE POINTS		$P(E_i)$	y
E_1	SS	p^2	2
E_2	SF	pq	1
E_3	FS	qp	1
E_4	FF	q^2	0

y	$p(y)$
0	q^2
1	$2pq$
2	p^2

$$\sum_{y=0}^{2} p(y) = (q + p)^2 = (1)^2 = 1$$

The probabilities of the sample points are easily calculated because each point is an intersection of two independent events, the outcomes of the first and second trials. Thus $P(E_i)$ can be obtained by applying the multiplicative law of probability:

$$P(E_1) = P(SS) = P(S)P(S) = p^2,$$

$$P(E_2) = P(SF) = P(S)P(F) = pq,$$

$$P(E_3) = P(FS) = P(F)P(S) = pq,$$

$$P(E_4) = P(FF) = P(F)P(F) = q^2.$$

The value of y assigned to each sample point is given in the third column. The reader will note that the numerical event $y = 0$ contains sample point E_4, the event $y = 1$ contains sample points E_2 and E_3, and $y = 2$ contains sample point E_1. The probability distribution $p(y)$, presented to the right of Table 6.2, reveals a most interesting consequence; the probabilities $p(y)$ are terms of the expansion $(q + p)^2$.

Summing, we obtain

$$\sum_{y=0}^{2} p(y) = q^2 + 2pq + p^2$$

$$= (q + p)^2 = 1.$$

The point that we wish to make is now quite clear; the probability distribution for the binomial experiment consisting of n trials is obtained by expanding $(q + p)^n$. The proof of this statement is omitted but may be obtained by using combinations to count the appropriate sample points or can be rather easily proved by mathematical induction, a task that we leave to the student of mathematics. Those more easily convinced may acquire further evidence of the truth of our statement by observing the derivation of the probability distribution for a binomial experiment consisting of $n = 3$ trials presented in Table 6.3.

Table 6.3 *p(y) for a Binomial Experiment, n = 3*

	SAMPLE POINTS	$P(E_i)$	y		y	p(y)
E_1	SSS	p^3	3		0	q^3
E_2	SSF	p^2q	2		1	$3pq^2$
E_3	SFS	p^2q	2		2	$3p^2q$
E_4	SFF	pq^2	1		3	p^3
E_5	FSS	p^2q	2			
E_6	FSF	pq^2	1			
E_7	FFS	pq^2	1			
E_8	FFF	q^3	0			

$$\sum_{y=0}^{3} p(y) = (q + p)^3 = 1$$

Since the probability associated with a particular value of y is the term involving p to the power y in the expansion of $(q + p)^n$, we may write the probability distribution for the binomial experiment as

$$p(y) = C_y^n p^y q^{n-y},$$

$$= \frac{n!}{y!(n - y)!} p^y q^{n-y},$$

where y may take values 0, 1, 2, 3, 4, ..., *n.*

You recall from high school algebra that the factorial notation, $n!$, is a short way of writing $n! = n(n - 1)(n - 2) \cdots (3)(2)(1)$. Thus $3! = 3 \cdot 2 \cdot 1$ and $0!$ is defined to be equal to 1. The notation C_y^n is a short way of writing

$$C_y^n = \frac{n!}{y!(n - y)!}$$

This notation is useful because it occurs so often when working with the binomial probability distribution.

Let us now consider a few examples.

Example 6.1 *Over a long period of time it has been observed that a given rifleman can hit a target on a single trial with probability equal to .8. If he fires four shots at the target,*

(a) *What is the probability that he will hit the target exactly two times?*

Solution   *Assuming that the trials are independent and that p remains constant from trial to trial, n = 4, p = .8, and*

$$p(y) = C_y^4(.8)^y(.2)^{4-y},$$

$$p(2) = C_2^4(.8)^2(.2)^{4-2}$$

$$= \frac{4!}{2!2!}(.64)(.04)$$

$$= .1536.$$

(b) *What is the probability that he will hit the target at least two times?*

Solution

$$P(\text{at least two}) = p(2) + p(3) + p(4)$$

$$= 1 - p(0) - p(1)$$

$$= 1 - C_0^4(.8)^0(.2)^4 - C_1^4(.8)(.2)^3$$

$$= 1 - .0016 - .0256$$

$$= .9728.$$

(c) *What is the probability that he will hit the target exactly four times?*

Solution

$$p(4) = C_4^4(.8)^4(.2)^0$$

$$= \frac{4!}{4!0!}(.8)^4(1)$$

$$= .4096.$$

Note that these probabilities would be incorrect if the rifleman could observe the location of each hit on the target; in that case, the trials would be dependent and p would likely increase from trial to trial.

Example 6.2   *Large lots of incoming product at a manufacturing plant are inspected for defectives by means of a sampling scheme. Ten items are to be examined and the lot rejected if two or more defectives are observed. If a lot contains exactly 5 percent defectives, what is the probability that the lot will be accepted? Rejected? Assume independence between successive draws from the lot.*

Solution   *If y equals the number of defectives observed, then n = 10 and the probability of observing a defective on a single trial will be p = .05. Then*

$$p(y) = C_y^{10}(.05)^y(.95)^{10-y}$$

and

$$P(\text{accept}) = p(0) + p(1) = C_0^{10}(.05)^0(.95)^{10} + C_1^{10}(.05)^1(.95)^9$$

$$= .914,$$

$$P(\text{reject}) = 1 - p(\text{accept})$$

$$= 1 - .914$$

$$= .086.$$

Example 6.3   *A new serum was tested to determine its effectiveness in preventing the common cold. Ten people were injected with the serum and observed for a period of 1 year. Eight survived the winter without a cold. Suppose it is known that when a serum is not used, the probability of surviving a winter without a cold is .5 and that whether an individual survives a winter without a cold is independent of the state of health of any other subject. What is the probability of observing eight or more survivors, given that the serum is ineffective in increasing the bodily resistance to colds?*

Solution   *Assuming that the vaccine is ineffective, the probability of surviving the winter without a cold is* $p = .5$. *The probability distribution for* y, *the number of survivors, is*

$$p(y) = C_y^{10}(.5)^y(.5)^{10-y} = C_y^{10}(.5)^{10},$$

$$P(8 \text{ or more}) = p(8) + p(9) + p(10)$$

$$= C_8^{10}(.5)^{10} + C_9^{10}(.5)^{10} + C_{10}^{10}(.5)^{10}$$

$$= .055.$$

Calculation of the binomial probabilities, $p(y)$, can be tedious. Fortunately, these probabilities have been calculated and are available in tables listed in the References at the end of the chapter. An abbreviated tabulation of the sum of $p(y)$ for $y = 0, 1, 2, \ldots, a$ is given in Table 1, Appendix, for $n = 5, 10, 15, 20,$ and 25. We shall illustrate the use of Table 1 with an example.

Example 6.4   *It is known from experience that 40 percent of all orders received by a shipping company are placed by the Mallon Company. If* $n = 10$ *orders are received by the shipping company, find the probability that*

(a) Not more than six are received from the Mallon Company.
(b) Exactly four orders are received from the Mallon Company.

Solution   *The above example describes a binomial experiment with* $n = 10$, $p = .4$, *and the binomial random variable,* y, *representing the number of orders received by the shipping company which were sent by the Mallon Company. We must find* $P(y \le 6)$ *and* $p(4)$.

(a)   P(*not more than 6 orders received from Mallon*)

$$= P(y = 0, 1, 2, 3, 4, 5, \text{ or } 6) = \sum_{y=0}^{6} p(y)$$

$$= .945.$$

(b)   P(*exactly 4 orders received from Mallon*)

$$= P(y = 4)$$

$$= \sum_{y=0}^{4} p(y) - \sum_{y=0}^{3} p(y)$$

$$= .633 - .382$$

$$= .251.$$

Examples 6.1, 6.2, and 6.3 illustrate the use of the binomial probability distribution in calculating the probability associated with values of y, the number of successes in n trials defined for the binomial experiment. Thus we note that the probability distribution, $p(y) = C_y^n p^y q^{n-y}$, provides a simple formula for calculating the probabilities of numerical events, y, applicable to a broad class of experiments that occur in everyday life. This statement must be accompanied by a word of caution. The important point, of course, is that each physical application must be carefully checked against the defining characteristics of the binomial experiment, Section 6.2, to determine whether the binomial experiment is a valid model for the application of interest.

6.4 The Mean and Variance for the Binomial Probability Distribution

Having derived the theoretical frequency distribution for the population associated with the binomial random variable, y, it would seem desirable to find formulas for its expected value and variance. Specifically, we would like to describe this theoretical distribution utilizing the mean and variance (or standard deviation) as measures of central tendency and variation. We shall have further use for these quantities in Chapter 8.

Our approach to the acquisition of formulas for μ and σ^2 will be similar to that employed in Section 6.2 for the determination of the probability distribution, $p(y)$. We shall use the methods of Chapter 5 to obtain these expectations; that is, $E(y)$ and $E(y - \mu)^2$, for the simple cases $n = 1$, 2, and 3, and then give the formulas for the general case without proof. The interested reader may derive the formulas for the general case involving n trials by using the summation theorems of Chapter 2, some algebraic manipulation, and a bit of ingenuity.

The expected value of y for $n = 1$ and 2 can be derived using the probabilities given in Tables 6.1 and 6.2 along with the definition of an expectation presented in Section 5.6. For $n = 1$ we obtain

$$\mu = E(y) = \sum_{y=0}^{1} yp(y) = (0)(q) + (1)(p) = p.$$

For $n = 2$,

$$\mu = E(y) = \sum_{y=0}^{2} yp(y) = (0)(q^2) + (1)(2pq) + (2)(p^2)$$

$$= 2p(q + p) = 2p.$$

The reader using Table 6.3 can quickly show that $E(y)$ for $n = 3$ trials is equal to $3p$ and would surmise that this pattern would hold in general. Indeed, it can be shown that the expected value of y for a binomial experiment consisting of n trials is

$$E(y) = np.$$

Similarly, we may obtain the variance of y for $n = 1$ and 2 trials as follows.

For $n = 1$,

$$\sigma^2 = E(y - \mu)^2 = \sum_{y=0}^{1} (y - \mu)^2 p(y) = (0 - p)^2(q) + (1 - p)^2(p)$$

$$= p^2 q + q^2 p = pq(q + p)$$

$$= pq.$$

For $n = 2$,

$$\sigma^2 = E(y - \mu)^2 = \sum_{y=0}^{2} (y - \mu)^2 p(y)$$

$$= (0 - 2p)^2(q^2) + (1 - 2p)^2(2pq) + (2 - 2p)^2(p^2)$$

$$= 4p^2 q^2 + (1 - 4p + 4p^2)(2pq) + 4(1 - p)^2 p^2.$$

Using the substitution $q = 1 - p$ and a bit of algebraic manipulation, we find that the above reduces to

$$\sigma^2 = 2pq.$$

The reader may verify that the variance of y for $n = 3$ trials is $3pq$. In general, for n trials it can be shown that the variance of y is

$$\sigma^2 = npq.$$

As we have previously mentioned, these formulas can now be employed to compute the mean and variance for the binomial variable, y. Thus we can say something concerning the center of the distribution as well as the variability of y.

6.5   Lot Acceptance Sampling

The reader will note that Examples 6.1 through 6.3 were problems in probability rather than statistics. The composition of the binomial population, characterized by p, the probability of a success on a single trial, was assumed known and we were interested in calculating the probability of certain numerical events. Let us now reverse the procedure; that is, let us assume that we possess a sample from the population and wish to make inferences concerning p. The physical settings for Examples 6.2 and 6.3 supply excellent practical situations in which the ultimate objective was statistical inference. We shall consider these two problems in greater detail in the succeeding sections.

Example 6.2 describes a plan for accepting or rejecting large lots of incoming items in a manufacturing plant. The objective is to screen the lots to eliminate those containing a high fraction of defective items. For example, suppose that a manufacturer purchases large lots, each containing 1,000 ball bearings of a specific type. He is unwilling to pay for defective bearings and hence will accept lots containing no more than $p = .05$ fraction defective. Thus a good lot is defined as one for which $p \leq .05$ and,correspondingly, an unacceptable lot would contain fraction defective $p > .05$. The manufacturer wishes to identify unacceptable lots so that they can be returned to the supplier.

One way to detect unacceptable lots would be to inspect every item in the lot. This procedure is not only costly but is also imperfect. That is, inspector fatigue as well as other human factors permit defective items to pass through the screen undetected. A less costly and effective means of screening is to reject or accept lots on the basis of a sample. Thus a sample of n items is drawn from the lot, inspected, and the number of defectives, y, is recorded. The lot is accepted if the number of defectives is less than or equal to a preselected number, a, called the acceptance number. If y exceeds a, the lot is rejected and returned to the supplier.

Every sampling plan is defined by a sample size n and an acceptance number a. Changing one or both of these numbers changes the sampling plan and the characteristics of the screen. These characteristics are measured by the probability of accepting a lot of a specified fraction defective as indicated in Example 6.2. For the ball-bearing illustration, we would like the probability of accepting a lot to be very small if $p > .05$ and the lot is consequently unacceptable. On the other hand, we would like to accept lots with a high probability if $p < .05$. We shall illustrate with an example.

Example 6.5   *Consider the following sampling plan for the purchaser of ball bearings. A sample of $n = 25$ bearings will be selected at random from a lot, and the. lot will be accepted if the number of defectives is less than or equal to $a = 1$. Use Table 1, Appendix, to find the probability of accepting lots containing the following fraction defectives:*

(a) $p = .10$.
(b) $p = .30$.
(c) $p = .01$.

Solution $P(accepting\ a\ lot) = P(y = 0, 1) = \sum\limits_{y=0}^{1} p(y)$.

Consulting Table 1, we find the probabilities of acceptance to be

(a)   .271.
(b)   .002.
(c)   .974.

Note that this sampling plan offers a fairly high risk of accepting a lot containing 10 percent defective. (The probability of acceptance for $p = .10$ is .271.) The manufacturer can decrease the probability of accepting by increasing the sample size n, by decreasing a, or both. The effect on the probability of lot acceptance of varying n and a will be illustrated in the Exercises at the end of the chapter.

The reader will note that lot acceptance sampling is an excellent example of statistical inference. Information contained in the sample is employed to infer the nature of p, the lot (population) fraction defective. Thus if the number of defectives in the sample is large, $y > a$, we infer that $p > .05$ and reject the lot. If $y < a$, we accept the lot. In essence, rejecting or accepting a lot is equivalent to making an inference about a population parameter, p.

6.6   A Test of an Hypothesis

The cold vaccine problem, Example 6.3, is illustrative of a statistical test of an hypothesis. The practical question to be answered concerns the effectiveness of the vaccine. Do the data contained in the sample present sufficient evidence to indicate that the vaccine is effective?

The reasoning employed in testing an hypothesis bears a striking resemblance to the procedure used in a court trial. In trying a man for theft, the court assumes the accused innocent until proved guilty. The prosecution collects and presents all available evidence in an attempt to contradict the "not-guilty" hypothesis and hence to obtain a conviction. The statistical problem portrays the vaccine as the accused. The hypothesis to be tested, called the null hypothesis, is that the vaccine is ineffective. The evidence in the case is contained in the sample drawn from the population of potential vaccine customers. The experimenter, playing the role of the prosecutor, believes that his vaccine is really effective and hence attempts to use the evidence contained in a sample to reject the null hypothesis and thereby to support his contention that the vaccine is, in fact, a very successful cold vaccine. The reader will recognize this procedure as an essential feature of the scientific method where all theories proposed must be compared with reality.

Intuitively, we would select the number of survivors, y, as a measure of the quantity of evidence in the sample. If y were large, we would be inclined to reject the null hypothesis and conclude that the vaccine is effective. On the other hand, a small value of y would provide little evidence to support the rejection of the null hypothesis. As a matter of fact, if the null hypothesis were true and the vaccine were ineffective, the probability of surviving a winter without a cold would be $p = 1/2$ and the average value of y would be

$$E(y) = np = 10(1/2) = 5.$$

Most individuals utilizing their own built-in decision makers would have little difficulty arriving at a decision for the case $y = 10$ or $y = 5, 4, 3, 2,$ or 1, which, on the surface, appear to provide substantial evidence to support rejection or acceptance, respectively. But what can be said concerning less obvious results, say $y = 7$, 8, or 9? Clearly, whether we employ a subjective or an objective decision-making procedure, we would choose the procedure that gave the smallest probability of making an incorrect decision.

The statistician would test the null hypothesis in an objective manner similar to our intuitive procedure. The device he employs to perform the test, called a test statistic, is calculated from information contained in the sample. In our example, the number of survivors, y, would suffice for a test statistic. We would then consider all possible values which the test statistic may assume, for example, $y = 0, 1,$ $2, \ldots, 9, 10$. These values would be divided into two groups, one called the rejection region and the other the acceptance region. An experiment is then conducted and the test statistic, y, observed. If y takes a value in the rejection region, the hypothesis is rejected. Otherwise, it is accepted. For example, we might choose $y = 8, 9$, or 10 as the rejection region and assign the remaining values of y to the acceptance region. Since we observed $y = 8$ survivors, we would reject the null hypothesis that the vaccine is ineffective and conclude that the probability of surviving the winter without a cold is greater than $p = 1/2$ when the vaccine is used. What is the probability that we will reject the null hypothesis when, in fact, it is true? The probability of falsely rejecting the null hypothesis is the probability that y will equal 8, 9, or 10, given that $p = 1/2$, and this is indeed the probability computed in Example 6.3 and found to equal .055. Since we have decided to reject the null hypothesis and note that this probability is small, we are reasonably confident that we have made the correct decision.

Upon reflection, the reader will observe that the manufacturer is faced with two possible types of error. On the one hand, he might reject the null hypothesis and falsely conclude that the vaccine was effective. Proceeding with a more thorough and expensive testing program or a pilot-plant production of the vaccine would result in a financial loss. On the other hand, he might decide not to reject the null hypothesis and falsely conclude that the vaccine was ineffective. This error would result in the loss of potential profits that could be derived through the sale of a successful vaccine.

Definition

A *type I error* for a statistical test is the error incurred by rejecting the null hypothesis when it is true. The probability of making a type I error is denoted by the symbol α.

The probability, α, will increase or decrease as we increase or decrease the size of the rejection region, Inasmuch as α measures the risk of falsely rejecting, we might ask why we do not choose the rejection region as small as possible. For example, why not choose $y = 10$ as the rejection region? Unfortunately, decreasing α increases the probability of not rejecting when the null hypothesis is false and an alternative hypothesis is true. This second type of error is called the type II error for a statistical test.

Definition

A *type II error* for a statistical test is the error incurred by accepting (not rejecting) the null hypothesis when it is false and some alternative hypothesis is true. The probability of making a type II error is denoted by the symbol β.

For a fixed sample size, n, the probabilities α and β are inversely related; as one increases, the other decreases. Increasing the sample size provides more information upon which to base the decision and hence reduces both α and β. In an experimental situation, the probabilities of type I and type II errors for a test measure the risk of making an incorrect decision. The experimenter selects values for these probabilities, and the rejection region and sample size are chosen accordingly.

A discussion of the theory of tests of hypotheses may seem a bit premature at this point, but it provides an introduction to a line of reasoning that is sometimes difficult to grasp and which is best presented when it is allowed to incubate in the mind of the student over a period of time. Thus, some of the exercises at the end of Chapter 6 involve the use of the binomial probability distribution and, at the same time, lead the student to utilize the reasoning involved in statistical tests of hypotheses. We shall take occasion to expand upon these ideas through examples and exercises in Chapter 7 and will discuss in detail the topic of statistical tests of hypotheses in Chapter 8 and succeeding chapters.

6.7   The Poisson Distribution

If, in a binomial experiment, the sample size n is quite large and p is small, the binomial probabilities are often approximated by the Poisson distribution

$$
\begin{aligned}
p(y) &= \frac{(np)^y e^{-np}}{y!} \\
&= \frac{(\mu)^y e^{-\mu}}{y!}, \qquad y = 0, 1, 2, 3, \ldots,
\end{aligned}
$$

where μ is the mean of the binomial distribution. The term $e = 2.71828\ldots$ and is the base of natural logarithms. For the student's convenience, $e^{-\mu}$ has been computed in Table 2, Appendix, for values of μ from 0 through 10 in increments of size .1.

Binomial tables are seldom available for n greater than 100, but many applications of a binomial experiment with $n = 100$ or more exist in business and economics. Consequently, we need simple, easy-to-compute approximation procedures for calculating binomial probabilities. The Poisson probability distribution provides good approximations to the binomial probabilities when n is large and $\mu = np$ is small, preferably with $np \le 7$. An approximation procedure suitable for larger values of $\mu = np$ will be presented in Chapter 7.

To illustrate the Poisson approximation procedure, consider the following application. Suppose that a life insurance company insures the lives of 5,000 men of age 42. If actuarial studies show the probability of any 42-year-old man dying in a given year to be .001, the exact probability the company will have to pay $y = 4$ claims during a given year is given by the binomial distribution as

$$P(y = 4) = p(4) = \frac{5{,}000!}{4!\,4{,}996!}(.001)^4(.999)^{4996},$$

for which tabulated binomial tables are not available. To compute $P(y = 4)$ by hand is out of the question, but the Poisson distribution can be used to provide a good approximation to $P(y = 4)$. Computing $\mu = np = (5{,}000)(.001) = 5$ and substituting into the formula for the Poisson probability distribution,

$$P(4) \approx \frac{(\mu)^4 e^{-\mu}}{4!}$$

$$= \frac{(5)^4 e^{-5}}{4!}$$

$$= \frac{(625)(.0067)}{24}$$

$$= .1745.$$

Example 6.6 *Suppose that a large food processing and canning plant has 20 automatic canning machines in operation at all times. If the probability that an individual canning machine breaks down during a given day is .05, find the probability that during a given day two canning machines fail. Use the binomial distribution to compute the exact probability and then compute the Poisson approximation.*

Solution   *This is a binomial experiment with* $n = 20$ *and* $p = .05$. *The expected number of machine breakdowns in a given day is* $\mu = np = 20(.05) = 1.0$. *Thus, using the binomial distribution and the binomial tables (Table 1, Appendix),*

$$P(y = 2) = p(2) = \frac{20!}{2!\,18!}(.05)^2(.95)^{18}$$

$$= \sum_{y=0}^{2} p(y) - \sum_{y=0}^{1} p(y)$$

$$= .925 - .736$$

$$= .189.$$

Using the Poisson distribution to approximate this binomial experimental outcome, we find that

$$P(y = 2) \approx p(2) = \frac{(1)^2 e^{-1}}{2!}$$

$$= \frac{.367879}{2}$$

from Table 2, Appendix. Thus, rounded to three decimal places,

$$P(y = 2) \approx p(2) = .184.$$

You can see that the Poisson approximation, .184, is quite close to the exact value of the binomial probability, .189. The larger the value of n (for a fixed value of $\mu = np$), the better will be the Poisson approximation. *

Example 6.7   *A manufacturer of power lawn mowers buys 1-horsepower two-cycle engines in lots of 1,000 from a supplier. He then equips each of the mowers produced by his plant with one of the engines. Past history shows that the probability of any one engine purchased from the supplier proving unsatisfactory is .001. In a shipment of 1,000 engines, what is the probability that none are defective? One is defective? Two are? Three are? Four are?*

Solution   *This is a binomial experiment with $n = 1,000$ and $p = .001$. Then the expected number of defectives in a shipment of $n = 1,000$ engines is $\mu = np = (1,000)(.001) = 1$. Since this is a binomial experiment, the probability of y defective engines in the shipment may be approximated by*

$$p(y) = \frac{(\mu)^y e^{-\mu}}{y!}$$

$$= \frac{(1)^y e^{-1}}{y!} = \frac{e^{-1}}{y!}$$

[since $(1)^y = 1$ for any value of y]. Therefore

$$p(0) \approx \frac{e^{-1}}{0!} = \frac{.368}{1} = .368,$$

$$p(1) \approx \frac{e^{-1}}{1!} = \frac{.368}{1} = .368,$$

$$p(2) \approx \frac{e^{-1}}{2!} = \frac{.368}{2} = .184,$$

$$p(3) \approx \frac{e^{-1}}{3!} = \frac{.368}{6} = .061,$$

$$p(4) \approx \frac{e^{-1}}{4!} = \frac{.368}{24} = .015.$$

* See Feller (1960), Chap. 6, references.

Notice that p(y) exists for any integer value of y greater than zero. However, p(y) decreases as y increases, and usually drops off to a negligible amount for y greater than 4 or 5. This can be seen from the formula for p(y) when one recognizes that the denominator y! will increase at a more rapid rate than the numerator, $(\mu)^y e^{-\mu}$. Also, the tailing off of p(y) for increasing y is consistent with the intent of the Poisson distribution—to provide a probability model for count data where the counts represent numbers of "rare events."

The Poisson probability distribution provides a good model for the count data resulting from any experiment where the count y represents the number of rare events observed in a given unit of time or space.

The Poisson probability distribution, therefore, has numerous applications other than approximating certain binomial probabilities. Some examples of experiments for which the random variable y can be considered a Poisson random variable are

1. The number of calls received by a switchboard during a given small period of time.

2. The number of claims against an insurance company during a given week.

3. The number of arrivals at a checkout stand during a given minute.

4. The number of machine breakdowns during a given day.

5. The number of sales by a real estate agent in a given day.

In each example, y represents the number of rather uncommon, rare events during a period of time over which an average of μ such events can be expected to occur. The only assumptions of the Poisson distribution used to model experiments such as those just described are that the counts or events occur randomly and independently of one another.

Example 6.8   *Arrivals at a gasoline service station occur randomly and independently of one another at the average rate of one every 10 minutes.*

   (a)   *Find the probability of no arrivals during a given half-hour.*

   (b)   *Find the probability of at least three arrivals during a given hour.*

Solution

   (a)   *If arrivals occur at the rate of one every 10 minutes, then one could expect $\mu = 3$ arrivals in a 30-minute (half-hour) period. Therefore, the*

probability of no arrivals in a given half-hour is

$$p(0) = \frac{(3)^0 e^{-3}}{0!} = \frac{e^{-3}}{1} = .050.$$

(b)   *During a given hour, one could expect $\mu = 6$ arrivals. Since*

$$P(y \geq 3) = \sum_{y=3}^{\infty} p(y) = 1 - p(0) - p(1) - p(2)$$

where

$$p(0) = \frac{(6)^0 e^{-6}}{0!} = .0025,$$

$$p(1) = \frac{(6)^1 e^{-6}}{1!} = (6)(.0025) = .0150,$$

$$p(2) = \frac{(6)^2 e^{-6}}{2!} = \frac{(36)(.0025)}{2} = .0450,$$

then

$$P(y \geq 3) = 1 - .0025 - .0150 - .0450$$

$$= 1 - .0625$$

$$= .9375.$$

Example 6.8 illustrates an area of study in business analysis known as queueing theory or waiting-line theory. In queueing theory it is of interest to study customer waiting times at service facilities, service times, downtime, and the probability the service facilities will be "swamped" in order to determine whether an additional service facility should be added, a current one dropped, or adjustments made in the current service facilities. The probabilities needed to answer these questions are derived from Poisson arrival probabilities. For a complete discussion of queueing theory, see Saaty (1961) or Hillier and Lieberman (1967).

Example 6.9   *Experience has shown that on days of advertised sales, the Castle Department Store can expect an average of three arrivals per minute at the cashier's stand. If a single cashier can handle a maximum of four customers per minute, what is the probability that during any given minute on a sale day* *the cashier will be swamped? Assume that arriving customers to the cashier follow a Poisson probability distribution.*

Solution *The probability the cashier will be swamped is the probability that the number of arrivals during any given minute, y, exceeds 4. Since y is a Poisson random variable with mean arrival rate $\mu = 3$ per minute,*

$$P(y > 4) = \sum_{y=5}^{\infty} p(y) = 1 - p(0) - p(1) - p(2) - p(3) - p(4)$$

$$= 1 - \frac{(3)^0 e^{-3}}{0!} - \frac{(3)^1 e^{-3}}{1!} - \frac{(3)^2 e^{-3}}{2!}$$

$$- \frac{(3)^3 e^{-3}}{3!} - \frac{(3)^4 e^{-3}}{4!}$$

$$= 1 - e^{-3}\left(1 + 3 + \frac{9}{2} + \frac{27}{6} + \frac{81}{24}\right)$$

$$= 1 - (.050)(16.375)$$

$$= 1 - .819$$

$$= .181.$$

Therefore, the chances are about one in six that during any given minute during a special sale, the single cashier will not be able to adequately handle the arriving customers.

6.8 Summary

A binomial experiment is typical of a large class of useful experiments encountered in real life, which satisfy, to a reasonable degree of approximation, the five defining characteristics stated in Section 6.2. The number of successes, y, observed in n trials is a discrete random variable with probability distribution

$$p(y) = C_y^n p^y q^{n-y},$$

where $q = 1 - p$ and $y = 0, 1, 2, 3, \ldots, n$. Statistically speaking, we are interested in making inferences concerning p, the parameter of a binomial population, as exemplified by the test of the effectiveness of the cold vaccine, Section 6.6, and the lot acceptance sampling problem, Example 6.5, Section 6.5, and later in Section 11.6.

If the sample size n is large and p is small, the binomial probabilities are often approximated by the Poisson distribution

$$p(y) = \frac{(\mu)^y e^{-\mu}}{y!}, \qquad y = 0, 1, 2, \ldots$$

and where μ is the mean of the random variable, y. The Poisson distribution is also useful in the case where count data represent the number of rare events observed in a given unit of time or space.

Exercises

1. List the five identifying characteristics of the binomial distribution.

2. Which of the following business problems can be modeled by the binomial distribution? For those which are not modeled by the binomial distribution, explain why they are not.
   (a) Determination of the probability that 5 of 10 assembly machines break down in a given day when the probability any will break down in a day is .15.
   (b) Determination of the probability that at least one assembly machine will break down in a given day when the probability any will break down in a given day is .15.
   (c) Determination of the probability of selecting 2 defective transistors in a sample of 5 transistors drawn from a bin containing 100 transistors of which 10 are defective.
   (d) Determination of the probability of selecting 2 defective transistors in a sample of 5 transistors, drawn from an assembly line in which each transistor produced is defective with probability .1.
   (e) Determination of the probability of selecting only 2 men in a group of 6 selected from a committee consisting of 10 men and 4 women.

3. A salesman figures that each contact results in a sale with probability 1/2. On a given day, he contacts three prospective clients. Let y equal the number of contacts who actually sign a sales contract with the salesman.
   (a) Use the formula for the binomial probability distribution to calculate the probabilities associated with $y = 0, 1, 2$, and 3.
   (b) Construct a probability distribution similar to Figure 5.1.
   (c) Find the expected value and standard deviation of y, using the formulas

$$E(y) = np,$$

$$\sigma = \sqrt{npq}.$$

   (d) Using the probability distribution (b), find the fraction of the population measurements lying within one standard deviation of the mean. Repeat for two standard deviations. How do your results agree with Tchebysheff's theorem and the empirical rule? Of what practical use are these results?

4. Suppose that another salesman figures that each of his contacts results in a sale with probability 1/10. Follow instructions (a), (b), (c), and (d) as stated in Exercise 3. Note that the probability distribution loses its symmetry and becomes skewed when p is not equal to 1/2.

5. The probability that a single radar set will detect an enemy plane is .9. If we have 5 radar sets, what is the probability that exactly 4 sets will detect the plane? (Assume that the sets operate independently of each other.) At least one set?

6. It is known that 10 percent of a brand of television tubes will burn out before their guarantee has expired. If 1,000 tubes are sold, find the expected value and variance of y, the number of original tubes that must be replaced. Within what limits would y be expected to fall? (*Hint*: Use Tchebysheff's theorem.)

7. Suppose that the four engines of a commercial aircraft are arranged to operate independently and that the probability of in-flight failure of a single engine is .01. What is the probability that, on a given flight,
   (a) No failures are observed?
   (b) No more than one failure is observed?

8. An old, established, family-owned company has decided to "go public." It has been reported that 90 percent of the brokerage houses are recommending the issue to their clients. Assuming this to be true, find
   (a) The probability of contacting two brokerage houses at random and finding that neither of them recommend purchase of this new stock issue.
   (b) The probability of contacting four brokerage houses at random and finding no more than two recommending purchase of the new stock issue.

9. A sampling plan is a rule for determining whether or not to accept a lot of items based on a sample selected from the lot. The plan specifies that a sample of n items is selected from the lot and that the lot is accepted if a preselected number, a, or fewer defectives are found within the sample. A buyer and seller agree to use a sampling plan with sample size $n = 5$ and acceptance number $a = 0$. What is the probability that the buyer would accept a lot having fraction defective
   (a) $p = 0$?   (b) $p = .1$?   (c) $p = .3$?
   (d) $p = .5$?   (e) $p = 1$?

10. Repeat Exercise 9 for $n = 5$, $a = 1$.

11. Repeat Exercise 9 for $n = 10$, $a = 1$.

12. Repeat Exercise 9 for $n = 25$, $a = 3$.

13. A gasoline service station offers their gasoline for sale at a 2 cents per gallon discount if the customer pays in cash and does not use his credit card. Past evidence has shown that 40 percent of all customers choose to pay in cash. During a given day, 25 customers buy gasoline at the service station. Find the probability that
   (a) At least 10 pay in cash.
   (b) No more than 20 pay in cash.
   (c) More than 10 but less than 15 pay in cash.
   (Use Table 1, Appendix.)

14. It is known that 90 percent of those who purchase a color television will have no claims covered by the guarantee during the duration of the guarantee. Suppose that 20 customers each buy a color television set from a certain appliance dealer. What is the probability that at least two of these 20 customers will have claims against the guarantee? (Use Table 1, Appendix.)

15.   Referring to Exercise 14, what is the expected value and standard deviation of y, the number of claims from 20 buyers? Within what limits would y be expected to fall?

16.   The proportion of residential households in Burlington, Vermont, that are heated by natural gas is approximately .2. A randomly selected city block within the Burlington city limits has 20 residential households. Assume that the properties of a binomial experiment are satisfied and find the probability that
   (a) None of the households are heated by natural gas.
   (b) No more than 4 of the 20 are heated by natural gas.
   (c) Why might the binomial experiment not provide a good model for this sampling situation? (See Definition, Section 6.2.)

17.   Suppose that it is known that 1 of 10 undergraduate college textbooks is an outstanding financial success. A publisher has selected 10 new textbooks for publication. What is the probability that
   (a) Exactly one will be an outstanding financial success?
   (b) At least one?
   (c) At least two?

18.   A manufacturing process which produces electron tubes is known to have a 5 percent defective rate. If a sample of $n = 25$ is selected from the manufacturing process, find the probability that
   (a) No more than two defectives are found.
   (b) Exactly four defectives are found.
   (c) At least three defectives are found.

19.   It is known that 70 percent of all customers who enter the Palace Department Store are women. During a given hour, $n = 20$ customers are seen entering the Palace. Find the probability that
   (a) Exactly 75 percent of them are women,
   (b) At least 75 percent of them are women.

20.   A mail order magazine subscription service considers any mail advertisement successful if at least 20 percent of those receiving an advertisement respond favorably by ordering a subscription. What would have to be the probability that any recipient of an advertisement will respond favorably in order to have a probability of 90 percent that at least 20 percent of 25 recipients of an advertisement respond favorably?

21.   A retail variety store that advertises extensively by mail circulars expects a sale from 1 of every 20 mailings. If 25 prospects are randomly selected from a city-wide mailing
   (a) How many sales can they expect to result from this sample of 25?
   (b) What is the probability that no sales will result from mailings to this group of 25 prospects?
   (c) What is the probability at least three sales will result from mailings to the 25 prospects?
   (d) Suppose that the 25 prospects had been selected from a single city neighborhood. Would this satisfy the properties of a binomial experiment?

22.   A manufacturer of floor wax has developed two new brands, A and B, which he wishes to subject to a housewife evaluation to determine which of the two is superior. Both waxes, A and B, are applied to floor surfaces in each of 15 homes.
   (a) If there is actually no difference in the quality of the brands, what is the probability that 10 or more housewives would state a preference for brand A?
   (b) If there is actually no difference in the quality of the brands, what is the probability that 10 or more housewives would state a preference for brand A or brand B?

23.   A machine is said to be in control if the proportion of defective items manufactured by the machine is not greater than 10 percent. To check whether a machine is in control,

10 finished items are randomly selected from its output. The implicit hypothesis that the machine is in control will be rejected if three or more defectives are found.
(a) What is the probability of the type I error for this test?
(b) If the machine is really out of control and the probability of a defective is .3, what is the probability of the type II error for the test?

24. The ABC Auto Rental Company claims that 60 percent of all cars rented in Oakdale are rented from their firm. To test their allegation four people who recently rented a car in Oakdale were interviewed, and it was found that one had rented from the ABC Company. Does this result present sufficient evidence to contradict the ABC Company's allegation? Justify your answer statistically.

25. A packaging experiment was conducted by placing two different package designs for Wheat-O, a breakfast food, side by side on a supermarket shelf. The objective of the experiment was to see if buyers indicated a preference for one of the two package designs. In a given day, six customers purchased a package of Wheat-O from the supermarket, with one choosing package design No. 1 and five choosing design No. 2.
(a) State the hypothesis to be tested.
(b) Let y equal the number of buyers who choose the second package design. What is the value of α for the test if the rejection region includes $y = 0$ and $y = 6$?
(c) What is the value of β for the alternative $p = .8$ (that is, 80 percent of the buyers actually favor the second package design)?
(d) In the context of our problem, give a practical interpretation of the type I error and the type II error.

26. Continuing Exercise 22, let p equal the probability that a housewife will choose brand A in preference to B, and suppose that we wish to test the hypothesis that there is no observable difference between the brands—in other words, that $p = 1/2$. Let y, the number of times that A is preferred to B, be the test statistic.
(a) Calculate the value of α for the test if the rejection region is chosen to include $y = 0, 1, 14$, and 15.
(b) If p is really equal to .8, what is the value of β for the test defined in (a)? (Note that this is the probability that $y = 2, 3, \ldots, 12, 13$ given that $p = .8$.)

27. Continuing Exercise 26, suppose that the rejection region is enlarged to include $y = 0, 1, 2, 13, 14, 15$.
(a) What is the value of α for the test? Should this probability be larger or smaller than the answer given in Exercise 26?
(b) If p is really equal to .8, what is the value of β for the test? Compare with your answer to part (b), Exercise 26.

28. The number of defective electrical fuses proceeding from each of two production lines, A and B, was recorded daily for a period of 10 days with the following results:

DAY	A	B
1	172	201
2	165	179
3	206	159
4	184	192
5	174	177
6	142	170
7	190	182
8	169	179
9	161	169
10	200	210

Assume that both production lines produced the same daily output. Compare the number of defectives produced by A and B each day and let y equal the number of days when B exceeded A. Do the data present sufficient evidence to indicate that production line B produces more defectives, on the average, than A? State the null hypothesis to be tested and use y as a test statistic.

29. Suppose that a given type battery will operate for at least 20 hours with probability .7. A piece of equipment uses three such batteries. Let y be the number of batteries (out of three) lasting at least 20 hours.
(a) Write down the probability function for y.
(b) Find $p(3)$.
(c) Find $P(y \leq 2)$.

30. A shipment of 200 portable television sets is received by a retailer. To protect himself against a "bad" shipment, he will inspect 5 sets and accept the entire lot if he observes 0 or 1 defectives. Suppose that there are actually 20 defective sets in the shipment.
(a) What is the probability that he accepts the entire shipment?
(b) Given that the retailer accepts the entire lot, what is the probability that he observed exactly 1 defective set?

31. (a) Under what conditions can the Poisson distribution be used to approximate certain binomial probabilities?
(b) What other application does the Poisson distribution have other than to estimate certain binomial probabilities?

32. Which of the following business problems can be modeled by the Poisson distribution? For those which are not modeled by the Poisson distribution, explain why they are not.
(a) Determination of the probability that 2 of 10 city busses will break down during a given day when the probability that any one will break down is .01.
(b) Determination of the probability that an insurance company will not have to pay out on any fire damage claims during a year given that the company has insured 1,000 firms against fire damage and the probability any one of the firms incurs a fire during a given year is .002.
(c) Determination of the probability that a telephone switchboard receives at least five incoming calls during a given hour, when incoming calls normally arrive randomly and independently of one another at an average rate of one every 15 minutes.
(d) Determination of the probability that a salesman consummates at least 25 sales in 100 contacts knowing that the probability he consummates a sale on any contact is .4.

33. If the average number of accidents over a specified section of highway is two per week, calculate the probability that no accidents will occur during a given week. Assume accidents occur randomly and independently of one another.

34. Logging trucks have a special problem with tire failure because of the rough terrain they are often required to traverse. Suppose that a logging company with 100 trucks has reason to believe that the average number of trucks with at least one tire failure in a given day is 5. Find the probability that during a given day,
(a) None of the trucks have tire failure.
(b) Five have tire failure.
(c) Not more than three have tire failure.

35. Arrivals occur randomly and independently at a service station at an average rate of four per hour. If the service facility can handle at most five arrivals per hour, find the probability that the service facility is overloaded.

36. Refer to Exercise 34. Suppose that a truck has a mechanical breakdown during any given day with probability .01. For the company with 100 logging trucks mentioned above,

find the probability that during a given day

(a) None of the trucks has a mechanical breakdown.

(b) At least two of the trucks have a mechanical breakdown.

37. A telephone switchboard receives an average of 5 calls per minute. Assuming that the incoming calls constitute a Poisson distribution, find the probability that the switchboard receives no calls during a specified minute of time.

38. In a certain large manufacturing plant, serious industrial accidents occur randomly and independently of one another at the rate of 1 every 10 working days. Find the probability of no more than one serious accident in the plant over the next month (30 working days).

39. Refer to Exercises 34 and 36. Assuming that tire failures and mechanical breakdowns are independent occurrences in the 100 logging trucks, find the probability that during a given day, none of the 100 logging trucks has either a tire or a mechanical problem.

40. A manufacturer of small, electronic desk calculators knows from experience that 1 percent of all the calculators manufactured and sold by his firm are defective and will have to be replaced under the warranty. A large accounting firm purchased 500 calculators from the manufacturer for use by their employees. Find the probability that

(a) None of the calculators will have to be replaced.

(b) No more than four will have to be replaced.

(c) At least two will have to be replaced.

41. Refer to Exercise 40. What is the expected number of desk calculators purchased by the accounting firm which can be expected to fail and must be replaced under the warranty?

References

Feller, W., *An Introduction to Probability Theory and Its Applications*, Vol. 1, 3rd ed. New York: John Wiley & Sons, Inc., 1968. Chapter 6.

Hillier, F. S., and G. J. Lieberman, *Introduction to Operations Research*. San Francisco: Holden-Day, Inc., 1967. Chapter 10.

Mosteller, F., R. E. K. Rourke, and G. B. Thomas, Jr., *Probability with Statistical Applications*, 2nd ed. Reading, Mass.: Addison-Wesley Publishing Company, Inc., 1970. Chapter 7.

National Bureau of Standards, *Tables of the Binomial Probability Distribution*. Washington, D.C.: U.S. Government Printing Office, 1949.

Saaty, T. L., *Elements of Queueing Theory: With Applications*. New York: McGraw-Hill Book Company, 1961.

Spurr, W., and C. P. Bonini, *Statistical Analysis for Business Decisions*, Rev. ed. Homewood, Ill.: Richard D. Irwin, Inc., 1973. Chapter 8.

Chapter Seven

The Normal Probability
Distribution

7.1   Introduction

Continuous random variables, as noted in Section 5.5, are associated with sample spaces representing the infinitely large number of sample points contained on a line interval. The following provide common examples of continuous random variables:

1. The heights or weights of a group of people.

2. The length of life of a perishable product, such as a light bulb, a machine part, or a food product.

3. The time it takes for an individual to perform a task.

4. The measurement errors resulting from laboratory experiments.

In short, any random variable whose values are measurements, as opposed to counts, is a continuous random variable. Reviewing Section 5.5 we note that the probabilistic model for the frequency distribution of a continuous random variable involves the selection of a curve, usually smooth, called the probability distribution or probability density function. While these distributions may assume a variety of shapes, it is interesting to note that a very large number of random variables observed in nature possess a frequency distribution that is approximately bell-shaped or, as the statistician would say, is approximately a normal probability distribution.

Mathematically speaking, the normal probability density function is the equation of the bell-shaped curve shown in Figure 7.1.

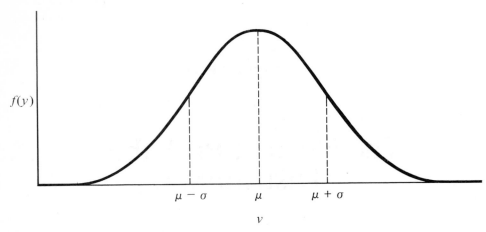

Figure 7.1   *Normal Probability Density Function*

$$f(y) = \frac{e^{-(y-\mu)^2/2\sigma^2}}{\sigma\sqrt{2\pi}}, \qquad -\infty < y < +\infty.$$

The symbols e and π represent irrational numbers whose values are approximately 2.7183 and 3.1416, respectively, while μ and σ are the population mean and standard deviation. The equation for the density function is constructed such that the area under the curve will represent probability. Hence the total area is equal to 1.

In practice, we seldom encounter variables which range in value from "minus infinity" to "plus infinity," whatever meaning we may wish to attach to these phrases. Certainly the height of humans, the weight of a specie of beetle, or the length of life of a light bulb does not satisfy this requirement. Nevertheless, a relative frequency histogram plotted for many types of measurements will generate a bell-shaped figure which may be approximated by the function shown in Figure 7.1. Why this particular phenomenon exists is a matter of conjecture. However, one explanation is provided by the central limit theorem, a theorem that may be regarded as the most important in statistics.

7.2   The Central Limit Theorem

The central limit theorem states that under rather general conditions, sums and means of samples of random measurements drawn from a population tend to possess, approximately, a bell-shaped distribution in repeated sampling. The significance of this statement is perhaps best illustrated by an example.

The Haberdashery Shop, a men's clothing store, is a retail outlet for Tailorcraft, a famous brand in men's suits. The Tailorcraft Company is interested in the average daily sales of its suits by The Haberdashery Shop. Samples of size $n = 5$, representing the number of Tailorcraft suits sold by The Haberdashery Shop each workday of a randomly selected week, are recorded within Table 7.1. Note that the number of suits sold each day during the first week selected is $y = 3, 5, 1, 3, 2$. The manager of The Haberdashery Shop assumes from his knowledge of past sales that the number of Tailorcraft suits sold per day is equiprobable to be any number from one through six. Calculate the sum of the five measurements as well as the sample mean, $\bar{y}$. For experimental purposes suppose that we have recorded the sales over 100 randomly chosen weeks (samples). The results for 100 samples are given in Table 7.1 along with the corresponding values of $\sum_{i=1}^{5} y_i$ and $\bar{y}$. Construct a frequency histogram for $\bar{y}$ $\left(\text{or } \sum_{i=1}^{5} y_i\right)$ for the 100 samples and observe the resulting distribution in Figure 7.2. You will observe an interesting result, that although the values of y in the population ($y = 1, 2, 3, 4, 5, 6$) are equiprobable and hence possess a probability distribution that is perfectly horizontal, the distribution of the sample means (or sums) chosen from the population forms a bell-shaped distribution. We shall add one additional comment without proof. If we should repeat the study outlined

Figure 7.2   *Histogram of Sample Means for the Sales of Tailorcraft Suits by The Haberdashery Shop*

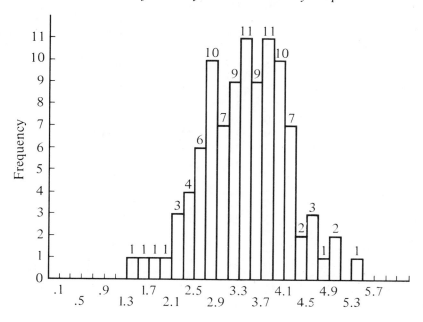

Table 7.1 *Sampling from the Population of Sales of
Tailorcraft Suits by The Haberdashery Shop*

SAMPLE NUMBER	SAMPLE MEASUREMENTS	$\sum y_i$	$\bar{y}$	SAMPLE NUMBER	SAMPLE MEASUREMENTS	$\sum y_i$	$\bar{y}$
1	3, 5, 1, 3, 2	14	2.8	43	2, 5, 3, 1, 4	15	3.0
2	3, 1, 1, 4, 6	15	3.0	44	4, 2, 3, 2, 1	12	2.4
3	1, 3, 1, 6, 1	12	2.4	45	4, 4, 5, 4, 4	21	4.2
4	4, 5, 3, 3, 2	17	3.4	46	5, 4, 5, 5, 4	23	4.6
5	3, 1, 3, 5, 2	14	2.8	47	6, 6, 6, 2, 1	21	4.2
6	2, 4, 4, 2, 4	16	3.2	48	2, 1, 5, 5, 4	17	3.4
7	4, 2, 5, 5, 3	19	3.8	49	6, 4, 3, 1, 5	19	3.8
8	3, 5, 5, 5, 5	23	4.6	50	4, 4, 4, 4, 4	20	4.0
9	6, 5, 5, 1, 6	23	4.6	51	2, 3, 5, 3, 2	15	3.0
10	5, 1, 6, 1, 6	19	3.8	52	1, 1, 1, 2, 4	9	1.8
11	1, 1, 1, 5, 3	11	2.2	53	2, 6, 3, 4, 5	20	4.0
12	3, 4, 2, 4, 4	17	3.4	54	1, 2, 2, 1, 1	7	1.4
13	2, 6, 1, 5, 4	18	3.6	55	2, 4, 4, 6, 2	18	3.6
14	6, 3, 4, 2, 5	20	4.0	56	3, 2, 5, 4, 5	19	3.8
15	2, 6, 2, 1, 5	16	3.2	57	2, 4, 2, 4, 5	17	3.4
16	1, 5, 1, 2, 5	14	2.8	58	5, 5, 4, 3, 2	19	3.8
17	3, 5, 1, 1, 2	12	2.4	59	5, 4, 4, 6, 3	22	4.4
18	3, 2, 4, 3, 5	17	3.4	60	3, 2, 5, 3, 1	14	2.8
19	5, 1, 6, 3, 1	16	3.2	61	2, 1, 4, 1, 3	11	2.2
20	1, 6, 4, 4, 1	16	3.2	62	4, 1, 1, 5, 2	13	2.6
21	6, 4, 2, 3, 5	20	4.0	63	2, 3, 1, 2, 3	11	2.2
22	1, 3, 5, 4, 1	14	2.8	64	2, 3, 3, 2, 6	16	3.2
23	2, 6, 5, 2, 6	21	4.2	65	4, 3, 5, 2, 6	20	4.0
24	3, 5, 1, 3, 5	17	3.4	66	3, 1, 3, 3, 4	14	2.8
25	5, 2, 4, 4, 3	18	3.6	67	4, 6, 1, 3, 6	20	4.0
26	6, 1, 1, 1, 6	15	3.0	68	2, 4, 6, 6, 3	21	4.2
27	1, 4, 1, 2, 6	14	2.8	69	4, 1, 6, 5, 5	21	4.2
28	3, 1, 2, 1, 5	12	2.4	70	6, 6, 6, 4, 5	27	5.4
29	1, 5, 5, 4, 5	20	4.0	71	2, 2, 5, 6, 3	18	3.6
30	4, 5, 3, 5, 2	19	3.8	72	6, 6, 6, 1, 6	25	5.0
31	4, 1, 6, 1, 1	13	2.6	73	4, 4, 4, 3, 1	16	3.2
32	3, 6, 4, 1, 2	16	3.2	74	4, 4, 5, 4, 2	19	3.8
33	3, 5, 5, 2, 2	17	3.4	75	4, 5, 4, 1, 4	18	3.6
34	1, 1, 5, 6, 3	16	3.2	76	5, 3, 2, 3, 4	17	3.4
35	2, 6, 1, 6, 2	17	3.4	77	1, 3, 3, 1, 5	13	2.6
36	2, 4, 3, 1, 3	13	2.6	78	4, 1, 5, 5, 3	18	3.6
37	1, 5, 1, 5, 2	14	2.8	79	4, 5, 6, 5, 4	24	4.8
38	6, 6, 5, 3, 3	22	4.4	80	1, 5, 3, 4, 2	15	3.0
39	3, 3, 5, 2, 1	14	2.8	81	4, 3, 4, 6, 3	20	4.0
40	2, 6, 6, 6, 5	25	5.0	82	5, 4, 2, 1, 6	18	3.6
41	5, 5, 2, 3, 4	19	3.8	83	1, 3, 2, 2, 5	13	2.6
42	6, 4, 1, 6, 2	19	3.8	84	5, 4, 1, 4, 6	20	4.0

Table 7.1   *Continued*

SAMPLE NUMBER	SAMPLE MEASUREMENTS	$\sum y_i$	$\bar{y}$	SAMPLE NUMBER	SAMPLE MEASUREMENTS	$\sum y_i$	$\bar{y}$
85	2, 4, 2, 5, 5	18	3.6	93	6, 3, 1, 5, 2	17	3.4
86	1, 6, 3, 1, 6	17	3.4	94	1, 3, 6, 4, 2	16	3.2
87	2, 2, 4, 3, 2	13	2.6	95	6, 1, 4, 2, 2	15	3.0
88	4, 4, 5, 4, 4	21	4.2	96	1, 1, 2, 3, 1	8	1.6
89	2, 5, 4, 3, 4	18	3.6	97	6, 2, 5, 1, 6	20	4.0
90	5, 1, 6, 4, 3	19	3.8	98	3, 1, 1, 4, 1	10	2.0
91	5, 2, 5, 6, 3	21	4.2	99	5, 2, 1, 6, 1	15	3.0
92	6, 4, 1, 2, 1	14	2.8	100	2, 4, 3, 4, 6	19	3.8

above by grouping together two week's sales as one sample to obtain a larger sample size, $n = 10$, we would find that the distribution of the sample means tends to become more nearly bell-shaped.

You will note that a proper evaluation of the form of the probability distribution of the sample means would require an infinitely large number of samples, or, at the very least, far more than the 100 samples contained in our experiment. Nevertheless, the 100 samples illustrate the basic idea involved in the central limit theorem, which may be stated as follows.

The Central Limit Theorem

If random samples of n observations are drawn from a population with finite mean, μ, and standard deviation, σ, then, when n is large, the sample mean, $\bar{y}$, will be approximately normally distributed with mean equal to μ and standard deviation $\sigma/\sqrt{n}$. The approximation will become more and more accurate as n becomes large.

Note that the central limit theorem could be restated to apply to the sum of the sample measurements, $\sum_{i=1}^{n} y_i$, which would also tend to possess a normal distribution, in repeated sampling, with mean equal to $n\mu$ and standard deviation $\sqrt{n}\sigma$, as n becomes large.

The reader will note that the mean and standard deviation of the distribution of sample means are definitely related to the mean and standard deviation of the sampled population as well as to the sample size, n. We shall forego discussion of this point for the moment and consider the relevance of the central limit theorem to our previous work.

The significance of the central limit theorem is twofold. First, it explains why some measurements tend to possess, approximately, a normal distribution. We might imagine the height of a human as being composed of a number of elements, each random, associated with such things as the height of the mother, the height of the father, the activity of a particular gland, the environment, and diet. If each of these effects tends to add to the others to yield the measurement of height, then height is the sum of a number of random variables and the central limit theorem may become effective and yield a distribution of heights that is approximately normal. All of this is conjecture, of course, because we really do not know the true situation that exists. Nevertheless, the central limit theorem, along with other theorems dealing with normally distributed random variables, provides an explanation of the rather common occurrence of normally distributed random variables in nature.

The second and most important contribution of the central limit theorem is in statistical inference. Many estimators that are used to make inferences about population parameters are sums or averages of the sample measurements. When this is true and when the sample size, n, is sufficiently large, we would expect the estimator to possess (approximately) a normal probability distribution in repeated sampling according to the central limit theorem.

We can then use the empirical rule discussed in Chapter 3 to describe the behavior of the inference maker. This aspect of the central limit theorem will be utilized in Section 7.4 as well as in later chapters dealing with statistical inference.

One disturbing feature of the central limit theorem, and of most approximation procedures, is that we must have some idea of how large the sample size n must be for the approximation to give useful results. Unfortunately, there is no clear-cut answer to this question, as the appropriate value for n will depend upon the population probability distribution as well as the use we shall make of the approximation. Although the preceding comment sidesteps the difficulty and suggests that we must rely solely upon experience, we may take comfort in the results of The Tailorcraft Company's sales analysis discussed previously in this section. Note that the distribution of $\bar{y}$, in repeated sampling, based upon a sample of only $n = 5$

Figure 7.3   *Frequency Distributions for $\bar{y}$ for Two Different Probability Distributions; $n = 2, 5, 10, 25$*

Case 1   Case 2

The Population Frequency Distributions

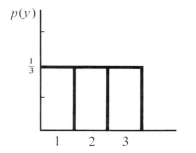
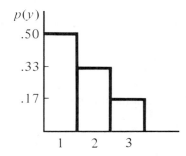

Figure 7.3   *Continued*

The Sampling Distributions

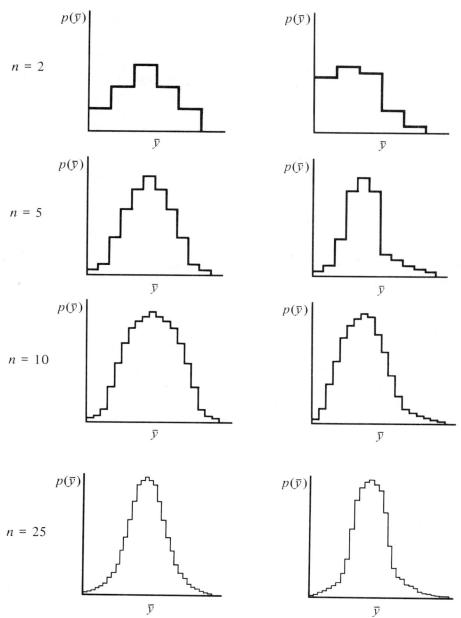

measurements, tends to be approximately bell-shaped. Generally speaking, the central limit theorem functions very well, even for small samples, but this is not always true.

In Figure 7.3, frequency distributions for $\bar{y}$ are shown for two different probability distributions, the uniform distribution on the left and a nonsymmetric distribution on the right, for sample sizes ranging (down the page) from $n = 2$ to $n = 25$. The sample means for each frequency histogram were obtained by drawing a large number of samples from the population, each of fixed sample size, and then computing $\bar{y}$ for each. Figure 7.3 illustrates two significant characteristics of the central limit theorem. The first is the somewhat remarkable fact that the central limit theorem functions regardless of the shape of the underlying population frequency distribution. Clearly, neither of the population frequency distributions, depicted in the first row of Figure 7.3, is bell-shaped. But, in both case 1 and case 2, the frequency distributions of the sample mean $\bar{y}$ are effectively approximated by the normal distribution, when the sample size is sufficiently large. Note how the frequency distribution for $\bar{y}$ approaches a bell shape as the sample size increases from $n = 2$ to $n = 25$ (moving from top to the bottom of Figure 7.3).

A second point to note is that the distribution of $\bar{y}$ for case 1 is closely approximated by a smooth, bell-shaped curve for samples as small as $n = 10$, but a much larger sample size is required to gain an effective normal approximation to the distribution of $\bar{y}$ for case 2. This is explained by the fact that when the probability distribution of y is symmetric about its mean μ, the central limit theorem will function very well for small sample sizes, often $n = 10$ or less. However, when the population frequency distribution is skewed (nonsymmetric), larger sample sizes are required to cause an effective approximation to the distribution of $\bar{y}$ by the normal probability distribution.

Some authors offer as a rule of thumb a required minimal sample size of $n = 30$ to guarantee an effective normal approximation regardless of the shape of the population frequency distribution. However, there are cases [the binomial experiment when either p or $(1 - p)$ is small is such a case] where $n = 30$ may be much too small. Consequently, we shall avoid reliance on such a rule. The appropriate sample size n will be given for specific applications of the central limit theorem as they are encountered in Section 7.5 and later in the text.

7.3   Random Samples

In previous sections we have referred to representative samples, sampling in a "random manner," and "random samples" without attempting an explicit definition of these phrases. You will note that the central limit theorem, as stated above, applies only when the sampling is conducted in a random manner. What is a random sample and why, in general, is the method of sampling important to our objective of statistical inference? The latter question, being more basic, will be answered first. We might consider the decision-making procedures discussed in Chapter 6 in connection with lot acceptance sampling and the test of an hypothesis concerning the effectiveness of the cold vaccine. In each case a sample was drawn from the population of interest in order to make an inference (a decision in each of these examples) concerning a parameter of the population.

If, after sampling, we observe what we consider to be a highly improbable result (that is, an improbable sample, assuming the null hypothesis to be true), we reject the hypothesis. If the sample is quite probable, assuming the null hypothesis to be true, we do not reject. In other words, we must know the probability of the observed sample in order to arrive at a statistical inference. Reiterating a statement made in Chapter 4, probability reasons from the population to the sample. Statistics, on the other hand, reverses the procedure, using probability as a vehicle to make inferences about the population based upon information contained in a sample. It should be reasonably clear that the sampling procedure will affect the probability of observing a particular sample and hence must be carefully considered.

Suppose that a sample of n measurements is drawn from a population consisting of N total measurements. How many different samples of n measurements can be drawn from the population? In effect, we ask how many different combinations of n measurements can be selected from the population. This was shown in Chapter 4 to be

$$C_n^N = \frac{N!}{n!(N-n)!}.$$

Definition

Suppose that a sample of n measurements is selected from a finite population of N measurements. If the sampling is conducted in such a way that each of the C_n^N samples has an equal probability of being selected, the sampling is said to be random and the result is said to be a random sample.

Perfect random sampling is difficult to achieve in practice. If the population is not too large, we might place each of the N numbers on a poker chip, mix the total, and select a sample of n chips. The numbers on the poker chips would specify the measurements to appear in the sample. Other techniques are available when the population is large.

In many situations, the population is conceptual, as in an observation made during a laboratory experiment. Here the population is envisioned to be the infinitely large number of measurements obtained when the experiment is repeated over and over again. If we wish a sample of $n = 10$ measurements from this population, we repeat the experiment 10 times and hope that the results represent, to a reasonable degree of approximation, a random sample.

Definition

Suppose that a sample of n measurements is selected from an infinite population of measurements. If the sampling is conducted in such a way that every combination of n measurements from the population has an equal probability of being selected, the sampling is said to be random and the result is said to be a random sample

---

While the primary purpose of this discussion has been to clarify the meaning of a random sample, we would like to mention that some sampling techniques are partly systematic and partly random. For instance, if we wish to determine the voting preference of the nation in a presidential election, we would not likely choose a random sample from the population of voters. Just due to pure chance, all the voters appearing in the sample might be drawn from a single city, say San Francisco, which might not be at all representative of the population. We would prefer a random selection of voters from smaller political districts, perhaps states, allotting a specified number to each state. The information from the randomly selected sub-samples drawn from the respective states would be combined to form a prediction concerning the entire population of voters in the country. The purpose of systematic sampling, as in the design of experiments in general, is to obtain a maximum of information for a fixed sample size. This, we recall, was one of the five elements of a statistical problem discussed in Chapter 1.

7.4   Tabulated Areas of the Normal Probability Distribution

The reader will note that the equation for the normal probability distribution, Section 7.1, is dependent upon the numerical values of μ and σ and that by supplying various values for these parameters, we could generate an infinitely large number of bell-shaped normal distributions. A separate table of areas for each of these curves is obviously impractical; rather we would like one table of areas applicable to all. The easiest way to do this is to work with areas lying within a specified number of standard deviations of the mean, as was done in the case of the empirical rule. For instance, we know that approximately .68 of the area will lie within one standard deviation of the mean, .95 within two, and almost all within three. What fraction of the total area will lie within .7 standard deviation, for instance? This question, as well as others, will be answered by Table 3, Appendix.

Inasmuch as the normal curve is symmetrical about the mean, we may simplify our table of areas by listing the areas between the mean μ and a specified number z of standard deviation to the right of μ. The distance from the mean to a given value of y is $(y - \mu)$. Expressing this distance in units of standard deviation σ, we obtain

$$z = \frac{y - \mu}{\sigma}.$$

Note that there is a one-to-one correspondence between z and y and, particularly, that $z = 0$ when $y = \mu$. The probability distribution for z is often called the standardized normal distribution, because its mean is equal to zero and its standard deviation is equal to 1. It is shown in Figure 7.4. The area under the normal curve between the mean, $z = 0$, and a specified value of z, say z_0, is recorded in Table 3, Appendix, and is shown as the shaded area in Figure 7.4.

Since the normal distribution is symmetrical and the total area under the curve is equal to 1, half of the area will lie to the right of the mean and half to the left. Areas to the left of the mean can be calculated by using the corresponding, and equal, area to the right of the mean.

Referring to Table 3, Appendix, we note that z, correct to the nearest tenth, is recorded in the left-hand column. The second decimal place for z, corresponding to hundredths, is given across the top row. Thus the area between the mean and $z = .7$ standard deviation to the right, read in the second column of the table opposite $z = .7$, is found to equal .2580. Similarly, the area between the mean and $z = 1.0$ is .3413. The area lying within one standard deviation on either side of the mean would be two times the quantity .3413, or .6826. The area lying within two standard deviations of the mean, correct to four decimal places, is $2(.4772) = .9544$. These numbers provide the approximate values, 68 percent and 95 percent, used in the empirical rule, Chapter 3. We conclude this section with some examples.

Figure 7.4   *Standardized Normal Distribution*

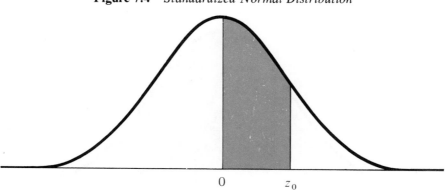

Example 7.1   *Find the value of z, say z_0, such that exactly (to four decimal places) .95 of the area is within $\pm z_0$ standard deviation of the mean; that is, find the z_0 such that $P(\mu - z_0\sigma < y < \mu + z_0\sigma) = .95$.*

Solution   *Half of the total area, .95, will lie to the left of the mean and half to the right because the normal distribution is symmetrical. Thus we seek the value, z_0, corresponding to an area equal to .475. The area .475 falls in the row corresponding to $z = 1.9$ and the .06 column. Hence $z_0 = 1.96$. Note that this is very close to the approximate value, $z = 2$, used in the empirical rule.*

Example 7.2   *Find the area between $z = -.5$ and $z = 1.0$ as shown in Figure 7.5.*

Solution   *The area required is equal to the sum of A_1 and A_2 shown in Figure 7.5. From Table 3 we read $A_2 = .3413$. The area A_1 would equal the corresponding area between $z = 0$ and $z = .5$, or $A_1 = .1915$. Thus the total area is equal to the probability*

$$P(-.5 \leq z \leq 1.0) = P(0 \leq z \leq .5) + P(0 \leq z \leq 1.0)$$
$$= A_1 + A_2$$
$$= .1915 + .3413$$
$$= .5328.$$

Example 7.3   *Let y be a normally distributed random variable with mean equal to 10 and standard deviation equal to 2. Find the probability that y will lie between 11 and 13.6.*

Figure 7.5   *Area Under the Normal Curve in Example 7.2*

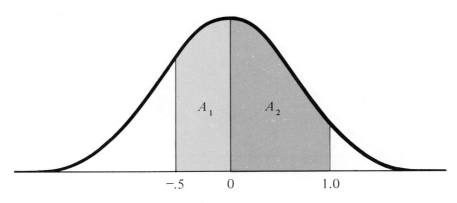

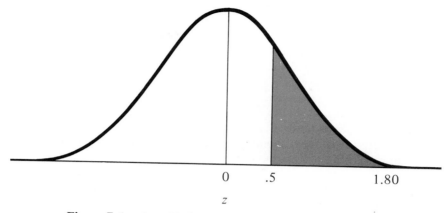

Figure 7.6   *Area Under the Normal Curve in Example 7.3*

Solution   *As a first step, we must calculate the values of z corresponding to $y_1 = 11$ and $y_2 = 13.6$. Thus*

$$z_1 = \frac{y_1 - \mu}{\sigma} = \frac{11 - 10}{2} = .5,$$

$$z_2 = \frac{y_2 - \mu}{\sigma} = \frac{13.6 - 10}{2} = 1.80.$$

The probability desired is therefore the area lying between z_1 and z_2, as shown in Figure 7.6. The areas between $z = 0$ and z_1, $A_1 = .1915$, and $z = 0$ and z_2, $A_2 = .4641$, are easily obtained from Table 3. The probability is equal to the difference between A_1 and A_2; that is,

$$P(11 < y < 13.6) = P(.5 \leq z \leq 1.80)$$
$$= A_2 - A_1$$
$$= .4641 - .1915 = .2726.$$

7.5   The Normal Approximation to the Binomial Distribution

In Chapter 6 we considered several applications of the binomial probability distribution, all of which required that we calculate the probability that y, the number of successes in n trials, would fall in a given region. For the most part we restricted our attention to examples where n was small because of the tedious calculations necessary in the computations of $p(y)$. Let us now consider the problem of calculating $p(y)$, or the probability that y will fall in a given region, when n is large, say $n = 1,000$. A direct calculation of $p(y)$ for large values of n is not an impossibility, but it does provide a formidable task which we would prefer to avoid. Fortunately, the central limit theorem provides a solution to this dilemma since we may view y, the number of successes in n trials, as a sum that satisfies the conditions of the central limit theorem. Each trial results in either 0 or 1 success with probability q and p, respectively. Therefore, each of the n trials may be regarded as an independent observation drawn from a simpler binomial experiment consisting of one trial, and y, the total number of successes in n trials, is the sum of these n independent observations. Then, if n is sufficiently large, the binomial variable, y, will be approximately normally distributed with mean and variance (obtained in Chapter 6) np and npq, respectively. We may then use areas under a fitted normal curve to approximate the binomial probabilities.

For instance, consider a binomial probability distribution for y when $n = 10$ and $p = 1/2$. Then $\mu = np = 10(1/2) = 5$ and $\sigma = \sqrt{npq} = \sqrt{2.5} = 1.58$. Figure 7.7 shows the corresponding binomial probability distribution and the approximating normal curve on the same graph. A visual comparison of the figures would suggest that the approximation is reasonably good, even though a small sample, $n = 10$, was necessary for this graphic illustration.

The probability that $y = 2$, 3, or 4 is exactly equal to the area of the three rectangles lying over $y = 2$, 3, and 4. We may approximate this probability with the area under the normal curve from $y = 1.5$ to $y = 4.5$, which is shaded in Figure 7.7. Note that the area under the normal curve between 2.0 and 4.0 would not provide a good approximation to the probability that $y = 2$, 3, or 4 because it excludes half of the probability rectangles corresponding to $y = 2$ and $y = 4$. Thus it is important to remember to approximate the entire areas for $y = 2$ and $y = 4$ by including the area over the interval 1.5 to 4.5.

Although the normal probability distribution provides a reasonably good approximation to the binomial probability distribution, Figure 7.7, this will not always be the case. When n is small and p is near 0 or 1, the binomial probability distribution will be nonsymmetrical; that is, its mean will be located near 0 or n. For example, when p is near zero, most values of y will be small, producing a distribution that is concentrated near $y = 0$ and tails gradually toward n. Certainly, when this is true, the normal distribution, symmetrical and bell-shaped, will provide a poor approximation to the binomial probability distribution. How, then, can we tell whether n and p are such that the binomial distribution will be symmetrical?

Recalling the empirical rule, Chapter 3, approximately 95 percent of the measurements associated with a normal distribution will lie within two standard deviations of the mean and almost all will lie within three. We would suspect that the binomial distribution would be nearly symmetrical if the distribution were able to spread out a distance equal to two standard deviations on either side of the mean and this is, in fact, the case. Hence, to determine when the normal approximation will be adequate, calculate $\mu = np$ and $\sigma = \sqrt{npq}$. If the interval $\mu \pm 2\sigma$ lies within the

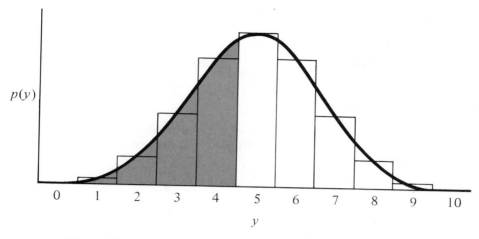

$p(y)$

0   1   2   3   4   5   6   7   8   9   10

y

Figure 7.7   *Comparison of a Binomial Probability Distribution and the Approximating Normal Distribution, $n = 10, p = 1/2$*

binomial bounds, 0 and n, the approximation will be reasonably good. Note that this criterion is satisfied for the example of Figure 7.7.

Example 7.4   *Refer to the binomial experiment illustrated in Figure 7.7, where $n = 10, p = .5$. Calculate the probability that $y = 2, 3,$ or 4 correct to three places using Table 1, Appendix. Then calculate the corresponding normal approximation to this probability.*

Solution   *The exact probability, P_1, can be calculated using Table 1(a), Appendix. Thus*

$$P_1 = \sum_{y=2}^{4} p(y) = \sum_{y=0}^{4} p(y) - \sum_{y=0}^{1} p(y)$$

$$= .377 - .011$$

$$= .366.$$

The normal approximation, as noted earlier in this section, would require the area lying between $y_1 = 1.5$ and $y_2 = 4.5$, where $\mu = 5$ and $\sigma = 1.58$. Thus

$$\sum_{y=2}^{4} p(y) \approx P(z_1 \leq z \leq z_2) = P_2$$

where

$$z_1 = \frac{y_1 - \mu}{\sigma} = \frac{1.5 - 5}{1.58} = -2.22,$$

$$z_2 = \frac{y_2 - \mu}{\sigma} = \frac{4.5 - 5}{1.58} = -.32.$$

The probability, P_2, is shown in Figure 7.8. The area between $z = 0$ and $z = 2.22$ is $A_1 = .4868$. Likewise, the area between $z = 0$ and $z = .32$ is $A_2 = .1255$. It is obvious from Figure 7.8 that

$$P_2 = P(z_1 \le z \le z_2)$$

$$= P(-2.22 \le z \le -.32)$$

$$= A_1 - A_2$$

$$= .4868 - .1255 = .3613.$$

Note that the normal approximation is quite close to the binomial probability obtained from Table 1.

Example 7.5   *The production line in a large manufacturing plant produces items of which 10 percent are defective. In a random sample of 100 items selected from the production line, what is the probability that we would find exactly $y = 9$ defectives?*

Solution   *The exact probability of observing $y = 9$ "successes" in $n = 100$ independent trials of a binomial experiment with a probability of success $p = .1$ at each trial is found by evaluating*

$$p(9) = C_9^{100}(.1)^9(.9)^{91}.$$

Since this form is very tedious to evaluate, we shall employ the normal approximation method. The mean and variance of the binomial distribution are

$$\mu = np = 100(.1) = 10,$$
$$\sigma = \sqrt{npq} = \sqrt{100(.1)(.9)} = 3.$$

The probability of exactly 9 successes would be approximated by the area under the normal curve between z_1 and z_2, where

$$z_1 = \frac{8.5 - 10}{3} = -.5$$

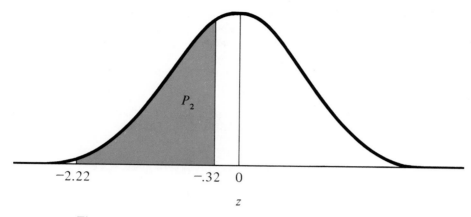

Figure 7.8   *Area Under the Normal Curve in Example 7.4*

and

$$z_2 = \frac{9.5 - 10}{3} = -.17$$

(see Figure 7.9). The area between $z_1 = -.5$ *and* $z_2 = -.17$, *and hence the probability of exactly 9 defectives, is approximately equal to*

$$p(9) \approx P(z_1 \leq z \leq z_2) = P(-.5 \leq z \leq -.17)$$
$$= .1915 - .0675$$
$$= .1240.$$

Figure 7.9   *Area Under the Normal Curve in Example 7.5*

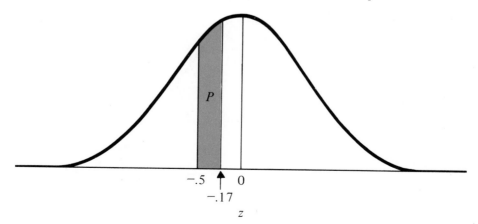

Example 7.6   *The reliability of an electrical fuse can be stated as the probability that a fuse, chosen at random from production, will function under the conditions for which it has been designed. A random sample of 1,000 fuses was tested and $y = 27$ defectives were observed. Calculate the probability of observing 27 or more defectives, assuming that the fuse reliability is .98.*

Solution   *The probability of observing a defective when a single fuse is tested is $p = .02$, given that the fuse reliability is .98. Then*

$$\mu = np = 1,000(.02) = 20,$$

$$\sigma = \sqrt{npq} = \sqrt{1,000(.02)(.98)} = 4.43.$$

The probability of 27 or more defective fuses, given $n = 1,000$, is

$$P = P(y \geq 27),$$

$$P = P(27) + P(28) + P(29) + \cdots + P(999) + P(1,000).$$

The normal approximation to P would be the area under the normal curve to the right of $y = 26.5$. (Note that we must use $y = 26.5$ rather than $y = 27$ so as to include the entire probability rectangle associated with $y = 27$.) The z value corresponding to $y = 26.5$ is

$$z = \frac{y - \mu}{\sigma} = \frac{26.5 - 20}{4.43} = \frac{6.5}{4.43} = 1.47,$$

and the area between $z = 0$ and $z = 1.47$ is equal to .4292, as shown in Figure 7.10. Since the total area to the right of the mean is equal to .5,

$$P = P(y \geq 27) \approx P(z \geq 1.47) = .5 - .4292$$

$$= .0708.$$

Figure 7.10   *Normal Approximation to the Binomial in Example 7.6*

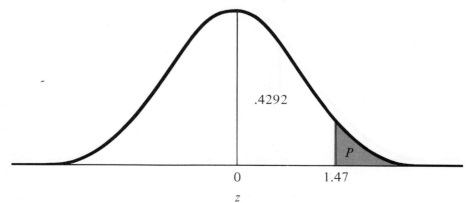

.4292

P

0   1.47

z

Example 7.7   *A new serum was tested to determine its effectiveness in preventing the common cold. One hundred people were injected with the serum and observed for a period of 1 year. Sixty-eight survived the winter without a cold. Suppose that according to prior information it is known that the probability of surviving the winter without a cold is equal to .5 when the serum is not used. On the basis of the results of the above experiment, what conclusions would you make regarding the effectiveness of the serum?*

Solution   *Translating the question into an hypothesis concerning the parameter of the binomial population, we wish to test the null hypothesis that p, the probability of survival on a single trial, is equal to .5. Assume that the content of the serum is such that it could not increase the susceptibility to colds. Then the alternative to the null hypothesis would reject the null hypothesis when y, the number of survivors, is large.*

Since the normal approximation to the binomial will be adequate for this example, we would interpret a large and improbable value of y to be one that lies several standard deviations away from the hypothesized mean, $\mu = np = 100(.5) = 50$.

Noting that

$$\sigma = \sqrt{npq} = \sqrt{(100)(.5)(.5)} = 5,$$

we may arrive at a conclusion without bothering to locate a specific rejection region. The observed value of y, 68, lies more than 3σ away from the hypothesized mean, $\mu = 50$. Specifically, y lies

$$z = \frac{y - \mu}{\sigma} = \frac{68 - 50}{5} = 3.6$$

standard deviations away from the hypothesized mean. This result is so improbable, assuming the serum ineffective, that we would reject the null hypothesis and conclude that the probability of surviving a winter without a cold is greater than $p = .5$ when the serum is used. (The reader will observe that the area above $z = 3.6$ is so small that it is not included in Table 3, Appendix.)

Rejecting the null hypothesis raises additional questions. How effective is the serum and is it sufficiently effective, from an economic point of view, to warrant commercial production? The former question leads to an estimation problem, a topic discussed in Chapter 8, while the latter, involving a business decision, would utilize the results of our experiments as well as a study of consumer demand, sales and production costs, and so forth, to achieve an answer useful to the drug company.

Example 7.8   *The probability of a type I error, α, and location of the rejection region for a statistical test of an hypothesis are usually specified before the data are collected. Suppose that we wish to test the null hypothesis, $p = .5$, in a*

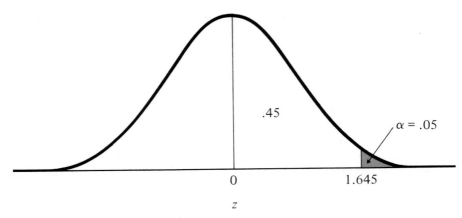

Figure 7.11   *Location of the Rejection Region*
in Example 7.8

situation identical to the cold serum problem in Example 7.7. Find the appropriate rejection region for the test if we wish α to be approximately equal to
.05. (*See Figure* 7.11.)

Solution   *We have previously stated in Example* 7.7 *that y, the number of
survivors, would be used as a test statistic and that the rejection region would
be located in the upper tail of the probability distribution for y. Desiring* α
approximately equal to .05, *we seek a value of y, say* y_α, *such that*

$$P(y \geq y_\alpha) \approx .05.$$

(*Note: The symbol* ≈ *means "approximately equal to."*) *This can be determined
by first finding the corresponding* z_α *which gives the number of standard
deviations between the mean,* μ = 50, *and* y_α. *Since the total area to the right of
z* = 0 *is* .5, *the area between z* = 0 *and* z_α *will equal* .45 (*see Figure* 7.11).
Checking Table 3, *we find that z* = 1.64 *corresponds to an area equal to*
.4495 *and z* = 1.65 *to an area of* .4505. *A linear interpolation between these
values would give*

$$z_\alpha = 1.645.$$

Recall the relation between z and y,

$$z_\alpha = \frac{y_\alpha - \mu}{\sigma},$$

and substitute $z_\alpha = 1.645$ into the expression. Then

$$1.645 = \frac{y_\alpha - 50}{5}.$$

Solving for y_α we obtain

$$y_\alpha = 58.225.$$

Obviously, we cannot observe $y = 58.225$ survivors; hence we must choose 58 or 59 as the point where the rejection region commences.

Suppose that we decide to reject when y is greater than or equal to 59. Then the actual probability of the type I error, α, for the test is

$$P(y \geq 59) = \alpha,$$

which can be approximated by using the area under the normal curve above $y = 58.5$, a problem similar to that encountered in Example 7.6. The z value corresponding to $y = 58.5$ is

$$z = \frac{y - \mu}{\sigma} = \frac{58.5 - 50}{5} = 1.7,$$

and the tabulated area between $z = 0$ to $z = 1.7$ is .4554:

$$\alpha = .5 - .4554$$
$$= .0446.$$

While the method described above provides a more accurate value for α, there is very little practical difference between an α of .0446 and one equal to .05. When n is large, time and effort may be saved by using z as a test statistic rather than y. This method was employed in Example 7.8. We would then reject the null hypothesis when z is greater than or equal to 1.645.

Example 7.9   *A cigarette manufacturer believes that approximately 10 percent of all smokers favor his product, brand A. To test this belief, 2,500 smokers are selected at random from the population of cigarette smokers and questioned concerning their cigarette brand preference. A total of $y = 218$ express a preference for brand A. Do these data provide sufficient evidence to contradict the hypothesis that 10 percent of all smokers favor brand A? Conduct a statistical test using an α equal to .05.*

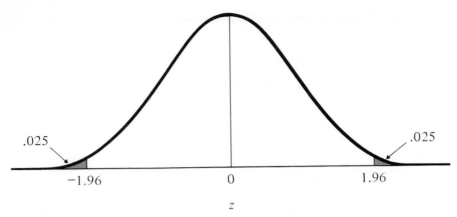

Figure 7.12 *Location of the Rejection Region in Example 7.9*

Solution *We wish to test the null hypothesis that p, the probability that a single smoker prefers brand A, is equal to .1 against the alternative that p is greater than or less than .1. The rejection region corresponding to an α = .05 would be located as shown in Figure 7.12. We would reject the null hypothesis when z > 1.96 or z < −1.96. In other words, we would reject when y lies more than approximately two standard deviations away from its hypothesized mean. Note that half of α is placed in one tail of the distribution and half in the other because we wish to reject the null hypothesis when p is either larger or smaller than p = .1. This is called a two-tailed statistical test in contrast to the one-tailed test discussed in Examples 7.7 and 7.8 when the alternative to the null hypothesis was only that p was larger than the hypothesized value.*

   Assuming the null hypothesis to be true, the mean and standard deviations for y are

$$\mu = np = (2{,}500)(.1) = 250,$$

$$\sigma = \sqrt{npq} = \sqrt{(2{,}500)(.1)(.9)} = 15.$$

The z value corresponding to the observed y = 218 is

$$z = \frac{y - \mu}{\sigma} = \frac{218 - 250}{15} = \frac{-32}{15} = -2.13.$$

   *Noting that z falls in the rejection region, we would reject the null hypothesis and conclude that less than 10 percent of all smokers prefer brand A.**

---

* To be exact, one should make the half unit correction for continuity when calculating z. For large *n* the correction will have little effect on either the computed value of z or on the test conclusion.

What is the probability that we have made an incorrect decision? The answer, of course, is either 1 or 0, depending upon whether our decision was correct or incorrect in this specific case. However, we know that if this statistical test were employed over and over again, the probability of rejecting the null hypothesis when it is true is only $\alpha = .05$. Hence we are reasonably certain that we have made the correct decision.

7.6   Summary

Many continuous random variables observed in nature possess a probability distribution that is bell-shaped and may be approximated by the normal probability distribution discussed in Section 7.1. The common occurrence of normally distributed random variables may be partly explained by the central limit theorem, which states that, under rather general conditions, the sum or the mean of a random sample of n measurements drawn from a population will be approximately normally distributed in repeated sampling when n is large.

As a case in point, the number of successes, y, associated with a binomial experiment may be regarded as a sum of n sample measurements that will possess, approximately, a normal probability distribution when n, the total number of trials, is large. This application of the central limit theorem provides a method for calculating, with reasonable accuracy, the probabilities of the binomial probability distribution by using corresponding areas under the normal probability distribution. Since the opportunities for the application of the binomial probability distribution within business are numerous, the normal approximation to the binomial is an essential topic in our study of business statistics. While other applications of the central limit theorem and the normal distribution will be encountered in succeeding chapters, we particularly note that the central limit theorem provides justification for the use of the empirical rule, Chapter 3. Furthermore, we observe that the contents of this chapter provide an extension and refinement of the thought embodied in the empirical rule.

Exercises

1.   A sample of $n = 4$ supermarkets is to be selected from a total of nine in a small community. Give the number of different samples that might be selected. If the sampling is random, what is the probability that a given sample will be selected?

2.   Let y equal the number of charge purchases made in a month by a credit customer of the Palace Department Store. The mean value of y and the standard deviation are known to be $\mu = 5.2$ and $\sigma = 1.9$, respectively. Suppose that a sampling experiment involving the random selection of $n = 5$ customer accounts from the credit files of the Palace

Department Store is repeated over and over again for an infinitely large number of times where the selected file is replaced after recording the number of charge purchases in the past month. From each sample of five measurements, the sample mean is computed. Find the mean and standard deviation for this distribution of sample means. (*Hint:* See the central limit theorem.)

3. Using Table 3, calculate the area under the normal curve between
    (a) $z = 0$ and $z = 1.2$. (b) $z = 0$ and $z = -.9$.

4. Repeat Exercise 3 for
    (a) $z = 0$ and $z = 1.6$. (b) $z = 0$ and $z = .75$.

5. Repeat Exercise 3 for
    (a) $z = 0$ and $z = 1.45$. (b) $z = 0$ and $z = -.42$.

6. Repeat Exercise 3 for
    (a) $z = 0$ and $z = -1.44$. (b) $z = 0$ and $z = 2.01$.

7. Repeat Exercise 3 for
    (a) $z = .3$ and $z = 1.56$. (b) $z = .2$ and $z = -.2$.

8. Repeat Exercise 3 for
    (a) $z = 1.21$ and $z = 1.75$. (b) $z = -1.3$ and $z = 1.74$.

9. Find the probability that z is greater than $-.75$.

10. Find the probability that z is less than 1.35.

11. Find a z_0 such that $P(z > z_0) = .5$.

12. Find a z_0 such that $P(z < z_0) = .8643$.

13. Find the probability that z lies between $z = .6$ and $z = 1.67$.

14. Find a z_0 such that $P(z < z_0) = .05$.

15. Find a z_0 such that $P(-z_0 < z < z_0) = .90$.

16. Find a z_0 such that $P(-z_0 < z < z_0) = .99$.

17. An auditor has found that the credit records of a large mail order house are normally distributed and show an average account billing error of $0 and a standard deviation of $1. (Billing errors may be positive or negative according to whether the purchaser was overcharged or undercharged.) If one credit account is randomly selected from the files of the mail order house, find the probability that it will contain a billing error
    (a) Between $0 and $1.50. (b) Between $-$2.00 and $0.
    (c) At least $1.75. (d) Which is not an overcharge.
    (e) Between $-$1.50 and $1.25. (f) Between $-$2.00 and $-$1.00.

18. The loan department of the First National Bank has found that home loans they have issued over the past year are normally distributed with a mean of $20,000 and a standard deviation of $2,500. One home loan account issued by the bank during the past year is randomly selected from the files of the loan department. Find the probability the amount of the loan was
    (a) $20,000 or less. (b) At least $20,000.
    (c) Between $15,000 and $22,000. (d) Between $17,000 and $19,000.
    (e) Between $21,000 and $25,000. (f) Less than $16,000.

19. The number of customers entering a certain restaurant in any given day is approximately normally distributed with mean $\mu = 40$ and standard deviation $\sigma = 11$. Find the

probability that during a given day
(a) At least 40 customers arrive.
(b) At least 45 customers arrive.
(c) Between 35 and 45 customers arrive.

20. All prospective employees of the U.S. Treasury Department are required to pass a special civil service examination before they are hired. Over a period of time, the examination scores have been normally distributed with a mean $\mu = 85$ and standard deviation $\sigma = 4$. Suppose that $n = 50$ applicants for a job with the Treasury Department sit for the test.
(a) What proportion can be expected to obtain an examination score of 90 or greater?
(b) An examination score of less than 80 is considered failing. What is the probability an individual will fail the examination?
(c) Of the 50 sitting for the examination, what is the expected number who will pass?

21. The scores on a company's personnel placement examination are normally distributed with a mean and standard deviation equal to 500 and 100, respectively. If Jones scored 650, what fraction of those taking the exam can be expected to exceed Jones' score?

22. Refer to Exercise 21. If personnel obtain a score of 375 or less, their employment with the firm is terminated. What percentage of those taking the examination can be expected to obtain a score causing their termination of employment with the firm?

23. The length of life of an automatic washer is approximately normally distributed with mean and standard deviation equal to 3.1 and 1.2 years, respectively. If this type of washer is guaranteed for 1 year, what fraction of original sales will require replacement?

24. The average length of time required to complete the civil service examination for prospective U.S. Treasury Department employees was found to equal 70 minutes, with a standard deviation of 12 minutes. When should the examination be terminated if the examination supervisor wishes to allow sufficient time for 90 percent of the applicants to complete the test? (Assume that the time required to complete the examination is normally distributed.)

25. The Midstate Paper Company employs two salesmen, Less and Moore. Less averages $20,000 in sales per month with standard deviation $8,000 while Moore averages $35,000 in sales per month with standard deviation $5,000. During a given month Moore's sales amounted to $43,000. How great would Less's sales volume have to be in order for it to be equivalently as great as Moore's sales volume? (Assume that monthly sales volumes for both men are normally distributed.)

26. The week's end closing prices of two securities were observed over a long period of time. The closing prices of security A averaged $50 with a standard deviation of $2.50, while those of security B averaged $95 with a standard deviation of $6.00. At the end of a given week, the closing price of security A was $59. Assume that the week's end closing prices for both securities are normally distributed.
(a) How great would the closing price of security B have to be to exhibit as great an increase as that exhibited by security A?
(b) Which security involves the greater risk to its owner? Why?

27. Consider a binomial experiment with $n = 25$, $p = .4$. Calculate $P(8 \leq y \leq 11)$ using
(a) The binomial probabilities, Table 1, Appendix.
(b) The normal approximation to the binomial.

28. Consider a binomial experiment with $n = 25$, $p = .2$. Calculate $P(y \leq 4)$ using
(a) Table 1, Appendix.
(b) The normal approximation to the binomial.

29.   It is generally assumed by a television manufacturer that 40 percent of all new TV sets sold in the city of Oakdale bear his firm's brand. In a given week, $n = 25$ Oakdale residents have been known to buy a new TV set. Find the probability that at least 8 but not more than 11 of the buyers purchased a set from the manufacturer in question, using successively
      (a) The binomial probabilities, Table 1, Appendix.
      (b) The normal approximation to the binomial.

30.   An assembly machine is known to produce items of which 10 percent are defective. Suppose that a sample of $n = 20$ is selected from the output of this machine. Using the normal approximation to the binomial, calculate
      (a) The probability of two to four defectives, inclusive, in the sample.
      (b) The probability of no more than four defectives in the sample.

31.   The mayor or Oakdale believes that 50 percent of the population of Oakdale favor fluoridation of the city's drinking water. During a given day, the mayor has his secretary randomly telephone $n = 100$ Oakdale residents and ask their opinion regarding fluoridation; given that the mayor's original assumption is correct, find
      (a) The probability that at least 60 indicate they favor fluoridation,
      (b) The probability that at least 50 but not more than 55 indicate they do not favor fluoridation.

32.   A salesman has found that, on the average, the probability of a sale on a single contact is equal to .3. If the salesman contacts 50 customers, what is the probability that at least 10 will buy? (Assume that y, the number of sales, follows a binomial probability distribution.)

33.   Voters in a certain city were sampled concerning their voting preference in a primary election. Suppose that candidate A could win if he could poll 40 percent of the vote. If 920 of a sample of 2,500 voters favored A, does this contradict the hypothesis that A will win?

34.   One thousand flash bulbs were selected from a large production lot and tested. Sixty-three were found to be defective. Does the sample present sufficient evidence to indicate that more than 5 percent of the bulbs in the lot are defective?

35.   A newly designed portable radio was styled on the assumption that 50 percent of all purchasers are female. If a random sample of 400 purchasers is selected, what is the probability that the number of female purchasers in the sample will be greater than 175?

36.   An airline finds that 5 percent of the persons making reservations on a certain flight will not show up for the flight. If the airline sells 160 tickets for a flight with only 155 seats, what is the probability that a seat will be available for every person holding a reservation and planning to fly?

37.   It is known from experience that 10 percent of those who register their intent to attend a certain convention do not show up. Suppose that 100 people indicate an intent to attend. Find the probability that
      (a) Two or more fail to show.
      (b) No more than three fail to show.

38.   It is known that 30 percent of all calls coming into a telephone exchange are long-distance calls. If 200 calls come into the exchange, what is the probability that at least 50 will be long-distance calls?

39.   A machine operation produces bearings whose diameters are normally distributed with mean and standard deviation equal to .498 and .002, respectively. If specifications

require that the bearing diameter equal .500 inch plus or minus .004 inch, what fraction of the production will be unacceptable?

40. A soft drink machine can be regulated so that it discharges an average of μ ounces per cup. If the ounces of fill are normally distributed with standard deviation equal to .3 ounce, give the setting for μ so that 8-ounce cups will overflow only 1 percent of the time.

41. Refer to Exercise 35. Suppose we wish to test the hypothesis that 50 percent of all purchasers are female against the alternative that this percentage is less than 50. To do this we shall select a random sample of 400 purchasers and reject the hypothesis if the number of female purchasers in the sample test is less than or equal to 175.
    (a) Find α for this test.
    (b) Find β if the true fraction of female purchasers is .4.

42. A manufacturing plant utilizes 3,000 electric light bulbs that have a length of life which is normally distributed with mean and standard deviation equal to 500 and 50 hours, respectively. In order to minimize the number of bulbs that burn out during operating hours, all the bulbs are replaced after a given period of operation. How often should the bulbs be replaced if we wish no more than 1 percent of the bulbs to burn out between replacement periods?

43. An advertising agency has stated that 20 percent of all television viewers watch a particular program. In a random sample of 1,000 viewers, $y = 184$ viewers were watching the program. Do these data present sufficient evidence to contradict the advertiser's claim?

44. The length of life of a certain fuse is known to be normally distributed with mean 1,000 hours and standard deviation 50 hours. Find the probability that one of the fuses chosen at random will last between 1,020 and 1,110 hours.

45. A certain kind of automobile battery is known to have a length of life which is normally distributed with mean 1,200 days and standard deviation 100 days. How long should the guarantee time be if the manufacturer wants to replace only 10 percent of the batteries sold?

46. The probability that a certain kind of component will fail in 1,000 hours or less is .20. Let y be the random number of components that fail in a sample of size 100.
    (a) What is the expected value of y?
    (b) What is the standard deviation of y?
    (c) Using the normal approximation, find $P(y < 30)$.

47. A purchaser of electric relays is supplied by two suppliers A and B. It is known that 2 out of every 3 relays used by the company come from supplier A. If 75 relays are selected at random from those in use by the company, find the probability that at most 48 of these relays come from supplier A. Assume that the company uses a large number of relays.

48. A national poll claims that 60 percent of all American voters favor a popular vote for presidential nominees. Investigation indicates that only 100 voters were sampled and, of those, $y = 54$ favored the popular vote. Suppose that the fraction of voters, p, favoring a popular vote is actually .6. Find the probability that $y \leq 54$ given that $p = .60$.

49. The average personal yearly income in a given state is $6,200, with a standard deviation of $400.
    (a) If a sample of 64 people is randomly chosen from this state, find the probability that the mean income for the sample exceeds $6,300.
    (b) If a second independent sample of 64 people is randomly chosen from this state, find the probability that both sample means exceed $6,300.

References

Alder, H. L., and E. B. Roessler, *Introduction to Probability and Statistics.* 5th ed. San Francisco: W. H. Freeman and Company, 1972. Chapter 7.

Hoel, P. G., *Elementary Statistics,* 3rd ed. New York: John Wiley & Sons, Inc., 1971. Chapter 4.

Mack, S. F., *Elementary Statistics.* New York: Holt, Rinehart and Winston, Inc., 1960. Chapter 5.

Chapter Eight

Statistical Inference

8.1   Introduction

    Inference, specifically decision making and prediction, is centuries old and plays an important role in our individual lives. Each of us is faced with daily personal decisions and situations that require predictions concerning the future. The government is concerned with predicting the flow of gold to Europe. The broker wishes knowledge concerning the behavior of the stock market. The metallurgist seeks to use the results of an experiment to infer whether or not a new type of steel is more resistant to temperature changes than another. The housewife wishes to know whether detergent A is more effective than detergent B in her washing machine. These inferences are supposedly based upon relevant bits of available information which we call observations or data.

    In many practical situations the relevant information is abundant, seemingly inconsistent, and, in many respects, overwhelming. As a result, our carefully considered decision or prediction is often little better than an outright guess. One need only refer to the "Market Views" section of the *Wall Street Journal* to observe the diversity of expert opinion concerning future stock market behavior. Similarly, a visual analysis of data by scientists and engineers will often yield conflicting opinions regarding conclusions to be drawn from an experiment. While many individuals tend to feel that their own built-in inference-making equipment is quite good, experience would suggest that most people are incapable of utilizing large amounts of data, mentally weighing each bit of relevant information, and arriving at a good inference. (You may test your individual inference-making equipment using the exercises in this chapter and the next. Scan the data and make an inference before using the appropriate statistical procedure. Compare the results.) Certainly, a study of inference-making systems is desirable, and this is the objective of the mathematical statistician. Although we have purposely touched upon some of the notions involved in statistical inference in preceding chapters, it will be beneficial to organize our knowledge at this point as we attempt an elementary presentation of some of the basic ideas involved in statistical inference.

> *The objective of statistics is to make inferences about a population based upon information contained in a sample.*

Inasmuch as populations are characterized by numerical descriptive measures called parameters, statistical inference is concerned with making inferences about population parameters. Typical population parameters are the mean, the standard deviation, and the area under the probability distribution above or below some value of the random variable or the area between two values of the variable. Indeed, the practical problems mentioned in the first paragraph of this section can be restated in the framework of a population with a specified parameter of interest.

Methods for making inference about parameters fall into one of two categories. We may make decisions concerning the value of the parameter, as exemplified by the lot acceptance sampling and test of an hypothesis described in Chapter 6. Or, we may estimate or predict the value of the parameter. While some statisticians view estimation as a decision-making problem, it will be convenient for us to retain the two categories and, particularly, to concentrate on estimation and tests of hypotheses.

A statement of the objective and the types of statistical inference would be incomplete without reference to a measure of goodness of inferential procedures. We may define numerous objective methods for making inferences in addition to our own individual procedures based upon intuition. Certainly a measure of goodness must be defined so that one procedure may be compared with another. More than that, we would like to state the goodness of a particular inference in a given physical situation. Thus, to predict that the price of a stock will be $80 next Monday would be insufficient and would stimulate few of us to take action to buy or sell. Indeed, we ask whether the estimate is correct to within a plus or minus $1, $2, or $10.

> *Statistical inference in a practical situation contains two elements: (1) the inference and (2) a measure of its goodness.*

Before concluding this introductory discussion of inference, it would be well to dispose of a question that frequently disturbs the beginner. Which method of inference should be used; that is, should the parameter be estimated or should we test an hypothesis concerning its value? The answer to this question is dictated by the practical question which has been posed and is often determined by personal preference. Some people like to test theories concerning parameters, while others prefer to express their inference as an estimate. We shall find that there are actually two methods of estimation, the choice of which, once again, is a matter of personal preference. Inasmuch as both estimation and tests of hypotheses are frequently used in scientific literature, we would be remiss in excluding one or the other from our discussion.

8.2   Types of Estimators

Estimation procedures may be divided into two types, point estimation and interval estimation. Suppose that we wish to estimate the annual salary of a particular employee of the Mallon Company. The estimate might be given as a single dollar value, for instance $7,500, or we might estimate that the salary would be contained in an interval, say $7,200 to $7,800. The first type of estimate is called a point estimate because a single number, representing the estimate, may be associated with a point on a line. The second type, involving two points and defining an interval on a line, is called an interval estimate. We shall consider each of these methods of estimation in turn.

A point-estimation procedure utilizes information in a sample to arrive at a single number or point which estimates the parameter of interest. The actual estimation is accomplished by an estimator. An estimator is a rule that tells us how to calculate the estimate based upon information in the sample; it is generally expressed as a formula. For example, the sample mean,

$$\bar{y} = \frac{\sum\limits_{i=1}^{n} y_i}{n},$$

is an estimator of the population mean μ and explains exactly how the actual numerical value of the estimate may be obtained once the sample values, $y_1, y_2, \ldots, y_n$, are known. On the other hand, an interval estimator uses the data in the sample to calculate two points which are intended to enclose the true value of the parameter estimated.

An investigation of the reasoning used in calculating the goodness of a point estimator is facilitated by considering an analogy. Point estimation is similar, in many respects, to firing a revolver at a target. The estimator, which generates estimates, is analogous to the revolver; a particular estimate is analogous to the bullet, and the parameter of interest, to the bull's-eye. Drawing a sample from the population and estimating the value of the parameter is equivalent to firing a single shot at the target.

Suppose that a man fires a single shot at a target and the shot pierces the bull's-eye. Do we conclude that he is an excellent shot? Obviously, the answer is no, because not one of us would consent to hold the target while a second shot is fired. On the other hand, if 1 million shots in succession hit the bull's-eye, we might acquire sufficient confidence in the marksman to hold the target for the next shot, if the compensation were adequate. The point we wish to make is certainly clear. We cannot evaluate the goodness of an estimation procedure on the basis of a single estimate; rather, we must observe the results when the estimation procedure is used over and over again, many many times—we then observe how closely the shots are distributed about the bull's-eye. In fact, since the estimates are numbers, we would evaluate the goodness of the estimator by constructing a frequency distribution of the estimates obtained in repeated sampling and note how closely the distribution centers about the parameter of interest.

Table 8.1   *Sample Means from Samples of Size n = 10 Selected from the Sales of Tailorcraft Suits by The Haberdashery Shop*

SAMPLE NUMBER	$\sum y_i$	$\bar{y}$	SAMPLE NUMBER	$\sum y_i$	$\bar{y}$
1	29	2.9	26	24	2.4
2	29	2.9	27	27	2.7
3	30	3.0	28	37	3.7
4	42	4.2	29	36	3.6
5	42	4.2	30	36	3.6
6	28	2.8	31	24	2.4
7	38	3.8	32	27	2.7
8	30	3.0	33	34	3.4
9	29	2.9	34	41	4.1
10	32	3.2	35	48	4.8
11	34	3.4	36	43	4.3
12	38	3.8	37	35	3.5
13	33	3.3	38	35	3.5
14	26	2.6	39	31	3.1
15	39	3.9	40	39	3.9
16	29	2.9	41	38	3.8
17	33	3.3	42	33	3.3
18	30	3.0	43	35	3.5
19	37	3.7	44	34	3.4
20	39	3.9	45	37	3.7
21	38	3.8	46	35	3.5
22	27	2.7	47	33	3.3
23	44	4.4	48	23	2.3
24	38	3.8	49	30	3.0
25	39	3.9	50	34	3.4

This point is aptly illustrated by considering the results of the sales-record study for The Haberdashery Shop, Section 7.2, where 100 samples of $n = 5$ observations were drawn from the population of all past sales records for which the population possessed a mean and standard deviation equal to $\mu = 3.5$ and $\sigma = 1.71$, respectively. The distribution of 100 sample means, each representing an estimate, is given in Figure 7.2. A glance at the distribution tells us that the estimates tend to pile up about the mean, $\mu = 3.5$, and also gives an indication as to the error of estimation that might be expected. If larger samples were selected, the distribution of sample means would appear to be even more concentrated around 3.5, suggesting a smaller error of estimation of the mean.

Suppose that we return to the sales records of The Haberdashery Shop and record samples of size $n = 10$ by letting each sample consist of the sales of Tailorcraft suits over two consecutive weeks (10 consecutive business days). That is, the first sample consists of the sample measurements 3, 5, 1, 3, 2 from the first week and 3, 1, 1, 4, 6 from the second week. Likewise, the second sample consists of the sales during the third and fourth weeks. The sample means $\bar{y}$ from the 50 samples of size $n = 10$ taken from Table 7.1 are listed in Table 8.1.

To further emphasize our point, Table 8.2 lists the sample means for samples of size $n = 25$ selected from the sales records of The Haberdashery Shop. In this case each sample consists of the sales over 5 consecutive weeks.

Table 8.2   *Sample Means from Samples of Size n = 25 Selected from the Sales of Tailorcraft Suits by The Haberdashery Shop*

SAMPLE NUMBER	$\sum y_i$	$\bar{y}$	SAMPLE NUMBER	$\sum y_i$	$\bar{y}$
1	72	2.88	11	69	2.76
2	100	4.00	12	91	3.64
3	82	3.28	13	71	2.84
4	75	3.00	14	103	4.12
5	90	3.60	15	96	3.84
6	80	3.20	16	87	3.48
7	79	3.16	17	89	3.56
8	89	3.56	18	88	3.52
9	86	3.44	19	83	3.32
10	100	4.00	20	72	2.86

Table 8.3 and Figure 8.1 show clearly the point of our discussion.

The larger the sample size, the more concentrated is the sampling distribution of sample means $\bar{y}$, and hence the more likely it is that $\bar{y}$ is close to the population mean μ.

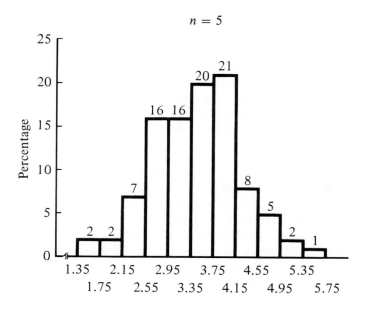

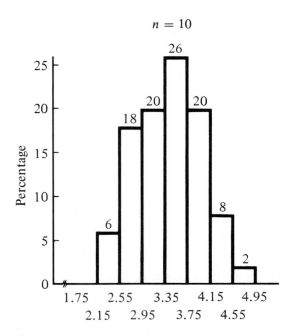

Figure 8.1   *Percentage Histogram of Sample Means for Samples of Size n = 5, n = 10, and n = 25 Selected from the Sales Records of The Haberdashery Shop*

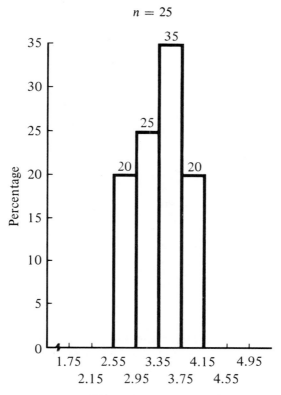

Figure 8.1   *Continued*

The reasoning behind this phenomenon is easily explained. The larger the size of the sample selected, the more likely it is that the sample will contain offsetting large and small sample values. Note, for instance, that in the case with samples of size $n = 25$, no samples were found for which the sample mean was less than 2.55 or greater than 4.15. However, of the 100 samples of size $n = 5$, 11 percent had a sample mean less than 2.55 and 16 percent had sample means greater than 4.15, showing that in at least 27 percent of the samples of size $n = 5$ we are obtaining very inaccurate estimates of the true population mean, $\mu = 3.5$.

   In recapitulation, suppose that we discuss the idea of estimation in general terms, not necessarily specifying that we are trying to estimate the population mean μ. Suppose that the estimation problem involves estimating some population parameter, which, for convenience, we shall call θ. The estimator of θ will be indicated by the symbol $\hat{\theta}$, where the "hat" indicates that we are estimating the parameter immediately beneath. Now, with the revolver-firing example in mind, we see that the desirable properties of a good estimator are quite obvious. We would like the

Table 8.3   *Percentage of Sample Means Falling in 11 Different Intervals for Samples of Size n = 5, n = 10, and n = 25 Selected from the Sales Records of The Haberdashery Shop*

	SAMPLE SIZE		
INTERVAL	$n = 5$	$n = 10$	$n = 25$
1.35–1.75	2	0	0
1.75–2.15	2	0	0
2.15–2.55	7	6	0
2.55–2.95	16	18	20
2.95–3.35	16	20	25
3.35–3.75	20	26	35
3.75–4.15	21	20	20
4.15–4.55	8	8	0
4.55–4.95	5	2	0
4.95–5.35	2	0	0
5.35–5.75	1	0	0

distribution of estimates to center about the parameter estimated as shown in Figure 8.2 and, in addition, we would like the spread of the distribution to be as small as possible. In other words, we would like the mean or expected value of the distribution of estimates to equal the parameter estimated.

Estimators which satisfy this property, that is,

$$E(\hat{\theta}) = \theta,$$

Figure 8.2   *Distribution of Estimates*

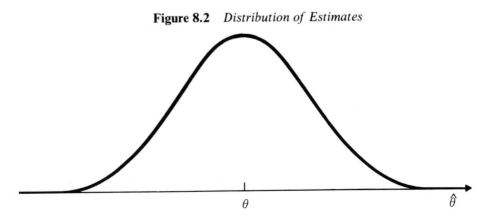

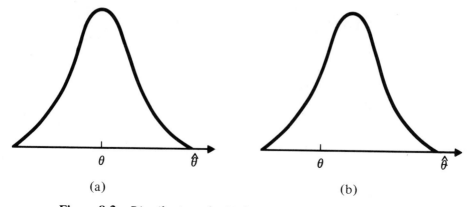

Figure 8.3 *Distributions for Unbiased and Biased Estimators*

are said to be unbiased. Otherwise, they are said to be biased. The frequency distributions for an unbiased estimator and a biased estimator are shown in Figure 8.3(a) and (b), respectively.

Also, we desire the variance or standard deviation for the estimator—that is, the distribution of estimates—to be a minimum. Thus the distribution of estimates in Figure 8.4(a) is preferable to that shown in Figure 8.4(b).

The goodness of an interval estimator is analyzed in much the same manner as is a point estimator. Samples of the same size are repeatedly drawn from the population and the interval estimate is calculated on each occasion. This process will generate a large number of intervals rather than points. A good interval estimate would successively enclose the true value of the parameter a large fraction of the time. This fraction is called the confidence coefficient for the estimator; the estimator itself is often called a confidence interval.

Figure 8.4 *Comparison of Estimator Variability*

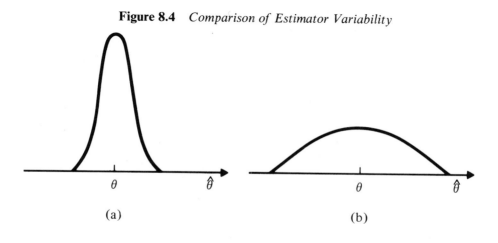

The selection of a "best" estimator—the proper formula to use in calculating the estimates—involves the comparison of various methods of estimation. This is the task of the theoretical statistician and is beyond the scope of this text. Throughout the remainder of this chapter and succeeding chapters, populations and parameters of interest will be defined and the appropriate estimator indicated along with its expected value and standard deviation.

8.3   Point Estimation of a Population Mean

Practical problems often lead to the estimation of a population mean μ. We are concerned with the average achievement of college students in a particular university, in the average strength of a new type of steel, in the average number of deaths per capita in a given social class, and in the average demands of a new product. Conveniently, the estimation of μ serves as a very practical application of statistical inference as well as an excellent illustration of the principles of estimation discussed in Section 8.2. Many estimators are available for estimating the population mean, μ, including the sample median, the average between largest and smallest measurements in the sample, and the sample mean, $\bar{y}$. Each would generate a probability distribution in repeated sampling and, depending upon the population and practical problem involved, would possess certain advantages and disadvantages. Although the sample median and the average of the sample extremes are easier to calculate, the sample mean, $\bar{y}$, is usually superior in that, for some populations, its variance is a minimum and, furthermore, regardless of the population, it is always unbiased.

Figure 8.5   *Distribution of $\bar{y}$ for Large n*

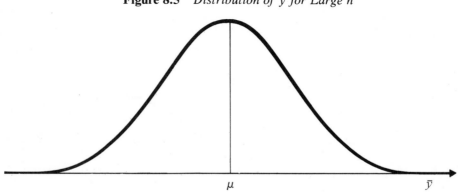

Three facts emerge from a study of the probability distribution of $\bar{y}$ in repeated random sampling of n measurements from a population with mean equal to μ and variance equal to σ^2. Regardless of the probability distribution of the population,

---

1. *The expected value of $\bar{y}$ is equal to μ, the population mean.*

2. *The standard deviation of $\bar{y}$ is equal to*

$$\sigma_{\bar{y}} = \frac{\sigma}{\sqrt{n}} \sqrt{\frac{N - n}{N - 1}},$$

where N is equal to the number of measurements in the population. In the following discussion we shall assume that N is large relative to the sample size, n, and hence that $\sqrt{(N - n)/(N - 1)}$ is approximately equal to 1. Then

$$\sigma_{\bar{y}} = \frac{\sigma}{\sqrt{n}}.$$

3. *When n is large, $\bar{y}$ will be approximately normally distributed according to the central limit theorem (assuming that μ and σ are finite numbers).*

Thus $\bar{y}$ is an unbiased estimator of μ with a standard deviation which is proportional to the population standard deviation, σ, and inversely proportional to the square root of the sample size, n. While we give no proof of these results, we suggest that they are intuitively reasonable. Certainly, the more variable the population data, measured by σ, the more variable will be $\bar{y}$. On the other hand, more information will be available for estimating as n becomes large. Hence the estimates should fall closer to μ, and $\sigma_{\bar{y}}$ should decrease.

In addition to knowledge of the mean and standard deviation of the probability distribution for $\bar{y}$, the central limit theorem provides information of its form. That is, when the sample size, n, is large, the distribution of $\bar{y}$ will be approximately normal. This distribution is shown in Figure 8.5.

With the above results in mind, suppose that we draw a single sample of $n = 5$ observations from the sales records of The Haberdashery Shop, from the study described in Section 7.2, and calculate the sample mean $\bar{y}$. How good will be this estimate of μ; that is, how far will it deviate from the mean, $\mu = 3.5$? Although we cannot state that $\bar{y}$ will *definitely* lie within a specified distance of μ, Tchebysheff's theorem states that if we were to draw many samples from the population, at least three-fourths of the estimates would lie within $2\sigma_{\bar{y}}$ of the mean of the distribution of $\bar{y}$'s, that is, μ. We have noted previously (Section 8.2) that $\sigma = 1.71$. Therefore,

$$2\sigma_{\bar{y}} = 2\sigma/\sqrt{n} = \frac{2(1.71)}{\sqrt{5}} = \frac{2(1.71)}{2.24} = 1.53.$$

Better than that, we would expect the sample means to be approximately normally distributed according to the central limit theorem, in which case approximately 95 percent of the estimates would lie within $2\sigma_{\bar{y}}$ or 1.53 of μ. A glance at Figure 7.2 will confirm this supposition.

The quantity $2\sigma_{\bar{y}}$ is an approximate bound on the error of estimation. We take this to imply that at least three-fourths of the estimates, and most likely 95 percent, will deviate from the mean less than $2\sigma_{\bar{y}}$. The use of two standard deviations rather than three is not sacred, but two would seem a reasonable choice for most practical problems.

Consider the following example of point estimation.

Example 8.1 *Suppose that we wish to estimate the average daily yield of a chemical manufactured in a chemical plant. The daily yield, recorded for $n = 50$ days, produced a mean and standard deviation equal to*

$$\bar{y} = 871 \text{ tons,}$$

$$s = 21 \text{ tons.}$$

Estimate the average daily yield, μ.

Solution *The estimate of the daily yield is then $\bar{y} = 871$ tons. The bound on the error of estimation is*

$$2\sigma_{\bar{y}} = 2\sigma/\sqrt{n} = 2\sigma/\sqrt{50}.$$

Although σ is unknown, we may approximate its value by using s, the estimator of σ. Thus the bound on the error of estimation is approximately

$$2s/\sqrt{n} = \frac{2(21)}{\sqrt{50}} = \frac{42}{7.07} = 5.94.$$

We would feel fairly confident that our estimate of 871 tons is within 5.94 tons of the true average yield.

Example 8.1 deserves further comment in regard to two points. The erroneous use of 2σ as a bound on the error of estimation, rather than $2\sigma_{\bar{y}}$, is common to beginners. Certainly, if we wish to discuss the distribution of $\bar{y}$, we must use its standard deviation, $\sigma_{\bar{y}}$, to describe its variability. Care must be taken not to confuse the descriptive measures of one distribution with another.

A second point of interest concerns the use of s to approximate σ. This approximation will be reasonably good when n is large, say 30 or greater. If the sample size is small, two techniques are available. Sometimes experience or data obtained from previous experiments will provide a good estimate of σ. When this is not available, we may resort to a small-sample procedure described in Chapter 9. The choice of $n = 30$ as the division between "large" and "small" samples is arbitrary. The reasoning for its selection will become apparent in Chapter 9.

8.4   Interval Estimation of a Population Mean

Constructing an interval estimate is like attempting to rope a steer. In this case, the parameter that you wish to estimate corresponds to the steer and the interval to the loop formed by the cowboy's lariat. Each time you draw a sample, you construct a confidence interval for a parameter and you hope to "rope it," that is,

Figure 8.6   *Ten Confidence Intervals for Mean Weekly Profit (each based on a sample of n = 20 observations)*

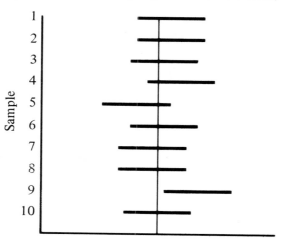

include it in the interval. You will not be successful for every sample. The probability that an interval will enclose the estimated parameter is the confidence
coefficient.

To consider a practical example, suppose that you wish to estimate the mean
profit per week of a small company. If we were to draw 10 samples, each containing
$n = 20$ weekly profit observations, and construct a confidence interval for the
population mean μ for each sample, the intervals might appear as shown in Figure
8.6. The horizontal line segments represent the 10 intervals and the vertical line
represents the location of the true mean weekly profit. Note that all but one of the
intervals enclose μ for these particular samples. Having grasped the concept of a
confidence interval, let us now consider how to find the confidence interval for a
population mean μ based on a random sample of n observations.

The interval estimator, or confidence interval, for a population mean may be
easily obtained from the results of Section 8.3. It is possible that $\bar{y}$ might lie either
above or below the population mean, although we would not expect it to deviate
more than approximately $2\sigma_{\bar{y}}$ from μ. Hence, if we choose $(\bar{y} - 2\sigma_{\bar{y}})$ as the lower
point of the interval, called the lower confidence limit, or LCL, and $(\bar{y} + 2\sigma_{\bar{y}})$ as
the upper point, or upper confidence limit, UCL, the interval most probably will
enclose the true population mean μ. In fact, if n is large and the distribution of $\bar{y}$ is
approximately normal, we would expect approximately 95 percent of the intervals
obtained in repeated sampling to enclose the population mean μ. Two possible
distributions, each with means located a distance $2\sigma_{\bar{y}}$ from $\bar{y}$, are shown in Figure
8.7, the corresponding confidence limits being indicated by dashed lines.

The confidence interval described is called a large-sample confidence interval
(or the confidence limits) because n must be large enough for the central limit theorem
to be effective and hence for the distribution of $\bar{y}$ to be approximately normal.
Inasmuch as σ is usually unknown, the sample standard deviation must be used to
estimate σ. As a rule of thumb, this confidence interval would be appropriate when
$n = 30$ or more.

The confidence coefficient, .95, corresponds to $\pm 2\sigma_{\bar{y}}$, or, more exactly, $1.96\sigma_{\bar{y}}$.
Recalling that .90 of the measurements in a normal distribution will fall within
$z = 1.645$ standard deviations of the mean (Table 3, Appendix II), we could con-

Figure 8.7   *Confidence Limits for μ*

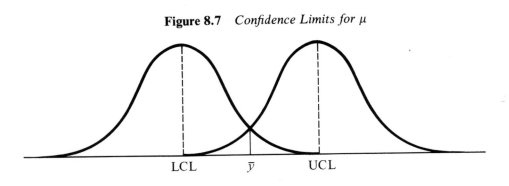

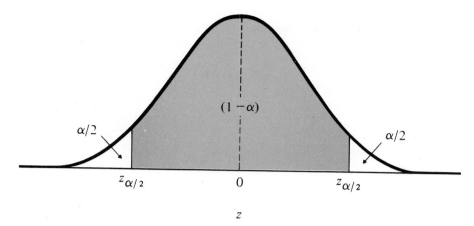

Figure 8.8   *Location of z*

struct 90 percent confidence intervals by using

$$\text{LCL} = \bar{y} - 1.645\sigma_{\bar{y}} = \bar{y} - 1.645\sigma/\sqrt{n}$$

and

$$\text{UCL} = \bar{y} + 1.645\sigma_{\bar{y}} = \bar{y} + 1.645\sigma/\sqrt{n}.$$

In general, we may construct confidence intervals corresponding to any desired confidence coefficient, say $(1 - \alpha)$, using

$$\bar{y} \pm z_{\alpha/2}\sigma/\sqrt{n}.$$

We shall define the quantity $z_{\alpha/2}$ to be the value in the z table, such that the area to the right of $z_{\alpha/2}$ is equal to $\alpha/2$ (see Figure 8.8); that is, $P(z > z_{\alpha/2}) = \alpha/2$. Thus a confidence coefficient equal to .95 would imply $\alpha = .05$ and $z_{.025} = 1.96$. The value of z employed for a 90 percent confidence interval would be $z_{.05} = 1.645$.

Example 8.2   *Find a 90 percent confidence interval for the population mean of Example 8.1. Recall that $\bar{y} = 871$ tons and $s = 21$ tons.*

Solution   *The 90 percent confidence limits would be*

$$\bar{y} \pm 1.645\sigma/\sqrt{n}.$$

Using s to estimate σ, we obtain

$$871 \pm (1.645)\frac{21}{\sqrt{50}},$$

or

$$871 \pm 4.89.$$

Therefore, we estimate that the average day yield μ lies in the interval 866.11 to 875.89 tons. The confidence coefficient, .90, implies that in repeated sampling, 90 percent of the confidence intervals similarly formed would enclose μ.

Example 8.3   *A sample of n = 100 employees from the Mallon Company was selected and the annual salary for each was recorded. The mean and standard deviation of their salaries were found to be*

$$\bar{y} = \$7,750$$

and

$$s = \$900.$$

Find the 95 percent confidence interval for the population average salary μ.

Solution   *The 95 percent confidence limits would be*

$$\bar{y} \pm 1.96\sigma/\sqrt{n}.$$

Using s to estimate σ, we obtain

$$\$7,750 \pm (1.96)\frac{\$900}{\sqrt{100}},$$

or

$$\$7,750 \pm \$176.40.$$

Thus the average salary for the employees of the Mallon Company is contained within the interval $7,573.60 to $7,926.40 with confidence coefficient .95.

Note that the width of the confidence interval increases as the confidence coefficient increases, a result that is in agreement with our intuition. Certainly if we wish to be more confident that the interval will enclose μ, we would increase the width of the interval. Confidence limits corresponding to some of the commonly used confidence coefficients are tabulated in Table 8.4.

Table 8.4   *Confidence Limits for μ*

CONFIDENCE COEFFICIENT	$z_{\alpha/2}$	LCL	UCL
.90	1.645	$\bar{y} - 1.645\sigma/\sqrt{n}$	$\bar{y} + 1.645\sigma/\sqrt{n}$
.95	1.96	$\bar{y} - 1.96\sigma/\sqrt{n}$	$\bar{y} + 1.96\sigma/\sqrt{n}$
.99	2.58	$\bar{y} - 2.58\sigma/\sqrt{n}$	$\bar{y} + 2.58\sigma/\sqrt{n}$

The choice of the confidence coefficient to be used in a given situation is made by the experimenter and will depend upon the degree of confidence that he wishes to place in his estimate. As we have pointed out, the larger the confidence coefficient, the wider the interval. As a result of this freedom of choice, it has become the custom of many experimenters to use a .95 confidence coefficient, although there is no logical foundation for its popularity.

The frequent use of the .95 confidence coefficient introduces a question asked by many beginners. Should one use $z = 1.96$ or $z = 2$ in the confidence interval? The answer is that it does not really make much difference which value is used. The value $z = 1.96$ is more exact for a .95 confidence coefficient, but the error introduced by using $z = 2$ will be very small. The use of $z = 2$ simplifies the calculations, particularly when the computing is done manually. We shall agree to use two standard deviations when placing bounds on the error of a point estimator but will use $z = 1.96$ when constructing a confidence interval, simply to remind the reader that this is the z value obtained from the table of areas under the normal curve.

Note the fine distinction between point estimators and interval estimators. Note also that in placing bounds on the error of a point estimate, for all practical purposes we are constructing an interval estimate when a population mean is being estimated. While this close relationship will exist for most of the parameters estimated in this text, a word of defense of our separation of point and interval estimation is in order. For instance, it is not obvious that the best point estimator will fall in the middle of the best interval estimator—in many cases it does not. Furthermore, it is not a foregone conclusion that the best interval estimator will even be a function of the best point estimator. Although these problems are of a theoretical nature, they are important and worth mentioning. From a practical point of view, the two methods are closely related and the choice between the point and the interval estimator in an actual problem depends upon the preference of the experimenter.

8.5   Estimation from Large Samples

Estimation of a population mean, Sections 8.3 and 8.4, sets the stage for the other estimation problems to be discussed in this chapter. A thread of unity runs through all, which, once it is observed, will simplify the learning process for the beginner. The following conditions will be satisfied for all estimation problems discussed in this chapter. Each point estimator of a parameter, say θ, will be unbiased. That is, the mean of the distribution of estimates obtained in repeated sampling will equal the parameter estimated. The standard deviation of the estimator will be given so that we may place a two-standard-deviation, $2\sigma_\theta$, bound on the error of estimation.

In each case, by the central limit theorem, the point estimate will be approximately normally distributed when n is large, and the probability that the error of estimation will be less than the bound, $2\sigma_\theta$, will be approximately .95.

The corresponding interval estimators will assume that the sample is large enough for the central limit theorem to produce normality in the distribution of the point estimator of θ as well as to provide a good estimate of any other unknown (for example, σ). Then the confidence intervals for any confidence coefficient, $1 - \alpha$, will equal

$$\hat{\theta} \pm z_{\alpha/2}\sigma_{\hat{\theta}}.$$

8.6   Estimating the Difference Between Two Means

A problem of equal importance to the estimation of population means is the comparison of two population means. For instance, we might wish to compare the effectiveness of two teaching methods. Students would be randomly divided into two groups, the first subjected to method 1 and the second to method 2. We would then make inferences concerning the difference in average student achievement as measured by some testing procedure.

Or, we might wish to compare the average yield in a chemical plant using raw materials furnished by two suppliers, *A* and *B*. Samples of daily yield, one for each of the two raw materials, would be recorded and used to make inferences concerning the difference in mean yield.

Each of these examples postulates two populations, the first with mean and variance μ_1 and σ_1^2, and the second with mean and variance μ_2 and σ_2^2. A random sample of n_1 measurements is drawn from population I and n_2 from population II, where the samples are assumed to have been drawn independently of one another. Finally, the estimates of the population parameters, $\bar{y}_1$, s_1^2, $\bar{y}_2$, and s_2^2, are calculated from the sample data.

The point estimator of the difference between the population means, $(\mu_1 - \mu_2)$, is $(\bar{y}_1 - \bar{y}_2)$, the difference between the sample means. If repeated pairs of samples on n_1 and n_2 measurements are drawn from the two populations and the estimate, $(\bar{y}_1 - \bar{y}_2)$, calculated for each pair, a distribution of estimates will result. The mean and standard deviation of the estimator, $(\bar{y}_1 - \bar{y}_2)$, will be

$$E(\bar{y}_1 - \bar{y}_2) = \mu_1 - \mu_2,$$

$$\sigma_{(\bar{y}_1 - \bar{y}_2)} = \sqrt{\frac{\sigma_1^2}{n_1} + \frac{\sigma_2^2}{n_2}}.$$

Furthermore, as pointed out in Section 8.5, when n_1 and n_2 are large, say 30 or more, the estimates will be approximately normally distributed in repeated sampling.

Although the formula for the standard deviation of $(\bar{y}_1 - \bar{y}_2)$ may appear to be complicated, a result derived in mathematical statistics will assist in its memorization. Certainly the variability of a difference between two independent random variables would seem, intuitively, to be greater than the variability of either of the two variables, since one may be extremely large at the same time that the other is extremely small. Hence each contributes a portion of its variability to the variability of the difference. This intuitive explanation is supported by a theorem in mathematical statistics which states that the variance of either the sum or the difference of two independent random variables is equal to the sum of their respective variances. That is,

$$\sigma_{(y_1 + y_2)}^2 = \sigma_1^2 + \sigma_2^2$$

and

$$\sigma_{(y_1 - y_2)}^2 = \sigma_1^2 + \sigma_2^2.$$

Therefore,

$$\sigma_{(\bar{y}_1 - \bar{y}_2)}^2 = \sigma_{\bar{y}_1}^2 + \sigma_{\bar{y}_2}^2 = \frac{\sigma_1^2}{n_1} + \frac{\sigma_2^2}{n_2},$$

and the standard deviation is

$$\sigma_{(\bar{y}_1 - \bar{y}_2)} = \sqrt{\frac{\sigma_1^2}{n_1} + \frac{\sigma_2^2}{n_2}}.$$

We shall have occasion to use this result again in Section 8.8.
The bound on the error of the point estimate is

$$2\sqrt{\frac{\sigma_1^2}{n_1} + \frac{\sigma_2^2}{n_2}}.$$

The sample variance s_1^2 and s_2^2 may be used to estimate σ_1^2 and σ_2^2 when these parameters are unknown. This approximation will be reasonably good where n_1 and n_2 are each equal to 30 or more.

Example 8.4   *A comparison of the wearing quality of two types of automobile tires was obtained by road-testing samples of $n_1 = n_2 = 100$ tires for each type. The number of miles until wear-out was recorded, where wear-out was defined as a specific amount of tire wear. The test results were as follows:*

$$\bar{y}_1 = 26{,}400 \; miles, \qquad \bar{y}_2 = 25{,}100 \; miles;$$
$$s_1^2 = 1{,}440{,}000, \qquad s_2^2 = 1{,}960{,}000.$$

Estimate the difference in mean time to wear-out, and place bounds on the error of estimation.

Solution   *The point estimate of $(\mu_1 - \mu_2)$ is*

$$(\bar{y}_1 - \bar{y}_2) = 26{,}400 - 25{,}100 = 1{,}300 \; miles$$

Thus

$$\sigma_{(\bar{y}_1 - \bar{y}_2)} = \sqrt{\frac{\sigma_1^2}{n_1} + \frac{\sigma_2^2}{n_2}}$$

$$\approx \sqrt{\frac{s_1^2}{n_1} + \frac{s_2^2}{n_1}} = \sqrt{\frac{1{,}440{,}000}{100} + \frac{1{,}960{,}000}{100}}$$

$$= \sqrt{34{,}000} = 184 \; miles.$$

We would expect the error of estimation to be less than $2\sigma_{(\bar{y}_1 - \bar{y}_2)} = 368$ miles. Therefore, it would appear that tire type 1 is superior to type 2 in wearing quality when subjected to the road test.

A confidence interval for $(\mu_1 - \mu_2)$ with confidence coefficient $(1 - \alpha)$ can be obtained by using

$$(\bar{y}_1 - \bar{y}_2) \pm z_{\alpha/2}\sqrt{\frac{\sigma_1^2}{n_1} + \frac{\sigma_2^2}{n_2}}.$$

As a rule of thumb, we shall require both n_1 and n_2 to be equal to 30 or more in order that s_1^2 and s_2^2 provide good estimates of their respective population variances.

Example 8.5   *Place a confidence interval on the difference in mean time to wear-out for the problem described in Example 8.4. Use a confidence co-efficient of .99.*

Solution   *The confidence interval will be*

$$(\bar{y}_1 - \bar{y}_2) \pm 2.58\sqrt{\frac{\sigma_1^2}{n_1} + \frac{\sigma_2^2}{n_2}}.$$

Using the results of Example 8.4, we find that the confidence interval is

$$1,300 \pm 2.58(184).$$

Therefore, LCL = 825, UCL = 1,775, *and the difference in mean time to wear-out is estimated to lie between these two points. Note that the confidence interval is wider than the* $\pm 2\sigma_{(\bar{y}_1 - \bar{y}_2)}$ *used in Example 8.4, because we have chosen a larger confidence coefficient.*

8.7   Estimating the Parameter of a Binomial Population

The best point estimator of the binomial parameter p is also the estimator that would be chosen intuitively. That is, the estimator $\hat{p}$ would equal

$$\hat{p} = \frac{y}{n},$$

the total number of successes divided by the total number of trials. By "best" we mean that $\hat{p}$ is unbiased and possesses a minimum variance compared with other possible estimators.

We recall that, according to the central limit theorem, y is approximately normally distributed when n is large. Inasmuch as n is a constant, we would suspect that $\hat{p}$ is also normally distributed when n is large, and this is indeed true. Furthermore, the expected value and standard deviation of p can be shown to equal

$$E(\hat{p}) = p,$$

$$\sigma_{\hat{p}} = \sqrt{\frac{pq}{n}}.$$

Bounds on the error of a point estimate will be

$$\pm 2 \sqrt{\frac{pq}{n}}$$

and the $(1 - \alpha)$ percent confidence interval, appropriate for large n, is

$$\hat{p} \pm z_{\alpha/2} \sqrt{\frac{\hat{p}\hat{q}}{n}}.$$

The sample size will be considered large when we can assume that the distribution of $\hat{p}$ is approximately normal. These conditions were discussed in Section 8.4.

The only difficulty encountered in our procedure will be in calculating $\sigma_{\hat{p}}$, which involves p (and $q = 1 - p$), an unknown. The reader will note that we have substituted $\hat{p}$ for the parameter p in the standard deviation, $\sqrt{pq/n}$. When n is large, little error will be introduced by this substitution. As a matter of fact, the standard deviation changes only slightly as p changes. This can be observed in Table 8.5, where $\sqrt{pq}$ is recorded for several values of p. Note that $\sqrt{pq}$ changes very little as p changes, especially when p is near .5.

Table 8.5   *Some Calculated Values of $\sqrt{pq}$*

p	$\sqrt{pq}$
.5	.50
.4	.49
.3	.46
.2	.40
.1	.30

Example 8.6   *A random sample of n = 100 voters in a community produced y = 59 voters in favor of candidate A. Estimate the fraction of the voting population favoring A and place a bound on the error of estimation.*

Solution   *The point estimate is*

$$\hat{p} = \frac{y}{n} = \frac{59}{100} = .59,$$

and the bound on the error of estimation is

$$2\sigma_{\hat{p}} = 2\sqrt{\frac{\hat{p}\hat{q}}{n}} = 2\sqrt{\frac{(.59)(.41)}{100}} = .098.$$

A 95 percent confidence interval for p would be

$$\hat{p} \pm 1.96\sqrt{\frac{\hat{p}\hat{q}}{n}}$$

or

$$.59 \pm 1.96(.049).$$

Thus we would estimate that p lies in the interval .494 to .686 with confidence coefficient .95.

8.8   Estimating the Difference Between Two Binomial Populations

The fourth and final estimation problem considered in this chapter is the estimation of the difference between the parameters of two binomial populations. Assume that the two populations I and II possess parameters p_1 and p_2, respectively. Independent random samples consisting of n_1 and n_2 trials are drawn from the population and the estimates $\hat{p}_1$ and $\hat{p}_2$ are calculated.

The point estimator of $(p_1 - p_2), (\hat{p}_1 - \hat{p}_2)$, is an unbiased estimator—that is,

$$E(\hat{p}_1 - \hat{p}_2) = p_1 - p_2,$$

with standard deviation

$$\sigma_{(\hat{p}_1 - \hat{p}_2)} = \sqrt{\frac{p_1 q_1}{n_1} + \frac{p_2 q_2}{n_2}}.$$

Note that in accordance with Section 8.6 the variance of $(\hat{p}_1 - \hat{p}_2)$ is equal to the sum of the variances of $\hat{p}_1$ and $\hat{p}_2$. Therefore, the bound on the error of estimation is

$$\pm 2 \sqrt{\frac{p_1 q_1}{n_1} + \frac{p_2 q_2}{n_2}},$$

where the estimates, $\hat{p}_1$ and $\hat{p}_2$, may be substituted for p_1 and p_2.

The $(1 - \alpha)$ confidence interval, appropriate when n_1 and n_2 are large, is

$$(\hat{p}_1 - \hat{p}_2) \pm z_{\alpha/2} \sqrt{\frac{\hat{p}_1 \hat{q}_1}{n_1} + \frac{\hat{p}_2 \hat{q}_2}{n_2}}.$$

Example 8.7 *A manufacturer of fly sprays wishes to compare two new concoctions, I and II. Two rooms of equal size, each containing 1,000 flies, are employed in the experiment, one treated with fly spray I and the other treated with an equal amount of fly spray II. A total of 825 and 760 flies succumbs to sprays I and II, respectively. Estimate the difference in the rate of kill for the two sprays when used in the last environment.*

Solution *The point estimate of $(p_1 - p_2)$ is*

$$(\hat{p}_1 - \hat{p}_2) = .825 - .760 = .065.$$

The bound on the error of estimation is

$$2 \sqrt{\frac{p_1 q_1}{n_1} + \frac{p_2 q_2}{n_2}} \approx 2 \sqrt{\frac{(.825)(.175)}{1,000} + \frac{(.76)(.24)}{1,000}}$$

$$= .036.$$

The corresponding confidence interval, using confidence coefficient .95, is

$$(\hat{p}_1 - \hat{p}_2) \pm 1.96 \sqrt{\frac{\hat{p}_1 \hat{q}_1}{n_1} + \frac{\hat{p}_2 \hat{q}_2}{n_2}}.$$

The resulting confidence interval is

$$.065 \pm .035.$$

Hence we estimate that the difference between the rates of kill, $(p_1 - p_2)$, *will fall in the interval .030 to .100. We are fairly confident of this estimate, because we know that if our sampling procedure were repeated over and over again, each time generating an interval estimate, approximately 95 percent of the estimates would enclose the quantity* $(p_1 - p_2)$.

8.9   Choosing the Sample Size

The design of an experiment is essentially a plan for purchasing a quantity of information which, like any other commodity, may be acquired at varying prices depending upon the manner in which the data are obtained. Some measurements contain a large amount of information concerning the parameter of interest; others may contain little or none. Since the sole product of research is information, it behooves us to make its purchase at minimum cost.

The sampling procedure, or experimental design as it is usually called, affects the quantity of information per measurement. This, along with the sample size, n, controls the total amount of relevant information in a sample. With few exceptions we shall be concerned with the simplest sampling situation, random sampling from a relatively large population, and will devote our attention to the selection of the sample size, n.

The researcher makes little progress in planning an experiment before encountering the problem of selecting the sample size. Indeed, perhaps one of the most frequent questions asked of the statistician is: How many measurements should be included in the sample? Unfortunately, the statistician cannot answer this question without knowing how much information the experimenter wishes to buy. Certainly, the total amount of information in the sample will affect the measure of goodness of the method of inference and must be specified by the experimenter. Referring specifically to estimation, we would like to know how accurate the experimenter wishes his estimate to be. This may be stated by specifying a bound on the error of estimation.

For instance, suppose that we wish to estimate the average daily yield of a chemical, μ (Example 8.1), and we wish the error of estimation to be less than 4 tons with a probability of .95. Since approximately 95 percent of the sample means will lie within $2\sigma_{\bar{y}}$ of μ in repeated sampling, we are asking that $2\sigma_{\bar{y}}$ equal 4 tons (see Figure 8.9). Then

$$2\sigma_{\bar{y}} = 4,$$

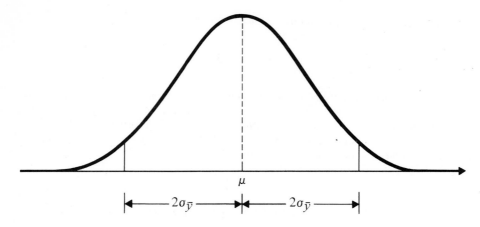

Figure 8.9 *Approximate Distribution of $\hat{y}$ for Large Samples*

or

$$2\sigma/\sqrt{n} = 4.$$

Solving for n, we obtain

$$n = \frac{\sigma^2}{4}$$

The reader will quickly note that we cannot obtain a numerical value for n unless the population standard deviation σ is known. And, certainly, this is exactly what we should expect because the variability of $\bar{y}$ depends upon the variability of the population from which the sample was drawn.

Lacking an exact value for σ, we would use the best approximation available, such as an estimate, s, obtained from a previous sample or knowledge of the range in which the measurements will fall. Since the range is approximately equal to 4σ (the empirical rule), one-fourth of the range will provide an approximate value for σ. For our example we would use the results of Example 8.1, which provided a reasonably accurate estimate of σ equal to $s = 21$. Then

$$n = \frac{\sigma^2}{4} \approx \frac{(21)^2}{4} = 110.25,$$

or

$$n = 111.$$

Using a sample size $n = 111$, we would be reasonably certain (with probability approximately equal to .95) that our estimate will lie within $2\sigma_{\bar{y}} = 4$ tons of the true average daily yield.

Actually we should expect the error of estimation to be much less than 4 tons. According to the empirical rule, the probability is approximately equal to .68 that the error of estimation would be less than $\sigma_{\bar{y}} = 2$ tons. The reader will note that the probabilities .95 and .68 used in these statements will be inexact, owing to the fact that s was substituted for σ. Although this method of choosing the sample size is only approximate for a specified desired accuracy of estimation, it is the best available and is certainly better than selecting the sample size on the basis of our intuition.

The method of choosing the sample size for all the large-sample estimation procedures discussed in preceding sections is identical to that described above. The experimenter must specify a desired bound on the error of estimation and an associated confidence level, $1 - \alpha$. For example, if the parameter is θ and the desired bound is B, we should equate

$$z_{\alpha/2}\sigma_{\hat{\theta}} = B,$$

where $z_{\alpha/2}$ is the z value defined in Section 8.4; that is,

$$P(z > z_{\alpha/2}) = \alpha/2.$$

We shall illustrate with examples.

Example 8.8   *The reaction of an individual to a stimulus in a psychological experiment may take one of two forms, A or B. If an experimeter wishes to estimate the probability p that a person will react in favor of A, how many people must be included in the experiment? Assume that he will be satisfied if the error of estimation is less than .04 with probability equal to .90. Assume also that he expects p to lie somewhere in the neighborhood of .6.*

Solution   *Since the confidence coefficient is $1 - \alpha = .90$, α must equal .10 and $\alpha/2 = .05$. The z value corresponding to an area equal to .05 in the upper tail of the z distribution is $z_{\alpha/2} = 1.645$. We then require*

$$1.645\sigma_{\hat{p}} = .04,$$

or

$$1.645\sqrt{\frac{pq}{n}} = .04.$$

Since the variability of $\hat{p}$ is dependent upon p, which is unknown, we must use the guessed value of $p = .6$ provided by the experimenter as an approximation. Then

$$1.645\sqrt{\frac{(.6)(.4)}{n}} = .04,$$

or

$$n = 406.$$

Example 8.9   *An experimenter wishes to compare the effectiveness of two methods of training industrial employees to perform a certain assembly operation. A number of employees is to be divided into two equal groups, the first receiving training method 1 and the second training method 2. Each will perform the assembly operation, and the length of assembly time will be recorded. It is expected that the measurements for both groups will have a range of approximately 8 minutes. If the estimate of the difference in mean time to assemble is desired correct to within 1 minute with probability approximately equal to .95, how many workers must be included in each training group?*

Solution   *Equating $2\sigma_{(\bar{y}_1 - \bar{y}_2)}$ to 1 minute, we obtain*

$$2\sqrt{\frac{\sigma_1^2}{n_1} + \frac{\sigma_2^2}{n_2}} = 1.$$

Or, since we desire n_1 to equal n_2, we may let $n_1 = n_2 = n$ and obtain the equation

$$2\sqrt{\frac{\sigma_1^2}{n} + \frac{\sigma_2^2}{n}} = 1.$$

As noted above, the variability of each method of assembly is approximately the same and hence $\sigma_1^2 = \sigma_2^2 = \sigma^2$. Since the range, equal to 8 minutes, is approximately equal to 4σ, then

$$4\sigma = 8$$

and

$$\sigma = 2.$$

Substituting this value for σ_1 and σ_2 in the above equation, we obtain

$$2\sqrt{\frac{(2)^2}{n} + \frac{(2)^2}{n}} = 1.$$

Solving, we have $n = 32$. Thus each group should contain $n = 32$ members.

8.10   A Statistical Test of an Hypothesis

The basic reasoning employed in a statistical test of an hypothesis was out-lined in Section 6.6 in connection with the test of the effectiveness of a cold vaccine. In this section we shall attempt a condensation of the basic points involved and refer the reader to Section 6.6 for an intuitive presentation of the subject.

The objective of a statistical test is to test an hypothesis concerning the values of one or more population parameters. A statistical test involves four elements:

1. *Null hypothesis.*
2. *Test statistic.*
3. *Rejection region.*
4. *Alternative hypothesis.*

Note that the specification of these four elements defines a particular test and that changing one or more creates a new test.

The null hypothesis, indicated symbolically as H_0, states the hypothesis to be tested. Thus H_0 will specify hypothesized values for one or more population param-eters. For example, we might wish to test the hypothesis that a population mean is equal to 50, or that two population means, say μ_1 and μ_2, are equal.

The decision to reject or accept the null hypothesis is based upon information contained in a sample drawn from the population of interest. The sample values are used to compute a single number, corresponding to a line, which operates as a decision maker and which is called the test statistic. The entire set of values which the test statistic may assume is divided into two sets or regions, one corresponding to the rejection region and the other to the acceptance region. If the test statistic computed from a particular sample assumes a value in the rejection region, the null hypothesis is rejected. If the test statistic falls in the acceptance region, the null hypothesis is accepted.

The decision procedure described above is subject to two types of errors which are prevalent in a two-choice decision problem. We may reject the null hypothesis when, in fact. it is true, or we may accept H_0 when it is false and some alternative hypothesis is true. These errors are called the type I and type II errors, respectively, for the statistical test.

Definition

A type I error for a statistical test is the error incurred by rejecting the null hypothesis when it is true. The probability of making a type I error is denoted by the symbol α.

A type II error for a statistical test is the error incurred by accepting (not rejecting) the null hypothesis when it is false and some alternative hypothesis is true. The probability of making a type II error is denoted by the symbol β.

The two states for the null hypothesis, that is, true or false, along with the two decisions which the experimenter may make are indicated in the two-way table, Table 8.6. The occurrences of the type I and type II errors are indicated in the appropriate cells.

Table 8.6   *Decision Table*

	NULL HYPOTHESIS	
DECISION	TRUE	FALSE
Reject H_0	Type I error	Correct decision
Accept H_0	Correct decision	Type II error

The goodness of a statistical test of an hypothesis is measured by the probabilities of making a type I or a type II error, denoted by the symbols α and β, respectively. These probabilities, calculated for the elementary statistical tests presented in the Exercises for Chapter 6, illustrate the basic relationship among α, β, and the sample size n. Since α is the probability that the test statistic will fall in the rejection region, assuming H_0 to be true, an increase in the size of the rejection region will increase α and, at the same time, decrease β for a fixed sample size. Reducing the size of the rejection region will decrease α and increase β. If the sample size n is increased, more information will be available upon which to base the decision and both α and β will decrease.

The probability of making a type II error, β, varies depending upon the true value of the population parameter. For instance, suppose that we wish to test the null hypothesis that the binomial parameter p is equal to $p_0 = .4$. (We shall use a subscript 0 to indicate the parameter value specified in the null hypothesis, H_0.) Furthermore, suppose that H_0 is false and that p is really equal to an alternative value, say p_a. Which will be more easily detected, a $p_a = .4001$ or a $p_a = 1.0$? Certainly, if p is really equal to 1.0, every single trial will result in a success and the sample results will produce strong evidence to support a rejection of $H_0 : p_0 = .4$. On the other hand, $p_a = .4001$ lies so close to $p_0 = .4$ that it would be extremely difficult to detect without a very large sample. In other words, the probability of accepting H_0, β, will vary depending upon the difference between the true value of p and the hypothesized value, p_0. A graph of the probability of a type II error, β, as a function of the true value of the parameter is called the operating characteristic curve for the statistical test. Note that the operating characteristic curves for the lot acceptance sampling plans, Chapter 6, were really graphs expressing β as a function of p.

Since the rejection region is specified and remains constant for a given test, α will also remain constant and, as in a lot acceptance sampling, the operating characteristic curve will describe the characteristics of the statistical test. An increase in the sample size, n, will decrease β and reduce its value for all alternative values of the parameter tested. Thus we will possess an operating characteristic curve corresponding to each sample size. This property of the operating characteristic curve was illustrated in the Exercises for Chapter 6.

Ideally, the experimenter will have in mind some values, α and β, which measure the risks of the respective errors he is willing to tolerate. He will also have in mind some deviation from the hypothesized value of the parameter, which he considers of *practical* importance and which he wishes to detect. The rejection region for the test will then be located in accordance with the specified value of α. Finally, he will choose the sample size necessary to achieve an acceptable value of β for the specified deviation that he wishes to detect. This could be done by consulting the operating characteristic curves, corresponding to various sample sizes, for the chosen test.

We will observe in the next section that the alternative hypothesis, denoted by the symbol H_a, assists in the location of the rejection region.

8.11 A Large-Sample Statistical Test

Large-sample tests of hypotheses concerning the population parameters discussed in Sections 8.3 to 8.9 are based upon a normally distributed test statistic and for that reason may be regarded as one and the same test. We shall present the

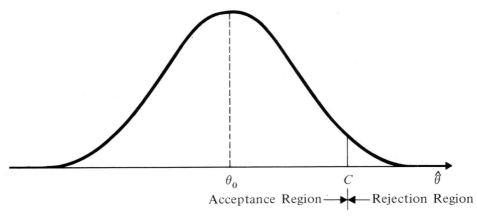

Figure 8.10 *Distribution of $\hat{\theta}$ When H_0 Is True*

reasoning in a very general manner, referring to the parameter of interest as θ. Thus, we could imagine θ as representing μ, $(\mu_1 - \mu_2)$, p, or $(p_1 - p_2)$. The specific tests for each will be illustrated by examples.

Suppose that we wish to test an hypothesis concerning a parameter θ and that an unbiased point estimator, $\hat{\theta}$, is available and known to be normally distributed with standard deviation $\sigma_{\hat{\theta}}$. If the null hypothesis,

$$H_0 : \theta = \theta_0,$$

is true, then $\hat{\theta}$ will be normally distributed about θ_0 as shown in Figure 8.10.

Suppose that, from a *practical* point of view, we are primarily concerned with the rejection of H_0 when θ is greater than θ_0. Then the alternative hypothesis would be $H_a : \theta > \theta_0$ and we would reject the null hypothesis when $\hat{\theta}$ is too large. "Too large," of course, means too many standard deviations, $\sigma_{\hat{\theta}}$, away from θ_0. The rejection region for the test is shown in Figure 8.10. The value of $\hat{\theta}$, C, which separates the rejection and acceptance regions is called the critical value of the test statistic. The probability of rejecting, assuming the null hypothesis to be true, would equal the area under the normal curve lying above the rejection region. Thus if we desire $\alpha = .05$, we would reject when $\hat{\theta}$ is more than $1.645\sigma_{\hat{\theta}}$ to the right of θ_0. A test rejecting in one tail of the distribution of the test statistic is called a one-tailed statistical test

If we wish to detect departures either greater than or less than θ_0, the alternative hypothesis would be

$$H_a : \theta \neq \theta_0,$$

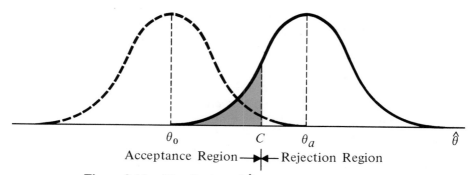

Figure 8.11   *Distribution of $\hat{\theta}$ When H_0 Is False and $\theta = \theta_a$*

that is,

$$\theta > \theta_0$$

or

$$\theta < \theta_0.$$

The probability of a type I error, α, would be equally divided between the two tails of the normal distribution, resulting in a two-tailed statistical test.

The calculation of β for the one-tailed statistical test described above can be facilitated by considering Figure 8.11.

When H_0 is false and $\theta = \theta_a$, the test statistic, $\hat{\theta}$, will be normally distributed about a mean θ_a rather than θ_0. The distribution of $\hat{\theta}$, assuming $\theta = \theta_a$, is shown by the solid line. The hypothesized distribution of $\hat{\theta}$, shown by dashed lines, locates the rejection region and the critical value of $\hat{\theta}$, C. Since β is the probability of accepting H_0, given $\theta = \theta_a$, β would equal the area under the solid curve located above the acceptance region. This area, which is shaded, could be easily calculated using the methods described in Chapter 7.

The reader will quickly note that all the point estimators discussed in the preceding section satisfy the requirements of the test described above when the sample size, n, is large. That is, the sample size must be large enough so that the point estimator will be approximately normally distributed, by the central limit theorem, and also must permit a reasonably good estimate of its standard deviation. We may therefore test hypotheses concerning μ, p, $(\mu_1 - \mu_2)$, and $(p_1 - p_2)$.

The mechanics of testing are simplified by using

$$z = \frac{\hat{\theta} - \theta_0}{\sigma_{\hat{\theta}}}$$

as a test statistic as noted in Example 7.8. Note that z is simply the deviation of a normally distributed random variable, $\hat{\theta}$, from θ_0 expressed in units of $\sigma_{\hat{\theta}}$. Thus for a two-tailed test with $\alpha = .05$ we would reject H_0 when $z > 1.96$ or $z < -1.96$, since $P(z < -1.96 \text{ or } z > 1.96) = .05$.

As we have previously stated, the method of inference used in a given situation will often depend upon the preference of the experimenter. Some people wish to express an inference as an estimate; others prefer to test an hypothesis concerning the parameter of interest. The following example will demonstrate the use of the z test in testing an hypothesis concerning a population mean and, at the same time, it will illustrate the close relationship between the statistical test and the large-sample confidence intervals discussed in the preceding sections.

Example 8.10   *Refer to Example 8.1. Test the hypothesis that the average daily yield of the chemical is $\mu = 880$ tons per day against the alternative that μ is either greater or less than 880 tons per day. The sample (Example 8.1), based on $n = 50$ measurements, yielded $\bar{y} = 871$ and $s = 21$ tons.*

Solution   *The null hypothesis and alternative are $H_0 : \mu = 880$ and $H_a : \mu \neq 880$. The point estimate for μ is $\bar{y}$. Therefore, the test statistic is*

$$z = \frac{\bar{y} - \mu_0}{\sigma_{\bar{y}}} = \frac{\bar{y} - \mu_0}{\sigma/\sqrt{n}}.$$

Using s to approximate σ, we obtain

$$z = \frac{871 - 880}{21/\sqrt{50}} = -3.03.$$

For $\alpha = .05$, the rejection region is $z > 1.96$ or $z < -1.96$. Since the calculated value of z falls in the rejection region, we reject the hypothesis that $\mu = 880$ tons and conclude that it is less. The probability of rejecting, assuming H_0 to be true, is only $\alpha = .05$. Hence we are reasonably confident that our decision is correct.

The statistical test based upon a normally distributed test statistic, with given α, and the $(1 - \alpha)$ percent confidence interval, Section 8.5, are clearly related. The interval $\bar{y} \pm 1.96\sigma/\sqrt{n}$, or approximately 871 ± 5.82, is constructed such that, in repeated sampling, $(1 - \alpha)$ of the intervals will enclose μ. Noting that $\mu = 880$ does not fall in the interval, we would be inclined to reject $\mu = 880$ as a likely value and conclude that the mean daily yield was, indeed, less. The following example will demonstrate the calculation of β for the statistical test, Example 8.10.

Example 8.11   *Referring to Example 8.10, calculate the probability β of accepting H_0 when μ is actually equal to 870 tons.*

Solution   *The acceptance region for the test, Example 8.10, is located in the interval $\mu_0 \pm 1.96\sigma_{\bar{y}}$. Substituting numerical values, we obtain*

$$880 \pm 1.96(21/\sqrt{50}),$$

or

$$874.18 \text{ to } 885.82.$$

The probability of accepting H_0, given $\mu = 870$, is equal to the area under the frequency distribution for the test statistic, $\bar{y}$, above the interval 874.18 to 885.82. Since $\bar{y}$ will be normally distributed with mean equal to 870 and $\sigma_{\bar{y}} = 21/\sqrt{50} = 2.97$, β is equal to the area under the normal curve located to the right of 874.18 (see Figure 8.12). Calculating the z value corresponding to 874.18, we obtain

$$z = \frac{\bar{y} - \mu}{\sigma/\sqrt{n}} = \frac{874.18 - 870}{21/\sqrt{50}} = 1.41.$$

We see from Table 3, Appendix, that the area between $z = 0$ and $z = 1.41$ is .4207. Therefore,

$$\beta = P \ (accept \ H_0 | \mu = 870)$$

$$= P \ (z > 1.41)$$

$$= .5 - .4207 = .0793.$$

Figure 8.12   *Calculating β in Example 8.11*

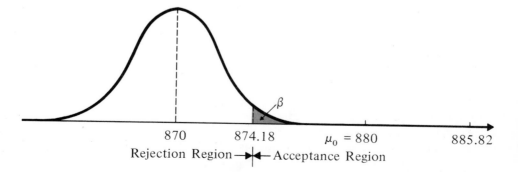

870   874.18 $\mu_0 = 880$ 885.82

Rejection Region ➝|⬅ Acceptance Region

Thus the probability of accepting H_0, given that μ is really equal to 870, is .0793 or, approximately, 8 chances in 100.

Example 8.12   *It is known that approximately 1 in 10 smokers favors cigarette brand A. After a promotional campaign in a given sales region, a sample of 200 cigarette smokers were interviewed to determine the effectiveness of the campaign. The result of the survey showed that a total of 26 people expressed a preference for brand A. Do these data present sufficient evidence to indicate an increase in the acceptance of brand A in the region? (Note that, for all practical purposes, this problem is identical to the cold serum problem given in Example 7.7.)*

Solution   *It is assumed that the sample satisfies the requirements of a binomial experiment. The question posed may be answered by testing the hypothesis*

$$H_0 : p = .10$$

against the alternative

$$H_a : p > .10.$$

A one-tailed statistical test would be utilized, because we are primarily concerned with detecting a value of p greater than .10. For this situation it can be shown that the probability of a type II error, β, is minimized by placing the entire rejection region in the upper tail of the distribution of the test statistic. The point estimator of p is $\hat{p} = y/n$ and the test statistic would be

$$z = \frac{\hat{p} - p_0}{\sigma_{\hat{p}}} = \frac{\hat{p} - p_0}{\sqrt{p_0 q_0/n}}.$$

Or, multiplying numerator and denominator by n, we obtain

$$z = \frac{y - np_0}{\sqrt{np_0 q_0}},$$

which is the test statistic used in Example 7.7. Note that the two test statistics are equivalent.

Once again we require a value of p so that $\sigma_{\hat{p}} = \sqrt{pq/n}$, appearing in the denominator of z, may be calculated. Since we have hypothesized that $p = p_0$, it would seem reasonable to use p_0 as an approximation for p. Note that this differs from the estimation procedure where, lacking knowledge of p, we chose $\hat{p}$ as the best approximation. This apparent inconsistency will have a negligible effect on the inference, whether it is the result of a test or an estimation, when n is large.

Choosing $\alpha = .05$, we would reject H_0 when $z > 1.645$. Substituting the numerical values into the test statistic, we obtain

$$z = \frac{\hat{p} - p_0}{\sqrt{p_0 q_0/n}} = \frac{.13 - .10}{\sqrt{\dfrac{(.10)(.90)}{200}}} = 1.41.$$

The calculated value, $z = 1.41$, does not fall in the rejection region and hence we do not reject H_0.

Do we accept H_0? No, not until we have stated some alternative value of p which is larger than $p_0 = .10$ and which is considered to be of practical significance. The probability of a type II error, β, should be calculated for this alternative. If β is sufficiently small, we would accept H_0 and would do so with the risk of an erroneous decision fully known.

Examples 8.10 and 8.12 illustrate an important point. If the data present sufficient evidence to reject H_0, the probability of an erroneous conclusion, α, is known in advance because α is used in locating the rejection region. Since α is usually small, we are fairly certain that we have made a correct decision. On the other hand, if the data present insufficient evidence to reject H_0, the conclusions are not so obvious. It does not necessarily follow that p is equal to p_0 when we fail to reject the null hypothesis. Rather, we conclude that there is insufficient evidence in the sample to indicate that p is greater than p_0. In Example 8.12, at the $\alpha = .05$ significance level, we would have failed to reject any hypothesized value for p greater than $p = .095$. We could have assumed that p is not significantly greater than .095, .097, .10, .13, or any other value greater than .095. However, only one of these values, $p = .10$, has a special importance in the context of the problem. Ideally, following the statistical test procedures outlined in Section 8.10, we would have specified a practically significant alternative, p_a, in advance and chosen n such that β would be small. Unfortunately, many experiments are not conducted in this ideal manner. Someone chooses a sample size and the experimenter or statistician is left to evaluate the evidence.

The calculation of β is not too difficult for the statistical test procedure outlined in this section but may be extremely difficult, if not beyond the capability of the beginner, in other test situations. A much simpler procedure for the beginner *to not reject H_0* , rather than to accept it ; then *estimate* using a confidence interval. The interval will give the experimenter a range of possible values for *p*.

Example 8.13   *A university investigation, conducted to determine whether car ownership was detrimental to academic achievement, was based upon two random samples of 100 male students, each drawn from the student body. The grade-point average for the $n_1 = 100$ non-car owners possessed an average and variance equal to $\bar{y}_1 = 2.70$ and $s_1^2 = .36$ as opposed to a $\bar{y}_2 = 2.54$ and $s_2^2 = .40$ for the $n_2 = 100$ car owners. Do the data present sufficient evidence to indicate a difference in the mean achievement between car owners and non-car owners?*

Solution   *We wish to test the null hypothesis that the difference between two population means, $(\mu_1 - \mu_2)$, equals some specified value, say D_0. (For our example we would hypothesize that $D_0 = 0$.)*
   Recall that $(\bar{y}_1 - \bar{y}_2)$ is an unbiased point estimator of $(\mu_1 - \mu_2)$ which will be approximately normally distributed in repeated sampling when n_1 and n_2 are large. Furthermore, the standard deviation of $(\bar{y}_1 - \bar{y}_2)$ is

$$\sigma_{(\bar{y}_1 - \bar{y}_2)} = \sqrt{\frac{\sigma_1^2}{n_1} + \frac{\sigma_2^2}{n_2}}.$$

Then

$$z = \frac{(\bar{y}_1 - \bar{y}_2) - D_0}{\sqrt{\dfrac{\sigma_1^2}{n_1} + \dfrac{\sigma_2^2}{n_2}}}$$

will serve as a test statistic when σ_1^2 and σ_2^2 are known or when s_1^2 and s_2^2 provide a good approximation for σ_1^2 and σ_2^2 (that is, when n_1 and n_2 are larger than 30).
   For our example,

$$H_0 : \mu_1 - \mu_2 = D_0 = 0,$$

against

$$H_a : \mu_1 - \mu_2 \neq 0.$$

Substituting into the formula for the test statistic, we obtain

$$z = \frac{(\bar{y}_1 - \bar{y}_2) - D_0}{\sqrt{\dfrac{\sigma_1^2}{n_1} + \dfrac{\sigma_2^2}{n_2}}} = \frac{2.70 - 2.54}{\sqrt{\dfrac{.36}{100} + \dfrac{.40}{100}}} = 1.83.$$

Using a two-tailed test with $\alpha = .05$, we would reject when $z > 1.96$ or $z < -1.96$. Since z does not fall in the rejection region, we do not reject the null hypothesis.

Note, however, that if we choose $\alpha = .10$, the rejection region would be $z > 1.645$ or $z < -1.645$ and the null hypothesis would be rejected.

The decision to reject or accept would, of course, depend upon the risk that we would be willing to tolerate. If we choose $\alpha = .05$, the null hypothesis would not be rejected, but we could not accept H_0 (that is, $\mu_1 = \mu_2$) without investigating the probability of a type II error. If α were chosen equal to .10, the null hypothesis would be rejected. With no other information given, we would be inclined to reject the null hypothesis that there is no difference in the average academic achievement of car owners versus non-car owners. The chance of rejecting H_0, assuming H_0 true, is only $\alpha = .10$ and hence we would be inclined to think that we have made a reasonably good decision.

Example 8.14   *The records of a hospital show that 52 men in a sample of 1,000 men versus 23 women in a sample of 1,000 women were admitted because of heart disease. Do these data present sufficient evidence to indicate a higher rate of heart disease among men admitted to the hospital?*

Solution   *We shall assume that the number of patients admitted for heart disease will follow approximately a binomial probability distribution for both men and women with parameters p_1 and p_2, respectively. Stated generally, we wish to test the hypothesis that a difference exists between p_1 and p_2, say $(p_1 - p_2) = D_0$. (For our example, we wish to test the hypothesis that $D_0 = 0$.) Recall that for large samples, the point estimator of $(p_1 - p_2)$, $(\hat{p}_1 - \hat{p}_2)$, is approximately normally distributed in repeated sampling with mean equal to $(p_1 - p_2)$ and standard deviation*

$$\sigma_{(\hat{p}_1 - \hat{p}_2)} = \sqrt{\frac{p_1 q_1}{n_1} + \frac{p_2 q_2}{n_2}}.$$

Then

$$z = \frac{(\hat{p}_1 - \hat{p}_2) - (p_1 - p_2)}{\sigma_{(\hat{p}_1 - \hat{p}_2)}}$$

would possess a standardized normal distribution in repeated sampling. Hence z could be employed as a test statistic to test

$$H_0 : (p_1 - p_2) = D_0$$

when suitable approximations are used for p_1 and p_2 which appear in $\sigma_{(\hat{p}_1 - \hat{p}_2)}$. Approximations are available for two cases.

Case 1: *If we hypothesize that p_1 equals p_2, that is,*

$$H_0 : p_1 = p_2,$$

or

$$(p_1 - p_2) = 0,$$

then $p_1 = p_2 = p$ and the best estimate of p is obtained by pooling the data from both samples. Thus, if y_1 and y_2 are the numbers of successes obtained from the two samples, then

$$\hat{p} = \frac{y_1 + y_2}{n_1 + n_2}.$$

The test statistic would be

$$z = \frac{(\hat{p}_1 - \hat{p}_2) - 0}{\sqrt{\dfrac{\hat{p}\hat{q}}{n_1} + \dfrac{\hat{p}\hat{q}}{n_2}}}$$

or

$$z = \frac{\hat{p}_1 - \hat{p}_2}{\sqrt{\hat{p}\hat{q}\left(\dfrac{1}{n_1} + \dfrac{1}{n_2}\right)}}.$$

Case 2: *On the other hand, if we hypothesize that D_0 is not equal to zero, that is,*

$$H_0 : (p_1 - p_2) = D_0,$$

where $D_0 \neq 0$, then the best estimates of p_1 and p_2 are $\hat{p}_1$ and $\hat{p}_2$, respectively. The test statistic would be

$$z = \frac{(\hat{p}_1 - \hat{p}_2) - D_0}{\sqrt{\dfrac{\hat{p}_1 \hat{q}_1}{n_1} + \dfrac{\hat{p}_2 \hat{q}_2}{n_2}}}.$$

For most practical problems involving the comparison of two binomial populations the experimenter will wish to test the null hypothesis that $(p_1 - p_2) = D_0 = 0$. For our example we test

$$H_0 : (p_1 - p_2) = 0$$

against the alternative

$$H_a : (p_1 - p_2) > 0.$$

Note that a one-tailed statistical test will be employed because, if a difference exists, we wish to detect $p_1 > p_2$. Choosing $\alpha = .05$, we will reject H_0 when $z > 1.645$.
   The pooled estimate of p required for $\sigma_{(\hat{p}_1 - \hat{p}_2)}$ is

$$\hat{p} = \frac{y_1 + y_2}{n_1 + n_2} = \frac{52 + 23}{1,000 + 1,000} = .0375.$$

The test statistic is

$$z = \frac{\hat{p}_1 - \hat{p}_2}{\sqrt{\hat{p}\hat{q}\left(\dfrac{1}{n_1} + \dfrac{1}{n_2}\right)}} = \frac{.052 - .023}{\sqrt{(.0375)(.9625)\left(\dfrac{1}{1,000} + \dfrac{1}{1,000}\right)}},$$

or

$$z = 3.41.$$

Since the computed value of z falls in the rejection region, we reject the hypothesis that $p_1 = p_2$ and conclude that the data present sufficient evidence to indicate that the percentage of men entering the hospital because of heart disease is higher than that of women. Note that this does not imply that the incidence of heart disease is higher in men. Perhaps fewer women enter the hospital when afflicted with the disease!

8.12   Some Comments on the Theory of Tests of Hypotheses

The theory of a statistical test of an hypothesis outlined in Section 8.10 is indeed a very clearcut procedure enabling the experimenter to either reject or accept the null hypothesis with measured risks, α and β. Unfortunately, the theoretical framework does not suffice for all practical situations.

The crux of the theory requires that we be able to specify a meaningful alternative hypothesis that permits the calculation of the probability of a type II error, β, for all alternative values of the parameter(s). This indeed can be done for many statistical tests, including the test discussed in Section 8.10, although the calculation of β for various alternatives and sample sizes may, in some cases, be a formidable task. On the other hand, it is extremely difficult, in some test situations, to clearly specify alternatives to H_0 which have *practical* significance. This may occur when we wish to test an hypothesis concerning the values of a set of parameters, a situation that we shall encounter in Chapter 16 in analyzing enumerative data.

The obstacle that we mention does not invalidate the use of statistical tests. Rather, it urges caution in drawing conclusions when insufficient evidence is available to reject the null hypothesis. It, together with the difficulty encountered in the calculation and tabulation for β for other than the simplest statistical tests, justifies skirting this issue in an introductory text. Hence, we shall agree to adopt the procedure described in Example 8.11 when tabulated values of β (the operating characteristic curve) are unavailable for the test. When the test statistic falls in the acceptance region, we will "not reject" rather than "accept." Further conclusions may be made by calculating an interval estimate for the parameter or by consulting one of the several published statistical handbooks for tabulated values of β. We will not be too surprised to learn that these tabulations are inaccessible, if not completely unavailable, for some of the more complicated statistical tests.

The probability of making a type I error, α, is often called the significance level of the statistical test, a term that originated in the following way. The probability of the observed value of the test statistic, or some value even more contradictory to the null hypothesis, measures, in a sense, the weight of evidence favoring rejection. Some experimenters report test results as being significant (we would reject) at the 5 percent significance level but not at the 1 percent level. This means that we would reject H_0 if α were .05 but not if it were .01. This line of thought does not conflict with the procedure of choosing the test in advance of the data collection. Rather, it presents a convenient way of publishing the statistical results of a scientific investigation, permitting the reader to choose his own α and β as he pleases.

Finally, we might comment on the choice between a one- or two-tailed test for a given situation. We emphasize that this choice is dictated by the practical aspects of the problem and will depend upon the alternative value of the parameter, say θ, which the experimenter is trying to detect. If we were to sustain a large financial loss if θ were greater than θ_0, but not if it were less, we would concentrate our attention on the detection of values of θ greater than θ_0. Hence we would reject in the upper tail of the distribution for the test statistics previously discussed. On the other hand, if we are equally interested in detecting values of θ that are either less than or greater than θ_0, we would employ a two-tailed test.

8.13 Summary

The material presented in Chapter 8 has been directed toward two objectives. First, we wanted to discuss the various methods of inference along with procedures for evaluating their goodness. Second, we wished to present a number of estimation procedures and statistical tests of hypotheses which, owing to the central limit theorem, make use of the results of Chapter 7. The resulting techniques possess practical value and, at the same time, illustrate the principles involved in statistical inference.

Inferences concerning the parameter(s) of a population may be made by estimating or testing hypotheses concerning their value. A parameter may be estimated using either a point or an interval estimator with the confidence coefficient and width of the interval measuring the goodness of the procedure.

A statistical test of an hypothesis or theory concerning the population parameter(s), ideally, will result in its rejection or acceptance. Practically, we may be forced to view this decision in terms of rejection or nonrejection. The probabilities of making the two possible incorrect decisions, resulting in type I and type II errors, measure the goodness of the decision procedure. While a test of an hypothesis may be best suited for some physical situations (for example, lot acceptance sampling), it would seem that estimation would be the eventual goal of many experimental investigations and hence would be desirable if one were permitted an option in his choice of a method of inference.

All the confidence intervals and statistical tests described in this chapter were based upon the central limit theorem and hence apply to large samples. When n is large, each of the respective estimators and test statistics will possess, for all practical purposes, a normal distribution in repeated sampling. This result, along with the properties of the normal distribution studied in Chapter 7, permits the construction of the confidence intervals and the calculation of α and β for the statistical tests.

Exercises

1. Define and discuss the following concepts with regard to their importance or relation to statistical inference:
    (a) The central limit theorem.
    (b) Type I and type II errors.
    (c) The probabilities α and β.
    (d) The level of significance.
    (e) A confidence interval.
    (f) The z test.

2.   Distinguish between a one-tailed test and a two-tailed test of an hypothesis.

3.   In each of the following hypothesis-testing situations, suggest whether a one-tailed test or a two-tailed test of an hypothesis is appropriate. In each case, justify your answer and then write the null and alternative hypotheses.

   (a)   A study by an economist to determine whether the unemployment level has changed significantly during the past year.

   (b)   A study to check the assumption of a credit manager who claims that the average account balance of credit customers for a certain store is at least $50.

   (c)   A marketing research study to determine whether the proportion of buyers who favor your product is greater than the proportion who favor the product of your competitor.

   (d)   A study to determine whether the average salary of employees from the Ford Motor Company differs significantly from the average salary of a General Motors employee.

   (e)   A study to determine whether pension benefits at a certain large firm have increased significantly during the past year.

4.   The mean and standard deviations for the life of a random sample of 100 light bulbs were calculated to be 1,280 and 142 hours, respectively. Estimate the mean life of the population of light bulbs from which the sample was drawn and place bounds on the error of estimation.

5.   Suppose that the population mean, Exercise 4, were really 1,285 hours with $\sigma = 150$ hours. What is the probability that the mean of a random sample of $n = 100$ measurements would exceed 1,300 hours?

6.   A new type of photoflash bulb was tested to estimate the probability, p, that the new bulb would produce the required light output at the appropriate time. A sample of 1,000 bulbs was tested and 920 were observed to function according to specifications. Estimate p and place bounds on the error of estimation.

7.   Using a confidence coefficient equal to .90, place a confidence interval on the mean life of the light bulbs of Exercise 4.

8.   Place a confidence interval on p of Exercise 6, using a confidence coefficient equal to .99. Interpret this interval.

9.   A random sample of 400 radio tubes was tested and 40 tubes were found to be defective. With confidence coefficient equal to .90, estimate the interval within which the true fraction defective lies.

10.   It is desired to estimate the mean hourly yield for a process manufacturing an antibiotic. The process is observed for 100 hourly periods chosen at random, with the following results:

$$\bar{y} = 34 \text{ oz/hr}; \qquad s = 3.$$

Estimate the mean hourly yield for the process using a 95 percent confidence interval.

11.   The mean and standard deviation of 49 randomly selected purchases on credit by the credit customers of a large department store were found to be $6.50 and $2.10, respectively. Find a 98 percent confidence interval for the mean of the population of all credit purchases of the store.

12.   The percentage of pages containing at least one typing mistake was recorded for a secretary using first a standard typewriter and then an electric typewriter. Using the standard typewriter, 64 of 200 typewritten pages contained at least one typing mistake,

while on the electric typewriter, 36 of 180 pages contained at least one mistake. Estimate the difference in the percentage of typewritten pages typed by the secretary containing at least one mistake using the standard and electric typewriter. Place bounds on the error of estimation.

13. Sixty out of 87 housewives prefer detergent A. If the 87 housewives represent a random sample from the population of all potential purchasers, estimate the fraction of total housewives favoring detergent A. (Use a 90 percent confidence interval.)

14. In examining the credit accounts of a department store, an auditor selected a random sample of 64 accounts and found the average account error to be $-\$42$, with a standard deviation of $16. Construct a confidence interval for the true average account error using a confidence coefficient equal to .95.

15. A hospital wished to estimate the average number of days required for treatment of patients between the ages of 25 and 34. A random sample of 500 hospital patients between these ages produced a mean and standard deviation equal to 5.4 and 3.1 days, respectively. Estimate the mean length of stay for the population of patients from which the sample was drawn. Place bounds on the error of estimation.

16. An experiment was conducted to compare the depth of penetration for two different hydraulic mining nozzles. The rock structure and the length of drilling time were the same for both nozzles. With nozzle A the average penetration was 10.8 inches with a standard deviation of 1.2 inches for a sample of 50 holes. With nozzle B the average and standard deviation of the penetration measurements were 9.1 and 1.6 inches, respectively, for a sample of 80 holes. Estimate the difference in mean penetration rate and place bounds on the error of estimation.

17. Construct a confidence interval for the difference between the population means of Exercise 16, using a confidence coefficient equal to .90.

18. In a poll taken among the stockholders of a company, 300 of 500 men favored the decision to adopt a new product line, whereas 64 of 100 women stockholders favored. Estimate the difference in the fractions favoring the decision and place a bound upon the error of estimation.

19. Past experience shows that the standard deviation of the yearly income of textile workers in a certain state is $400. How large a sample of textile workers would one need to take if one wished to estimate the population mean to within $50.00 with a probability of .95 of being correct? Given that the mean of the sample in this problem is $4,800, determine 95 percent confidence intervals for the population mean.

20. How many voters must be included in a sample collected to estimate the fraction of the popular vote favorable to a presidential candidate in a national election if the estimate is desired correct to within .005? Assume that the true fraction will lie somewhere in the neighborhood of .5.

21. A quality-control engineer wants to estimate the fraction of defectives in a large lot of light bulbs. From previous experience, he feels that the actual fraction of defectives should be somewhere around .2. How large a sample should he take if he wants to estimate the true fraction to within .01 using a 95 percent confidence interval?

22. A dean of men wishes to estimate the average cost of the freshman year at a particular college correct to within $200.00, with a probability of .95. If a random sample of freshmen is to be selected and requested to keep financial data, how many must be included in the sample? Assume that the dean knows only that the range of expenditure will vary from approximately $2,200 to $4,000.

23.   In the past, a chemical plant has produced an average of 1,100 pounds of chemical per day. A random sample of 260 operating days from the past year shows the following:

$$\bar{y} = 1,060 \text{ lb/day},$$

$$s = 340 \text{ lb/day}.$$

It is desired to test whether or not the average daily production has dropped significantly over the past year.
(a) Give the appropriate null and alternative hypotheses.
(b) If z is used as a test statistic, determine the rejection region corresponding to a level of significance $\alpha = .05$.
(c) Do the data provide sufficient evidence to indicate a drop in average daily production?

24.   It is required to estimate the fraction of automobiles on Florida highways that have defective brakes.
(a) A random sample of $n = 100$ automobiles is selected for inspection. Of these 20 are found to have defective brakes. Construct a 95 percent confidence interval for the fraction of automobiles on Florida highways having defective brakes.
(b) Suppose that a more accurate estimate than the one found in (a) is wanted. How large a sample would be necessary to reduce the bound on error to .04?

25.   It is known from past observation that the standard deviation of the incomes of the credit customers of a large department store is $250. How large a sample must be selected from all the credit customers of the department store to be fairly sure (probability .95) that the sample mean does not differ from the true population by more than $100 in absolute value?

26.   It is desired to estimate the difference in the average time to assemble an electronic component for two factory workers to within 2 minutes with a probability of .95. If the standard deviation of the assembly times is approximately equal to 6 minutes for each worker, how many component assembly times must be observed for each worker? (Assume that the number of component assembly times observed for each worker will be the same.)

27.   A television station claims that their 6 o'clock evening news reaches 50 percent of the viewing audience in their area. A firm who is considering the purchase of advertising time during the 6 o'clock time slot wishes to test the validity of the station's claim. How large a sample should the firm select if they want to be about 95 percent confident that the estimated proportion of the viewing audience is correct to within 5 percent?

28.   The daily wages in a particular industry are normally distributed with a mean of $13.20 and a standard deviation of $2.50. If a company in this industry randomly samples 40 of their workers and finds the average wage to be $12.20, can this company be accused of paying inferior wages at the 1 percent level of significance? Interpret your results.

29.   Two sets of 50 elementary school children are taught to read by two different methods. At the conclusion of the instructional period, a reading test gives the results $\bar{y}_1 = 74$, $\bar{y}_2 = 71$, $s_1 = 9$, $s_2 = 10$. Test to see whether there is evidence of a real difference between the two population means. (Use $\alpha = .10$.)

30.   A manufacturer of automatic washers provides a particular model in one of three colors, A, B, or C. Of the first 1,000 washers sold, it is noticed that 400 of the washers were of color A. Would you conclude that customers have a preference for color A? Assume that about an equal number of color B and color C washers have been sold. (Use $\alpha = .01$.)

31. A manufacturer claims that at least 20 percent of the public prefers his product. A sample of 100 persons is taken to check his claim. With $\alpha = .05$, how small would the sample percentage need to be before the claim could be rightfully refuted? (*Note:* This would require a one-tailed test of an hypothesis.)

32. Refer to Exercise 31. Sixteen people in the sample of 100 consumers expressed a preference for the manufacturer's product. Does this present sufficient evidence to reject the manufacturer's claim? (Test at the 10 percent level of significance.)

33. Refer to Exercise 27. Suppose that a sample of 100 television viewers are selected from the potential viewing audience of the television station and 38 indicate that they watch the station's 6 o'clock evening news. Is this sufficient evidence to refute the claim of the television station that their 6 o'clock evening news reaches 50 percent of the viewing audience? (Test at the 1 percent level of significance.)

34. A marketing representative wishes to determine the acceptability of a new product in a particular community. If he could feel confident that about 50 percent of the community's residents would buy his company's product, the marketing representative would suggest that it be marketed in that community. A random sample of $n = 64$ is selected from the target community with 24 of those sampled stating that they would buy the product. Should the marketing representative suggest the product be marketed in the target community? (Use a significance level of .05.)

35. The braking ability was compared for two types of 1973 automobiles. Random samples of 64 automobiles were tested for each type. The recorded measurement was the distance required to stop when the brakes were applied at 40 miles per hour. The computed sample means and variances were

$$\bar{y}_1 = 118, \qquad \bar{y}_2 = 109,$$
$$s_1^2 = 102, \qquad s_2^2 = 87.$$

Do the data provide sufficient evidence to indicate a difference in the mean stopping distance for the two types of automobiles?

36. A test of the breaking strengths of two different types of cables was conducted using samples of $n_1 = n_2 = 100$ pieces of each type of cable.

CABLE 1	CABLE 2
$\bar{y}_1 = 1,925$	$\bar{y}_2 = 1,905$
$s_1 = 40$	$s_2 = 30$

Do the data provide sufficient evidence to indicate a difference between the mean breaking strengths of the two cables? (Use $\alpha = .10$.)

37. A survey of buying habits was conducted in Boston and Seattle. In Boston, 200 housewives were interviewed, and it was found that they spend an average of $120 on food per month with a standard deviation of $25, whereas in Seattle 175 housewives reported an average monthly food expenditure of $130 with a standard deviation of $35. Using a significance level of .05, test the hypothesis that there is no difference in the average amount spent on food per month between housewives in Boston and Seattle. Interpret your results.

38.   To test the effects of a new fertilizer on wheat production, a tract of land was divided into 60 squares of equal areas, all portions having similar qualities in respect to soil, exposure to sunlight, and so on. The new fertilizer was applied to 30 squares and the old fertilizer was applied to the remaining squares. The mean number of bushels of wheat harvested per square of land using the new fertilizer was 18 bushels with a standard deviation of .6 bushel. The corresponding mean and standard deviation for the squares using the old fertilizer were 17 bushels and .5 bushel, respectively. Using a significance level of .05, test the hypothesis that there is no difference between the fertilizers against the alternative that the new fertilizer is better than the old.

39.   A manufacturer claims that at least 95 percent of the equipment that he supplied to a factory conformed to specification. An examination of a sample of 700 pieces of equipment reveals that 53 were faulty. Test his claim at a significance level of .05. Interpret your results.

40.   Refer to Exercise 4. Test the hypothesis that the average length of life of the light bulbs is equal to 1,300 hours against the alternative that the mean is less. (Use $\alpha = .05$.)

41.   Refer to Exercise 16. Do the data present sufficient evidence to indicate a difference in the mean depth of penetration obtained using the two nozzles?

42.   Random samples of 200 bolts manufactured by machine A and 200 bolts manufactured by machine B showed 16 and 8 defective bolts, respectively. Do these data present sufficient evidence to suggest a difference in the performance of the machines? (Use a .05 level of significance.)

43.   The mean lifetime of a sample of 100 fluorescent bulbs produced by a company is computed to be 1,570 hours with a standard deviation of 120 hours. If μ is the mean lifetime of all the bulbs produced by the company, test the hypothesis $\mu = 1,600$ hours against the alternative hypothesis $\mu < 1,600$, using a level of significance of .05.

44.   In comparing the mean weight loss for two diets the following sample data were obtained:

	DIET 1	DIET 2
Sample size, n	40	40
Sample mean, $\bar{y}$	10 lb	8 lb
Sample variance, s^2	4.3	5.7

Do the data provide sufficient evidence to indicate that diet 1 produces a greater mean weight loss than diet 2? (Use $\alpha = .05$.)

45.   To estimate the proportion of unemployed workers in Panama, an economist selected at random 400 persons from the working class. Of these, 25 were unemployed.
(a) Estimate the true proportion of unemployed workers and place bounds on the error of estimation.
(b) How many persons must be sampled in order to reduce the bound on error to .02?

46.   A random sample of 36 cigarettes of a certain brand were tested for nicotine content. The sample gave a mean of 22 and a standard deviation of 4 milligrams. Find a 98 percent confidence interval for μ, the true mean nicotine content of the brand.

47.   Presently 20 percent of potential customers buy a certain brand of soap, say brand A. In order to increase sales, an extensive advertising campaign will be conducted. At the end of the campaign, a sample of 400 potential customers will be interviewed to determine if the campaign was successful.

(a) State H_0 and H_a in terms of p, the probability that a customer prefers soap brand A.

(b) It is decided to conclude that the advertising campaign was a success if at least 92 out of the 400 customers interviewed prefer brand A. Find α. (Use the normal approximation to the binomial distribution to evaluate the desired probability.)

48. Suppose that the true fraction p in favor of the death penalty is the same for Democrats as it is for Republicans. Independent random samples are selected, one consisting of 800 Republicans and the other of 800 Democrats. Find the probability that the sample fraction of Republicans favoring the death penalty exceeds that of the Democrats by more than .03 if the true proportion who favor the death penalty is $p = .5$. What is this probability if $p = .1$?

49. Mr. Sands believes that the fraction p_1 of Republicans in favor of the death penalty is greater than the fraction p_2 of Democrats in favor of the death penalty. He acquired independent random samples of 200 Republicans and 200 Democrats and found 46 Republicans and 34 Democrats favoring the death penalty. Does this evidence provide statistical support at the .05 level of significance for Mr. Sands's belief?

50. A magazine subscription service in a city containing 25,000 households is interested in estimating the average number of magazine subscriptions by the residents of each household. Suppose that we let y equal the number of magazine subscriptions held by the residents of a sample household. In a random sample of 401 households selected from the city, it was found that

$$\sum_{i=1}^{401} y_i = 785 \quad \text{and} \quad \sum_{i=1}^{401} y_i^2 = 2{,}015.$$

(a) Find a point estimate for the average number of magazine subscriptions per resident household in the city.

(b) Does the point estimate computed in (a) supply the reader with any measure of confidence in its closeness to μ, the unknown mean number of magazine subscriptions per resident household in the entire city? Explain.

(c) Place bounds on the error of estimation of μ.

(d) Suppose that the magazine subscription service wishes to be 99 percent confident that they obtain an interval estimate which contains μ. Find an interval estimate that bounds μ with 99 percent confidence. What is the meaning of this interval estimate?

(e) Without gathering additional sample information, how can the magazine subscription service reduce the width of the confidence interval for μ? What price must be paid for the reduction?

(f) If a separate sample of $n = 401$ households were sampled, would you expect the 99 percent confidence interval for μ based on the "new" sample to be the same as the interval estimate computed in (d) for the original sample? Explain.

(g) If the two sets of sample observations are combined, what will be the effect on the width of the resulting confidence interval (for a fixed confidence level)?

(h) Based on the results obtained in part (d) and from the known number of households in the city, find a 99 percent confidence interval for the *total* number of magazine subscriptions by all the residents of the city.

(i) The director of the magazine subscription service has issued the following statement: "We shall undertake an extensive sales campaign in the city unless there is sufficient evidence to indicate that the average number of subscriptions per household is 1.8 or greater. We are further willing to assume no more than 5 percent chance of failing to undertake the sales campaign when we should have." Based on the sample information, should the subscription service undertake a sales campaign in the city?

References

Dixon, W. J., and F. J. Massey, Jr., *Introduction to Statistical Analysis.* 3rd ed. New York: McGraw-Hill Book Company, 1969. Chapters 6 and 7.

Freund, J. E., and F. J. Williams; revised by B. Perles and C. Sullivan, *Modern Business Statistics.* Englewood Cliffs, N.J.: Prentice-Hall, Inc., 1969. Chapters 9, 10, and 11.

Hoel, P. G., and R. J. Jessen, *Basic Statistics for Business and Economics.* New York: John Wiley & Sons, Inc., 1971. Chapters 6 and 7.

Chapter Nine

Inference from Small Samples

9.1 Introduction

Large-sample methods for making inferences concerning population means and the difference between two means were discussed with examples in Chapter 8. Frequently, such function as cost and available time limit the size of the sample that can be acquired. When this occurs, the large-sample procedures of Chapter 8 are inadequate and other tests and estimation procedures must be used. In this chapter we shall study several small-sample inferential procedures which are closely related to the large-sample methods presented in Chapter 8. Specifically, we shall consider methods for estimating and testing hypotheses concerning population means, the difference between two means, a population variance, and a comparison of two population variances. Small-sample tests and confidence intervals for binomial parameters will be omitted from our discussion.

9.2 Student's t Distribution

We introduce our topic by considering the following problem. A very costly experiment has been conducted to evaluate a new process for producing synthetic diamonds. Six diamonds have been generated by the new process with recorded weights of .46, .61, .52, .48, .57, and .54 carat.

A study of the process costs indicates that the average weight of the diamonds must be greater than .5 carat if the process is to be operated at a profitable level. Do the six diamond-weight measurements present sufficient evidence to indicate that the average weight of the diamonds produced by the process is in excess of .5 carat?

Recall that, according to the central limit theorem,

$$z = \frac{\bar{y} - \mu}{\sigma/\sqrt{n}}$$

possesses approximately a normal distribution in repeated sampling when n is large. For $\alpha = .05$, we would employ a one-tailed statistical test and reject when $z > 1.645$. This, of course, assumes that σ is known or that a good estimate, s, is available and is based upon a reasonably large sample (we have suggested $n \geq 30$). Unfortunately, the latter requirement will not be satisfied for the $n = 6$ diamond-weight measurements. How, then, may we test the hypothesis that $\mu = .5$ against the alternative that $\mu > .5$?

The problem we pose is not new; it received serious attention by statisticians and experimenters at the turn of the century. If a sample standard deviation s were substituted for σ in z, would the resulting quantity possess approximately a standard-ized normal distribution in repeat sampling? More specifically, would the rejection region $z > 1.645$ be appropriate—that is, would approximately 5 percent of the values of the test statistic, computed in repeated sampling, exceed 1.645? The answer to these questions, not unlike many of the problems encountered in the sciences, may be resolved by experimentation. In other words, we could draw a small sample, say $n = 6$ measurements, and compute the value of the test statistic. Then we would repeat this process over and over again a very large number of times and construct a frequency distribution for the computed values of the test statistic. The general shape of the distribution and the location of the rejection region would then be evident.

The distribution of

$$t = \frac{\bar{y} - \mu}{s/\sqrt{n}}$$

for samples drawn from a normally distributed population was discovered by W. S. Gosset and published (1908) under the pen name "Student." He referred to the quantity under study as t and it has ever since been known as Student's t. We omit the complicated mathematical expression for the density function for t but describe some of its characteristics.

The distribution of the test statistic

$$t = \frac{\bar{y} - \mu}{s/\sqrt{n}}$$

in repeated sampling is, like z, mound-shaped and perfectly symmetrical about $t = 0$. Unlike z, it is much more variable, tailing rapidly out to the right and left, a phenomenon that may be readily explained. The variability of z in repeated sampling is due solely to $\bar{y}$; the other quantities appearing in z (n and σ) are non-random. On the other hand, the variability of t is contributed by two random quantities, $\bar{y}$ and s, which can be shown to be independent of one another. When $\bar{y}$ is very large, s may be very small, and vice versa. As a result, t will be more variable than z in repeated sampling. Finally, as we might surmise, the variability of t decreases as n increases because the estimate of σ, s, will be based upon more and more information. When n is infinitely large, the t and z distributions will be identical. Gosset discovered that the distribution of t depended upon the sample size n.

The divisor of the sum of squares of deviations $(n - 1)$ that appears in the formula for s^2 is called the number of degrees of freedom associated with s^2. The origin of the term "degrees of freedom" is linked to the statistical theory underlying the probability distribution of s^2. We shall not pursue this point further except to note that one may say that the test statistic t is based upon a sample of n measurements or that it possesses $(n - 1)$ degrees of freedom.

The critical values of t which separate the rejection and acceptance regions for the statistical test are presented in Table 4, Appendix. The tabulated value, t_α, records the value of t such that an area α lies to its right, as shown in Figure 9.1. The sample size n is shown in the first column of the table, and the t_α, corresponding

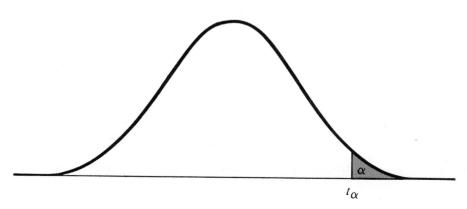

Tabulated Values for Student's t

to various values of α, appear in the top row. Thus, if we wish to find the value of t, such that 5 percent of the area lies to its right, we would use the column marked $t_{.05}$. The critical value of t for our example, found in the $t_{.05}$ column opposite $n = 6$, is $t = 2.015$. Thus we would reject $H_0 : \mu = .5$ when $t > 2.015$. Observe that we may use either the sample size, n, or the degrees of freedom, d.f. (shown in the last column of Table 4), to locate the critical value of t.

Note that the critical value of t will always be larger than the corresponding critical value of z for a specified α. For example, where $\alpha = .05$, the critical value of t for $n = 2$ is $t = 6.314$, which is very large when compared with the corresponding $z = 1.645$. Proceeding down the $t_{.05}$ column, we note that the critical value of t decreases, reflecting the effect of a larger sample size on the estimation of σ. Finally, when n is infinitely large, the critical value of t will equal 1.645.

The reason for choosing $n = 30$ as the dividing line between large and small samples is apparent. For $n = 30$, the critical value of $t_{.05} = 1.699$ is numerically quite close to $z_{.05} = 1.645$. For a two-tailed test based upon $n = 30$ measurements and $\alpha = .05$, we would place .025 in each tail of the t distribution and reject $H_0 : \mu = \mu_0$ when $t > 2.045$ or $t < -2.045$. Note that this is very close to the $z_{.025} = 1.96$ employed in the z test.

It is important to note that the Student's t and corresponding tabulated critical values are based upon the assumption that the sampled population possesses a normal probability distribution. This indeed is a very restrictive assumption because, in many sampling situations, the properties of the population will be completely unknown and may be nonnormal. If this were to affect seriously the distribution of the t statistic, the application of the t test would be very limited. Fortunately, this point is of little consequence, as it can be shown that the distribution of the t statistic is relatively stable for populations that are nonnormal but possess a mound-shaped probability distribution. This property of the t statistic and the common occurrence of mound-shaped distributions of data in nature enhance the value of Student's t for use in statistical inference.

Second, we should note that $\bar{y}$ and s^2 must be independent (in a probabilistic sense) in order that the quantity

$$\frac{\bar{y} - \mu}{s/\sqrt{n}}$$

possess a t distribution in repeated sampling. As mentioned previously, this requirement will automatically be satisfied when the sample has been randomly drawn from a normal population.

Having discussed the origin of Student's t and the tabulated critical values (Table 4, Appendix II) we now return to the problem of making an inference about the mean diamond weight based upon our sample of $n = 6$ measurements. Prior to considering the solution, the reader may wish to test his built-in inference-making equipment by glancing at the six measurements and arriving at a conclusion concerning the significance of the data.

9.3   Small-Sample Inferences Concerning a Population Mean

The statistical test of an hypothesis concerning a population mean may be stated as follows:

$$H_0 : \mu = \mu_0.$$

$$\text{Test statistic} : t = \frac{\bar{y} - \mu_0}{s/\sqrt{n}}.$$

Alternative Hypothesis H_a: *Specified by the experimenter, depending upon the alternative values of μ which he wishes to detect.*
Rejection Region: *See the critical values of t, Table 4, Appendix.*

The mean and standard deviation for the six diamond weights are .53 and .0559, respectively, and the elements of the test as defined above are

$$H_0 : \mu = .5.$$

$$\text{Test statistic} : t = \frac{\bar{y} - \mu_0}{s/\sqrt{n}} = \frac{.53 - .5}{.0559/\sqrt{6}} = 1.31.$$

$$H_a : \mu > .5.$$

Rejection Region: *The rejection region for $\alpha = .05$ is $t > 2.015$.*

Noting that the calculated value of the test statistic does not fall in the rejection region, we do not reject H_0. This implies that the data do not present sufficient evidence to indicate that the mean diamond weight exceeds .5 carat.

The calculation of the probability of a type II error, β, for the t test is difficult and is beyond the scope of this test. Therefore, we shall avoid this problem and obtain an interval estimate for μ as noted in Section 8.12.

We recall that the large-sample confidence interval for μ is

$$\bar{y} \pm z_{\alpha/2} \sigma/\sqrt{n},$$

where $z_{\alpha/2} = 1.96$ for a confidence coefficient equal to .95. This result assumes that σ is known and simply involves a measurement of $1.96\sigma_{\bar{y}}$ (or approximately $2\sigma_{\bar{y}}$)

on either side of $\bar{y}$ in conformity with the empirical rule. When σ is unknown and must be estimated by a small-sample standard deviation s, the large-sample confidence interval based on z will not enclose μ 95 percent of the time in repeated sampling. While we omit the derivation, it seems fairly clear that the corresponding small confidence interval for μ will be

$$\bar{y} \pm t_{\alpha/2} s/\sqrt{n},$$

where $s/\sqrt{n}$ is the estimated standard deviation of $\bar{y}$.

For our example,

$$\bar{y} \pm t_{\alpha/2} s/\sqrt{n} = .53 \pm 2.571 \frac{.0559}{\sqrt{6}},$$

or

$$.53 \pm .059.$$

The interval estimate for μ is, therefore, .471 to .589 with confidence coefficient equal to .95. If the experimenter wishes to detect a small increase in mean diamond weight in excess of .5 carat, the width of the interval must be reduced by obtaining more diamond-weight measurements. This will decrease both $1/\sqrt{n}$ and $t_{\alpha/2}$ and thereby decrease the width of the interval. Or, looking at it from the standpoint of a statistical test of an hypothesis, more information will be available upon which to base a decision, and the probability of making a type II error will decrease.

Example 9.1 *A manufacturer of gunpowder has developed a new powder that is designed to produce a muzzle velocity equal to 3,000 feet per second. Eight shells are loaded with the charge and the muzzle velocities measured. The resulting velocities are shown in Table 9.1.*

Table 9.1

MUZZLE VELOCITY	FT/SEC
3,005	2,995
2,925	3,005
2,935	2,935
2,965	2,905

Do the data present sufficient evidence to indicate that the average velocity differs from 3,000 feet per second?

Solution   *Testing the null hypothesis that $\mu = 3{,}000$ feet per second against the alternative that μ is either greater than or less than 3,000 feet per second will result in a two-tailed statistical test. Thus*

$$H_0 : \mu = 3{,}000,$$

$$H_a : \mu \neq 3{,}000.$$

Using $\alpha = .05$ and placing .025 in each tail of the t distribution, we find that the critical value of t for $n = 8$ measurements (or seven degrees of freedom) is $t = 2.365$. Hence we shall reject H_0 if $t > 2.365$ or $t < -2.365$. (Recall that the t distribution is symmetrical about $t = 0$.)

The sample mean and standard deviation for the recorded data are

$$\bar{y} = 2{,}959 \qquad and \qquad s = 39.4.$$

Then

$$t = \frac{\bar{y} - \mu_0}{s/\sqrt{n}} = \frac{2{,}959 - 3{,}000}{39.4/\sqrt{8}} = -2.94.$$

Since the observed value of t falls in the rejection region, we will reject H_0 and conclude that the average velocity is less than 3,000 feet per second. Furthermore, we will be reasonably confident that we have made the correct decision. Using our procedure, we should erroneously reject H_0 only $\alpha = .05$ of the time in repeated applications of the statistical test.

A confidence interval will provide additional information concerning μ. Calculating

$$\bar{y} \pm t_{\alpha/2} s/\sqrt{n},$$

we obtain

$$2{,}959 \pm (2.365)\frac{39.4}{\sqrt{8}},$$

or

$$2{,}959 \pm 33.$$

Thus we estimate the average muzzle velocity to lie in the interval 2,926 to 2,992 feet per second. A more accurate estimate can be obtained by increasing the sample size.

9.4   Small-Sample Inferences Concerning the Difference Between Two Means

The physical setting for the problem which we consider is identical to that discussed in Section 8.6. Independent random samples of n_1 and n_2 measurements, respectively, are drawn from two populations, which possess means and variances μ_1, σ_1^2 and μ_2, σ_2^2. Our objective is to make inferences concerning the difference between the two population means, $\mu_1 - \mu_2$.

The following small-sample methods for testing hypotheses and placing a confidence interval on the difference between two means are, like the case for a single mean, founded upon assumptions regarding the probability distributions of the sampled populations. Specifically, we shall assume that both populations possess a normal probability distribution and, also, that the population variances, σ_1^2 and σ_2^2, are equal. In other words, we assume that the variability of the measurements in the two populations is the same and can be measured by a common variance, which we shall designate as σ^2; that is, $\sigma_1^2 = \sigma_2^2 = \sigma^2$.

The point estimator of $\mu_1 - \mu_2$, $(\bar{y}_1 - \bar{y}_2)$, the difference between the sample means, was discussed in Section 8.8, where it was observed to be unbiased and to possess a standard deviation

$$\sigma_{(\bar{y}_1 - \bar{y}_2)} = \sqrt{\frac{\sigma_1^2}{n_1} + \frac{\sigma_2^2}{n_2}}$$

in repeated sampling. This result was used in placing bounds on the error of estimation, the construction of a large-sample confidence interval, and the z-test statistic

$$z = \frac{(\bar{y}_1 - \bar{y}_2) - D_0}{\sqrt{\dfrac{\sigma_1^2}{n_1} + \dfrac{\sigma_2^2}{n_2}}}$$

for testing an hypothesis, $H_0 : \mu_1 - \mu_2 = D_0$. Utilizing the assumption that $\sigma_1^2 = \sigma_2^2 = \sigma^2$, the z-test statistic could be simplified as follows:

$$z = \frac{(\bar{y}_1 - \bar{y}_2) - D_0}{\sqrt{\dfrac{\sigma^2}{n_1} + \dfrac{\sigma^2}{n_2}}} = \frac{(\bar{y} - \bar{y}_2) - D_0}{\sigma \sqrt{\dfrac{1}{n_1} + \dfrac{1}{n_2}}}.$$

For small-sample tests of the hypotheses $H_0: \mu_1 - \mu_2 = D_0$, where D_0 is the hypothesized difference between the means, it would seem reasonable to use the test statistic

$$t = \frac{(\bar{y}_1 - \bar{y}_2) - D_0}{s\sqrt{\dfrac{1}{n_1} + \dfrac{1}{n_2}}};$$

that is, we would substitute a sample standard deviation s for σ. Surprisingly enough, this test statistic will possess a Student's t distribution in repeated sampling when the stated assumptions are satisfied, a fact that can be proved mathematically or verified by experimental sampling from two normal populations.

The estimate, s, to be used in the t statistic could be either s_1 or s_2, the standard deviations for the two samples, although the use of either would be wasteful since both estimate σ. Since we wish to obtain the best estimate available, it seems reasonable to use an estimator that will pool the information from both samples. This estimator, utilizing the sums of squares of the deviations about the mean for both samples, is

$$s^2 = \frac{\displaystyle\sum_{i=1}^{n_1} (y_i - \bar{y}_1)^2 + \sum_{i=1}^{n_2} (y_i - \bar{y}_2)^2}{n_1 + n_2 - 2},$$

where

$$s_1^2 = \frac{\displaystyle\sum_{i=1}^{n_1} (y_i - \bar{y}_1)^2}{n_1 - 1}$$

and

$$s_2^2 = \frac{\displaystyle\sum_{i=1}^{n_2} (y_i - \bar{y}_2)^2}{n_2 - 1}.$$

Note that the pooled estimator may also be written as

$$s^2 = \frac{(n_1 - 1)s_1^2 + (n_2 - 1)s_2^2}{n_1 + n_2 - 2}.$$

As in the case for the single sample, the denominator in the formula for s^2, $(n_1 + n_2 - 2)$, is called the "number of degrees of freedom" associated with s^2. It can be proved mathematically that the expected value of the pooled estimator, s^2, is equal to σ^2 and hence that s^2 is an unbiased estimator of the common population variance. Finally, we note that the divisors of the sums of squares of deviations in s_1^2 and s_2^2, $(n_1 - 1)$ and $(n_2 - 1)$, respectively, are the numbers of degrees of freedom associated with these two independent estimators of σ^2. It is interesting to note that an estimator using the pooled information from both samples would possess $(n_1 - 1) + (n_2 - 1)$, or $(n_1 + n_2 - 2)$, degrees of freedom.

Summarizing, the small-sample statistical test for the difference between two means is as follows:

$$H_0 : \mu_1 - \mu_2 = D_0,$$

$$\text{Test Statistic} : t = \frac{(\bar{y}_1 - \bar{y}_2) - D_0}{s\sqrt{\dfrac{1}{n_1} + \dfrac{1}{n_2}}}.$$

The alternative hypothesis, H_a, and α would be specified by the experimenter and would be used to locate the critical value of t for the rejection region. s is the square root of s^2, the pooled estimator of σ^2.

The critial value of t can be obtained from Table 4, Appendix, with one slight adjustment to the procedure outlined in Section 9.2. Now that we are utilizing information from two samples to estimate σ^2, we can no longer use the first column indicating sample size, n, to locate the critical value for t. Rather, we shall use the last column on the right, marked d.f., for degrees of freedom. Thus if $n_1 = 10$ and $n_2 = 12$, we would use the t value corresponding to $(n_1 + n_2 - 2) = 20$ degrees of freedom. The following example will serve as an illustration.

Example 9.2   *An assembly operation in a manufacturing plant requires approximately a 1-month training period for a new employee to reach maximum efficiency. A new method of training was suggested and a test conducted to compare the new method with the standard procedure. Two groups of nine new employees were trained for a period of 3 weeks, one group using the new method and the other following standard training procedure. The length of time in minutes required for each employee to assemble the device was recorded at the end of the 3-week period. These measurements appear in Table 9.2. Do the data present sufficient evidence to indicate that the mean time to assemble at the end of the 3-week training period is less for the new training procedure?*

Table 9.2

STANDARD PROCEDURE	NEW PROCEDURE
32	35
37	31
35	29
28	25
41	34
44	40
35	27
31	32
34	31

Solution *Let μ_1 and μ_2 equal the mean time to assemble for the standard and the new assembly procedures, respectively. Also, assume that the variability in mean time to assemble is essentially a function of individual differences, that the population distributions of measurements are approximately normal, and that the variability for the two populations of measurements will be approximately equal.*

The sample means and sum of squares of deviations are

$$\bar{y}_1 = 35.22,$$

$$\sum_{i=1}^{9} (y_i - \bar{y}_1)^2 = 195.56;$$

$$\bar{y}_2 = 31.56,$$

$$\sum_{i=1}^{9} (y_i - \bar{y}_2)^2 = 160.22.$$

Then the pooled estimate of the common variance is

$$s^2 = \frac{\sum_{i=1}^{9} (y_i - \bar{y}_1)^2 + \sum_{i=1}^{9} (y_i - \bar{y}_2)^2}{n_1 + n_2 - 2}$$

$$= \frac{195.56 + 160.22}{9 + 9 - 2}$$

$$= 22.24,$$

and the standard deviation is $s = 4.72$.

The null hypothesis to be tested is

$$H_0 : \mu_1 - \mu_2 = 0.$$

Suppose that we are concerned only with detecting whether or not the new method reduces the assembly time and, therefore, that the alternative hypothesis is

$$H_a : \mu_1 - \mu_2 > 0.$$

This would imply that we should use a one-tailed statistical test and that the rejection region for the test will be located in the upper tail of the t distribution. Referring to Table 4, Appendix II, we note that the critical value of t for $\alpha = .05$ and $(n_1 + n_2 - 2) = 16$ degrees of freedom is 1.746. Therefore, we shall reject when $t > 1.746$.
The calculated value of the test statistic is

$$t = \frac{(\bar{y}_1 - \bar{y}_2)}{s\sqrt{\dfrac{1}{n_1} + \dfrac{1}{n_2}}} = \frac{35.22 - 31.56}{4.71\sqrt{\dfrac{1}{9} + \dfrac{1}{9}}}$$

$$= 1.64.$$

Comparing this with the critical value, $t = 1.746$, we note that the calculated value does not fall in the rejection region. Therefore, we must conclude that there is insufficient evidence to indicate that the new method of training is superior at the .05 level of significance.

The small-sample confidence interval for $(\mu_1 - \mu_2)$ is based upon the same assumptions as was the statistical test procedure. This confidence interval, with confidence coefficient $(1 - \alpha)$, is given by the formula

$$(\bar{y}_1 - \bar{y}_2) \pm t_{\alpha/2} s\sqrt{\frac{1}{n_1} + \frac{1}{n_2}}.$$

Note the similarity in the procedures for constructing the confidence intervals for a single mean, Section 9.2, and the difference between two means. In both cases the interval is constructed by using the appropriate point estimator and then adding and subtracting an amount equal to $t_{\alpha/2}$ times the estimated standard deviation of the point estimator.

Example 9.3   *Find an interval estimate for* $(\mu_1 - \mu_2)$*, Example 9.2, using a confidence coefficient equal to .95.*

Solution   *Substituting into the formula*

$$(\bar{y}_1 - \bar{y}_2) \pm t_{\alpha/2} s \sqrt{\frac{1}{n_1} + \frac{1}{n_2}},$$

we find the interval estimate (or 95 percent confidence interval) to be

$$(35.22 - 31.56) \pm (2.120)(4.72) \sqrt{\frac{1}{9} + \frac{1}{9}}$$

or

$$3.66 \pm 4.71.$$

Thus we estimate the difference in mean time to assemble, $(\mu_1 - \mu_2)$*, to fall in the interval* -1.05 *to* 8.37*. Note that the interval width is considerable and that it seems advisable to increase the size of the samples and reestimate.*

Before concluding our discussion it is necessary to comment on the two assumptions upon which our inferential procedures are based. Moderate departures from the assumption that the populations possess a normal probability distribution do not seriously affect the distribution of the test statistic and the confidence coefficient for the corresponding confidence interval. On the other hand, the population variances should be nearly equal in order that the aforementioned procedures be valid.

If there is reason to believe that the population variances are unequal, an adjustment must be made in the test procedures and the corresponding confidence interval. We omit a discussion of these techniques but refer the interested reader to Li (1961) or Anderson and Bancroft (1952).

A procedure will be presented in Section 9.7 for testing an hypothesis concerning the equality of two population variances.

9.5   A Paired-Difference Test

A manufacturer wished to compare the wearing qualities of two different types of automobile tires, A and B. To make the comparison, a tire of type A and one of type B were randomly assigned and mounted on the rear wheels of each of five automobiles. The automobiles were then operated for a specified number of miles and the amount of wear was recorded for each tire. These measurements appear in Table 9.3. Do the data present sufficient evidence to indicate a difference in average wear for the two tire types?

Table 9.3

AUTOMOBILE	A	B
1	10.6	10.2
2	9.8	9.4
3	12.3	11.8
4	9.7	9.1
5	8.8	8.3

$$\bar{y}_1 = 10.24 \qquad \bar{y}_2 = 9.76$$

Analyzing the data, we note that the difference between the two sample means is $(\bar{y}_1 - \bar{y}_2) = .48$, a rather small quantity, considering the variability of the data and the small number of measurements involved. At first glance it would seem that there is little evidence to indicate a difference between the population means, a conjecture that we may check by the method outlined in Section 9.3.

The pooled estimate of the common variance, σ^2, is

$$s^2 = \frac{\sum\limits_{i=1}^{n_1} (y_i - \bar{y}_1)^2 + \sum\limits_{i=1}^{n_2} (y_i - \bar{y}_2)^2}{n_1 + n_2 - 2} = \frac{6.932 + 7.052}{5 + 5 - 2} = 1.748$$

and

$$s = 1.32.$$

The calculated value of t used to test the hypothesis that $\mu_1 = \mu_2$ is

$$t = \frac{\bar{y}_1 - \bar{y}_2}{s\sqrt{\dfrac{1}{n} + \dfrac{1}{n}}} = \frac{10.24 - 9.76}{1.32\sqrt{\dfrac{1}{5} + \dfrac{1}{5}}} = .58,$$

a value that is not nearly large enough to reject the hypothesis that $\mu_1 = \mu_2$.

The corresponding 95 percent confidence interval is

$$(\bar{y}_1 - \bar{y}_2) \pm t_{\alpha/2} s \sqrt{\frac{1}{n_1} + \frac{1}{n_2}} = (10.24 - 9.76) \pm (2.306)(1.32) \sqrt{\frac{1}{5} + \frac{1}{5}},$$

or -1.45 to 2.41. Note that the interval is quite wide, considering the small difference between the sample means.

A second glance at the data reveals a marked inconsistency with this conclusion. We note that the wear measurement for type A is larger than the corresponding value for type B for each of the five automobiles. These differences, recorded as $d = A - B$, are shown in Table 9.4.

Table 9.4

AUTOMOBILE	$d = A - B$
1	.4
2	.4
3	.5
4	.6
5	.5

$$\bar{d} = .48$$

Suppose that we were to use y, the number of times that A is larger than B, as a test statistic, as was done in Exercise 22, Chapter 6. Then the probability that A would be larger than B on a given automobile, assuming no difference between the wearing quality of the tires, would be $p = 1/2$, and y would be a binomial random variable.

If we choose $y = 0$ and $y = 5$ as the rejection region for a two-tailed test, then $\alpha = p(0) + P(5) = 2(1/2)^5 = 1/16$. We would then reject $H_0 : \mu_1 = \mu_2$ with a probability of a type I error equal to $\alpha = 1/16$. Certainly this is evidence to indicate that a difference exists in the mean wear of the two tire types.

The reader will note that we have employed two different statistical tests to test the same hypothesis. Is it not peculiar that the t test, which utilizes more information (the actual sample measurements) than the binomial test, fails to supply sufficient evidence for rejection of the hypothesis $\mu_1 = \mu_2$?

The explanation of this seeming inconsistency is quite simple. The t test described in Section 9.3 is not the proper statistical test to be used for our example. The statistical test procedure, Section 9.3, requires that the two samples be; independent and random. Certainly, the independence requirement was violated by the manner in which the experiment was conducted. The (pair of) measurements, an A

and a *B*, for a particular automobile are definitely related. A glance at the data will show that the readings are of approximately the same magnitude for a particular automobile but vary from one automobile to another. This, of course, is exactly what we might expect. Tire wear, in a large part, is determined by driver habits, the balance of the wheels, and the road surface. Since each automobile has a different driver, we would expect a large amount of variability in the data from one automobile to another.

   The familiarity that we have gained with interval estimation has shown that the width of the large and small confidence intervals will depend upon the magnitude of the standard deviation of the point estimator of the parameter. The smaller its value, the better the estimate and the more likely that the test statistic will reject the null hypothesis if it is, in fact, false. Knowledge of this phenomenon was utilized in designing the tire-wear experiment.

   The experimenter realized that the wear measurements would vary greatly from auto to auto and that this variability could not be separated from the data if the tires were assigned to the 10 wheels in a random manner. (A random assignment of the tires would have implied that the data be analyzed according to the procedure of Section 9.3). Instead, a comparison of the wear between the tire types *A* and *B* made on each automobile resulted in the five difference measurements. This design eliminates the effect of the car-to-car variability and yields more information on the mean difference in the wearing quality for the two tire types.

   The proper analysis of the data would utilize the five difference measurements to test the hypothesis that the average difference is equal to zero, a statement that is equivalent to $H_0 : \mu_1 = \mu_2$ against $H_a : \mu_1 \neq \mu_2$.

   You may verify that the average and standard deviation of the five difference measurements are

$$\bar{d} = .48,$$

$$s_d = .0837.$$

Then

$$H_0 : \mu_d = 0$$

and

$$t = \frac{\bar{d} - 0}{s_d / \sqrt{n}} = \frac{.48}{.0837 / \sqrt{5}} = 12.8.$$

   The critical value of *t* for a two-tailed statistical test, $\alpha = .05$ and four degrees of freedom, is 2.776. Certainly, the observed value of $t = 12.8$ is extremely large and highly significant. Hence we would conclude that the average amount of wear for tire type B is less than that for type A.

A 95 percent confidence interval for the difference between the mean wear would be

$$\bar{d} \pm t_{\alpha/2} s_d / \sqrt{n} = .48 \pm (2.776)\frac{.0837}{\sqrt{5}}$$

or $.48 \pm .10$.

The statistical design of the tire experiment represents a simple example of a randomized block design and the resulting statistical test is often called a paired-difference test The reader will note that the pairing occurred when the experiment was planned and not after the data were collected Comparisons of tire wear were made within relatively homogeneous blocks (automobiles) with the tire types randomly assigned to the two automobile wheels.

An indication of the gain in the amount of information obtained by blocking the tire experiment may be observed by comparing the calculated confidence interval for the unpaired (and incorrect) analysis with the interval obtained for the paired-difference analysis. The confidence interval for $(\mu_1 - \mu_2)$ that might have been calculated, had the tires been randomly assigned to the 10 wheels (unpaired), is unknown but probably would have been of the same magnitude as the interval -1.45 to 2.41, calculated by analyzing the observed data in an unpaired manner. Pairing the tire types on the automobiles (blocking) and the resulting analysis of the differences produced the interval estimate $.38$ to $.58$. Note the difference in the width of the intervals, which indicates the very sizable increase in information obtained by blocking in this experiment.

While blocking proved to be very beneficial in the tire experiment, this may not always be the case. We observe that the degrees of freedom available for estimating σ^2 are less for the paired than for the corresponding unpaired experiment. If there were actually no difference between the blocks, the reduction in the degrees of freedom would produce a moderate increase in the $t_{\alpha/2}$ employed in the confidence interval and hence increase the width of the interval. This, of course, did not occur in the tire experiment because the large reduction in the standard deviation of $\bar{d}$ more than compensated for the loss in degrees of freedom.

9.6   Inference Concerning a Population Variance

We have seen in the preceding sections that an estimate of the population variance, σ^2, is fundamental to procedures for making inferences about the population means. Moreover, there are many practical situations where σ^2 is the primary objective of an experimental investigation; thus it assumes a position of far greater importance than that of the population mean.

Scientific measuring instruments must provide unbiased readings with a very small error of measurement. An aircraft altimeter that measured the correct altitude on the *average* would be of little value if the standard deviation of the error of measurement were 5,000 feet. Indeed, bias in a measuring instrument can often be corrected, but the precision of the instrument, measured by the standard deviation of the error of measurement, is usually a function of the design of the instrument itself and cannot be controlled.

Machined parts in manufactured process must be produced with minimum variability in order to reduce out-of-size, and hence defective, products. In general, it is desirable to maintain a minimum variance in the measurements of the quality characteristics of an industrial product in order to achieve process control and therefore minimize the percentage of poor-quality product.

The sample variance,

$$s^2 = \frac{\sum_{i=1}^{n} (y_i - \bar{y})^2}{n-1},$$

is an unbiased estimator of the population variance σ^2. The distribution of sample variances generated by repeated sampling will have a probability distribution that commences at $s^2 = 0$ (since s^2 cannot be negative) with a mean equal to σ^2. Unlike the distribution of $\bar{y}$, the distribution of s^2 is nonsymmetrical, the exact form being dependent upon the probability distribution of the population.

For the methodology that follows we shall assume that the sample is drawn from a normal population and that s^2 is based upon a random sample of n measurements. Or, using the terminology of Section 9.2, we would say that s^2 possesses $(n-1)$ degrees of freedom.

The next and obvious step would be to consider the distribution of s^2 in repeated sampling from a specified normal distribution—one with a specific mean and variance—and to tabulate the critical values of s^2 for some of the commonly used tail areas. If this is done, we will find that the distribution of s^2 is independent of the population mean μ, but possesses a distribution for each sample size and each value of σ^2. This task would be quite laborious, but fortunately it may be simplified by standardizing, as was done by using z in the normal tables.

The quantity

$$\chi^2 = \frac{(n-1)s^2}{\sigma^2},$$

called a chi-square variable by statisticians, admirably suits our purposes. Its distribution in repeated sampling is called, as we might suspect, a chi-square probability distribution. The equation of the density function for the chi-square distribution is well known to statisticians, who have tabulated critical values corresponding to various tail areas of the distribution. These values are presented in Table 5, Appendix.

The shape of the chi-square distribution, like that of the t distribution, will vary with the sample size or, equivalently, with the degrees of freedom associated with s^2. Thus Table 5 is constructed in exactly the same manner as the t table, with the degrees of freedom shown in the last column. The symbol χ_α^2 indicates that the tabulated χ^2 value is such that an area, α, lies to its right. Stated in probabilistic terms,

$$P(\chi^2 > \chi_\alpha^2) = \alpha.$$

Thus 99 percent of the area under the χ^2 distribution would lie to the right of $\chi_{.99}^2$. We note that the extreme values of χ^2 must be tabulated for both the lower and upper tails of the distribution because it is nonsymmetrical.

You can check your ability to use the table by verifying the following statements. The probability that χ^2, based upon $n = 16$ measurements, will exceed 24.9958 is .05. For a sample of $n = 6$ measurements, 95 percent of the area under the χ^2 distribution will lie to the right of $\chi^2 = 1.145476$.

The statistical test of a null hypothesis concerning a population variance,

$$H_0 : \sigma^2 = \sigma_0^2,$$

will employ the test statistic

$$\chi^2 = \frac{(n-1)s^2}{\sigma_0^2}.$$

If σ^2 is really greater than the hypothesized value, σ_0^2, the test statistic will be large and will probably fall toward the upper tail of the distribution. If $\sigma^2 < \sigma_0^2$, the test statistic will tend to be small and will probably fall toward the lower tail of the χ^2 distribution. As in other statistical tests, we may use either a one- or two-tailed statistical test, depending upon the alternative hypothesis that we choose. We shall illustrate with an example.

Example 9.4   *A cement manufacturer claimed that concrete prepared from his product would possess a relatively stable compressive strength and that the strength, measured in kilograms per square centimeter, would lie within a range of 40 kilograms per square centimeter. A sample of $n = 10$ measurements* *produced a mean and variance equal to*

$$\bar{y} = 312,$$

$$s^2 = 195,$$

respectively. Do these data present sufficient evidence to reject the manu-facturer's claim?

Solution   *As stated, the manufacturer claimed that the range of the strength measurements would equal 40 kilograms per square centimeter. We will suppose that he meant that the measurements would lie within this range 95 percent of the time and therefore that the range would equal approximately 4σ and that $\sigma = 10$. We would then wish to test the null hypothesis*

$$H_0 : \sigma^2 = (10)^2 = 100$$

against the alternative

$$H_a : \sigma^2 > 100.$$

The alternative hypothesis would require a one-tailed statistical test with the entire rejection region located in the upper tail of the χ^2 distribution. The critical value of χ^2 for $\alpha = .05, n = 10$, is $\chi^2 = 16.9190$, which implies that we will reject H_0 if the test statistic exceeds this value.
Calculating, we obtain

$$\chi^2 = \frac{(n-1)s^2}{\sigma_0^2} = \frac{1,755}{100} = 17.55.$$

Since the value of the test statistic falls in the rejection region, we conclude that the null hypothesis is false and that the range of concrete strength measurements will exceed the manufacturer's claim.

A confidence interval for σ^2 with a $(1 - \alpha)$ confidence coefficient can be shown to be

$$\frac{(n-1)s^2}{\chi_U^2} < \sigma^2 < \frac{(n-1)s^2}{\chi_L^2},$$

where χ_L^2 and χ_U^2 are the lower and upper χ^2 values which would locate one-half of α in each tail.

For example, a 90 percent confidence interval for σ^2, Example 9.4, would use

$$\chi_L^2 = \chi_{.95}^2 = 3.32511,$$
$$\chi_U^2 = \chi_{.05}^2 = 16.9190.$$

Then the interval estimate for σ^2 would be

$$\frac{(9)(195)}{16.9190} < \sigma^2 < \frac{(9)(195)}{3.32511},$$

or

$$103.73 < \sigma^2 < 527.82.$$

Example 9.5   *An experimenter is convinced that his measuring equipment possesses a variability measured by a standard deviation, $\sigma = 2$. During an experiment he recorded the measurements 4.1, 5.2, and 10.2. Do these data disagree with his assumption? Test the hypothesis, $H_0 : \sigma = 2$ or $\sigma^2 = 4$, and place a 90 percent confidence interval on σ^2.*

Solution   *The calculated sample variance is $s^2 = 10.57$. If we wish to detect $\sigma^2 > 4$ as well as $\sigma^2 < 4$, we should employ a two-tailed test. Using $\alpha = .10$ and placing .05 in each tail, we will reject when $\chi^2 > 5.99147$ or $\chi^2 < .102587$. The calculated value of the test statistic is*

$$\chi^2 = \frac{(n-1)s^2}{\sigma_0^2} = \frac{(2)(10.57)}{4} = 5.29.$$

Since the test statistic does not fall in the rejection region, the data do not provide sufficient evidence to reject the null hypothesis, $H_0 : \sigma^2 = 4$.

The corresponding 90 percent confidence interval is

$$\frac{(n-1)s^2}{\chi_U^2} < \sigma^2 < \frac{(n-1)s^2}{\chi_L^2}.$$

The values of χ_L^2 and χ_U^2 are

$$\chi_L^2 = \chi_{.95}^2 = .102587,$$

$$\chi_U^2 = \chi_{.05}^2 = 5.99147.$$

Substituting these values into the formula for the interval estimate, we obtain

$$\frac{2(10.57)}{5.99147} < \sigma^2 < \frac{2(10.57)}{.102587},$$

or

$$3.53 < \sigma^2 < 207.2.$$

9.7   Comparing Two Population Variances

The need for statistical methods to compare two population variances is readily apparent from the discussion in Section 9.6. We may frequently wish to compare the precision of one measuring device with that of another, the stability of one manufacturing process with that of another, or even the variability in the grading procedure of one college professor with that of another.

Intuitively, we might compare two population variances, σ_1^2 and σ_2^2, using the ratio of the sample variances s_1^2/s_2^2. If s_1^2/s_2^2 is nearly equal to 1, we would find little evidence to indicate that σ_1^2 and σ_2^2 are unequal. On the other hand, a very large or small value for s_1^2/s_2^2 would provide evidence of a difference in the population variances.

How large or small must s_1^2/s_2^2 be in order that sufficient evidence exists to reject the null hypothesis.

$$H_0 : \sigma_1^2 = \sigma_2^2?$$

The answer to this question may be readily acquired by studying the distribution of s_1^2/s_2^2 in repeated sampling.

When independent random samples are drawn from two normal populations with equal variances, that is, $\sigma_1^2 = \sigma_2^2$, then s_1^2/s_2^2 possesses a probability distribution in repeated sampling that is known to statisticians as an *F* distribution. We need not concern ourselves with the equation of the density function for *F* except to state that, as we might surmise, it is reasonably complex. For our purposes it will suffice to accept the fact that the distribution is well known and that critical values have been tabulated. These appear in Tables 6 and 7, Appendix.

The shape of the *F* distribution is nonsymmetrical and will depend upon the number of degrees of freedom associated with s_1^2 and s_2^2. We shall represent these quantities as v_1 and v_2, respectively. This fact complicates the tabulation of critical values for the *F* distribution and necessitates the construction of a table for each value that we may choose for a tail area, α. Tables 6 and 7 present critical values corresponding to $\alpha = .05$ and $.01$, respectively.

For example, Table 6 records the value $F_{.05}$ such that the probability that *F* will exceed $F_{.05}$ is $.05$. Another way of saying this is that 5 percent of the area under the *F* distribution lies to the right of $F_{.05}$. The degrees of freedom for s_1^2, v_1 are indicated across the top of the table while the degrees of freedom for s_2^2, v_2 appear in the first column on the left.

Referring to Table 6, we note that $F_{.05}$ for sampling sizes $n_1 = 7$ and $n_2 = 10$ (that is, $v_1 = 6$, $v_2 = 9$) is 3.37. Likewise, the critical value, $F_{.05}$, for sample size $n_1 = 9$ and $n_2 = 16$ ($v_1 = 8$, $v_2 = 15$) is 2.64.

In a similar manner, the critical values for a tail area, $\alpha = .01$, are presented in Table 7. Thus

$$P(F > F_{.01}) = .01.$$

The statistical test of the null hypothesis,

$$H_0 : \sigma_1^2 = \sigma_2^2,$$

utilizes the test statistic

$$F = s_1^2/s_2^2.$$

When the alternative hypothesis implies a one-tailed test, that is,

$$H_a : \sigma_1^2 > \sigma_2^2,$$

we may use the tables directly. However, when the alternative hypothesis requires a two-tailed test,

$$H_a : \sigma_1^2 \neq \sigma_2^2,$$

we note that the rejection region will be divided between the lower and upper tails of the *F* distribution and that tables of critical values for the lower tail are conspicuously missing. The reason for their absence is not difficult to explain.

We are at liberty to identify either of the two populations as population I. If the population with the larger sample variance is designated as population II, then $s_2^2 > s_1^2$ and we shall be concerned with rejection in the lower tail of the *F* distribution. Since the identification of the population is arbitrary, we may avoid this difficulty by designating the population with the larger variance as population I.

Always place the larger sample variance in the numerator of

$$F = s_1^2/s_2^2$$

and designate that population as I.

Then, since the area in the right-hand tail will represent only $\alpha/2$, we double this value to obtain the correct value for the probability of a type I error, α. Hence, if we use Table 6 for a two-tailed test, the probability of a type I error will be $\alpha = .10$. We will illustrate with examples.

Example 9.6   *Two samples consisting of 10 and 8 measurements each were observed to possess sample variances equal to $s_1^2 = 7.14$ and $s_2^2 = 3.21$, respectively. Do the sample variances present sufficient evidence to indicate that the population variances are unequal?*

Solution   *Assume that the populations possess probability distributions that are reasonably mound-shaped and hence will satisfy, for all practical purposes, the assumption that the populations are normal.*

We wish to test the null hypothesis,

$$H_0 : \sigma_1^2 = \sigma_2^2,$$

against the alternative,

$$H_a : \sigma_1^2 \neq \sigma_2^2.$$

Using Table 6 and doubling the tail area, we will reject when $F > 3.68$ with $\alpha = .10$ since $n_1 = 10$ and $n_2 = 8$.

The calculated value of the test statistic is

$$F = \frac{s_1^2}{s_2^2} = \frac{7.14}{3.21} = 2.22.$$

Noting that the test statistic does not fall in the rejection region, we do not reject $H_0 : \sigma_1^2 = \sigma_2^2$. Thus there is insufficient evidence to indicate a difference between the population variances.

Example 9.7   *The variability in the amount of impurities present in a batch of a chemical used for a particular process depends upon the length of time the process is in operation. A manufacturer using two production lines, 1 and 2, has made a slight adjustment to process 2, hoping to reduce the variability as well as the average amount of impurities in the chemical. Samples of $n_1 = 25$ and $n_2 = 25$ measurements from the two batches yield means and variances as follows:*

$$\bar{y}_1 = 3.2,$$
$$s_1^2 = 1.04;$$
$$\bar{y}_2 = 3.0,$$
$$s_2^2 = .51.$$

Do the data present sufficient evidence to indicate that the process variability is less for process 2? Test the null hypothesis, $H_0 : \sigma_1^2 = \sigma_2^2$.

Solution   *Testing the null hypothesis,*

$$H_0 : \sigma_1^2 = \sigma_2^2,$$

against the alternative,

$$H_a : \sigma_1^2 > \sigma_2^2,$$

at an $\alpha = .05$ significance level, we shall reject H_0 when F is greater than $F_{.05} = 1.98$; that is, we shall employ a one-tailed statistical test.
   We readily observe that the calculated value of the test statistic,

$$F = \frac{s_1^2}{s_2^2} = \frac{1.04}{.51} = 2.04,$$

falls in the rejection region, and hence we conclude that the variability of process 2 is less than for process 1.

The test for the equality of two population variances does not assume that the means are equal, but we might notice that the process averages in both Examples 9.6 and 9.7 are nearly equal. What the test does examine is the comparative uniformity of individual values within each population. For instance, in Example 9.6 if we had rejected our hypothesis, we would have concluded that the closing prices of one stock are significantly more volatile than the closing prices of the other. Thus one would conclude that even though the average prices of the two stocks are nearly equal, one stock involves more risk than the other, as indicated by its larger variance. Our hypothesis of equal variances was not rejected, though, suggesting that about an equal amount of risk is assumed by owning either stock.

9.8 Summary

It is important to note that the t, χ^2, and F statistics employed in the small-sample statistical methods discussed in the preceding sections are based upon the assumption that the sampled populations possess a normal probability distribution. This requirement will be satisfied for many types of experimental measurements.

The reader will observe the close relationship connecting Student's t and the z statistic and therefore the similarity of the methods for testing hypotheses and the construction of confidence intervals. The χ^2 and F statistics employed in making inferences concerning population variances do not, of course, follow this pattern, but the reasoning employed in the construction of the statistical tests and confidence intervals is identical for all the methods we have presented.

Exercises

1. Why is the z test usually inappropriate as a test statistic when the sample size is small?

2. What assumptions are made when Student's t test is employed to test an hypothesis concerning a population mean? What is the result if these assumptions are not valid but Student's t test is used anyway?

3. A chemical process has produced, on the average, 800 tons of chemical per day. The daily yields for the past week are 785, 805, 790, 793, and 802 tons. Do these data indicate that the average yield is less than 800 tons and hence that something is wrong with the process? Test at the 5 percent level of significance.

4. Find a 90 percent confidence interval for the mean yield in Exercise 3.

5. Refer to Exercises 3 and 4. How large should the sample be in order that the width of the confidence interval be reduced to approximately 5 tons?

6. A random sample of $n = 20$ secretaries selected from a large city produced an average hourly wage of $\bar{y} = \$2.65$ and a standard deviation of $s = \$.37$. Find a 95 percent confidence interval for the mean hourly rate for secretaries in the city.

7. A random sampling of $n = 24$ items in a supermarket showed a difference between the actual versus the recorded inventories of the items. The mean and standard deviation of the differences between actual versus recorded values for the 24 items were $-\$37.14$ and $\$6.42$, respectively. Find a 95 percent confidence interval for the mean difference between actual versus recorded value per item in the supermarket.

8. The files of 19 employees of the Mallon Company were randomly selected from the files of all Mallon employees available in Mallon's personnel office. For each employee selected, the number of work days they were absent from their job in the past year, including vacation and sick leave, was recorded. The mean and standard deviation for the sample were found to be 24.7 and 1.8, respectively.
   (a) Find a 98 percent confidence interval for the mean of the population of all Mallon employees.
   (b) Give a practical interpretation of the confidence interval calculated in part (a).

9. A coin-operated soft-drink machine was designed to discharge, on the average, 7 ounces of beverage per cup. To test the machine, 10 cupfuls of beverage were drawn from the machine and measured. The mean and standard deviation of the 10 measurements were 7.1 and .12 ounces, respectively. Do these data present sufficient evidence to indicate that the mean discharge differs from 7 ounces? Test at the 10 percent level of significance.

10. Find a 90 percent confidence interval for the mean discharge in Exercise 9.

11. A building contractor has built a large number of houses of about the same size and value. The contractor claims that the average value of these houses (or similar houses that he might have built) does not exceed $25,000. A real estate appraiser randomly selected five of the new houses built by the contractor and assessed their values as $24,500, $27,000, $26,000, $25,000, and $25,500. Do the five appraisals contradict the building contractor's claim regarding the average value of his houses? Test at the $\alpha = .05$ level of significance.

12. Owing to the variability of trade-in allowance, the profit per new car sold by an automobile dealer varies from car to car. The profit per sale, tabulated for the past week, was (in hundreds of dollars)

2.1	6.2
3.0	4.5
1.2	5.1

    Do these data present sufficient evidence to indicate that the average profit per sale is less than $480? (Test at the $\alpha = .05$ level of significance.)

13. Find a 90 percent confidence interval for the mean profit per sale in Exercise 12.

14. A cigarette manufacturer claimed that his cigarettes contained no more than 25 milligrams of nicotine. A sample of 16 cigarettes yielded a mean and standard deviation equal to 26.4 and 2, respectively. Do the data provide sufficient evidence to refute the manufacturer's claim? (Use $\alpha = .10$.)

15. Refer to Exercise 14. Estimate the mean nicotine content of this brand of cigarette using a 90 percent confidence interval.

16.   The vice-president of a large commercial banking chain has recorded the percentage gain in demand deposit accounts for 17 of the branch banks during the past year. The average gain computed from the sample was 11.3 percent and the standard deviation equaled 3.4 percent.
(a) Find a 90 percent confidence interval for the mean growth rate of demand deposits for the banking chain during the past year.
(b) Give a practical interpretation of the confidence interval calculated in part (a).

17.   A manufacturer of television sets claimed that his product possessed an average defect-free life of 3 years. Three households in a community have purchased the sets and all three sets are observed to fail before three years, with failure times equal to 2.5, 1.9, and 2.9 years, respectively. Do these data present sufficient evidence to contradict the manufacturer's claim? (Test at the $\alpha = .05$ level of significance.)

18.   Calculate a 90 percent confidence interval for the mean life of the television sets in Exercise 17.

19.   Refer to Exercises 17 and 18. Approximately how many observations would be required to estimate the mean life of the television sets correct to within two-tenths of a year with probability equal to .90?

20.   What assumptions are made about the populations from which independent random samples are obtained when utilizing the t distribution in making small-sample inferences concerning the difference in population means?

21.   A production process has two assembly machines which perform identical operations on different assembly lines. As a result of their constant use, machine breakdowns occur quite frequently. The time between 11 consecutive breakdowns was recorded for each machine. Suppose that the time between breakdowns for each machine is normally distributed with a common variance, σ^2. The sample means and variance of recorded times between breakdowns are as follows:

MACHINE 1	MACHINE 2
$\bar{y}_1 = 60.4$ min	$\bar{y}_2 = 65.3$ min
$s_1^2 = 31.40$	$s_2^2 = 44.82$

Do the data present sufficient evidence to indicate a difference between the population mean machine breakdown times? (Test at the $\alpha = .10$ level of significance.)

22.   A cannery prints "weight 16 ounces" on its label. The quality-control supervisor selects 9 cans at random and weighs them. He finds $\bar{y} = 15.7$ and $s = .5$. Do the data present sufficient evidence to indicate that the weight is less than that claimed on the label? (Use $\alpha = .05$.)

23.   The following data were collected on lost-time accidents (the figures given are mean man-hours lost per month over a period of 1 year) both before and after an industrial safety program was put into effect. Data were recorded for six industrial plants.

	PLANT NUMBER					
	1	2	3	4	5	6
Before program	38	64	42	70	58	30
After program	31	58	43	65	52	29

Do the data present sufficient evidence to indicate whether the safety program was effective in reducing lost-time accidents? (Use $\alpha = .10$.)

24. A magazine subscription service conducts two sales training programs for prospective salesmen. Each salesman participates in one training program or the other, but not both. To measure the efficiency of each training program, a company representative randomly selected a group of salesmen and recorded the number of sales they had consummated in the past month. The sample means and variances computed from the sales data are as follows:

	TRAINING PROGRAM 1	TRAINING PROGRAM 2
No. salesmen	11	14
$\bar{y}$	64	69
s^2	52	71

Do the data present sufficient evidence to indicate a difference in the mean number of monthly sales for the populations associated with the two sales training programs? Test at the $\alpha = .05$ level of significance.

25. Five secretaries were selected at random from among the secretaries of a large insurance company. The typing speed (words per minute) was recorded for each secretary on an electric typewriter and on a standard typewriter. The following results were obtained:

SECRETARY	ELECTRIC TYPEWRITER	STANDARD TYPEWRITER
1	82	73
2	77	69
3	79	75
4	68	62
5	84	71

Does this evidence justify the conclusion that the secretaries' typing speed is greater with an electric typewriter than with a standard typewriter? (Use $\alpha = .10$.)

26. A comparison of the time before recognition of the product for two different color advertising layouts of a common product produced the following results (in seconds) when applied to a random sample of 16 people.

LAYOUT 1	LAYOUT 2
1	4
3	2
2	3
1	3
2	1
1	2
3	3
2	3

(a) Do the data present sufficient evidence to indicate a difference in mean recognition time for the two layouts? (Test at the $\alpha = .05$ level of significance.)
(b) Obtain a 90 percent confidence interval for $(\mu_1 - \mu_2)$.
(c) Give a practical interpretation for the confidence interval in part (b).

27.   Refer to Exercise 26. Suppose that the product recognition experiment had been conducted using people as blocks and making a comparison of recognition time within each person, that is, each of the eight persons would be subject to both layouts in a random order. The data for the experiment (in seconds) are as follows:

PERSON	LAYOUT 1	LAYOUT 2
1	3	4
2	1	2
3	1	3
4	2	1
5	1	2
6	2	3
7	3	3
8	1	3

(a) Do the data present sufficient evidence to indicate a difference in mean recognition time for the two layouts? Test at the $\alpha = .05$ level of significance.

(b) Obtain a 95 percent confidence interval for $(\mu_1 - \mu_2)$.

(c) Give a practical interpretation for the confidence interval obtained in part (b).

28.   Analyze the data in Exercise 27 as though the experiment had been conducted in an unpaired manner. Calculate a 95 percent confidence interval for $(\mu_1 - \mu_2)$ and compare it with the old obtained in part (b) of Exercise 27. Does it appear that blocking increased the amount of information available in the experiment?

29.   An auditor for a hardware store chain wished to compare the efficiency of two different auditing techniques. To do so he selected a sample of nine store accounts, applied auditing technique A, then selected another nine store accounts and applied auditing technique B. The number of material (accounting) errors found in each store's account is shown in the table. Determine whether there is evidence of a difference in the mean number of accounting errors detected by the two auditing techniques. Test at the $\alpha = .10$ level of significance.

A	B
125	89
116	101
133	97
115	95
123	94
120	102
132	98
128	106
121	98
$\sum y = 1,113$	880
$\bar{y} = 123.7$	97.8
$\sum y_i^2 = 137,973$	86,240

30.   Would the amount of information extracted from the data in Exercise 29 be increased by pairing successive observations and analyzing the differences? Suppose we assume that only nine store accounts were selected and that the data from Exercise 29 represent a paired experiment giving the number of accounting errors found in each of the nine store accounts using each of the two auditing techniques.

(a) Calculate a 90 percent confidence interval for $(\mu_1 - \mu_2)$ assuming the data of Exercise 29 are from a paired experiment.

(b) Calculate a 90 percent confidence interval for $(\mu_1 - \mu_2)$ assuming the data of Exercise 29 are from an unpaired experiment.

(c) Compare the widths of the intervals.

31. When should one employ a paired-difference analysis in making inferences concerning the difference between two means?

32. An experiment was conducted to compare the density of cakes prepared from two cake mixes, A and B. Six cake pans received batter A and six received batter B. Expecting a variation in oven temperature the experimenter placed an A and a B side by side at six different locations within the oven. The six paired observations are as follows (in ounces per cubic inch).

A	B
.135	.129
.102	.120
.098	.112
.141	.152
.131	.135
.144	.163

Do the data present sufficient evidence to indicate a difference in the average density for cakes prepared using the two types of batter? (Test at the $\alpha = .05$ level of significance.)

33. Place a 95 percent confidence interval on the difference between the average densities for the two mixes in Exercise 32. Then give a practical interpretation to this confidence interval.

34. Two plastics, each produced by a different process, were tested for ultimate strength. The measurements given represent breaking load in units of 100 pounds per square inch:

PLASTIC 1	PLASTIC 2
15.3	21.2
18.7	22.4
22.3	18.3
17.6	19.3
19.1	17.1
14.8	27.7

(a) Do the data present sufficient evidence to indicate a difference between the mean ultimate strength for the plastics? (Use $\alpha = .05$.)

(b) How many observations would be required to estimate $(\mu_1 - \mu_2)$ correct to within 500 pounds per square inch with a probability of .90?

35. Refer to Exercise 3. Find a 90 percent confidence interval for σ^2, the variance of the population of daily yields.

36. A manufacturer of a machine to package soap powder claimed that his machine could load cartons at a given weight with a range of no more than $\frac{2}{5}$ ounce. The mean and variance of a sample of eight 3-pound boxes were found to equal 3.1 and .018 pound, respectively.

(a) Test the hypothesis that the variance of the population of weight measurements is $\sigma^2 = .01$ against the alternative, $\sigma^2 > .01$. (Use an $\alpha = .05$ level of significance.)

(b) Find a 90 percent confidence interval for σ^2.

(c) Give a practical interpretation for the confidence interval obtained in part (b).

37. A dairy is in the market for a new bottle-filling machine and is considering models A and B manufactured by company A and company B, respectively. If ruggedness, cost, and convenience are comparable in the two models, the deciding factor is the variability of fills (the model producing fills with the smaller variance being preferred.) Let σ_1^2 and σ_2^2 be the fill variances for models A and B, respectively, and consider various tests of the null hypothesis. Obtaining samples of fills from the two machines and utilizing the test statistic s_1^2/s_2^2, one would set up as rejection region an upper-tail area, lower-tail area, or two-tailed area of the F distribution, depending on his point of view. Which type of rejection region would be most favored by the following persons:

(a) The manager of the dairy? Why?

(b) A salesman for company A? Why?

(c) A salesman for company B? Why?

38. Refer to Exercise 37. Wishing to demonstrate that the variability of fills is less for model A than for model B, a salesman for company A acquired a sample of 30 fills from a machine of model A and a sample of 10 fills from a machine of model B. The sample variances were $s_1^2 = .027$ and $s_2^2 = .065$, respectively. Does this result provide statistical support at the .05 level of significance for the salesman's claim?

39. A precision instrument is guaranteed to be accurate to within 2 units. A sample of four instrument readings on the same object yielded the measurements 353, 351, 351, and 355. Test the null hypothesis that $\sigma = .7$ against the alternative, $\sigma > .7$. (Conduct the test at the $\alpha = .05$ level of significance.)

40. The temperature of operation of two paint-drying ovens associated with two manufacturing production lines was recorded for 20 days. (Pairing was ignored.) The means and variance of the two samples are

$$\bar{y}_1 = 164, \qquad \bar{y}_2 = 168,$$
$$s_1^2 = 81, \qquad s_2^2 = 172.$$

Do the data present sufficient evidence to indicate a difference in temperature variability for the two ovens? (Test the hypothesis that $\sigma_1^2 = \sigma_2^2$ at the $\alpha = .10$ level of significance.)

41. A market analyst wishes to see whether shelf location affects the sales of his product. He believes that placement of his product at eye level will result in greater sales than if the product is placed on a lower shelf. The following data represent the number of sales of the market analyst's product in four different stores. Sales were observed over 2 weeks with product placement at eye level one week and on a lower shelf the other week.

	NO. SOLD	
STORE	LOWER SHELF	EYE-LEVEL SHELF
1	27	33
2	22	23
3	32	38
4	32	33

Test at the 5 percent level of significance to determine whether placement of the product at eye level significantly increases sales.

42. The office of the Lane County Assessor is considering the use of a computer valuation model for obtaining the assessed valuations for each of the residential dwellings of Lane County. The assessor is interested in seeing how assessed valuations obtained from the model compare with assessments made by an "expert" valuer. To note the comparison, the assessor randomly selected 10 residential dwellings from Lane County, computed their assessed valuation using the computer model, and obtained an assessed valuation for each from an expert valuer. The results are as follows:

| | ASSESSED VALUATIONS | |
DWELLING	COMPUTER MODEL	EXPERT VALUER
1	$21,000	$20,000
2	37,500	36,000
3	42,000	40,000
4	28,000	28,500
5	30,000	31,000
6	36,500	35,000
7	44,500	44,000
8	23,000	24,500
9	46,000	44,000
10	30,000	29,500

(a) What is the advantage of conducting the experiment as a paired experiment by blocking on the houses?

(b) What would be the effect of testing the hypothesis $H_0 : \mu_1 = \mu_2$ against the alternative $H_a : \mu_1 \neq \mu_2$ by using the methods of Section 9.4 and assuming that the two sets of values constitute two independent samples? Would such an analysis be (theoretically) incorrect?

(c) Analyzing the problem as a paired-difference experiment, do the sample data present sufficient evidence to indicate a difference in mean assessed valuation for the two assessment procedures? (Let $\alpha = .05$.)

(d) Obtain a 95 percent confidence interval for $(\mu_1 - \mu_2)$. Interpret this interval.

(e) Suppose that the above sample information is truly representative of all 40,000 residential dwelling units in Lane County. Furthermore, assume that the expert valuer is giving as true a measure as is possible for each residential dwelling unit he is asked to value. What is the estimated gain (loss) in *total* Lane County property valuation by using the computer model for valuation instead of hiring the more reliable, but also slower and more expensive, expert valuer?

(f) Obtain a 95 percent confidence interval for the gain (loss) in total Lane County property valuation by using the computer valuation model.

(g) Property taxes are assessed in Lane County at the annual rate of 3 percent of the assessed valuation of the residential dwelling. What estimated additional (lesser) amount of property tax revenue can Lane County expect to incur by using the computer valuation model?

(h) Obtain a 95 percent confidence interval for the additional (lesser) amount of property tax revenue Lane County is expected to receive if they decide to use the computer valuation model instead of hiring an expert valuer.

References

Anderson, R. L., and T. A. Bancroft, *Statistical Theory in Research*. New York: McGraw-Hill Book Company, 1952. Chapter 7.

Freund, J. E., and F. J. Williams; revised by B. Perles and C. Sullivan, *Modern Business Statistics*. Englewood Cliffs, N.J.: Prentice-Hall, Inc., 1969. Chapters 9, 10, and 11.

Hoel, P. G., and R. J. Jessen, *Basic Statistics for Business and Economics*. New York: John Wiley & Sons, Inc., 1971. Chapter 7.

Li, J. C. R., *Introduction to Statistical Inference*. Ann Arbor, Mich.: J. W. Edwards, Publisher, Inc., 1961. Chapter 10.

Chapter Ten

Decision Making Under Uncertainty

10.1 Introduction

A statistical test of an hypothesis is a decision-making procedure that employs the probabilities of the two types of errors, α and β, to evaluate the goodness of a test. Although not explicitly stated, certain losses would probably be associated with each type of error, and the expected loss could be a more practical criterion for comparing two statistical test procedures. In this chapter we present an elementary discussion of the modern concepts of decision making. This new theory utilizes the concept of gain (or loss) associated with every possible decision available to the decision maker and selects the decision that maximizes his expected gain.

Modern decision making attempts to formally integrate the personal preferences and perceptions of the decision maker into the decision analysis. The decision maker is thus forced to assume a more active role in the decision-making process. In the end, he relies more on rules consistent with his logic and personal behavior and less on the mechanical use of a set of formulas and tabulated probabilities.

Classical hypothesis testing, on the other hand, often tends to cause an arbitrary reliance on rules and formulas. This arbitrariness is best evidenced by the almost religious zeal attached to the significance level, $\alpha = .05$. Great care should be taken when selecting the error probabilities, α and β, in a statistical test of an hypothesis. These probabilities should certainly consider losses associated with the errors which they define as well as any prior information that may not be formally involved with the sample data used to calculate the test statistic. Modern decision making allows for the separate, formal, and consistent treatment of payoffs; prior information detached from the sample; and the decision maker's personal preferences without requiring him to rely on any arbitrary α value.

In summary, modern decision making (sometimes called Bayesian decision theory or decision analysis) is not really in conflict with classical hypothesis testing procedures at all. The difference is simply in the degree of formality of decision-making procedures employed and whether the decision maker himself plays an active or a passive role in the formulation of the decision.

10.2   Certainty Versus Uncertainty

In most decision-making situations, the decision maker must choose one of several possible actions or alternatives. Usually the alternatives and their associated payoffs are known in advance to the decision maker. An investor choosing one from several investment opportunities, a store owner determining how many of a certain type of commodity to stock, and a company executive making capital budgeting decisions are all examples of a business decision maker selecting from a multitude of alternatives. However, it is not known which alternative will be best in each case unless the decision maker also knows with certainty the values of the economic variables that affect profit. We call these variables states of nature since they represent different events that may occur or states over which the decision maker has no control.

Generally, the states of nature in a decision problem are denoted by the symbols $s_1, s_2, \ldots, s_k$. That is, the first state of nature is denoted by s_1, the second by the symbol s_2, and so forth. It is assumed that the states of nature are mutually exclusive (no two states can be in effect at the same time) and collectively exhaustive (all possible states are included within the analysis).

If n actions or alternatives are available to the decision maker, they are generally labeled $a_1, a_2, \ldots, a_n$. It is also assumed that the alternatives constitute a mutually exclusive, collectively exhaustive set.

The exact identity of the alternatives and states of nature associated with a decision-making situation is unique to that problem. An investor may wish to invest a certain sum of money in a savings account, a treasury bond, or a number of shares of a mutual fund. His available alternatives would be the investment of his money in one of the three mentioned investment opportunities while the states of nature that may influence his economic payoffs would be the possible states of the securities market in the near future. Another investor may wish to invest none, part, or all of the same or a different sum of money among the same three investment opportunities. His alternatives would include all possible splits of his investment sum among the three investment opportunities and may be practically endless. In such cases alternatives may have to be grouped and others eliminated in order to arrive at an analytical solution to the decision-making problem. In any decision-making problem, the ingenuity and perceptiveness of the decision maker are required to identify his available actions or alternatives and their associated payoffs and the states of nature that may affect the outcome.

When the state of nature, s_k, which will be in effect is known, or, if unknown, has no influence on the outcome of the alternatives, we say that the decision maker is operating under certainty. Otherwise, we say the decision is made under uncertainty.

Decision making under certainty is the simpler of the two techniques. The decision maker simply evaluates the outcome of each alternative and selects the one that best meets his objective. Under uncertainty, the task is at best complicated. Probability theory and mathematical expectation offer tools through which logical procedures for selecting the best alternative can be established. Statistics provides the structure to reach the decision, but the decision maker must inject his intuition and knowledge of the problem into the decision-making framework in order to arrive at the decision which is both theoretically justifiable and intuitively appealing. A good theoretical framework and a commonsense approach are both essential ingredients for decision making under uncertainty. One cannot function properly without the other.

To understand these ideas, consider an investor who wishes to invest $1,000 in one of three possible investment opportunities. Investment A is a savings plan with a commercial bank returning 6 percent annual interest, and investment B is a government bond returning the equivalent of $4\frac{1}{2}$ percent annual interest. These two investments involve no risk, and hence no uncertainty to the investor.

Suppose that investment C consists of the shares of a mutual fund with a wide diversity of available holdings from the securities market. The annual return from an investment in C is dependent upon the uncertain behavior of the mutual fund under varying economic conditions.

Assuming that the investor will invest his $1,000 either in one of the aforementioned investment opportunities or not invest at all, his available actions are as follows:

a_1:   Do not invest.
a_2:   Select investment A, the 6 percent commercial bank savings plan.
a_3:   Select investment B, the $4\frac{1}{2}$ percent government bond.
a_4:   Select investment C, the uncertain mutual fund.

Actions a_1, a_2, and a_3 do not involve uncertainty as the outcomes associated with the selection of any of these actions do not depend upon the uncertain market conditions. We could therefore say it is clear that action a_2 dominates actions a_1 and a_3. In general, one action is said to dominate another when the second action is never preferred to the first, regardless of the state of nature. Unless the investor attaches patriotic considerations to the selection of the government bond, investment B would never be selected when investment A is available. Similarly, action a_1, which provides for no growth of the principal amount, is clearly inferior to the risk-free positive-growth investment alternatives, actions a_2 and a_3.

Investment C, the mutual fund investment, is another matter. This alternative (a_4) is associated with an uncertain outcome that, depending on the state of the economy, may produce either a negative return or a positive return. Thus there exists no immediately apparent dominance relationship between action a_4 and action a_2 (the best among the actions involving no uncertainty, a_1, a_2, and a_3).

Suppose that the investor believes that if the market is "down" in the next year, an investment in the mutual fund would lose 10 percent; if the market "stays the same," the investment stays the same; and if the market is "up," the investment would gain 20 percent. The investor has thus defined the states of nature for his investment decision-making problem as

s_1:   the market is down,
s_2:   the market has remained unchanged,
s_3:   the market is up.

A study of the market combined with economic expectations for the coming year lead the investor to attach subjective probabilities of 1/4, 1/4, and 1/2, respectively, to the states of nature, s_1, s_2, and s_3. The question of interest is then: How can the investor use the foregoing information regarding investments *A*, *B*, and *C* and the expected market behavior as an aid to select the investment which best satisfies his objectives?

10.3   Analysis of the Decision Problem

In any problem involving the choice of one from many alternatives, we first must identify all the actions we may take and all the states of nature whose occurrence may influence our decision. The action to take none of the listed alternatives whose outcome is known with certainty may also be included within this list. Associated with each action is a list of payoffs to the decision maker. These are the value consequences to him should he take a specific action, given that each of the states of nature occurs. Of course, if an action does not involve risk, the payoff will be the same no matter which state of nature occurs.

The payoffs associated with each possible outcome in a decision problem are listed in a payoff table, which is defined as follows:

Definition

A *payoff table* is a listing in tabular form of the value payoffs associated with all possible actions under every state of nature in a decision problem.

The payoff table is usually displayed in grid form, with the states of nature assuming the role of the columns, and the actions, the rows. If we label the actions $a_1, a_2, \ldots, a_n$ and the states of nature $s_1, s_2, \ldots, s_k$, a payoff table for a decision problem would appear as shown in Table 10.1. A payoff is entered in each of the $(n)(k)$ cells of the payoff table, one for the payoff associated with each action under every possible state of nature.

Table 10.1   *Payoff Table*

STATES OF NATURE

ACTIONS	s_1	s_2	s_3	$\cdots$	s_k
a_1					
a_2					
a_3					
$\vdots$					
a_n					

It is important at this point to digress for a moment and examine what is meant by the concept of a "payoff." What is the decision maker attempting to accomplish? Assuming that he is a rational decision maker, he will process the list of alternatives and select the action that best satisfies his objectives. The payoffs he assigns to each possible outcome must be assessed in value units consistent with his objectives.

These value units may, in fact, not be measurable in monetary units at all. Or, the value consequences may be represented in a payoff table as some measure combining profit and a subjective measure such as "possible environmental impact."

The following problem settings should illustrate the importance of sometimes satisfying a goal by other than short-term profit maximization. A doctor is faced with the problem of treating a group of factory employees all of whom exhibit a rash on their upper bodies. He does not know the source of the rash, but for similar rashes he knows that an inexpensive medicated lotion works quite well. He also has access to a new experimental, but costly, drug which may prove effective. Ten patients are administered the lotion and 10 are given the experimental drug. After 3 days, those given the new drug are all back at work and completely free of the effects of the rash. Nine of the 10 patients administered the lotion are cured within 6 days, but the lotion does not effectively cure the tenth patient at all. The new experimental drug is then administered to all future employees who exhibit the rash. Clearly, the cost of administering the new drug is incidental in this case. Cure rate and time lost from the job were the measures of payoff considered.

A company is considering building a subsidiary plant in one of two locations. The most costly location for building is in an area with chronic unemployment and low per capita income. The more expensive site location is chosen. Thus the company executives have sought to maximize some social goal, perhaps identified as the firm's public image, instead of minimizing building costs. Payoff has been measured in social value units or public image units and is represented accordingly in the payoff table.

Defense planning is made using a probability of damage payoff measure to rank alternatives. Timber companies adopt a payoff model combining timber harvesting costs and environmental considerations, such as clear-cutting versus selective harvesting. Scientific expeditions measure payoff on an arbitrary scale in terms of the comparative worth of expected findings to the scientific community and the public.

An example of the construction of a value model follows. This example involves the selection of one from among three alternatives under certainty.

Example 10.1   *A recent college graduate has three firm job offers in hand. All three jobs appear to involve interesting and stimulating job activities. The offers are from companies A, B, and C, where company A is located in a large Eastern city, company B in a large Midwestern city, and company C in a small Western city. The monetary offers are all within $100 of $12,000, so the size of the offer is an inconsequential measure of comparative value to associate with each offer. Construct a payoff model and find payoff measures for each company offer.*

Solution   *The graduate selects job location, promotional opportunities, and job fringe benefits as the valid measures of value payoff to associate with each offer. He subjectively assigns a rating on a 0-to-10 scale to measure the value contribution for each component of payoff for each offer. These are shown in Table 10.2.*

Table 10.2

	COMPANY *A*	COMPANY *B*	COMPANY *C*
Job location	6	4	10
Promotional opportunities	6	9	5
Fringe benefits	7	6	4

To combine the components of payoff, the graduate asks himself: What are the relative measures of importance of these three components of payoff? Suppose he assumes that job location is most important and twice as important as either promotional opportunities or fringe benefits. He thus assigns a weight of 2 to the job location scaled values and weights of 1 to promotional opportunities and fringe benefits, to obtain the following payoff measures:

$$payoff \ (company \ A) = \ 6(2) + 6(1) + 7(1) = 25,$$

$$payoff \ (company \ B) = \ 4(2) + 9(1) + 6(1) = 23,$$

$$payoff \ (company \ C) = 10(2) + 5(1) + 4(1) = 29.$$

It is clear that before a decision maker can rationally evaluate a set of alternatives, he must clearly identify his goals and objectives. Having done this, a payoff measure is selected that can effectively rank the outcomes according to the amount by which they satisfy his goals and objectives. The payoff measure is thus unique to the decision maker and his preferences and certainly unique to each new problem setting.

Advanced methods can and do handle most classes of nonmonetary outcomes in a decision analysis. However, these methods are reserved for a later course. For economy of time and space, the examples in this chapter will assume an analysis involving monetary payoff, measurable by the profit or opportunity loss associated with each possible outcome.

Definition

The opportunity loss $L_{i,j}$ *for selecting action* a_i, *given that state of nature* s_j *is in effect, is the difference between the maximum profit that could be realized if* s_j *occurs and the profit obtained by selecting action* a_i.

The opportunity loss is zero at the optimal action for each state of nature. A nonzero opportunity loss does not necessarily imply an accounting loss but only that the decision maker had the opportunity to realize $L_{i,j}$ more in profit had he selected the best action instead of action a_i. The concept of an opportunity loss (sometimes called the regret) need not be concerned with lost profits. In a general sense, an opportunity loss is a measure of the amount of payoff that has been foregone by taking a particular action a_i under state of nature s_j.

A payoff table displaying the opportunity losses in a decision analysis is called an opportunity-loss table, and one showing profits is called a profit table

The decision consists of selecting from the list of possible alternatives the action that best satisfies the decision maker's objectives. This decision is called the optimal decision. Various economic objectives and the decision processes necessary to accomplish these objectives will be examined in Sections 10.4, 10.7, and 10.8.

Example 10.2   *For the investment problem discussed in Section 10.2, construct the opportunity-loss table.*

Solution   *Define the actions "select no investment," "select investment A," "select investment B," and "select investment C" as* a_1, a_2, a_3, *and* a_4, *respec-*

tively. Also, let s_1, s_2, and s_3 represent the state of the securities market as "down," "about the same," and "up," respectively.

Actions a_1, a_2, and a_3 are not affected by the states of nature, but action a_4 is. The resultant profits associated with this problem are listed in Table 10.3.

Table 10.3   *Profit Table for the Investment Problem (in dollar units)*

	STATE OF NATURE		
ACTION	s_1 (DOWN)	s_2 (THE SAME)	s_3 (UP)
a_1 (none)	0	0	0
a_2 (A)	60	60	60
a_3 (B)	45	45	45
a_4 (C)	−100	0	200

We can see that if state of nature s_1 or s_2 is in effect, the best action is to select a_2, the 6 percent savings plan. If the securities market is up, the $200 profit for investing in investment C far exceeds what we could realize by selecting any other action.

From the definition of opportunity loss given earlier and from the information within Table 10.3, we can now construct the opportunity-loss table. It is given in Table 10.4.

Table 10.4   *Opportunity-Loss Table for the Investment Problem*

	STATE OF NATURE		
ACTION	s_1 (DOWN)	s_2 (THE SAME)	s_3 (UP)
a_1 (none)	60	60	200
a_2 (A)	0	0	140
a_3 (B)	15	15	155
a_4 (C)	160	60	0

Example 10.3   *A retailer must decide each morning how many of a perishable commodity to include in his inventory. The commodities cost him $2 per unit and are sold for $5 per unit, realizing a profit of $3 per unit. Any unsold items at the day's end are a total loss to the retailer. By recording the daily demand for this commodity over a long period of time, the retailer was able to construct*

the following probability distribution on the daily demand level(s):

s_i	$p(s_i)$
0	0
1	0.5
2	0.3
3	0.2
4 *or more*	0

Construct the opportunity-loss table.

Solution   *In this problem, the states of nature are the demand levels and the actions are the possible inventory levels.*

The profits associated with each action are as in Table 10.5, where inventory levels 1, 2, and 3 are denoted by a_1, a_2, and a_3, respectively. Similarly, the

Table 10.5 *Profit Table for the Demand-Inventory Problem*

ACTION (INVENTORY)	STATE OF NATURE (DEMAND)		
	$s_1(1)$	$s_2(2)$	$s_3(3)$
$a_1(1)$	3	3	3
$a_2(2)$	1	6	6
$a_3(3)$	−1	4	9

demand levels are labeled s_1, s_2, and s_3. It then follows directly that the opportunity losses would be as exhibited in Table 10.6.

Table 10.6 *Opportunity-Loss Table for the Demand-Inventory Problem*

ACTION (INVENTORY)	STATE OF NATURE (DEMAND)		
	$s_1(1)$	$s_2(2)$	$s_3(3)$
$a_1(1)$	0	3	6
$a_2(2)$	2	0	3
$a_3(3)$	4	2	0

In the investment problem, Section 10.2, the states of nature that will be in effect have no bearing on the outcome of investments A and B. But with investment C, the unknown state of nature which will be in effect does influence the outcome. Hopefully, this illustrates the importance of an earlier remark. Personal judgment and subjective reasoning are required of the decision maker to identify the relevant states of nature and to place precise probabilities on their occurrence. The intuition, perception, and judgment of the decision maker are thus an integral part of the analysis in modern decision making.

Definition

 The probabilities representing the chances of occurrence of the identifiable states of nature in a decision problem before gathering any sample information are called prior probabilities.

How should the prior probabilities be determined? As indicated in Example 10.2, we may sometimes be able to estimate the probabilities of different states of nature from previous experience. Our probability estimate may then just be the relative frequency of occurrence of that particular state of nature in the past. However, in other decision problems our feeling about which states of nature are more likely to occur cannot be summarized solely in such historical relative frequencies. In those cases, some other method of assessing prior probabilities is required. [See Howard (1966) or Winkler (1972) for some techniques available in eliciting personal opinion concerning the prior probabilities.]

In short, there is no simple answer to the question of how to select the prior probabilities. Realizing that the optimal action is often quite sensitive to only a slight change in the set of prior probabilities, the decision maker seeks a precise and meaningful set of prior probabilities. To accomplish this end, he uses all available information at his disposal and relies on his judgment and experience to process that information and identify, as well as possible, his prior probabilities

We shall not expand on the necessary aspects of the subjective elements of our decision framework and will assume now that they have been formulated. The discussion in the remainder of this chapter presents some logical procedures for selecting the best action after all states of nature have been identified and their associated payoffs and probabilities have been computed.

10.4   Expected Monetary Value Decisions

One decision-making procedure, which employs both the payoff table and the prior probabilities associated with the states of nature to arrive at a decision, is called the expected monetary value decision procedure.

> **Definition**
>
> An *expected monetary value* decision is the selection of an available action based on either the expected opportunity loss or the expected profit of the action.

The optimal expected monetary value decision is the selection of the action associated with the minimum expected opportunity loss or the action associated with the maximum expected profit, depending upon the decision maker's objective. We shall note later that expected opportunity loss decisions and expected profit decisions are always associated with the same optimal decision.

The concept of expected monetary value is an application of mathematical expectation, Section 5.6, where opportunity loss or profit is the random variable and the prior probabilities represent the probability distribution associated with the random variable. The expected opportunity loss for each action a_i is found by evaluating

$$E(L_i) = \sum_{\text{all } j} L_{i,j} p(s_j), \qquad i = 1, 2, \ldots,$$

where $L_{i,j}$ is the opportunity loss for selecting action a_i given that state of nature s_j occurs and $p(s_j)$ is the prior probability assigned to state of nature s_j. If we are interested in computing the expected profits for each action, the analysis would be the same except that we would substitute the profits, $P_{i,j}$, for the opportunity losses, $L_{i,j}$, in the above formula. The following examples should clarify the computational procedures involved with the excepted monetary value decision procedure.

Example 10.4 *Find the optimal decision that minimizes the investor's expected opportunity loss, Example 10.2.*

Solution *Our prior probabilities associated with the states of nature s_1, s_2, and s_3 are $p(s_1) = 1/4$, $p(s_2) = 1/4$, and $p(s_3) = 1/2$. Thus the expected opportunity losses are*

$$E(L_1) = \$60\left(\frac{1}{4}\right) + \$60\left(\frac{1}{4}\right) + \$200\left(\frac{1}{2}\right) = \$130,$$

$$E(L_2) = \$0\left(\frac{1}{4}\right) + \$0\left(\frac{1}{4}\right) + \$140\left(\frac{1}{2}\right) = \$70,$$

$$E(L_3) = \$15\left(\frac{1}{4}\right) + \$15\left(\frac{1}{4}\right) + \$155\left(\frac{1}{2}\right) = \$85,$$

and

$$E(L_4) = \$160\left(\frac{1}{4}\right) + \$60\left(\frac{1}{4}\right) + \$0\left(\frac{1}{2}\right) = \$55.$$

Action a_4, the mutual fund investment, is the optimal expected monetary value decision, since its expected opportunity loss is less than that for any other action.

Actions a_1 and a_3 could have been eliminated from the analysis at the begining, since their payoffs are never better than those for a_2. They were retained in our example for illustrative purposes.

As an aside, suppose that we compute the expected profits for each action of Example 10.2. If P_i represent the profit realized by selecting action a_i, then we find

$$E(P_1) = \$0\left(\frac{1}{4}\right) + \$0\left(\frac{1}{4}\right) + \$0\left(\frac{1}{2}\right) = \$0,$$

$$E(P_2) = \$60\left(\frac{1}{4}\right) + \$60\left(\frac{1}{4}\right) + \$60\left(\frac{1}{2}\right) = \$60,$$

$$E(P_3) = \$4\left(\frac{1}{4}\right) + \$45\left(\frac{1}{4}\right) + \$45\left(\frac{1}{2}\right) = \$45,$$

and

$$E(P_4) = -\$100\left(\frac{1}{4}\right) + \$0\left(\frac{1}{4}\right) + \$200\left(\frac{1}{2}\right) = \$75.$$

Consistent with our analysis based on opportunity losses, action a_4 is best, since it is associated with the maximum expected profit. This is no accident but is an occurrence that will always result. A proof of this assertion follows from the definition of opportunity loss. The difference between the expected opportunity losses of any two actions is equal in magnitude but opposite in sign from the difference between their expected profits. For instance, in Example 10.2, if we look at actions a_2 and a_4,

$$E(L_4) - E(L_2) = \$55 - \$70 = -\$15$$

$$E(P_4) - E(P_2) = \$75 - \$60 = \$15.$$

Under either method, action a_4 is \$15 better than a_2.

Example 10.5   *Find the inventory level that minimizes the expected oppor-tunity loss for the demand-inventory problem, Example* 10.3.

Solution   *The historical frequencies of demand, the prior probabilities for this case, are given in Example 10.3. The expected opportunity losses are found by evaluating*

$$E(L_i) = \sum_{j=1}^{3} L_{i,j} p(s_j)$$

for each inventory level, i = 1, 2, 3.
    The expected opportunity losses at each inventory level are

$$E(L_1) = \$0(.5) + \$3(.3) + \$6(.2) = \$2.10,$$
$$E(L_2) = \$2(.5) + \$0(.3) + \$3(.2) = \$1.60,$$

and

$$E(L_3) = \$4(.5) + \$2(.3) + \$0(.2) = \$2.60.$$

Thus the retailer's optimal decision is to stock 2 units of the commodity.

Note that in our second example the prior distribution assigned to the states of nature was constructed empirically from historical data. However, sub-jectivity and intuition are also implicit in this case, as evidenced by the fact that past historical frequencies are believed to adequately depict the future. In any decision problem, the prior probabilities reflect all available information, both empirical and subjective, related to the likelihoods of occurrence of the states of nature.

10.5   Justification of Expected Monetary Value Decisions

Expected profit or opportunity-loss decisions are most easily interpreted if we look at the decision in the long run. If the optimal action is repeated time after time, the average of the opportunity losses incurred using one procedure would be less than if the decision maker employed some other decision-making scheme. In our second example, this idea is easy to see. If the retailer stocks 2 units every day, his average of all daily opportunity losses will be a minimum and will be about $1.60, less than the average loss incurred by stocking 1 or 3 units each day.

In an experiment that cannot necessarily be repeated, such as the investment problem, Section 10.2, or a capital budgeting problem, expected monetary value decisions are not so easily justified. For the investment problem, we would expect the average profit for investment C to be $75, or a return of $7\frac{1}{2}$ percent on the investment. Thus the expected monetary value decision maker selects investment C, since its expected return of $7\frac{1}{2}$ percent is greater than the sure returns of 6 percent for investment A and $4\frac{1}{2}$ percent for investment B.

The best way of interpreting nonrepetitive expected monetary value decisions is by examining the expected opportunity losses. The expected opportunity loss associated with the optimal decision represents the loss to be expected if we select the optimal decision. This does not imply that the opportunity loss we will actually realize by selecting the optimal decision will equal this value. Often it is impossible for this value ever to be realized. Recalling Example 10.4, the optimal decision was to select action a_4 with an associated expected opportunity loss of $55. Note, however, that if action a_4 is selected, the only possible opportunity losses that can be realized are $160, $60, and $0, none of which equals the expected opportunity loss, $55.

What is implied is that the minimum expected opportunity loss measures the expected cost of uncertainty due to our uncertain knowledge about which state of nature will be in effect. If the opportunity presented itself, we should be willing to pay up to the amount of the cost of uncertainty to obtain information identifying the state of nature that will be in effect. Minimizing our expected cost of uncertainty seems to be a logical objective, and this is what we are doing by selecting the action associated with the maximum expected profit and minimum expected opportunity loss.

Another way of justifying the use of this decision method is to examine the components of the expected monetary value. The profit or loss values are economic outcomes, while their relative frequencies of occurrence are the prior probabilities assigned to the states of nature. Thus an expected monetary analysis provides a model that combines both real economic data and qualitative or subjective information available to the decision maker related to the outcome of the economic data. It is the only decision-making model available to us at this time which incorporates all available information into the decision. Also, it makes the decision maker more than just an impartial observer by forcing him to construct meaningful prior probabilities to associate with the states of nature. This latter concept is the most important and often the most difficult task in decision making under uncertainty.

A reassessment of the values assigned to the prior probabilities often changes the optimum decision. Suppose that the investor confronted with the investment problem, Section 10.2, after reconsidering his prior beliefs, decides to assign as prior probabilities

$$p(s_1) = \frac{1}{4}, \qquad p(s_2) = \frac{1}{2}, \qquad p(s_3) = \frac{1}{4}.$$

His expected profit for investment C is now

$$E(P_4) = -\$100\left(\frac{1}{4}\right) + \$0\left(\frac{1}{2}\right) + \$200\left(\frac{1}{4}\right) = \$25,$$

while the expected profits for investments A and B remain \$60 and \$45, respectively. Hence, under the new set of prior probabilities, investment C is only third best behind the "new" optimum decision to select investment A.

Expected monetary value decisions, since they employ probabilities in the decision analysis, assume that the priors assigned to the states of nature are the true probabilities for the problem. The optimal expected monetary value decision is meaningful only in terms of its associated prior probabilities. If the decision maker does not have complete confidence in the prior probabilities that he has assigned to the states of nature, he should try other likely sets of priors in order to examine the sensitivity of the decision to the selection of the prior probabilities.

10.6   The Economic Impact of Uncertainty

Ideally, one would like to know in advance which state of nature will be in effect. In the investment problem, knowing the market will be "down" or "about the same," the decision maker would select investment A, the 6 percent commercial bank savings account; knowing the market will be "up," his best course of action would be to select investment C, the mutual fund investment. In the demand-inventory example, if he knows which demand level will be in effect, he selects an inventory level to exactly meet demand.

Under normal conditions, uncertainty prevails and the decision maker must act according to his best information and interests. Not knowing the state of nature that will be in effect, he cannot expect a return as great as that he could expect if the true state of nature were known.

Using an expected monetary value approach, the decision maker, in the face of uncertainty, selects the alternative that maximizes his expected profit and minimizes his expected opportunity loss. We shall now formally define a concept that was earlier only mentioned in passing.

Definition

The expected opportunity loss associated with the optimal decision is called the cost of uncertainty.

The cost of uncertainty is the maximum amount the decision maker would pay to know precisely the state of nature that will be in effect. It is then the value the decision maker would place on perfect information (information removing all uncertainty) offered to him. The cost of uncertainty is sometimes called the expected value of perfect information or simply EVPI.

In Example 10.4 the optimal decision is to select action a_4 with expected opportunity loss $E(L_4) = \$55$. We were shown in Example 10.5 that action a_2, with expected opportunity loss $E(L_2) = \$1.60$, is best. These two values are the costs of uncertainty associated with, respectively, the investment problem and the demand-inventory problem. In each case these values represent the maximum amount the decision maker would be willing to pay to know precisely the state of nature that will be in effect.

To better understand the concept of the cost of uncertainty or EVPI, let us focus on Example 10.4, the investment problem. Suppose that the decision maker knows with certainty which state of nature will be in effect. If he knows that the state will be s_1 or s_2, he selects action a_2, as the opportunity losses for selecting a_2 under states s_1 and s_2 are the least. Similarly, if he knows that state of nature s_3 will be in effect, he selects action a_4. In each case the opportunity loss is zero, so the decision maker's expected opportunity loss under certainty is

$$E(L_0) = \$0\left(\frac{1}{4}\right) + \$0\left(\frac{1}{4}\right) + \$0\left(\frac{1}{2}\right) = \$0.$$

The best the decision maker can expect under uncertainty is the expected opportunity loss of $55 by selecting the optimal action, a_4. Therefore, the effect of uncertainty of market conditions costs the investor, on the average, $55 each time he faces an investment decision such as the one outlined in Section 10.2.

The cost of uncertainty or EVPI may be more easily interpreted if defined in terms of expected profits. Under certainty of the state of nature, the decision maker can expect a profit of

$$E(P_0) = \$60\left(\frac{1}{4}\right) + \$60\left(\frac{1}{4}\right) + \$200\left(\frac{1}{2}\right) = \$130,$$

by selecting action a_2 under states s_1 and s_2 and action a_4 under state of nature s_3. This represents his expected profit under perfect information.

The best the investor can expect under uncertainty is $75, the expected profit associated with the optimal decision, action a_4. The difference between expected profits under certainty and uncertainty is $130 - $75 = $55, the EVPI. The cost of uncertainty or, equivalently, the EVPI is then the amount of profits foregone or additional losses incurred due to uncertain conditions affecting the outcome of a decision problem

Suppose that the investor has the opportunity to hire the services of the Securities Consulting Agency (SCA). This group would survey many market experts to determine whether they believe the securities market will fall, stay about the same, or rise within the next year. The consensus of the survey would then be sold by the SCA to the investor.

How much should the investor pay for the SCA report? If the SCA provides perfect market information, the investor would pay up to $55 for the report, but no more. That is, the value of the perfect information supplied by the SCA does not exceed $55. The reasoning behind this limiting value is easy to see. For instance, if the decision maker should pay $60 to the SCA for perfect market information, his expected profit would be $130 (the expected profit for perfect information) minus $60 (the cost of buying the perfect information), or $70. But an expected profit of $70 is $5 less than the $75 expected profit by taking action a_4 under uncertainty and using no auxiliary information.

Naturally the investor does not expect perfect market information from the SCA. Thus the amount he should pay for the SCA report is some amount less than $55, an amount that is determined from the measures of reliability of the SCA market analysis techniques. The concept of placing a value on imperfect sample information will be demonstrated in the following section.

10.7   Decision Making That Involves Sample Information

From the definition and discussion of the prior probabilities in Sections 10.3 and 10.5, it was said they are acquired either by subjective selection or by computation from historical data. No current information describing the chance of occurrence of the states of nature was assumed to be available.

Perhaps observational information or other evidence may be available to the decision maker either for purchase or at the cost of experimentation. For instance, a retailer whose business is dependent upon the weather may consult a meteorologist before making his decision, or an investor may hire a market consultant before investing. Market research surveys before the release of a new product represent another area in which the decision maker seeks additional information. In each instance the decision maker is acquiring information relative to the occurrence of the states of nature from a source other than that from which the priors were computed.

If such information is available, Bayes' law can be employed to revise the prior probabilities to reflect the new information. These revised probabilities are called posterior probabilities

Definition

The posterior probability $p(s_k|x)$ represents the chance of occurrence of the state of nature, s_k, given the experimental information, x. This probability is

$$p(s_k|x) = \frac{p(x|s_k)p(s_k)}{\sum\limits_{\text{all } i} p(x|s_i)p(s_i)}.$$

The probabilities $p(x|s_i)$ are the conditional probabilities of observing the observational information x under the states of nature s_i, and the probabilities $p(s_i)$ are the priors. The notation used here for Bayes' law is different from what was presented in Chapter 4. The careful reader will note their equivalence.

The expected monetary value decisions are formulated the same as before except that we use the posterior probabilities in place of the priors. If our objective is to minimize the expected opportunity loss, the quantity is computed for each action, a_i. As before, the optimal decision is to select the action associated with the smallest expected opportunity loss.

$$E(L_i) = \sum\limits_{\text{all } j} L_{i,j}p(s_j|x), \qquad i = 1, 2, \dots.$$

Example 10.6   *It is known that an assembly machine operates either at a 5 or a 10 percent defective rate. When believed to be running at the 10 percent defective rate, the machine is judged out of control, shut down, and readjusted. From past history the machine is known to run at the 5 percent defective rate 90 percent of the time. A sample of $n = 20$ has been selected from the output of the machine and $y = 2$ defectives have been observed. Based on both the prior and sample information, what is the probability the assembly machine is in control (5 percent defective rate)?*

Solution   *The states of nature in this example relate to the possible assembly machine defective rates. Thus the states of nature are*

$$s_1 = .05 \quad and \quad s_2 = .10,$$

with assumed prior probabilities of occurrence of .90 and .10, respectively. We want to use these priors, in light of the observed sample information, to find the posterior probability associated with state s_1.

In this example the "experimental information x" is the observation of $y = 2$ defectives from a sample of $n = 20$ items selected from the output of the assembly machine. It is necessary that we find the probability that the experimental information x could arise under each state of nature s_j. This can be accomplished by referring to the tables for the binomial probability distribution (Table 1, Appendix). Under state of nature $s_1 = .05$, we find

$$p(x|.05) = p(n = 20, y = 2|.05)$$
$$= .925 - .736$$
$$= .189.$$

Similarly, under state of nature $s_2 = .10$ we find

$$p(x|.10) = .285.$$

Now we are ready to employ Bayes' law to find the posterior probability the machine is in control (s_1) based on both the prior and experimental information.

Table 10.7   *Columnar Approach to Use of Bayes' Law, Example 10.6*

(1) STATES OF NATURE s_j	(2) PRIORS $p(s_j)$	(3) EXPERIMENTAL INFORMATION $p(x|s_j)$	(4) PRODUCT $p(s_j)p(x|s_j)$	(5) POSTERIORS $p(s_j|x)$
s_1 .05	.9	.189	.1701	.86
s_2 .10	.1	.285	.0285	.14
	1.0		.1986	1.00

The application of Bayes' law is most clearly illustrated by using a columnar approach (see Table 10.7). Using a columnar approach, the states of nature, their associated prior probabilities, and the probabilities the experimental information x could arise under each state of nature are listed in the first three columns. In column (4) we compute the product of the corresponding entries from columns (2) and (3). These values measure the joint probabilities, $p(x|s_j)$. We then sum the entries within column (4). This sum is the term in the denominator of the formula for Bayes' law and measures the marginal probability of observing the experimental information, x. The posterior probabilities, column (5), are thus obtained by taking each entry within column (4) and dividing it by

the sum of the entries from column (4). This simply rescales the joint proba-
bilities of column (4) causing them to sum to 1.00. For instance,

$$p(s_1|x) = \frac{.1701}{.1986} \quad while \ p(s_2|x) = \frac{.0285}{.1986}.$$

Even though we found 10 percent of the sample items to be defective (2 of 20),
the posterior probability that the machine is running at the 10 percent defective
rate (out of control) is only .14, very little greater than the prior probability
the machine is out of control. Therefore, the probability the machine is not
running out of control is .86.

In review of the solution to Example 10.6, the careful reader will note that
the columnar approach is nothing but a restructuring of Bayes' law and is bound
to give the same numerical answers as would be obtained by plugging the proper
numbers into the formula for Bayes' law. For those who are not convinced of this
fact, Example 10.6 should be repeated using the formula-plugging approach instead
of the columnar approach.

The experimental information x often presents itself other than as sample
information. It may be in the form of an expert opinion, the result of an engineering
survey or a structural test, or the observance of a sudden, unpredictable economic
trend. How can such information best be used to help us in the task of decision
making under conditions involving uncertainty? We must first evaluate the reliability of the information and then incorporate these measures of reliability into
the decision analysis with the other problem data.

The discussion involving the hypothetical Securities Consulting Agency
presented in the previous section offers a case in point. Notice that the "experimental information" in this example is in the form of an opinion; based on their
studies, SCA will indicate the market condition (state of nature) which they believe
will occur. In this example the experimental information, x, may then present
itself at any of three levels. That is, SCA may report

$$x_1 = \text{"the market will be down,"}$$

$$x_2 = \text{"the market will remain at the same level,"}$$

or

$$x_3 = \text{"the market will be up."}$$

The probabilities, $p(x|s_j)$, should be rewritten as $p(x_i|s_j)$ to recognize the different
possible responses, x_i, $i = 1, 2, 3$, which may be given by the SCA. These probabilities measure the reliability of the experimental information, x_i, provided by

the SCA. If the information provides complete certainty, then

$$p(x_i|s_j) = \begin{cases} 1 & \text{if } i = j, \\ 0 & \text{if } i \neq j. \end{cases}$$

The further removed the $p(x_i|s_j)$ values are from these limits, the less reliable, and hence the less valuable, is the experimental information that is available.

Example 10.7   *Reconsider the investment problem, Example 10.2. Suppose that the investor is considering hiring the services of the Securities Consulting Agency, the group discussed in Section 10.6. In the past when SCA has conducted a market survey for a client the results shown in Table 10.8 have been noted. For example, $p(x_1| s_2) = .15$ is the probability that SCA concludes the market will drop when it actually stays the same. Find the investor's best decision based on the expected opportunity losses associated with each possible response from the SCA.*

Table 10.8   *Conditional Probabilities Indicating the Reliability of SCA Market Surveys, $p(x_i|s_j)$*

| | STATE OF NATURE | | |
RESPONSE (x)	s_1 (DOWN)	s_2 (THE SAME)	s_3 (UP)
x_1 (down)	.60	.15	.05
x_2 (the same)	.30	.50	.25
x_3 (up)	.10	.35	.70

Solution   *Recall from Table 10.1 that regardless of which state of nature is in effect, action a_2 guarantees a greater profit than either action a_1 or action a_3. Thus we could ignore actions a_1 and a_3, which are dominated by a_2, reducing the investor's decision to one of choosing either action a_2 or action a_4, depending on the information received from the SCA. An analysis of the investor's problem involves three decisions, one for each response "down," "stay the same," or "up" from the SCA. We need first to compute the revised probabilities, the posteriors, for each response. If the SCA suggests that the market will drop, we employ Bayes' law using the columnar approach and find (see Table 10.9)*

$$p(s_1|x_1) = 12/17, \qquad p(s_2|x_1) = 3/17, \qquad p(s_3|x_1) = 2/17.$$

Table 10.9   *Columnar Approach for
Using Bayes' Law, Example 10.7*

(1)	(2)	(3)	(4)	(5)
s_j	$p(s_j)$	$p(x_1\|s_j)$	$p(s_j)p(x_1\|s_j)$	$p(s_j\|x_1)$
s_1 (down)	1/4	.60	.1500	.706 = 12/17
s_2 (the same)	1/4	.15	.0375	.176 = 3/17
s_3 (up)	1/2	.05	.0250	.118 = 2/17
			.2125	1.000 = 17/17

*Similarly, under the response from SCA that the market will stay the same,
we would find*

$$p(s_1|x_2) = 3/13, \qquad p(s_2|x_2) = 5/13, \qquad p(s_3|x_2) = 5/13,$$

and if they say it will rise,

$$p(s_1|x_3) = 2/37, \qquad p(s_2|x_3) = 7/37, \qquad p(s_3|x_3) = 28/37.$$

Now suppose that the SCA reports that the market will drop. Then, using
*the opportunity-loss values from Table 10.4, the expected opportunity losses
associated with actions a_2 and a_4 are*

$$E(L_2) = \$0\left(\frac{12}{17}\right) + \$0\left(\frac{3}{17}\right) + \$140\left(\frac{2}{17}\right) = \$16.47$$

and

$$E(L_4) = \$160\left(\frac{12}{17}\right) + \$60\left(\frac{3}{17}\right) + \$0\left(\frac{2}{17}\right) = \$123.53.$$

*Thus, if SCA suggests the market will drop, the investors should choose the
6 percent savings plan, action a_2. The expected opportunity losses for the
other two SCA responses have been computed and are listed in Table 10.10.
The investor's optimal decisions are easily read from this table. He should
select action a_2 if "down" or "the same" is reported, but he should select a_4
if the SCA reports the market will be "up" in the coming year.*

Table 10.10   *Expected Opportunity Losses for Example 10.7*

RESPONSES FROM THE SCA

ACTION	DOWN	THE SAME	UP
a_2	\$16.47	\$53.85	\$105.95
a_4	\$123.53	\$60.00	\$20.00

The value of revising our prior probabilities and arriving at this more complex solution is twofold. First, the independent source of information we are using to compute the posterior probabilities gives us a check that the values we assign to the prior probabilities of the states of nature are near what the true values should be. That is, we are updating our guesses with someone else's guesses or with experimental evidence. This procedure allows us to incorporate all available information into our decision model. As a second point, related to the first, the additional information will allow us to tailor our decision to the specific outcome of the experimental evidence. Thus instead of having a single decision, we have a whole array of decisions corresponding to the nature of the experimental evidence. In the investment problem, each response from the SCA initiates a decision by the investor. Thus he is able to "partition" his decision and obtain the most use possible from the additional information.

What is the value of the sample information? Certainly the investor would not pay as much as \$55 for the sample information, but how much should he be willing to pay?

Although it was not mentioned earlier, we could show that

$$p(x_i) = \sum_{\text{all } j} p(x_i|s_j)p(s_j), \qquad i = 1, 2, \ldots,$$

which is the sum of the entries within column (4) by use of the columnar approach. Therefore, the probability the SCA report will indicate that the market will be "down" (x_1) is

$$p(x_1) = (.6)(1/4) + (.15)(1/4) + (.05)(1/2) = .2125.$$

Similarly, the probabilities that their report will indicate the market will be "about the same" (x_2) and "up" (x_3) can be found using the same formula and are, respectively,

$$p(x_2) = .3250$$

and

$$p(x_3) = .4625.$$

Returning to Example 10.7, we recall that when the SCA reports x_1 = down or x_2 = the same, the investor should select action a_2. However, when the report suggests x_3 = up, action a_4 is best. Referring back to Table 10.10, we can see that the investor's expected opportunity loss using the SCA service is then

$$E(L) = \$16.47p(x_1) + \$53.85p(x_2) + \$20.00p(x_3)$$
$$= \$16.47(.2125) + \$53.85(.3250) + \$20.00(.4625)$$
$$= \$30.25.$$

Thus the experimental information is worth, at most,

$$\$55.00 - \$30.25 = \$24.75,$$

since the experimental information has effectively reduced the investor's expected cost of uncertainty by that amount. This value, called the expected value of sample information (EVSI), represents the maximum amount the investor would pay for the SCA market service. Under no conditions would the investor pay more than $24.75. For any amount less than $24.75 which he pays for the SCA report, the investor incurs a net savings by buying the additional information.

10.8   Other Topics in Modern Decision Making

Over the past fifteen years, modern decision making has evolved from a controversial set of rules of thumb into a rigorous discipline involving techniques now generally accepted by both the theoretician and the practitioner. Only the most important topics involved with modern decision making have been included in the chapter up to this point. Other topics and techniques of lesser importance will be introduced in this section. For a complete discussion of modern decision making, the reader is referred to Schlaifer (1969) or Winkler (1972).

Decisions Ignoring Prior Information

Occasionally, the attitude toward risk of the decision maker suggests that a limit exists on the amount of money he can afford to lose. Such an individual may be typified by an investor with a very small bankroll or a retailer on the verge of bankruptcy. The prior probabilities attached to the states of nature are ignored by such individuals even if the probabilities associated with unfavorable states are extremely small. He looks only at the magnitudes of the losses for each action, shows virtually no interest in the magnitude of potential profits, and makes his decision without computing an expected monetary value. A decision criterion that satisfies a conservative economic objective such as described above is provided by the minimax decision.

Definition

The minimax decision is the selection of the action whose maximum possible opportunity loss is a minimum.

The minimax decision maker is saying that in order to remain competitive in his business he must, at all costs, avoid the large opportunity losses. He is minimizing his maximum opportunity loss and, by so doing, usually rejecting those alternatives associated with the greatest possible return. He thus assures himself of at best a stable financial position.

Example 10.8   *Find the minimax decision for the investment problem, Example 10.2.*

Solution   *The maximum opportunity losses associated with each action are*

Action	a_1	a_2	a_3	a_4
Max. opp. loss	$200	$140	$155	$160

Thus the minimax decision is to select action a_2, the 6 percent savings plan.

Another decision criterion is the maximax decision method, which selects the action that maximizes the maximum possible profit. The individual who employs this technique has a very small aversion toward risk and might be categorized as a gambler. He stands a great chance of losing everything but is concerned only with the possibility of making a quick fortune.

Maximin, maximizing the minimum profit, is similar in nature but somewhat more conservative than maximax.

All these techniques have two common traits. First, the decision maker employing minimax, maximax, or maximin strategies tends to totally ignore prior information relating to the probabilities of occurrence of the states of nature. His attitudes toward risk make some economic payoffs appear attractive and others unattractive regardless of the occurrence of the states of nature. The second similarity is that minimax, maximax, or maximin decisions are usually one-shot decisions. If they were not, the "averaging effect" of employing minimax, maximax, or maximin continuously could tend to deplete one's profits, since whether accepted or not, the states of nature do occur according to some probability distribution.

The expected monetary value decision and the minimax, maximax, or maximin decisions are often the same. This only occurs by chance and does not imply any similarity between objectives. The basic difference is that the expected monetary value decisions incorporate prior information (probabilities) into the decision model while the others ignore this information.

Decision Trees

A tree diagram is a useful device to illustrate a multistage probability problem. When used in a decision analysis application, the tree diagram is called a decision tree .

Decision trees are most useful for multistage decision problems, especially decision problems sequenced over time. The decision tree graphically X-rays the decision problem and displays the anatomy of the decision. The decision tree becomes more useful as the decision problem becomes more complex, by focusing attention on the interrelationship of activities and events over time.

In order to properly clarify interpretation of the tree, decision points are represented by squares while chance points, points over which the decision maker has no control, are represented by circles. At the base of the tree are the available first-stage alternatives. From each alternative, the decision tree constructs the chronological path, leading through chance points and other decision points, to each assumed possible terminal outcome. Payoffs associated with each path and probabilities of occurrence associated with the chance events are shown on the tree.

In Figure 10.1 a decision tree has been used to illustrate the investment problem. Notice that the anatomy of the problem appears on the tree according to how its activities relate over time. Before the investor decides between actions a_2 and a_4 (a_1 and a_3 have been eliminated because of their dominance by a_2), he must first decide whether or not to buy the SCA report at a cost of $\$C$. His stage 1 activity, and hence the base of the decision tree, is the decision problem involving the experimental information offered by the SCA report. Each branch of the tree illustrates a possible sequence of activities from that initial decision to each possible terminal outcome.

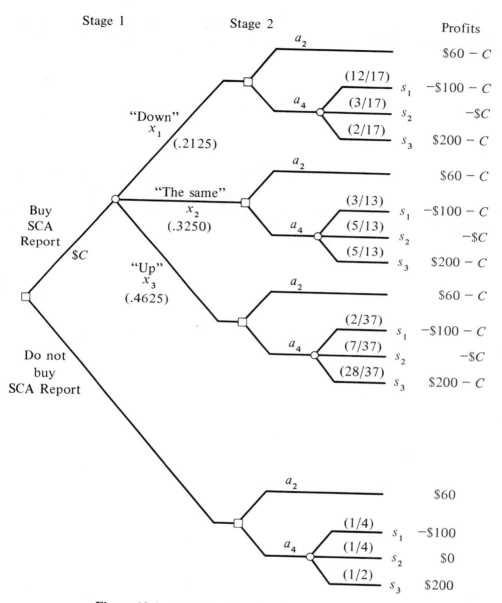

Stage 1

Stage 2

Profits

a_2 $60 - C$

(12/17) s_1 $-\$100 - C$

a_4 (3/17) s_2 $-\$C$

"Down" x_1 (2/17) s_3 $\$200 - C$

(.2125)

a_2 $60 - C$

"The same" x_2 (3/13) s_1 $-\$100 - C$

(.3250) a_4 (5/13) s_2 $-\$C$

Buy SCA Report

(5/13) s_3 $\$200 - C$

$\$C$

"Up" x_3 a_2 $60 - C$

(.4625)

(2/37) s_1 $-\$100 - C$

a_4 (7/37) s_2 $-\$C$

(28/37) s_3 $\$200 - C$

Do not buy SCA Report

a_2 $60

(1/4) s_1 $-\$100

a_4 (1/4) s_2 $0

(1/2) s_3 $200

Figure 10.1   *Decision Tree for the Investment Problem,*
Example 10.8

There is no rigid set of rules for constructing a decision tree. The only
requirements are that the decision tree illustrate the anatomy of the decision problem
while properly ordering the problem activities over time. The decision maker then

has a clear picture of the decision problem and can proceed, working from the terminal outcomes backward toward the base of the tree, to find the set of decisions that best satisfies his objectives.

The Utility for Money

Suppose the owner of a $20,000 home has been informed by insurance actuaries that his home stands a $1:200$ chance of being destroyed by fire during a given year. If the home owner can purchase a fire insurance policy to cover the possible loss of his home due to fire for an annual premium of $150, should he make the purchase?

The payoffs associated with each action available to the home owner are as follows:

	FIRE s_1	NO FIRE s_2
Buy insurance a_1	$-\$150$	$-\$150$
No insurance a_2	$-\$20,000$	$\$0$

His expected gains (payoffs) for selecting each available action are, respectively,

$$E(P_1) = -\$150(1/200) - \$150(199/200) = -\$150$$

and

$$E(P_2) = -\$20,000(1/200) + \$0(199/200) = -\$100.$$

Based solely on expected monetary value criteria, the home owner would not buy the insurance. However, we can be certain that most any rational individual would buy such an insurance policy.

The problem is that it is often inappropriate to perform a decision analysis based solely on expected monetary value considerations. An expected monetary value decision carries the implicit assumptions that the value of a dollar does not differ from one person to the next and that the value of D dollars is equal to D times the value of a single dollar. These assumptions are invalid when we consider that we each have different measures of personal wealth and thus financial limits beyond which we are not willing to venture.

The theory of utility prescribes a method whereby the outcomes of a decision problem can be scaled according to their relative value to the decision maker.

The scaler units collectively describe the decision maker's utility curve. The decision analysis is then performed by substituting utility values for monetary values and computing the expected utility associated with each action. Maximization of utility then ensures maximization of value to the decision maker in terms of how he perceives the comparative personal measures of value of the possible outcomes associated with his decision problem. The actual assessment of utility for an individual is a complex activity involving the quantification of his subjective feelings toward risk and will not be discussed in this text. For detailed discussions of some modern developments in utility assessment, the reader is referred to Raiffa (1968) or Winkler (1972).

Utility measures are needed primarily when the decision problem contains some possible outcomes which, if incurred, may place the decision maker in financial jeopardy. As opposed to adopting a minimax decision, the decision maker may choose to rescale the monetary outcomes according to his preferences and perform an expected utility value analysis. This allows him full utilization of all available resources, including probability measures associated with the uncertain events which the minimax decision ignores, and provides a decision that is guaranteed to maximize his personal interpretation of value.

10.9   Summary

Decision making under uncertainty is characterized by a decision maker selecting from among many alternatives, some of which have uncertain outcomes. He must determine which among the alternatives available to him best satisfies his objective.

Usually the objective is involved with an expected monetary value decision. If so, the decision maker must act as follows:

1. List all possible actions that he may take and all the states of nature that may affect the outcomes of those actions.

2. List the payoffs associated with each action under every state of nature.

3. Determine meaningful probabilities to assign to the states of nature as their likelihoods of occurrence.

4. Compute the expected profit or expected opportunity loss for each action.

5. Select the action associated with the maximum expected profit or the minimum expected opportunity loss, both of which arrive at the same decision.

If additional information is available to the decision maker, Bayes' law can be employed to revise the prior probabilities based on experimental information. The posterior probabilities then reflect all available information, both subjective and experimental, relevant to the likelihood of occurrence of the states of nature.

Exercises

1. How are the decision-making methods of Chapter 10 different from the decision-making methods of Chapters 8 and 9?

2. Discuss the following terms and concepts with regard to our studies within Chapter 10:
    (a) Decision making under certainty
    (b) Decision making under uncertainty
    (c) Opportunity loss
    (d) Expected monetary value decision
    (e) Minimax decision
    (f) Expected value of perfect information
    (g) Posterior probabilities
    (h) Payoff
    (i) Expected value of sample information
    (j) Utility

3. What is the justification for using an expected monetary value objective in decision problems involving uncertainty?

4. For each of the following business-decision-making problems, list the actions available to the businessman and the states of nature that might result to affect his payoff.
    (a) The marketing of a new brand of soft drink in a Midwestern state.
    (b) The replacement of manually operated packaging machines by a fully automated machine.
    (c) The leasing of a computer by a commercial bank to process checks and handle internal accounting.
    (d) Deciding whether or not to bid on a construction contract to build an office building.
    (e) The pricing of a newly developed power lawn mower.
    (f) The investment of a company pension fund.

5. Refer to Exercise 4 and indicate whether the outcomes associated with the businessman's available actions in (a) through (f) are known with certainty or involve uncertainty. Do any of the six decision-making problems involve an exercise of decision making under certainty?

6. A contractor is faced with the opportunity to bid on a construction job to repave 10 miles of a federal highway. From what source does the contractor gather information to help him construct meaningful prior probabilities on the states of nature, namely, which competitors will submit bids, the type of highway to be repaved, and the wear characteristics of the highway? How would he use this information to construct meaningful priors?

7. Gregson owns and operates a small magazine and book store in a town where no other magazine and book store exists ; thus competition is not a problem. However, Gregson must still attempt to gauge the demand for each different magazine and book before ordering.
    (a) Is the problem of estimating the demand level for a magazine or book an exercise in decision making under certainty or uncertainty?
    (b) What information does Gregson consider before determining the number of copies of a magazine or book that he should have in stock?
    (c) If Gregson's objective is to select the inventory level that maximizes his expected profit, how would he use the information obtained from part (b) to place meaningful prior probabilities on the possible demand levels?

8. Refer to Exercise 4 and indicate whether a minimax decision or an expected monetary value decision would be appropriate for each of the decision making situations (a) through (f). Defend your selection in each situation.

9. An owner of a newsstand believes the demand for one of his magazines to be as follows:

DEMAND	PROBABILITY OF DEMAND
4	.20
5	.15
6	.35
7	.30

Each copy costs 20 cents and sells for 60 cents. Assume that he cannot return unsold copies.
(a) Construct the profit table.
(b) Construct the opportunity-loss table.
(c) Find the minimax decision.
(d) Find the inventory level that maximizes the owner's expected daily profits.
(e) What is the owner's average daily profit if he selects the inventory level determined in part (d)?

10. A businessman is trying to decide whether to take one of two contracts or neither one. He has simplified the situation somewhat and feels it is sufficient to imagine that the contracts provide the following alternatives:

CONTRACT *A*		CONTRACT *B*	
PROFIT	PROBABILITY	PROFIT	PROBABILITY
$100,000	.2		
50,000	.4	$40,000	.3
0	.3	10,000	.4
− 30,000	.1	− 10,000	.3

(a) Which contract should the businessman select if he wishes to maximize his expected profit?
(b) What is the expected profit associated with the optimal decision?
(c) Give a practical interpretation for the expected profit from part (b). Is it actually the profit the businessman can expect if he selects the "optimal" contract?

11. A retail trade association is considering publishing a quarterly trade journal describing the activities of the firms within their association. The journal is a feasible undertaking only if a sufficient number of members agree to subscribe. The association believes that the following probabilities adequately represent the chance that a given percentage of the trade association membership will subscribe to the journal:

Percentage	p	.30	.40	.50	.60
Probability	$P(p)$	.1	.3	.4	.2

$7 + 5 = 13$

Suppose there are 1,000 members in the trade association and that fixed costs of printing the journal will amount to $160 per quarter with a variable cost of $.25 per journal. How much would the trade association have to charge per journal in order to break even?

12. The Chemical Corporation is interested in determining the potential loss on a binding purchase contract that will be in effect at the end of the fiscal year. The corporation produces a chemical compound which deteriorates and must be discarded if it is not sold by the end of the month during which it was produced. The total variable cost of the manufactured compound is $25 per unit and it is sold for $40 per unit. The compound can be purchased from a competitor for $40 per unit plus $5 freight per unit. It is estimated that failure to fill orders would result in the complete loss of customers placing orders for the compound. The corporation has sold the compound for the past 30 months. Demand has been irregular and sales per month during this time have been

UNITS SOLD PER MONTH	NUMBER OF MONTHS
4,000	6
5,000	15
6,000	9

(a) Find the probability of sales of 4,000, 5,000, or 6,000 units in any month.
(b) Assuming that all orders will be filled, construct the profit table and the opportunity-loss table.
(c) What is the expected monthly income of the corporation if 5,000 units are manufactured every month and all orders are filled?
(d) What is the inventory level that maximizes the corporation's expected monthly income?

13. George Smith will buy a 1-year term life insurance policy from either firm A or firm B. Firm A offers a $10,000 policy for $200, while firm B offers a $25,000 policy for $250. Actuarial tables suggest that those of Smith's age have a probability of .99 of living through the next year.
(a) Construct Smith's payoff (profit) table, listing the actions that he may take and the states of nature that may result.
(b) Which policy maximizes Smith's expected gain?
(c) Recalling our discussion of similar problems from Section 5.6, criticize the premiums placed on each of the policies.

14. A building contractor is considering whether or not to submit a bid on a contract to build a large, modern apartment complex. Analysis of the proposed plan and other preliminary planning required by the contractor and his firm before submitting a bid on this contract would cost the building firm $50,000. If they bid, they will submit a bid large enough to realize a $250,000 profit for themselves (including the cost of preliminary planning). If the contractor's objective is to maximize his expected profit, how large must be the probability of his winning the contract before he will decide to submit a bid on the apartment contract?

15. A manufacturer of electric power tools is contemplating the purchase of $\frac{1}{4}$-horsepower electric motors from a Japanese manufacturer. The motors are currently produced internally and, from experience, it is known that about 97 percent of all internally produced motors are nondefective. The product from the Japanese manufacturer,

although available at a unit cost of 50 cents less than the cost to produce a motor internally, has an uncertain quality. Based on best available information, the following probability distribution describes the quality (fraction defective) of motors available from the Japanese manufacturer:

FRACTION DEFECTIVE	PROBABILITY
.01	.3
.05	.5
.10	.2

The cost to the power tool manufacturer of having to replace or repair a power tool with a defective motor is estimated to be $10 per tool. Assuming that the manufacturer will need 50,000 electric motors during the next year, should he purchase the motors from the Japanese supplier or manufacture them internally?

16. The Electronics Corporation produces electron tubes for use in transmitting equipment. Currently, the principal material used for the tube casings is made of di-essolan. The management is considering the use of tetra-essolan for the casings to be used on production runs where a relatively low proportion of the tubes are defective. Tetra-essolan is more expensive than di-essolan but is also more attractive to the consumer. There is great difficulty determining in advance of a production run what the proportion of defective tubes will be, so it is not certain which would be the best material to use for the casings. After considerable research, the corporation has determined that the following information best describes the relationship among proportion defective, their associated probabilities of occurrence (priors), and the dollar profits per production run using each of the casing materials.

PROPORTION OF TUBES DEFECTIVE PER PRODUCTION RUN	PRIOR PROBABILITY OF PROPORTION DEFECTIVE	CASING MATERIAL	
		DI-ESSOLAN	TETRA-ESSOLAN
.01	.5	$50	$180
.05	.2	80	100
.10	.2	120	70
.20	.1	160	40

(a) If management's objective is to maximize their expected profits, which casing material should they use?
(b) What is the expected profit associated with the optimal decision?
(c) How much would the corporation be willing to pay to know the exact proportion of tubes that will be defective in advance of a production run?

17. A building contractor must decide how many speculative homes to build. Each home would be of the same design and would cost the contractor $20,000 to build. He plans to sell each for $25,000 but intends to auction off unsold homes at the end of 6 months to recover construction costs. Auction prices on homes of the design proposed by the contractor have been bringing $17,500. Suppose that the contractor's prior beliefs regarding the likelihood of selling any number of the speculative homes within 6 months

are as follows:

NO. SPECULATIVE HOMES SOLD WITHIN 6 MONTHS	PROBABILITY
0	.05
1	.15
2	.45
3	.25
4	.10
5 or more	0

If the contractor's objective is to maximize his expected return, how many of the speculative homes should he build?

18. A newspaper publisher is considering distributing a newspaper in Bay City. His potential profits depend upon which of two methods of distribution he chooses for the distribution of his newspaper in Bay City and the proportion of the 50,000 Bay City households that subscribe to his newspaper. The daily profits associated with each method of distribution under every assumed likely proportion of subscribing households are as follows:

NO. HOUSEHOLDS SUBSCRIBING	PROPORTION SUBSCRIBING p	$P(p)$	DAILY PROFITS METHOD A	METHOD B
20,000	.4	.3	$1,000	$1,200
25,000	.5	.5	1,400	1,500
30,000	.6	.2	2,100	1,800

(a) Based only on the above information, what is the best method of distribution for the publisher?
(b) How much would the publisher be willing to pay to know the exact proportion of households who would subscribe to his newspaper?

19. The manager of a manufacturing plant that produces an item for which demand has been quite variable must decide whether to buy a new assembly machine or to have their current assembly machine repaired at a cost of $500. The new machine would cost $7,000 and would assemble finished items at a cost of $.60 per unit, while their current machine incurs a variable cost of $1.10 per unit. Units are produced as demand occurs so that management will not be left with unsold merchandise. The selling price of each unit of production is $2.00 and the manager believes that demand will occur according to the following probability distribution:

REMAINING DEMAND	PROBABILITY
5,000	.2
10,000	.4
25,000	.3
50,000	.1

(a) Construct the profit table, listing the actions and possible states of nature.
(b) If the manager's objective is to maximize the expected profits to the manufacturing plant, what is his optimal decision?

(c) What is the expected profit associated with the optimal decision?

(d) Give a practical interpretation to the expected profit calculated in part (c).

20. Refer to Exercise 19 and suppose that a new machine is also available which would cost $2,000 and incur a variable cost of $1 per unit in the process of assembling a finished unit. Thus the manager can choose from among three machines, two new ones and the old one. If his objective is to maximize the manufacturing plant's expected profit, what is the manager's optimal decision?

21. Refer to Exercise 15. Before deciding whether or not to purchase the 50,000 motors from the Japanese supplier, suppose that the power tool manufacturer obtains a sample of 25 motors from the Japanese supplier, subjects the motors to a rigorous battery of tests, and finds three of them to be defective. Based on the information contained in Exercise 15 and this sample information, should the manufacturer buy from the Japanese supplier?

22. Refer to Exercise 16 and suppose that the Electronics Corporation has decided to select a sample of 25 finished tubes from the production process before deciding whether or not to switch to tetra-essolan for the remainder of a day's production run. Three defective tubes are found in the sample. From the tables for the binomial distribution (Table 1, Appendix), the probability of observing three defectives in a sample of size $n = 25$, given that the fraction defective within the population is p_D, has been determined and is given for each possible value of p_D:

p_D	$P(n = 25, 3 \text{ defectives}|p_D)$
.01	.002
.05	.093
.10	.227
.20	.142

(a) Using Bayes' law, construct the posterior probabilities associated with the fraction defective (p_D) levels.

(b) Incorporating both the prior and sample information, should the Electronics Corporation use di-essolan or tetra-essolan for the casings during that day?

(c) How much would the Electronics Corporation have been willing to pay to obtain the given sample information? Explain.

23. Refer to Exercises 16 and 22. Suppose that during another day a sample of $n = 25$ finished tubes is selected from the process and that two defectives are found. Use the binomial probability tables (Table 1, Appendix) to compute the probability of observing two defectives in a sample of size $n = 25$, given that the fraction defective within the population is .01, .05, .10, and .20. With regard to the sample information of observing two defectives in a sample of size $n = 25$ and their associated probabilities for each p_D level, answer the questions posed in Exercise 22.

24. A sampling plan is defined as a decision rule, whereby the decision maker selects a sample of n items and makes one decision if less than or equal to a defectives are observed but makes a complementary decision if greater than a defectives are observed in the sample. With regard to the results of Exercises 22 and 23, suggest a sampling plan for the Electronics Corporation using a sample size of $n = 25$.

25. Refer to Exercise 18. Suppose that the newspaper decides to conduct a door-to-door survey of a sample of Bay City households before deciding on his method of distribution. If in a sample of 25 households 14 indicate they would subscribe to his newspaper, what is the publisher's best method of distribution?

26.   A publisher is considering marketing a new monthly magazine BLASH (Buy Low and Sell High) with articles and other information of special interest to investors. Based upon past experience and his perceptions of potential demand for a monthly such as BLASH, the publisher has established the following profit table to represent his annual profits under three assumed possible levels of buyer response.

	ANNUAL PROFITS	
BUYER RESPONSE	DO NOT PUBLISH	PUBLISH
Poor (R_1)	$0	$- \$2,500,000$
Fair (R_2)	0	500,000
Good (R_3)	0	3,000,000

The publisher estimates the probabilities of occurrence of the three buyer responses to be $P(R_1) = .5$, $P(R_2) = .2$, and $P(R_3) = .3$. Should the publisher go ahead with the project and publish BLASH?

27.   Refer to Exercise 26. Suppose the publisher recognizes that competition would be very fierce owing to the presence of many current and successful publications dealing with the same subject as BLASH. He thus wishes to test market BLASH and base his decision on information other than his own experience and perceptions. A test market will result in either an unfavorable reaction (O_1) or a favorable reaction (O_2). Based upon historical experience from market tests on other publications, the publisher has established the following conditional probabilities given buyer response:

$$P(O_1|R_1) = .9, \qquad P(O_1|R_2) = .4, \qquad P(O_1|R_3) = .3,$$
$$P(O_2|R_1) = .1, \qquad P(O_2|R_2) = .6, \qquad P(O_2|R_3) = .7.$$

(a) What is the publisher's best decision if the market test is "unfavorable"?
(b) What is the publisher's best decision if the market test is "favorable"?
(c) Construct a decision tree to illustrate the publisher's decision problem.

28.   Shown is a set of utility values that have been assessed for the associated dollar-valued outcomes by a decision maker.

Dollar-valued outcome	$-\$10,000$	$-\$5,000$	$-\$1,000$	$0	$5,000	$10,000	$25,000
Utility	0	.45	.50	.55	.70	.80	1.0

If the decision maker wishes to maximize his expected utility, how should he act on each of the following investment problems?
(a) The investment of $1,000 in an oil drilling venture returning either a $10,000 profit or nothing. The probability of success in the oil drilling venture is estimated to be .1.
(b) The investment of $10,000 in a new motel–restaurant facility. Depending on the success of the project, the investment is estimated to return a $25,000 profit with probability .2, a $5,000 profit with probability .3, lose $5,000 with probability .4, or lose the entire $10,000 investment with probability .1.

References

Hadley, G., *Introduction to Probability and Statistical Decision Theory*. San Francisco: Holden-Day, Inc., 1967. Chapters 3, 4, 8, and 9.

Howard, R., "Decision Analysis: Applied Decision Theory," *Proceedings, Fourth International Conference on Operational Research*, 1966.

Jedamus, P., and R. J. Frame, *Business Decision Theory*. New York: McGraw-Hill Book Company, 1969.

Raiffa, H., *Decision Analysis*. Reading, Mass.: Addison-Wesley Publishing Company, Inc., 1968.

Schlaifer, R., *Analysis of Decisions Under Uncertainty*. New York: McGraw-Hill Book Company, 1969.

Winkler, R. L., *An Introduction to Bayesian Inference and Decision*. New York: Holt, Rinehart and Winston, Inc., 1972.

Chapter Eleven

Quality Control

11.1 Introduction

A product is regarded as acceptable if it coincides with the manufacturer's product description and satisfies the demands of the consumer. For instance, a 16-ounce can of motor oil that contains exactly 16 ounces, or a lot of bolts all $2\frac{1}{2}$ inches long and of the same diameter, would satisfy the manufacturer's specifications and be acceptable products to the consumer. However, 2-pound cans of coffee that contain 25 to 35 ounces of coffee probably would not be acceptable.

Manufacturers are always attempting to improve the quality and design of their product. When they have developed what they consider a superior product, they then seek uniformity in its production. Uniformity gives the consumer a guarantee that quality characteristics of the product are as described by the manufacturer. Indeed, uniformity is demanded by consumers for all goods and services. The manufacturer who does not meet this demand can expect to lose the consumer's confidence and hence lose his business.

Statistical quality control is designed to detect departures from product specifications and to indicate the need for remedial action in the manufacturing process. Literally, quality control is an ongoing control of the outgoing quality of the product.

Two types of variables affect a process, those which can and those which cannot be controlled. The associated variations are called controllable and random respectively. Such factors as machine wear, machine adjustment, and the operator's skill may contribute to the controllable variation and may be detected by a quality-control study. Ideally, if the controllable variation is detected and corrective action is taken, the total variation affecting the manufacturing process can be reduced to only random variation. The process is then said to be in a state of statistical control

Quality control had its origin in Great Britain in the 1920s but did not gain prominence on a large scale until World War II. Then came production goals that exceeded the normal output of American industry and taxed the capabilities of both men and machines. As peak production was achieved, the quality of production dropped and consequently motivated the development of new and efficient methods of quality control. Most of the modern concepts of quality control evolved during this wartime period.

Quality-control techniques are currently used by almost every manufacturing enterprise to minimize internal waste and maintain a uniformly high quality product. Furthermore, applications are not limited to manufacturing processes. They can be applied to assist in controlling error within any process involving a continuous operation. For instance, they can be employed to control the errors of a cashier in a large department store, control a secretary's typing errors, or even control the errors and improve the consistency of an athletic team.

Product quality during the production process is monitored by a control chart. The control chart is based on sample information, measurable or qualitative, extracted from the process at different points in time. If the product is measurable by length, weight, potency, cost, and so forth, its quality is monitored by constructing control charts to plot the means and ranges or standard deviations of the sample information. A control chart designed to monitor a process with measurable characteristics is called a control chart for variables.

A sample for a process whose characteristics are not measurable is called an attribute sample. Sampling industrial products for defectives is the most common type of attribute sampling. Control charts designed to monitor such qualitative data are called control charts for attributes, the most common of which is the p chart. You may wish to refer to Chapter 6 to review the discussion of the binomial experiment and sampling for defectives.

11.2   Control Charts

A control chart such as the one illustrated in Figure 11.1 is a graph on which is plotted a sample average, sample range, fraction defective, or some other sample statistic calculated from samples collected periodically over time. For example, suppose a process fills cans with antifreeze and the observed statistic is the average weight of a sample of five cans. Then the control chart would show the average weight for five cans plotted at equal intervals of time, say each hour, and would yield a series of points as shown in Figure 11.1.

The reasoning behind the control chart is quite logical. When the loading machine is operating properly, the sample means oscillate within a band whose boundaries are located $3\sigma_{\bar{x}}$ from the process mean.* The process mean will depend

---

* Because of the central limit theorem, which states that the distribution of sample means is approximately mound-shaped, and by the empirical rule, almost all the sample means generated by the process will be contained within three standard deviations of the process mean.

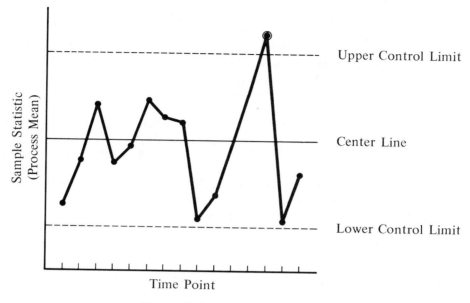

Figure 11.1   *Typical Control Chart*

on the setting of the loading machine, and the distance between the upper and lower control limits depends on $\sigma_{\bar{x}} = \sigma/\sqrt{n}$. For a fixed sample size, $\sigma_{\bar{x}}$ is proportional to σ or, equivalently, the variability in the load per can. If something should happen to the fill machine so that the load per can decreased, the average of the sample of five loads would likely fall below and very possibly more than three standard deviations below the process mean. This would indicate that either we have observed a rare event or something has happened to the fill machine. Thus, a signal is given to the engineers to investigate the process, check the setting on the machine, and make certain that the equipment is operating properly. If, in fact, the process mean or variability has changed, the process is said to be out of control and corrective action is taken to return the process to its original operating condition.

The control chart is characterized by three lines. The central line represents the average value of the plotted statistic for a large number of samples. At least 25 samples of 4 observations each should be used to locate the mean for the control chart statistic, and one must be certain that the samples have been drawn during a period of time when the process is judged to be "in control." The lower and upper lines, called the lower control limit (LCL) and the upper control limit (UCL), respectively, are lines located three standard deviations (of the statistic) away from the center line. Then, based on the empirical rule, values of the sample statistic computed at each point in time should fall within the control limits with a very high probability. If a point falls outside the limits, we have observed an event that will occur roughly 1 time in a 100, or else the process characteristics have changed and the process is judged to be "out of control." Thus the control chart provides a very rough and useful tool for judging whether a process requires investigation and possibly corrective action. Typical control charts are those constructed for the sample mean, the sample range, or the sample fraction defective. The sample mean is monitored to detect a change in the mean of a quality that is characteristic of the product. The sample range is likewise kept under continuous observation to detect shifts in variability of men or machines associated with the process. Similarly, the production manager will wish to keep a check on the fraction defective to make sure that this quantity stays within the boundaries of process capability.

The control chart not only indicates when a process may be out of control but also may suggest the cause of the difficulty. For example, a slowly decreasing sample average quality over time, as shown in Figure 11.2, may indicate that parts of a machine are wearing, or it could indicate fatigue on the part of an operator. Similar comments might also be made if the process mean tended to trend upward over time. A line has been sketched through the points on Figure 11.2 to indicate the trend of the process. In a case such as this, impending trouble can often be detected and corrected before the process is seriously out of control. An upward trend in the range of the sample observations could indicate a tendency toward increased process variation and could again possibly be traced through the process machinery or personnel. Clues provided by the control chart may not be obvious to the layman but will frequently be quite meaningful to the process engineer. He is familiar with the

Figure 11.2   *Control Chart for a Process with a Decreasing Average Quality*

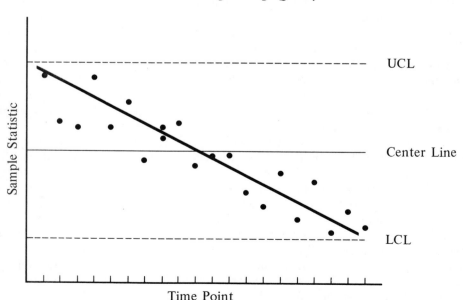

equipment and personnel associated with the process and more likely will be able to identify sources of process difficulty.

One other point is worth mentioning before we proceed to a discussion of specific types of control charts and illustrative examples. You should clearly note the difference between manufacturer's specifications and control limits for a quality characteristic of a product. Specifications are limits on a quality characteristic, set by either the manufacturer or his customer, to identify a good product. Specifications give limits within which the manufacturer wishes a quality characteristic to fall and represent a standard of quality set by either himself or his customer. Generally speaking, a product that does not meet specifications is considered unacceptable and is usually shipped back to the supplier. Thus specifications give limits within which we desire the product quality characteristic to fall. In contrast, control limits are determined by the capabilities of the process and indicate what the process is actually producing rather than what we want it to produce. For example, a customer purchasing cans of antifreeze might specify that loads per can must exceed 31 fluid ounces or be declared unacceptable. This specification interval, 31 fluid ounces and beyond, indicates an interval in which the manufacturer desires the load to fall. In contrast, the fill machine might be set so as to discharge a mean load of 32 plus or minus 1.6 fluid ounces. This interval indicates the distribution of loads that the fill machine is capable of producing as it is currently adjusted and implies that many cans will not meet the process specification of 31 ounces or more.

Specifications can be stated in terms of the actual unit of measurement, for example, fluid ounces of load per can, or they can be given as specifications on some statistics computed from samples drawn from shipments of antifreeze. Thus one might specify that the mean load for a sample of five cans exceed 31.5 ounces.

Figure 11.3   (a)*Process Whose Control Limits Are Contained Within the Specification Interval; (b) Process Whose Control Limits Are Overlapping the Specification Interval*

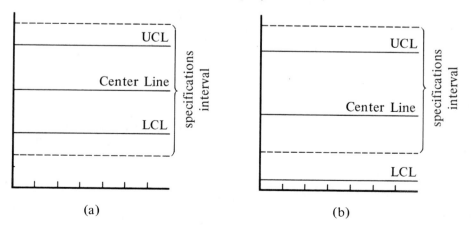

(a)   (b)

Figure 11.3 shows control charts with specification limits superimposed as dashed lines. Figure 11.3(a) is a control chart for a process in which the control limits lie within the specification limits. Almost all the product for this process satisfies the manufacturer's specifications. In contrast, Figure 11.3(b) gives the control chart for a process in which the lower control limit lies outside the specification limits. One would expect this process to yield some unacceptable product.

To summarize, specification limits characterize a product quality goal. Control limits are a measure of reality, that is, a measure of process quality capability.

11.3   Control Charts for Variables

Control charts designed to monitor the measurable characteristics of a production process are the mean chart ($\overline{X}$ chart) and the range chart (R chart). To be consistent with the literature, we shall denote the variable sample measurement by the random variable $\overline{X}$, even though in earlier chapters we have consistently used $\bar{y}$ to represent the random variable. We shall demonstrate the use of each chart by referring to an illustrative example.

Suppose that a corporation that manufactures field rifles for the Department of Defense operates a production line that turns out finished firing pins. Since it is desirable for the rifles to be uniform in operation, the firing pins must meet certain stated specifications. For purpose of illustration, suppose the specifications for the firing pins are that they be 1 inch plus or minus .08 inch in length. To monitor this process an inspector randomly selects five firing pins from the production line, measures their length, and repeats this process at 10-minute intervals.

The control charts for monitoring the average and interval variability of an ongoing production process whose individual items possess measurable characteristics are defined below:

Definition

A mean chart, or $\overline{X}$ chart, is a control chart on which are plotted the means of samples drawn from the production process at equally spaced points in time.

The mean chart provides an ongoing check of the average product quality. However, an average may consist of very different measurements. Thus the mean chart may not tell us much about the interval variability of the process.

Definition

A *range chart*, or R chart, is a control chart on which are plotted the ranges of successive samples drawn from the production process at equally spaced points in time.

The range of a sample is the difference between the largest and the smallest measurement in the sample and it gives a picture of the variability within the process. Suppose, for the firing-pin example, that the quality-control inspector selects a sample whose measurements (lengths of the five firing pins) are .1 inch, .3 inch, .2 inch, 2.5 inches, and 2.4 inches. The range of the given sample is (2.5 inches − .1 inch) = 2.4 inches. A range this wide probably would not be associated with a process in control and would not meet the product specifications of 1 inch plus or minus .08 inch. Hence, even though the average quality for this one sample appears to be acceptable, the data suggest an unacceptable lack of uniformity in the production process.

We might recall from Chapter 3 that a good measure of variability is the standard deviation. In quality-control studies, the size of the sample selected from the process at each sampling interval is seldom as large as 10. For small sample sizes, the range is almost as good an estimator of σ as the standard deviation, and it is much easier to compute. As a consequence, quality-control studies in practice use R charts almost exclusively as a measure of process variability.

Logically at this point one might ask how we construct the UCL, the LCL, and the center line. We shall present the limits most commonly used in practice. From the central limit theorem, Section 7.2, we know that the distribution of sample means is approximately bell-shaped. Hence the control limits within which most sample means will fall are

$$UCL = \bar{\bar{X}} + \frac{3\sigma_x}{\sqrt{n}}$$

and

$$LCL = \bar{\bar{X}} - \frac{3\sigma_x}{\sqrt{n}},$$

where $\bar{\bar{X}}$ is the overall mean of a large set of sample data collected over a period of time, n is the size of the sample selected at each time point, and σ_x is the process standard deviation. As is usually the case, the true standard deviation is not known and should be replaced by its estimate, s_X.*

The UCL and LCL for the R chart are

$$\text{UCL} = \bar{R} + 3\sigma_R$$

and

$$\text{LCL} = \bar{R} - 3\sigma_R,$$

where $\bar{R}$ is the average of all the sample ranges and σ_R is the standard deviation of the range. As before, the true standard deviation, σ_R, is replaced by its estimate, s_R. We should remark at this point that the LCL for an R chart is relatively meaningless as a control. If the range at some point is very small, uniformity, not excess variation within the process, is implied. Since the uniformity is what we seek, corrective action should not be taken when the range of a sample is smaller than its LCL unless the sample mean at that point in time exceeds one of its control limits.

Having estimated the standards our process is capable of maintaining, we then use those standards to monitor the process over time. Standards should be set only when we have obtained enough sample information on the process when it is in control, or else the control limits may not be able to do the job for which they are designed.

> **Example 11.1**   *For the example discussed earlier of the production process manufacturing firing pins, perform a quality-control study by employing both the $\bar{X}$ chart and the R chart to study the sample data. The sample data*

---

* Suppose that we select samples from the process of k different points in time, each sample consisting of n randomly selected items. The sample means will be denoted by $\bar{X}_1, \bar{X}_2, \bar{X}_3, \ldots, \bar{X}_k$ and the ranges by $R_1, R_2, R_3, \ldots, R_k$. Then the overall mean is found by computing

$$\bar{\bar{X}} = \frac{\bar{X}_1 + \bar{X}_2 + \cdots + \bar{X}_k}{k},$$

and the average range is

$$\bar{R} = \frac{R_1 + R_2 + \cdots + R_k}{k}.$$

The standard deviations s_X and s_R are computed as follows:

$$s_X = \sqrt{\frac{\sum\limits_{i=1}^{k} \sum\limits_{j=1}^{n} (x_{ij} - \bar{\bar{X}})^2}{nk - 1}} \quad \text{and} \quad s_R = \sqrt{\frac{\sum\limits_{i=1}^{k} (R_i - \bar{R})^2}{k - 1}},$$

where x_{ij} denotes the measurement of the jth item from the ith sample.

given in Table 11.1 represent 30 samples of five measurements each, selected at 10-minute intervals from the output of the manufacturing process while it is deemed in control. Each measurement is recorded as the difference in one-hundredths of an inch between the actual measured length and 1 inch. Suppose the data were available for only the first 25 time points for use in constructing control charts. Use the data for the first 25 time points to construct an $\bar{X}$ chart and an R chart, and then use the charts to monitor the data from the next five samples.

Table 11.1   *Firing-Pin Lengths*[a]

| SAMPLE NUMBER | OBSERVATION NUMBER | | | | | $\bar{X}$ MEAN | R RANGE |
	1	2	3	4	5		
1	5	3	−1	0	3	2.0	6
2	−1	1	2	1	−3	0	5
3	−7	−4	1	−2	−3	−3.0	8
4	−2	1	3	−1	2	.6	5
5	2	−1	−1	0	−2	−.4	4
6	3	5	1	−1	2	2.0	6
7	1	−4	−2	0	−3	−1.6	5
8	−2	1	2	−1	−3	−.6	5
9	1	−4	−6	−1	2	−1.6	8
10	0	2	−1	3	1	1.0	4
11	2	−1	4	0	−2	.6	6
12	7	0	−3	2	1	1.4	10
13	3	3	−2	1	2	1.4	5
14	−1	−4	2	6	1	.8	10
15	2	0	−5	−2	1	−.8	7
16	−1	4	−2	0	−3	−.4	7
17	−3	−1	−1	−2	0	−1.4	3
18	−2	2	3	−1	6	1.6	8
19	1	1	−2	−3	−2	−1.0	4
20	6	−2	−2	4	0	1.2	8
21	3	1	−4	−2	0	−.4	7
22	−2	5	6	−1	−2	1.2	8
23	−8	−5	0	−1	1	−2.6	9
24	0	−4	2	3	−1	0	7
25	5	−2	−4	0	2	.2	9
26	3	1	−3	2	2	1.0	6
27	−1	6	5	9	−4	3.0	13
28	3	7	2	4	8	4.8	6
29	8	1	−1	3	7	3.6	9
30	−4	2	0	−3	2	−.6	6

[a]The measurements represent the difference, in one-hundredths of an inch, between the actual measured length and 1 inch.

Solution   *The sample mean $\overline{X}$ and the range R have been computed for each of the 30 samples and are listed in the two right-hand columns. The center lines for the mean chart and the range chart are found by computing, respectively,*

$$\sum_{i=1}^{25} \overline{X}_i/25 = .2/25 = .008$$

and

$$\sum_{i=1}^{25} R_i/25 = 164/25 = 6.56.$$

In order to construct the control limits for each chart, we need an estimate for the variance, $\sigma_{\overline{X}}^2$, and the variance, σ_R^2. Employing the formulas for their estimation given earlier, we find

$$s_{\overline{X}}^2 = 7.9493 \quad and \quad s_R^2 = 3.84$$

and the standard deviations are

$$s_{\overline{X}} = 2.82 \quad and \quad s_R = 1.96$$

The upper and lower control limits for the mean chart are then

$$UCL = .008 + \frac{3(2.82)}{\sqrt{5}} = 3.830$$

and

$$LCL = .008 - \frac{3(2.82)}{\sqrt{5}} = -3.782.$$

For the range chart, the control limits are

$$UCL = 6.56 + 3(1.96) = 12.44$$

and

$$LCL = 6.56 - 3(1.96) = .68.$$

Figures 11.4 and 11.5 illustrate the mean and range charts for the data. For the data from the process assumed to be in control, the data from the first 25 periods, no sample statistic appears outside the control limits in either chart. However, at the twenty-seventh time point, the sample range is outside the upper control limit of the range chart, and at the twenty-eighth time point the sample mean is outside the upper control limit of the mean chart. Thus the process may have been out of control at the twenty-seventh and twenty-eighth time points, and action should have been taken to locate the source of the implied controllable variation.

We do not wish to imply that if the process mean is out of control, the range chart will also indicate the presence of an excess of controllable variation. This happens only by coincidence. We can notice in Figure 11.4, though, that the sample averages are much larger than the process mean during the time period from twenty-seven through twenty-nine. Hence the indication of a large, but still acceptable, sample mean and an unacceptable sample range at the twenty-seventh time period might suggest that a change has occurred in the process and the average of the process measurements will soon be out of control.

Finally, we should check to see if the process is meeting the product specifications of the buyer. The specifications state that the firing pins be 1 inch plus or

Figure 11.4 $\bar{X}$ *Chart for Example* 11.1

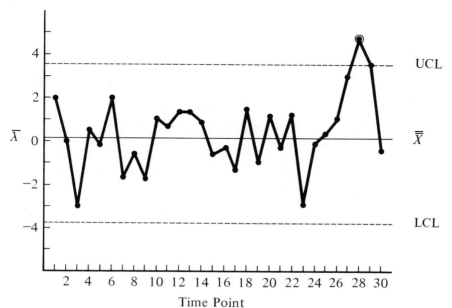

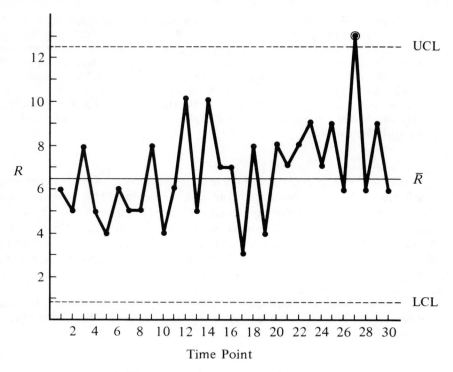

Figure 11.5   *R Chart for Example* 11.1

Figure 11.6   *Specification Interval and Distribution of Process Values for Example* 11.1

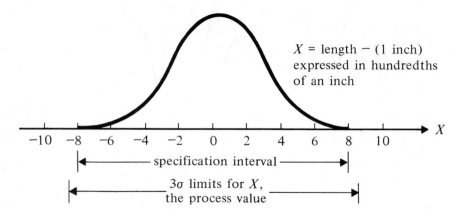

X = length − (1 inch) expressed in hundredths of an inch

specification interval

3σ limits for X, the process value

minus .08 inch in length. Since the sample measurements were obtained as the difference, in one-hundredths of an inch, between the observed length and 1 inch, the specification interval for X will be -8 to 8.

Suppose we know from previous experience that the distribution of firing pin lengths is approximately normal. Then the chance that this process is capable of meeting the stated specifications is found by calculating the probability that a randomly selected firing pin will fall within the specification interval using the normal curve areas, Table 3, Appendix. The probability that the process meets specifications when the process is in control is (see Chapter 7)

$$P(-8 < X < 8) = P\left(\frac{-8 - \mu_X}{\sigma_X} < z < \frac{8 - \mu_X}{\sigma_X}\right)$$

Using the sample variance, $s_X^2 = 7.9493$, to approximate σ_X^2, we have

$$P(-8 < X < 8) = P\left(\frac{-8 - .008}{\sqrt{7.9493}} < z < \frac{8 - .008}{\sqrt{7.9493}}\right)$$

$$= P(-2.855 < z < 2.821)$$

$$= .9955$$

Hence the probability that a randomly selected firing pin does not meet specifications when the process is in control is very small, and it is highly unlikely that the shipment of firing pins will fail to meet the stated specifications of the Department of Defense.

Figure 11.6 should clarify this notion for the reader. As long as the specification interval contains practically the entire distribution of process values, the chances the specifications will not be met when the process is in control are very small.

Example 11.2   *A production process at a food processing plant is designed to fill 1-quart (32 fluid ounces) containers with a mixed fruit juice. A sampling inspector randomly selected four filled containers at each of 25 different points in time and measured their content. From the sample information, he observed the process mean and standard deviation to be*

$$\overline{X} = 30.8 \text{ fluid ounces}$$

and

$$s_X = 1.20 \text{ fluid ounces,}$$

respectively. The individual measurements will not be included within our discussion.
  (*a*) *What are the control limits for controlling the average quality or content of this process?*
  (*b*) *How do we interpret these limits?*

Solution   *The standard line is set at 30.8 fluid ounces (not at 32 fluid ounces) and the control limits are*

$$UCL = 30.8 + 3(1.20)/\sqrt{4} = 32.6 \ fluid \ ounces$$

and

$$LCL = 30.8 - 3(1.20)/\sqrt{4} = 29.0 \ fluid \ ounces.$$

If the average for a sample selected in the future falls outside these interval limits, the process is assumed to be out of control.

11.4   The Proportion Defective Chart for Attribute Data

If our production process consists of items that do not necessarily conform to measurable specifications and can be classified as either "good" or "defective," the $\bar{X}$ chart and R chart are inappropriate. We would find examples of such production processes in an assembly line producing transistors that are either operable or inoperable or an assembly line producing light bulbs that either work or do not work. In each case, an item is acceptable if it meets its intended objective and unacceptable otherwise, with product measure being of minor importance.

The sampling procedure for attribute data is the same as that conducted for measurable data except that the observations assume a different form. A sample of a predetermined size, say n, is selected at each of many different, equally spaced time intervals. For each sample, the proportion of defective items within the sample is noted instead of some measurable characteristic. A specially designed control chart is available for monitoring such a process.

Definition

A proportion defective chart, or p chart, is a control chart on which is plotted the proportion of defectives found in samples drawn from the production process at equally spaced points over time.

The *p* chart is used to control the *proportion of defective units* that are being produced by the manufacturing process. We are assuming that our problem of attribute sampling can be modeled by the binomial distribution. In this section we shall denote the proportion defective observed in a single sample as $\hat{p}$ and call $\bar{p}$ the estimate of *p* utilizing *all available samples*. Thus

$$\bar{p} = \frac{\text{total number of defectives in all samples}}{\text{total number of observations in all samples}},$$

and, as we recall from Chapter 6, if *p* is the true proportion defective at each trial in a binomial experiment, then the standard deviation of $\hat{p}$ is

$$\sigma_{\hat{p}} = \sqrt{\frac{p(1 - p)}{n}} \approx \sqrt{\frac{\bar{p}(1 - \bar{p})}{n}},$$

where *n* is the size of the sample selected at each sampling interval. Applying the central limit theorem (Section 7.2), when the sample size is large, the sampling distribution of $\hat{p}$ can be approximated by a normal distribution with a mean equal to $\bar{p}$ and a standard deviation equal to $\sigma_{\hat{p}}$. Note that $\bar{p}$ is not the true population-proportion defective, but $\bar{p}$ should be very close to *p* if the sample size, *n*, is large (say, $n \geq 50$).

The upper and lower limits for the *p* chart are found by forming the 3σ probability limits around $\bar{p}$; that is,

$$\text{UCL}_p = \bar{p} + 3\sqrt{\frac{\bar{p}(1 - \bar{p})}{n}}$$

and

$$\text{LCL}_p = \bar{p} - 3\sqrt{\frac{\bar{p}(1 - \bar{p})}{n}}.$$

As with the control charts for variables, the values $\bar{p}$, UCL_p, and LCL_p need not be recomputed with each additional set of data, but should be revised periodically to reflect the current state of the process. We should also exclude from the computation of $\bar{p}$ any sample data obtained during a point in time at which the process was found to be out of control and producing an excessively large proportion of defectives. Unlike the procedure with the control charts for variables, we need not have as many as 25 samples before constructing the control limits if the size of the sample selected at each sampling interval is large. In general, the larger the sample size, the smaller the number of samples required; the more samples selected, the smaller the required sample size at each sampling interval.

Example 11.3   *In one of the production lines at an automobile assembly plant, side panel and door windows are produced. A window is categorized as defective if it contains any scratches, cracks, bubbles, or other obvious visual imperfections. A quality control engineer samples the output of the production line once every day by randomly selecting 100 items and noting the number of defectives. The results of the last 20 days are shown in Table 11.2. Construct a p chart and check to see if the process is within control.*

Solution   *From the data in Table 11.2, we have a total of 90 defectives out of 2,000 observations. Thus the average for the process is*

$$\bar{p} = \frac{90}{2,000} = .045,$$

Table 11.2   *Number of Defective Door Windows Observed in Each of 20 Daily Samples for an Automobile Assembly Plant, Example 11.3, Each Sample of Size n = 100*

SAMPLE NUMBER	SAMPLE SIZE	NO. DEFECTIVES	$\hat{p}$
1	100	8	.08
2	100	5	.05
3	100	3	.03
4	100	9	.09
5	100	4	.04
6	100	5	.05
7	100	8	.08
8	100	5	.05
9	100	3	.03
10	100	6	.06
11	100	4	.04
12	100	3	.03
13	100	5	.05
14	100	6	.06
15	100	2	.02
16	100	5	.05
17	100	0	.00
18	100	3	.03
19	100	4	.04
20	100	2	.02
Total	2,000	90	

and the control limits are

$$UCL_p = .045 + 3\sqrt{\frac{(.045)(1 - .045)}{100}} = .107$$

and

$$LCL_p = .045 - 3\sqrt{\frac{(.045)(1 - .045)}{100}} = -.017$$

Since the LCL_p is less than zero, we set it equal to zero. However, the lower control limit for the p chart, like the lower control limit for the R chart, is essentially meaningless because a small sample proportion is an indication that the process is extremely efficient.

Figure 11.7 illustrates the p chart for this example. We note that none of the samples contains a proportion defective greater than the UCL_p. However, we can see that there appears to be a distinct downward trend in the proportion defective

Figure 11.7   *p Chart for Example 11.3*

over time. If, as it appears, the average quality of the process has recently improved, it would be advisable to compute $\bar{p}$ from only the most recent samples. This would give a control chart with closer, more sensitive control limits and one that allows a smaller number of observed defectives before rejecting a process as out of control.

Another way the quality-control engineer may obtain a p chart with narrower control limits is by increasing the size of the sample selected at each point in time. Technically, this is valid because increasing n decreases the size of the standard deviation,

$$\sigma_p = \sqrt{\frac{\bar{p}(1 - \bar{p})}{n}}.$$

It is logically valid because increasing the amount of sample information should also increase the precision of our estimates. Hence the observed $\bar{p}$ from a large sample size should be a more accurate estimate of the true $\bar{p}$ than an estimate obtained from a small sample.

11.5   The *c* Chart

Often, the object of a quality-control study is to monitor the number of defects per unit and not the proportion of units possessing defects. In such cases we may find that a natural sampling unit cannot be identified, the sampling is very complex, or the defects per unit are quite varied in nature. For instance, one might be interested in the number of errors per page typed by a secretary, the number of imperfections in a finished roll of steel, or the number of imperfections in a man's suit. In the latter two cases an acceptable item may be one that contains imperfections, as long as the number of imperfections per unit is small. Quite likely, every roll of finished steel contains at least one imperfection if we consider every possible cause of defect from wrinkles to surface scratches to nonuniformity in thickness.

It is essential that the exact form of the sampling unit, whether it is a natural or an artificial sampling unit, and the exact nature of what comprises a defect be precisely defined. That is, we want to be observing only the number of imperfections per man's suit—not the number of imperfections per suit one day, the number of imperfections on five women's dresses the next, and only the number of buttons missing on each suit the next. The quality of rolls of finished steel would be assessed by sampling a segment of a roll, say the first 10 feet, and noting the number of imperfections.

The number of defects per sampled unit, denoted by the symbol c, is monitored using a c chart.

> **Definition**
>
> *A c chart is a control chart on which is plotted the number of defects per sampling unit from samples drawn from a production process at equally spaced points over time.*

The number of defects per sampled unit, c, will possess a distribution that can be closely approximated by the Poisson probability distribution. This distribution possesses the property that its mean and variance are equal. (Refer back to Chapter 6.)

Like the $\bar{X}$, R, and p control charts, the construction of the c chart is based on the empirical rule. That is, control limits are located $3\sigma_c$ away from the process mean. The center line of the c chart is estimated by the average number of defects, $\bar{c}$, computed over a large number of sampled units, say 100 or more. Since σ_c^2 can be also estimated by $\bar{c}$, we locate the upper and lower control limits at

$$\text{UCL} = \bar{c} + 3\sqrt{\bar{c}},$$

and

$$\text{LCL} = \bar{c} - 3\sqrt{\bar{c}}.$$

Sometimes a manufacturer may wish to construct a control chart for the average number of defects, $\bar{c}$, based on a sample of n units. For example, he might wish to sample $n = 3$ units at each time point and plot the average number of defects per unit. Then the center line and control limits will be

$$\bar{c} = \text{average of the number of defects for at least 100 sampled units,}$$

$$\text{UCL} = \bar{c} + 3\sqrt{\frac{\bar{c}}{n}},$$

and

$$\text{LCL} = \bar{c} - 3\sqrt{\frac{\bar{c}}{n}}.$$

Example 11.4   *The copy editor for a daily newspaper, in an attempt to control copy and typesetting errors, has decided to employ a quality-control study.*

For each of the last 100 days' newspapers, he has randomly selected 10 pages and recorded number of errors. The total number of errors observed on the selected pages of 100 newspapers was 1,360. (a) Construct the c chart by which the copy editor can monitor future error rates. (b) Suppose that the results for the next 20 days are as shown in Table 11.3. Plot the data on the chart to determine whether the process remains in control.

Solution

(a) $\bar{c}$, UCL_c, and LCL_c are calculated as follows:

$$\bar{c} = 13.6,$$

$$UCL_c = 13.6 + 3\sqrt{13.6} = 24.67,$$

and

$$LCL_c = 13.6 - 3\sqrt{13.6} = 2.53.$$

(b) *From the c chart, Figure 11.8, we see that, according to current standards, the newspaper contains an allowable number of errors if the number of errors per 10 pages does not exceed 24. At no time during the last 20 days did the process appear to be out of control.*

Table 11.3   *Number of Errors Observed on 10 Randomly Selected Pages over 20 Consecutive Days for the Newspaper Problem, Example 11.4*

DAY	NO. ERRORS
1	11
2	14
3	20
4	13
5	16
6	14
7	18
8	9
9	19
10	12
11	13
12	7
13	11
14	22
15	4
16	13
17	12
18	10
19	18
20	16

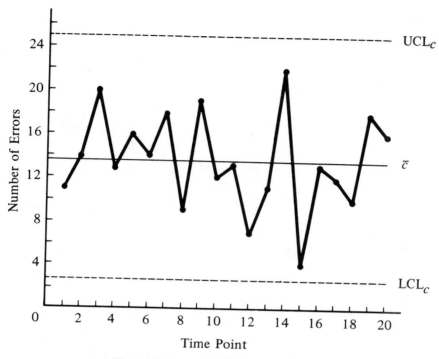

Figure 11.8   *c Chart for Example* 11.4

11.6   Lot Acceptance Sampling for Defectives

A manufacturing plant may be regarded as an operation that transforms raw materials into a finished product, the raw materials entering the rear door of the plant and the product moving out the front. To operate efficiently, a manufacturer desires to minimize the amount of defective raw material and, in the interest of quality, minimize the number of defective products shipped to his customers. To accomplish this objective, he will erect a "screen" at both doors in an attempt to prevent defectives from passing through.

Control of the quality of products shipped to customers is accomplished by the quality-control methods of Sections 11.2 through 11.5. However, control-chart methods are not appropriate for screening incoming raw materials.

To simplify our discussion, consider the screening of incoming raw materials consisting of large lots (boxes) of items such as bolts, nails, and bearings. Diagrammatically, the screen would function in the manner indicated in Figure 11.9. The lots would proceed to the rear door of the plant, would be accepted if the fraction

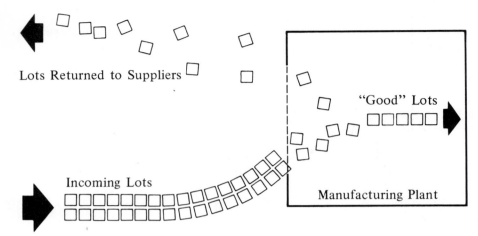

Figure 11.9 *Screening for Defectives*

defective were small, and would be returned to the supplier if the fraction defective were large.

A screen could be constructed in a number of ways, the most obvious and seemingly perfect solution being a complete and careful inspection of each single item received. Unfortunately, the cost of total inspection is often enormous and hence unfeasible. A second disadvantage, not readily apparent, is that, even with complete inspection, defective items seem to slip through the screen. People become bored and lose perception when subjected to long hours of inspecting, particularly when the operation is conducted at high speed. Thus nondefective items are often rejected and defective items accepted. The final disadvantage of total inspection is that some tests are by their very nature destructive. Testing a photoflash bulb to determine the quantity of light produced destroys the bulb. If all bulbs were tested in this manner, the manufacturers would have none left to sell.

A second type of screen, relatively inexpensive and lacking the tedium of total inspection, involves the use of a statistical sampling plan similar to the plan described in Example 6.5. A sample of n items is chosen at random from the lot of items and inspected for defectives. If the number of defectives, y, is less than or equal to a predetermined number, a, called the acceptance number, the lot is accepted. Otherwise, the lot is rejected and returned to the supplier. The purpose of a sampling plan is not to control the quality of the supplier's materials, but to enable the manufacturer to make a decision to accept or reject the supplier's lot. The acceptance number of the plan described in Example 6.5 was $a = 1$.

The reader will note that this sampling plan operates in a completely objective manner and results in an inference concerning the population of items contained in the lot. In effect, the sampler is testing the hypothesis that the population fraction defective, p, is less than or equal to a breakeven proportion, p_B. The breakeven proportion is the value of *p* at which the costs for accepting and rejecting the lot are equal. If the lot is rejected, we infer that the fraction defective, *p*, is too large; if the lot is accepted, we infer that $p \leq p_B$ and acceptable for use in the manufacturing process. A type I error occurs when the manufacturer rejects the lot and actually *p* is small and less than p_B. This leads to the shipment of a "good" lot back to the supplier and as a consequence a financial loss to him. The probability of a type I error is frequently called the producer's risk.

A type II error occurs when the lot is accepted and when it actually contains a high fraction defective. That is, *p* is actually greater than p_B. The manufacturer accepting the lot (which should have been rejected) receives more defective items than expected. The probability or risk associated with a type II error is called the consumer's risk.

If we suppose the breakeven proportion to be $p_B = .05$, the correct decision would be to

accept the lot if $p \leq .05$,

reject the lot if $p > .05$.

A producer's risk. the probability of rejecting when we should accept, is associated with every value of *p* less than .05. Similarly, a consumer's risk, the probability of accepting when we should reject, is associated with every *p* greater than .05. We

Figure 11.10   *Operating Characteristic Curve for the Sampling Plan*
n = 20, a = 2

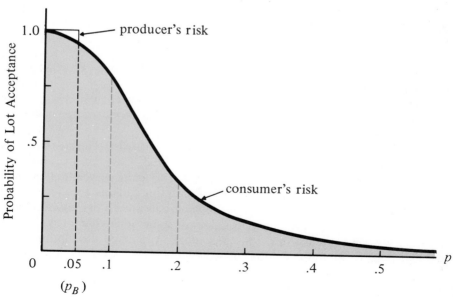

now consider the problem of selecting a sampling plan, that is, a sample size *n* and an acceptance number, *a*, that will correctly accept or reject lots a high fraction of the time and hence ensure that the consumer's and producer's risks are small.

Quality-control engineers characterize the goodness of a sampling plan by calculating the probability of lot acceptance for various lot fractions defective. The result is presented in a graphic form and is called the operating characteristic curve for the sampling plan. The operating characteristic curve for the sampling plan *n* = 20, *a* = 2 is shown in Figure 11.10. The producer's risk and the consumer's risk are shown in the areas in which each apply. Since the operating characteristic curve plots the probability of lot acceptance, the producer's risk is (1 − probability of acceptance) at each value of *p* less than our assumed value for the breakeven proportion, p_B = .05. You will note that the probability of acceptance always drops as the fraction defective increases, a result that is in agreement with our intuition.

For the sampling plan depicted in Figure 11.10, we know we want to accept all lots with a fraction defective less than or equal to *p* = .05 and reject those with *p* > .05. Thus, if the lot fraction defective is *p* = .10 or *p* = .20, we want to reject the lot and return it to the supplier. If the true lot fraction defective is *p* = .10, the operating characteristic curve shows us that the probability is about .70 that two or less defectives in a sample of twenty will be found, indicating erroneously that the lot should be accepted. Hence, if *p* = .10, by employing an *n* = 20, *a* = 2 sampling rule, the manufacturer as a consumer has a 70 percent chance of accepting a lot he should reject. If the true lot fraction defective is *p* = .20, the manufacturer's probability of accepting the lot when he should reject under the *n* = 20, *a* = 2 sampling rule is reduced to about 20 percent. Intuitively, the consumer's risk is less when *p* = .20 than when *p* = .10, since the more defectives there are in the lot, the less likely is the chance that two or less defectives are found in a sample of 20 items selected from the lot, and hence the greater is his chance of rejecting the lots that he should reject.

In order for the screen (the sampling plan) to operate satisfactorily, we would like the probability of accepting lots with a low fraction defective to be high and the probability of accepting lots with a high fraction defective to be low. Ideally, the operating characteristic curve for a perfect decision rule (screen) would be as shown in Figure 11.11. This sampling plan would ensure the decision maker that it would be impossible for him to ever accept or reject in error.

Such a plan is impossible unless we sample the entire lot. The best we can do is to adjust *n* and *a* until an acceptable plan is found. Cost considerations will include three items: the cost of sampling, the cost of rejecting a good lot (and hence shipping it back to the supplier), and the cost of accepting bad lots. Ideally, we would select *n* and place limits on the amount of allowable consumer's risk and producer's risk so as to minimize the largest expected loss or some other characteristic of the mean loss. We omit discussion of this procedure. A detailed description of this approach can be found in the writings of Schlaifer (1961).

Let us consider a less ideal situation to develop the logic in selecting *n* and *a*. Suppose that the maximum sample size we can select is predetermined by the

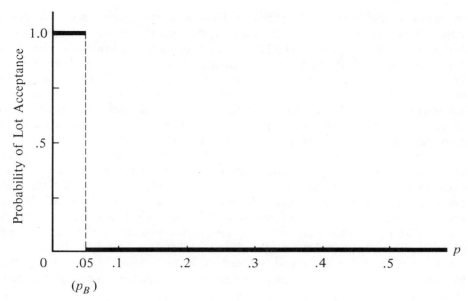

Figure 11.11   *Operating Characteristic Curve for
a Perfect Sampling Plan*

Figure 11.12   *Operating Characteristic Curves for the
Sampling Plans* $(n = 20, a = 0)$, $(n = 20, a = 1)$, $(n = 20, a = 2)$

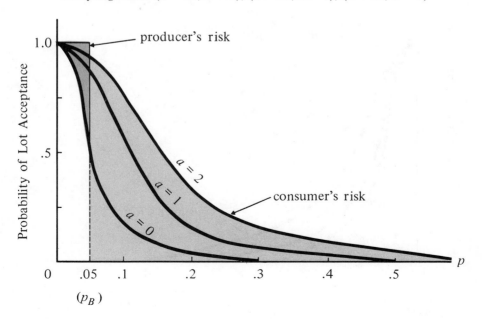

amount of money available for sampling. Thus, we may be given *n* and be forced to adjust the acceptance level *a* to find the plan most suitable to our objectives. For a sample of size *n* = 20, Figure 11.12 shows the operating characteristic curve for the sampling plans with acceptance levels 0, 1, and 2. As we decrease *a*, we decrease the consumer's risk at the expense of increasing the producer's risk. Increasing *a* for a fixed *n* has an opposite effect. So, we see, we cannot always have our cake and eat it, too. For a given number of pieces of data, here *n* = 20, we can squeeze out only so much information. If we wish to decrease the risk in one part of our problem, we must be willing to inherit more risk in another part.

If we increase *n* and adjust *a* appropriately, both risks can be lowered. Figure 11.13 shows the operating characteristic curve for three sampling plans. With each decision rule, the sampling plan calls for us to accept if 5 percent or less of the items are defective. In our assumed example, our breakeven proportion was .05. It need not be true that the sampling plan rejects if the fraction defective within the sample is greater than p_B. All that need be true is that the risks associated with our sampling plan be as small as possible under the given sample size *n*. Logically, the larger the sample size, the more likely will our sample fraction defective be near the true fraction defective *p*. However, large samples are more expensive to obtain than small samples.

Figure 11.13 *Operating Characteristic Curves for the Sampling Plans* ($n = 20, a = 1$), ($n = 40, a = 2$), ($n = 80, a = 4$)

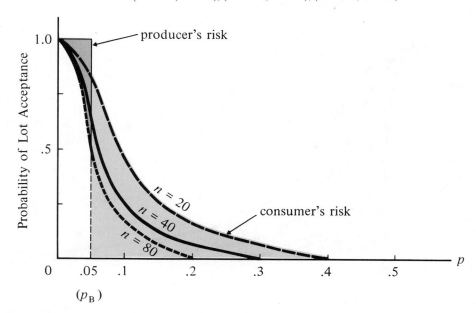

Example 11.5   *Calculate the probability of lot acceptance for a sampling plan with sample size $n = 5$ and acceptance number $a = 0$ for lot fraction defective $p = .1, .3,$ and .5. Sketch the operating characteristic curve for the plan.*

Solution

$$P(\text{accept}) = p(0) = C_0^5 p^0 q^5 = q^5,$$

$$P(\text{accept} \mid p = .1) = (.9)^5 = .590,$$

$$P(\text{accept} \mid p = .3) = (.7)^5 = .168,$$

$$P(\text{accept} \mid p = .5) = (.5)^5 = .031.$$

A sketch of the operating characteristic curve can be obtained by plotting the three points obtained from the above calculation. In addition, we know that the probability of acceptance must equal 1 when $p = 0$ and must equal zero when $p = 1$. The operating characteristic curve is given in Figure 11.14.

Calculating the binomial probabilities is a tedious task when n is large. To simplify our calculations, the sum of the binomial probabilities from $y = 0$ to $y = a$ is presented in Table 1, Appendix, for sample sizes $n = 5, 10, 20,$ and 25. We will use Table 1 in the following example.

Figure 11.14   *Operating Characteristic Curve ($n = 5, a = 0$)*

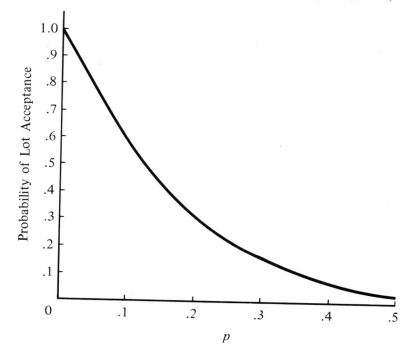

Example 11.6   *Construct the operating characteristic curve for a sampling plan with n = 15, a = 1.*

Solution   *The probability of lot acceptance will be calculated for p = .1, .2, .3, and .5.*

$$P(\text{accept}) = p(0) + p(1) = \sum_{y=0}^{a=1} p(y),$$

$$P(\text{accept} \mid p = .1) = .549,$$
$$P(\text{accept} \mid p = .2) = .167,$$
$$P(\text{accept} \mid p = .3) = .035,$$
$$P(\text{accept} \mid p = .5) = .000.$$

The operating characteristic curve for the sampling plan is given in Figure 11.15.

Sampling inspection plans are widely used in industry. Each sampling plan possesses its own unique operating characteristic curve which characterizes the

Figure 11.15   *Operating Characteristic Curve (n = 15, a = 1)*

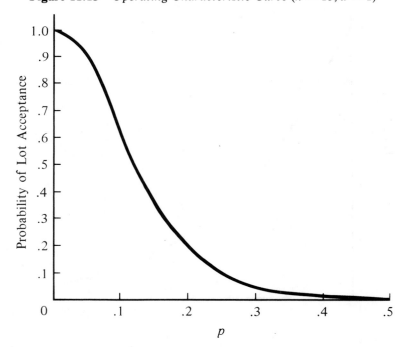

plan and, in a sense, describes the size of the holes in the screen. The quality-control engineer will choose the plan that satisfies the requirements of his situation. Increasing the acceptance number increases the probability of acceptance and hence increases the size of the holes in the screen. Increasing the sample size provides more information upon which to base the decision and hence improves the discriminatory power of the decision procedure. When n is large, the operating characteristic curve will drop rapidly as p increases. You can verify these remarks by working the appropriate exercises at the end of the chapter.

11.7   Lot Acceptance Sampling for Continuous Random Variables

The methods of Section 11.6 assume that each unit of the supplier's lot can be classified as "good" or "defective." If interest is on some measurable characteristic of each unit or an average measure of the entire lot, these methods are not appropriate. For instance, instead of counting the number of defective tires received from the tire manufacturer, an automobile manufacturer may measure the maximum stress in pounds of each tire before failure. Some lots may not be measurable in terms of specific individual sampling units. A construction engineer purchases large rolls of steel cable which must meet stress requirements and a gasoline distributor purchases large shipments of gasoline which must meet octane requirements. In such cases artificial sampling units are built by the construction engineer, who might test the stress of 10-foot lengths of the cable, and by the gasoline distributor, who computes the octane rating in different 1 gallon units from the shipment.

In lot acceptance sampling for a continuous random variable, y, we are primarily interested in monitoring the process mean, μ_y. Two possible values for the process mean are determined, μ_0 and μ_1, such that if the mean is as high as μ_0, we would want the probability of accepting the lot to be very high; if the mean is as low as μ_1, we would want the probability of rejecting the lot to be very high. The value μ_0 is called the acceptable quality level (AQL) and μ_1 is called the lot tolerance fraction defective (LTFD). The second term is somewhat misleading, since with continuous random variables we are not dealing with "fractions defective."

The real or artificial sampling units are selected and our test is the simple test of an hypothesis

$$H_0 : \mu_y = \mu_0$$

against the alternative,

$$H_a : \mu_y = \mu_1.$$

From the central limit theorem, Section 7.2, we know that for samples of moderate size n is large and the sampling distribution of the sample mean, $\bar{y}$, is approximately normal. As we recall from Chapter 8, a test for our hypothesis is to reject the null hypothesis and reject the lot if

$$\bar{y} < \mu_0 - z_\alpha \sigma / \sqrt{n}.$$

Otherwise, the lot is accepted. The standard deviation σ is the standard deviation of all the measurements in the lot and may have to be estimated by s_y, an estimate computed from the sample measurements. The normal deviate, z_α, is the standard normal tabulated value corresponding to α, the probability of rejecting the lot when it should be accepted. Another way of viewing α is that $(1 - \alpha)$ is the probability that we demand for accepting the lot if the true average is as high as μ_0, the AQL.

   The sample size may be selected arbitrarily or selected to satisfy certain probabilities of making correct decisions. If $(1 - \beta)$ is the probability demanded for rejecting the lot if the true process mean is as low as μ_1, the LTFD, then

$$n = \left[\frac{\sigma(z_\alpha - z_{1-\beta})}{\mu_0 - \mu_1} \right]^2$$

is the sample size which guarantees that

1. $(1 - \alpha)$ percent of the time we will accept lots whose process mean μ_y is at least as large as the AQL, μ_0.

2. $(1 - \beta)$ percent of the time we will reject lots whose process mean $\mu_y \le \mu_1$, the LTFD.

Within the formula, σ is the standard deviation of the process measurements, z_α is the standard normal tabulated value corresponding to α (obtained from $1 - \alpha$), and $z_{1-\beta}$ is the standard normal tabulated value corresponding to $1 - \beta$. Essentially, α measures our risk of rejecting lots we should accept, and β, the risk of accepting lots we should reject. If the computed sample size is too large because of economic or other reasons, we may obtain a smaller n by increasing one or the other or both of our allowable risks, α and β.

Example 11.7   *A construction engineer buys steel cable in large rolls to use in supporting equipment and temporary structures during the process of constructing permanent structures. He selects an AQL of 200 lb breaking strength and an LTFD of 180-lb breaking strength. Also, he wants to be 95 percent sure that he accepts rolls of cable with an average breaking strength of at least 200 lb and 95 percent sure that he rejects those with average breaking strength of not more than 180 lb. His sample consists of the breaking strengths recorded from having* *tested 10-foot sections of the cable. What is the "best" sample size and decision rule for the construction engineer? Assume that $\sigma = 50$ lb.*

Solution   *The required probability of accepting the lot when $\mu_y \geq 200$ lb is .95, and the required probability of rejecting the lot when $\mu_y \leq 180$ lb is .95. Thus $\alpha = .05$ and $1 - \beta = .95$, and from Table 4, Appendix,*

$$z_\alpha = 1.645 \quad \text{and} \quad z_{1-\beta} = -1.645.$$

Since $\sigma = 50$ lb, $\mu_0 = 200$ lb, and $\mu_1 = 180$ lb, the required sample size is

$$n = \left[\frac{(50)(1.645 + 1.645)}{200 - 180}\right]^2 = 67.65.$$

Therefore, the decision rule is for the construction engineer to reject lots if the average of 68 sample measurements is less than

$$\mu_0 - z_\alpha\sigma/\sqrt{n},$$

or

$$200 - 1.645\,(50)/\sqrt{68} = 190 \; lb$$

and to accept lots whose average is

$$\bar{y} \geq 190 \; lb.$$

11.8   Other Quality-Control Techniques

The statistical methods used by the practicing quality-control engineer are numerous and varied. We have touched upon only the most basic tools in this chapter. Other quality-control techniques should at least be mentioned to give the reader a complete picture of the capabilities of a quality-control study.

The Runs Test

The nonparametric runs test gives a test for randomness of a sequence of process values over time. If a control chart indicates a long run of sample values on one side or the other of the process standard, the runs test can be employed to determine whether or not the evidence is inconsistent with the assumption that the sample values are distributed randomly about the process standard. For instance, if the runs test indicates that the average quality of the process is deteriorating over time, corrective action should be taken to control the average quality before the process is out of control. A decreasing fraction defective in the *p* chart might indicate the beneficial effects of a quality-control study. The student is encouraged to read Section 17.7 at this time to gain a better appreciation for the use of a runs test in a quality-control study.

Sequential Sampling

In the lot acceptance sampling problem for attribute data, an (n, a) decision rule is adopted which states that we will sample *n* items and accept the lot if we observe *a* or fewer defectives. In sequential sampling, the items are selected one at a time. After each item is selected, a decision is made to accept the lot, to reject the lot, or to select another item. A sequential sampling plan allows the sampling inspector to reach a final decision to accept or reject the lot with, on the average, fewer total observations than the conventional (n, a) method. However, the savings in sampling may be more than offset by the computational difficulties required by the sequential rule. Those interested in exploring the details of sequential sampling should refer to Grant (1964).

AOQ Studies

Suppose that every incoming lot from the supplier has a fraction defective, *p*. Furthermore, assume that lots which are rejected by the sampling plan are submitted to 100 percent sampling such that every defective is replaced by a nondefective item from the supplier. If the manufacturer applies the same (n, a) sampling plan to each incoming lot, he can expect to accept each lot with a probability of $P_a(p)$ and reject each lot with a probability of $1 - P_a(p)$. That is, $P_a(p)$ is the fraction of total lots accepted by the plan. Since the lot can be viewed as a group of Bernoulli random variables, each being either a defective or a nondefective,

$$P_a(p) = \sum_{i=0}^{a} C_i^n p^i (1 - p)^{n-i}.$$

The fraction defective in each incoming lot will be either *p*, if the lot is accepted, or 0, if the lot is rejected. For all lots received by the manufacturer from the supplier, the supplier's average outgoing quality is

$$AOQ = p[P_a(p)].$$

The AOQ is the long-run average fraction defective for each lot received from the supplier.

The AOQ is dependent upon the sampling plan (n, a) and the fraction defective p within the manufacturer's incoming lots. For a given sampling plan (n, a) the AOQ is small for small and large values of p and tends to increase and reach its maximum near $p = a/n$. The maximum value of the AOQ is often referred to as the average outgoing quality limit (AOQL) of the supplier. The AOQL is the maximum fraction of defective items to be expected in the long run by the manufacturer if he employs a specific (n, a) rule regardless of the value of p

Bayesian Considerations

In our study of control charts we inferred that the control limits form approximately a 99 percent probability interval around the process standard. When the size of the sample selected at each time point is small, which is the common case in the use of control charts for variable data, a 99 percent probability interval allows for a very high probability of a type II error, the error incurred by assuming the process is in control when actually it is out of control. Control limits should be selected that balance the probabilities of type I and type II errors and the losses associated with each. Also, the control limits might be based partly on past information relevant to our process. Bayes' law, Section 4.10, allows us to combine prior information with experimental evidence to construct meaningful probabilities on whether our process does or does not possess an excess of controllable variation.

The Bayesian decision theory concepts of Chapter 10 can also be applied to the lot acceptance sampling problem. The possible levels of the fraction defective, p, are assumed to be the states of nature in a decision problem to which we assign a (possibly subjective) probability distribution. The decision to accept or reject the lot may be made with or without the aid of sample information selected from the lot. The decision theory approach allows the decision maker to incorporate information relevant to the value of p into the model. However, the method also requires the decision maker to determine the losses associated with taking the action to accept or reject the lot at each possible value of p, often an excessively difficult task. The details of the decision theory approach to lot acceptance sampling are given in Schlaifer (1961).

11.9   Summary

Quality-control techniques are employed to identify the presence of controllable variations within the production process. An excess of controllable variation may be accompanied by a lack of uniformity in the product design, a deterioration in its average quality, or, in the case of attribute data, an increase in the fraction of defective items produced. A quality-control chart can tell us, with a high degree of assurance, when an excess of controllable variation exists, but it cannot identify the factors within the process responsible for this excess.

The decision to accept or reject an incoming lot from a supplier is determined by a sampling plan (n, a). By this plan, n items are selected randomly from the incoming lot and a decision is made to accept the lot if less than or equal to a defectives are found. The (n, a) sampling plan is selected which strikes a fair balance between the risk to the producer of having a good lot rejected and the risk to the consumer of accepting a bad lot.

Exercises

1. Distinguish between quality control and inspection.

2. Distinguish between controllable variation and random variation in an ongoing production process.

3. Discuss the following terms with regard to our study of quality-control methods:
   (a) The center line of a control chart.
   (b) The upper and lower control limits of a control chart.
   (c) An ongoing production process that has been found to be out of control.
   (d) An (n, a) sampling plan.
   (e) An operating characteristics curve for a sampling plan.
   (f) The AQL and LTFD.
   (g) A sequential sampling plan.

4. What would be the intent of a study and what statistics would be measured using each of the following types of quality-control charts? Give an example of a business problem where each chart would be useful in a quality-control study.
   (a) An $\bar{X}$ chart.
   (b) An R chart.
   (c) A p chart.
   (d) A c chart.

5. A bottle manufacturer has observed that over a period of time when his manufacturing process was assumed to be in control, the average weight of the finished bottles was 5.2 ounces with a standard deviation of .3 ounce. The observed data were gathered in samples of six bottles selected from the production process at 50 points in time. The average range of all the samples was found to be .6 ounce and the standard deviation of ranges was .2. During each of the next 5 days, samples of size $n = 6$ were selected from the manufacturing process, with the following results:

DAY	$\bar{X}$	R
1	5.70	.43
2	5.32	.51
3	6.21	1.25
4	6.09	.98
5	5.63	.60

(a) Construct the $\bar{X}$ chart and the R chart from the data during which the process was assumed to be in control and plot data for the last 5 days.

(b) Use the control charts constructed in part (a) to monitor the process for the simple data from the next 5 days.

(c) Does the production of bottles appear to be out of control during any of these 5 days? Interpret your results.

6. Refer to Exercise 5 and suppose that past experience has shown the distribution of weights to be approximately normal. Suppose that a soft drink bottler specifies that the bottles he purchases from the manufacturer must weigh at least 4.8 ounces but not more than 5.5 ounces each. If the manufacturing process is in control, find:
(a) The probability that a single bottle will meet the stated specifications.
(b) The number of bottles in a shipment of 10,000 bottles from the manfacturer that can be expected not to meet the bottler's stated specifications.

7. A quality-control engineer wants to establish an $\bar{X}$ chart and an R chart to monitor the production of a precision instrument. Every hour, during a time when the production process is known to be in control, the engineer randomly selected five instruments from the production process and measured their thicknesses. After 25 hours the sum of his 125 thickness measurements totaled 305 mm, the sum of the 25 range measurements totaled 42 mm, and the standard deviations for the measurements and their ranges were, respectively, $s_x = .42$ mm and $s_R = .5$.
(a) Construct the control limits and the center line for the $\bar{X}$ chart and the R chart based on the above data.
(b) How great would the mean of a sample of five measurements have to be before the production process would be assumed to be out of control? Does the range value also have to exceed its control limits at the same time that a mean value does for a process to be assumed out of control?

8. A buyer of precision instruments from the manufacturer described within Exercise 7 specifies that all instruments he buys must have thicknesses not in excess of 3 mm. If he buys a lot of 1,000 of the precision instruments from the manufacturer during a time when the manufacturer's production process is in control:
(a) If past experience indicates that the distribution of thicknesses is approximately normal, what is the probability that a single instrument will meet his specifications?
(b) What is the expected number of instruments in the lot that will meet the buyer's specifications?

9. The following table lists the number of defective 60-watt light bulbs found in samples of 100 light bulbs selected over 25 days from a manufacturing process. Assume that during these 25 days the manufacturing process was not producing an excessively large fraction of defectives.

DAY	DEFECTIVES	DAY	DEFECTIVES
1	4	14	4
2	2	15	0
3	5	16	2
4	8	17	3
5	3	18	1
6	4	19	4
7	4	20	0
8	5	21	2
9	6	22	2
10	1	23	3
11	2	24	5
12	4	25	3
13	3		

(a) Construct a *p* chart to monitor the manufacturing process and plot the data.

(b) How large must the fraction of defective items be in a sample selected from the manufacturing process before the process is assumed to be out of control?

(c) During a given day suppose that a sample of 100 items is selected from the manufacturing process and that 15 defective bulbs are found. If a decision is made to shut down the manufacturing process in an attempt to locate the source of the implied controllable variation, explain how this decision might lead to erroneous conclusions.

10.   A hardware store chain purchases large shipments of light bulbs from the manufacturer described in Exercise 9 and specifies that each shipment must contain no more than 4 percent defectives. When the manufacturing process is in control, what is the probability that the hardware store's specifications are met after selecting a sample of $n = 100$ bulbs?

11.   Refer to Exercise 9. During a given week, the numbers of defective bulbs in each of 5 samples of 100 were found to be 2, 4, 9, 7, and 11. Is there reason to believe that the production process has been producing an excess proportion of defectives at any time during the week?

12.   A production process yields a long-run fraction defective of .03 when within control. Once each hour, 100 items are selected from the production process, their measurements are recorded, and the fraction of defectives is noted.

(a) Construct the control limits for the *p* chart to monitor the production process.

(b) Suppose that the true fraction of defectives within the production process suddenly shifts to .06. What is the probability that the shift will be detected in the first sample selected from the production process?

13.   A manufacturing process is designed to produce electron tubes and is known to have an average defective rate of 5 percent when in control. A buyer of electron tubes from the manufacturer specifies that shipments he receives must contain no more than 7 percent defectives. If the buyer places an order for 100 electron tubes at a time when the manufacturing process is known to be in control, what is the probability that his specifications will be met?

14.   The following represent the number of imperfections (scratches, chips, cracks, blisters) noted in 25 finished (4 × 8) walnut wall panels : 7, 5, 4, 10, 9, 5, 6, 3, 8, 8, 3, 5, 4, 9, 3, 3, 2, 4, 1, 5, 7, 3, 2, 6, 3. The total number of defects on 75 finished panels previously inspected was 375.

(a) Assume that the manufacturing process was in statistical control during the period when the above data were gathered and construct a *c* chart to monitor the process (use the total number of defects for the 100 panels to construct the chart). Plot the number of defects listed above for the 25 panels.

(b) If one wall panel is found to have more imperfections than the upper control limit allows, should the quality-control engineer assume that the manufacturing process is out of control, or should he wait until he finds repeated panels with an excessive number of imperfections before he assumes that the process is out of control? Explain.

15.   A quality-control engineer wishes to study the alternative sampling plans $n = 5, a = 1$ and $n = 25, a = 5$. On the same sheet of graph paper, construct the operating characteristic curve for both plans, making use of acceptance probabilities at $p = .05, p = .10, p = .20, p = .30,$ and $p = .40$ in each case.

(a) If you were a seller producing lots with fraction defective ranging from $p = 0$ to $p = .10$, which of the two sampling plans would you prefer?

(b) If you were a buyer wishing to be protected against accepting lots with fraction defective exceeding $p = .30$, which of the two sampling plans would you prefer?

16. A radio and television manufacturer who buys large lots of transistors from an electronics supplier wishes to accept all lots for which the fraction defective is less than 6 percent. The manufacturer's sampling inspector selects $n = 25$ transistors from each lot shipped by the supplier and notes the number of defectives.

    (a) On the same sheet of graph paper, construct the operating characteristic curves for the sampling plans $n = 25$, $a = 1$, 2, and 3.

    (b) Which sampling plan best protects the supplier from having acceptable lots rejected and returned by the manufacturer?

    (c) Which sampling plan best protects the manufacturer from accepting lots for which the fraction of defectives exceeds 6 percent?

    (d) How might the sampling inspector arrive at an acceptance level that compromises between the risk to the producer and the risk to the consumer?

17. A buyer and a seller agree to use sampling plan ($n = 15$, $a = 1$) or sampling plan ($n = 10$, $a = 0$.) Under each of these plans, determine the probability that the buyer would accept the lot if the fraction defective of the lot is

    (a) $p = .05$ (b) $p = .10$ (c) $p = .20$

    (d) $p = .40$ (e) $p = 1.0$

    Construct the operating characteristic curve for each of the plans.

18. (a) How does the sample size affect the operating characteristics curve?

    (b) Holding the sample size fixed, how is the operating characteristics curve affected by increasing the acceptance number, a?

19. Refer to Exercise 16 and assume that the manufacturer wishes the probability to be at least .90 of his accepting lots containing 1 percent defective and the probability to be about .90 of rejecting any lot with 10 percent or more defective. If the manufacturer's sampling inspector samples $n = 25$ items from the supplier's incoming shipments, what is the acceptance level (a) that meets the above requirements?

20. An independent gasoline distributor purchases gasoline by the tanker load from the major oil companies. However, he suspects that the major oil companies often attempt to ship him a gasoline of inferior grade and keep the higher-quality gasoline for their own franchised stations. As a check on the octane level of each incoming shipment, the distributor selects 1-quart units from the tanker and measures the octane rating of each unit. If he wishes the probability to be at least .90 that he rejects a shipment whose octane rating is 90 or less and wishes the probability to be at least .90 that he accepts shipments whose rating is 95 or more, find the sample size and decision rule that meet the distributor's demands. Assume from past experience that it is known that the standard deviation of octane ratings is 8.1.

21. An aircraft manufacturer purchases rivets in lots of 50,000 from a supplier. To be usable, all rivets must be approximately 1 inch in length. The manufacturer wishes to accept lots whose rivets have an average length of 1.0 inch with a probability of .98 and to reject with a probability of .95 any lot whose average rivet length is either below .9 inch or above 1.1 inches. Past experience suggests the standard deviation of rivet lengths from the supplier is .12 inch. Find the sample size and decision rule that meet the manufacturer's demands.

22. Suppose that every incoming lot from a supplier has a fraction defective of 5 percent and assume that lots which are rejected by the manufacturer's sampling plan are submitted to 100 percent inspection such that every defective is replaced by a nondefective item from the supplier. Find the average outgoing quality for the sampling plans:

    (a) $n = 25$, $a = 1$ (b) $n = 25$, $a = 2$

    (c) $n = 20$, $a = 1$ (d) $n = 10$, $a = 1$

References

Cowden, D. J., *Statistical Methods in Quality Control*. Englewood Cliffs, N.J.: Prentice-Hall, Inc., 1957.

Duncan, A. J., *Quality Control and Industrial Statistics*. 3rd ed. Homewood, Ill.: Richard D. Irwin, Inc., 1965.

Grant, E. L., *Statistical Quality Control*, 3rd ed. New York: McGraw-Hill Book Company, 1964.

Hadley, G., *Introduction to Business Statistics*. San Francisco: Holden-Day, Inc., 1968.

Schlaifer, R., *Introduction to Statistics for Business Decisions*. New York: McGraw-Hill Book Company, 1961.

Chapter Twelve

Linear Regression and Correlation

12.1   Introduction

An estimation problem of particular importance in almost any field of study is the problem of *forecasting*, or *predicting*, the value of a process variable from known, related variables. Practical examples of prediction problems are numerous in business, industry, and the sciences. The stockbroker wishes to predict stock market behavior as a function of a number of "key indices" which are observable. The sales manager of a chain of retail stores wishes to predict the monthly sales volume of each store from the number of credit customers and the amount spent on advertising. The manager of a manufacturing plant would like to relate yield of a chemical to a number of process variables. He will then use the prediction equation to find the settings for the controllable process variables that would provide the maximum yield of the chemical. The personnel director of a corporation, like the admissions director of a university, wishes to test and measure individual characteristics so that he may hire the person best suited for a job. The political scientist may wish to relate success in a political campaign to the characteristics of a candidate, his opposition, and various campaign issues and promotional techniques. Certainly, all the prediction problems are, in many respects, one and the same.

The statistical approach to each problem is, in a sense, a formalization of the procedure we might follow intuitively. Suppose that a security analyst is attempting to predict the price of a firm's securities on the securities market from the Dow Jones Industrial Average, the prime interest rate, and the sales volume for the firm over the past month. He could expect the security price to rise as the Dow Jones Average and the sales volume rise. However, a rise in the prime interest rate would tend to drive money out of the securities market and into the more risk-free investments and hence would be accompanied by a decrease in security prices. Even though each of the above variables seems to individually influence the security price in some way, when observed together these variables may have an interactive effect which influences the security price differently from the way either does alone. For instance, how would a firm's security price be affected if a rise in sales volume were accompanied by an increase in the prime interest rate? The true relationship in this case could probably best be seen by introducing another variable into the model, say the amount of new debt undertaken by the firm in the past month, which would be related to both the prime interest rate and the sales volume. Carrying this line of thought to the ultimate and idealistic extreme, we would expect the price of a firm's securities to be a mathematical function of the foregoing variables plus any others that may influence price and be easily measurable. Ideally, we would like to possess a mathematical equation that relates the price of a particular firm's securities to all relevant variables so that the equation could be used for prediction.

Observe that the problem we have defined is of a very general nature. We are interested in a random variable, y, that is related to a number of independent predictor variables, $x_1, x_2, x_3, \ldots$. The variable y for our example would be the price of a particular firm's securities at a point in time, and the independent predictor variables might be

$$x_1 = \text{Dow Jones Industrial Average,}$$

$$x_2 = \text{prime interest rate,}$$

$$x_3 = \text{last month's retail sales volume,}$$

and so on. The ultimate objective would be to measure $x_1, x_2, x_3, \ldots$ for a particular firm, substitute these values into the prediction equation, and thereby predict the

Table 12.1   *Advertising Expenditures and Sales Volumes for the Morgan Company During 10 Randomly Selected Months*

MONTH	ADVERTISING EXPENDITURES x (IN THOUSANDS OF DOLLARS)	SALES VOLUME y (IN THOUSANDS OF DOLLARS)
1	1.2	101
2	.8	92
3	1.0	110
4	1.3	120
5	.7	90
6	.8	82
7	1.0	93
8	.6	75
9	.9	91
10	1.1	105

price of the firm's securities. In order to accomplish this end, we must first locate the related variables $x_1, x_2, x_3, \ldots$ and obtain a measure of the strength of their relationship to y. Then we must construct a good prediction equation that will express y as a function of the selected independent, predictor variables.

In this chapter we shall be concerned primarily with the reasoning involved in acquiring a prediction equation based upon one or more independent variables. We shall restrict our attention to the simple problem of predicting y as a linear function of a single variable and observe that the solution for the multivariate problem, for example predicting the price of a firm's securities, will consist of a generalization of our technique. Since the methodology for the multivariate predictor is fairly complex, as will later become apparent, it is omitted from the discussion.

12.2   A Simple Linear Probabilistic Model

We shall introduce our topic by considering the problem of predicting the gross monthly sales volume for the Morgan Company, a large, metropolitan, retail hardware store. As the predictor variable we shall use the amount spent by the Morgan Company on advertising during the month of interest. As noted in Section 12.1, we wish to determine whether advertising is actually worthwhile—that is, whether advertising is actually related to the firm's sales volume—and, in addition, we wish to obtain an equation that may be useful for prediction purposes. The evidence, presented in Table 12.1, represents a sample of advertising expenditures and the associated sales volumes for the Morgan Company during 10 randomly selected months during which they were in operation. We shall assume that the advertising expenditures and sales volumes for these 10 months constitute a random sample of measurements for all past and immediate future months' operations for the Morgan Company.

Our initial approach to the analysis of the data of Table 12.1 is to plot the data as points on a graph, representing a month's sales volume as y and the corresponding advertising expenditure as x. The graph shown in Figure 12.1 is called a scatter diagram. You will quickly observe that y appears to increase as x increases. (Could this arrangement of the points occur by chance even if x and y were unrelated?)

One method of obtaining a prediction equation relating y to x would be to place a ruler on the graph and move it about until it seems to pass through the points and provide what we might regard as the "best fit" to the data. Indeed, if we were to draw a line through the points, it would appear that our prediction problem was solved. Certainly, we may now use the graph to predict the Morgan Company's monthly sales volume as a function of the amount budgeted for advertising during

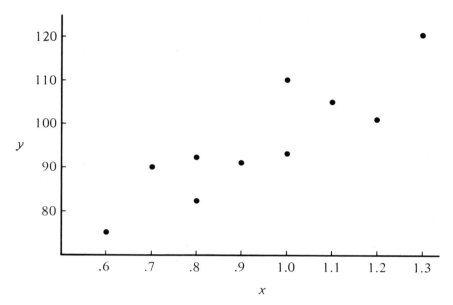

Figure 12.1   *Plot of the Data of Table* 12.1

that month. Furthermore, we note that we have chosen a mathematical model expressing the supposed functional relation between y and x.

You will recall several facts concerning the graphing of mathematical functions. First, the mathematical equation of a straight line is

$$y = \beta_0 + \beta_1 x,$$

where β_0 is the y intercept and β_1 is the slope of the line. Second, the line which we may graph corresponding to any linear equation is unique. Each equation will correspond to only one line and vice versa. Thus when we draw a line through the points, we have automatically chosen a mathematical equation,

$$y = \beta_0 + \beta_1 x,$$

where β_0 and β_1 have unique numerical values.

The linear model, $y = \beta_0 + \beta_1 x$, is said to be a deterministic mathematical model, because when a value of x is substituted into the equation, the value of y is determined and no allowance is made for error. Fitting a straight line through a set of points by eye produces a deterministic model. Many other examples of deterministic mathematical models may be found by leafing through the pages of elementary chemistry, physics, or engineering textbooks.

Deterministic models are quite suitable for explaining physical phenomena and predicting when the error of prediction is negligible for practical purposes. Thus Newton's law, which expresses the relation between the force F imparted by a moving body with mass m and acceleration a given by the deterministic model,

$$F = ma,$$

predicts force with very little error for most practical applications. "Very little" is, of course, a relative concept. An error of .1 inch in forming an I beam for a bridge is extremely small but would be impossibly large in the manufacture of parts for a wrist watch. Thus in many physical situations the error of prediction cannot be ignored. Indeed, consistent with our stated philosophy, we would hesitate to place much confidence in a prediction unaccompanied by a measure of its goodness. For this reason, a visual choice of a line to relate the advertising expenditures to the sales volume would be of limited utility.

In contrast to the deterministic model, we might employ a probabilistic mathematical model to explain some physical phenomenon. As we might suspect, probabilistic mathematical models contain one or more random elements with specified probability distributions. For our example we shall relate the sales volume to the advertising expenditures by the equation

$$y = \beta_0 + \beta_1 x + \varepsilon,$$

Figure 12.2   *Linear Probabilistic Model*

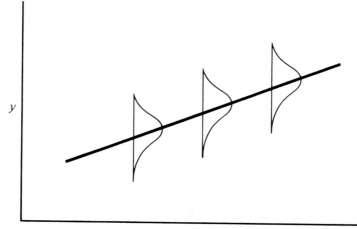

where ε is assumed to be a random variable with expected value equal to zero and variance equal to σ^2. In addition, we shall assume that any pair ε_i and ε_j, corresponding to two observations y_i and y_j, are independent. In other words, we assume that the average or expected value of y is linearly related to x and that observed values of y will deviate above and below this line by a random amount ε. Furthermore, we have assumed that the distribution of errors about the line will be identical, regardless of the value of x, and that any pair of errors will be independent of one another. The assumed line, giving the expected value of y for a given value of x, is indicated in Figure 12.2. The probability distribution of the random error ε is shown for several values of x. Note that σ measures the spread of these identical distributions of random errors.

Let us now consider the problem of finding the prediction equation, or regression line, as it is commonly known in statistics.

12.3   The Method of Least Squares

The statistical procedure for finding the "best-fitting" straight line for a set of points seems to be in many respects a formalization of the procedure employed when we fit a line by eye. For instance, when we visually fit a line to a set of data, we move the ruler until we think that we have minimized the deviations of the points from the prospective line. If we denote the predicted value of y obtained from the fitted line as $\hat{y}$, then the prediction equation will be

$$\hat{y} = \hat{\beta}_0 + \hat{\beta}_1 x,$$

where $\hat{\beta}_0$ and $\hat{\beta}_1$ represent estimates of the true β_0 and β_1. This line for the data of Table 12.1 is shown in Figure 12.3. The vertical lines drawn from the prediction line to each point represent the deviations of the points from the predicted value of y. Thus the deviation of the ith point is

$$y_i - \hat{y}_i,$$

where

$$\hat{y}_i = \hat{\beta}_0 + \hat{\beta}_1 x_i.$$

Having decided that in some manner or other we shall attempt to minimize the deviations of the points in choosing the best-fitting line, we must now define what we mean by "best." That is, we wish to define a criterion for "best fit" that will seem intuitively reasonable, is objective, and under certain conditions will give the best prediction of y for a given value of x

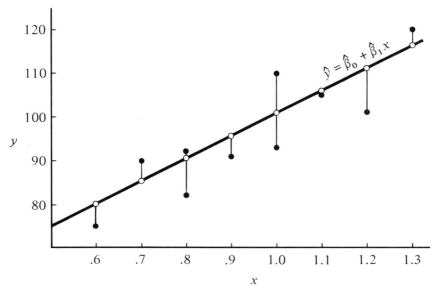

Figure 12.3   *Linear Prediction Equation*

We shall employ a criterion of goodness that is known as the principle of least squares and which may be stated as follows. Choose as the "best-fitting" line that one that minimizes the sum of squares of the deviations of the observed values of y from those predicted. Expressed mathematically, we wish to minimize

$$\text{SSE} = \sum_{i=1}^{n} (y_i - \hat{y}_i)^2.$$

The term SSE represents the sum of squares of deviations or, as it is commonly called, the sum of squares for error.

Substituting for $\hat{y}_i$ in SSE, we obtain

$$\text{SSE} = \sum_{i=1}^{n} [y_i - (\hat{\beta}_0 + \hat{\beta}_1 x_i)]^2.$$

The method for finding the numerical values of $\hat{\beta}_0$ and $\hat{\beta}_1$ that minimize SSE utilizes differential calculus and hence is beyond the scope of this text. We simply state that it can be shown that $\hat{\beta}_0$ and $\hat{\beta}_1$ are the solutions of the following pair of simultaneous linear equations:

$$\hat{\beta}_1 = \frac{\sum\limits_{i=1}^{n}(x_i - \bar{x})(y_i - \bar{y})}{\sum\limits_{i=1}^{n}(x_i - \bar{x})^2} = \frac{n\sum\limits_{i=1}^{n}x_iy_i - \left(\sum\limits_{i=1}^{n}x_i\right)\left(\sum\limits_{i=1}^{n}y_i\right)}{n\sum\limits_{i=1}^{n}x_i^2 - \left(\sum\limits_{i=1}^{n}x_i\right)^2}$$

and

$$\hat{\beta}_0 = \bar{y} - \hat{\beta}_1\bar{x}.$$

These are known as the least-squares equations The calculation of $\hat{\beta}_0$ and $\hat{\beta}_1$ for the data of Table 12.1 is simplified by the use of Table 12.2.

Table 12.2   *Calculations for the Data of Table 12.1*

y_i	x_i	x_i^2	x_iy_i	y_i^2
101	1.2	1.44	121.2	10,201
92	.8	.64	73.6	8,464
110	1.0	1.00	110.0	12,100
120	1.3	1.69	156.0	14,400
90	.7	.49	63.0	8,100
82	.8	.64	65.6	6,724
93	1.0	1.00	93.0	8,649
75	.6	.36	45.0	5,625
91	.9	.81	81.9	8,281
105	1.1	1.21	115.5	11,025
Sum 959	9.4	9.28	924.8	93,569

Substituting the appropriate sums from Table 12.2 into the least-squares equations we obtain

$$\hat{\beta}_1 = \frac{n\sum\limits_{i=1}^{n}x_iy_i - \left(\sum\limits_{i=1}^{n}x_i\right)\left(\sum\limits_{i=1}^{n}y_i\right)}{n\sum\limits_{i=1}^{n}x_i^2 - \left(\sum\limits_{i=1}^{n}x_i\right)^2}$$

$$= \frac{10(924.8) - (9.4)(959)}{10(9.28) - (9.4)^2} = 52.567$$

and

$$\hat{\beta}_0 = \bar{y} - \hat{\beta}_1\bar{x} = 95.9 - (52.567)(.94)$$
$$= 95.9 - 49.41 = 46.49.$$

Then, according to the principle of least squares, the best-fitting straight line (often called the regression line) relating the advertising expenditures to the sales volume is

$$\hat{y} = \hat{\beta}_0 + \hat{\beta}_1 x,$$

or

$$\hat{y} = 46.49 + 52.57x.$$

The graph of this equation is shown in Figure 12.3.
   We may now predict y for a given value of x by referring to Figure 12.3 or by substituting into the prediction equation. For example, if the Morgan Company has budgeted $1,000 for advertising in a month, their predicted sales volume would be

$$\hat{y} = \hat{\beta}_0 + \hat{\beta}_1 x = 46.49 + (52.57)(1.0) = 99.06,$$

or, after decoding, $99,060.
   Our next and obvious step is to place a bound upon our error of estimation. We shall consider this and related problems in succeeding sections.

12.4   Calculating s^2, an Estimator of σ^2

Recall that we constructed a probabilistic model for y in Section 12.2,

$$y = \beta_0 + \beta_1 x + \varepsilon,$$

where ε is a random error with mean value equal to 0 and variance equal to σ^2. Thus each observed value of y is subject to a random error, ε, which will enter into the computations of $\hat{\beta}_0$ and $\hat{\beta}_1$ and will introduce errors in these estimates. Further, if we use the least-squares line,

$$\hat{y} = \hat{\beta}_0 + \hat{\beta}_1 x$$

to predict some future value of y, the random errors will affect the error of prediction. Consequently, the variability of the random errors, measured by σ^2, plays an important role when estimating or predicting using the least-squares line.
   The first step toward acquiring a bound on a prediction error requires that we estimate σ^2, the variance of the random error ε. For this purpose it seems reasonable to use SSE, the sum of squares of deviation (sum of squares for error) about the

predicted line. Indeed, it can be shown that

$$\hat{\sigma}^2 = s^2 = \frac{\text{SSE}}{n-2}$$

provides a good estimator for σ^2 which will be unbiased and be based upon $(n-2)$ degrees of freedom.

The sum of squares of deviations, SSE, may be calculated directly by using the prediction equation to calculate $\hat{y}$ for each point, then calculating the deviations $(y_i - \hat{y}_i)$, and finally calculating

$$\text{SSE} = \sum_{i=1}^{n} (y_i - \hat{y}_i)^2.$$

This tends to be a tedious procedure and is rather poor from a computational point of view, because the numerous subtractions tend to introduce computational rounding errors. An easier and computationally better procedure is to use the formula

$$\text{SSE} = \sum_{i=1}^{n} (y_i - \bar{y})^2 - \frac{\hat{\beta}_1}{n}\left[n\sum_{i=1}^{n} x_i y_i - \left(\sum_{i=1}^{n} x_i\right)\left(\sum_{i=1}^{n} y_i\right)\right].$$

Observe that the quantity in the brackets is simply the numerator used in the calculation of $\hat{\beta}_1$ and hence has already been computed. Furthermore, note that it is desirable to retain a large number of digits (preferably all) in the calculations to avoid serious rounding errors in the final answer.

Substituting into this formula we find that SSE for the data of Table 12.1 is

$$\text{SSE} = \sum_{i=1}^{n} (y_i - \bar{y})^2 - \frac{\hat{\beta}_1}{n}\left[n\sum_{i=1}^{n} x_i y_i - \left(\sum_{i=1}^{n} x_i\right)\left(\sum_{i=1}^{n} y_i\right)\right]$$

$$= 1{,}600.9 - \frac{52.57}{10}\left[(10)(924.8) - (9.4)(959)\right]$$

$$= 373.92.$$

Then

$$s^2 = \frac{\text{SSE}}{n-2} = \frac{373.92}{8} = 46.74.$$

12.5   Inferences Concerning the Slope of Line β_1

The initial inference desired in studying the relationship between y and x concerns the existence of the relationship. That is, do the data present sufficient evidence to indicate that y and x are linearly related over the region of observation? Or, is it quite probable that when y and x are completely unrelated the points would fall on the graph in a manner similar to that observed in Figure 12.1?

The practical question we pose concerns the value of β_1, which is the average change in y for a 1-unit change in x. Stating that y and x are not linearly related is equivalent to saying that $\beta_1 = 0$. We should first test the hypothesis that $\beta_1 = 0$ against the alternative that $\beta_1 \neq 0$. As we might suspect, the estimator, $\hat{\beta}_1$, is extremely useful in constructing a test statistic for this hypothesis. Therefore, we wish to examine the distribution of estimates, $\hat{\beta}_1$, that would be obtained when samples, each containing n points, are repeatedly drawn from the population of interest. If we assume that the random error, ε, is normally distributed, in addition to the previously stated assumptions, it can be shown that both $\hat{\beta}_0$ and $\hat{\beta}_1$ will be normally distributed in repeated sampling and that the expected value and variance of $\hat{\beta}_1$ will be

$$E(\hat{\beta}_1) = \beta_1,$$

$$\sigma_{\hat{\beta}_1}^2 = \frac{\sigma^2}{\sum\limits_{i=1}^{n} (x_i - \bar{x})^2}.$$

Thus $\hat{\beta}_1$ is an unbiased estimator of β_1; we know its standard deviation, and hence we can construct a z statistic in the manner described in Section 8.11. Then

$$z = \frac{\hat{\beta}_1 - \beta_1}{\sigma_{\hat{\beta}_1}} = \frac{\hat{\beta}_1 - \beta_1}{\sigma \bigg/ \sqrt{\sum\limits_{i=1}^{n} (x_i - \bar{x})^2}}$$

would possess a standardized normal distribution in repeated sampling. Since the actual value of σ^2 is unknown, we should obtain the estimated standard deviation of β_1, which is

$$s \bigg/ \sqrt{\sum\limits_{i=1}^{n} (x_i - \bar{x})^2}.$$

Substituting s for σ in z, we obtain, as in Chapter 9, a test statistic,

$$t = \frac{\hat{\beta}_1 - \beta_1}{s \bigg/ \sqrt{\sum_{i=1}^{n}(x_i - \bar{x})^2}} = \frac{\hat{\beta}_1 - \beta_1}{s}\sqrt{\sum_{i=1}^{n}(x_i - \bar{x})^2},$$

which can be shown to follow a Student's t distribution in repeated sampling with $(n - 2)$ degrees of freedom. Note that the number of degrees of freedom associated with s^2 determines the number of degrees of freedom associated with t. We observe that the test of an hypothesis that β_1 equals some particular numerical value, say $\beta_1 = 0$, is the familiar t test encountered in Chapter 9.

For example, suppose that we wish to test the null hypothesis

$$H_0:\beta_1 = 0$$

against

$$H_a:\beta_1 \neq 0$$

for the sales volume and advertising expenditure data in Table 12.1. The test statistic will be

$$t = \frac{\hat{\beta}_1 - 0}{s}\sqrt{\sum_{i=1}^{n}(x_i - \bar{x})^2},$$

and if we choose $\alpha = .05$, we will reject H_0 when $t > 2.306$ or $t < -2.306$. The critical value of t is obtained from the t table using $(n - 2) = 8$ degrees of freedom. Substituting into the test statistic, we obtain

$$t = \frac{\hat{\beta}_1}{s}\sqrt{\sum_{i=1}^{n}(x_i - \bar{x})^2} = \frac{52.57}{6.84}\sqrt{.444}$$

or

$$t = 5.12.$$

Observing that the test statistic exceeds the critical value of t, we shall reject the null hypothesis, $\beta_1 = 0$, and conclude that there is evidence to indicate that the gross monthly sales volume is linearly related to the advertising expenditures.

Once we have decided that x and y are linearly related, we are interested in examining this relationship in detail. If x increases by 1 unit, what is the predicted change in y and how much confidence can be placed in the estimate? In other words, we require an estimate of the slope β_1. The reader will not be surprised to observe a continuity in the procedures of Chapters 9 and 12. That is, the $(1 - \alpha)$ confidence interval for β_1 can be shown to be

$$\hat{\beta}_1 \pm t_{\alpha/2}(\text{estimated } \sigma_{\hat{\beta}_1})$$

or

$$\hat{\beta}_1 \pm \frac{t_{\alpha/2}s}{\sqrt{\sum_{i=1}^{n}(x_i - \bar{x})^2}}.$$

The 95 percent confidence interval for β_1 based upon the data of Table 12.1 is

$$\hat{\beta}_1 \pm \frac{t_{.025}s}{\sqrt{\sum_{i=1}^{n}(x_i - \bar{x})^2}}.$$

Substituting, we obtain

$$52.57 \pm \frac{(2.306)(6.84)}{\sqrt{.444}}$$

or

$$52.57 \pm 23.68.$$

Several points concerning the interpretation of our results deserve particular attention. As we have noted, β_1 is the slope of the assumed line over the region of observation and indicates the linear change in y for a 1-unit change in x. If we do not reject the null hypothesis, $\beta_1 = 0$, it does not mean that x and y are unrelated. In the first place, we must be concerned with the probability of committing a type II error, that is, accepting when H_0 is false. Second, it is possible that x and y might be perfectly related in a curvilinear, but not linear, manner. For example, Figure 12.4 depicts a curvilinear relationship between y and x over the domain of x, $a \le x \le f$. We note that a straight line would provide a good predictor of y if fitted over a small interval in the x domain, say $b \le x \le c$. The resulting line would be line 1. On the other hand, if we attempt to fit a line over the region $b \le x \le d$, β_1 will equal zero and the best fit to the data will be the horizontal line 2. This would occur even though all the points fell perfectly on the curve and y and x possessed a functional relation as defined in Section 12.2. We must take care in drawing conclusions if we do not find evidence to indicate that β_1 differs from zero. Perhaps we have chosen the wrong type of probabilistic model for the physical situation.

Note that the comments contain a second implication. If the data provide values of x in an interval $b \le x \le c$, then the calculated prediction equation is appropriate only over this region. Obviously, extrapolation in predicting y for

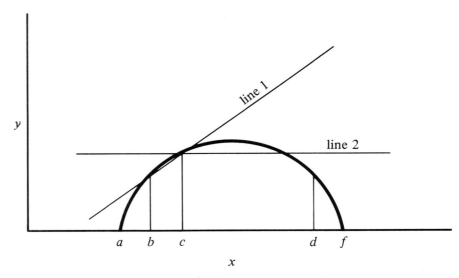

Figure 12.4   *Curvilinear Relation*

values of x outside the region $b \le x \le c$ for the situation indicated in Figure 12.4 would result in a serious prediction error.

Finally, if the data present sufficient evidence to indicate that β_1 differs from zero, we do not conclude that the true relationship between y and x is linear. Undoubtedly, y is a function of a number of variables which demonstrate their existence to a greater or lesser degree in terms of the random error ε that appears in the model. This, of course, is why we have been obliged to use a probabilistic model in the first place. Large errors of prediction imply curvatures in the true relation between y and x, the presence of other important variables that do not appear in the model, or, as most often is the case, both. All we can say is that we have evidence to indicate that y changes as x changes and that we may obtain a better prediction of y by using x and the linear predictor than simply using $\bar{y}$ and ignoring x. Note that this does not imply a causal relationship between x and y. Some third variable may have caused the change in both x and y, producing the relationship that we have observed.

12.6   Estimating the Expected Value of y for a Given Value of x

Let us assume that x and y are linearly related according to the probabilistic model defined in Section 12.2 and therefore that $E(y|x) = \beta_0 + \beta_1 x$ represents the expected value of y for a given value of x. Since the fitted line

$$\hat{y} = \hat{\beta}_0 + \hat{\beta}_1 x$$

attempts to estimate the true linear relation (that is, we estimate β_0 and β_1), $\hat{y}$ would be used to estimate the expected value of y as well as a particular value of y for a given value of x. It seems quite reasonable to assume that the error of estimation would differ for these two cases. In this situation we consider the estimation of the expected value of y for a given value of x.

Observe the two lines in Figure 12.5. The first line represents the line of means for the true relationship.

$$E(y|x) = \beta_0 + \beta_1 x,$$

and the second is the fitted prediction equation,

$$\hat{y} = \hat{\beta}_0 + \hat{\beta}_1 x.$$

[Note that the symbol $E(y|x)$ means the expected value of y for a *given* value of x.]

We readily observe that the error in predicting the expected value of y when $x = x_p$ will be the deviation between the two lines above the point x_p and that

Figure 12.5   *Expected and Predicted Values for y*

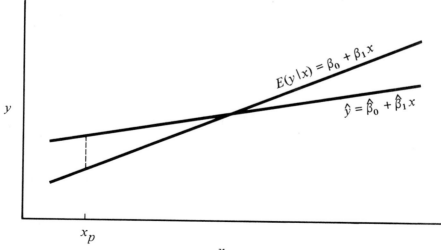

this error will increase as we move to the end points of the interval over which x has been measured. It can be shown that the predicted value,

$$\hat{y} = \hat{\beta}_0 + \hat{\beta}_1 x,$$

is an unbiased estimator of $E(y|x)$, that is, $E(y) = \beta_0 + \beta_1 x$, and that it will be normally distributed with variance

$$\sigma_{\hat{y}}^2 = \sigma^2 \left[\frac{1}{n} + \frac{(x_p - \bar{x})^2}{\sum\limits_{i=1}^{n} (x_i - \bar{x})^2} \right]$$

The corresponding estimated variance of y would use s^2 to replace σ^2 in the expression above.

The results outlined above may be used to test an hypothesis concerning the average or expected value of y for a given value of x, say x_p.* (This, of course, would also enable us to test an hypothesis concerning the y intercept, β_0, which is the special case where $x_p = 0$.) The null hypothesis would be

$$H_0 : E(y|x = x_p) = E_0,$$

where E_0 is the hypothesized numerical value of $E(y)$ when $x = x_p$. Once again, it can be shown that the quantity

$$t = \frac{\hat{y} - E_0}{\text{estimated } \sigma_{\hat{y}}}$$

$$= \frac{\hat{y} - E_0}{s \sqrt{\dfrac{1}{n} + \dfrac{(x_p - \bar{x})^2}{\sum\limits_{i=1}^{n} (x_i - \bar{x})^2}}}$$

follows a Student's t distribution in repeated sampling with $(n - 2)$ degrees of freedom. The statistical test is conducted in exactly the same manner as the other t test previously discussed.

* See cautionary comments in Section 12.5. It is best if x_p lies within the range of the observed values of x.

The corresponding $(1 - \alpha)$ confidence interval for the expected value of y, given $x = x_p$, is

$$\hat{y} \pm t_{\alpha/2}s\sqrt{\frac{1}{n} + \frac{(x_p - \bar{x})^2}{\sum\limits_{i=1}^{n}(x_i - \bar{x})^2}}.$$

For example, if we wish to estimate the average gross sales volume for all months in which the advertising expenditures were \$1,000, or $x_p = 1.0$, we would obtain

$$\hat{y} = \hat{\beta}_0 + \hat{\beta}_1 x,$$

or

$$\hat{y} = 46.49 + (52.57)(1.0) = 99.06$$
$$= \$99{,}060.$$

The 95 percent confidence interval would be

$$99.06 \pm (2.306)(6.84)\sqrt{\frac{1}{10} + \frac{(1.0 - .94)^2}{.444}},$$

or

$$99.06 \pm 5.19,$$

which is equivalent to

$$\$99{,}060 \pm \$5{,}190.$$

12.7   Predicting a Particular Value of y for a Given Value of x

Suppose that the prediction equation obtained for the 10 measurements in Table 12.1 were used to predict the Morgan Company's sales volume for a month selected at random.

Although the expected value of y for a particular value of x is of interest for our example (Table 12.1), we are primarily interested in *using* the prediction equation, $\hat{y} = \hat{\beta}_0 + \hat{\beta}_1 x$, based upon our observed data to predict the sales volume for a month during which the Morgan Company is or has been in operation. If the Morgan Company's advertising expenditures during the month of interest were x_p, we intuitively see that the error of prediction (the deviation between $\hat{y}$ and the actual sales volume, y, which will occur during that month) is composed of two elements. Since the sales volume will equal

$$y = \beta_0 + \beta_1 x_p + \varepsilon,$$

$(y - \hat{y})$ will equal the deviation between $\hat{y}$ and the expected value of y, described in Section 12.6, *plus* the random amount ε which represents the deviation of a month's sales volume from the expected value. Thus the variability in the error for predicting a single value of y will exceed the variability for predicting the expected value of y.

It can be shown that the variance of the error of predicting a particular value of y when $x = x_p$, that is, $(y - \hat{y})$, is

$$\sigma^2 \left[1 + \frac{1}{n} + \frac{(x_p - \bar{x})^2}{\sum\limits_{i=1}^{n} (x_i - \bar{x})^2} \right].$$

When n is very large, the second and third terms under the radical will become small and the variance of the prediction error will approach σ^2. These results may be used to construct the following prediction interval for y, given $x = x_p$:

$$\hat{y} \pm t_{\alpha/2} s \sqrt{1 + \frac{1}{n} + \frac{(x_p - \bar{x})^2}{\sum\limits_{i=1}^{n} (x_i - \bar{x})^2}}.$$

For example, if in a particular month the advertising expenditures were \$1,000, then $x_p = 1.0$ and we would predict that the sales volume would be

$$99.06 \pm (2.306)(6.84) \sqrt{1 + \frac{1}{10} + \frac{(1.0 - .94)^2}{.444}},$$

or

$$99.06 \pm 16.60$$

or

$$\$99,060 \pm \$16,600.$$

Note that in a practical situation we would probably have data on the sales volume and advertising expenditures from more than the $n = 10$ months indicated in Table

12.1. More data would reduce somewhat the width of the bound on the error of prediction by decreasing the quantity under the square-root sign in the above expression.

12.8   A Coefficient of Correlation

It is sometimes desirable to obtain an indicator of the strength of the linear relationship between two variables, y and x, that will be independent of their respective scales of measurement. We shall call this a measure of the linear correlation between y and x.

The measure of linear correlation commonly used in statistics is called the coefficient of correlation between y and x. This quantity, denoted by the symbol r, is computed as follows:

$$r = \frac{\sum\limits_{i=1}^{n} (x_i - \bar{x})(y_i - \bar{y})}{\sqrt{\sum\limits_{i=1}^{n} (x_i - \bar{x})^2 \sum\limits_{i=1}^{n} (y_i - \bar{y})^2}}$$

$$= \frac{n \sum\limits_{i=1}^{n} x_i y_i - \left(\sum\limits_{i=1}^{n} x_i\right)\left(\sum\limits_{i=1}^{n} y_i\right)}{\sqrt{\left[n \sum\limits_{i=1}^{n} x_i^2 - \left(\sum\limits_{i=1}^{n} x_i\right)^2\right]\left[n \sum\limits_{i=1}^{n} y_i^2 - \left(\sum\limits_{i=1}^{n} y_i\right)^2\right]}}$$

The second expression is easier to use computationally, since many of these quantities will have been computed in the calculation of $\hat{\beta}_1$.

The coefficient of correlation for the sales volume advertising expenditure data, Table 12.1, may be obtained by using the formula for r and the quantities

$$\left[n \sum\limits_{i=1}^{n} x_i y_i - \left(\sum\limits_{i=1}^{n} x_i\right)\left(\sum\limits_{i=1}^{n} y_i\right)\right] = 233.4$$

and

$$\left[n \sum\limits_{i=1}^{n} x_i^2 - \left(\sum\limits_{i=1}^{n} x_i\right)^2\right] = 4.44,$$

which were previously computed. Then

$$r = \frac{n \sum\limits_{i=1}^{n} x_i y_i - \left(\sum\limits_{i=1}^{n} x_i \right) \left(\sum\limits_{i=1}^{n} y_i \right)}{\sqrt{\left[n \sum\limits_{i=1}^{n} x_i^2 - \left(\sum\limits_{i=1}^{n} x_i \right)^2 \right] \left[n \sum\limits_{i=1}^{n} y_i^2 - \left(\sum\limits_{i=1}^{n} y_i \right)^2 \right]}}$$

$$= \frac{233.4}{\sqrt{(4.44)(16,009)}}$$

$$= .88.$$

A study of the coefficient of correlation, r, yields rather interesting results and explains the reason for its selection as a measure of linear correlation. We note that the denominators used in calculating r and $\hat{\beta}_1$ will always be positive since they both involve sums of squares of numbers. Since the numerator used in calculating r is identical to the numerator of the formula for the slope $\hat{\beta}_1$, the coefficient of correlation r will assume exactly the same sign as $\hat{\beta}_1$ and will equal zero when $\hat{\beta}_1 = 0$. Thus $r = 0$ implies no linear correlation between y and x. A positive value for r will imply that the line slopes upward to the right; a negative value indicates that it slopes downward to the right.

The interpretation of r as a descriptive statistic is usually in terms of r^2 (called the coefficient of determination), since with a bit of algebraic manipulation we can show that

$$r^2 = 1 - \frac{\text{SSE}}{\sum\limits_{i=1}^{n} (y_i - \bar{y})^2}$$

$$= \frac{\sum\limits_{i=1}^{n} (y_i - \bar{y})^2 - \text{SSE}}{\sum\limits_{i=1}^{n} (y_i - \bar{y})^2}.$$

In other words, r^2 will lie in the interval

$$0 \le r^2 \le 1$$

and r will equal $+1$ or -1 only when all the points fall exactly on the fitted line, that is, when SSE equals zero.

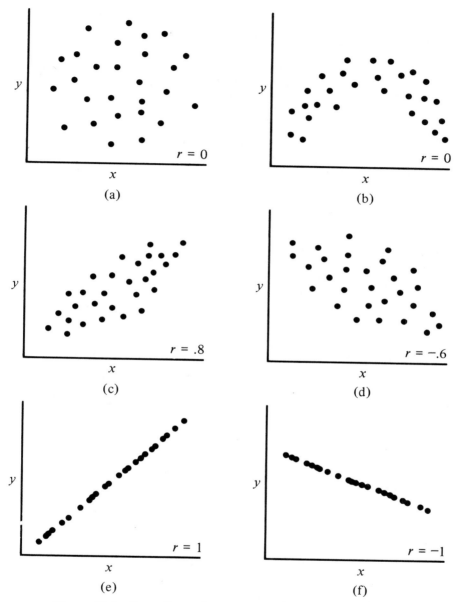

Figure 12.6   *Some Typical Scatter Diagrams and Their Associated Correlation Coefficients*

Figure 12.6 shows six typical scatter diagrams and their associated correlation coefficients. Note that $r = 0$ implies no linear correlation, not simply "no correlation." A pronounced quadratic pattern may exist as in Figure 12.6(b) but its (linear) correlation coefficient may equal 0. In general, we can say that r measures the linear association of the two variables y and x. When $r = 1$ or -1, all the points fall on a straight line; when $r = 0$, they are scattered and give no evidence of a linear relation. Any other value of r suggests the degree to which the points tend to be linearly related.

A better understanding of the meaning of r^2 can be obtained by considering an example. Suppose the data suggest a linear relationship between y and x and that you fit a least-squares line through the data as shown in Figure 12.7(a). Note the deviations shown by the vertical line segments between the fitted line and the data points and imagine the magnitude of SSE, the sum of squares of these deviations. Now suppose that you do not assume that

$$y = \beta_0 + \beta_1 x + \varepsilon$$

but rather that x contributes no information for predicting y. Then you would drop the term $\beta_1 x$ out of the model and would expect y to equal

$$y = \beta_0 + \varepsilon,$$

where, as before, $E(\varepsilon) = 0$. As you might suspect, the least-squares prediction of some new value of y for this model is the sample mean, $\hat{y} = \bar{y}$. This prediction line is shown in Figure 12.7(b) along with the vertical lines representing the errors of prediction. Compare the magnitude of the deviations of the data points from the line

$$\hat{y} = \hat{\beta}_0 + \hat{\beta}_1 x$$

Figure 12.7   *Two Models Fit to the Same Data*

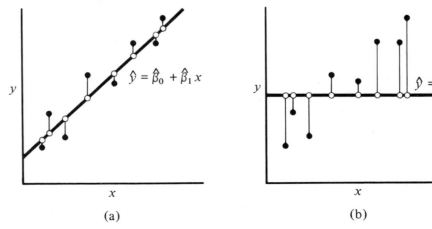

(a)

(b)

for Figure 12.7(a) with those about the line

$$\hat{y} = \bar{y}$$

of Figure 12.7(b). This subjective comparison can be expressed in a more objective way by comparing the sums of squares for error for the two models (prediction equations), that is, SSE and

$$\sum_{i=1}^{n} (y_i - \bar{y})^2.$$

This comparison appears as a ratio in the expression for r^2; thus

$$r^2 = 1 - \frac{\text{SSE}}{\sum_{i=1}^{n} (y_i - \bar{y})^2} = \frac{\sum_{i=1}^{n} (y_i - \bar{y})^2 - \text{SSE}}{\sum_{i=1}^{n} (y_i - \bar{y})^2}.$$

Note that the numerator of the expression on the right is the difference between the error sums of squares for the two fitted lines in Figure 12.7. Therefore, r^2 is equal to the ratio of the reduction in the sum of squares of deviations obtained by using the linear model to the total sum of squares of deviations about the sample mean $\bar{y}$, which would be the predictor of y if x were ignored. Thus r^2, the coefficient of determination, would seem to give a more meaningful interpretation of the strength of the relation between y and x than would the correlation coefficient r.

The reader will observe that the sample correlation coefficient r is an estimator of a population correlation coefficient ρ which would be obtained if the coefficient of correlation were calculated using all the points in the population. A discussion of a test of an hypothesis concerning the value of ρ is omitted as well as a bound on the error of estimation. Ordinarily, we would be interested in testing the null hypothesis that $\rho = 0$, and since this is equivalent to the hypothesis that $\beta_1 = 0$, we have already considered this problem. If the evidence in the sample suggests that y and x are related, it seems appropriate to redirect our attention to the objective of our search—the acquisition of a predictor for y—and to be more interested in the significance of β_1, and the interval estimates for a particular value of y, the $E(y|x)$ and β_1.

While r gives a rather nice measure of the goodness of fit of the least-squares line to the fitted data, its use in making inferences concerning ρ appears to be of dubious practical value in many situations. It seems unlikely that a phenomenon y, observed in the physical sciences and especially in economics, would be a function of a single variable. Thus the correlation coefficient between the monthly sales volume of a firm and any one variable probably would be quite small and of questionable value. A larger reduction in SSE could possibly be obtained by constructing a predictor of y based upon a set of variables $x_1, x_2, \ldots$.

One further reminder is worthwhile concerning the interpretation of r. It is not uncommon for researchers in some fields to speak proudly of sample correlation coefficients r in the neighborhood of .5 (and, in some cases, as low as .1) as being indicative of a "relation" between y and x. Certainly, even if these values were accurate estimates of ρ, only a very weak relation would be indicated. A value $r = .5$ implies that the use of x in predicting y reduces the sum of squares of deviations about the prediction line by only $r^2 = .25$, or 25 percent. A correlation coefficient, $r = .1$, implies only an $r^2 = .01$ or 1 percent reduction in the total sum of squares of deviations that could be explained by x.

If the linear coefficient of correlation between y and each of two variables, x_1 and x_2, were calculated to be .4 and .5, respectively, it does not follow that a predictor using both variables would account for a $(.4)^2 + (.5)^2 = .41$ or a 41 percent reduction in the sum of squares of deviation. Actually, x_1 and x_2 might be highly correlated and therefore contribute virtually the same information for the prediction of y.

Finally, we remind the reader that r is a measure of linear correlation and that x and y could be perfectly related by a curvilinear function when the observed value of r is equal to zero.

12.9   The Additivity of Sums of Squares

An important property of a regression analysis is that it tends to partition the total sum of squares of deviations,

$$\sum_{i=1}^{n} (y_i - \bar{y})^2,$$

into two parts, one attributable to the sum of squares of deviations of the y values about the fitted line SSE, and another that represents the reduction in the sum of squares of deviations that results from information contributed by the auxiliary variable, x.

To understand the partitioning of sums of squares, note that a regression analysis tends to partition the deviation of each measurement from its mean $(y_i - \bar{y})$ into two parts. Thus

$$(y_i - \bar{y}) = (y_i - \hat{y}_i) + (\hat{y}_i - \bar{y}).$$

The partitioning of $(y_i - \bar{y})$ can be seen in Figure 12.8.

Taking the sum of squared deviations over all observations for each expression within the partitioning of $(y_i - \bar{y})$, it can be shown that

$$\sum_{i=1}^{n} (y_i - \bar{y})^2 = \sum_{i=1}^{n} (\hat{y}_i - \bar{y})^2 + \sum_{i=1}^{n} (y_i - \hat{y}_i)^2.$$

Thus the total sum of squares of y (called total SS) can be partitioned into two components:

---

total SS = SSR + SSE,

where

$$SSR = \sum_{i=1}^{n} (\hat{y}_i - \bar{y})^2$$

= *sum of squares due to regression,*

which is the amount of total variation explained by the auxiliary variable x, and

$$SSE = \sum_{i=1}^{n} (y_i - \hat{y}_i)^2$$

= *sum of squares for error,*

the amount of total variation unexplained by the auxiliary variable x.

The partitioning of the sums of squares is important for two reasons. It gives an important additive relationship for the sums of squares,

$$\text{total SS} = \text{SSR} + \text{SSE},$$

that can often reduce computational effort in a regression analysis. (You can compute two of the quantities and obtain the third by subtraction.) Second, it helps to explain the contribution of the auxiliary variable x in providing information for the prediction of y. Finally, note that you can write r^2 as

$$r^2 = \frac{\text{total SS} - \text{SSE}}{\text{total SS}} = \frac{\text{SSR}}{\text{total SS}}.$$

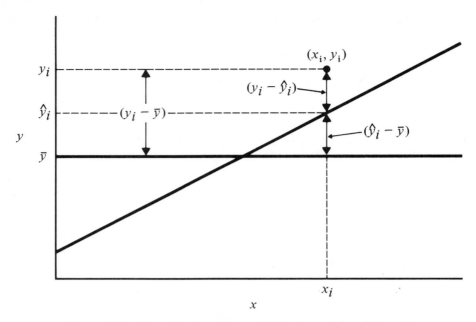

Figure 12.8   *Partitioning of* $(y_i - \bar{y})$ *into* $(y_i - \hat{y}_i)$ *and* $(\hat{y}_i - \bar{y})$

12.10   A Multivariate Prediction Model

A prediction equation based upon a number of variables, $x_1, x_2, \ldots, x_k$, could be obtained by the method of least squares in exactly the same manner as that employed for the simple linear model. For example, we might wish to fit the model

$$y = \beta_0 + \beta_1 x_1 + \beta_2 x_2 + \beta_3 x_3 + \varepsilon,$$

where y is the price of a firm's securities at the end of some month, x_1 is earnings per share during the past fiscal year, x_2 is the gross sales volume for the firm during the preceding month, and x_3 is the firm's profit margin during the past month. (Note that we could add other variables as well as the squares, cubes, and cross products of x_1, x_2, and x_3.)

We would need a random sample of the recorded values for y, x_1, x_2, and x_3 for n randomly selected months during which the firm of interest was in operation. The set of measurements y, x_1, x_2, x_3 for each of the n months could be regarded as the coordinates of a point in four-dimensional space. Then, ideally, we would like to possess a multidimensional "ruler" (in our case, a plane) that we could visually move about among the n points until the deviations of the observed values of y from the predicted would in some sense be a minimum. Although we cannot graph points in four dimensions, you can readily see that this device is provided by the method of least squares, which, mathematically, performs this task for us.

The sum of squares of deviations of the observed value of y from the fitted model would be

$$\text{SSE} = \sum_{i=1}^{n} (y_i - \hat{y}_i)^2$$

$$= \sum_{i=1}^{n} [y_i - (\hat{\beta}_0 + \hat{\beta}_1 x_{1i} + \hat{\beta}_2 x_{2i} + \hat{\beta}_3 x_{3i})]^2,$$

where $\hat{y} = \hat{\beta}_0 + \hat{\beta}_1 x_1 + \hat{\beta}_2 x_2 + \hat{\beta}_3 x_3$ is the fitted model and $\hat{\beta}_0$, $\hat{\beta}_1$, $\hat{\beta}_2$, and $\hat{\beta}_3$ are estimates of the model parameters. We would then use the calculus to find the estimates, $\hat{\beta}_0$, $\hat{\beta}_1$, $\hat{\beta}_2$, and $\hat{\beta}_3$, that make SSE a minimum. The estimates, as for the simple linear model, would be obtained as the solution of a set of four simultaneous linear equations known as the least-squares equations.

In the above case, with three independent variables, x_1, x_2, and x_3, the least-squares equations (sometimes called normal equations) give four linear equations in the four unknowns $\hat{\beta}_0$, $\hat{\beta}_1$, $\hat{\beta}_2$, and $\hat{\beta}_3$. The four least-squares equations, which we do not derive but simply state, are

$$\hat{\beta}_0 n + \hat{\beta}_1 \sum x_1 + \hat{\beta}_2 \sum x_2 + \hat{\beta}_3 \sum x_3 = \sum y,$$
$$\hat{\beta}_0 \sum x_1 + \hat{\beta}_1 \sum x_1^2 + \hat{\beta}_2 \sum x_1 x_2 + \hat{\beta}_3 \sum x_1 x_3 = \sum x_1 y,$$
$$\hat{\beta}_0 \sum x_2 + \hat{\beta}_1 \sum x_1 x_2 + \hat{\beta}_2 \sum x_2^2 + \hat{\beta}_3 \sum x_2 x_3 = \sum x_2 y,$$
$$\hat{\beta}_0 \sum x_3 + \hat{\beta}_1 \sum x_1 x_3 + \hat{\beta}_2 \sum x_2 x_3 + \hat{\beta}_3 \sum x_3^2 = \sum x_3 y,$$

where each summation sign indicates that the quantity within the summation sign is to be summed over all data points, $i = 1, 2, \ldots, n$.

Note the pattern formed by the terms in the least-squares equations above and you will surmise a truth—that this pattern holds for any number of independent variables. For the regression model

$$y = \beta_0 + \beta_1 x_1 + \beta_2 x_2 + \varepsilon$$

with two independent variables, the three least-squares equations in the three unknowns $\hat{\beta}_0$, $\hat{\beta}_1$, and $\hat{\beta}_2$ are

$$\hat{\beta}_0 n + \hat{\beta}_1 \sum x_1 + \hat{\beta}_2 \sum x_2 = \sum y,$$
$$\hat{\beta}_0 \sum x_1 + \hat{\beta}_1 \sum x_1^2 + \hat{\beta}_2 \sum x_1 x_2 = \sum x_1 y,$$
$$\hat{\beta}_0 \sum x_2 + \hat{\beta}_1 \sum x_1 x_2 + \hat{\beta}_2 \sum x_2^2 = \sum x_2 y.$$

Note the location of these terms in the equations for the three-variable model.

Now block out the appropriate terms for the simple model

$$y = \beta_0 + \beta_1 x_1 + \varepsilon$$

with one independent variable, x. The two least-squares equations in the two unknowns $\hat{\beta}_0$ and $\hat{\beta}_1$ are

$$\hat{\beta}_0 n + \hat{\beta}_1 \sum x = \sum y,$$
$$\hat{\beta}_0 \sum x + \hat{\beta}_1 \sum x^2 = \sum xy.$$

Solving these two equations for the unknowns gives exactly the same values for $\hat{\beta}_0$ and $\hat{\beta}_1$ as would be obtained by using the formulas for $\hat{\beta}_0$ and $\hat{\beta}_1$ on page 330.

By an extension of the preceding discussion, for a regression model with k independent variables, there will be $(k + 1)$ least-squares equations in the $(k + 1)$ unknowns, $\hat{\beta}_0, \hat{\beta}_1, \hat{\beta}_2, \ldots, \hat{\beta}_k$. The form of the $(k + 1)$ least-squares equations can be established from the pattern set by the least-squares equations for the models with one, two, and three independent variables.

12.11   Solving the Least-Squares Equations

Solution of the least-squares equations for $\hat{\beta}_0, \hat{\beta}_1, \hat{\beta}_2, \ldots, \hat{\beta}_k$ guarantees that the resultant estimates, substituted into the prediction equation,

$$\hat{y}_i = \hat{\beta}_0 + \hat{\beta}_1 x_{1i} + \hat{\beta}_2 x_{2i} + \cdots + \hat{\beta}_k x_{ki},$$

minimize the sum of square deviations

$$SSE = \sum_{i=1}^{n} (y_i - \hat{y}_i)^2.$$

That is, no other set of estimates for the betas will provide a smaller SSE.
A set of m equations in m unknowns is commonly solved

1. By expressing the simultaneous equations in matrix form and solving by means of matrix algebra (employing matrix inverse and matrix multiplication operations), or

2. By a process of elimination, individually solving for each unknown.

Both approaches become quite tedious when the number of equations, and hence the number of unknowns, exceeds three. Preprogrammed routines are available and should be employed in these cases.

Example 12.1   *The owner of an automobile dealership believes the relationship between the number of new cars sold by his agency in a given month, y, is related to the number of his agency's full-page newspaper advertisements during the month, x, by the model*

$$y = \beta_0 + \beta_1 x_1 + \beta_2 x_2 + \varepsilon,$$

where $x_1 = x$ and $x_2 = x^2$. Over a period of 6 months, he noticed the following results:

	MONTH					
	1	2	3	4	5	6
y	10	10	15	20	30	40
x	0	1	2	2	3	4

Fit the model $y = \beta_0 + \beta_1 x_1 + \beta_2 x_2 + \varepsilon$ to the data by solving the least-squares equations to obtain estimates of the unknown parameters $\beta_0, \beta_1, and \beta_2$.

Solution   *The model $y = \beta_0 + \beta_1 x_1 + \beta_2 x_2 + \varepsilon$, or, equivalently, the model $y = \beta_0 + \beta_1 x + \beta_2 x^2 + \varepsilon$, is an example of a second-order polynomial. It requires the solution of three least-squares equations in the three unknowns $\hat{\beta}_0, \hat{\beta}_1, and \hat{\beta}_2$. In Table 12.3, the necessary elements are calculated from the data so that the least-squares equations for this problem can be identified.*

Table 12.3   *Calculations for the Data of Example 12.1*

MONTH i	y_i	x_{1i}	x_{2i}	x_{1i}^2	x_{2i}^2	$x_{1i}x_{2i}$	$x_{1i}y_i$	$x_{2i}y_i$
1	10	0	0	0	0	0	0	0
2	10	1	1	1	1	1	10	10
3	15	2	4	4	16	8	30	60
4	20	2	4	4	16	8	40	80
5	30	3	9	9	81	27	90	270
6	40	4	16	16	256	64	160	640
Sum	125	12	34	34	370	108	330	1,060

Remember, for the calculations within Table 12.3, $x_{1i} = x_i$ and $x_{2i} = x_i^2$. Therefore, $x_{1i}^2 = x_i^2$, $x_{2i}^2 = x_i^4$, $x_{1i}x_{2i} = x_i^3$, $x_{1i}y_i = x_iy_i$, and $x_{2i}y_i = x_i^2y_i$.
   Substituting the appropriate sums from Table 12.3 into the least-squares equations, we find

(I) $$6\hat{\beta}_0 + 12\hat{\beta}_1 + 34\hat{\beta}_2 = 125,$$

(II) $$12\hat{\beta}_0 + 34\hat{\beta}_1 + 108\hat{\beta}_2 = 330,$$

(III) $$34\hat{\beta}_0 + 108\hat{\beta}_1 + 370\hat{\beta}_2 = 1{,}060.$$

For convenience we have labeled the three least-squares equations as (I), (II), and (III). We shall now employ the process of elimination to solve for the unknowns, $\hat{\beta}_0$, $\hat{\beta}_1$, and $\hat{\beta}_2$.
   Suppose that we subtract 2(I) from equation (II). We then have

$$10\hat{\beta}_1 + 40\hat{\beta}_2 = 80$$

or

$$\hat{\beta}_1 = 8 - 4\hat{\beta}_2.$$

Now subtract (34/6)(I) from equation (III) and you will find that

$$40\hat{\beta}_1 + 177.33\hat{\beta}_2 = 351.67$$

or

$$\hat{\beta}_1 = 8.79 - 4.43\hat{\beta}_2.$$

We now have eliminated $\hat{\beta}_0$ and have two equations in two unknowns. Setting these two equations equal to one another, we can solve for $\hat{\beta}_2$;

$$8 - 4\hat{\beta}_2 = 8.79 - 4.43\hat{\beta}_2$$

or

$$.43\hat{\beta}_2 = .79.$$

Thus $\hat{\beta}_2 = 1.84$.
   From an earlier equation,

$$\hat{\beta}_1 = 8 - 4\hat{\beta}_2$$
$$= 8 - 4(1.84)$$
$$= .64.$$

Returning to equation (I), we find that it can be rewritten as

$$\hat{\beta}_0 = \tfrac{1}{6}(125 - 12\hat{\beta}_1 - 34\hat{\beta}_2).$$

Therefore,

$$\hat{\beta}_0 = \tfrac{1}{6}[125 - 12(.64) - 34(1.84)]$$
$$= \tfrac{1}{6}(54.76)$$
$$= 9.13.$$

The equation for predicting monthly sales (y) from the number of full-page newspaper advertisements during the month (x) and the quadratic term $x_2 = x^2$ is

$$\hat{y} = 9.13 + .64x_1 + 1.84x_2.$$

The errors of prediction can be found by substituting the predictor variables x_1 and x_2 into the prediction equation and computing the estimated sales, $\hat{y}$. For month 1,

$$\hat{y}_1 = 9.13 + .64(0) + 1.84(0)$$
$$= 9.13.$$

Therefore, the error of prediction for month 1 is

$$e_1 = y_1 - \hat{y}_1$$
$$= 10 - 9.13$$
$$= .87.$$

The estimated sales, $\hat{y}_i$, and errors of prediction are as follows:

y_i	10	10	15	20	30	40
$\hat{y}_i$	9.13	11.61	17.77	17.77	27.61	41.13
e_i	.87	−1.61	−2.77	2.23	2.39	−1.13

The sum of squared errors is

$$\text{SSE} = \sum_{i=1}^{6} (y_i - \hat{y}_i)^2 = \sum_{i=1}^{6} e_i^2 = 22.9838.$$

We are guaranteed that no other values could be found to estimate the unknown parameters β_0, β_1, and β_2 which would result in an SSE smaller than 22.9838.

The graph for the equation

$$\hat{y} = 9.13 + .64x_1 + 1.84x_2 \qquad (x_1 = x, x_2 = x^2)$$

is shown in Figure 12.9. Note that the straight-line model

$$y = \beta_0 + \beta_1 x + \varepsilon$$

would have provided a much poorer fit to the data points than the polynomial model that was used.

For a prediction model with three or more independent variables, it is practically imperative that one employ an electronic computer to estimate the unknown regression parameters, $\beta_0, \beta_1, \beta_2, \ldots, \beta_k$. Almost every computing facility has access to at least one "canned" regression-analysis program which requires that the user need only execute the proper commands to activate the program and then to submit his problem data.

To illustrate, we shall consider a study designed to examine the role of television viewing in the lives of a select group of people over 65 years of age. The purpose of the study was to provide guidelines for developing television programming that will adequately meet the special needs of this audience. A sample of $n = 25$ senior citizens was selected and from each senior citizen was obtained $y =$ the

Figure 12.9 *Plot of the Data and the Prediction Model from Example 12.1*

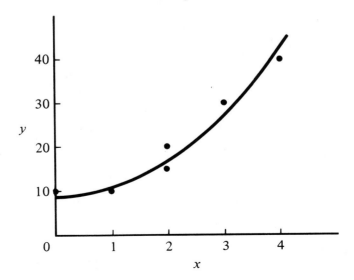

average number of hours per day spent watching television, x_1 = his marital status (x_1 = 1 if the interviewee is living with his spouse, x_1 = 0 if not), x_2 = his age, and x_3 = his number of years' education.* The data are listed in Table 12.4.

Table 12.4   *Daily Hours Spent Watching Television, Marital Status, Age, and Years of Education of 25 Randomly Selected Senior Citizens*

INDIVIDUAL	HOURS y	MARITAL STATUS x_1	AGE x_2	EDUCATION x_3
1	.5	1	73	14
2	.5	1	66	16
3	.7	0	65	15
4	.8	0	65	16
5	.8	1	68	9
6	.9	1	69	10
7	1.1	1	82	12
8	1.6	1	83	12
9	1.6	1	81	12
10	2.0	0	72	10
11	2.5	1	69	8
12	2.8	0	71	16
13	2.8	0	71	12
14	3.0	0	80	9
15	3.0	0	73	6
16	3.0	0	75	6
17	3.2	0	76	10
18	3.2	0	78	6
19	3.3	1	79	6
20	3.3	0	79	4
21	3.4	1	78	6
22	3.5	0	76	9
23	3.6	0	65	12
24	3.7	0	72	12
25	3.7	0	80	6

* Variable x_1 is an example of a *dummy variable*, a frequently employed independent variable designed to include the effect of a *qualitative* factor into a regression model. Dummy variables serve to partition the regression model into two separate components,

$$\hat{y} = (\hat{\beta}_0 + \hat{\beta}_1) + \hat{\beta}_2 x_2 + \hat{\beta}_3 x_3$$

and

$$\hat{y} = \hat{\beta}_0 + \hat{\beta}_2 x_2 + \hat{\beta}_3 x_3,$$

the former modeling response in the presence of the qualitative factor, the other, in its absence.

Table 12.5 *Computer Output for Senior Citizen Television Viewing Data, Table 12.4*

MULTIPLE R	.7918
R SQUARE	.6269
STD. ERROR OF EST.	.7524

ANALYSIS OF VARIANCE

	DF	SUM OF SQUARES	MEAN SQUARE	F RATIO
REGRESSION	3	19.972	6.657	11.760
RESIDUAL	21	11.888	.566	

INDIVIDUAL ANALYSIS OF VARIABLES

VARIABLE	COEFFICIENT	STD. ERROR	F VALUE
(CONSTANT	1.41411)		
MARITAL STATUS	−1.17396	.31445	13.9380
AGE	.03971	.03191	1.5480
YEARS EDUCATION	−.15106	.05023	9.0456

The objective of this study is to relate y, the average daily hours spent watching television, to the descriptive variables x_1, x_2, and x_3 defined earlier. For purposes of simplicity, we shall select the prediction model

$$y = \beta_0 + \beta_1 x_1 + \beta_2 x_2 + \beta_3 x_3 + \varepsilon,$$

which provides for four least-squares equations in the four unknowns $\beta_0, \beta_1, \beta_2,$ and β_3. The least-squares equations are

$$25\hat{\beta}_0 + 10\hat{\beta}_1 + 1{,}846\hat{\beta}_2 + 254\hat{\beta}_3 = 58.5,$$
$$10\hat{\beta}_0 + 10\hat{\beta}_1 + 748\hat{\beta}_2 + 105\hat{\beta}_3 = 16.2,$$
$$1{,}846\hat{\beta}_0 + 748\hat{\beta}_1 + 137086\hat{\beta}_2 + 18{,}509\hat{\beta}_3 = 4{,}376.0,$$
$$254\hat{\beta}_0 + 105\hat{\beta}_1 + 18{,}509\hat{\beta}_2 + 2{,}892\hat{\beta}_3 = 533.4.$$

Solving for the four unknowns by hand would likely be a tedious, time-consuming task.

Table 12.5 reproduces the computer output obtained by applying a commonly used regression-analysis program to the data of Table 12.4. The most important quantities appearing within the output may be interpreted as follows:

1. *Multiple R.* The multiple correlation of independent variables x_1, x_2, and x_3 together with the dependent variable, y. The multiple R is the multivariate counterpart to the simple correlation r defined within Section 12.8.

2. R^2 (coefficient of determination). The proportion of variation in y explained by the independent variables x_1, x_2, and x_3. As with r^2 of Section 12.8, we find

$$R^2 = \frac{\text{SSR}}{\text{total SS}} = \frac{\text{SSR}}{\text{SSR} + \text{SSE}},$$

so R^2 ranges between 0 and $+1$. R^2 is an important and commonly used measure of the strength of a multiple regression relationship; the closer R^2 is to $+1$, the stronger the assumed relationship. In our example,

$$R^2 = \frac{19.972}{19.972 + 11.888} = \frac{19.972}{31.860} = .6269,$$

indicating that about 63 percent of the variation in hours spent watching television can be explained by the independent variables x_1, x_2, and x_3.

3. *F ratio.* Test statistic for the hypothesis

$$H_0 : \beta_1 = \beta_2 = \beta_3 = 0,$$

against the alternative hypothesis,

H_a : at least one of the parameters β_1, β_2, and β_3 is not equal to zero.

Or, equivalently, H_a implies that at least one of the independent variables is linearly related to the dependent variable y. H_0 implies the converse. H_0 is rejected if the F ratio exceeds the tabulated F with 3 and 21 degrees of freedom [in general, k and $(n - k - 1)$ d.f.], where k is the number of independent variables in the model] at a preselected level of significance, α. From Table 6, Appendix, at the 5 percent level, the critical F with 3 and 21 d.f. is 3.07; thus we reject the hypothesis H_0 and assume that at least one independent variable contributes information for the prediction of y.

4. *Variable coefficients.* The solution of the least-squares equations for $\hat{\beta}_0$, $\hat{\beta}_1$, $\hat{\beta}_2$, and $\hat{\beta}_3$. The prediction equation is

$$\hat{y} = 1.41411 - 1.17396x_1 + .03971x_2 - .15106x_3,$$

which relates y to x_1, x_2, and x_3 for the 25 subjects within the experiment. Note that the equation suggests that, all other influences being equal, a 1-unit increase in x_3 (an additional year of education) implies that the person watches television an average of .15106 less hours per week. Analogous interpretations follow for the other two independent variables, x_1 and x_2.

5. *Standard error*. The estimated standard deviations, $s_{\hat{\beta}_1}$, $s_{\hat{\beta}_2}$, and $s_{\hat{\beta}_3}$, respectively, of the regression coefficient estimates, $\hat{\beta}_1$, $\hat{\beta}_2$, and $\hat{\beta}_3$. These statistics allow for the construction of $(1 - \alpha)$ confidence intervals for the regression coefficients, the parameters β_1, β_2, and β_3. For instance, the $(1 - \alpha)$ confidence interval for β_1 would be

$$\hat{\beta}_1 \pm t_{\alpha/2} s_{\hat{\beta}_1},$$

where the t statistic is associated with 21 d.f. [in general, $(n - k - 1)$d.f.]. The 95 percent confidence interval for β_1 is then

or
$$-1.17396 \pm (2.080)(.31445)$$
$$-1.17396 \pm .65406.$$

6. *F value*. Test statistic for the hypothesis that the regression coefficient (the beta) for a specific independent variable is equal to 0. Rejecting indicates that the associated independent variable contributes information for the prediction of y. Rejection occurs if the F value exceeds the tabulated F with 1 and 21 d.f. [in general, 1 and $(n - k - 1)$d.f.] at a preassumed level of significance. From Table 6, Appendix, at $\alpha = .05$ the critical F for 1 and 21 d.f. is 4.32. Thus we have sufficient evidence at the 5 percent level of significance to indicate that marital status and years of education contribute information for the prediction of y (television viewing hours) but that age does not.

12.12   Further Comments on Multiple Regression

Since independent variable x_2, the subject's age, has a small F value, should x_2 be dropped from the model (and consequently the analysis)? To answer this question, perhaps we should first ask why one would ever want to delete an independent variable from the model. Two important reasons are that it contributes nothing for the prediction of y, or that its associated measurements are costly to record. Certainly recording one's age is not as expensive a task as, say, obtaining precise survey information for particular land values in a real estate application. Thus, cost is not a limiting factor in the senior citizen television viewing study.

In directing our attention to the first point, one must bear in mind that the F values provide a test statistic for the conditional hypothesis concerning the significance of the associated independent variable in the presence of the other independent variables. Even though an independent variable may alone be highly correlated with y, because of interrelationships with other independent variables, its F value may be small. However, the variable may still serve a useful purpose.

For instance, prior beliefs might suggest that age together with marital status has a positive effect on the dependent variable, daily television viewing time. That is, the older the subject, the less likely he is living with his spouse, and, thus, the more free time he is likely to have for such activities as television viewing.

Variable x_2, age, may be acting in a catalytic manner with variable x_1, marital status. Even though x_2, in the presence of x_1 and x_3, shows a weak relationship to y, it is likely enhancing the relationship between x_1, x_2 and x_3, *collectively* and y. This could only be proved conclusively, however, by first deleting x_2 from the analysis and noting the reduction in the coefficient of determination, R^2.

Logic, prior beliefs, and cost considerations must all be used to supplement the information provided by the F values in order to determine which variables should be kept in the equation. Logic may also suggest the addition of untried variables in the analysis. Additional variables need not be restricted to quantifiable descriptive factors such as the subject's annual income but can also include descriptive qualitative factors such as job status, included in the model by using a dummy variable.

Variable transformations, such as the quadratic term for an independent variable or exponential transformations of independent variables are often useful in demand and other econometric analyses. First-order models (with each predictor variable used only in its actual form) should be used only as a first approximation. Separate visual plots of each predictor variable against y may suggest apparent quadratic, cubic, logistic, trigonometric or other relationships which, if included as a separate predictor, give a more reliable prediction equation. If two independent variables, x_1 and x_2, are thought to be highly related, a separate predictor variable, $x_3 = x_1 x_2$, often improves predictive accuracy.

In most applications of regression analysis, many different combinations of independent variables are tried, defining many different regression (prediction) models. An often-employed measure of the adequacy of a regression (prediction) model suggests that the "best" model is one with the largest measure for R^2, the coefficient of determination. But a word of caution is in order. R^2 can be artificially forced toward 1.0 by allowing the number of predictor variables, k, to approach the sample size, n. Thus the coefficient of determination is meaningful only when the ratio (k/n) is sufficiently small, with "sufficiently small" usually interpreted as .25 or less. Thus to properly interpret our results, we would like to restrict the number of predictor variables to be less than $n/4$.

A final word of caution should be offered to extend a comment of Section 12.5 regarding the one-independent-variable regression model. The calculated prediction equation based on a set of independent variables, $x_1, x_2, \ldots$, is appropriate only over the range of sample values of $x_1, x_2, \ldots$ used in the analysis. Extrapolation beyond this range may lead to errors such as those mentioned within Section 12.5.

12.13   Summary

Although it was not stressed, you may have observed that the prediction of a particular value of a random variable, y, was considered for the most elementary situation in Chapters 8 and 9. Thus, if we possessed no information concerning variables related to y, the sole information available for predicting y would be provided by its probability distribution. As we noted in Chapter 5, the probability that y falls between two specific values, say y_1 and y_2, equals the area under the probability distribution curve over the interval $y_1 \le y \le y_2$. And, if we were to select randomly one member of the population, we should in all likelihood choose μ, or some other measure of central tendency, as the most likely value of y to be observed. Thus we wish to estimate μ, and this problem was considered in Chapters 8 and 9.

Chapter 12 is concerned with the problem of predicting y when auxiliary information is available on other variables, say $x_1, x_2, x_3, \ldots$, which are related to y and hence assist in its prediction. We have concentrated primarily on the problem of predicting y as a linear function of a single variable, x, which provides the simplest extension of the prediction problem beyond that considered in Chapters 8 and 9.

Exercises

1.   What assumptions are necessary to use the prediction equation $\hat{y} = \hat{\beta}_0 + \hat{\beta}_1 x$ to predict the value of a dependent variable, y, from a predictor variable, x?

2.   Define and discuss the following concepts as they relate to our study of linear regression and correlation analysis:
(a) The method of least squares.
(b) The slope of the simple linear model.
(c) A curvilinear probabilistic model.
(d) The variance of the random error of the regression equation.
(e) A confidence interval for the expected value of y, given $x = x_p$.
(f) The coefficient of correlation between y and x.
(g) The reduction in sum of squares of deviation obtained by using the linear model.
(h) A multivariate prediction equation.

3.   For what configurations of sample points will s^2 be zero?

4.   For what parameter is s^2 an unbiased estimator? Explain how this parameter enters into the description of the probabilistic model $y = \beta_0 + \beta_1 x + \varepsilon$.

5.   Given the linear equation $y = 6 + 3x$:
(a) Give the y intercept and slope for the line.
(b) Graph the line corresponding to the equation.

6.   Follow the instructions given in Exercise 5 for the linear equation $2x - 3y - 5 = 0$.

7.   Given five points whose coordinates are

y	0	0	1	1	3
x	-2	-1	0	1	2

(a) Find the least-squares line for the data.
(b) As a check on the calculations in (a), plot the five points and graph the line.
(c) Calculate s^2.
(d) Do the data present sufficient evidence to indicate that y and x are linearly related? (Test the hypothesis that $\beta_i = 0$, using $\alpha = .05$.)

8.   The following data represent the number of workdays absent during the past year, y, and the number of years employed by the company, x, for seven employees randomly selected from a large company.

y	2	0	5	6	4	9	2
x	7	8	2	3	5	3	7

(a) Find the least-squares line for the data.
(b) As a check on the calculations in (a), plot the seven points and graph the line.
(c) Calculate s^2.
(d) Do the data present sufficient evidence to indicate that y and x are linearly related? (Test the hypothesis that $\beta_1 = 0$, using $\alpha = .05$.)

9.   An experiment was conducted in a supermarket to observe the relation between the amount of display space allotted to a brand of coffee (brand A) and its weekly sales. The amount of space allotted to brand A was varied over 3-, 6-, and 9-square-foot displays in a random manner over 12 weeks while the space allotted to competing brands was maintained at a constant 3 square feet for each. The following data were observed:

Weekly sales y (dollars)	526	421	581	630	412	560	434	443	590	570	346	672
Space alloted x (ft^2)	6	3	6	9	3	9	6	3	9	6	3	9

(a) Find the least-squares line appropriate for these data.
(b) Plot the points and graph the least-squares line as a check on your calculations.
(c) Calculate s^2.

10.   Do the data in Exercise 9 present sufficient evidence to indicate that sales for brand A are linearly related to display area when the display area varies between 3 and 9 square feet? (Test using $\alpha = .05$.) Would you expect the relation between y and x to be linear if x were varied over a wider range (say $x = 1$ to $x = 30$)?

11.   Find a 95 percent confidence interval for the slope of the line in Exercise 9. Of what use is this confidence interval? That is, give a practical interpretation to this confidence interval.

12.   Find a 90 percent confidence interval for the slope of the line in Exercise 8. Give a practical interpretation to this confidence interval.

13.   Refer to Exercise 8. Obtain a 90 percent confidence interval for the expected value of y when $x = 4$. Give a practical interpretation to this confidence interval.

14.   Refer to Exercise 9. On the average, how much coffee (brand A) would you expect to sell if a 6-square-foot display is employed? (Obtain a 95 percent confidence interval for the expected value of y given that x equals 6 square feet.) Assume that sales conditions and all other factors would be similar to those used in the experiment.

15.   Refer to Exercise 9. If a 3-square foot display of brand A were employed for the thirteenth week, what value would you predict for that week's sales? Construct an interval estimate of the predicted sales using a confidence coefficient equal to .90.

16.   Refer to Exercise 8. Given that $x = 2$, find an interval estimate for a particular value of y. Use a confidence coefficient equal to .90. Give a practical interpretation to this confidence interval.

17.   Discuss the following questions with regard to the study of the correlation between two variables.
      (a) How does the coefficient of correlation measure the strength of the linear relationship between two variables, y and x?
      (b) Describe the significance of the algebraic sign and the magnitude of r.
      (c) What is implied when the value of r is very close to zero?
      (d) What value does r assume if all the sample points fall on the same straight line if the line has a positive slope? If the line has a negative slope?

18.   Calculate the coefficient of correlation r for the data in Exercise 8. What is the significance of this particular value of r?

19.   Calculate the coefficient of correlation for the data in Exercise 9. How much of a reduction in SSE was obtained by using the least-squares predictor rather than $\bar{y}$ in predicting y for the data in Exercise 9?

20.   An economist wished to develop a model enabling him to examine the relationship between the Federal Reserve discount rate and bank debits. In the process of his study, the following data were obtained for the years 1962 through 1968:

Federal Reserve discount rate	y	3.00	3.38	3.88	4.38	4.50	4.25	5.25
Bank debits (trillions of $)	x	3.43	3.75	4.52	5.13	5.94	6.35	7.99

      (a) Find the least-squares prediction equation appropriate for the data.
      (b) Graph the points and the least-squares line as a check on your calculations.
      (c) Calculate s^2.

21.   Do the data in Exercise 20 present sufficient evidence to indicate that x is useful in predicting y? (Test using $\alpha = .01$.)

22.   Calculate r^2, the proportion of variation in Federal Reserve discount rates explained by bank debits, for the data in Exercise 20.

23.   Refer to Exercise 20. Obtain a 90 percent confidence interval for the expected Federal Reserve discount rate knowing that the bank debit level is 7 trillion dollars.

24. An experiment was conducted to observe the effect of an increase in temperature on the potency of an antibiotic. Three 1-ounce portions of the antibiotic were stored for equal lengths of time at each of the following temperatures: 30°, 50°, 70°, and 90°. The potency readings observed at the temperature of the experimental period were

Potency readings	38, 43, 29	32, 26, 33	19, 27, 23	14, 19, 21
Temperature	30	50	70	90

   (a) Find the least-squares appropriate for these data.
   (b) Plot the points and graph the lines as a check on your calculations.
   (c) Calculate s^2.

25. Refer to Exercise 24. Estimate the change in potency for a 1-unit change in temperature. Use a 90 percent confidence interval.

26. Refer to Exercise 24. Estimate the mean potency corresponding to a temperature of 50 degrees. Use a 90 percent confidence interval.

27. Refer to Exercise 24. Suppose that a batch of the antibiotic were stored at 50°F for the same length of time as the experimental period. Predict the potency of the batch at the end of the storage period. Use a 90 percent confidence interval.

28. Calculate the coefficient of correlation for the data in Exercise 24. How much reduction in SSE was obtained by using the least-squares predictor rather than $\bar{y}$ in predicting y for the data in Exercise 24?

29. A marketing research experiment was conducted to study the relationship between the length of time necessary for a buyer to reach a decision and the number of alternative package designs of a product presented. Brand names were eliminated from the packages to reduce the effects of brand preferences. The buyers made their selections using the manufacturer's product descriptions on the packages as the only buying guide. The length of time necessary to reach a decision is recorded for 15 participants in the marketing research study.

Length of decision time (sec)	5, 8, 8, 7, 9	7, 9, 8, 9, 10	10, 11, 10, 12, 9
No. alternatives	2	3	4

   (a) Find the least-squares line appropriate for these data.
   (b) Plot the points and graph the line as a check on your calculations.
   (c) Calculate s^2.
   (d) Do the data present sufficient evidence to indicate that the length of decision time is linearly related to the number of alternative package designs? (Test at the $\alpha = .05$ level of significance.)

30. In the accompanying table, x is the tensile force applied to a steel specimen in thousands of pounds and y is the resulting elongation in thousandths of an inch.

x	1	2	3	4	5
y	2	4	5	6	8

   (a) Assuming the regression of y on x to be linear, find the least-squares line for the data.

(b) Plot the points and graph the line found in (a) as a check on your calculations.
(c) Calculate SSE and *s* for the data.

31.   Refer to Exercise 30. Use a 95 percent prediction interval to predict the elongation if the experiment is to be run one more time at $x = 4$.

32.   Refer to Exercise 30. Construct a 90 percent confidence interval for the mean change in elongation of the specimen per thousand pounds of tensile stress.

33.   Refer to Exercise 30. If a force of 0 pounds is applied, the resulting elongation should be 0 units. Perform a test of an hypothesis to see if the line is consistent with the preceding statement. (Use $\alpha = .05$.)

34.   Refer to Exercise 30.
(a) Find the coefficient of correlation *r* for the above set of data.
(b) By what percentage has the sum of squares of error been reduced by using the linear predictor $\hat{y}$ rather than $\bar{y}$?

35.   A comparison of the undergraduate grade-point averages of 12 corporate employees with their scores on a managerial trainee examination produced the following results:

Exam score	*y*	76	89	83	79	91	95	82	69	66	75	80	88
G.P.A.	*x*	2.2	2.4	3.1	2.5	3.5	3.6	2.5	2.0	2.2	2.6	2.7	3.3

(a) Find the least-squares prediction equation appropriate for the data.
(b) Graph the points and the least-squares line as a check on your calculations.
(c) Calculate s^2.
(d) Do the data present sufficient evidence to indicate that *x* (undergraduate G.P.A.) is useful in predicting *y* (managerial trainee exam score)? (Test using $\alpha = .05$.)

36.   Calculate the coefficient of correlation for the data in Exercise 35. By what percentage was the sum of squares of deviations reduced by using the least-squares predictor $\hat{y} = \hat{\beta}_0 + \hat{\beta}_1 x$ rather than $\bar{y}$ as a predictor of *y* for the data in Exercise 35?

37.   Refer to Exercise 35. Obtain a 90 percent confidence interval for the expected examination score for all managerial trainees whose undergraduate G.P.A. was 2.6.

38.   Use the least-squares equation derived in Exercise 35 to predict the exam score for a particular managerial trainee whose undergraduate G.P.A. was 2.6. Obtain a 90 percent confidence interval for this individual's true exam score.

39.   Explain why the confidence intervals obtained in Exercises 37 and 38 are not the same.

Supplementary Exercises

The following exercises relate to the multivariate predictor model and may require extensive computational effort to arrive at a solution. These exercises can be deleted if only a review of the simple linear regression model is desired.

1.   Discuss the following terms as they relate to the multivariate predictor model:
(a) The coefficient of determination.
(b) The least-squares equations.
(c) A dummy variable.
(d) *F* tests.

2. Discuss the following statement: "First-order multivariate predictor models (with each predictor variable used only in its actual form) should be used only as first approximations to the final prediction model."

3. The owner of an automobile dealership undertook a study to determine the relationship between

y = number of new cars sold per month by his dealership,
x_1 = number of 10-minute local TV spot advertisements during the month,
x_2 = number of full-page newspaper advertisements during the month.

Over a period of 6 months, the owner noticed the following results:

	MONTH					
	1	2	3	4	5	6
y	10	10	20	30	40	40
x_1	0	1	2	2	3	4
x_2	1	0	2	3	3	3

Use the process of elimination to fit the model $y = \beta_0 + \beta_1 x_1 + \beta_2 x_2 + \varepsilon$ to the data by solving the least-squares equations for the unknown parameters $\hat{\beta}_0$, $\hat{\beta}_1$, and $\hat{\beta}_2$.

4. Refer to Supplementary Exercise 3. Using the fitted model, compute the errors of prediction for the 6 months during which the sample was gathered. Then
(a) Compute R^2, the coefficient of determination.
(b) Compute the sum of squared errors (SSE) and find the estimate of the variance of the predicted values of y given x_1 and x_2 by the formula

$$s^2 = \frac{SSE}{n - 3}.$$

5. A land developer was interested in creating a model to use for purposes of estimating the selling price of beach lots on the Oregon coast. To do so he recorded for each of 20 beach lots which has recently been sold:

y = sale price of the beach lot in $1,000 units,
x_1 = area of the lot (in hundreds of square feet),
x_2 = elevation of the lot,
x_3 = slope of the lot.

The land developer then employed a regression-analysis computer program and obtained the following output:

MULTIPLE R   .8854
R SQUARE   .7838
STD. ERROR OF EST.   .6075

ANALYSIS OF VARIANCE

	DF	SUM OF SQUARES	MEAN SQUARE	F RATIO
REGRESSION	3	21.409	7.136	19.345
RESIDUAL	16	5.903	.369	

INDIVIDUAL ANALYSIS OF VARIABLES

VARIABLE	COEFFICIENT	STD. ERROR	F VALUE
(CONSTANT	−2.491)		
AREA	.099	.058	2.935
ELEVATION	.029	.006	23.327
SLOPE	.086	.031	7.841

(a) Give the prediction equation for the linear model relating selling price to the area, elevation, and slope of a beach lot.

(b) What percentage of the variation in selling price is explained by the three predictor variables?

(c) Test the hypothesis that none of the predictor variables is a useful predictor of y in the presence of another predictor. Let $\alpha = .05$.

(d) Which predictor variable shows the strongest predictive relationship to selling price in the presence of the other variables? Explain.

(e) Which predictor variable shows the weakest predictive relationship to selling price in the presence of the other variables? Explain.

6.   Refer to Supplementary Exercise 5. Find a 90 percent confidence interval for the regression parameter relating "area" to "selling price" in the presence of "elevation" and "slope." What is the meaning of this relationship?

7.   Refer to Supplementary Exercise 5. Estimate the selling price for an Oregon beach lot that is rectangular, 100 feet by 50 feet, 20 feet above sea level, and has a 5-degree slope toward the ocean.

8.   A frozen-foods processing company would like to develop a prediction model that can be used to predict the quarterly demand for its mixed-vegetable line. With a reliable model, the company can more effectively plan its budgets and production requirements, as well as estimate the inventory requirements of its different warehouses. The demand for mixed vegetables is believed to be a function of (1) the price of the product as offered by the company, (2) the average industry price, and (3) the quarterly advertising expenditure by all sources to promote the product. Thirty quarterly observations of these data are available and are listed in the table.

Quarter	y	x_1	x_2	x_3	Quarter	y	x_1	x_2	x_3
1	7.35	3.45	3.85	5.50	16	8.87	3.25	4.20	6.80
2	8.51	3.25	4.00	6.80	17	9.53	3.45	4.20	7.00
3	9.55	3.20	4.40	7.50	18	9.50	3.25	4.20	6.90
4	7.50	3.40	3.70	5.50	19	8.75	3.25	4.10	6.00
5	9.29	3.20	4.10	7.10	20	7.85	3.45	3.75	6.00
6	8.32	3.30	3.75	6.50	21	7.65	3.45	3.65	6.00
7	8.75	3.25	3.50	6.80	22	7.19	3.55	3.65	5.80
8	7.78	3.45	3.85	5.50	23	8.09	3.45	3.85	6.50
9	7.08	3.45	3.65	5.10	24	8.80	3.35	3.75	7.00
10	8.05	3.25	4.00	6.00	25	9.23	3.20	4.10	6.80
11	6.85	3.25	4.00	6.50	26	8.32	3.25	4.00	6.50
12	8.00	3.35	3.75	6.00	27	8.27	3.35	3.80	6.50
13	9.10	3.20	4.10	7.00	28	7.53	3.45	3.75	6.50
14	8.95	3.25	4.00	7.00	29	7.93	3.45	3.85	5.80
15	8.92	3.35	4.10	6.90	30	9.47	3.45	4.20	6.80

Use an available regression-analysis computer program to fit the linear model $y = \beta_0 + \beta_1 x_1 + \beta_2 x_2 + \beta_3 x_3 + \varepsilon$ to the data.

(a) Give the equation for the model to predict quarterly demand of the company's mixed vegetables from the company's price per case, the average industry price per case, and quarterly advertising expenditures.
(b) What proportion of the variation in the quarterly demand for the company's mixed vegetables is explained by the company's price, the average industry price, and quarterly advertising expenditures?

References

Anderson, R. L., and T. A. Bancroft, *Statistical Theory in Research*. New York: McGraw-Hill Book Company, 1952, Chapter 13.

Draper, N., and H. Smith, *Applied Regression Analysis*. New York: John Wiley & Sons, Inc., 1966.

Ezekiel, M., and K. A. Fox, *Methods of Correlation* and *Regression Analysis*, 3d ed. New York: John Wiley & Sons, Inc., 1959.

Li, J. C. R., *Introduction to Statistical Inference*. Ann Arbor, Mich.: J. W. Edwards, Publisher, Inc., 1961, Chapter 16.

Mendenhall, W., *An Introduction to Linear Models and the Design and Analysis of Experiments*. Belmont, Calif.: Wadsworth Publishing Company, Inc., 1967, Chapters 6 and 7.

Chapter Thirteen

The Analysis of Variance

13.1   Introduction

Many experiments are conducted to determine the effect of one or more variables on a response. A linear relationship between a response, y, and an independent variable, x, was studied in Chapter 12, and, in a more general sense, the comparison of means in Chapter 9 was a similar problem. For example, the comparison of the difference in the mean monthly sales volume for two different amounts spent on advertising is a study of the independent variable, advertising expenditures, which is a type of "stimulus," on a response, y, the mean rate of sales.

The preceding comments indicate that independent experimental variables may be one of two types, quantitative or qualitative. The former, as the name implies, are those familiar variables that are subject to a quantitative interpretation. Qualitative variables are not. Thus the monthly sales volume, annual income, number of employees, and daily demand represent four quantitative variables. In contrast, the "manufacturer" of automobile tires is a variable that is likely to be related to the wearing characteristics of tires, but there is no way to order or arrange five "manufacturers" on a continuum. Thus "manufacturers" would be a qualitative independent variable. Similarly, we may wish to determine whether the mean yield of chemical in a manufacturing operation varies depending upon the foreman managing the process and also whether it varies from one working shift to another. Four foremen, Jones, Smith, Adams, and Green, would represent "levels" or settings of a single qualitative variable, "foremen"; the three working shifts would identify levels of a second qualitative variable, "shifts."* The complete experiment would involve,

---

* The word "level" is usually used to denote the intensity for a quantitative independent variable. We use it in the present context to refer to the "settings" for either quantitative or qualitative independent variables.

therefore, a study of the effect of two independent qualitative variables, "foremen" and "shifts," on yield of chemical.

In this chapter we consider the comparison of more than two means, which, in the context of the previous discussion, implies a study of the effect of a single independent variable (quantitative or qualitative) on a response. We shall then extend the procedure to include the analysis of designed experiments involving two independent variables and discuss a generalization of the procedure for more than two independent variables.

13.2   The Analysis of Variance

The methodology for the analysis of experiments involving several independent variables can best be explained in terms of the linear probabilistic model of Chapter 12. Although elementary and unified, this approach is not susceptible to the condensation necessary for inclusion in an elementary text. Instead, we shall attempt an intuitive discussion using a procedure known as the analysis of variance Actually, the two approaches are connected and the analysis of variance can easily be explained in a general way in terms of the linear model. The interested reader may consult the introductory text by Mendenhall (1967).

As the name implies the analysis-of-variance procedure attempts to analyze the variation of a response and to assign portions of this variation to each of a set of independent variables The reasoning is that response variables vary only because of variation in a set of unknown independent variables. Since the experimenter will rarely, if ever, include all the variables affecting the response in his experiment, random variation in the response is observed even though all independent variables considered are held constant. The objective of the analysis of variance is to locate important independent variables in a study and to determine how they interact and affect the response.

The rationale underlying the analysis of variance can be indicated best with a symbolic discussion. The actual analysis of variance—that is, "how to do it"—can be illustrated with an example.

Recall that the variability of a set of *n* measurements is proportional to the sum of squares of deviations,

$$\sum_{i=1}^{n} (y_i - \bar{y})^2$$

and that this quantity is used to calculate the sample variance. The analysis of variance partitions the sum of squares of deviations, called the total sum of squares of deviations, into parts, each of which is attributed to one of the independent variables in the experiment, plus a remainder that is associated with random error. This may be shown diagrammatically as indicated in Figure 13.1 for three independent variables.

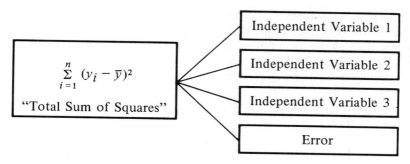

Figure 13.1   *Partitioning of the Total Sum of Squares of Deviations*

If a multivariable linear regression model were written for the response, as suggested in Section 12.9, the portion of the total sum of squares of deviations assigned to error would be the sum of squares of deviations of the y values about their respective predicted values obtained from the prediction equation, $\hat{y}$. You will recall that this quantity, represented by the sum of squares of deviations of the y values about a straight line, was denoted as SSE in Chapter 12.

Figure 13.2   *Graphic Portrayal of the Deviations of the y Values About Their Means*

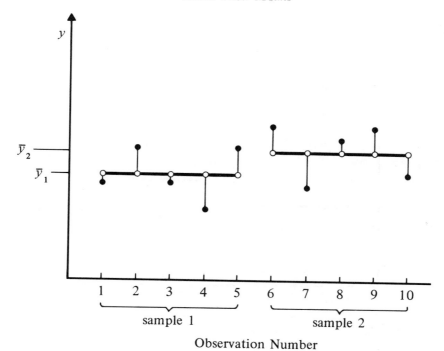

For the cases we consider, when the independent variables are unrelated to the response, it can be shown that each of the pieces of the total sum of squares of deviations, divided by an appropriate constant, provides an independent and unbiased estimator of σ^2, the variance of the experimental error. When a variable is highly related to the response, its portion (called the "sum of squares" for the variable)

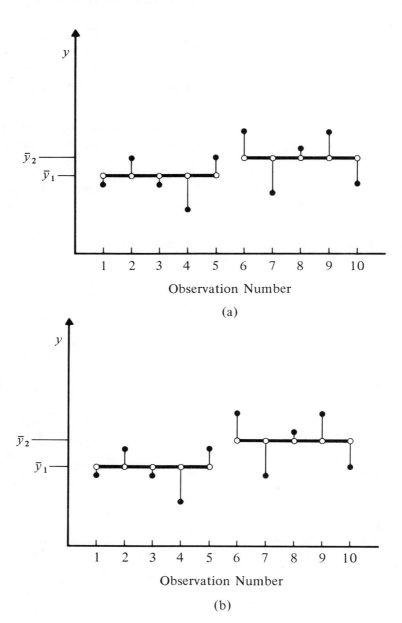

(a)

(b)

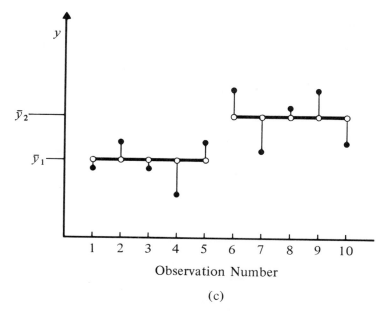

(c)

Figure 13.3   *Three Fictitious Sets of Measurements,* $n_1 = n_2 = 5$
(the Relative Positions of Points Within Each Set Is Held Constant)

will be inflated. This condition can be detected by comparing the estimate of σ^2 for a particular independent variable with that obtained from SSE using an F test (see Section 12.7). If the estimate for the independent variable is significantly larger, the F test will reject an hypothesis of "no effect for the independent variable" and produce evidence to indicate a relation to the response.

The logic behind an analysis of variance can be illustrated by considering a familiar example, the comparison of two population means for an unpaired experiment (completely randomized design), which was analyzed in Chapter 9 using a Student's t statistic. We shall commence by giving a graphic and intuitive explanation of the procedure.

Suppose that we have selected random samples of five observations each from two populations, I and II, and that the y values are plotted as shown in Figure 13.2. Note that the $n_1 = 5$ observations from population I lie to the left; the $n_2 = 5$ observations from population II lie to the right. The sample means, $\bar{y}_1$ and $\bar{y}_2$, are shown as horizontal lines in the figure and the deviations of the y values about their respective means are the vertical line segments. Now examine Figure 13.2. Do you think the data provide sufficient evidence to indicate a difference between the two population means? Before we explain, let us look at another figure.

The same two sets of five points are plotted in Figure 13.3 except that the relative distance between the two sets is greater in (b) than in (a) and even greater in (c). Therefore, the distance between $\bar{y}_1$ and $\bar{y}_2$ increases as you move from Figure 13.3(a) to (b) and then to (c), but the relative variation within each set is held constant.

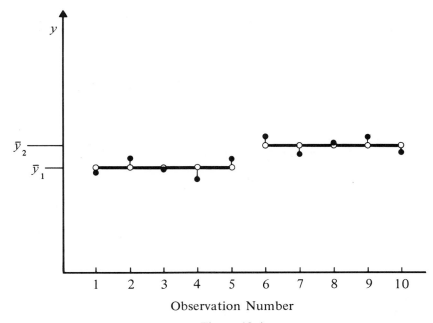

Figure 13.4

Now view the three plots, (a), (b), and (c), and decide which situation, (a), (b), or (c), provides the greatest evidence to indicate a difference between μ_1 and μ_2. We think you will choose Figure 13.3(c) because that plot shows the greatest difference between sample means in comparison with the variation of the points about their respective sample means. This latter variation was held constant for all three plots.

Note that the population means actually may differ for Figure 13.3(a) but this fact would not be apparent, because the variation of the points about their respective sample means is too large in comparison with the difference between $\bar{y}_1$ and $\bar{y}_2$. Figure 13.4 shows the same difference between sample means as for Figure 13.3(a), but the variation within samples has been reduced. Now it appears that a difference does exist between μ_1 and μ_2.

Now let us leave our intuitive discussion and consider the two sample comparison of means for sample sizes n_1 and n_2. Particularly, we shall want to see how the total sum of squares of deviations can be partitioned into portions corresponding to the difference between the means and another to the variation within the two samples. The total sum of squares of deviations of all $(n_1 + n_2)$ y values about the general mean is

$$\text{Total SS} = \sum_{i=1}^{2} \sum_{j=1}^{n_i} (y_{ij} - \bar{y})^2,$$

where $\bar{y}$ is the average of all $(n_1 + n_2)$ observations contained in the two samples. Then with a bit of algebra you can show that

$$\text{Total SS} = \sum_{i=1}^{2} \sum_{j=1}^{n_i} (y_{ij} - \bar{y})^2 = \underbrace{\sum_{i=1}^{2} n_i(\bar{y}_i - \bar{y})^2}_{\text{SST}} + \underbrace{\sum_{i=1}^{2} \sum_{j=1}^{n_i} (y_{ij} - \bar{y}_i)^2}_{\text{SSE}}$$

where $\bar{y}_i$ is the average of the observations in the ith sample, $i = 1, 2$. The first quantity to the right of the equal sign, called the sum of squares for treatments and denoted by the symbol SST, can be shown (with a bit of algebra) to equal

$$\text{SST} = \frac{n_1 n_2}{n_1 + n_2}(\bar{y}_1 - \bar{y}_2)^2.$$

Thus SST, which increases as the difference between $\bar{y}_1$ and $\bar{y}_2$ increases, measures the variation between the sample means. Consequently, SST would be larger for the data of Figure 13.3(c) than for Figure 13.3(a).

The second quantity to the right of the equal sign is the familiar pooled sum of squares of deviations computed in the t test of Section 9.4. It is the sum of the sum of squares of deviations of the y values about their respective sample means. This pooled sum of squares measures within sample variation, a variation that is usually attributed to experimental error, and is consequently called "sum of squares for error" (denoted by the symbol SSE).

The quantities SST and SSE measure the two kinds of variation that we viewed in the graphic representation of Figure 13.3, the variation between means and the variation within samples. The greater the variation between means (the larger SST) in comparison with the variation within samples (SSE), the greater the weight of evidence to indicate a difference between μ_1 and μ_2. How large is large? When will SST be large enough (relative to SSE) to indicate a real difference between μ_1 and μ_2?

As indicated in Chapter 9,

$$s^2 = \text{MSE} = \frac{\text{SSE}}{n_1 + n_2 - 2}$$

provides an unbiased estimator of σ^2. Also, when the null hypothesis is true (that is, $\mu_1 = \mu_2$), SST divided by an appropriate number of degrees of freedom yields a second unbiased estimator of σ^2, which we shall denote as MST. For this example, the number of degrees of freedom for MST is equal to 1.

When the null hypothesis is true (that is, $\mu_1 = \mu_2$), MSE (the mean square for error) and MST (the mean square for treatments) will estimate the same quantity and should be "roughly" of the same magnitude. When the null hypothesis is false and $\mu_1 \neq \mu_2$, MST will probably be larger than MSE.

The preceding discussion, along with a review of the variance ratio, Section 9.7, suggests the use of

$$\frac{\text{MST}}{\text{MSE}}$$

as a test statistic to test the hypothesis $\mu_1 = \mu_2$ against the alternative, $\mu_1 \neq \mu_2$. Indeed, when both populations are normally distributed, it can be shown that MST and MSE are independent in a probabilistic sense and

$$F = \frac{\text{MST}}{\text{MSE}}$$

follows the F probability distribution of Section 9.7. Disagreement with the null hypothesis is indicated by a large value of F, and hence the rejection region for a given α will be

$$F \geq F_\alpha.$$

Thus the analysis-of-variance test results in a one-tailed F test. The degrees of freedom for the F will be those associated with MST and MSE, which we will denote as v_1 and v_2, respectively. Although we have not indicated how one determines v_1 and v_2, in general, $v_1 = 1$ and $v_2 = (n_1 + n_2 - 2)$ for the two-sample experiment described.

If we test $H_0 : \mu_1 = \mu_2$ against $H_a : \mu_1 \neq \mu_2$ using the methods of Section 9.4, our test statistic is

$$t = \frac{\bar{y}_1 - \bar{y}_2}{\sqrt{s^2\left(\frac{1}{n_1} + \frac{1}{n_2}\right)}}$$

where the t statistic has $n_1 + n_2 - 2$ degrees of freedom. But

$$t^2 = \frac{(\bar{y}_1 - \bar{y}_2)^2}{s^2\left(\frac{1}{n_1} + \frac{1}{n_2}\right)} = \frac{\frac{n_1 n_2}{n_1 + n_2}(\bar{y}_1 - \bar{y}_2)^2}{s^2} = \frac{\text{MST}}{\text{MSE}} = F$$

[since $1/n_1 + 1/n_2 = (n_1 + n_2)/n_1 n_2$]. Thus we have an equivalent two-tailed test procedure: you can test the hypothesis $H_0 : \mu_1 = \mu_2$ against the alternative hypothesis $H_a : \mu_1 \neq \mu_2$, using either a Student's t statistic or an F statistic. However, the analysis-of-variance procedure will enable us to compare more than two population means (as we will see in Section 13.3). The t statistic of Section 9.4 does not.

Before proceeding to some illustrative examples, we should point out that our computations are often simplified by coding the data. By coding we mean that the data are transformed by adding a constant, multiplying a constant, or a combination of both to each observational value. Theorem 3.1 implies that if all the data are coded in the same way, the F values computed from the original data and the coded data are equal. The following example illustrates the use of coding in an analysis-of-variance problem.

Example 13.1   *The coded values for the hours of life of two brands of light bulbs are given below for samples of six bulbs drawn randomly from each of the two brands. The true values, in hundreds of hours, were coded by multiplying each by $(1/100)$ to give the coded values given in Table 13.1. Do the data present*

Table 13.1

BULB	A	B
1	6.1	9.1
2	7.1	8.2
3	7.8	8.6
4	6.9	6.9
5	7.6	7.5
6	8.2	7.9
Total	43.7	48.2

sufficient evidence to indicate a difference in mean lifetime for the two brands of light bulbs?

Solution   *Although the Student's t could be used as the test statistic for this example, we shall use our analysis-of-variance F test, since it is more general and can be used to compare more than two means.*

The two desired sums of squares of deviations* are

$$\text{SST} = n_1 \sum_{i=1}^{2} (\bar{y}_i - \bar{y})^2 = 6 \sum_{i=1}^{2} (\bar{y}_i - \bar{y})^2 = \frac{n_1}{2}(\bar{y}_1 - \bar{y}_2)^2 = \frac{6}{2}\left(\frac{43.7}{6} - \frac{48.2}{6}\right)^2$$

$$= 1.6875,$$

$$\text{SSE} = \sum_{i=1}^{2} \sum_{j=1}^{6} (y_{ij} - \bar{y}_i)^2 = \sum_{j=1}^{6} (y_{1j} - \bar{y}_1)^2 + \sum_{j=1}^{6} (y_{2j} - \bar{y}_2)^2$$

$$= 5.8617.$$

* *Note:* These formulas apply to the special case where $n_1 = n_2$.

(The reader may verify that SSE *is the pooled sum of squares of the deviations for the two samples discussed in Section 9.4. Also, note that Total* SS = SST + SSE.*) The mean squares for treatment and error are, respectively,*

$$MST = \frac{SST}{1} = 1.6875,$$

$$MSE = \frac{SSE}{2n_1 - 2} = \frac{5.8617}{10} = .5862.$$

To test the null hypothesis $\mu_1 = \mu_2$, *we compute the test statistic*

$$F = \frac{MST}{MSE} = \frac{1.6875}{.5862} = 2.88.$$

The critical value of the F statistic for $\alpha = .05$ *is 4.96. Although the mean square for treatments is almost three times as large as the mean square for error, it is not large enough to reject the null hypothesis. Consequently, there is not sufficient evidence to indicate a difference between* μ_1 *and* μ_2.

    As noted, the purpose of the preceding example was to illustrate the computations involved in a simple analysis of variance. The F test for comparing two means is equivalent to a Student's t test, because an F statistic with one degree of freedom in the numerator is equal to t^2. *Had the t test been used for this example, we would have found* $t = -1.6967$, *which we see satisfies the relationship* $t^2 = (-1.6967)^2 = 2.88 = F$. *This relationship also holds for the critical values. The reader can easily verify that the square of* $t_{.025} = 2.228$ *(used for the two-tailed test with* $\alpha = .05$ *and* $v = 10$ *degrees of freedom) is equal to* $F_{.05} = 4.96$.

Of what value is the Total SS? The answer is that it provides an easy way to compute SSE. Since the total SS partitions into SST and SSE, that is,

$$Total\ SS = SST + SSE,$$

then

$$SSE = Total\ SS - SST.$$

Both the total SS and SST are easy to compute. Hence one can easily find SSE by substituting into the expression above. For this example

$$
\text{Total SS} = \sum_{i=1}^{2} \sum_{j=1}^{6} (y_{ij} - \bar{y})^2 = \sum_{i=1}^{2} \sum_{j=1}^{6} y_{ij}^2 - \frac{\left(\sum_{i=1}^{2} \sum_{j=1}^{6} y_{ij} \right)^2}{12}
$$

$$
= (\text{sum of squares of all } y \text{ values}) - \frac{(\text{total of all } y \text{ values})^2}{12}
$$

$$
= 711.35 - \frac{(91.9)^2}{12} = 7.5492.
$$

Then

$$
\begin{aligned}
\text{SSE} &= \text{Total SS} - \text{SST} \\
&= 7.5492 - 1.6875 \\
&= 5.8617.
\end{aligned}
$$

This is exactly the same value obtained by the tedious computation and pooling of the sums of squares of deviations from the individual samples.

13.3   A Comparison of More Than Two Means

An analysis of variance to detect a difference in a set of more than two population means is a simple generalization of the analysis of variance of Section 13.2. The random selection of independent samples from p populations is known as a completely randomized experimental design

Assume that independent random samples have been drawn from p normal populations with means $\mu_1, \mu_2, \ldots, \mu_p$, respectively, and variance σ^2. Thus all populations are assumed to possess equal variances. And, to be completely general, we allow the sample sizes to be unequal and let n_i, $i = 1, 2, \ldots, p$, be the number in the sample drawn from the ith population. The total number of observations in the experiment will be $n = n_1 + n_2 + \cdots + n_p$.

Let y_{ij} denote the measured response on the jth experiment unit in the ith sample and let T_i and $\bar{T}_i$ represent the total and the mean, respectively, for the observations in the ith sample. (The modification in the symbols for sample totals and averages will simplify the computing formulas for the sums of squares.) Then, as in the analysis of variance involving two means,

$$
\text{Total SS} = \text{SST} + \text{SSE},
$$

where

$$\text{Total SS} = \sum_{i=1}^{p} \sum_{j=1}^{n_i} (y_{ij} - \bar{y})^2 = \sum_{i=1}^{p} \sum_{j=1}^{n_i} y_{ij}^2 - \text{CM}$$

$$= (\text{sum of squares of all } y \text{ values}) - \text{CM}$$

and

$$\text{CM} = \frac{(\text{total of all observations})^2}{n} = \frac{\left(\displaystyle\sum_{i=1}^{p} \sum_{j=1}^{n_i} y_{ij} \right)^2}{n} = n\bar{y}^2$$

(the term CM denotes "correction for the mean"),

$$\text{SST} = \sum_{i=1}^{p} n_i (\bar{T}_i - \bar{y})^2 = \sum_{i=1}^{p} \frac{T_i^2}{n_i} - \text{CM}$$

$$= (\text{sum of squares of the treatment totals with each square divided by the number of observations in that particular total}) - \text{CM}$$

$$\text{SSE} = \text{Total SS} - \text{SST}.$$

Although the easy way to compute SSE is by subtraction as shown above, it is interesting to note that SSE is the pooled sum of squares for all p samples and is equal to

$$\text{SSE} = \sum_{i=1}^{p} \sum_{j=1}^{n_i} (y_{ij} - \bar{T}_i)^2.$$

The unbiased estimator of σ^2 based on $(n_1 + n_2 + \cdots + n_p - p)$ degrees of freedom is

$$s^2 = \text{MSE} = \frac{\text{SSE}}{n_1 + n_2 + \cdots + n_p - p}.$$

The mean-square treatments will possess $(p - 1)$ degrees of freedom, that is, one less than the number of means, and

$$\text{MST} = \frac{\text{SST}}{p - 1}.$$

To test the null hypothesis

$$H_0 : \mu_1 = \mu_2 = \cdots = \mu_p$$

against the alternative that at least one of the equalities does not hold, MST is compared with MSE using the F statistic based upon $v_1 = p - 1$ and $v_2 = \left(\sum_{i=1}^{p} n_i - p \right) = n - p$ degrees of freedom. The null hypothesis will be rejected if

$$F = \frac{\text{MST}}{\text{MSE}} > F_\alpha,$$

where F_α is the critical value of F, based on $(p - 1)$ and $(n - p)$ degrees of freedom, for probability of a type I error, α.

Intuitively, the greater the difference between the observed treatment means, $\overline{T}_1, \overline{T}_2, \ldots, \overline{T}_p$, the greater will be the evidence to indicate a difference between their corresponding population means. It can be seen from the above expression that SST $= 0$ when all the observed treatment means are identical because then $\overline{T}_1 = \overline{T}_2 = \cdots = \overline{T}_p = \bar{y}$, and the deviations appearing in SST, $(\overline{T}_i - \bar{y})$, $i = 1, 2, \ldots, p$, will equal zero. As the treatment means get farther apart, the deviations $(\overline{T}_i - \bar{y})$ will increase in absolute value and SST will increase in magnitude. Consequently, the larger the value of SST, the greater will be the weight of evidence favoring a rejection of the null hypothesis. This same line of reasoning will apply to the F tests employed in the analysis of variance for all designed experiments.

The test is summarized as follows:

F Test for Comparing p Population Means

$H_0 : \mu_1 = \mu_2 = \cdots = \mu_p$
$H_a :$ *One or more pairs of population means differ*

Test Statistic: $F = \dfrac{\text{MST}}{\text{MSE}}$

where F is based on $v_1 = (p - 1)$ and $v_2 = (n - p)$ degrees of freedom.
Rejection Region: *Reject if $F > F_\alpha$, where F_α lies in the upper tail of the F distribution (with $v_1 = p - 1$ and $v_2 = n - p$) and satisfies the expression*

$$P(F > F_\alpha) = \alpha.$$

The assumptions underlying the analysis-of-variance F tests should receive particular attention. The samples are assumed to have been randomly selected from the p populations in an independent manner. The populations are assumed to be normally distributed with equal variances σ^2 and means $\mu_1, \mu_2, \ldots, \mu_p$. Moderate departures from these assumptions will not seriously affect the properties of the test. This is particularly true of the normality assumption.

Example 13.2   *Four groups of salesmen for a magazine sales agency were subjected to different sales training programs. Because there were some dropouts during the training programs, the number of trainees varied from group to group. At the end of the training programs, each salesman was randomly assigned a sales area from a group of sales areas that were judged to have equivalent sales potentials. The number of sales made by each of the four groups of salesmen during the first week after completing the training program is listed in Table 13.2. Do the data present sufficient evidence to indicate a difference in the mean achievement for the four training programs?*

Table 13.2

	1	2	3	4
	65	75	59	94
	87	69	78	89
	73	83	67	80
	79	81	62	88
	81	72	83	
	69	79	76	
		90		
T_i	454	549	425	351
$\bar{T}_i$	75.67	78.43	70.83	87.75

Solution

$$CM = \frac{\left(\sum_{i=1}^{4} \sum_{j=1}^{n_i} y_{ij} \right)^2}{n} = \frac{(\text{total of all observations})^2}{n}$$

$$= \frac{(1{,}779)^2}{23} = 137{,}601.8,$$

$$Total\ SS = \sum_{i=1}^{4} \sum_{j=1}^{n_i} y_{ij}^2 - CM$$

$$= (\text{sum of squares of all } y \text{ values}) - CM$$
$$= (65)^2 + (87)^2 + (73)^2 + \cdots + (88)^2 - CM$$
$$= 139{,}511 - 137{,}601.8$$
$$= 1{,}909.2,$$

$$SST = \sum_{i=1}^{4} \frac{T_i^2}{n_i} - CM$$

$$= \text{(sum of squares of the treatment totals with each square divided by}$$
$$\text{the number of observations in that particular total)} - \text{CM}$$

$$= \frac{(454)^2}{6} + \frac{(549)^2}{7} + \frac{(425)^2}{6} + \frac{(351)^2}{4} - \text{CM}$$

$$= 138{,}314.4 - 137{,}601.8$$

$$= 712.6,$$

$$\text{SSE} = \text{total SS} - \text{SST} = 1{,}196.6.$$

The mean squares for treatment and error are

$$\text{MST} = \frac{\text{SST}}{p-1} = \frac{712.6}{3} = 237.5,$$

$$\text{MSE} = \frac{\text{SSE}}{n_1 + n_2 + \cdots + n_p - p} = \frac{\text{SSE}}{n-p} = \frac{1{,}196.6}{19} = 63.0.$$

The test statistic for testing the hypothesis, $\mu_1 = \mu_2 = \mu_3 = \mu_4$, *is*

$$F = \frac{\text{MST}}{\text{MSE}} = \frac{237.5}{63.0} = 3.77,$$

where

$$v_1 = (p-1) = 3,$$

$$v_2 = \sum_{i=1}^{p} n_i - 4 = 19.$$

The critical value of F for $\alpha = .05$ *is* $F_{.05} = 3.13$. *Since the computed value of F exceeds* $F_{.05}$, *we reject the null hypothesis and conclude that the evidence is sufficient to indicate a difference in mean achievement for the four training programs.*

You may feel that the above conclusion could have been made on the basis of visual observation of the treatment means. It is not difficult to construct a set of data that will lead the "visual" decision maker to erroneous results.

13.4 Analysis-of-Variance Table for a Completely Randomized Design

The calculations of the analysis of variance are usually displayed in an analysis-of-variance (ANOVA or AOV) table. The table for the design of Section

Table 13.3 *ANOVA Table for a Comparison of Means*

SOURCE	d.f.	SS	MS	F
Treatments	$p - 1$	SST	$MST = SST/(p - 1)$	MST/MSE
Error	$n - p$	SSE	$MSE = SSE/(n - p)$	
Total	$n - 1$	Total SS		

13.3 involving p treatment means is shown in Table 13.3. Column 1 shows the source of each sum of squares of deviations; column 2 gives the respective degrees of freedom; columns 3 and 4 give the corresponding sums of squares and mean squares, respectively. A calculated value of F, comparing MST and MSE, is usually shown in column 5. Note that the degrees of freedom and sums of squares add to their respective totals.

The ANOVA table for Example 13.2, shown in Table 13.4, gives a compact presentation of the appropriate computed quantities for the analysis of variance.

Table 13.4 *ANOVA Table for Example 13.2*

SOURCE	d.f.	SS	MS	F
Treatments	3	712.6	237.5	3.77
Error	19	1,196.6	63.0	
Total	22	1,909.2		

13.5 Estimation for the Completely Randomized Design

Confidence intervals for a single treatment mean and the difference between a pair of treatment means, Section 13.3, are identical to those given in Chapter 9. The confidence interval for the mean of treatment i or the difference between treatments i and j are, respectively,

$$\bar{T}_i \pm t_{\alpha/2} s/\sqrt{n_i}$$

and

$$(\bar{T}_i - \bar{T}_j) \pm t_{\alpha/2} s \sqrt{\frac{1}{n_i} + \frac{1}{n_j}},$$

where

$$s = \sqrt{s^2} = \sqrt{\mathrm{MSE}} = \sqrt{\frac{\mathrm{SSE}}{n_1 + n_2 + \cdots + n_p - p}}$$

and $t_{\alpha/2}$ is based upon $(n - p)$ degrees of freedom.

Note that the confidence intervals stated above are appropriate for single treatment means or a comparison of a pair of means selected prior to observation of the data. The stated confidence coefficients are based on random sampling. If one were to look at the data and always compare the largest and smallest sample means, the assumption of randomness would be disturbed. Certainly the difference between the largest and smallest sample means is expected to be larger than for a pair selected at random.

Example 13.3   *Find a 95 percent confidence interval for the mean number of sales for those trained in training program 1, Example 13.2.*

Solution   *The 95 percent confidence interval for the mean number of sales is*

$$\bar{T}_1 \pm t_{.025} s/\sqrt{6},$$

or

$$75.67 \pm \frac{(2.093)(7.94)}{\sqrt{6}},$$

or

$$75.67 \pm 6.78.$$

Example 13.4 *Find a 95 percent confidence interval for the difference in mean sales for training programs 1 and 4, Example 13.2.*

Solution *The 95 percent confidence interval for* $(\mu_1 - \mu_4)$ *is*

$$(\bar{T}_1 - \bar{T}_4) \pm (2.093)(7.94)\sqrt{\frac{1}{6} + \frac{1}{4}},$$

or

$$-12.08 \pm 10.73.$$

13.6 A Randomized Block Design

The randomized block design is a generalization of the paired-difference design, Section 9.5. The purpose of this design is to make comparisons between a set of treatments within blocks of relatively homogeneous experimental material. In Section 9.5 two treatments (types of automobile tires) were compared within the relative homogeneity of a single automobile, which eliminated auto-to-auto variability.

The difference between a randomized block design and the completely randomized design can be demonstrated by considering an experiment to compare the effect of product display (treatments) on sales in a marketing analysis. Product display may be defined as packaging variations or arrangements within the market-place.

Suppose that four package designs are selected as the treatments and we wish to study their effect on sales within 10 supermarkets. The 10 supermarkets could then be randomly assigned as distributors for each of the four package designs. Random assignment of the supermarkets to treatments (or vice versa) randomly distributes errors due to interval variability of the supermarkets to the four treatments and yields four samples that are, for all practical purposes, random and independent. This would be a completely randomized experimental design and would require the analysis of Section 13.3.

The confidence interval for a comparison of means using the completely randomized design is dependent upon s, the estimated standard deviation of the experimental error. If one were able to reduce σ, the value of s would probably decrease and the confidence interval would narrow, indicating an increase in information in the experiment. This would imply that a reduction is required in the magnitude of the random experimental errors that occur when making repeated measurements for a given treatment.

The random experimental error is composed of a number of components. Some of these are due to the differences between the supermarkets, to the failure of consecutive sales records for the product within a supermarket to be identical (due to variation in the supermarket's advertising and changing patterns of its customers' buying behavior), to the failure of the marketing research director to administer consistently the program from supermarket to supermarket, and, finally, to errors in recording the actual sales records in each store. Reduction of any of these causes of error will increase the information in the experiment.

The store-to-store variation in the above experiment can be eliminated by using the supermarkets as blocks. Thus, each supermarket would receive each of the four package designs (treatments) assigned in a random sequence. The resulting randomized block design would appear symbolically as in Figure 13.5. Each display in a single store is an experimental unit. We see four units (squares) assigned to each store in Figure 13.2, where it is assumed that the displays are run in a time sequence in the order shown from top to bottom. The circled number appearing in a given square is the package design (treatment) to be used for that display. In store number 1, the package design displays are run in the order 2, 1, 4, 3. With the randomized block design only 10 supermarkets are required to acquire 10 sales measurements per treatment, whereas 40 would be required using the completely randomized design. Note that each treatment occurs exactly once in each block.

The word "randomized" in the name of the design implies that the treatments are randomly assigned within the block. For our experiment, position within the block would pertain to the position in the sequence when assigning a particular

Figure 13.5   *Randomized Block Design*

Supermarkets (Blocks)

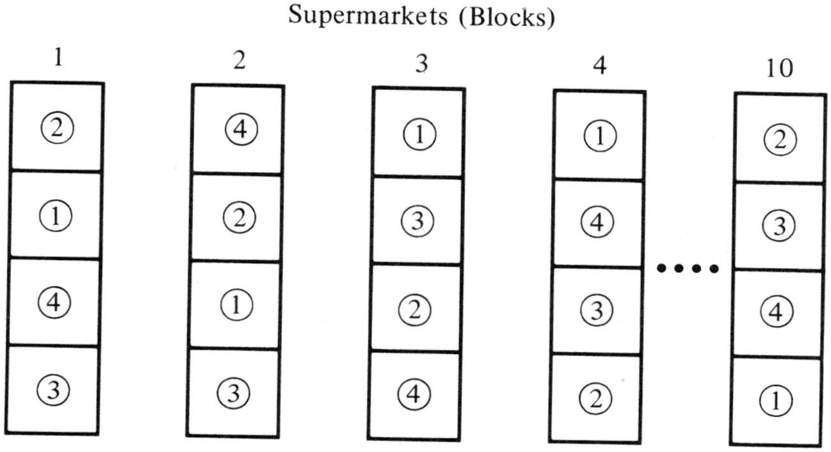

package design to a given supermarket over time. For instance, the experiment may be conducted over a period of 4 weeks with each store being randomly assigned a different package design to sell each week. The purpose of the randomization (that is, position in the block) is to eliminate bias due to time. For example, if the product to be studied is packaged turkey stuffing mix, sales are likely to be very high during the Thanksgiving week. Randomizing within the supermarkets will tend to minimize the chance of one package design appearing very favorable primarily because of its selection as the design to market by all the supermarkets during Thanksgiving week. However, it is well to note that if a sizable and identical trend in sales (response) does exist within blocks, more error might be introduced by blocking than that implied by store-to-store variability. If this were the case, the blocks would not be "relatively homogeneous" as formerly thought, and the randomized block design would not be appropriate.

Blocks may represent time, location, or experimental material. If three treatments are to be compared and there is a suspected trend in the mean response over time, a substantial part of the time-trend variation may be removed by blocking. All three treatments would be randomly applied to experimental units in one small block of time. This procedure would be repeated in succeeding blocks of time until the required amount of data is collected. As we have seen, a comparison of the sale of competitive or differently designed products in supermarkets should be made within supermarkets, thus using the supermarkets as blocks and removing store-to-store variability. An experiment designed to test and compare subject response to a set of stimuli uses the subjects as blocks to minimize the chance of bias due to fatigue or learning. Animal experiments in agriculture and medicine often utilize animal litters as blocks, applying all the treatments, one each, to animals within a litter. Because of heredity, animals within a litter are more homogeneous than those between litters. This type of blocking removes the litter-to-litter variation just as the stimulus–response experiment is designed to remove the subject-to-subject variation and the market preference experiment is designed to remove store-to-store variation.

13.7   The Analysis of Variance for a Randomized Block Design

The randomized block design implies the presence of two qualitative independent variables, "blocks" and "treatments." Consequently, the total sum of squares of deviations of the response measurements about their mean may be partitioned into three parts, the sums of squares for blocks, treatments, and error.

Denote the total and average of all observations in block i as B_i and $\bar{B}_i$, respectively. Similarly, let T_j and $\bar{T}_j$ denote the total and mean of all observations receiving treatment j. Then, for a randomized block design involving b blocks and p treatments,

$$\text{Total SS} = \text{SSB} + \text{SST} + \text{SSE}$$

$$= \sum_{i=1}^{b} \sum_{j=1}^{p} (y_{ij} - \bar{y})^2 = \sum_{i=1}^{b} \sum_{j=1}^{p} y_{ij}^2 - \text{CM}$$

$$= (\text{sum of squares of all } y \text{ values}) - \text{CM},$$

$$\text{SSB} = p \sum_{i=1}^{b} (\bar{B}_i - \bar{y})^2 = \frac{\sum_{i=1}^{b} B_i^2}{p} - \text{CM}$$

$$= \frac{\text{sum of squares of all block totals}}{\text{number of observations in a single total}} - \text{CM},$$

$$\text{SST} = b \sum_{j=1}^{p} (\bar{T}_j - \bar{y})^2 = \frac{\sum_{j=1}^{p} T_j^2}{b} - \text{CM}$$

$$= \frac{\text{sum of squares of all treatment totals}}{\text{number of observations in a single total}} - \text{CM},$$

where

$$\bar{y} = (\text{average of all } n = bp \text{ observations}) = \frac{\sum_{i=1}^{b} \sum_{j=1}^{p} y_{ij}}{n}$$

and

$$\text{CM} = \frac{(\text{total of all observations})^2}{n} = \frac{\left(\sum_{i=1}^{b} \sum_{j=1}^{p} y_{ij} \right)^2}{n}.$$

The analysis of variance for the randomized block design is presented in Table 13.5. The degrees of freedom associated with each sum of squares is shown in the second column. Mean squares are calculated by dividing the sums of squares by their respective degrees of freedom. Note that the degrees of freedom for blocks, treatments, and error always sum to $(n - 1)$.

Table 13.5   *ANOVA Table for a Randomized Block Design*

SOURCE	d.f.	SS	MS
Blocks	$b - 1$	SSB	$\text{MSB} = \text{SSB}/(b - 1)$
Treatments	$p - 1$	SST	$\text{MST} = \text{SST}/(p - 1)$
Error	$n - b - p + 1$	SSE	$\text{MSE} = \dfrac{\text{SSE}}{n - b - p + 1}$
Total	$n - 1$	Total SS	

To test the null hypothesis "there is no difference in treatment means" we use the F statistic,

$$F = \frac{\text{MST}}{\text{MSE}},$$

and reject if $F > F_\alpha$ based on $v_1 = (p - 1)$ and $v_2 = (n - b - p + 1)$ degrees of freedom. [Since $n = bp$, v_2 may also be written as $v_2 = (b - 1)(p - 1)$.]

Blocking not only reduces the experimental error, it also provides an opportunity to see whether evidence exists to indicate a difference in the mean response for blocks. Under the null hypothesis that there is no difference in mean response for blocks, MSB provides an unbiased estimator of σ^2 based on $(b - 1)$ degrees of freedom. Where a real difference exists in the treatment means, MSB will probably be inflated in comparison with MSE, and

$$F = \frac{\text{MSB}}{\text{MSE}}$$

provides a test statistic. As in the test for treatments, the rejection region for the test will be

$$F > F_\alpha,$$

based on $v_1 = b - 1$ and $v_2 = n - b - p + 1$ degrees of freedom.

Example 13.5   *A consumer-preference study involving three different package designs (treatments) was laid out in a randomized block design among four supermarkets (blocks). The data shown in Figure 13.6 represent the number of*

Supermarkets

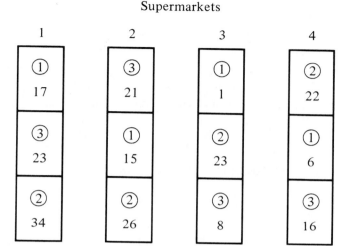

Figure 13.6

units sold for each package design within each supermarket during each of three given weeks. Do the data present sufficient evidence to indicate a difference in the mean sales for each package design (treatment)? Do they present sufficient evidence to indicate a difference in mean sales for the supermarkets?

Solution   *The treatment and block totals are as follows:*

$$T_1 = 39 \qquad T_2 = 105 \qquad T_3 = 68$$
$$B_1 = 74 \qquad B_2 = 62 \qquad B_3 = 32 \qquad B_4 = 44$$

The sums of squares for the analysis of variance are shown individually below, and jointly on the analysis-of-variance table (Table 13.6). Thus

$$CM = \frac{(\text{total})^2}{n} = \frac{(212)^2}{12} = 3{,}745.33$$

$$\text{Total SS} = \sum_{i=1}^{4} \sum_{j=1}^{3} (y_{ij} - \bar{y})^2 = \sum_{i=1}^{4} \sum_{j=1}^{3} y_{ij}^2 - CM$$

$$= (\text{sum of squares of all } y \text{ values}) - CM$$

$$= (17)^2 + (23)^2 + \cdots + (16)^2 - CM$$

$$= 4{,}686 - 3{,}745.33 = 940.67,$$

$$\text{SSB} = \frac{\sum\limits_{i=1}^{4} B_i^2}{3} - \text{CM}$$

$$= \frac{\text{sum of squares of all block totals}}{\text{number of observations in a single total}} - \text{CM}$$

$$= \frac{(74)^2 + (62)^2 + (32)^2 + (44)^2}{3} - \text{CM}$$

$$= 4{,}093.33 - 3{,}745.33 = 348.00,$$

$$\text{SST} = \frac{\sum\limits_{j=1}^{3} T_j^2}{4} - \text{CM}$$

$$= \frac{\text{sum of squares of all treatment totals}}{\text{number of observations in a single total}} - \text{CM}$$

$$= \frac{(39)^2 + (105)^2 + (68)^2}{4} - \text{CM}$$

$$= 4{,}292.5 - 3{,}745.33 = 547.17,$$

$$\text{SSE} = \text{Total SS} - \text{SSB} - \text{SST}$$

$$= 940.67 - 348.00 - 547.17 = 45.50.$$

Table 13.6   *ANOVA Table*

SOURCE	d.f.	SS	MS	F
Blocks	3	348.00	116.00	15.30
Treatments	2	547.17	273.58	36.09
Error	6	45.50	7.58	
Total	11	940.67		

We use the ratio of mean-square treatments to mean-square error to test an hypothesis of no difference in the expected response for treatments. Thus

$$F = \frac{\text{MST}}{\text{MSE}} = \frac{273.58}{7.58} = 36.09.$$

The critical value of the F statistic ($\alpha = .05$) for $v_1 = 2$ and $v_2 = 6$ degrees of freedom is $F_{.05} = 5.14$. Since the computed value of F exceeds the critical value, there is sufficient evidence to reject the null hypothesis and conclude that a real difference does exist in the expected sales for the three package designs.

A similar test may be conducted for the null hypothesis that no difference exists in the mean sales for supermarkets. Rejection of this hypothesis would imply that store-to-store variability does exist and that blocking is desirable. The computed value of F based on $v_1 = 3$ and $v_2 = 6$ degrees of freedom is

$$F = \frac{\text{MSB}}{\text{MSE}} = \frac{116.00}{7.58} = 15.30.$$

Since this value of F exceeds the corresponding tabulated critical value, $F_{.05} = 4.76$, we reject the null hypothesis and conclude that a real difference exists in the expected sales in the four supermarkets; that is, the data present sufficient evidence to support our decision to block with respect to supermarkets.

13.8   Estimation for the Randomized Block Design

The confidence interval for the difference between a pair of means is similar to that for the completely randomized design, Section 13.5. It is

$$(\bar{T}_i - \bar{T}_j) \pm t_{\alpha/2} s \sqrt{\frac{2}{b}},$$

where $n_i = n_j = b$, the number of observations contained in a treatment mean. The difference between the confidence intervals for the completely randomized and the randomized block designs is that s, appearing in the expressions above, will probably be smaller for the randomized block design.

Similarly, one may construct a $(1 - \alpha)$ percent confidence interval for the difference between a pair of block means. Each block contains p observations corresponding to the p treatments. Therefore, the confidence interval is

$$(\bar{B}_i - \bar{B}_j) \pm t_{\alpha/2} s \sqrt{\frac{2}{p}}.$$

Example 13.6   *From the problem described within Example 13.5, construct a 90 percent confidence interval for the difference between the expected sales from package designs 1 and 2, that is, for the difference between treatments 1 and 2.*

Solution   *The confidence interval for the difference in mean response for a pair of treatments is*

$$(\overline{T}_i - \overline{T}_j) \pm t_{\alpha/2} s \sqrt{\frac{2}{b}},$$

where, for our example, $t_{.050}$ is based upon 6 degrees of freedom. Then

$$(26.25 - 9.75) \pm (1.943)(2.75) \sqrt{\frac{2}{4}},$$

or

$$16.50 \pm 3.78.$$

Thus we estimate the difference between mean sales for the two package designs to lie in the interval 12.72 to 20.28. A much smaller confidence interval can be acquired by increasing b, the number of supermarkets included in the experiment.

13.9   Summary

The completely randomized and the randomized block designs are illustrations of two experiments involving one and two qualitative independent variables, respectively. The analysis of variance partitions the total sum of squares of deviations of the response measurements about their mean into portions associated with each independent variable and the experimental error. The former may be compared with the sum of squares for error, using mean squares and the F statistic, to see whether the mean squares for the independent variables are unusually large and thereby indicate an effect on the response.

This chapter has presented a brief introduction to the analysis of variance and its associated subject, the design of experiments. Experiments can be designed to investigate the effect of many quantitative and qualitative variables on a response. These may be variables of primary interest to the experimenter as well as nuisance variables, such as blocks, which we attempt to separate from the experimental error. They are subject to an analysis of variance when properly designed. A more extensive coverage of the basic concepts of experimental design and the analysis of experiments will be found in the references.

Exercises

1. State the assumptions underlying the following experimental design models:
   (a) A completely randomized design.
   (b) A randomized block design.

2. (a) Discuss the advantages of blocking.
   (b) What happens to these advantages as you increase the size of the blocks (the number of experimental units per block)?

3. A cab company is conducting a study of three brands of tires before determining which brand to order for all their cabs. The study involved selecting four different tires from each brand and randomly assigning them to the left front wheel of 12 different cabs. The wear is recorded after 10,000 miles of use. The wear noted at the end of the test period is given in terms of the millimeters of tread wear:

BRAND A	BRAND B	BRAND C
462	250	319
421	336	425
470	322	460
411	268	380

   Assume that the requirements for a completely randomized design are met and analyze the data. State whether there is statistical support at the $\alpha = .05$ level for the conclusion that the three brands of tires differ in resistance to wear.

4. A study was undertaken to compare the productivity of the operators of four identical assembly machines. Production records were examined for three randomly selected days where the days of record were not necessarily the same for any two assembly machine operators. The data are as follows:

OPERATOR 1	OPERATOR 2	OPERATOR 3	OPERATOR 4
230	220	215	225
220	210	215	215
225	220	220	225

   Assuming that the requirements for a completely randomized design are met, analyze the data. State whether there is statistical support at the $\alpha = .05$ level of significance for the conclusion that the four assembly machine operators differ in average daily productivity.

5. Refer to Exercise 4. Let μ_1 and μ_2 denote the mean production rates of operators 1 and 2, respectively.
   (a) Find a 90 percent confidence interval for μ_1. Interpret this interval.
   (b) Find a 95 percent confidence interval for $\mu_1 - \mu_2$. Interpret this interval.

6. A trucking company wished to compare three makes of trucks before ordering an entire fleet of one of the makes. Prices for each of the makes were about the same and thus were ignored in the comparison. Five trucks of each make were run 5,000 miles each and the average cost of operation per mile was noted for each truck. However,

because of driver illness, accidents, and tire failure, two make B and two make C trucks did not complete the 5,000-mile test. For those that did finish, the following results were observed:

MAKE A	MAKE B	MAKE C
7.3	5.4	7.9
8.3	7.4	9.5
7.6	7.1	8.7
6.8		
8.0		

(a) Perform an analysis of variance for this experiment.
(b) Do the data provide sufficient evidence to indicate a difference in the average cost per mile of operation for the three makes of trucks? (Use $\alpha = .01$.)
(c) Is there an advantage having the same number of measurements within each treatment in a completely randomized design? Explain.

7.   Refer to Exercise 6. Let μ_A and μ_B, respectively, denote the mean cost per mile of operating a truck of make A and make B.
(a) Find a 95 percent confidence interval for μ_A.
(b) Find a 95 percent confidence interval for μ_B.
(c) Find a 95 percent confidence interval for $\mu_A - \mu_B$.
(d) Is it correct to assume that the confidence interval computed in part (c) can be obtained as the difference between the confidence intervals found in parts (a) and (b)? Explain.

8.   A study has been initiated to investigate the cleaning ability of three laundry detergents. Four different brands of automatic washing machines are to be used in the experiment with each of the three laundry detergents tested in each of the four washers. Thus, 12 combinations will exist within the experiment. Twelve stacks of laundry, containing an equal amount of soil, are to be laundered. At the completion of each wash load, the laundry is to be tested by a meter for "whiteness" and the results are to be recorded.
(a) Is this a randomized block design? Explain.
(b) Suppose that *two* stacks of soiled laundry are to be subjected to each of the three detergents in each of the four washing machines. What type of experimental design is this?

9.   Suppose that a marketing executive undertook a study to examine the comparative effect of three different promotional techniques (treatments) in four different sales areas (blocks) and obtained the following results:

SOURCE	d.f.	SS
Blocks	3	0.03
Treatments	2	7.48
Error	6	3.90
Total	11	11.41

State precisely the conclusions that you would derive from the analysis-of-variance table. (Perform all tests at the 5 percent level of significance.)

10.   A dealer has in stock three cars (cars A, B, and C) of the same make and model. Wishing to compare these cars in gasoline consumption, a customer arranged to test each car

with each of three brands of gasoline (brands A, B, and C). In each trial, 1 gallon of gasoline was put in an empty tank and the car was driven without stopping until it ran out of gasoline. The following table shows the number of miles covered in each of the nine trials.

BRAND OF GASOLINE	CAR A	CAR B	CAR C
A	22.4	17.0	19.2
B	20.8	19.4	20.2
C	21.5	18.7	21.2

(a) Should the customer conclude that the three cars differ in gasoline mileage? (Test at the $\alpha = .05$ level.)
(b) Do the data indicate that the brand of gasoline affects gasoline mileage? (Test at the $\alpha = .05$ level.)

11. Refer to Exercise 10. Suppose that gasoline mileage is unrelated to brand of gasoline; carry out an analysis of the data appropriate for a completely randomized design with three treatments.
(a) Should a customer conclude that the three cars differ in gasoline mileage? (Test at the $\alpha = .05$ level.)
(b) Comparing your answer for part (a) in Exercise 10 with your answer for part (a) above, can you suggest a reason why blocking may be unwise in certain cases?

12. A study was undertaken to determine the relative typing speeds of eight secretaries on four different brands of typewriters. Each secretary was assigned to each of the typewriters and her average typing speed in words per minute for 10 minutes of typing was recorded. The order of assignment of typewriters to each secretary was conducted in a random manner. The data obtained are as follows:

TYPEWRITER BRAND	SECRETARY							
	1	2	3	4	5	6	7	8
A	79	80	77	75	82	77	78	76
B	74	79	73	70	76	78	72	74
C	82	86	80	79	81	80	80	84
D	79	81	77	78	82	77	77	78

(a) Identify the design used for this experiment and justify your diagnosis.
(b) Perform an analysis of variance on the data.
(c) Do the data provide sufficient evidence to indicate that the mean typing speed for the secretaries varies from brand to brand of typewriters? (Test using $\alpha = .05$.)
(d) Why was the order of assignment of typewriters to each secretary conducted in a random manner? In general, what is the advantage of randomly assigning the treatments to the blocks?

13. Refer to Exercise 12. Let μ_C and μ_D, respectively, denote the mean typing speeds for using typewriter C and typewriter D. Find a 99 percent confidence interval for $(\mu_C - \mu_D)$. Interpret this interval.

14. A zoning commission has been formed to estimate the average appraisal value of houses in a residential suburb of a city. The commission is considering using one of three different appraisal models in their appraisal efforts. To test for consistency among the three appraisal models, each model is separately used to generate an appraisal value for

each of five different residential dwellings. The results are as follows:

DWELLING

APPRAISAL MODEL	1	2	3	4	5
A	$21,000	$37,000	$28,000	$37,000	$30,000
B	22,500	40,000	27,500	39,000	33,000
C	19,000	35,000	27,500	36,000	31,000

Without any specific directives, perform an analysis of the above data. What are your conclusions? What recommendations would you make to the zoning commission about the relative merits of the three appraisal models? (*Hint:* Code the data.)

15.   A portion of a questionnaire was constructed to enable judges to evaluate four proposed site locations. The judges, selected from the executive group and upper and middle management of the company, were asked to respond concerning their perceptions of accessibility of each site to primary markets, transportation facilities, state corporation regulations, and living desirability of the area relative to each proposed site. Their responses were then collated and coded on a 0 to 20 scale. The data obtained are as follows:

JUDGES

SITES	1	2	3	4	5	6	7	8
1	9	10	7	5	12	7	8	6
2	4	9	3	0	6	8	2	4
3	12	16	10	9	11	10	10	14
4	9	11	7	8	12	7	7	8

(a) The primary objective of this was to compare site locations. Give the type of design employed for this experiment and justify your diagnosis.
(b) Perform an analysis of variance on the data.
(c) Do the data provide sufficient evidence to indicate that the mean coded scores vary from site to site? (Test using $\alpha = .05$.)
(d) Suppose that the data did provide sufficient evidence to indicate differences among the mean coded questionnaire scores associated with the four sites. Would this imply that the questionnaire was able to detect a difference in preferences for the building sites?

16.   A completely randomized design was conducted to compare the effect of five different advertising layouts on product recognition time. Twenty-seven people were employed in the experiment. Regardless of their results of the analysis of variance, it is desired to compare layouts A and D. The results of the experiment were as follows (time in seconds):

LAYOUT

	A	B	C	D	E
	.8	.7	1.2	1.0	.6
	.6	.8	1.0	.9	.4
	.6	.5	.9	.9	.4
	.5	.5	1.2	1.1	.7
		.6	1.3	.7	.3
		.9	.8		
		.7			
Total	2.5	4.7	6.4	4.6	2.4
Mean	.625	.671	1.067	.920	.48

(a) Conduct an analysis of variance and test for a difference in mean recognition time resulting from the five advertising layouts.

(b) Compare layouts A and D to see if there is a difference in mean recognition time.

17. The experiment in Exercise 16 might have been more effectively conducted using a randomized block design with subjects as blocks since we would expect mean recognition time to vary from one person to another. Four people were used in a new experiment, and each person was shown each of the five advertising layouts in a random order. The results are as follows (time in seconds):

| | LAYOUT | | | | |
SUBJECT	A	B	C	D	E
1	.7	.8	1.0	1.0	.5
2	.6	.6	1.1	1.0	.6
3	.9	1.0	1.2	1.1	.6
4	.6	.8	.9	1.0	.4

Conduct an analysis of variance and test for differences in treatments (advertising layouts). (Test at the $\alpha = .05$ level.)

References

Guenther, W. C., *Analysis of Variance*. Englewood Cliffs, N.J.: Prentice-Hall, Inc., 1964.

Hicks, C. R., *Fundamental Concepts in the Design of Experiments*. New York: Holt, Rinehart and Winston, Inc., 1964.

Li, J. C. R., *Introduction to Statistical Inference*. Ann Arbor, Mich.: J. W. Edwards, Publisher, Inc., 1961.

Mendenhall, W., *An Introduction to Linear Models and the Design and Analysis of Experiments*. Belmont, Calif.: Wadsworth Publishing Company, Inc., 1967.

Chapter Fourteen

Elements of Time-Series Analysis

14.1 Introduction

The businessman is constantly faced with variables whose values are random over time. Time as either an independent experimental variable or as an added dimension to other variables of interest may help or hinder him in his decision-making processes. We have seen in preceding chapters that many unmeasured and uncontrolled variables may cause a response to vary over time and thereby inflate the experimental error. The undesirable effect of time can be reduced by using blocking designs (such as the randomized block design, Chapter 13) and making experimental treatment comparisons within relatively homogeneous blocks of time. In other decision-making situations, time may be one of the most important variables. This usually occurs in problems of the type described in Chapter 12, where we wish to estimate the expected value of y or to predict a new value of y at a future point in time after having observed the pattern of the values of y during past and present time periods. For example, an investor is interested in predicting future security prices, a store manager is interested in the effect of time on demand for his product, and the marketing manager is interested in the pattern of sales over time. In a sense, everyone who plans for the future by attempting to budget his time and resources is concerned with processes that are random over time. If we believe that interest rates will drop in the near future, it may be wise to rent now and buy a home later. The skier plans his vacations during the winter because he knows that the seasonal weather pattern calls for the greatest snowfall to occur during the winter.

Any sequence of measurements taken on a variable process over time is called a time series. The time series is usually represented by the mathematical equation listing the process values as a function of time, or equivalently, as a curve on a graph whose vertical coordinate gives the value of the random response plotted against time on the horizontal axis. In Figure 14.1 we note a time series that plots U.S. Treasury bill rates as a function of time between the years 1925 and 1968. The same information could have been shown in tabular form, but the pattern of change over time would have been much more obscure. It is the pattern generated by the time series and not necessarily the individual values which offers the planning device. An individual who is planning a long-term investment portfolio will want to buy treasury bills only at times when the rates are projected to be high. Projecting the treasury-bill rates into the future implies extending the trends, cycles, and other elements of the pattern from the time series of Figure 14.1.

Applications of time-series analytical techniques are not limited to business problems concerned solely with economic data. Demand analyses are very common in marketing research problems. Quality-control studies are also common business applications of time-series analyses. By employing computer feedback systems, modern industrial process control theory utilizes multiple time series to keep the industrial manufacturing process "in control" and to correct and adjust the process when it is found to be "out of control." Furthermore, such a study enables the manufacturer to move to positions of higher product quality and yield and to greater manufacturing profits.

The analysis of time series, that is, the utilization of sample data for purposes of inference (estimation, decision making, and prediction) is a complicated and difficult subject. Response measurements appearing in a time series are usually correlated, with the correlation increasing as the time interval between a pair of measurements decreases. Consequently, time-series data will often defy the basic assumptions of independence required for the methods described in preceding

Figure 14.1 *U.S. Treasury Bill Rates from 1925 to 1968*

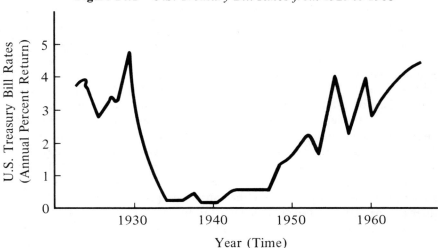

chapters. Indeed, the methodology of time-series analysis is in an embryonic state in comparison with that for the static (time-independent) case with which we are so familiar. For this reason, published time-series analyses often appear to be based on highly subjective methods, and predictions (forecasts) are most often unaccompanied by a measure of goodness. Perhaps a second reason for the rather primitive techniques often employed in the analysis of time series is the mathematical complexity of the theory underlying the more sophisticated and newer methodologies. The mathematical background required for an understanding of some of the more powerful methods of time-series analysis places the subject beyond the grasp of many nonmathematically trained forecasters.

The preceding comments are intended to introduce the subject of time-series analysis and also to explain the absence of a single method of analysis. We shall begin by first exploring the components of a time series which together determine its pattern. In Chapter 15 we shall examine some of the available techniques for extending the pattern of the time series and forecasting future process values. Because of the importance of forecasting in modern business decision making, our emphasis in the study of time-series methods will be placed on the analytical methods of Chapter 15 as opposed to the descriptive methods of this chapter.

14.2 Components of Time Series

Statisticians often think of a time series as the addition of four meaningful *component series:*

---

1. *Long-term trend.*
2. *Cyclical effect.*
3. *Seasonal effect.*
4. *Random variation.*

Long-term trends are often present in time series because of the steady increase in population, gross national product, the effect of competition, or other factors, that fail to produce sudden changes in response but produce a steady and gradual change over time. A time series with an upward long-term trend would be similar to the increase in the population of the United States from 1900 until 1969, as shown in Figure 14.2.

Cyclical effects in a time series are apparent when the response rises and falls in a gentle, wavelike manner about a long-term trend curve like the unemployment rate in the United States from 1900 to 1969, illustrated in Figure 14.3. The unemployment rate does not seem to follow an increasing or decreasing trend over time but

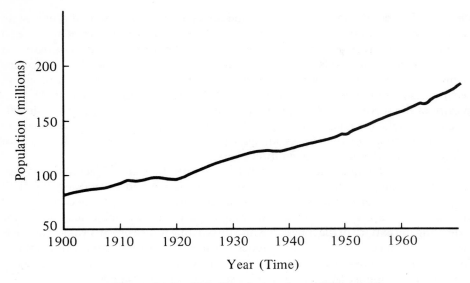

Figure 14.2   *U.S. Population from* 1900 *to* 1969

appears to fluctuate with general conditions of the economy, demands from the military service, and the onset of automation. Generally, cyclic effects in a time series can be caused by pulsations in the demand for a product, business cycles, stockpiling, and, particularly, the inability of supply to meet exactly the require-

Figure 14.3   *Unemployment Rate in the United States from* 1900 *to* 1969

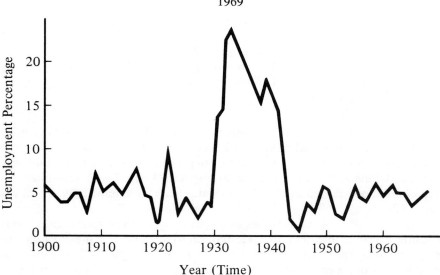

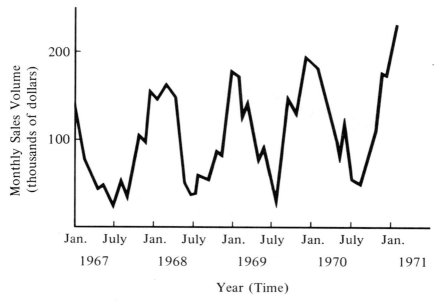

Figure 14.4   *Monthly Retail Sales Volume of the Palace Department Store from 1967 to 1971*

ments of customer demand when the time series is a plot of economic values over time. For a noneconomic time series, cyclic effects are usually the effect of governmental, economic, or political policies.

Seasonal effects in time series are those rises and falls that always occur at a particular time of the year. For example, auto sales and earnings tend to decrease during August and September because of the changeover to new models, while the sales of television sets rise in the month of December. The essential difference between seasonal and cyclic effects is that seasonal effects are predictable, occurring at a given interval of time from the last occurrence, while cyclic effects are completely unpredictable. A time-series component suggesting seasonal effects is illustrated by the sales of a department store, shown in Figure 14.4.

The fourth component of a time series is random variation. This component represents the random upward and downward movement of the series after adjustment for the long-term trend, the cyclic effect, and the seasonal effect. Random variation, which might appear as the variation from the increasing, linear trend in Figure 14.5, is the unexplained shifting and bobbing of the series over the short-term period. Political events, weather, and an amalgamation of many human actions tend to cause random and unexpected changes in a time series.

All time series contain random variation. In addition, a time series may contain none, one, two, or all of the three components, long-term trend, cyclic effect, and seasonal effect.

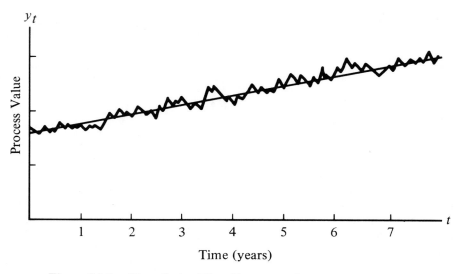

Figure 14.5 *Time Series That Shows Random Variation from an Increasing Linear Trend*

With most time-series processes it is not easy to distinguish between the components. Often, seasonal and cyclic effects or the three components, long-term trend and cyclic and seasonal effects, have become so integrated that they are

Figure 14.6 *Monthly Retail Sales Volume for the Palace Department Store from 1967 to 1971*

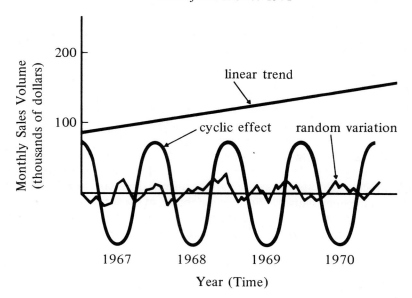

inseparable. On the other hand, if the components appear to be distinguishable, it is not difficult to separate them. For instance, the monthly sales of the Palace Department Store, Figure 14.4, illustrate a seasonal effect and a long-term trend with superimposed random variation. The long-term trend and seasonal effect, when identified, could be subtracted from the process values. The remainder is attributable to random variation. An illustration of how this might be accomplished is shown in Figure 14.6.

The communications engineer refers to the long-term trend and the cylic and seasonal effects as the signal of the time series. We shall use this terminology for purposes of discussion. Since the signal is the part of the time series that is deterministic, it is important for purposes of prediction to be able to separate the signal from random variation, called noise by the communication engineer. Determination of future process values would simply amount to the statistician adding together the extended patterns of the known components of the signal with the projected random variation. Since the random variation is at best probabilistic, accurate estimation of future process values can be expected only when the magnitude of the random variation, as measured by its variance, is small. Otherwise, the oscillations of the random variation over time may overwhelm the effect of the signal components or even cancel them out entirely. Such a process is illustrated in Figure 14.7, where the seasonal effect and long-term trend from Figure 14.6 are combined with a random variation with a large variance. The resultant time-series process illustrates only the long-term trend, the seasonal effect having been "hidden" by the random variation.

Figure 14.7   *Time Series Whose Seasonal Effect Has Been Hidden by the Presence of Random Variation with Excessively Large Variance*

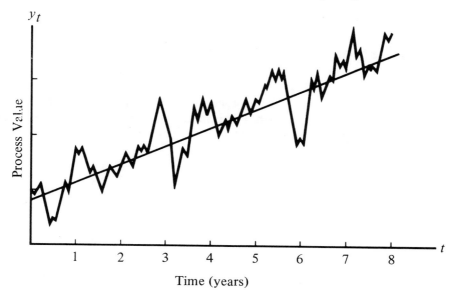

Even if the proper signal is discovered and projected, the predicted process values may be inaccurate if the magnitude of the random variation is great. In such a case the best we can do is to give a probability interval for the predicted process value, where the probability interval is based on the supposed probability distribution of the random variation.

14.3   Smoothing Methods

Traditional methods of time series analysis have rested heavily on smoothing techniques that attempt to cancel out the effect of random variation and presumably reveal the components that are being sought. Smoothing can be accomplished by utilizing a moving average of the response measurements over a set number of time periods. Thus one might average the monthly sales of a company over a 4-month period and plot the average at the midpoint of the 4-month time interval. The next point in the series would be obtained by adding to the 4-month total the next month's sales in the series, dropping the sales from the earliest month of the previous 4 and computing a new 4-month average. Thus the time series of moving averages would show a point for each month that would be the calculated average response for a specified time interval below and above the given month. The net effect is to transform the original sales time series to a moving-average series that is smoother (less subject to rapid oscillations) and more likely to reveal the underlying trend or cycles in the pattern of sales over time.

The moving average $\bar{y}_t$ at time point t of the response measurements over M time periods is found by computing

$$\bar{y}_t = \frac{y_{t-(M-1)/2} + y_{t+1-(M-1)/2} + y_{t+2-(M-1)/2} + \cdots + y_{t+(M-1)/2}}{M},$$

where M is an odd number and y_t is the process response at time t, y_{t-1} is the process response at time $t - 1$, and so forth. For instance, if the moving average is to be computed over three period intervals ($M = 3$), the first few moving averages would be computed as follows:

$$\bar{y}_2 = \frac{y_1 + y_2 + y_3}{3},$$

$$\bar{y}_3 = \frac{y_2 + y_3 + y_4}{3},$$

$$\bar{y}_4 = \frac{y_3 + y_4 + y_5}{3},$$

and so forth. The moving-average formula can be simplified by rewriting it in the recursive form

$$\bar{y}_t = \bar{y}_{t-1} + \frac{\text{next observation} - \text{most remote observation}}{M}$$

since all we are doing at each step is to recompute the average by adding in the next observation and dropping the observation from M periods in the past.

It is often constructive to compute the moving average over an odd number of time periods so we have actual values of comparison. If M is an even number, the moving averages would occur between the time points instead of at the time points. The primary disadvantage of using a moving average for smoothing is that unless $M = 1$, we do not have a smoothed value corresponding to each process value. For instance, if we compute the moving averages over each $M = 5$ consecutive responses of the time series, there would be no smoothed value corresponding to the first two nor the last two process values. With a large number of response measurements, this is no problem, but it may be a serious consideration when the number of response measurements is small.

Another smoothing scheme, which is more efficient than the moving average in the sense that it computes a smoothed value corresponding to each response measurement, is the process of exponential smoothing. The exponentially smoothed process value at time period t is denoted by S_t. The smoothing scheme begins by assigning $S_1 = y_1$ at the first period. For the second time period,

$$S_2 = \alpha y_2 + (1 - \alpha)S_1,$$

and for any succeeding time period t, the smoothed value S_t is found by computing

$$S_t = \alpha y_t + (1 - \alpha)S_{t-1}, \qquad 0 \le \alpha \le 1.$$

This equation is called the basic equation of exponential smoothing and the constant α is called the smoothing constant.

Where the moving-average smoothing scheme formed averages over M time periods, S_t computes an average from all past process values $y_t, y_{t-1}, \ldots, y_1$, where y_t is the value at the time period t, y_{t-1} is the value at time period $t - 1$, and y_1 is the process value from the first time period where data are available. This can be seen if we expand the basic equation and find by a process of induction

$$\begin{aligned} S_t &= \alpha y_t + (1 - \alpha)S_{t-1} \\ &= \alpha y_t + (1 - \alpha)\alpha y_{t-1} + (1 - \alpha)^2 S_{t-2} \\ &\;\;\vdots \\ &= \alpha \sum_{i=0}^{t-2} (1 - \alpha)^i y_{t-i} + (1 - \alpha)^{t-1} y_1. \end{aligned}$$

Even though remote responses are not dropped in an exponential smoothing scheme as they are in a moving average, their contribution to the smoothed value S_t becomes less at each successive time point. The speed at which remote responses are dampened out is determined by the selection of the smoothing constant, α. For values of α near 1, remote responses are dampened out quickly; for α near 0, they are dampened out slowly.

   The theory of selection of the "best" smoothing constant, α, is omitted because it requires more than an elementary knowledge of mathematics. Although it is beyond the scope of this text, we shall make some general remarks about its selection. When the underlying process is quite volatile (the magnitude of the random variation is large), we would like to average out the effects of the random variation quickly. Thus we would select a small smoothing constant so that the smoothed value S_t will reflect S_{t-1}, the averaged process values from the first $t-1$ time periods, to a greater extent than it reflects the "noisy" measurement y_t. Similarly, for a moderately stable process, a large smoothing constant would be selected. The following example illustrates the use of three different smoothing models on a rather volatile time series.

Example 14.1   *The week's end closing prices for the securities of the Color-Vision Company, a manufacturer of color television sets, have been recorded over a period of 30 consecutive weeks. Find the 5-week moving-average time series and the exponentially smoothed time series using smoothing constants $\alpha = .1$ and $\alpha = .5$.*

Solution   *The original process values, y_t (week's end closing prices for each of the 30 weeks), the 5-week moving averages, $\bar{y}_t$, and the exponentially smoothed time series, S_t for $\alpha = .1$ and $\alpha = .5$ are listed in Table 14.1. The moving averages were found by computing*

$$\bar{y}_t = \frac{y_{t-2} + y_{t-1} + y_t + y_{t+1} + y_{t+2}}{5}$$

for each of the time periods $t = 3, 4, \ldots, 28$. For instance, the seventh moving average value, $\bar{y}_7$, was found to be

$$\bar{y}_7 = \frac{y_5 + y_6 + y_7 + y_8 + y_9}{5}$$

$$= \frac{64 + 65 + 72 + 78 + 75}{5}$$

$$= 70.8.$$

The original time series and the moving-average time series are shown together in Figure 14.8.

Table 14.1   *Original and Smoothed Week's End Closing Prices for the Securities of the Color-Vision Company over 30 Consecutive Weeks**

t	y_t	$\bar{y}_t$	$S_t(\alpha = .1)$	$S_t(\alpha = .5)$
1	71		71.0	71.0
2	70		70.9	70.5
3	69	68.4	70.7	69.8
4	68	67.2	70.4	68.9
5	64	67.6	69.8	66.5
6	65	69.4	69.3	65.8
7	72	70.8	69.6	68.9
8	78	73.0	70.4	73.5
9	75	75.0	70.9	74.3
10	75	74.6	71.3	74.7
11	75	74.0	71.7	74.9
12	70	74.0	71.5	72.5
13	75	73.8	71.9	73.8
14	75	74.4	72.2	74.4
15	74	77.6	72.4	74.2
16	78	79.0	73.0	76.0
17	86	79.0	74.3	81.0
18	82	78.8	75.1	81.5
19	75	77.6	75.1	78.3
20	73	75.0	74.9	75.7
21	72	73.2	74.6	73.8
22	73	73.4	74.4	73.4
23	72	75.4	74.2	72.7
24	77	77.2	74.5	74.9
25	83	78.8	75.3	79.0
26	81	81.4	75.9	80.0
27	81	83.0	76.4	80.5
28	85	83.2	77.3	82.8
29	85		78.1	83.9
30	84		78.7	83.9

* All smoothed values have been rounded to the nearest tenth of a unit.

The exponentially smoothed time series employing a smoothing constant $\alpha = .1$ was computed by first setting

$$S_1 = 71.0,$$

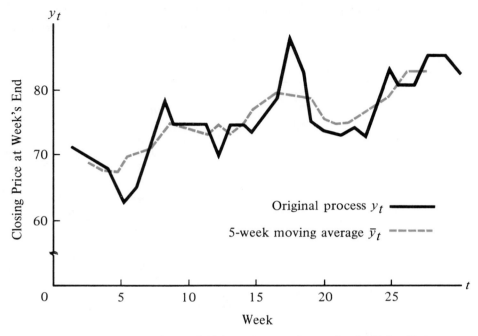

Figure 14.8   *Week's End Closing Security Prices for the Color-Vision Company over 30 Weeks with the 5-Week Moving-Average Process Superimposed*

and then

$$S_2 = (.1)(70) + (1 - .1)(71.0)$$
$$= 70.9,$$
$$S_3 = (.1)(69) + (1 - .1)(70.9)$$
$$= 70.7,$$

and so forth. In a similar manner, each of the values for the exponentially smoothed time series with $\alpha = .5$ *are found by first setting*

$$S_1 = 71.0$$

and then computing

$$S_t = (.5)y_t + (1 - .5)S_{t-1},$$

*for each of the time periods t = 2, 3, 4, . . . , 30. The original time series is
plotted together with both of the exponentially smoothed time series in Figure
14.9.*

Observe that in both Figures 14.8 and 14.9, the smoothed time series appear
more stable than the original series. However, the 5-week moving-average series and
the exponentially smoothed time series with $\alpha = .5$ appear to be much less stable than
the exponentially smoothed series with $\alpha = .1$. The latter series, although under-
shooting the original series much of the time, appears to suggest the presence of a
linear trend with a cyclic effect. Hence the true components of the original series
(if a linear trend and a cyclic effect are the true components) most readily become
apparent when the original series is smoothed by an exponential smoothing scheme
employing a small smoothing constant. This is not a generalization, however; the
small smoothing constant yields the best results for the data used here.

Perhaps the major advantage of smoothing techniques is typified by the old
saying that a picture is worth a thousand words. Moving averages and exponentially
smoothed time series sometimes makes trends, cycles, and seasonal effects more

Figure 14.9 *Week's End Closing Security Prices for the Color-
Vision Company over 30 Weeks with the Two Exponentially
Smoothed Processes Superimposed*

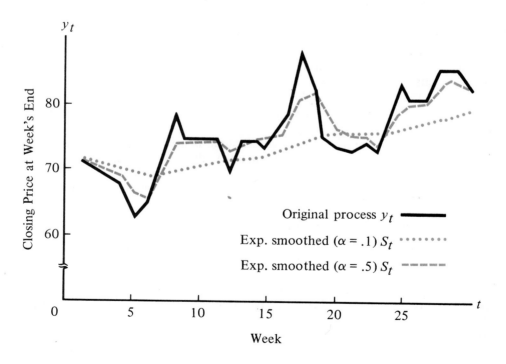

visible to the eye and consequently lead to a simple and useful description of the time-series process for the businessman or economist. When presented as simply a description of the time series (as is often the case), smoothing techniques often ignore the basic objective of statistics, inference, and leave this difficult task to the reader. Thus we still seek techniques for estimation and prediction that are accompanied by measures of goodness. We shall investigate such methods in Chapter 15.

14.4   Adjustment of Seasonal Data

Suppose that one is interested in examining short-term trends or the effect of an assumed business cycle on the time series representing his business activity. This is a difficult, if not impossible, task if the time series exhibits a pronounced seasonal component, since the seasonal fluctuations tend to overwhelm the other components. If the seasonal component can be removed from the time series, identification, examination, and interpretation of trends and cycles is greatly simplified.

The most common method for removing the seasonal component from a time series containing a seasonal component is by employing a moving-average model with M equal to the number of time points in one complete seasonal period. In most all seasonal time series, the seasonal period is either 4 or 12 time periods. The former are time series consisting of quarterly data, like quarterly jewelry or toy sales, typically relatively constant during the first three quarters of each year but much higher during the fourth quarter owing to the effect of the Christmas market. When the time points are months and the time series is seasonal, the seasonal period is almost always 12 months. Sales of soft drinks, beer, and golf equipment follow the seasons—sales are high during the warm months, low during the cool months. The demand and sales for air conditioners, clothing, skiing equipment, gardening equipment, airline travel, and many other items also follow a 12-month seasonal pattern.

The moving-average smoothing technique is used to remove the seasonal component from a time series by performing the following computations:

1. Let M equal the number of time periods in one complete seasonal period.

2. Compute the M-period moving average for the time series.

3. If M is an even number, center the moving-average values by averaging together adjacent moving averages.

The obvious disadvantage of the moving-average deseasonalization method is that $M/2$ observations are lost at the beginning and at the end of the time series. Typically, this is not a serious problem if the time series contains a sufficient number of measurements. A rule of thumb is that we should have at least three complete

seasons represented within the time series before the moving-average deseasonalization methods are applied.

To illustrate the moving-average deseasonalization technique, consider the
time series of monthly sales of the Bush Brewing company for the years 1968–1970,
as shown in the first column of Table 14.2. Looking ahead to Figure 14.10, we can
see that this time series follows a 12-month seasonal pattern. Thus we shall let
$M = 12$.

The first moving-average value will fall between June and July of 1968 as
$M = 12$ is an even number. We can find this first moving-average value as

$$\bar{y}_{\text{June-July}} = \frac{\begin{array}{c} 19.6 + 18.6 + 23.2 + 24.5 + 27.7 + 30.0 + 28.7 + 33.8 \\ + 25.1 + 22.1 + 21.8 + 20.9 \end{array}}{12}$$

$$= \frac{296}{12} = 24.667.$$

Similarly, we can find

$$\bar{y}_{\text{July-Aug}} = \frac{296}{12} + \frac{23.3 - 19.6}{12} = \frac{299.7}{12} = 24.975.$$

Notice that the July–August value was computed using the short-cut procedure
introduced in Section 14.3. The short-cut procedure cannot be used to compute
the first moving average but can be used to compute every moving average after
the first. Centering, so that we have a moving average uniquely associated with each
observation in the time series (except the first six and last six observations, which are
lost by employing the moving average), we find,

$$\bar{y}_{\text{July}} = \frac{24.667 + 24.975}{2} = 24.821.$$

Taking the process one step further, we find

$$\bar{y}_{\text{Aug-Sept}} = \frac{299.7}{12} + \frac{20.1 - 18.6}{12} = \frac{301.2}{12} = 25.1$$

and

$$\bar{y}_{\text{Aug}} = \frac{\bar{y}_{\text{July-Aug}} + \bar{y}_{\text{Aug-Sept}}}{2} = \frac{24.975 + 25.1}{2} = 25.038.$$

The remaining 22 moving averages have been computed and are listed within
Table 14.2.

Table 14.2   *Actual and 12-Month Moving-Average Time Series of Sales of Bush Brewing Company, 1968–1970*

Time	Actual Sales	12-Month Moving Average	Centered Moving Average
1968			
January	19.6		
February	18.6		
March	23.2		
April	24.5		
May	27.7		
June	30.0		
July	28.7	24.667	24.821
August	33.8	24.975	25.038
September	25.1	25.100	25.304
October	22.1	25.508	25.596
November	21.8	25.683	25.721
December	20.9	25.758	25.896
		26.033	
1969			
January	23.3		26.267
February	20.1	26.500	26.300
March	28.1	26.100	26.152
April	26.6	26.208	26.333
May	28.6	26.458	26.479
June	33.3	26.500	26.475
July	34.3	26.450	26.502
August	29.0	26.558	26.670
September	26.4	26.783	26.795
October	25.1	26.808	26.833
November	22.3	26.858	26.858
December	20.3	26.858	26.691
		26.525	
1970			
January	24.6		26.691
February	22.8	26.858	26.983
March	28.4	27.108	27.045
April	27.2	26.983	27.097
May	28.6	27.200	27.196
June	29.3	27.192	27.242
July	38.3	27.292	
August	32.0		
September	24.9		
October	27.7		
November	22.2		
December	21.5		

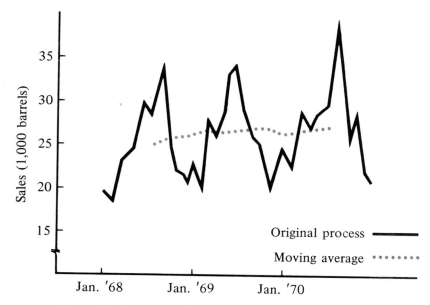

Figure 14.10 *Sales Volume for the Bush Brewing Company for the Years* 1968, 1969, *and* 1970 *with a Superimposed* 12-*Month Moving Average*

In Figure 14.10 we have plotted the original time series of sales by Bush Brewing Company for the years 1968–1970 and have superimposed the 12-month moving average. Having smoothed out the seasonal fluctuations, the moving average exhibits only a linear growth trend. No short-term trends or business cycles appear in existence for the period 1968–1970. In the final analysis, the Bush Brewing Company's sales manager can assume that sales of his firm's products are increasing relatively over time but fluctuate seasonally over the year, exhibiting greater than average sales during the warm months, and lesser than average sales during the cooler months. The only other factors affecting the Bush time series can be considered of minimal importance and very short-lived, allowing for their categorization as random variation.

14.5   Index Numbers

Because of the variability in the buying power of the dollar over time, it is necessary to deflate some values and inflate others in order to make meaningful comparisons. For example, to compare the relative cost of a 4-year college education today and in 1940, we would first have to determine the buying power of the dollar today as compared with the buying power of a 1940 dollar. Index numbers are computed for such purposes and are used every day by businessmen and economists to make meaningful comparisons over time. Their use is not limited strictly to monetary comparisons, but for business problems, application of index numbers to other than monetary processes is uncommon.

Definition

An *index number* is a ratio or an average of ratios expressed as a percentage. Two or more time periods are involved, one of which is the base time period. The value at the base time period serves as the standard point of comparison, while the values at the other time periods are used to show the percentage change in value from the standard value of the base period.

The concept of an index number is most easily illustrated through an example.

Example 14.2   *Suppose that we wish to compare the average hourly wages for a journeyman electrician in 1950, 1955, 1960, 1965, and 1970, using 1950 as the base year. The average hourly wages and their computed index numbers for each of the five years are listed in Table 14.3.*

Table 14.3   *Average Hourly Wages for Journeyman Electricians for 5 Years*

YEAR	AVERAGE HOURLY WAGES	WAGE INDEX (1950 BASE)
1950	$2.00	100
1955	2.85	142.5
1960	3.90	195
1965	5.25	262.5
1970	6.00	300

The wage index for each year is computed by evaluating the ratio

$$I_k = \frac{(\text{average hourly wages in year } k)(100)}{\text{average hourly wages in 1950}}.$$

Each wage index is a percentage that indicates the percentage of 1950 wages earned in the year of interest.

Definition

A list of index numbers for two or more periods of time, where each index number employs the same base year, is called an *index time series*.

The above example is an index time series for the years 1950, 1955, 1960, 1965, and 1970. An index time series is simply a transformation of the original time series to one giving each year's process value as a percentage of the value for the base year.

A commonly used index to compare two sets of prices from a wide variety of items is called a simple aggregate index.

Definition

A simple aggregate index is the ratio of an aggregate (sum) of commodity prices for a given year, k, to an aggregate of the prices of the same commodities in some base year, expressed as a percentage.

This index is computed by evaluating

$$I_k = \frac{\sum_{i=1}^{n} p_{ki}}{\sum_{i=1}^{n} p_{0i}}(100),$$

where the p_{ki}'s are the prices in year k of i items, where i ranges from 1 to n, and the p_{0i}'s are the base-year prices of the same i items.

Example 14.3   *The average consumer prices in cents per pound for certain staple food items in 1955 and 1970 are given in Table 14.4.*

Table 14.4

ITEM	1955	1970
Sugar	10	13
Wheat flour	10	15
Butter	83	79
Sirloin steak	80	135
Ground beef	40	80
Frying chicken	45	85

The aggregate price index is then

$$I_{1970} = \frac{13 + 15 + 79 + 135 + 80 + 85}{10 + 10 + 83 + 80 + 40 + 45}(100)$$

$$= \frac{407}{268}(100) = 152,$$

which implies that the prices of these six items in 1970 are 52 percent higher than they were in 1955.

The simple aggregate index has as its greatest weakness the fact that changes in the measuring units may drastically affect the value of the index. In the above example, suppose that we had considered the prices of 10-pound bags of sugar and wheat flour instead of the prices of these items per pound. If the 10-pound prices were $1.00 and $1.30 for the sugar and $1.00 and $1.50 for the flour, then our price index would be

$$I_{1970} = \frac{659}{448}(100) = 147,$$

indicating 5 percent less of an increase in prices than indicated by our former index value. By changing the scale of measurement of some of the units being measured within the simple aggregate index, the statistician could derive almost any index value at his discretion. This lack of objectivity of the simple index tends to discount its usefulness for making meaningful comparisons.

An index that gives a more uniform measure of comparison is called a weighted aggregate index.

Definition

A *weighted aggregate index* is the ratio of an aggregate of weighted commodity prices for a given year, k, to an aggregate of the weighted prices of the same commodities in some base year, expressed as a percentage.

In this case the prices do not necessarily contribute equally to the value of the index. Each price is weighted (multiplied) by the quantity of the item produced or the number of units purchased or consumed so as to include each item considered by the index according to its importance in the aggregate of prices of the items being described by the index. The index is found by computing

$$I_k = \frac{\sum\limits_{i=1}^{n} p_{ki}q_{ki}}{\sum\limits_{i=1}^{n} p_{oi}q_{oi}}(100),$$

where the q_{ki}'s and the q_{0i}'s are the quantities associated with the n prices for the reference year and the base year, respectively.

The U.S. Department of Labor uses a special form of a weighted aggregate index for several of its published indices. This index is called the Laspeyres Index and is found by computing

$$L = \frac{\sum\limits_{i=1}^{n} p_{ki}q_{0i}}{\sum\limits_{i=1}^{n} p_{0i}q_{0i}}(100).$$

The reasoning behind using base-year quantities as the weights for the reference-year prices is that the base-year quantities do not change from year to year. Thus we can make more meaningful comparisons of the change in prices and buying power over time, since we are considering only the change in price per given number of units and not changing the number of units. By using the base-year quantities, though, we tend to give too much weight to the commodities whose prices have increased, since an increase in price will often be accompanied by a decrease in the quantity consumed or purchased. However, if essential or staple items are being considered, the effect of using only the base-year weights on the value of the index should be small. Since it is often difficult and expensive to obtain the quantities for each time period, it may be a worthwhile tradeoff to give up some accuracy of the computed index value by employing the Laspeyres Index.

Example 14.4   *The average consumer prices for certain staple food items from Example 14.3 are listed in Table 14.5. Also, we are given the average amount of each item recommended as necessary to sustain a family of four in 1955. Find the Laspeyres Index to measure the amount of change of the 1970 prices on these items from 1955 to 1970.*

Table 14.5

ITEM	1955 PRICE p_0	1970 PRICE p_k	1955 QUANTITY q_0
Sugar	10	13	25
Wheat flour	10	15	60
Butter	83	79	50
Sirloin steak	80	135	25
Ground beef	40	80	120
Frying chicken	45	85	40

Solution   *The Laspeyres Index is*

$$L = \frac{13(25) + 15(60) + 79(50) + 135(25) + 80(120) + 85(40)}{10(25) + 10(60) + 83(50) + 80(25) + 40(120) + 45(40)}(100)$$

$$= \frac{21{,}550}{13{,}600}(100) = 158.$$

Thus the cost for these staple food items in 1970 is 58 percent higher than the cost for these items in 1955, when considering the total annual food expenditures.

Other less frequently used weighted aggregative price indices are the Paasche Index and Fisher's Ideal Index The Paasche Index uses the reference-year rather than the base-year quantities as weights for the weighted index. Other than that, the computational procedure is the same for the Laspeyres and the Paasche Indexes. Previously we mentioned that the Laspeyres Index tends to "overweight" commodities whose prices have increased. Analogously, the Paasche Index tends to "underweight" commodities whose prices have increased. Hence we might suspect that the price index should be somewhere between these two indexes. This is the supposition behind the use of Fisher's Ideal Index.

The Fisher Index is the geometric mean of the Laspeyres and the Paasche Indexes. Computationally,

$$\text{Fisher's Index} = \sqrt{(\text{Laspeyres Index})(\text{Paasche Index})}$$

$$= (100)\sqrt{\frac{\sum p_{ki}q_{0i}}{\sum p_{0i}q_{0i}}\frac{\sum p_{ki}q_{ki}}{\sum p_{0i}q_{ki}}}.$$

Although the Fisher Index would seem to measure the price index more accurately than the Laspeyres or the Paasche Index, it is seldom used in practice. The Fisher Index, since it is a function of the Paasche Index, requires a new set of quantities at each time period. These are often difficult and expensive to obtain. Also, the Fisher Index does not give a uniform index for purposes of comparison in an index time series. That is, like the Paasche Index, the Fisher Index does not hold the quantity measure constant as does the Laspeyres Index. Thus the Laspeyres Index, or some form of the Laspeyres Index, is used at the practical exclusion of other types of indexes when the business statistician chooses to use a weighted aggregate index.

Two important price indexes computed regularly by the Bureau of Labor Statistics are the Consumer Price Index and the Wholesale Price Index. Both may be somewhat misleading and deserve some explanation. The Consumer Price Index (CPI) is computed and published monthly. It is computed from data gathered from a random sample of clerical workers' and wage earners' family expenditures from across the country. About 300 different items from food products to clothing to rent to luxuries to fees paid to doctors and dentists are sampled for each family selected. A weighted aggregate index is computed using the information gathered in the period 1957–1959 as the base information. The computed index is then published as the Consumer Price Index. The CPI is used as a factor to deflate Gross National Product and other measures of economic wealth to "cancel out" the effect of inflation or deflation. Also, other price indexes, such as the Retail Price Index, are computed as a function of the CPI.

Now let us interpret the CPI as a price deflator or as a cost-of-living indicator. The CPI is not representative of all American families but only those from which the sample data have been collected — clerical workers and wage earners. The CPI says little or nothing about the cost of living for a professional person. In addition, the CPI is restricted in attention to clerical workers and wage earners of moderate income, as those included within the sample are of moderate income. Thus the CPI "market basket index" does not reflect purchases of families at the lowest and highest extremes of the income scale, even though they may be families of clerical workers and wage earners. A further limiting factor of the CPI is that it ignores taxation and product-quality changes over time. It would be almost impossible to select an index that would be perfectly representative in every way, so, recognizing its limitations, we use the CPI as a measure, if not a valid measure, of the changes in prices of goods and services for American families.

The Wholesale Price Index (WPI) is computed from information obtained by sampling the producers' selling prices of about 2,000 different items in the primary markets. Agricultural commodities, raw materials, fabricated products, and many manufactured items are included. The WPI is a weighted aggregate index computed and published monthly by the Bureau of Labor Statistics. Its base period is 1957–1959.

Many industrial contracts, especially those with the Department of Defense, allow for adjustment of the contract price and payments according to the change in the WPI. This allows the contractor and the buyer to negotiate and plan in terms of some constant dollar amounts. The primary difficulty is that the WPI is not really an indicator of wholesale prices at all but represents the change in producers' selling prices. In many instances, this makes no difference, but the name of the index, the Wholesale Price Index, may in itself be misleading and cause the businessman to form unwarranted conclusions.

Security market indexes, such as the Dow Jones Industrial Average, are computed differently from the wage and price indexes previously described. They might better be described as averages of a group of individual time series rather than as indicators of change of value or price.

The Dow Jones Industrial Average pretends to compute the average of the daily closing prices of the securities of 30 predetermined industrial firms. The computations become involved, though, when financial occurrences such as mergers and stock splits take place. For the sake of discussion, suppose that the Dow Jones average consists of the securities of only two firms, one whose stock is valued at $20 per share, the other valued at $30. The Dow Jones average would be

$$\frac{1}{2}(\$20 + \$30) = \$25.$$

During the next day, suppose that a stock split occurs with the firm whose securities were valued at $20 per share. Now each security from the first firm is worth only $10 and the Dow Jones average, ignoring the stock split, would be

$$\frac{1}{2}(\$10 + \$30) = \$20.$$

To consider the effect of the split, the Dow Jones average finds the divisor d such that

$$\frac{1}{d}(\$10 + \$30) = \$25,$$

where $25 was the average before the split. Here $d = 1.6$. If during the day of the stock split, the first security increased in price to $12 per share while the other remained at $30, the new Dow Jones average would be computed as

$$\frac{1}{1.6}(\$12 + \$30) = \$26.25.$$

Each time stock dividends are declared, a merger occurs, or a stock split takes place, the Dow Jones Industrial Average becomes less meaningful because of the continual adjustment of the divisor term, d. Although the divisor started out as 30 (since the Dow Jones average is computed from the security prices of 30 firms), it is now about 4.5 and will continue to decrease as more stock splits, mergers, and other financial happenings occur. Actually the Dow Jones average is not an average at all. Its usefulness as a measure of market value has diminished and will continue to diminish with time.

14.6   Summary

A time series is a sequence of measurements taken on a process that varies over time. It is usually represented in graphical form with its process values listed on the vertical axis plotted against time on the horizontal axis. One may think of a time series as consisting of components such as a long-term trend, a cyclic effect, or a seasonal effect. Any or none of the components may be present in a time series. In addition, all time series possess random variation, which tends to obscure the non-random components of the series. Smoothing methods may sometimes reveal the underlying components in a time series by "canceling out" the effects of random variation.

The values from a time series are often misleading, especially those which occur in monetary units. Index numbers are used to deflate some monetary values and inflate others so that meaningful monetary comparisons can be made over time. Index numbers measure the change in price or value of a single or an aggregate of commodities from some base time period to a reference time period. Weighted indexes, which multiply the commodity prices by a predetermined factor, are the most commonly used type of index numbers. Most price indexes computed regularly by the Bureau of Labor Statistics are weighted indexes.

Care must be taken to interpret an index number or series properly. Many commonly used indexes, such as the Consumer Price Index, the Wholesale Price Index, and the Dow Jones Industrial Average, do not portend what their titles might imply. One must examine the exact intent of an index, the identity of the commodities that are included within the index, and the weights associated with each commodity included within the index before meaningful conclusions can be made.

Exercises

1. List and define the components of a time series.

2. Which of the time-series components would you expect to be present in each of the following series?
    (a) The week's end closing values of the Dow Jones Industrial Average from Jan. 1, 1965, to Jan. 1, 1974.
    (b) The gross monthly sales volume of Sears Roebuck and Company from January 1960 to January 1974.
    (c) The gross monthly sales volume of the Miller Brewing Company from June 1960 to June 1974.
    (d) The annual sales of life insurance in the United States from 1950 to 1975.
    (e) The monthly farm employment in the United States from January 1955 to January 1975.

3. The following data represent the gross monthly sales volume (in thousands of dollars) of The Pharmaceutical Company from January 1972 to January 1974.

1972		1973	
TIME	SALES	TIME	SALES
Jan.	18.0	Jan.	23.3
Feb.	18.5	Feb.	22.6
Mar.	19.2	Mar.	23.1
Apr.	19.0	Apr.	20.9
May	17.8	May	20.2
June	19.5	June	22.5
July	20.0	July	24.1
Aug.	20.7	Aug.	25.0
Sept.	19.1	Sept.	25.2
Oct.	19.6	Oct.	23.8
Nov.	20.8	Nov.	25.7
Dec.	21.0	Dec.	26.3

(a) Plot the sales values against time and construct the time series.
(b) Which time-series components appear to exist within the sales pattern?

4.   Refer to Exercise 3 and smooth the monthly sales values by computing a 3-month moving-average series. Plot the smoothed series and the original series on the same sheet of graph paper. What conclusions do you draw?

5.   Refer to Exercise 3 and smooth the monthly sales volumes by computing
(a) An exponentially smoothed series employing the smoothing constant $\alpha = .1$.
(b) An exponentially smoothed series employing the smoothing constant $\alpha = .25$.
(c) On a sheet of graph paper, superimpose the two smoothed series on the original series. What conclusions do you draw?

6.   Refer to Exercise 3 and break down the original series into its components as was done in Figure 14.6 for the sales of the Palace Department Store. Is it always possible to separate the components of a time series? Explain.

7.   The table lists the monthly sales (in thousands of dollars) of a women's apparel shop over the years 1970 through 1974. Remove the seasonal component from these data by applying a 12-month moving average to the data. Plot the original series and the de-seasonalized series together on the same piece of graph paper. After removing the seasonal component, what inherent components do these data appear to possess?

	1970	1971	1972	1973	1974
January	12.3327	13.3708	14.3747	14.5151	15.1144
February	12.9585	14.6156	15.9360	14.6323	15.3555
March	15.7480	17.4000	16.8129	16.4262	18.6998
April	15.5027	16.2574	15.2642	15.7848	17.1827
May	16.1040	17.6280	17.8682	18.1914	18.2053
June	16.9076	16.4033	16.4432	16.9352	18.6406
July	14.2196	14.8934	15.1211	16.3979	17.2713
August	15.6731	16.7835	16.9940	17.4069	17.1966
September	16.9057	16.5715	16.0469	16.5623	17.4080
October	18.5070	22.3205	20.8081	21.5474	21.2315
November	20.8645	23.8217	22.0516	21.2594	21.5733
December	23.8468	25.1588	24.3519	25.8063	27.5733

8.   Refer to the sales data from the women's apparel shop, Exercise 7. Smooth the monthly sales volumes over the 5-year period 1970–1974 by computing
(a) An exponentially smoothed series employing the smoothing constant $\alpha = .1$.
(b) An exponentially smoothed series employing the smoothing constant $\alpha = .4$.
(c) On a sheet of graph paper, superimpose the two smoothed series on the original series. What conclusions do you draw?

9.   Refer to Exercises 7 and 8. Does the 12-month moving-average model used in Exercise 7 appear to more effectively eliminate the seasonal pattern from the women's apparel data than either of the exponential smoothing models from Exercise 8? Would a moving-average model with an M other than 12 have eliminated the seasonal component as well? Explain.

10. For each of the following decision-making situations, explain how an individual might construct and use an index number as an aid in arriving at a conclusion.
(a) A public utility company wishes to increase its rates by the amount of inflation in the economy of its area since rates were last set. The current rates were established in 1968.

(b) A homeowner wishes to establish a selling price for his home which cost him $25,000 in 1960.

(c) The owner of a small hardware store would like to know how the growth in sales of his store over the past 5 years compares with the growth in sales of a large competing hardware chain.

(d) An individual would like to know the real buying power of a dollar he currently earns in comparison with the buying power of a dollar he earned 10 years ago.

11. Criticize the following uses of index numbers:

(a) The portfolio manager for a pension fund must decide whether to invest a large sum in a corporate bond account or in a mutual fund. If the Dow Jones Industrial Average drops by more than five points in the next week, he will invest in the corporate bond account. Otherwise, he will elect the mutual fund investment.

(b) A business economist observes that the Consumer Price Index has risen from 105.2 in 1965 to 131.6 in 1975. He concludes that living costs have increased by 26.4 percent during that time.

(c) A government contractor notices that the Wholesale Price Index has increased by 13 percent over the past 2 years. Thus he asks the government for a 13 percent increase in the contractual payoff.

(d) A lumber wholesaler is interested in the real increase in sales he has incurred over the past 5 years. To measure the increase, he computes a Laspeyres weighted aggregate index, considering all types of lumber he handles, using the current and 5-year-old board-foot selling prices and the quantities of each type of lumber he sold 5 years ago.

12. Suppose that the cost-of-living indicators imply that living costs have risen 43 percent from 1960 to 1974. If Bob Owen's annual income has risen from $12,500 in 1960 to $16,400 in 1974, has his "real" income actually risen?

13. The costs in cents per pound of six common meat products for 5 consecutive years are listed below:

YEAR	GROUND BEEF	ROUND STEAK	RIB ROAST	HAM	FRYING CHICKEN	PORK CHOPS
1970	42	87	100	98	45	110
1971	48	88	105	105	49	95
1972	52	92	110	100	55	105
1973	57	100	120	97	62	112
1974	60	105	129	89	69	125

Using 1970 as the base year, compute

(a) The simple price index for each type of meat for each of the 5 years.

(b) The simple aggregate index of meat prices for each of the 5 years.

14. Refer to Exercise 13. In 1970, the average family of four bought 115 lb of ground beef, 75 lb of round steak, 50 lb of rib roast, 50 lb of ham, 100 lb of frying chicken, and 80 lb of pork chops. Compute the Laspeyres weighted aggregate index for the meat prices over the past 5 years.

15. Refer to Exercise 13. In 1974 the average family of four consumed 135 lb of ground beef, 70 lb of round steak, 50 lb of rib roast, 35 lb of ham, 110 lb of frying chicken, and 75 lb of pork chops. Compute the Paasche weighted aggregate index for the meat prices in 1974 using 1970 as the base year.

16. Refer to Exercises 14 and 15. Compute Fisher's Ideal Index for the meat prices in 1974 using 1970 as the base year. Discuss the significance of this index.

17.   A power company was interested in examining the relative costs of heating over a 4-year period. In their study, the power company contacted a sample of householders who heat by electric heat, use an oil furnace, or heat by natural gas and obtained the average quantity each householder used per month. (Quantities were obtained from utility company records.) The results are as follows:

	UNIT PRICE				AVERAGE MONTHLY USAGE			
	1970	1971	1972	1973	1970	1971	1972	1973
Electricity	1.50	1.50	1.70	1.72	67	75	68	70
Oil	.22	.29	.30	.32	230	263	225	237
Gas	7.50	8.00	8.20	8.20	6.8	7.2	6.9	7.0

(a) Find the Laspeyres weighted aggregate index for the 1971, 1972, and 1973 average monthly heating costs using 1970 as the base year.
(b) Find the Paasche weighted aggregate index for the years 1971, 1972, and 1973 average monthly heating costs using 1970 as the base year.

18.   Refer to Exercise 17. Compute Fisher's Ideal Index for the average monthly heating costs during 1971, 1972, and 1973 using 1970 as the base year. What conclusions do you draw about the relative heating costs over the 4-year period 1970–1973, based upon the Laspeyres, Paasche, and Fisher Ideal indexes? If the results were contradictory, which index would you consider the most reliable? Explain.

19.   Refer to Exercise 17. Separately compute a Laspeyres Index for each method of heating over the three years 1971, 1972, and 1973 using 1970 as the base year. Which method of heating has increased in cost the most rapidly? Which has shown the least relative cost increase?

20.   A small manufacturing plant produces power lawn mowers, hand-operated lawn mowers, and small power garden tillers. During the past 3 years, their sales volume and average selling price per unit have been:

	SELLING PRICES				NUMBER UNITS SOLD		
	1972	1973	1974		1972	1973	1974
Power mower	$60	65	71	Power mower	10,000	12,500	17,000
Hand mower	24	27	30	Hand mower	7,650	7,800	8,550
Tiller	53	60	65	Tiller	2,400	2,650	2,200

(a) Find the Laspeyres weighted aggregate index for the 1973 and 1974 selling prices of the production of the manufacturing plant. (Use 1972 as the base year.)
(b) Find the Paasche weighted aggregate index for the 1973 and 1974 selling prices of the production of the manufacturing plant. (Use 1972 as the base year.)

References

Doody, F. S., *Introduction to the Use of Economic Indicators*. New York: Random House, Inc., 1965.

Freund, J. E., and F. J. Williams; revised by B. Perles and C. Sullivan, *Modern Business Statistics*. Englewood Cliffs, N.J.: Prentice-Hall, Inc., 1969. Chapters 15 and 16.

Spurr, W. A., and C. P. Bonini, *Statistical Analysis for Business Decisions*. Rev. ed. Homewood, Ill.: Richard D. Irwin, Inc., 1973. Chapter 18.

U.S. Department of Commerce. *Business Statistics*, biennial supplement to the *Survey of Current Business*. Washington, D.C.: U.S. Government Printing Office, 1967 et seq.

Chapter Fifteen

Forecasting Models

15.1   Introduction

We all exist in an environment governed by time. It is thus a common goal for business organizations, public organizations, and individuals to allocate available time among competing resources in some optimal manner. This is accomplished by making forecasts of future activities and taking the proper actions as suggested by these forecasts.

In business and public administration, the organization is usually concerned with both short-term and long-term forecasts. The short-term forecast is usually planned to look no more than one year into the future and involves forecasting sales, price changes, and customer demand, which in turn reflect upon the need for seasonal employment, short-term capital expenditures, and inventory management procedures. The long-term forecast usually looks from 2 to 10 years into the future and is used as a planning model for product line and capital investment decisions, as indicated by changing demand patterns.

Naturally, the further a forecast is projected into the future, the more speculative it becomes. But since the future is *always* uncertain, one cannot expect complete accuracy to be associated with any forecast. The time series underlying the process to be forecast is bound to be influenced by many causal factors—some forcing the time series up while conflicting factors act to force the series down. Nevertheless, it is essential for the businessman to make forecasts of his future business activity in order to efficiently budget his time and resources. He cannot hope to account for every possible factor that may cause the process of interest to rise or fall over time. All that can be expected is that the benefits gained by forecasting offset the opportunity cost for not forecasting. It is important to note that such benefits are not limited to real monetary savings but may imply a sharpening of the businessman's thinking to consider the interplay of the events that affect the movement of the time series under study.

We recall from Section 14.3 that smoothing methods may sometimes reveal trends and seasonal and cyclic effects in the time series. Forecasting by extending these patterns is a very speculative procedure. One must first assume that the past is a mirror of the future, that past trends and cycles will continue into the future. This is seldom the case. Thus one must not only smooth the data and try to extend the signal components into the future but also predict the impact of unknown factors such as political events, research, changing buyer behavior, and new product development.

Statistical forecasting methods at best provide a starting point for predicting future business activity. If the time series of business activity is very volatile, if patterns of movement over time are not distinguishable, and if economic, social, and political events appear uncertain, statistics may be of no use in developing forecasts. Even if none of these factors appears to be a problem, the presence of random variation alone suggests that forecasts will be less than accurate for each successive period into the future.

In the end, mathematical forecasting procedures and judgment must work hand in hand. Subjective evaluations must be made of floating currencies on import–export trade, the effect of a strike of our labor force, the effect of a competitor's new promotional campaign, and so forth, and these subjective evaluations must (in turn) be used to "condition" the forecast obtained from the mathematical model. As long as uncertainty is involved with future business and economic activity, forecasting must be recognized as an art that becomes more perfect as the forecaster gains experience and the ability to adapt his procedures to meet the changing environment of the firm.

15.2   Probabilistic Forecasting Models

The linear model of Section 12.10 will sometimes provide a suitable probabilistic model for establishing the long-term trend for a time series. For example, a long-term upward or downward trend similar to that implied in Figure 15.1 (a) might be isolated by fitting the straight line,

$$y = \beta_0 + \beta_1 x + \varepsilon,$$

where the independent variable $x =$ the unit of time, using the procedures of Chapter 12. A curvilinear long-term trend, as shown in (b), could be modeled using a parabolic function,

$$y = \beta_0 + \beta_1 x + \beta_2 x^2 + \varepsilon.$$

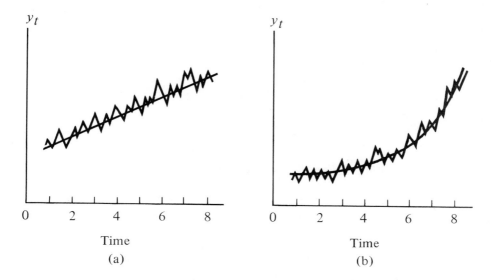

Figure 15.1   *Time Series with Linear and Curvilinear
Long-Term Trends*

The corresponding prediction function, $\hat{y} = \hat{\beta}_0 + \hat{\beta}_1 x + \hat{\beta}_2 x^2$, could be determined by using the method of least squares in the manner illustrated by Example 12.1.

The assumption of independence of the random error, ε, associated with successive measurements will not usually be satisfied, and consequently the probabilistic statements associated with the estimation of $E(y)$ or prediction of y will be in error. One would suspect that they would be conservative and that knowledge of the actual pattern of correlation would permit more accurate estimation and prediction. If the response is an average over a period of time, the correlation of adjacent response measurements will be reduced and will quite possibly satisfy adequately the assumption of independence implied in the least-squared inferential procedures.

Other linear models (linear in the unknown "weights," $\beta_0, \beta_1, \beta_2$, etc.) can be constructed and fit to data generated by economic time series using the method of least squares. For example, the yearly production of steel, y, is a function of its price, the price of competitive structural materials, the production of competitive products during the preceding year, the amount of steel purchased during the immediately preceding years (to measure current inventory), and many other variables. A linear model relating these independent variables to steel production might be

$$y = \beta_0 + \beta_1 x_1 + \beta_2 x_2 + \beta_3 x_3 + \cdots + \beta_k x_k + \varepsilon,$$

where

x_1 = time,

x_2 = price of steel,

$x_3 = x_2^2$ (allowing curvature in the response curve as a function of price),

x_4 = production of aluminum during previous year,

x_5 = price of aluminum,

x_6 = steel production during previous year,

$\vdots$

$x_k = x_2 x_5$ (an interaction effect between steel and aluminum prices).

One could even include variables of the type, say, $x_7 = \sin(2\pi x_1/3)$, which would be a cyclic effect due to time with a period of 3 years. In other words, the model builder has unlimited room for ingenuity in constructing the linear model. The test of the model is how well it agrees with his sample data and then, more importantly, how well it continues to forecast the future.

In building a forecasting model, the procedure is usually to begin with a large number of variables that might be closely related to the response. Combinations of these variables are used to form models that are fit to the sample data using the method of least squares. Speaking in a very general sense, the procedure is continued until one obtains a model that predicts with a relatively small error of prediction. The retained model is then tested by comparing predicted and observed response measurements collected at future points in time.

The fitting of a regression model to data by the method of least squares was discussed in Chapter 12. The computation involved in fitting a multi-independent variable linear model is extensive and sometimes practically impossible on a desk calculator. One is well advised to employ an available preprogrammed multiple regression-analysis computer program, as discussed in Section 12.9, for such an analysis. Owing to the advent of the computer, least-squares computations, unmanageable 20 years ago, can now be obtained in seconds. This gives modern-day managers a distinct advantage over their predecessors by allowing them to derive forecast models to assist in program planning, budgeting, and control.

15.3   A Least-Squares, Sinusoidal Model

In Figure 14.9 the week's end security prices for the Color-Vision Company were plotted against time. One can notice "peaks" in the time series at the eighth, seventeenth, and twenty-eighth and twenty-ninth time points and "valleys" at the fifth, twelfth, and twenty-third time points. Very roughly, one could infer that these peaks and valleys suggest that the time series follows a cyclic pattern with 10 time points as the period of one complete cycle. We shall assume that the security prices for the Color-Vision Company follow this pattern and construct an appropriate least-squares model to forecast the prices over time.

The model we shall use is*

$$y_t = \beta_0 + \beta_1 t + \beta_2 \cos\left(\frac{2\pi t}{10}\right) + \beta_3 \sin\left(\frac{2\pi t}{10}\right) + \beta_4 t \cos\left(\frac{2\pi t}{10}\right) + \beta_5 t \sin\left(\frac{2\pi t}{10}\right) + \varepsilon.$$

Notice that this model is a special form of the multivariate predictor model (see Section 12.9),

$$y = \beta_0 + \beta_1 x_1 + \beta_2 x_2 + \beta_3 x_3 + \beta_4 x_4 + \beta_5 x_5 + \varepsilon,$$

where

$$x_1 = t, \text{ the index of time,}$$

$$x_2 = \cos(2\pi t/10),$$

$$x_3 = \sin(2\pi t/10),$$

$$x_4 = t \cos(2\pi t/10),$$

$$x_5 = t \sin(2\pi t/10).$$

The linear term $\beta_1 t$ should reflect the linear trend of the series with time, while the terms $\cos(2\pi t/10)$ and $\sin(2\pi t/10)$ give a cyclic effect with a period of 10 weeks to the forecasted prices. The inclusion of the terms $t \cos(2\pi t/10)$ and $t \sin(2\pi t/10)$ allows the amplitudes (heights) of the cyclic function to change over time, a necessary requirement since the peaks in the time series of Figure 14.9 are of varying heights. A multiple linear regression model with periodic (trigonometric) terms for the independent variables, such as the one suggested above, is called a sinusoidal model.

A sinusoidal model is merely one of many types of models that are adaptable to the method of least squares. It is especially useful here because of the cyclic effects that appear to exist within the Color-Vision prices over time but is primarily used as an illustration of how nonlinear functions of the independent variables may be combined linearly to produce a least-squares forecasting equation.

---

* The notation $(2\pi t/10)$ refers to the number of radians at which the associated trigonometric term must be evaluated. Since one complete cycle equals 2π radians, $(2\pi t/10)$ at $t = 3$ would imply that the cosine must be evaluated at a point 3/10 of the way through its complete cycle. Thus $\cos(2\pi 3/10) = -.30$.

The forecasting model computed by the method of least squares as the best-fit equation to the Color-Vision data is

$$\hat{y}_t = 68.46 + .44t + 3.98 \cos\left(\frac{2\pi t}{10}\right) - .22 \sin\left(\frac{2\pi t}{10}\right) - .20t \cos\left(\frac{2\pi t}{10}\right)$$

$$- .19t \sin\left(\frac{2\pi t}{10}\right),$$

where $\hat{y}_t$ is the forecast price at the end of week t, for $t = 1, 2, 3, \ldots, 30$. The original data, the forecast prices, and the forecast errors are shown in Table 15.1.

How well does this model forecast the week's end security prices of the Color-Vision Company? The observed and forecasted prices listed in Table 15.1 are plotted against time in Figure 15.2. It appears that the least-squares forecasting equation we have selected is not too responsive to the sudden changes of value in the original series. It must be remembered that the observed and forecasted security prices should agree to some extent because the observed prices were used in determining the best fitting model according to the least-squares theory. In spite of this we would regard

Figure 15.2   *Least-Squares Forecasts for the Week's End Security Prices of the Color-Vision Company*

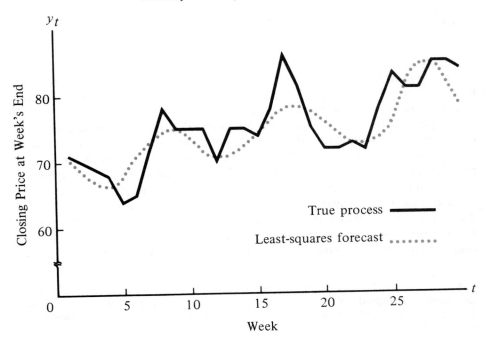

Table 15.1   *Actual and Forecasted Week's End Security Prices for the Color-Vision Company; Forecasts Determined by a Least-Squares, Sinusoidal Forecasting Model*

WEEK (t)	COS	SIN	t COS	t SIN	ACTUAL VALUES y_t	FORECAST $\hat{y}_t$	FORECAST ERROR $e_t = y_t - \hat{y}_t$
1	.80	.58	.80	.58	71	71.71	− .71
2	.30	.95	.61	1.90	70	69.85	.15
3	−.30	.95	−.92	2.85	69	68.03	.97
4	−.80	.58	−3.23	2.35	68	67.11	.89
5	−1.00	.00	−5.00	.00	64	67.69	−3.69
6	−.80	−.58	−4.85	−3.52	65	69.70	−4.70
7	−.30	−.95	−2.16	−6.65	72	72.27	−.27
8	.30	−.95	2.47	−7.60	78	74.34	3.66
9	.80	−.58	7.28	−5.29	75	75.27	−.27
10	1.00	.00	10.00	.00	75	74.80	.20
11	.80	.58	8.89	6.46	75	73.29	1.71
12	.30	.95	3.70	11.41	70	71.75	−1.75
13	−.30	.95	−4.01	12.36	75	71.17	3.83
14	−.80	.58	−11.32	8.22	75	71.97	3.03
15	−1.00	.00	−15.00	.00	74	74.07	−.07
16	−.80	−.58	−12.94	−9.40	78	76.83	1.17
17	−.30	−.95	−5.25	−16.16	86	79.09	6.91
18	.30	−.95	5.56	−17.11	82	79.91	2.09
19	.80	−.58	15.37	−11.16	75	79.12	−4.12
20	1.00	.00	20.00	.00	72	77.13	−4.13
21	.80	.58	16.98	12.34	72	74.87	−2.87
22	.30	.95	6.79	20.92	73	73.64	−.64
23	−.30	.95	−7.10	21.87	72	74.31	−2.31
24	−.80	.58	−19.41	14.10	77	76.83	.17
25	−1.00	.00	−25.00	.00	83	80.45	2.55
26	−.80	−.58	−21.03	−15.28	81	83.96	−2.96
27	−.30	−.95	−8.34	−25.67	81	85.91	−4.91
28	.30	−.95	8.65	−26.62	85	85.48	−.48
29	.80	−.58	23.46	−17.04	85	82.98	2.02
30	1.00	.00	30.00	.00	84	79.47	4.53

the agreement to be good, considering the simplicity of the linear model used. The sinusoidal model has been introduced simply to illustrate the usefulness of artificial trigonometric variables as predictors in a probabilistic forecasting model. In a real application, these artificial variables would almost always be supplemented by measurable predictors such as last week's sales or a market index, resulting in a more accurate forecasting equation than the one we have obtained. We should note that the addition of extra terms in a least-squares model can only give us greater forecast accuracy and cannot decrease our forecast accuracy. If the term introduced as a predictor variable is redundant, it will simply be "weighted out" by acquiring a small associated regression coefficient in the least-squares forecasting equation. [Note that the coefficient of the sin $(2\pi t/10)$ term in our preceding model was only .17. Thus sin $(2\pi t/10)$ does not contribute much to the value of $\hat{y}_t$.] The ultimate criterion of goodness of the forecasting model, of course, is how well the model forecasts the future.

Forecasting always requires extrapolation beyond the interval of time in which the sample data were collected, a procedure that can lead to errors of prediction considerably larger than those expected according to least-squares theory. This is occasionally caused by a change in the basic form of the linear model relating y to the original independent variables but most often is due to the omission of one or more independent variables that may well have remained stable over the interval of time in which the sample data were collected. Taxation policies, research expenditures, political developments, and buyer behavior are examples of variables that may remain stable over the sample collection period but may cause abrupt and relatively large forecast errors when their values exhibit sudden changes during the forecast period.

One almost always fails to include in the model one or more "dormant" variables, with the result that forecasts far into the future may be subject to large errors. In spite of this, the least-squares forecasting equation, with the relatively crude least-squares bound on the error of prediction, is a very useful tool. This is particularly true for short-term forecasting, where relative stability persists in the system for at least a short period of time. The important point to keep in mind is that large errors can occur when extrapolating.

15.4 The Autoregressive Forecasting Model

Linear models accounting for correlations between adjacent observations in a time series are called autoregressive models. Thus, if y_t and y_{t+1} are the responses at times t and $(t+1)$, respectively, we might write

$$y_{t+1} = \beta_0 + \beta_1 x + \varepsilon,$$

where

$$x = y_t.$$

Thus we are using knowledge of the response at time period t to predict the response at time $(t+1)$. We refer to the above model as the first-order autoregressive model. The general pth-order autoregressive equation is written as

$$y_{t+1} = \beta_0 + \beta_1 y_t + \beta_2 y_{t-1} + \beta_3 y_{t-2} + \cdots + \beta_p y_{t-p+1} + \varepsilon.$$

An autoregressive model of order greater than 1 is necessary to include information in the model due to the correlation between observations separated by more than one unit of time. For instance, the sales volume of the Palace Department Store, illustrated in Figure 14.4, seems to indicate an obvious annual (12-month) cycle. Thus a "good" autoregressive model for forecasting the future sales of the Palace Department Store might be

$$y_{t+1} = \beta_0 + \beta_1 y_t + \beta_2 y_{t-5} + \beta_3 y_{t-11} + \varepsilon,$$

where $\beta_1 y_t$ is the effect on the next month's sales caused by last month's sales volume, $\beta_2 y_{t-5}$ is the 6-month effect, and $\beta_3 y_{t-11}$ is the 12-month effect. The 6-month effect was chosen because of an assumed significant strong negative relationship of sales for months separated by 6 months—high sales in December, low sales in June, moderately high in November and January, moderately low in May and July. The 12-month effect is more apparent. Sales are always high in December, always low in June, always moderately high in November and January, and always moderately low in May and July. Thus there is an apparent high positive correlation between the sales for the same month for different years.

The autoregressive model need not be restricted to a linear relationship. For example, we could use

$$y_{t+1} = \beta_0 + \beta_1 x + \beta_2 x^2 + \varepsilon,$$

where $x = y_t$ if we have reason to believe that each response is a quadratic function of the most recent response.

The equation that best forecasts the future values of a random process from its past values or other related variables is not easily determined. The autoregressive model suggests that if a high correlation exists between the values of a random process at constant intervals of time, then the autoregressive model may be appropriate for forecasting.

The only way we can determine whether the autoregressive model, or any other forecasting model, is a good forecasting model is to use each to develop forecasts. The one that returns the most accurate forecasts, as measured by the smallness of SSE, where

$$\text{SSE} = \sum_{all\ t} (y_t - \hat{y}_t)^2,$$

is the one that should be best for our purposes.

Autoregressive models can be fitted to time-series data using the method of generalized least squares. Essentially, this amounts to letting the lagged process responses, $y_t, y_{t-1}, y_{t-2}, \ldots, y_{t-p}$, assume the role of the independent variables in the linear regression model. Then we solve for estimates of the regression parameters β_0, β_1, ..., β_{p+1} by least-squares methods as outlined for the general linear regression model in Chapter 12. The theory of inference associated with autoregressive models is beyond the scope of this text but can be found in Box and Jenkins (1969).

The autoregressive model

$$y_{t+1} = \beta_0 + \beta_1 y_t + \beta_2 y_{t-1} + \varepsilon$$

was fitted to the week's end security prices of the Color-Vision Company. A second-order autoregressive model was selected only to motivate the use of an autoregressive model, not to suggest that the second-order model is the "best" autoregressive model for forecasting the Color-Vision prices. The second-order autoregressive equation for forecasting the security prices one week ahead of available data is

$$\hat{y}_{t+1} = 18.74 + 1.03 y_t - .28 y_{t-1},$$

where y_t is the most recent week's end security price and y_{t-1} is the next most recent week's end price. To see how well the model fits the data, we compute the estimated price $\hat{y}_{t+1}$ for each week where actual observed closing prices exist for the two preceding weeks. For instance, the predicted price at the end of the tenth week is

$$\hat{y}_{10} = 18.74 + 1.03 y_9 - .28 y_8$$
$$= 18.74 + 1.03(75) - .28(78)$$
$$= 74.15,$$

where the actual price at the end of the ninth week was 75 and the eighth week, 78. Table 15.2 lists the actual and autoregressive forecasts for the Color-Vision security prices, which are then plotted in Figure 15.3.

Figure 15.3 exhibits a very noticeable lag-one effect. That is, the fitted prices appear to be practically identical with the actual price from the previous time period. This relationship is due to the fact that the autoregressive model we have selected estimates future security prices as a function of only the two latest security prices. But since the correlation between prices separated by two time periods is small, the forecasted price is essentially a function of only the most recent observation. Thus a logical conclusion might be that the autoregressive model, at least the second-order autoregressive model we have chosen, is not a good model to use to forecast future Color-Vision security prices since the model does not appear to adequately fit the available past prices. However, in all 30 cases, the forecast error

Table 15.2   *Actual and Forecasted Week's End Security Prices for the Color-Vision Company; Forecasts Determined by a Second-Order Autoregressive Model**

WEEK (t)	y_{t-1}	y_{t-2}	TRUE VALUE y_t	FORECAST $\hat{y}_t$	FORECAST ERROR $e_t = y_t - \hat{y}_t$
1	70†	69†	71	71.81	−.81
2	71	70†	70	72.56	−2.56
3	70	71	69	71.26	−2.26
4	69	70	68	70.50	−2.50
5	68	69	64	69.75	−5.75
6	64	68	65	65.90	−.90
7	65	64	72	68.04	3.96
8	72	65	78	74.94	3.06
9	78	72	75	79.23	−4.23
10	75	78	75	74.15	.85
11	75	75	75	75.30	−.30
12	75	75	70	75.30	−5.30
13	70	75	75	70.14	4.86
14	75	70	75	76.69	−1.69
15	75	75	74	75.30	−1.30
16	74	75	78	74.27	3.73
17	78	74	86	78.68	7.32
18	86	78	82	85.82	−3.82
19	82	86	75	79.47	−4.47
20	75	82	73	73.36	−.36
21	73	75	72	73.24	−1.24
22	72	73	73	72.76	.24
23	73	72	72	74.07	−2.07
24	72	73	77	72.76	4.24
25	77	72	83	78.20	4.80
26	83	77	81	83.00	−2.00
27	81	83	81	79.27	1.73
28	81	81	85	79.83	5.17
29	85	81	85	83.96	1.04
30	85	85	84	82.84	1.16

*The forecasted values that appear may not be exactly those computed from the forecast equation because of rounding errors.

† The values of y_t for the two weeks preceding week 1 were 69 and 70, respectively.

is less than 10 percent of the true value, a standard of accuracy commonly required by management.

If the actual process we are attempting to forecast is quite stable, a first- or second-order autoregressive model should return fairly accurate forecasts. When the actual process is rather volatile, autoregressive forecasts may not be accurate. But

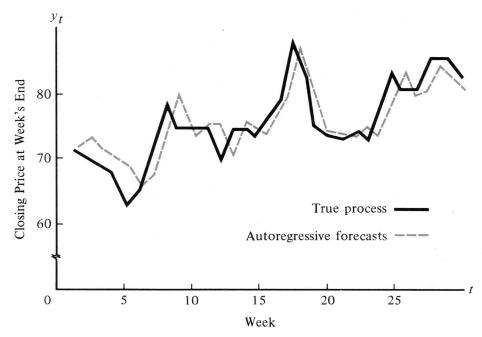

Figure 15.3   *Autoregressive Forecasts for the Week's End Security Prices of the Color-Vision Company*

we could hardly expect any forecasting model to predict accurately the future behavior of a volatile process. Some additional forecasting accuracy can be expected for each additional autoregressive term added to the autoregressive forecasting equation. However, inclusion of y_{t-2} into the autoregressive model

$$y_{t+1} = \beta_0 + \beta_1 y_t + \beta_2 y_{t-1} + \varepsilon$$

may not add enough in predictive accuracy to offset the cost and effort necessary to incorporate the extra term and its values over time into the model. Only the terms that add significantly to predictive accuracy should be incorporated into the model, where significance is measured by the relative sizes of the correlations between process values separated by constant intervals of time.

Time lags at which significant correlations exist are seldom determinable by only a visual inspection of the plot of the time series. In general one determines whether an autoregressive model is appropriate by computing a correlogram, a graphical display of the correlations existing between observations spaced by a constant interval of time. These time-lag correlations, called autocorrelations, are computed in a manner similar to the method of Section 12.8. If $y_1, y_2, \ldots, y_n$ are the values for n consecutive time periods in a time series, then the autocorrelation between the values separated by k time periods is

$$r_k = \frac{\sum\limits_{t=1}^{n} (y_t - \hat{y}_t)(y_{t+k} - \hat{y}_{t+k})}{\sum\limits_{t=1}^{n} (y_t - \hat{y}_t)^2}, \qquad -1 \le r_k \le 1,$$

where $\hat{y}_t$ is the value at time t of the linear trend equation fit to the time series. That is, by the linear regression methods of Chapter 12, the linear equation $\hat{y}_t = \hat{\alpha}_0 + \hat{\alpha}_1 t$ is fitted to the process values over time. The terms $\hat{y}_t$ are used in the computation of r_k to "cancel out" the effects that may exist of a linear trend over time. A correlogram for a time series may appear as shown in Figure 15.4. The autocorrelations for process values separated by one and four time periods appear to be greater than the other correlations. Thus an appropriate autoregressive forecasting function for this process might be

$$y_{t+1} = \beta_0 + \beta_1 y_t + \beta_2 y_{t-3} + \varepsilon.$$

Figure 15.4   *Correlogram for a Time Series*

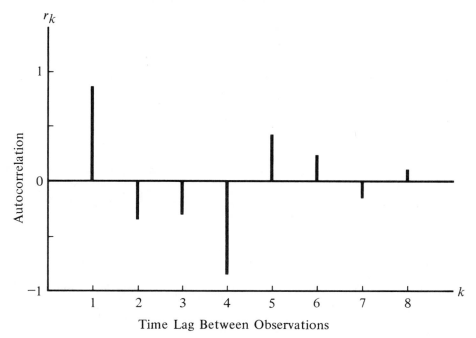

Time Lag Between Observations

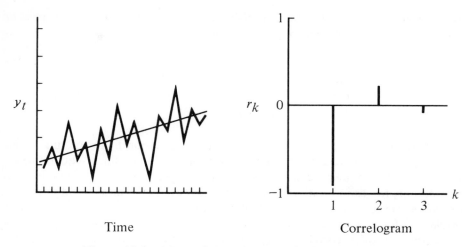

Figure 15.5 *Plot and Correlogram of a Time Series That Is
Very Unstable over Time*

We should note before concluding our discussion of autoregressive models
that a negative autocorrelation is just as meaningful as a positive one. We are
interested in the absolute magnitude $|r_k|$ and not its sign. A negative r_k implies that
when a process value is greater than the average trend, the value k time periods
ahead or behind that value tends to be less than the average trend. If significant,
such a relationship may be just as useful for purposes of prediction as when both
y_t and y_{t+k} are simultaneously either greater or less than the average trend. As an

Figure 15.6 *Plot and Correlogram of a Time Series That Is
Rather Stable over Time*

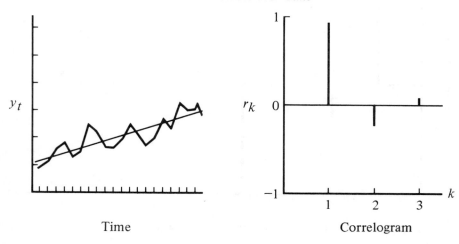

illustration, compare Figures 15.5 and 15.6. In Figure 15.5 we note a process that is highly unstable, returning a value for the time series on a different side of the average trend line each successive time period. Its autocorrelation value r_1 is negative. In Figure 15.6 the time series is more stable, does not alternate around the average trend as often, and has a positive autocorrelation value r_1. In either case, y_t would probably be a good predictor of y_{t+1} in a first-order autoregressive model.

15.5 An Exponential Smoothing Forecasting Model

In Section 14.3 we examined the use of smoothing techniques for "averaging out" the effects of random variation. It was mentioned that the smoothed series is a series of averages, each computed from available past data. In the case of the moving-average series, only the data from the past M periods were used for each value; with the exponentially smoothed series, all available past data were used for the computation of each smoothed value. Smoothing methods can also be used for forecasting. We shall present two forecasting models based on smoothing techniques, the others being left to the reader to explore if he should so desire.

Our first model is the multiple exponential smoothing forecasting model developed by Robert Goodell Brown. Suppose that we have the observations $y_1, y_2, \ldots, y_t$ from a time series. Our objective will be to compute a forecast of the process value y_{t+T}, which is T time points ahead of our available data. We shall assume that the relationship between the process value y_t and time t is an nth-degree polynomial,

$$y_t = \beta_0 + \beta_1 t + \frac{\beta_2}{2!} t^2 + \cdots + \frac{\beta_n}{n!} t^n + \varepsilon.$$

This is not a restrictive assumption at all, since almost all relationships could be satisfactorily fit by a polynomial that includes enough terms. Advanced mathematics could show us that the forecast of the process value y_{t+T} for an nth-degree polynomial is conveniently expressed by the Taylor series expansion around the latest observation as

$$\hat{y}_{t+T} = y_t^{(0)} + T y_t^{(1)} + \frac{T^2}{2!} y_t^{(2)} + \cdots + \frac{T^n}{n!} y_t^{(n)},$$

where $y_t^{(0)}, y_t^{(1)}, y_t^{(2)}, \ldots$ are the zeroth, first, and second derivatives, respectively, of the time series evaluated at time t.*

* The Taylor series expansion, developed by the English mathematician Brook Taylor in 1715, is a very useful technique for approximating the values of a function from its higher derivatives.

Brown's method gives a convenient way of expressing these complicated, seemingly meaningless derivatives in terms of smoothed statistics. If the time series appears constant with time, such as, perhaps, the average annual rainfall in Portland, Oregon, over the past 25 years, then we use the simple exponentially smoothed value S_t to forecast y_{t+T}. That is,

$$\hat{y}_{t+T} = S_t = \alpha y_t + (1 - \alpha)S_{t-1}.$$

If the process is linear over time, as was the illustration in Figure 14.2, the forecast is

$$\hat{y}_{t+T} = \left(2 + \frac{\alpha T}{1 - \alpha}\right)S_t - \left(1 + \frac{\alpha T}{1 - \alpha}\right)S_t(2),$$

where $S_t(2) = \alpha S_t + (1 - \alpha)S_{t-1}(2)$. The statistic $S_t(2)$ is called the double smoothed statistic and is a smoothing of the smoothed process values. That is, the series of $S_t(2)$ values is a smoothing of the series of S_t values where the observations, the y_t values, in the S_t series are the counterparts of the S_t values in the $S_t(2)$ series. The statistic $S_t(2)$ gives an indication of the trend of the averages, S_t, over time. Hence its inclusion in the model will account for a linear trend of y_t with time.

If the time series is not constant or linear over time, it is best to approximate its true polynomial relationship by a second-order polynomial. Otherwise, the computational difficulties involved in computing the forecasting equation are multiplied. Unless a time series is extremely volatile, second-degree polynomial forecasting methods work quite well. The suggested forecasting equation when the time series is neither constant nor linear with time is

$$\hat{y}_{t+T} = [6(1 - \alpha)^2 + (6 - 5\alpha)\alpha T + \alpha^2 T^2]\frac{S_t}{2(1 - \alpha)^2}$$

$$- [6(1 - \alpha)^2 + 2(5 - 4\alpha)\alpha T + 2\alpha^2 T^2]\frac{S_t(2)}{2(1 - \alpha)^2}$$

$$+ [2(1 - \alpha)^2 + (4 - 3\alpha)\alpha T + \alpha^2 T^2]\frac{S_t(3)}{2(1 - \alpha)^2}.$$

The triple-smoothed statistic $S_t(3)$ is, in a sense, describing the average rate of change of the average rates of change. It is found by computing

$$S_t(3) = \alpha S_t(2) + (1 - \alpha)S_{t-1}(3).$$

The forecasting equations listed earlier for the constant model, the linear model, and for the second-order polynomial model were presented without an explanation of their derivation. The derivations, in each case, are very involved and will be eliminated from our discussion. Those interested in the derivation of these forecasting equations are referred to Chapter 9 of Brown (1963).

The purpose of using the smoothed statistic S_t, $S_t(2)$, and $S_t(3)$ within Brown's method is to develop estimates for the coefficients in the polynomial model relating the process value y_t with time. This is performed recursively by continually updating the coefficients in the forecasting model as more data become available. That is, a different forecasting equation is acquired at every point in time, each based on all the available past and present process values. The recursions are initiated by assuming some value for $S_t(2)$ and $S_t(3)$ at the first time period, $t = 1$. A wise choice for these initial values is the first observation y_1. The values selected in the beginning are not critical, though, since their contribution to the forecasting equation will decrease as more data are incorporated into the model. The selection of the smoothing constant α is arbitrary, as explained in the discussion of smoothing methods within Section 14.3. The selection rule suggested for data smoothing is also recommended for the use of smoothing methods for forecasting. That is, if the process is volatile, a small value of α is selected; if the process is stable, a large α will probably give the most accurate forecasts. Some authors have suggested that the smoothing constant α change with time to reflect any new trends in the process. The benefits of such a plan, though, would probably be outweighed by the additional computational difficulties.

One might ask why Brown's method should be used when a least-squares model can be fitted to the data to represent the same polynomial relationship between y_t and time that is being assumed for Brown's method. The advantage of Brown's method is that it is a recursive method which develops a new forecasting model each time an additional observation is observed. One could also compute a new least-squares model with each new observation but the computational difficulties would be enormous. Least-squares models are usually of the type described in Sections 15.2 and 15.3, where one forecasting model is constructed from which forecasts are made without updating the model each time new observational information is obtained. Thus the multiple smoothing forecasting method of Brown is more efficient in that it incorporates more information into the forecasting model. Care should be taken, though, when we are attempting to forecast further than one time point ahead ($T > 1$). Unforeseeable events may cause the time series to react differently than it has ever reacted before. Thus, regardless of how much past data are incorporated into the model, we may not be able to forecast future process values accurately. The reader interested in the details of Brown's method of forecasting is again referred to Brown (1963).

Example 15.1   *Use Brown's method of multiple smoothing to forecast the week's end security prices of the Color-Vision Company. Assume that the actual polynomial relationship between y_t and time is at least a second-order polynomial. Let $T = 1$.*

Solution   *Since we are assuming that our process is neither constant nor linear with time, we shall employ the triple smoothing method to forecast the prices one time point ahead of available data. Since the process is rather volatile, as illustrated in Figure 14.8, we shall select* $\alpha = .2$. *Since* $T = 1$, *our forecasts are computed from the equation*

$$\hat{y}_{t+1} = [6(1 - .2)^2 + (6 - 5(.2))(.2) + (.2)^2]\frac{S_t}{2(1 - .2)^2}$$

$$- [6(1 - .2)^2 + 2(5 - 4(.2))(.2) + 2(.2)^2]\frac{S_t(2)}{2(1 - .2)^2}$$

$$+ [2(1 - .2)^2 + (4 - 3(.2))(.2) + (.2)^2]\frac{S_t(3)}{2(1 - .2)^2}$$

$$= 3.813S_t - 4.375S_t(2) + 1.563S_t(3).$$

At $t = 1$, *we have* $S_1 = 71$, $S_1(2) = 71$, *and* $S_1(3) = 71$, *since* $y_1 = 71$. *At each succeeding time period* $t = 2, 3, \ldots, 30$, *the smoothed statistics are found by computing*

$$S_t = (.2)y_t + (1 - .2)S_{t-1},$$

$$S_t(2) = (.2)S_t + (1 - .2)S_{t-1}(2),$$

Figure 15.7   *Exponential Smoothing Forecasts for the Week's End Security Prices of the Color-Vision Company*

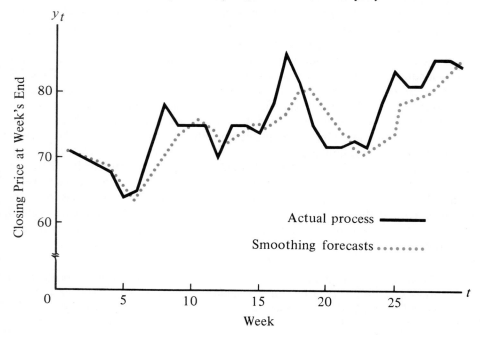

and

$$S_t(3) = (.2)S_t(2) + (1 - .2)S_{t-1}(3).$$

The smoothed statistics are then reentered into the forecasting model to obtain the forecast for the next time period.

The forecasts obtained by Brown's method and the true process values are listed in Table 15.3 and illustrated in Figure 15.7.

Table 15.3   *Actual and Forecasted Week's End Security Prices for the Color-Vision Company; Brown's Triple Smoothing Forecasting Method Was Used to Compute the Forecasts*

TIME t	ACTUAL PRICE y_t	FORECAST $\hat{y}_t$	FORECAST ERROR $e_t = y_t - \hat{y}_t$
1	71		
2	70	70.29	−.29
3	69	69.69	−.69
4	68	68.73	−.73
5	64	67.57	−3.57
6	65	64.52	.48
7	72	65.36	6.64
8	78	71.00	7.00
9	75	73.94	1.06
10	75	74.75	.25
11	75	75.71	−.71
12	70	75.13	−5.13
13	75	73.21	1.79
14	75	74.30	.70
15	74	74.88	−.88
16	78	74.54	3.46
17	86	76.63	9.37
18	82	82.61	−.61
19	75	83.67	−8.67
20	73	79.84	−6.84
21	72	76.07	−4.07
22	73	73.08	−.08
23	72	71.86	.14
24	77	70.60	6.40
25	83	72.94	10.06
26	81	78.05	2.95
27	81	79.97	1.03
28	85	81.03	3.97
29	85	83.92	1.08
30	84	85.51	−1.51

The multiple exponential smoothing model is often used as a tracking model to detect turning points in a time series. Identification of turning points is very useful

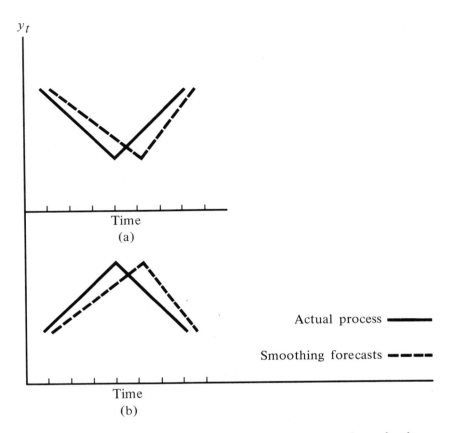

Figure 15.8   *Detection of Turning Points in a Time Series by the Multiple Exponential Smoothing Model*

when studying such time series as price movements, consumer buying habits, economic indicators like the floating value of currencies, or security price movements over time. The multiple exponential smoothing model is generally interpreted as having noted a time series that has bottomed out when the true process values cut over the smoothing forecasts, as illustrated in Figure 15.8(a). A process that has peaked out is noted when the true process values cut under the smoothing model forecasts. [See Figure 15.8(b).]

In Figure 15.7 the multiple exponential smoothing model identifies the time series of Color-Vision prices as having reached a low point (bottoming out) at periods 6, 13, 16, and 23. Peaks, when prices have reached a high point and should be on the way down, are noted at periods 11, 15, 18, and 30. If an investor with a typical buy-low-and-sell-high objective were to have purchased Color-Vision securities each time a low point was indicated by the model and sold the securities each time the prices peaked out, he would have made considerable profit over the period indicated. In fact, his average gain per share would have been $25 over the 30-week period.

Used simply as a forecasting model, the multiple exponential smoothing model with smoothing constant $\alpha = .2$ appears less reliable than the sinusoidal model for forecasting the security prices of the Color-Vision Company. This conclusion applies only to the security prices of the Color-Vision Company and should not be taken as a general rule to apply when selecting a forecasting model for a time series. A forecasting model that is appropriate for one time series may be totally inappropriate for generating forecasts of another time series.

15.6   The Exponentially Weighted Moving-Average Forecasting Model

One forecasting method has proved to be especially effective for generating forecasts of a process with a pronounced seasonal effect. This method, called the exponentially weighted moving average (EWMA) forecasting model, operates by separately estimating at each point in time the smoothed process average, the process trend, and the seasonal factor and then combining these three components to compute a forecast.

As we noted in Section 14.2, the seasonal effect is independent of a long-term trend and cyclic effects. Furthermore, since the seasonal effect is recurrent and periodic, it is predictable. Seasonality is a very common effect in business forecasting problems, especially as a component of the sales pattern of a firm. In most retailing enterprises, sales tend to be high around December; breweries and soft drink companies tend to have a sales pattern that follows the temperature—high sales when the weather is warm and low sales during cool weather; ski manufacturers have a sales pattern that peaks every winter. One could create a virtually endless list of examples of time series in business which exhibit a seasonal pattern. Thus the exponentially weighted moving average model is an extremely valuable aid to the business forecaster.

At each point in time the separate components of the time series which are estimated by the EWMA model are

1. The smoothed process average at time t:

$$S_t = (\alpha)\frac{y_t}{F_{t-L}} + (1 - \alpha)(S_{t-1} + R_{t-1}).$$

2. The updated trend gain at time t:

$$R_t = (\beta)(S_t - S_{t-1}) + (1 - \beta)R_{t-1}.$$

3. The updated seasonal factor at time t

$$F_t = (\gamma)\frac{y_t}{S_t} + (1 - \gamma)F_{t-L}.$$

Within these equations, α, β, and γ are smoothing constants, arbitrarily selected by the statistician and satisfying the properties

$$0 \leq \alpha \leq 1, \qquad 0 \leq \beta \leq 1, \qquad 0 \leq \gamma \leq 1.$$

The index L in the seasonal factor, F_{t-L}, is the seasonal period—the number of time points required for a repeat of the seasonal effect present in the time series, y_t is the true process value at time t, and the statistics S_{t-1} and R_{t-1} are the smoothed process average and trend factors, respectively, which were estimated at time period $t - 1$. These component equations are combined to give the forecast of the process value T time periods ahead of the most recent data (time period t) as

$$\hat{y}_{t+T} = (S_t + (T)R_t)F_{t-L+T}.$$

In each of the component equations, the model is computing an exponentially weighted moving average—hence the name of the model arises. Each component equation is estimating a factor that will be used in the forecast equation by weighting an estimate of that factor based on the most recent process value with the previous value of the factor. One can see how this is performed by examining Table 15.4. Educational psychologists refer to such updating schemes as those illustrated by the three component equations of our model as learning curves, since we are learning more about each component by incorporating new information into the estimation equations while still utilizing the available past information.

Table 15.4

COMPONENT (FACTOR)	ESTIMATE BASED ON MOST RECENT PROCESS VALUE	ESTIMATE BASED ON REMOTE VALUE
Smoothed average	$\dfrac{y_t}{F_{t-L}}$	$S_{t-1} + R_{t-1}$
Trend gain	$S_t - S_{t-1}$	R_{t-1}
Seasonal factor	$\dfrac{y_t}{S_t}$	F_{t-L}

Initial values must be determined for the statistics S and R so that we can compute S_t and R_t at time $t = 1$. Furthermore, initial values are needed for the seasonal factor, F_t, at each time point (each month, each week, etc.) of the entire seasonal period. The initial values are usually improved by using two or more complete seasonal periods of the data as a "warm-up" period before any forecasts are computed. For instance, if we are interested in analyzing and then forecasting the monthly sales of a retail department store, an initial value for S and R is selected and 12 seasonal factors (one for each month) are selected. These values are used to initiate the recursion of each equation. After two or more complete seasonal periods, the erroneous effects of the initial estimates for S, R, and the 12 values of F should be sufficiently dampened out. The rate at which the initial values are dampened out depends upon the selection of smoothing constants, α, β, and γ. As a general rule, α and β are small, usually about equal to .1, while the seasonal factor smoothing constant, γ, is best set at about .4. The statistician should not arbitrarily select the aforementioned values, though; he should try many combinations of values for α, β, and γ until a combination is found that generates sufficiently accurate forecasts. Note, however, that the number of combinations of possible values for α, β, and γ is exceedingly large.

Example 15.2 *The monthly sales volumes for the Bush Brewing Company are listed in Table 15.5 for the period of time from January 1, 1966, to January 1, 1971.*

Table 15.5 *Monthly Sales in Thousands of Barrels of the Bush Brewing Company from January 1, 1966, to January 1, 1971*

MONTH	SALES VOLUME (THOUSANDS OF BARRELS)				
	1966	1967	1968	1969	1970
January	18.7	18.3	19.6	23.3	24.6
February	15.6	17.6	18.6	20.1	22.8
March	18.3	24.1	23.2	28.1	28.4
April	19.6	21.8	24.5	26.6	27.2
May	21.4	23.3	27.7	28.6	28.6
June	28.9	28.7	30.0	33.3	29.3
July	24.5	30.0	28.7	34.3	38.3
August	24.5	29.1	33.8	29.0	32.0
September	21.9	23.5	25.1	26.4	24.9
October	20.1	21.6	22.1	25.1	27.7
November	17.9	21.6	21.8	22.3	22.2
December	17.9	19.8	20.9	20.3	21.5

Use the sales data from 1966 and 1967 to generate estimates for the smoothed process average, the trend factor, and the monthly seasonal factors. Beginning January 1, 1968, use the exponentially weighted moving-average method to forecast the sales of Bush Brewery 1 month ahead of available data.

Solution *We shall use the previously suggested smoothing constants, $\alpha = .1$, $\beta = .1$, and $\gamma = .4$, in the three recursive component equations. Initial estimates for the factors S and R and the 12 seasonal factors may be obtained as follows:*
(a) Let S_0, the initial value for the process average, be represented by the first process value, y_1. Thus $S_0 = 18.7$.

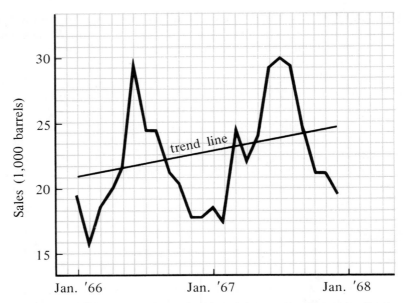

Figure 15.9   *Sales Volume for the Bush Brewing Company for the Years 1966 and 1967 Illustrating an Arbitrarily Drawn Trend Line*

(b) *On a sheet of graph paper, plot the available data for the time series. (In our problem, we are assuming that the monthly data from 1966 and 1967 are available as sample data.) With the aid of a ruler, draw a line through a plot of the available time-series data which, with eyeball accuracy, appears to depict the linear trend of the data. Such a line is illustrated for the Bush Brewing Company sales data in Figure 15.9.*

(c) *Let R_0, the initial value for the trend gain, be represented by the slope of the arbitrarily drawn trend line; that is, the average gain in trend (sales) per unit of time. The value of the trend line at $t = 1$ is 21; the value at $t = 24$ is 24. Thus*

$$R_0 = \frac{24 - 21}{24 - 1} = \frac{3}{23} = .13.$$

(d) *The initial monthly seasonal factors are found by evaluating the ratio*

$$\frac{actual\ sales\ volume\ for\ the\ month}{value\ of\ the\ trend\ for\ the\ month}$$

*for each month of the first entire seasonal pattern. For the Bush Brewing
Company, the first three seasonal indices are*

$$F_{\text{January}} = \frac{18.7}{21.0} = .89,$$

$$F_{\text{February}} = \frac{15.6}{21.13} = .74,$$

and

$$F_{\text{March}} = \frac{18.3}{21.26} = .86,$$

with the other monthly indexes calculated in a similar fashion.

*Using the initial values for the process average, the trend factor, and the
12 seasonal factors, the recursive component equations are initiated. At the
first time point, $t = 1$, we compute the statistics*

$$S_1 = \alpha\left(\frac{y_1}{F_{\text{Jan}}}\right) + (1 - \alpha)(S_0 + R_0)$$

$$= .1\left(\frac{18.7}{.89}\right) + .9(18.7 + .13)$$

$$= 19.05,$$

$$R_1 = \beta(S_1 - S_0) + (1 - \beta)R_0$$

$$= .1(19.05 - 18.7) + .9(.13)$$

$$= .15,$$

and

$$F_1 = \gamma\left(\frac{y_1}{S_1}\right) + (1 - \gamma)F_{\text{Jan}}$$

$$= .4\left(\frac{18.7}{19.05}\right) + .6(.89)$$

$$= .93.$$

At each succeeding month of the "smoothing period" (the first 24 months of data), the statistics

$$S_t = .1\left(\frac{y_t}{F_{t-12}}\right) + .9(S_{t-1} + R_{t-1}),$$

$$R_t = .1(S_t - S_{t-1}) + .9(R_{t-1}),$$

and

$$F_t = .4\left(\frac{y_t}{S_t}\right) + .6(F_{t-12})$$

are computed. Forecasting is begun at the twenty-fourth time period by computing the forecast, $\hat{y}_{25} = (S_{24} + R_{24})F_{13}$, of the sales during the twenty-fifth time period. Thereafter, forecasts are made 1 month ahead of available data by the forecast equation

$$\hat{y}_{t+1} = (S_t + R_t)F_{t-11}$$

for the time periods $t = 25, 26, \ldots, 60$. The 1-month-ahead forecasts and the actual monthly sales values for the Bush Brewing Company for the years 1968, 1969, and 1970 are listed in Table 15.6 and are plotted in Figure 15.10.

Figure 15.10   *Weighted Moving-Average Forecasts for the Monthly Sales of the Bush Brewing Company*

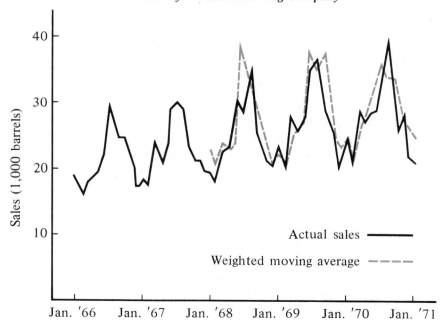

Table 15.6 *Actual and Forecasted Monthly Sales of the Bush*
Brewing Company; Forecasting Method: an Exponentially Weighted
Moving Average (listed values in thousands of barrels)

TIME	ACTUAL SALES y_t	FORECAST $\hat{y}_t$	FORECAST ERROR $e_t = y_t - \hat{y}_t$
1968			
January	19.6	22.7	−3.1
February	18.6	19.7	−1.1
March	23.2	24.2	−1.0
April	24.5	24.0	.5
May	27.7	26.0	1.7
June	30.0	34.2	−4.2
July	28.7	30.9	−2.2
August	33.8	30.1	3.7
September	25.1	26.2	−1.1
October	22.1	23.9	−1.8
November	21.8	22.0	−.2
December	20.9	21.2	−.3
1969			
January	23.3	22.6	.7
February	20.1	20.5	−.4
March	28.1	25.4	2.7
April	26.6	26.2	.4
May	28.6	28.7	−.1
June	33.3	35.0	−1.7
July	34.4	32.5	1.9
August	29.0	34.4	−5.4
September	26.4	27.4	−1.0
October	25.1	24.6	.5
November	22.3	23.4	−1.1
December	20.3	22.4	−2.1
1970			
January	24.6	24.1	.5
February	22.8	21.4	1.4
March	28.4	27.9	.5
April	27.2	27.5	−.3
May	28.6	29.8	−1.2
June	29.3	35.5	−6.2
July	38.3	33.7	4.6
August	32.0	33.1	−1.1
September	24.9	27.9	−3.0
October	27.7	25.3	2.4
November	22.2	23.7	−1.5
December	21.5	22.2	−.7

From Figure 15.10 and the forecast equation given above, we can note the dependence of the EWMA forecasting model on the seasonal factors. Notice, for example, the erratic up-and-down behavior of the true sales pattern during the summer of 1968. This same behavior is exhibited by the sales forecasts for the summer months of 1969, since the seasonal indices used in the forecast equations for the summer months of 1969 were computed during the summer months of 1968.

The Bush Brewing Company example emphasizes an earlier remark. *The EWMA forecasting model is an appropriate forecasting model only if the seasonal pattern is pronounced, regular, and predictable.* Otherwise, because of the inclusion of the seasonal factor as a multiplicative term in the forecast equation, an erratic behavior in the seasonal pattern will cause a similarly erratic and possibly erroneous response in the pattern of the forecasts during the following season.

15.7   A Growth Model

Growth processes often exhibit little or no cyclic or seasonal effect and the trend appears to be exponential. The earnings of Electromation, Inc. (Figure 15.11) exhibit this type of growth trend.

An exponential growth model suitable for data of the type exhibited in Figure 15.11 is

$$g = ae^{bx}\varepsilon',$$

where

$$x = \text{time},$$

$$\varepsilon' = \text{random error}.$$

Note that the larger the general level of earnings, as indicated by ae^{bx}, the larger will be the random error, since ε' is multiplied by this quantity.

The parameters a and b can be estimated by the method of least squares by taking the natural logarithm of the growth model. That is,

$$\ln g = \ln (ae^{bx}\varepsilon')$$

$$= \ln a + bx + \ln \varepsilon'.$$

If we let

$$y = \ln g,$$

$$\beta_0 = \ln a,$$

$$\beta_1 = b,$$

$$\varepsilon = \ln \varepsilon',$$

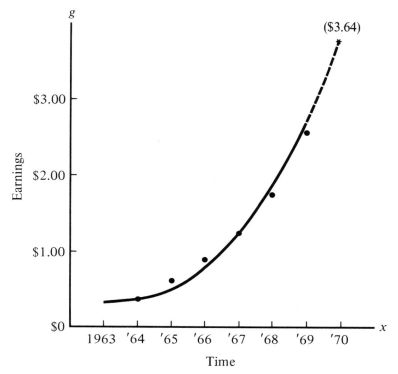

Figure 15.11   *Earnings of Electromation, Incorporated, and the Forecasted Earnings as Determined by a Growth Curve*

we have the straight-line linear model of Chapter 12,

$$y = \beta_0 + \beta_1 x + \varepsilon.$$

This transformation of the response measurements has the additional advantage of causing a relatively larger reduction in the random errors for large x and hence has a tendency to stabilize the variance of the random errors as required by the least-squares inferential procedures. We illustrate with an example.

Example 15.3   *Fit an exponential-type model to the earnings data (Figure 15.11) using the logarithmic transformation and the method of least squares. The data are shown in Table 15.7.*

Table 15.7

EARNINGS/SHARE g (DOLLARS)	TIME x	LN g y	ESTIMATE $\hat{y}$	$g = e^{\hat{y}}$
$ .25	1963	− 1.386	− 1.299	$ .27
.40	1964	− .916	− .929	.40
.62	1965	− .478	− .558	.57
.86	1966	− .151	− .188	.82
1.20	1967	.182	.182	1.20
1.78	1968	.577	.552	1.74
2.35	1969	.854	.922	2.52
	1970		1.293	3.64

Then, from Chapter 12,

$$\hat{\beta}_1 = \frac{n \sum_{i=1}^{n} x_i y_i - \sum_{i=1}^{n} x_i \sum_{i=1}^{n} y_i}{n \sum_{i=1}^{n} x_i^2 - \left(\sum_{i=1}^{n} x_i \right)^2} = .37021,$$

$$\hat{\beta}_0 = \bar{y} - \hat{\beta}_1 \bar{x} = -728.021,$$

and

$$\hat{y} = -728.021 + .37021x.$$

A comparison of the fitted growth curve and the data is shown in Figure 15.11.

The estimator of the parameter that measures rate of exponential growth is β_1, since $\beta_1 = b$. Confidence intervals for b can be obtained using the methods of Section 12.5.

Note that the expected value of y is equal to the expected value of $\ln g$. Confidence intervals can be obtained for $E(y)$ and prediction intervals for y using the methods of Sections 12.6 and 12.7, respectively, when the least-squares assumptions are satisfied. This procedure is followed by taking the antilogarithms of the limits in the confidence and prediction intervals of Sections 12.6 and 12.7. Unfortunately, we really wish to estimate $E(g)$, but $e^{E(y)}$ is not equal to $E(g)$. This difference will not be too great, and consequently confidence intervals obtained for $E(y)$ can be used to obtain approximate confidence intervals for $E(g)$. Prediction intervals for g can be approximated by transforming the prediction interval for y (Section 12.7), say

$$k_1 < y < k_2,$$

to

$$e^{k_1} < g < e^{k_2}.$$

Example 15.4   *Assume that the logarithms of the earnings, Example 15.3, are for all practical purposes independent and that the least-squares assumptions hold. Further, assume that the growth process will remain fairly stable during 1970. (This latter assumption is not likely to be satisfied—because of inflationary difficulties encountered in the 1969 state of the economy.) Find a 95 percent prediction interval for the earnings, g, in 1970.*

Solution   *From Section 12.7 we find that the prediction interval for y given* $x = x_p$ *is*

$$\hat{y} \pm t_{\alpha/2} s \sqrt{1 + \frac{1}{n} + \frac{(x_p - \bar{x})^2}{\sum\limits_{i=1}^{n} (x_i - \bar{x})^2}},$$

where

$$s = \sqrt{s^2} \quad \text{and} \quad s^2 = \sum_{i=1}^{n} \frac{(y_i - \hat{y}_i)^2}{n - 2}.$$

For our problem we have recorded earnings for the years 1963 through 1969. Thus n = 7. The actual earnings, y, and their estimates, ŷ, determined from the regression equation are listed in Example 15.3. Solving for the variance of the residuals, we find

$$s^2 = \frac{.0208}{7 - 2} = \frac{.0208}{5} = .00416.$$

Thus s = .064. Since we seek a 95 percent prediction interval, $t_{.05/2}$ *with 5 degrees of freedom is 2.571.*

Hence for the year $x_p = 1970$ *we would find the 95 percent prediction interval for y to be*

$$1.293 \pm (2.571)(.064) \sqrt{1 + \frac{1}{7} + \frac{(1970 - 1966)^2}{28}},$$

.   *or*

$$1.293 \pm .215.$$

Thus $k_1 = 1.078$ and $k_2 = 1.508$, so the 95 percent prediction interval for the earnings in 1970 is

$$e^{1.078} < g < e^{1.508},$$

or

$$\$2.94 < g < \$4.62.$$

15.8   Summary

Forecasting is a necessary task for the businessman in order for him to budget his time and resources. Forecasts provide a plan, however tentative, for the businessman to follow in order to achieve his objectives and remain competitive.

Forecasting methods are many and varied. Traditionally, forecasting has been quite subjective, without relying on rigorous mathematical forecasting models. The use of mathematical forecasting models has been suggested within this chapter, since the mathematical models can be

1. Designed to track the specific components (long-term trend, cyclic and seasonal effects, and so forth) within the time series under study.
2. Adapted to conform to the intuitive knowledge of the businessman about the time series.

This last point is especially important; it implies that the ingenuity of the business statistician is an essential factor in the selection of an appropriate forecasting model.

The ultimate criterion for the value of a forecasting model is how well it forecasts the future. Incumbent upon this criterion is the assumption that past behavior of the time series mirrors its future behavior. Dormant variables and other factors may cause a time series to react differently in the future than it has ever reacted before. Thus a model that "fits" the sample data well may perhaps not be a good model to forecast the future behavior of the time series.

Statistics provides only a starting point in the analysis of a time series and the adoption of a forecasting scheme. Statistical and mathematical models are limited and cannot provide a complete solution to forecasting problems as long as uncertainty exists within the problem.

Exercises

1. Discuss the importance of the following factors as they relate to our discussion of economic forecasting concepts and methods:
    (a) Sinusoidal model.
    (b) Seasonal factor.
    (c) Period of a cycle or seasonal factor.
    (d) Curvilinear, long-term trend.
    (e) Correlogram.
    (f) Smoothing constant.
    (g) Growth model.

2. Discuss the possible dangers of forecasting by extrapolating beyond the interval of time in which the sample data were collected.

3. Discuss the following statement: "Statistics, at least in its current state of development, comes somewhere between being of relatively little value and providing a complete solution of the problem of economic forecasting" (Freund and Williams, 1969, p. 427).

4. Of the forecasting methods discussed within Chapter 15, which would appear to be best designed to develop long-term forecasts? Which methods would you suggest for short-term forecasts? Explain.

5. For each of the following forecasting problems, suggest the forecast method you would recommend, defend the selection of your chosen method, and suggest the relevant data you might use in the forecast.
    (a) The unemployment rate in the United States for each of the next 12 months.
    (b) The total number of housing starts in the United States in the next calendar year.
    (c) The demand for electrical power for each of the next 20 years by the resident and commercial users in Topeka, Kansas.
    (d) The sales of skis and skiing equipment by a large sporting goods chain during each of the next 24 months.
    (e) The sales of term life insurance in the state of Georgia during the next calendar year.

6. A requirement for almost all forecasting methods is that the time-series data used within the model be evenly spaced over time. That is, the data occur in weekly intervals, monthly intervals, and so forth, and not at random intervals over time.
    (a) Why is this requirement necessary for most forecasting methods?
    (b) Of the forecasting methods discussed within Chapter 15, which do you suppose require that the data be evenly spaced over time?

7. What type of forecasting model would you choose to forecast each of the following time series? Explain.

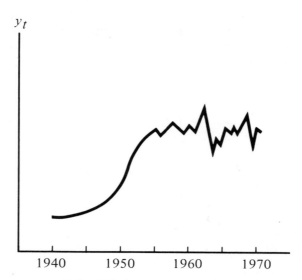

Dollar Value of All Premiums Written for
Glass Insurance in the United States

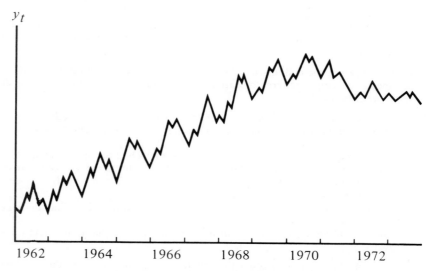

Number of Nonreturnable Beer Bottles Sold by
a Glass Container Manufacturer

8.   Refer to Exercise 7 and the time series depicting the number of nonreturnable beer
bottles sold by a glass container manufacturer. Clearly, this time series shows a linear
growth trend over time. However, currently we are experiencing the total removal of
nonreturnable containers from the markets of some states due to ecological considera-

tions. How does this relevant, but subjective, information affect our forecast model? Can we expect the linear growth trend to continue as it has in the past? How can the subjective information be incorporated into our total forecast model? Explain. [See Reinmuth and Geurts (1972).]

9. Employing the methods of Chapter 12, construct a linear forecasting model to fit the monthly sales volume data of The Pharmaceutical Company, Chapter 14, Exercise 3. Compare the forecast sales with the true monthly sales values by plotting both together on the same piece of graph paper.

10. Refer to Chapter 14, Exercise 3. Suppose a statistician claims that the sinusoidal forecasting model,

$$\hat{y}_t = 17.0 + .365t + 1.1 \sin\left(\frac{2\pi t}{6}\right),$$

which indicates the presence of a 6-month cycle in the sales pattern, is an efficient model for forecasting the sales of The Pharmaceutical Company. Let January 1972 be designated as time period $t = 1$, February 1972 as $t = 2$, and so forth. Using the above forecasting model, plot the forecast and actual sales of The Pharmaceutical Company. Does the suggested sinusoidal model appear to be a good forecasting equation for this problem?

11. Refer to Exercises 9 and 10. Is the sinusoidal model of Exercise 10 a better model for forecasting the monthly sales of The Pharmaceutical Company than the linear forecasting model from Exercise 9? Explain. (*Hint*: Compute the SSE associated with each forecasting model and select the model with the smallest SSE.)

12. For the exponentially weighted moving-average model (EWMA), discuss the selection of initial values for the three recursive equations involving S, R, and the L values of F. Why is a "warm-up" period needed for the values of S, R, and F before any forecasts are generated?

Supplementary Exercises

The following exercises require extensive computational effort for their solution. The student with access to an electronic computer and the ability to write computer programs may find it helpful to write his own programs to facilitate the solution of these exercises. The exercises may be eliminated if the student desires only a superficial overview of forecasting methods.

1. Refer to Chapter 14, Exercise 3. Fit a first-order autoregressive model,

$$y_t = \beta_0 + \beta_1 y_{t-1} + \varepsilon,$$

to the sales data from The Pharmaceutical Company by letting the 1-month-lagged sales values, y_{t-1}, assume the role of the independent variable, x, and employing the linear regression methods of Chapter 12. Compute the autoregressive forecasts and plot the autoregressive forecasts against the true monthly sales volumes.

2.   Refer to Chapter 14, Exercise 3. Assume that the true pattern of monthly sales of The Pharmaceutical Company over time is linear and use Brown's multiple exponential smoothing forecasting method to forecast the monthly sales 1 month ahead of available data. Plot the multiple exponential smoothing forecasts against the true monthly sales volumes. Let the smoothing constant $\alpha = .1$.

3.   Refer to Exercises 9 and 10 and Supplementary Exercises 1 and 2. Which of the four forecasting models computed in these four exercises represents the best model for forecasting the monthly sales of The Pharmaceutical Company? Explain.

4.   The following data represent the monthly revenue, in thousands of dollars, of a resort restaurant:

	1968	1969	1970
January	12.0	13.3	15.3
February	13.2	14.8	16.4
March	14.5	17.0	18.9
April	15.6	18.1	18.4
May	20.0	21.8	21.2
June	20.5	21.1	23.8
July	21.9	24.0	25.4
August	19.2	21.2	24.5
September	16.1	20.7	23.4
October	16.7	17.4	20.4
November	14.8	16.8	18.0
December	14.2	14.7	16.6

Assume that the pattern of revenues over time is neither constant nor linear. Use Brown's multiple exponential smoothing forecasting method to forecast the monthly revenue 1 month ahead of available data. Plot the forecast revenue against the true monthly revenue. Let the smoothing constant $\alpha = .1$.

5.   Refer to Supplementary Exercise 4. Use the exponentially weighted moving-average forecasting method to forecast the monthly revenue 1 month ahead of available data for the year 1970. Use the sales data from 1968 and 1969 to recursively generate good values for the smoothed statistics S, R, and the 12 values of F. Plot the forecast revenues for 1970 against the true revenues. Let the smoothing constants be $\alpha = .1$, $\beta = .1$, and $\gamma = .4$.

6.   Repeat Supplementary Exercise 5 by using the exponentially weighted moving average method to forecast the monthly revenue for 1970 three months ahead of available data.

7.   Refer to Chapter 14, Exercise 7. Use the exponentially weighted moving-average forecasting model to forecast monthly sales for the women's apparel shop 1 month ahead of available data for the years 1972, 1973, and 1974. Use the sales data from 1970 and 1971 to recursively generate good values for the smoothed statistics, S, R, and the 12 values of F. Plot the forecast sales for 1972, 1973, and 1974 against the true sales volumes. Let the smoothing constants be $\alpha = .1$, $\beta = .1$, and $\gamma = .4$.

8.   From the listing of company reports in your library, select a company and record their annual (or quarterly) sales over the past several years. Then use these recorded sales values as the dependent variable observations in a multiple-regression forecast model. Use your own discretion in selecting predictor variables for the regression model considering sinusoidal terms, functions of time, measurable independent variables obtained from an almanac or from the company reports, dummy variables, and variable

transformations. Fit the model using a preprogrammed regression-analysis computer program. How good was the fit of your model to the recorded sales values? Could your model have been improved by selecting other variables or deleting some that you have employed?

9. The following data represent the quarterly earnings per share for the shareholders of the Coca-Cola Company for the years 1960 through 1969.

	1960	1961	1962	1963	1964	1965	1966	1967	1968	1969
Q1	.13	.15	.16	.18	.22	.26	.31	.35	.38	.42
Q2	.21	.21	.24	.26	.31	.36	.42	.47	.51	.57
Q3	.26	.27	.30	.33	.39	.45	.52	.59	.66	.74
Q4	.12	.14	.16	.18	.22	.26	.31	.35	.38	*

* Earnings from $Q4$ of 1969 were not available.

It has been suggested by an executive of Coca-Cola that the sinusoidal regression model

$$y_t = \beta_0 + \beta_1 t + \beta_2 \sin\left(\frac{2\pi t}{4}\right) + \beta_3 \cos\left(\frac{2\pi t}{4}\right) + \varepsilon,$$

where y_t is the amount of earnings from quarter t and t is the index of time ranging from $t = 1$ for $Q1$ of 1960 to $t = 39$ for $Q3$ of 1969 provides a good model for forecasting Coke's quarterly earnings.

(a) Fit the above sinusoidal model to the earnings data. What are the estimates for the parameters in the forecast equation?

(b) How well does the sinusoidal model fit the earnings data? That is, how much of the variation in earnings can be explained by the model? (See Section 12.9.)

10. In examining a plot of the time series of quarterly earnings of Coca-Cola (see Supplementary Exercise 9), one can notice that the amplitudes of the seasonal patterns appear to be increasing over time. Thus a sinusoidal model such as

$$y_t = \beta_0 + \beta_1 t + \beta_2 \sin\left(\frac{2\pi t}{4}\right) + \beta_3 \cos\left(\frac{2\pi t}{4}\right) + \beta_4 t \sin\left(\frac{2\pi t}{4}\right) + \beta_5 t \cos\left(\frac{2\pi t}{4}\right) + \varepsilon$$

may provide a better fit to the Coca-Cola quarterly earnings.

(a) Fit the above sinusoidal model to the data from Exercise 9. What are the estimates for the parameters in the forecast equation?

(b) What greater proportion of variation is explained by the model of Supplementary Exercise 10 over the model of Supplementary Exercise 9?

11. Deposits are the lifeblood of commercial banks. They are the chief source of bank funds and provide the base for loans and other financial transactions of the bank. Thus, if a bank can effectively forecast deposits, they can accurately manage their investment activities to maintain a high degree of both liquidity and profitability. A San Francisco banking executive obtained the following data representing the level of demand deposits for the San Francisco city banks over the period 1965–1969. All figures are in billions of dollars.

	1965	1966	1967	1968	1969
January	13.48	14.50	15.29	15.94	16.04
February	13.08	13.80	14.57	15.11	15.19
March	13.37	13.94	14.63	15.11	15.15
April	13.88	14.55	15.15	15.46	15.88
May	13.16	14.05	14.55	14.93	15.13
June	13.63	14.53	15.07	15.39	15.53
July	13.80	14.58	15.45	15.69	16.00
August	13.76	14.33	15.04	15.49	15.44
September	14.18	14.97	15.70	15.69	15.60
October	14.27	14.69	15.06	15.66	16.06
November	14.65	15.11	15.57	15.95	16.15
December	15.09	15.49	16.12	16.29	16.33

(Source: U.S. Board of Governors of Federal Reserve System, *Deposits, Reserves, and Borrowings of Member Banks.*)

(a) Use the monthly data from 1965, 1966, and 1967 to develop initial estimates for the smoothing contants S, R, and the 12 values of F in the EWMA forecasting model as outlined in Example 15.2, Section 15.6. Let $\alpha = .1$, $\beta = .1$, and $\gamma = .4$.

(b) Using the monthly data from 1965, 1966, and 1967 as assumed past data, develop the EWMA forecasting model over this period and generate monthly forecasts for the 24 months of 1968 and 1969. Let the forecast lead period $T = 1$. (That is, develop forecasts one period in advance of available data.)

12. The following table represents the annual gross revenue for a manufacturer of a water-purification unit for the years 1963 through 1970:

Year	1963	1964	1965	1966	1967	1968	1969	1970
Revenue ($1,000)	21.1	19.4	23.0	26.9	29.1	40.5	64.3	101.2

(a) Using a log transformation on the annual revenues, fit a growth curve to the data. Plot the forecast values against the actual annual gross revenues.

(b) Estimate the gross revenue for the company for 1971.

References

Box, G. E. P., and G. M. Jenkins, *Time Series Analysis, Forecasting and Control.* San Francisco: Holden–Day, Inc., 1969.

Brown, R. G., *Smoothing, Forecasting, and Prediction of Discrete Time Series.* Englewood Cliffs, N.J.: Prentice-Hall, Inc., 1963.

Chambers, J., S. Mullick, and D. Smith, "How to Choose the Right Forecasting Model," *Harvard Business Review*, Vol. 49, July–August 1971, pp. 45–74.

Chisholm, R. K., and G. R. Whitaker, Jr., *Forecasting Methods.* Homewood, Ill.: Richard D. Irwin, Inc., 1971.

Freund, J. E., and F. J. Williams; revised by B. Perles and C. Sullivan, *Modern Business Statistics.* Englewood Cliffs, N.J.: Prentice-Hall, Inc., 1969.

Quenouille, M., *The Analysis of Multiple Tim e Series*. London: Charles Griffin & Company, Ltd., 1957.

Reinmuth, J. E., and M. D. Geurts, "A Bayesian Approach to Forecasting Effects of Atypical Situations," *Journal of Marketing Research*, Vol. 9 (1972), pp. 292–298.

Winters, P., "Forecasting Sales by Exponential Weighted Moving Averages," *Management Science Journal*, Vol. 6, No. 3 (April 1960), pp. 332–345.

Chapter Sixteen

Analysis of Enumerative Data

16.1   A Description of the Experiment

Many experiments, particularly in the social sciences, result in enumerative (or count) data. For instance, the classification of people into five income brackets would result in an enumeration or count corresponding to each of the five income classes. Or, we might be interested in studying the reaction of a mouse to a particular stimulus in a psychological experiment. If a mouse will react in one of three ways when the stimulus is applied and if a large number of mice were subjected to the stimulus, the experiment would yield three counts, indicating the number of mice falling in each of the reaction classes. Similarly, a traffic study might require a count and classification of the type of motor vehicles using a section of highway. An industrial process manufactures items that fall into one of three quality classes: acceptable, seconds, and rejects. A student of the arts might classify paintings in one of k categories according to style and period in order to study trends in style over time. We might wish to classify ideas in a philosophical study or style in the field of literature. The results of an advertising compaign would yield count data that indicate a classification of consumer reaction. Indeed, many observations in the physical sciences are not amenable to measurement on a continuous scale and result in enumerative or classificatory data.

The illustrations in the preceding paragraph exhibit, to a reasonable degree of approximation, the following characteristics, which define a *multinomial* experiment:

---

1. *The experiment consists of n identical trials.*

2. *The outcome of each trial falls into one of k classes or cells.*

3. *The probability that the outcome of a single trial will fall in a particular cell, say cell i, is p_i (i = 1,2,...,k), and remains the same from trial to trial. Note that*

$$p_1 + p_2 + p_3 + \cdots + p_k = 1.$$

4. *The trials are independent.*

5. *We are interested in $n_1, n_2, n_3, \ldots, n_k$, where n_i (i = 1, 2, ..., k) is equal to the number of trials in which the outcome falls in cell i. Note that $n_1 + n_2 + n_3 + \cdots + n_k = n$.*

The above experiment is analogous to tossing n balls at k boxes where each ball must fall in one of the boxes. The boxes are arranged such that the probability that a ball will fall in a box varies from box to box but remains the same for a particular box in repeated tosses. Finally, the balls are tossed in such a way that the trials are independent. At the conclusion of the experiment, we observe n_1 balls in the first box, n_2 in the second, ..., and n_k in the kth. The total number of balls is equal to

$$\sum_{i=1}^{k} n_i = n.$$

Note the similarity between the binomial and multinomial experiments and, in particular, that the binomial experiment represents the special case for the multinomial experiment when $k = 2$. The single parameter of the binomial experiment, p, is replaced by the k parameters, $p_1, p_2, \ldots, p_k$, of the multinomial. In this chapter, inferences concerning $p_1, p_2, \ldots, p_k$ will be expressed in terms of a statistical test of an hypothesis concerning their specific numerical values or their relationship one to another.

If we were to proceed as in Chapter 6, we would derive the probability of the observed sample $(n_1, n_2, \ldots, n_k)$ for use in calculating the probability of the type I and type II errors associated with a statistical test. Fortunately, we have been relieved of this chore by the British statistician Karl Pearson, who proposed a very useful test statistic for testing hypotheses concerning $p_1, p_2, \ldots, p_k$, and gave its approximate probability distribution in repeated sampling.

16.2   The Chi-Square Test

Suppose that $n = 100$ balls were tossed at the cells and that we knew that p_1 was equal to .1. How many balls would be expected to fall in the first cell? Referring to Chapter 6 and utilizing knowledge of the binomial experiment, we would calculate

$$E(n_1) = np_1 = 100(.1) = 10.$$

In like manner, the expected number falling in the remaining cells may be calculated using the formula

$$E(n_i) = np_i, \qquad i = 1, 2, \ldots, k.$$

Now suppose that we hypothesize values for $p_1, p_2, \ldots, p_k$ and calculate the expected value for each cell. Certainly, if our hypothesis is true, the cell counts, n_i, should not deviate greatly from their expected values, np_i $(i = 1, 2, \ldots, k)$. Hence it would seem intuitively reasonable to use a test statistic involving the k deviations,

$$n_i - np_i, \qquad i = 1, 2, \ldots, k.$$

In 1900 Karl Pearson proposed the following test statistic, which is a function of the square of the deviations of the observed counts from their expected values, weighted by the reciprocal of their expected value:

$$
\begin{aligned}
X^2 &= \sum_{i=1}^{k} \frac{[n_i - E(n_i)]^2}{E(n_i)} \\
&= \sum_{i=1}^{k} \frac{(n_i - np_i)^2}{np_i}.
\end{aligned}
$$

Although the mathematical proof is beyond the scope of this text, it can be shown that when n is large, X^2 will possess, approximately, a chi-square probability distribution in repeated sampling. Experience has shown that the cell counts, n_i, should not be too small in order that the chi-square distribution provide an adequate approximation to the distribution of X^2. As a rule of thumb, we shall require that all expected cell counts equal or exceed five, although Cochran (1952) has noted that this value can be as low as 1 for some situations.

You will recall the use of the chi-square probability distribution for testing an hypothesis concerning a population variance, σ^2, in Section 9.6. Particularly, we stated that the shape of the chi-square distribution would vary depending upon the number of degrees of freedom associated with s^2, and we discussed the use of Table 5, Appendix, which presents the critical values of χ^2 corresponding to various right-hand tail areas of the distribution. Therefore, we must know which χ^2 distribution to use—that is, the number of degrees of freedom—in approximating the distribution of X^2, and we must know whether to use a one-tailed or two-tailed test in locating the rejection region for the test. The latter problem may be solved directly. Since large deviations of the observed cell counts from those expected would tend to contradict the null hypothesis concerning the cell probabilities $p_1, p_2, \ldots, p_k$, we would reject the null hypothesis when X^2 is large and employ a one-tailed statistical test using the upper tail values of χ^2 to locate the rejection region.

The determination of the appropriate number of degrees of freedom to be employed for the test can be rather difficult and therefore will be specified for the physical applications described in the following sections. In addition, we will state the principle involved (and which is fundamental to the mathematical proof of the approximation) so that the reader may understand why the number of degrees of freedom changes with various applications. This states that the appropriate number of degrees of freedom will equal the number of cells, k, less one degree of freedom for each independent linear restriction placed upon the observed cell counts. For example, one linear restriction is always present because the sum of the cell counts must equal n; that is,

$$n_1 + n_2 + n_3 + \cdots + n_k = n.$$

Other restrictions will be introduced for some applications because of the necessity for estimating unknown parameters required in the calculation of the expected cell frequencies or because of the method in which the sample is collected. These will become apparent as we consider various practical examples.

16.3   A Test of an Hypothesis Concerning Specified Cell Probabilities

The simplest hypothesis concerning the cell probabilities would be one that specifies numerical values for each. For example, consider a customer-preference study where three different package designs are used to display the same product. We wish to test the hypothesis that the buyer has no preference concerning the choice of package design and, therefore, that

$$H_0 : p_1 = p_2 = p_3 = 1/3$$

against

$$H_a: \text{at least one } p_i \text{ is different from } 1/3,$$

where p_i is the probability a customer will choose package design i ($i = 1, 2,$ or 3). Suppose that the product to be packaged is a food product and that the three packages are displayed side by side in several supermarkets in a particular city. In one day's time it was noted that $n = 90$ customers purchased the product, of which $n_1 = 23$ purchased package design 1, $n_2 = 36$ purchased package design 2, and $n_3 = 31$ purchased package design 3. Symbolically, $n_1 = 23$, $n_2 = 36$, and $n_3 = 31$ represent the observed cell frequencies for cells 1, 2, and 3. The expected cell frequencies would be the same for each cell,

$$E(n_i) = np_i = 90(1/3) = 30.$$

Table 16.1 *Observed and Expected Cell Counts for the Customer-Preference Study*

	PACKAGE DESIGN		
	1	2	3
Observed cell frequency	$n_1 = 23$	$n_2 = 36$	$n_3 = 31$
Expected cell frequency	(30)	(30)	(30)

The observed and expected cell frequencies are presented in Table 16.1. Noting the discrepancy between the observed and expected cell frequency, we would wonder whether the data present sufficient evidence to warrant rejection of the hypothesis of no preference.

The chi-square test statistic for our example will possess $(k - 1) = 2$ degrees of freedom since the only linear restriction on the cell frequencies is that

$$n_1 + n_2 + \cdots + n_k = n,$$

or, for our example,

$$n_1 + n_2 + n_3 = 90.$$

Therefore, if we choose $\alpha = .05$, we would reject the null hypothesis when $X_2 > 5.991$ (see Table 5, Appendix).

Substituting into the formula for X^2, we obtain

$$X^2 = \sum_{i=1}^{k} \frac{[n_i - E(n_i)]^2}{E(n_i)} = \sum_{i=1}^{k} \frac{(n_i - np_i)^2}{np_i}$$

$$= \frac{(23 - 30)^2}{30} + \frac{(36 - 30)^2}{30} + \frac{(31 - 30)^2}{30}$$

$$= 2.87.$$

Since X^2 is less than the tabulated critical value of χ^2, the null hypothesis is not rejected and we conclude that the data do not present sufficient evidence to indicate that the buyers of the area have a preference for a particular package design.

16.4 Contingency Tables

A problem frequently encountered in the analysis of count data concerns the independence of two methods of classification of observed events. For example, we might wish to classify defects found on furniture produced in a manufacturing plant, first, according to the type of defect and, second, according to the production shift. Ostensibly, we wish to invesigate a contingency—a dependence between the two classifications. Do the proportions of various types of defects vary from shift to shift?

A total of $n = 309$ furniture defects was recorded and the defects were classified according to one of four types: A, B, C, or D. At the same time, each piece of furniture was identified according to the production shift in which it was manufactured. These counts are presented in Table 16.2, which is known as a contingency table. (*Note:* Numbers in parentheses are the expected cell frequencies.)

Table 16.2 *Contingency Table*

	TYPE OF DEFECT				
SHIFT	A	B	C	D	TOTAL
1	15 (22.51)	21 (20.99)	45 (38.94)	13 (11.56)	94
2	26 (22.99)	31 (21.44)	34 (39.77)	5 (11.81)	96
3	33 (28.50)	17 (26.57)	49 (49.29)	20 (14.63)	119
Total	74	69	128	38	309

Let p_A equal the unconditional probability that a defect will be of type A. Similarly, define p_B, p_C, and p_D as the probabilities of observing the three other types of defects. Then these probabilities, which we will call the column probabilities of Table 16.2, will satisfy the requirement

$$p_A + p_B + p_C + p_D = 1.$$

In like manner, let p_i $(i = 1, 2, \text{or } 3)$ equal the row probability that a defect will have occurred on shift i, where

$$p_1 + p_2 + p_3 = 1.$$

Then, if the two classifications are independent of each other, a cell probability will equal the product of its respective row and column probabilities in accordance with the multiplicative law of probability. For example, the probability that a particular defect will occur in shift 1 and be of type A is $(p_1)(p_A)$. Thus we observe that the numerical values of the cell probabilities are unspecified in the problem under consideration. The null hypothesis specifies only that each cell probability will equal the product of its respective row and column probabilities and therefore imply independence of the two classifications, while the alternative hypothesis is that this equality does not hold for at least one cell.

The analysis of the data obtained from a contingency table differs from the problem discussed in Section 16.3, because we must estimate the row and column probabilities in order to estimate the expected cell frequencies.

If proper estimates of the cell probabilities are obtained, the estimated expected cell frequencies may be substituted for the $E(n_i)$ in X^2, and X^2 will continue to possess a distribution in repeated sampling that is approximated by the chi-square probability distribution. The proof of this statement as well as a discussion of the methods for obtaining the estimates are beyond the scope of this text. Fortunately, the procedures for obtaining the estimates yield estimates that are intuitively obvious for our relatively simple applications.

It can be shown that the estimator of a column probability will equal the column total divided by $n = 309$. If we denote the total of column j as c_j, then

$$\hat{p}_A = \frac{c_1}{n} = \frac{74}{309},$$

$$\hat{p}_B = \frac{c_2}{n} = \frac{69}{309},$$

$$\hat{p}_C = \frac{c_3}{n} = \frac{128}{309},$$

$$\hat{p}_D = \frac{c_4}{n} = \frac{38}{309}.$$

Similarly, the row probabilities p_1, p_2, and p_3 may be estimated using the row totals r_1, r_2, and r_3:

$$\hat{p}_1 = \frac{r_1}{n} = \frac{94}{309},$$

$$\hat{p}_2 = \frac{r_2}{n} = \frac{96}{309},$$

and

$$\hat{p}_3 = \frac{r_3}{n} = \frac{119}{309}.$$

Denote the observed frequency of the cell in row i and column j of the contingency table as n_{ij}. Then the estimated expected value of n_{11} will be

$$\hat{E}(n_{11}) = n[\hat{p}_1 \cdot \hat{p}_A] = n\left(\frac{r_1}{n}\right)\left(\frac{c_1}{n}\right)$$

$$= \frac{r_1 c_1}{n},$$

where $(\hat{p}_1 \cdot \hat{p}_A)$ is the estimated cell probability. Similarly, we may find the estimated expected value for any other cell, say $\hat{E}(n_{23})$,

$$\hat{E}(n_{23}) = n[\hat{p}_2 \cdot \hat{p}_c] = n\left(\frac{r_2}{n}\right)\left(\frac{c_3}{n}\right)$$

$$= \frac{r_2 c_3}{n}.$$

In other words, we see that the estimated expected value of the observed cell frequency, n_{ij}, for a contingency table is equal to the product of its respective row and column totals divided by the total frequency; that is,

$$\hat{E}(n_{ij}) = \frac{r_i c_j}{n}.$$

The estimated expected cell frequencies for our example are shown in parentheses in Table 16.2.

We may now use the expected and observed cell frequencies shown in Table 16.2 to calculate the value of the test statistic:

$$X^2 = \sum_{i=1}^{12} \frac{[n_i - \hat{E}(n_i)]^2}{\hat{E}(n_i)}$$

$$= \frac{(15 - 22.51)^2}{22.51} + \frac{(26 - 22.99)^2}{22.99} + \cdots + \frac{(20 - 14.64)^2}{14.64}$$

$$= 19.17.$$

The only remaining obstacle involves the determination of the appropriate number of degrees of freedom associated with the test statistic. We will give this as a rule that we will attempt to justify. The degrees of freedom associated with a contingency table possessing r rows and c columns will always equal $(r - 1)(c - 1)$. Thus, for our example, we will compare X^2 with the critical value of χ^2 with $(r - 1)$ $(c - 1) = (3 - 1)(4 - 1) = 6$ degrees of freedom.

You will recall that the number of degrees of freedom associated with the X^2 statistic will equal the number of cells (in this case, $k = rc$) less one degree of freedom for each independent linear restriction placed upon the observed cell frequencies. The total number of cells for the data of Table 16.2 is $k = 12$. From this we subtract one degree of freedom because the sum of the observed cell frequencies must equal n; that is,

$$n_{11} + n_{12} + \cdots + n_{34} = 309.$$

In addition, we used the cell frequencies to estimate three of the four column probabilities. Note that the estimate of the fourth-column probability will be determined once we have estimated p_A, p_B, and p_C, because

$$p_A + p_B + p_C + p_D = 1.$$

Thus we lose $(c - 1) = 3$ degrees of freedom for estimating the column probabilities.

Finally, we used the cell frequencies to estimate $(r - 1) = 2$ row probabilities and therefore we lose $(r - 1) = 2$ additional degrees of freedom. The total number of degrees of freedom remaining will be

$$\text{d.f.} = 12 - 1 - 3 - 2 = 6.$$

And, in general, we see that the total number of degrees of freedom associated with an $r \times c$ contingency table will be

$$\text{d.f.} = rc - 1 - (c - 1) - (r - 1)$$
$$= (r - 1)(c - 1).$$

Therefore, if we use $\alpha = .05$, we will reject the null hypothesis that the two classifications are independent if $X^2 > 12.592$. Since the value of the test statistic, $X^2 = 19.17$, exceeds the critical value of χ^2, we will reject the null hypothesis. The data present sufficient evidence to indicate that the proportion of the various types of defects varies from shift to shift. A study of the production operations for the three shifts would probably reveal the cause.

Example 16.1   *A survey was conducted to evaluate the effectiveness of a new flu vaccine which had been administered in a small community. The vaccine was provided free of charge in a two-shot sequence over a period of 2 weeks to those wishing to avail themselves of it. Some people received the two-shot sequence, some appeared only for the first shot, and others received neither.*
   A survey of 1,000 local inhabitants in the following spring provided the information shown in Table 16.3. Do the data present sufficient evidence to indicate that the vaccine was successful in reducing the number of flu cases in the community?

Table 16.3   *Data Tabulation for Example* 16.1

	NO VACCINE	ONE SHOT	TWO SHOTS	TOTAL
Flu	24 (14.4)	9 (5.0)	13 (26.6)	46
No flu	289 (298.6)	100 (104.0)	565 (551.4)	954
Totals	313	109	578	1,000

Solution   *The question stated above asks whether the data provide sufficient evidence to indicate a dependence between the vaccine classification and the occurrence or nonoccurrence of flu. We therefore analyze the data as a contingency table.*
   The estimated expected cell frequencies may be calculated using the appropriate row and column totals,

$$\hat{E}(n_{ij}) = \frac{r_i c_j}{n}.$$

Thus

$$\hat{E}(n_{11}) = \frac{r_1 c_1}{n} = \frac{(46)(313)}{1{,}000} = 14.4,$$

$$\hat{E}(n_{12}) = \frac{r_1 c_2}{n} = \frac{(46)(109)}{1{,}000} = 5.0.$$

These values are shown in parentheses in Table 16.3.

The value of the test statistic, X^2, will now be computed and compared with the critical value of χ^2 possessing $(r - 1)(c - 1) = (1)(2) = 2$ degrees of freedom. Then, for $\alpha = .05$, we will reject the null hypothesis when $X^2 > 5.991$. Substituting into the formula for X^2, we obtain

$$X^2 = \frac{(24 - 14.4)^2}{14.4} + \frac{(289 - 298.6)^2}{298.6} + \cdots + \frac{(565 - 551.4)^2}{551.4}$$

$$= 17.35.$$

Observing that X^2 falls in the rejection region, we reject the null hypothesis of independence of the two classifications. A comparison of the percentage incidence of flu for each of the three categories would suggest that those receiving the two-shot sequence were less susceptible to the disease.

Further analysis of the data could be obtained by deleting one of the three categories, the second column, for example, to compare the effect of the vaccine with that of no vaccine. This could be done by using either a 2×2 contingency table or treating the two categories as two binomial populations and using the methods of Section 8.8. Or, we might wish to analyze the data by comparing the results of the two-shot vaccine sequence with those of the combined no-vaccine and one-shot groups. That is, we would combine the first two columns of the 2×3 table into one.

16.5   *r × c* Tables with Fixed Row or Column Totals

In the previous section we described the analysis of an $r \times c$ contingency table using examples which, for all practical purposes, fit the multinomial experiment described in Section 16.1. While the methods of collecting data in many surveys may obviously adhere to the requirements of a multinomial experiment, other methods do not. For example, we might not wish to sample randomly the population described in Example 16.1 because we might find that, owing to chance, one category is completely missing. For example, people who have received no flu shots might fail to appear in the sample. Thus we might decide beforehand to interview a specified number of people in each column category, thereby fixing the column totals in advance. While these restrictions tend to disturb somewhat our visualization of the experiment in the multinomial content, they have no effect on the analysis of the data. As long as we wish to test the hypothesis of independence of the two classifications, and none of the row or column probabilities is specified in advance, we may analyze the data as an $r \times c$ contingency table. It can be shown that the resulting X^2 will possess a probability distribution in repeated sampling that is approximated by a chi-square distribution with $(r - 1)(c - 1)$ degrees of freedom.

To illustrate, suppose that we wish to test an hypothesis concerning the equivalence of four binomial populations as indicated in the following example.

Example 16.2   *A survey of voter sentiment was conducted in four midcity political wards to compare the fraction of voters favoring candidate A. Random samples of 200 voters were polled in each of the four wards with results as shown in Table 16.4. Do the data present sufficient evidence to indicate that the fractions of voters favoring candidate A differ in the four wards?*

Table 16.4   *Data Tabulation for Example 16.2*

	WARD				
	1	2	3	4	TOTALS
Favor A	76 (59)	53 (59)	59 (59)	48 (59)	236
Do not favor A	124 (141)	147 (141)	141 (141)	152 (141)	564
Totals	200	200	200	200	800

Solution   *The reader will observe that the test of an hypothesis concerning the equivalence of the parameters of the four binomial populations corresponding to the four wards is identical to an hypothesis implying independence of the row and column classifications. Thus, if we denote the fraction of voters favoring A as p and hypothesize that p is the same for all four wards, we imply that the first- and second-row probabilities are equal to p and $(1 - p)$, respectively. The probability that a member of the same sample of $n = 800$ voters falls in a particular ward will equal one-quarter since this was fixed in advance. Then the cell probabilities for the table would be obtained by multipli-*

cation of the appropriate row and column probabilities under the null hypothesis and be equivalent to a test of independence of the two classifications.

The estimated expected cell frequencies, calculated using the row and column totals, appear in parentheses in Table 16.4. We see that

$$X^2 = \frac{\sum_{i=1}^{8} [n_i - \hat{E}(n_i)]^2}{E(n_i)}$$

$$= \frac{(76 - 59)^2}{59} + \frac{(124 - 141)^2}{141} + \cdots + \frac{(152 - 141)^2}{141}$$

$$= 10.72.$$

The critical value of χ^2 for $\alpha = .05$ and $(r - 1)(c - 1) = (1)(3) = 3$ degrees of freedom is 7.815. Since X^2 exceeds this critical value, we reject the null hypothesis and conclude that the fraction of voters favoring candidate A is not the same for all four wards.

16.6   Other Applications

The applications of the chi-square test in analyzing enumerative data described in Sections 16.3, 16.4, and 16.5 represent only a few of the interesting classificatory problems which may be approximated by the multinomial experiment and for which our method of analysis is appropriate. By and large, these applications are complicated to a greater or lesser degree because the numerical values of the cell probabilities are unspecified and hence require the estimation of one or more population parameters. Then, as in Sections 16.4 and 16.5, we can estimate the cell probabilities. Although we omit the mechanics of the statistical tests, several additional applications of the chi-square test are worth mention as a matter of interest.

For example, suppose that we wish to test an hypothesis stating that a population possesses a normal probability distribution. The cells of a sample frequency histogram (for example, Figure 3.2) would correspond to the k cells of the multinomial experiment, and the observed cell frequencies would be the number of measurements falling in each cell of the histogram. Given the hypothesized normal probability distribution for the population we could use the areas under the normal curve to calculate the theoretical cell probabilities and hence the expected cell frequencies. The difficulty arises when μ and σ are unspecified for the normal population and these parameters must be estimated to obtain the estimated cell probabilities. This difficulty, of course, can be surmounted.

The construction of a two-way table to investigate dependency between two classifications can be extended to three or more classifications. For example, if we wish to test the mutual independence of three classifications, we would employ a three-dimensional "table" or rectangular parallelepiped. The reasoning and methodology associated with the analysis of both the two- and three-way tables are identical, although the analysis of the three-way table is a bit more complex.

A third and interesting application of our methodology would be its use in the investigation of the rate of change of a multinomial (or binomial) population as a function of time. For example, we might study the decision-making ability of a human (or any animal) as he is subjected to an educational program and tested over time. If, for instance, he is tested at prescribed intervals of time and the test is of the yes-or-no type, yielding a number of correct answers, y, that would follow a binomial probability distribution, we would be interested in the behavior of the probability of a correct response, p, as a function of time. If the number of correct responses was recorded for c time periods, the data would fall in a $2 \times c$ table similar to that in Example 16.2 (Section 16.5). We would then be interested in testing the hypothesis that p is equal to a constant, that is, that no learning has occurred, and we would then proceed to more interesting hypotheses to determine whether the data present sufficient evidence to indicate a gradual (say, linear) change over time as opposed to an abrupt change at some point in time. The procedures we have described could be extended to decisions involving more than two alternatives.

You will observe that our learning example is common to business, to industry, and to many other fields, including the social sciences. For example, we might wish to study the rate of consumer acceptance of a new product for various types of advertising campaigns as a function of the length of time that the campaign has been in effect. Or, we might wish to study the trend in the lot fraction defective in a manufacturing process as a function of time. Both of these examples, as well as many others, require a study of the behavior of a binomial (or multinomial) process as a function of time.

The examples that we have just described are intended to suggest the relatively broad application of the chi-square analysis of enumerative data, a fact that should be borne in mind by the experimenter concerned with this type of data. The statistical test employing X^2 as a test statistic is often called a "goodness-of fit" test. Its application for some of these examples requires care in the determination of the appropriate estimates and the number of degrees of freedom for X^2, which, for some of these problems, may be rather complex.

16.7   Summary

The preceding material has been concerned with a test of an hypothesis regarding the cell probabilities associated with a multinomial experiment. When the number of observations, n, is large, the test statistic, X^2, can be shown to possess, approximately, a chi-square probability distribution in repeated sampling, the number of degrees of freedom being dependent upon the particular application. In general, we assume that n is large and that the minimum expected cell frequency is equal to or is greater than five.

Several words of caution concerning the use of the X^2 statistic as a method of analyzing enumerative-type data are appropriate. The determination of the correct number of degrees of freedom associated with the X^2 statistic is very important in locating the rejection region. If the number is incorrectly specified, erroneous conclusions might result. Also, note that nonrejection of the null hypothesis does not imply that it should be accepted. We would have difficulty in stating a meaningful alternative hypothesis for many practical applications and, therefore, would lack knowledge of the probability of making a type II error. For example, we hypothesize that the two classifications of a contingency table are independent. A specific alternative would have to specify some measure of dependence, which may or may not possess practical significance to the experimenter. Finally, if parameters are missing and the expected cell frequencies must be estimated, the estimators of missing parameters should be of a particular type in order that the test be valid. In other words, the application of the chi-square test for other than the simple applications outlined in Sections 16.3, 16.4, and 16.5 will require experience beyond the scope of this introductory presentation of the subject.

Exercises

1. List the characteristics of a multinomial experiment.

2. A city expressway utilizing four lanes in each direction was studied to see whether drivers preferred to drive on the inside lanes. A total of 1,000 automobiles were observed during the heavy early morning traffic and their respective lanes recorded. The results were as follows:

Lane	1	2	3	4
Observed count	294	276	238	192

   Do the data present sufficient evidence to indicate that some lanes were preferred over others? (Test the hypothesis that $p_1 = p_2 = p_3 = p_4 = 1/4$ using $\alpha = .05$.)

3. During a given day, the manager of a large supermarket observed the number of shoppers choosing each of the market's six checkout stands. The following results were observed:

Stand No.	1	2	3	4	5	6
Frequency	84	110	146	152	61	47

   Do these data present sufficient evidence to indicate that some checkout stands were preferred over others? (Use $\alpha = .05$.)

4. A quality-control engineer for a factory wishes to examine the operating efficiency of two assembly machine operators. The operators are in charge of the same machine but work during different shifts. During a given week, the number of good and defective finished items produced by the assembly machine while each operator was on duty were observed to be

	OPERATOR A	OPERATOR B
Good	551	416
Defective	16	17

Do these data present sufficient evidence to indicate that the operators work with about the same efficiency? (Test the hypothesis that the proportion of defective items produced by each operator is the same.)
(a) Test using the X^2 statistic. (Use $\alpha = .05$.)
(b) Use the z test from Section 8.11.

5. A study to determine the effectiveness of a drug (serum) for arthritis resulted in the comparison of two groups each consisting of 200 arthritic patients. One group was inoculated with the serum while the other received a placebo (an inoculation that appears to contain serum but actually is nonactive). After a period of time, each person in the study was asked to state whether his arthritic condition was improved. The following results were observed:

	TREATED	UNTREATED
Improved	117	74
Not improved	83	126

Do these data present sufficient evidence to indicate that the serum was effective in improving the condition of arthritic patients?
(a) Test using the X^2 statistic. (Use $\alpha = .05$.)
(b) Use the z test in Section 8.11.

6. A company selling air brushes is about to mount a new advertising campaign. Before doing so, they would like to determine if the campaign should be directed to the male or female market individually, or to both together. A sample of 1,750 users of their air brush found the following distribution of "regular" and "occasional" users by sex:

TYPE OF USER	MALE	FEMALE
Regular	170	465
Occasional	475	640

Do these data present sufficient evidence to indicate that the use of the air brush on an occasional or regular basis is related to the sex of the user? (Let $\alpha = .01$.)

7. A radio station conducted a survey to study the relationship between the number of radios per household and family income. The survey, based upon $n = 1,000$ interviews, produced the following results:

	FAMILY INCOME (IN DOLLARS)			
NO. RADIOS PER HOUSEHOLD	LESS THAN 4,000	4,000–7,000	7,000–10,000	MORE THAN 10,000
1	126	362	129	78
2	29	138	82	56

Do the data present sufficient evidence to indicate that the number of radios per household is dependent upon family income? (Test at $\alpha = .10$.)

8. A group of 306 people were interviewed to determine their opinion concerning a particular current American foreign-policy issue. At the same time, their political affiliation was recorded. The data are:

	APPROVE OF POLICY	DO NOT APPROVE OF POLICY	NO OPINION
Republicans	114	53	17
Democrats	87	27	8

Do the data present sufficient evidence to indicate a dependence between party affiliation and the opinion expressed for the sampled population?

9. A study was conducted to determine whether individuals earning over $20,000 per year use the services of an accountant in preparation of their income taxes at the same rate in different regions of the United States. Four states were selected as representative of the four regions, Northeast, South, Midwest, and West. From each state, a random selection of individuals with annual incomes in excess of $20,000 was obtained. Each individual was then asked whether or not he uses the services of an accountant in preparation of his income taxes. The results are:

	RHODE ISLAND	FLORIDA	IOWA	CALIFORNIA
Use an accountant	46	121	63	108
Prepares taxes himself	149	179	178	192

Do the data indicate a difference in the rate of use of the services of an accountant from one region to another? (Test using $\alpha = .05$.)

10. A survey of the opinions of the stockholders of a corporation regarding a proposed merger was studied to determine whether the resulting opinion was independent of the number of shares held. Two hundred stockholders were interviewed with the following results being observed:

	OPINION		
SHARES HELD	IN FAVOR	OPPOSED	UNDECIDED
Under 100	37	16	5
100–500	30	22	8
Over 500	32	44	6

Do these data present sufficient evidence to indicate that the opinions of the stockholders concerning the merger were dependent upon the number of shares held by the stockholder? (Test using $\alpha = .05$.)

11. The responses for the data in Exercise 10 were reclassified according to whether the stockholder was male or female.

	OPINION		
SEX	IN FAVOR	OPPOSED	UNDECIDED
Female	39	46	9
Male	60	36	10

Do these data present sufficient evidence to indicate that stockholder reaction to the proposed merger varied for the various opinion categories depending upon whether the stockholder was male or female? (Test using $\alpha = .05$.)

12. A manufacturer of buttons wished to determine whether the fraction of defective buttons produced by three machines varied from machine to machine. Samples of 400 buttons were selected from each of the three machines and the number of defectives counted for each sample. The results are as follows:

Machine No.	1	2	3
No. defectives	16	24	9

Do these data present sufficient evidence to indicate that the fraction of defective buttons varies from machine to machine? (Test using $\alpha = .05$.)

13. A carpet company was interested in comparing the fraction of new home builders favoring carpet over other floor coverings for homes in three different areas of a city. The objective was to decide how to allocate sales effort to the areas. A survey was conducted and the data are as follows:

	AREAS		
	1	2	3
Carpet	69	126	16
Other materials	78	99	27

Do the data indicate a difference in the percentage favoring carpet from one region of the city to another?

14. A survey was conducted by an auto repairman to determine whether various auto ills were dependent upon the make of the auto. His survey, restricted to this year's model, produced the following results:

	TYPE OF REPAIR		
MAKE	ELECTRICAL	FUEL SUPPLY	OTHER
A	17	19	7
B	14	7	9
C	6	21	12
D	33	44	19
E	7	9	6

Do these data present sufficient evidence to indicate a dependency between auto makes and type of repair for these new-model cars? Note that the repairman did not utilize all the information available when he conducted his survey. In conducting a study of this type, what other factors should be recorded?

15. An analysis of accident data was made to determine the distribution of numbers of fatal accidents for three different size automobiles. The data for 346 accidents are as follows:

	SIZE OF AUTO		
	SMALL	MEDIUM	LARGE
Fatal	67	26	16
Not fatal	128	63	46

Do the data indicate that the frequency of fatal accidents is dependent on the size of automobiles?

16. A printer was interested in examining the relationship between the number of printing errors and the type size used. He selected three different books recently printed by his company and each printed using a different type size. From each book he recorded the number of pages with printing errors and the number of error-free pages. The results are as follows:

	TYPE SIZE		
	A	B	C
Pages with errors	23	17	41
Pages without errors	241	183	210

Do the data indicate a dependence between type size and printing errors?

17. A manufacturer of floor polish conducted a consumer-preference experiment to see whether a new floor polish, *A*, was superior to those of four of his competitors. A sample of 100 housewives viewed five patches of flooring that had received the five polishes and each indicated the patch that she considered superior in appearance. The lighting, background, and so forth, were approximately the same for all five patches. The results of the survey are as follows:

Polish	A	B	C	D	E
Frequency	27	17	15	22	19

Do these data present sufficient evidence to indicate a preference for one or more of the polished patches of floor over the others? If one were to reject the hypothesis of "no preference" for this experiment, would this imply that polish *A* is superior to the others? Can you suggest a better method of conducting the experiment?

18. A sociologist conducted a survey to determine whether the incidence of various types of crime varied from one part of a particular city to another. The city was partitioned into three regions and the crimes classified as homicide, car theft, grand larceny, petty larceny, and other. An analysis of 1,599 cases produced the following results:

CITY REGION	HOMICIDE	AUTO THEFT	GRAND LARCENY (NEGLECTING AUTO THEFT)	PETTY LARCENY	OTHER
1	12	239	191	122	47
2	17	163	278	201	54
3	7	98	109	44	17

Do these data present sufficient evidence to indicate that the occurrence of various types of crime is dependent upon city region?

References

Anderson, R. L., and T. A. Bancroft, *Statistical Theory in Research*. New York: McGraw-Hill Book Company, 1952. Chapter 12.

Cochran, W. G., "The χ^2 Test of Goodness of Fit," *Annals of Mathematical Statistics*, Vol. 23 (1952), pp. 315–345.

Dixon, W. J., and F. J. Massey, Jr., *Introduction to Statistical Analysis*. 3rd ed. New York: McGraw-Hill Book Company, 1969. Chapter 13.

Chapter Seventeen

Nonparametric Statistics

17.1   Introduction

Some experiments yield response measurements that defy quantification. That is, they generate response measurements that can be ordered (ranked), but the location of the response on a scale of measurement is arbitrary. Although experiments of this type occur in almost all fields of study, they are particularly evident in social science research and in studies of consumer preference. For example, suppose that a judge is employed to evaluate and rank the sales abilities of four salesmen, the edibility and taste characteristics of five brands of cornflakes, or the relative appeal of five new automobile designs. Since it is clearly impossible to give an exact measure of sales competence, palatability of food, or design appeal, the response measurements are of a completely different character from those presented in preceding chapters. The judge's scale of measurement may be a Likert scale,* a semantic differential, or an ordinal scale of his own design.

Nonparametric statistical methods are not only useful for analyzing ranked data but also for the case where only directional differences are available. That is, a judge may indicate his preference between a pair of test items but not be willing or able to indicate a measure of the magnitude of his preference.

The word "nonparametric" evolves from the type of hypothesis usually tested when dealing with ranked data of the type described above. *Parametric hypotheses* are those concerned with the population parameters. *Nonparametric hypotheses* do not involve the population parameters but are concerned with the form of the population frequency distribution. Tests of hypotheses concerning the

*See the footnote on page 505.

binomial parameter p, the tests concerning μ, σ^2, and the analysis-of-variance tests were parametric. On the other hand, an hypothesis that a particular population possesses a normal distribution (without specification of parameter values) would be nonparametric. Similarly, an hypothesis that the distributions for two populations are identical would be nonparametric.

This latter hypothesis would be pertinent to the three ranking problems previously described. Even though we do not have an exact measure of sales competence, we can imagine that one exists and that in repeated performances a given salesman would generate a population of such measurements. An hypothesis that the four probability distributions for the populations (associated with the four salesmen) are identical would imply no difference in the sales ability of the salesmen. Similarly, we would imagine that a scale of palatability for cornflakes does exist (even if unknown to us) and that a population of responses representing the reactions of a very large set of prospective consumers corresponds to each brand. An hypothesis that the distributions of palatability for the five brands are identical implies no difference in consumer preference for these products.

The preceding illustrations suggest that the hypotheses not only are non-parametric but indicate that the underlying population distributions are unknown. Although Kendall and Stuart (1961) suggest that statistical procedures appropriate for this latter condition be called distribution-free, it has become common to classify statistical methods for either nonparametric hypotheses or populations of unknown distributional form as nonparametric methods—in spite of the fact that these two conditions are in many respects unrelated (one deals with the null hypothesis and the other with the dependence of a test procedure on knowledge of the population distributional forms). However, we will conform with common usage of the term "nonparametric statistical methods" and think of procedures applicable to situations where the form of the population distribution is unknown or where the case involves a nonparametric hypothesis.

Nonparametric statistical procedures apply to data other than those that are difficult to quantify. They are particularly useful in making inferences in situations where serious doubt exists about the assumptions underlying standard methodology. For example, the t test for comparing a pair of means, Section 9.4, is based on the assumption that both populations are normally distributed with equal variances. Now, admittedly, the experimenter will never know whether these assumptions hold in a practical situation, but he will often be reasonably certain that departures from the assumptions will be small enough so that the properties of his statistical procedure will be undisturbed. That is, α and β will be approximately what he thinks they are. On the other hand, it is not uncommon for the experimenter seriously to question his assumptions and wonder whether he is using a valid statistical procedure. This difficulty may be circumvented by using a nonparametric statistical test and thereby avoiding reliance on a very uncertain set of assumptions.

It is a hard fact of life that one rarely gets "something for nothing." Circumventing the assumptions usually requires a rephrasing of one's hypothesis, a price that often is not difficult to pay. Instead of hypothesizing that $\mu_1 = \mu_2$, we hypothesize that "the population distributions are identical." Note that the practical implications of the two hypotheses are not equivalent because the latter hypothesis is more restrictive. Two distributions could differ and still possess the same mean. A second and less obvious price exacted by the nonparametric procedures is that they usually use a smaller amount of information in the sample than do corresponding parametric methods. Consequently, they may be less efficient than a suitable parametric test. This means that in testing with a given α, the probability of a type II error, β, for a specified alternative may be larger for the nonparametric test. We shall have more to say on this point after giving an example of a nonparametric procedure.

We shall discuss only the most common situations where nonparametric methods are used. For a more complete treatment of the subject, the reader is referred to Siegel (1956) or Conover (1971).

17.2   A Comparison of Statistical Tests

When we have the choice between two statistical test procedures utilizing a given data set for the same hypothesis, how can the choice best be resolved? One method would be to hold the sample size and α constant for both procedures and compare β, the probability of a type II error. Actually, statisticians prefer a comparison of the power of a test where

$$\text{power} = 1 - \beta.$$

Since β is the probability of failing to reject the null hypothesis when it is false, the power of the test is the probability of rejecting the null hypothesis when it is false and some specified alternative is true. It is the probability that the test will do what it was designed to do, that is, detect a departure from the null hypothesis when a departure exists.

Probably the most common method of comparing two test procedures is in terms of the relative efficiency (also called power efficiency) of a pair of tests.

Definition
  The relative efficiency of two tests is the ratio of the sample sizes for the two test procedures required to achieve the same α and β for a given alternative to the null hypothesis.

This method of comparison is meaningful from a practical point of view but poses difficulties for some hypotheses because the number of alternatives may be infinitely large and difficult to tabulate. Which "relative efficiency" should one give in comparing the test procedures?

The asymptotic relative efficiency of a pair of tests is a quantity approached by the relative efficiency as the alternative hypothesis specifies parameter values closer and closer to the value implied by H_0. Although asymptotic relative efficiency will in general depend on α and β, in many important cases this is not so. This quantity is, indeed, compact, but is meaningless because the experimenter is not concerned with minute departures from the null hypothesis and actually is not dealing with infinitely large samples. Several other attempts to package the comparison of a pair of statistical tests in a single number have been proposed and are subject to the same criticism. To be useful, the method of comparison must consider the experimenter and his testing problem.

17.3 The Sign Test for Comparing Two Population Distributions

Suppose that we wish to compare consumer ratings (on a scale of 1 to 10) of two window cleaners. Six housewives are randomly selected from the pertinent consumer group and each rates one window treated with cleaner A and another by cleaner B. A 10 rating is "best." The data for this paired difference experiment (a randomized block design, two treatments per block) are shown in Table 17.1. Do the data present sufficient evidence to indicate a difference in consumer preference for the two cleaners?

Table 17.1 *Consumer Ratings*

HOUSEWIFE	A	B
1	10	7
2	7	5
3	8	7
4	5	2
5	7	6
6	9	6

No complicated statistical test is needed to answer the question. Indeed, we can use a rough-and-ready nonparametrics test procedure, known as the *sign test*, that can almost be performed "by eye." That is, we note that the rating for cleaner A exceeds the rating for B for all six housewives (thus the signs of the six differences are all positive). Assuming no difference between the cleaners, this result is equivalent to flipping a balanced coin six times and observing six heads (or tails). This probability, $(1/2)^6 + (1/2)^6 = 1/32$, is quite small. Hence we would likely reject an hypothesis that the distributions of consumer preferences, for the two cleaners, are identical.

Without emphasizing the point, we employed a nonparametric statistical test as an alternative procedure for determining whether evidence existed to indicate a difference in the mean wear for the two types of tires in the pair-difference experiment, Section 9.5. Each pair of responses was compared and y (the number of times A exceeded B) was used as the test statistic. This nonparametric test is called a sign test because y is the number of positive (or negative) signs associated with the differences. The implied null hypothesis is that the two population distributions are identical and the resulting technique is completely independent of the form of the distribution of differences. Thus, regardless of the distribution of differences, the probability that A exceeds B for a given pair will be $p = .5$ when the null hypothesis is true (that is, when the distributions for A and B are identical). Then y will possess a binomial probability distribution, and a rejection region for y can be obtained using the binomial probability distribution of Chapter 6. (We shall illustrate this point in the example that follows.)

Example 17.1   *In a market research experiment, a food-processing company undertook a study to determine the acceptability of a sugar substitute in their canned orange juice. Eleven families were given a liberal supply of both the current product (A) and the new one with the sugar substitute (B), asked to use them over a 4-week period, and to state their preference. The results are shown in Table 17.2.*

Table 17.2

FAMILY	PRODUCT A	B	PREFERRED PRODUCT
1	−	+	B
2	−	+	B
3	+	−	A
4	−	+	B
5	0	0	No preference
6	−	+	B
7	−	+	B
8	+	−	A
9	−	+	B
10	−	+	B
11	−	+	B

Assume that the 11 families are representative of potential users of the company's product. Let y equal the number of families preferring the current product (A). Do the data present sufficient evidence to indicate a preference for one of the two orange drinks, the orange juice with a sugar substitute (B) or the current orange juice (A)? State the null hypothesis to be tested and use y as a test statistic.

Solution   *Because each pair of preferences, A and B, corresponds to a particular family, we see that the data were collected using a paired difference experiment. Consequently, the observed responses are paired as they appear in the data tabulation. Let y be the number of times that a family indicates a preference for product A. Under the hypothesis that the two products are equally preferred, the probability p that A is preferred over B for a given family is p = .5. Or, equivalently, we wish to test an hypothesis that the binomial parameter p equals .5.* What should be done in case of ties between the paired responses? This difficulty is circumvented by omitting tied pairs and thereby reducing n, the number of pairs. *In this example the effective sample size is 10, not 11.*

Very large or very small values of y are most contradictory to the null hypothesis. Therefore, the rejection region for the test will be located by including the most extreme values of y that at the same time provide an α that is feasible for the test.

Suppose that we would like α to be somewhere on the order of .05 or .10. We would commence the selection of the rejection region by including y = 0 and y = 10 and calculate the α associated with this region using p(y) (the probability distribution for the binomial random variable, Chapter 6). With n = 10, p = .5,

$$\alpha = p(0) + p(10) = C_0^{10}(.5)^{10} + C_{10}^{10}(.5)^{10} = .002.$$

Since the value of α is too small, the region will be expanded by including the next pair of y values most contradictory to the null hypothesis, y = 1 and y = 9. The value of α for this region (y = 0, 1, 9, 10) may be obtained from Table 1, Appendix.

$$\alpha = p(0) + p(1) + p(9) + p(10) = .022.$$

This is also too small, so we again expand the region to include y = 0, 1, 2, 8, 9, 10. The reader may verify that the corresponding value of α is .11. Assuming that this value of α is acceptable to the experimenter (and the reader), we will employ y = 0, 1, 2, 8, 9, 10 as the rejection region for the test. (See Figure 17.1.)

From the data, we observe that y = 2 and therefore we reject the null hypothesis. We conclude that sufficient evidence exists to indicate that the population of buyers is not indifferent between the two products. In fact, it appears that a greater preference exists for product B, the orange juice with the sugar substitute. The probability of rejecting the null hypothesis when it is true is only α = .11, and therefore we are reasonably confident of our conclusion.

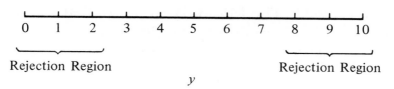

Figure 17.1   *Rejection Region for Example* 17.1

The experimenter in this example used the sign test as a rough and rapid tool for detecting a preference between two products. The rather large value of α is not likely to disturb him, because he can collect additional data (by allowing more families to conduct the experiment) if he is concerned about making a type I error in reaching his conclusion.

The sign test is most often employed for observations that have been randomly selected in pairs using a paired-difference experiment. This is because the paired design (a special case of the randomized block design) usually contains more information than a completely randomized design (two independent random samples) containing the same number of observations. However, the sign test can also be used to compare two population distributions where samples of equal size have been randomly, and independently, selected from the two populations. Then the pairs are formed by randomly matching each observation in sample A with an observation in sample B.

The values of α associated with the sign test can be obtained by using the normal approximation to the binomial probability distribution discussed in Section 7.5. The reader can verify (by comparison of exact probabilities with their approximations) that these approximations will be quite adequate for n as small as 10. This is due to the symmetry of the binomial probability distribution for $p = .5$. For $n \geq 25$, the z test of Chapters 7 and 8 will be quite adequate, where

$$z = \frac{y - np}{\sqrt{npq}} = \frac{y - n/2}{1/2\sqrt{n}}.$$

This would be testing the null hypothesis $p = .5$ against the alternative $p \neq .5$ and would utilize the familiar rejection regions of Chapter 8.

Summarizing, the sign test is a very easily applied nonparametric procedure for comparing two populations. No assumptions are made concerning the underlying population distributions. The value of the test statistic can be quickly obtained by a visual count and the rejection region can be easily located by using a table of binomial probabilities. Furthermore, the data need not be ordinal. That is, we only need to know which member of a pair is preferred. Although not the most efficient nonparametric test, the sign test is useful because of its ease of application.

17.4 The Mann–Whitney U Test for Comparing Two Population Distributions

The sign test for comparing two population distributions ignores the actual magnitudes of the paired observations and thereby discards information that would be useful in detecting a departure from the null hypothesis. A statistical test that partially circumvents this loss by utilizing the relative magnitudes of the observations was proposed by H. B. Mann and D. R. Whitney and is equivalent to a test proposed independently by F. Wilcoxon.

Assume that you have independent random samples of n_1 and n_2 observations, respectively, from the two populations. Then the Mann–Whitney statistic, U, is obtained by ordering all $(n_1 + n_2)$ observations according to their magnitude and counting the number of observations in sample A that precede each observation in sample B. The U statistic is the sum of these counts.

For example, suppose that eight observations from samples A and B are

$$25, \quad 26, \quad 27, \quad 28, \quad 29, \quad 31, \quad 32, \quad 35$$
$$A \quad\ A \quad\ A \quad\ B \quad\ B \quad\ A \quad\ B \quad\ B$$

The smallest B observation is 28, and $u_1 = 3$ observations from sample A precede it. Similarly, $u_2 = 3$ A observations precede the second B observation and $u_3 = 4$ and $u_4 = 4$ A observations precede the third and fourth B observations, respectively (32 and 35). Then

$$U = u_1 + u_2 + u_3 + u_4 = 14.$$

Very large or small values of U will imply a separation of the ordered A and B observations and will provide evidence to indicate a difference between the population distributions for A and B.

The probabilities required for calculating α for small samples (n_1 and $n_2 \leq 10$) are included in Table 8, Appendix. A large-sample approximation will be given at the end of this section. Entries in Table 8 are $P(U \leq U_0)$. For example, $P(U \leq 1) = .0238$ for $n_1 = 3$ and $n_2 = 6$. The rejection region for a two-tailed test would require doubling the tabulated one-tail probability to find α. Hence the Mann–Whitney U test procedure always requires calculating the smaller value of U and using the lower tail of the U distribution as the rejection region (see Figure 17.2).

If $n_1 = 6$ and $n_2 = 8$, one could use the smaller value of U and reject when $U \leq 9$. The tabulated value gives $P(U \leq 9) = .0296$. This probability must be doubled in calculating α to take into account the corresponding large values of U that would be included in the rejection region for a two-tailed test. Then $\alpha = .0592$.

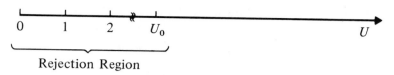

Rejection Region

Figure 17.2 *Rejection Region for the Mann–Whitney U Test*
(reject if $U \leq U_0$)

A shortcut procedure for calculating U can be obtained by ranking all $n_1 + n_2$ observations, letting the smallest observation have a rank of 1, the second smallest rank 2, and so on. Let T_A be the sum of the ranks for the measurements in sample A and T_B be the corresponding sum of ranks for sample B. Then it can be shown (proof omitted) that

$$U_A = n_1 n_2 + \frac{n_1(n_1 + 1)}{2} - T_A,$$

$$U_B = n_1 n_2 + \frac{n_2(n_2 + 1)}{2} - T_B,$$

where

$$U_A + U_B = n_1 n_2.$$

The first value of U will be the number of A observations preceding the B observations, and the second will be the total count of the B observations preceding the A's. For our example,

$$U_A = n_1 n_2 + \frac{n_1(n_1 + 1)}{2} - T_A$$

$$= (4)(4) + \frac{(4)(5)}{2} - 12 = 14$$

and

$$U_B = n_1 n_2 - U_A$$

$$= 16 - 14 = 2.$$

We have agreed to use the smaller sum and hence would use $U = 2$ as the observed value of the test statistic.

Ties in the observations can be handled by averaging the ranks that would have been assigned to the tied observations and assigning this average to each .If three observations are tied and are due to receive ranks 3, 4, 5, we would assign the rank of 4 to all three. The next observation in the sequence would receive the rank of 6, and ranks 3 and 5 would not appear. Similarly, if two observations are tied for ranks 3 and 4, each would receive a rank of 3.5, and ranks 3 and 4 would not appear.

Example 17.2 *Two sales training programs, A and B, were conducted by the Mallon Company. Four groups of 50 prospective sales personnel were trained within each training program. Two months after the completion of training, the number of salesmen remaining on the sales staff of the Mallon Company was observed. The results are as follows:*

A	B
28	33
31	29
27	35
25	30

Do these data present sufficient evidence to indicate a difference in the population distributions for A and B?

Solution *The ranks are shown below alongside the $(n_1 + n_2 = 8)$ measurements. The rank sums for the two samples are also shown.*

A	B
(3) 28	33 (7)
(6) 31	29 (4)
(2) 27	35 (8)
(1) 25	30 (5)

Rank sum	12	24

Then

$$U_A = n_1 n_2 + \frac{n_1(n_1 + 1)}{2} - T_A$$

$$= (4)(4) + \frac{(4)(4 + 1)}{2} - 12$$

$$= 14$$

and

$$U_B = n_1 n_2 - U_A = 16 - 14 = 2.$$

From Table 8, Appendix, for $n_1 = 4$ and $n_2 = 4$,

$$P(U \leq 2) = .0571.$$

Since .0571 is an acceptable value for α, we will select $U \leq 2$ as the rejection region for our test. Using the smaller value of U as the test statistic, $U = 2$, we reject the hypothesis that the population distributions for training programs A and B are identical.

Example 17.3   *Test the hypothesis of no difference in the distribution of the number of material errors found by the two different auditing techniques, Chapter 9, Exercise 29.*

Solution   *The data for this example are shown in Table 17.3. The rank associated with each observation is given alongside in parentheses. Observe that although this is not a blocked (paired) experiment, each A observation exceeds its corresponding B measurement. Thus, even though we do not have unique pairs, regardless as to how the A and B measurements might be paired, the A measurement would exceed its B counterpart in nine of nine pairs. The sign test would then indicate rejection of the hypothesis of no difference in the population distribution of the number of material errors detected by the two auditing techniques. Certainly this procedure, which required less than 30 seconds to discuss, was more rapid than the calculations involved in the Student's t test, Chapter 9. The concept is that if you can see something that is recognizable with the naked eye (the sign test), why use a microscope (the t test)?*

Table 17.3

A	B
(15) 125	89 (1)
(11) 116	101 (7)
(18) 133	97 (4)
(10) 115	95 (3)
(14) 123	94 (2)
(12) 120	102 (8)
(17) 132	98 (5.5)
(16) 128	106 (9)
(13) 121	98 (5.5)

Rank sum 126	45

Although we have tested our hypothesis using the sign test, we will show that the same result can be quickly obtained using the more powerful Mann–Whitney U test. Thus

$$n_1 = n_2 = 9$$

and

$$U_A = n_1 n_2 + \frac{n_1(n_1 + 1)}{2} - T_A = (9)(9) + \frac{(9)(10)}{2} - 126 = 0.$$

From Table 8, $P(U = 0)$ for $n_1 = n_2 = 9$ is .000. The value of α for a two-tailed test and a rejection region of $U = 0$ and $U = 81$ is $\alpha = .000$.

A simplified large-sample test can be obtained by using the familiar z statistic of Chapter 8. When the population distributions are identical, it can be shown that the U statistic has expected value and variance,

$$E(U) = \frac{n_1 n_2}{2}$$

and

$$V(U) = \frac{n_1 n_2 (n_1 + n_2 + 1)}{12},$$

and the distribution of

$$z = \frac{U - E(U)}{\sigma_U}$$

tends to normality with mean zero and variance equal to 1 as n_1 and n_2 become large. This approximation will be adequate when n_1 and n_2 are both larger than, say, 10. Thus for a two-tailed test with $\alpha = .05$, we would reject the null hypothesis if $|z| \geq 1.96$.

What constitutes an "adequate" approximation is a matter of opinion. The reader will observe that the z statistic will reach the same conclusion as the exact U test for Example 17.3. Thus

$$z = \frac{0 - \dfrac{(9)(9)}{2}}{\sqrt{\dfrac{(9)(9)(9 + 9 + 1)}{12}}} = \frac{-40.5}{\sqrt{128.25}} = -3.58.$$

This value of z falls in the rejection region ($|z| \geqslant 1.96$) and hence agrees with the sign test and the U test using the exact tabulated values for the rejection region.

Example 17.4   *A tax consultant wished to compare the ratio of assessed value to sales value for properties in two sections of a city. An analysis of 23 property sales, $n_1 = 11$ from section I, $n_2 = 13$ from section II, were randomly selected from the two sections of the city. The assumed value for each property was obtained from tax records and the ratio of assessed value to sales value was computed. The ratios for the two sections of the city are shown in Table 17.4. Ranks of the ratios are shown in parentheses.*

Table 17.4

(9)	.55	.49	(5)
(17.5)	.67	.68	(19)
(1)	.43	.59	(10.5)
(6.5)	.51	.72	(21)
(3.5)	.48	.67	(17.5)
(12)	.60	.75	(22.5)
(20)	.71	.65	(14.5)
(8)	.53	.77	(24)
(2)	.44	.62	(13)
(14.5)	.65	.48	(3.5)
(22.5)	.75	.59	(10.5)
		.51	(6.5)
$T_1 = 116.5$		.66	(16)

$$T_2 = 183.5$$

Do the data provide sufficient evidence to indicate a difference in the ratios of assessed to sale values for properties in the two sections of the city? Test a null hypothesis of "no difference" using $\alpha = .05$.

Solution   *Since n_1 and n_2 are both larger than 10, we shall use the z test. Then*

$$E(U) = \frac{n_1 n_2}{2} = \frac{(11)(13)}{2} = 71.5,$$

$$V(U) = \frac{n_1 n_2 (n_1 + n_2 + 1)}{12} = \frac{(11)(13)(11 + 13 + 1)}{12} = 297.92,$$

$$\sigma_U = \sqrt{297.92} = 17.3,$$

and the observed value of U is

$$U = n_1 n_2 + \frac{n_2(n_2 + 1)}{2} - T_2$$

$$= (11)(13) + \frac{(13)(14)}{2} - 183.5$$

$$= 50.5.$$

We shall test the null hypothesis that the distributions of ratios for the two sections of the city are identical against the alternative that they differ. Since this alternative implies a two-tailed test, we shall reject the null hypothesis if $|z| \geq 1.96$ ($\alpha = .05$).

The observed value of the test statistic is

$$z = \frac{U - E(U)}{\sigma_U} = \frac{50.5 - 71.5}{17.3} = -1.21.$$

Since z does not fall in the rejection region, there is not sufficient evidence to indicate a difference in the ratios of assessed to sales value for properties located in the two sections of the city.

Why use the Mann–Whitney U test for this example rather than the parametric test employing Student's t? Distributions of ratios often tend to be nonnormal and hence there is a good possibility the requirements of the Student's t test are not met.

Parameter-test procedures, using the z statistic (Section 8.6) or the t statistic (Section 9.4), are appropriate to test the hypothesis of "no difference" between the two population distributions if the assumptions underlying the tests are satisfied. If you have doubts on this point, the Mann–Whitney U statistic offers an efficient alternative. When the Mann–Whitney U test is applied to data that satisfy the assumptions of the t test, its relative efficiency approaches 95.5 percent as $n_1 + n_2$ increases and drops off only to about 95 percent for moderate-sized samples. The Mann–Whitney U test is thus a very efficient alternative to the t test while being much less restrictive in terms of assumed data requirements.

17.5   The Wilcoxon Rank Sum Test for a Paired Experiment

A Wilcoxon rank-sum test can be adapted to the paired-difference experiment of Section 9.5 by considering the paired differences of the two treatments A and B.

Under the null hypothesis of no differences in the distributions for A and B, the expected number of negative differences between pairs would be $n/2$ (where n is the number of pairs), and positive and negative differences of equal absolute magnitude should occur with equal probability. If one were to order the differences according to their absolute values and rank them from smallest to largest, the expected rank sums for the negative and positive differences would be equal. Sizable departures of the rank sum of the positive (or negative) differences from its expected value would provide evidence to indicate a difference between the distributions of responses for the two treatments, A and B.

The rank sum T of the positive (or negative) differences contains the information provided by the sign-test statistic and, in addition, gives information on the relative magnitude of the differences. For example, a low rank sum for negative differences indicates that both the number and absolute values of negative differences are small.

To carry out the Wilcoxon rank-sum test, let T equal the smaller sum of ranks taking the same sign and refer to Table 9, Appendix which gives critical values of T for specific values of α. If the observed T is less than or equal to the tabulated critical value corresponding to the chosen α, the null hypothesis is rejected

Hence the rejection region for the Wilcoxon rank-sum test is similar to that for the Mann–Whitney U test. If the critical value of T is T_0, you reject the null hypothesis when $T \leq T_0$ (as shown in Figure 17.3).

In calculating T, differences equal to zero are eliminated and the number of pairs, n, is reduced accordingly. Ties are treated in the same manner as for the unpaired comparisons of two distributions.

Figure 17.3   *Rejection Region for the Wilcoxon Rank-Sum Test for Paired Experiment (reject if $T \leq T_0$)*

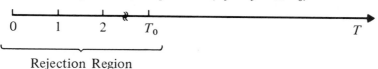

Example 17.5   *A frozen foods wholesaler undertook a study to compare consumer opinion of his line of frozen dinners (A) with those of his most active competitor (B). The study was conducted by having the purchasing manager of each of six nationwide supermarket chains respond on a 10-point Likert scale**

*A Likert scale is an instrument that associates ordinal values with qualitative attributes. In this example the attribute is "measure of acceptability," for which the associated Likert scale would appear as follows:

Impression   Very poor   Acceptable   Outstanding

1   2   3   4   5   6   7   8   9   10

The respondent is then asked to mark his response on the scale. His mark then defines an assumed measure of acceptability for the product in question.

according to their evaluation of the two products. In their analysis, the respondents were asked to consider price, package design, variety, company promotion, and time before spoilage when scoring each product on a Likert scale. The results are shown in Table 17.5. Do these data indicate that the population distributions of scaled responses differ significantly between product A and product B?

Table 17.5

RESPONDENT	LIKERT SCORE A	B	DIFFERENCE A − B	RANK
1	6.5	4.0	2.5	3
2	4.0	8.0	−4.0	4
3	5.5	6.5	−1.0	1.5
4	5.5	10.0	−4.5	5
5	7.0	8.0	−1.0	1.5
6	4.0	9.5	−5.5	6

Solution   The smaller rank sum is that for positive difference, and hence $T = 3$. From Table 9, the critical value of T for a two-tailed test, $\alpha = .10$, is $T = 2$. Since the observed value of T exceeds the critical value of T, there is not sufficient evidence to indicate a significant difference in the population distributions of scaled responses associated with the two products. (Values of T less than or equal to the critical value imply rejection.)

When n is large (say 25), T will be approximately normally distributed with mean and variance

$$E(T) = \frac{n(n + 1)}{4},$$

$$V(T) = \frac{n(n + 1)(2n + 1)}{24}.$$

Then the z statistic

$$z = \frac{T - E(T)}{\sigma_T} = \frac{T - \frac{n(n + 1)}{4}}{\sqrt{\frac{n(n + 1)(2n + 1)}{24}}}$$

can be used as a test statistic. Thus, for a two-tailed test and $\alpha = .05$, we would reject the hypothesis of "identical population distributions" when $|z| \geq 1.96$.

When the Wilcoxon test is used on a data set that actually satisfies the assumptions of the paired t test, the relative efficiency is about 95 percent for large samples. For small samples, the relative efficiency drops off very little. Thus, if any doubt exists about the applicability of the use of the t test for a paired experiment, the Wilcoxon test offers a very efficient alternative.

17.6   The Runs Test: A Test for Randomness

Consider a production process in which manufactured items emerge in sequence and each is classified as either defective (D) or nondefective (N). We have studied how one might compare the fraction defective over two equal time intervals using the normal deviate test, Chapter 8, and extended this to a test of an hypothesis of constant p over two or more time intervals using the chi-square test of Chapter 16. The purpose of these tests was to detect a change or trend in the fraction defective, p. We saw in the studies of quality control in Chapter 11 the effect of process quality-control methods on trends in the process average or fraction defective. Evidence to indicate increasing fraction defective might indicate the need for a process study to locate the source of difficulty. A decreasing value might suggest that a process quality-control program was having a beneficial effect in reducing the fraction defective.

Trends in fraction defective (or other quality measures) are not the only indication of lack of process control. A process may cause periodic runs of defectives with the average fraction defective remaining constant, for all practical purposes, over long periods of time. For example, photoflash lamps are manufactured on a rotating machine with a fixed number of positions for bulbs. A bulb is placed on the machine at a given position, the air is removed, oxygen is pumped into the bulb, and the glass base is flame sealed. If a machine contains 20 positions, and several adjacent positions are faulty (too much heat in the sealing process), surges of defective lamps will emerge from the process in a periodic manner. Tests to compare the process fraction defective over equal intervals of time will not detect this periodic difficulty in the process. The periodicity, indicated by runs of defectives, is indicative of non-randomness in the occurrence of defectives over time and can be detected by a test for randomness. The statistical test that we present, known as the runs test, is discussed in detail by Wald and Wolfowitz (1940). Other practical applications of the runs test will follow.

As the name implies, the runs test studies a sequence of events where each element in the sequence may assume one of two outcomes, say success (S) or failure (F). The runs test is thus applied to a binary sequence of n_1 "successes" and n_2 "failures." If we think of the sequences of items emerging from a manufacturing process as defective (*F*) or nondefective (*S*), the observation of 20 items might yield

$$S\,S\,S\,S\,S\,F\,F\,S\,S\,S\,F\,F\,F\,S\,S\,S\,S\,S\,S\,S.$$

We notice the groupings of defectives and nondefectives and wonder whether this implies nonrandomness and, consequently, lack of process control. A run is defined to be a maximal subsequence of like elements. For example, the first five successes are a subsequence of five like elements and it is maximal in the sense that it includes the maximum number of like elements before encountering an *F*. (The first four elements form a subsequence of like elements, but it is not maximal because the fifth element could also be included.) Consequently, the 20 elements shown above are arranged in five runs, the first containing five *S*'s, the second containing two *F*'s, and so on.

A very small or very large number of runs in a sequence would indicate nonrandomness. Therefore, we shall use *R* (the number of runs in a sequence) as a test statistic to test the null hypothesis that the elements are arranged in random sequence. The rejection region for the alternative, "the sequence is nonrandom," is $R \leq k_1$ and $R \geq k_2$, as indicated in Figure 17.4. A one-tailed test, using values of *R* in the upper tail, would be employed for an alternative hypothesis that "the expected value of *R* is larger than when randomness is present." This would imply an overmixing of the elements of the sequence. In contrast, a one-tailed test, using values of *R* in the lower tail, would be used for the alternative hypothesis that the expected value of *R* is less than when randomness is present. This alternative would be used if one knew that overmixing could not possibly occur and one could only expect a small number of runs (large groups of like elements). Or, it would be used if overmixing was unimportant from a practical point of view.

To illustrate the selection of the alternative hypothesis, consider a test of the null hypothesis that the sequence of defective and nondefective light bulbs emerging from a production line is random. Either a very small number of runs (excessive groupings of defectives) or a very large number (overmixing) could occur if specific positions on a machine were operating improperly. Thus, where it is desirable to detect either under or overmixing of defective and nondefective bulbs we would employ a two-tailed test. In contrast, suppose that a mutual fund manager wished to determine whether requests for refunds were occurring randomly or in spurts. Then we would test a null hypothesis of randomness against the alternative

Figure 17.4   *Rejection Region for the Runs Test*

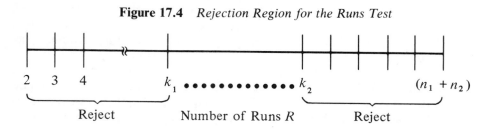

that the expected number of runs would be less than if randomness were present. This would call for locating the rejection region in the lower tail of Figure 17.4.

The values of $P(R \leq a)$ are given in Table 10 for all combinations of n_1 and n_2 where n_1 and n_2 are less than or equal to 10. These can be used to locate the rejection regions for a one- or two-tailed test. We will illustrate with an example.

Example 17.6 *A true–false examination is constructed with the answers running in the following sequence:*

$$T \, F \, F \, T \, F \, T \, F \, T \, T \, F \, T \, F \, F \, T \, F \, T \, F \, T \, T \, F.$$

Does this sequence indicate a depature from randomness in the arrangement of T and F answers?

Solution *The sequence contains $n_1 = 10\,T$ and $n_2 = 10\,F$ answers with $y = 16$ runs. Nonrandomness can be indicated by either an unusually small or an unusually large number of runs, and, consequently, we shall be concerned with a two-tailed test.*

Suppose that we wish to use α approximately equal to .05 with .025 or less in each tail of the rejection region. Then from Table 10 with $n_1 = n_2 = 10$, we note $P(R \leq 6) = .019$ and $P(R \leq 15) = .981$. Then $P(R \geq 16) = .019$, and we would reject the hypothesis of randomness if $R \leq 6$ or $R \geq 16$. Since $R = 16$ for the observed data, we conclude that evidence exists to indicate nonrandomness in the professor's arrangement of answers. His attempt to mix the answers was overdone.

A second application of the runs test is for detecting nonrandomness of a sequence of quantitative measurements over time. These sequences, known as time series, occur in many fields. For example, the measurement of a quality characteristic of an industrial product, blood pressure of a human, and the price of a stock on the stock market all vary over time. Departures in randomness in a series, caused either by trends or periodicities, can be detected by examining the deviations of the time-series measurements from their average. Negative and positive deviations could be denoted by S and F, respectively, and we could then test this time sequence of deviations for nonrandomness. We will illustrate with an example.

Example 17.7 *Paper is produced in a continuous process. Suppose that a brightness measurement, y, is made on the paper once every hour and that the results appear as shown in Figure 17.5.*

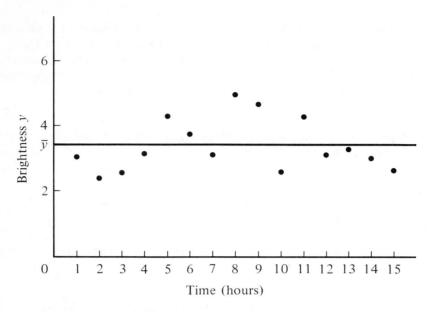

Figure 17.5   *Paper Brightness Versus Time*

The average for the 15 measurements, $\bar{y}$, appears as shown. Note the deviations about $\bar{y}$. Do these indicate a lack of randomness and thereby suggest periodicity in the process and lack of control?

Solution   *The sequence of negative (S) and positive (F) deviations as indicated in Figure 17.5 is*

$$S\,S\,S\,S\,F\,F\,S\,F\,F\,S\,F\,S\,S\,S\,S.$$

Then $n_1 = 10$, $n_2 = 5$, and $R = 7$. Consulting Table 10, $P(R \le 7) = .455$. This value of R is not improbable, assuming the hypothesis of randomness to be true. Consequently, there is not sufficient evidence to indicate nonrandomness in the sequence of brightness measurements.

The runs test can also be used to compare two population frequency distributions for a two-sample unpaired experiment. It provides an alternative to the Mann–Whitney U test, Section 17.4. If the measurements for the two samples are arranged in order of magnitude, they will form a sequence. The measurements for samples 1 and 2 can be denoted as S and F, respectively, and we are once again concerned with a test for randomness. If all measurements for sample 1 are smaller than those for sample 2, the sequence will result in $S\,S\,S\ldots S\,F\,F\,F\ldots F$, or $R = 2$ runs. A small value of R will provide evidence of a difference in population frequency distributions, and the rejection region chosen would be $R \leq a$. This rejection region would imply a one-tailed statistical test. An illustration of the application of the runs test to compare two population frequency distributions will be left as an exercise for the reader.

As in the case of the other nonparametric test statistics studied in earlier sections of this chapter, the probability distribution for R tends to normality as n_1 and n_2 become large. The approximation is good when n_1 and n_2 are both greater than 10. Consequently, we may use the z statistic as a large-sample test statistic where

$$z = \frac{R - E(R)}{\sqrt{V(R)}}$$

and

$$E(R) = \frac{2n_1 n_2}{n_1 + n_2} + 1,$$

$$V(R) = \frac{2n_1 n_2 (2n_1 n_2 - n_1 - n_2)}{(n_1 + n_2)^2 (n_1 + n_2 - 1)}$$

are the expected value of R and variance of R, respectively. The rejection region for a two-tailed test, $\alpha = .05$, is $|z| \geq 1.96$.

17.7   Rank Correlation Coefficient

In preceding sections we have used ranks to indicate the relative magnitude of observations in nonparametric tests for comparison of treatments. We shall now employ the same technique in testing for a monotonic relation between two ranked variables. A rank correlation provides a measure of the degree of linearity between the ranking variables or a measure of the degree of monotonicity between the variables being observed. Thus a rank correlation coefficient is frequently referred to as a coefficient of agreement for preference data. Two common rank correlation coefficients are the Spearman r_s and the Kendall τ. We will present the Spearman r_s because its computation is identical to that for the sample correlation coefficient, r, of Chapter 12. Kendall's rank correlation coefficient is discussed in detail in Kendall and Stuart (1961).

Suppose an individual who is in the market for a 24-inch color television set ranks the standard models for each of the eight major television manufacturers. His preferences are listed in Table 17.6 next to the manufacturer's suggested retail price for the set under consideration. Do the data suggest an agreement between the individual's preference rankings and the manufacturer's suggested retail prices? Or, one might express this question by asking whether a correlation exists between his preferences and the prices.

Table 17.6

MANUFACTURER	PREFERENCE	PRICE
1	7	$449.50
2	4	525.00
3	2	479.95
4	6	499.95
5	1	580.00
6	3	549.95
7	8	469.95
8	5	532.50

The two variables of interest are the preference rankings and price. The former is already in rank form, and the prices may be ranked similarly as shown in Table 17.7. The ranks for tied observations are obtained by averaging the ranks that the tied observations would occupy as for the Mann–Whitney U statistic. The Spearman

Table 17.7

MANUFACTURER	PREFERENCE RANKS (x_i)	PRICE RANKS (y_i)
1	7	1
2	4	5
3	2	3
4	6	4
5	1	8
6	3	7
7	8	2
8	5	6

rank correlation coefficient, r_s, is calculated using the ranks as the paired measurements on the two variables, x and y, in the formula for r, Chapter 12. Thus

$$r_s = \frac{n \sum\limits_{i=1}^{n} x_i y_i - \left(\sum\limits_{i=1}^{n} x_i\right)\left(\sum\limits_{i=1}^{n} y_i\right)}{\sqrt{\left[n \sum\limits_{i=1}^{n} x_i^2 - \left(\sum\limits_{i=1}^{n} x_i\right)^2\right]\left[n \sum\limits_{i=1}^{n} y_i^2 - \left(\sum\limits_{i=1}^{n} y_i\right)^2\right]}}.$$

When there are no ties in either the x observations or the y observations, the above expression for r_s algebraically reduces to the simpler expression,

$$r_s = 1 - \frac{6 \sum d_i^2}{n(n^2 - 1)}, \qquad where \ d_i = x_i - y_i.$$

If the number of ties is small in comparison with the number of data pairs, little error will result in using this shortcut formula for calculating r_s. We shall illustrate the use of the formula by an example.

Example 17.8 *Calculate r_s for the preference–price data shown in Table 17.7*

Solution   *The values of d_i and d_i^2, $i = 1, 2, \ldots, 8$, are shown in Table 17.8.*

MANUFACTURER	x_i	RANK y_i	RANK d_i	d_i^2
1	7	1	6	36
2	4	5	−1	1
3	2	3	−1	1
4	6	4	2	4
5	1	8	−7	49
6	3	7	−4	16
7	8	2	6	36
8	5	6	−1	1
				144

Substituting into the formula for r_s,

$$r_s = 1 - \frac{6 \sum_{i=1}^{n} d_i^2}{n(n^2 - 1)} = 1 - \frac{6(144)}{8(64 - 1)}$$

$$= -.714 .$$

The Spearman rank correlation coefficient may be employed as a test statistic to test an hypothesis of "no association" between two populations. We assume that the n pairs of observations, (x_i, y_i), have been randomly selected and therefore "no association between the populations" would imply a random assignment of the n ranks within each sample. Each random assignment (for the two samples) would represent a sample point associated with the experiment and a value of r_s could be calculated for each. Thus it is possible to calculate the probability that r_s assumes a large absolute value due solely to chance and thereby suggests an association between populations when none exists.

We shall spare the reader the details involved in calculating the probability that r_s exceeds some critical value, say r_0, and will present the critical values for $\alpha = .05, .025, .01$, and $.005$ in Table 11. The tabulated values give r_0 such that $P(r_s > r_0) \approx .05$ or $.01$ as indicated. Therefore they represent the critical values for a one-tailed test. The α for a two-tailed test would require doubling the tabulated probabilities.

Example 17.9   *Test an hypothesis of "no association" between the populations for Example 17.8 against the alternative that a correlation does exist.*

Solution   *The critical value of r_s for a one-tailed test with $\alpha = .05$ and $n = 8$ is .643. Let us assume that the correlation between the individual's preference rankings and the manufacturer's suggested retail prices could not possibly be positive. (That is, assume that a low preference rank means a television set is highly favorable and should be associated with a high price if the manufacturers' prices are indicators of quality, additional features, guarantee, and so forth.) The alternative hypothesis would be that the population, ρ, is less than zero, and we would be concerned with a one-tailed test. Thus α for the test would be the tabulated value .05, and we would reject the null hypothesis if $r_s \leq -.643$.*

The calculated value of the test statistic, $r_s = -.714$, is less than the critical value for $\alpha = .05$. Hence the null hypothesis of "no association" would be rejected at the $\alpha = .05$ level of significance. It appears that some agreement does exist between preference and price.

17.8   Some General Comments on Nonparametric Statistical Tests

The nonparametric statistical tests presented in the preceding pages represent only a few of the many nonparametric statistical measures of inference available. A much larger collection of nonparametric test procedures, along with worked examples, is given by Siegel (1956) and Conover (1971), and an extensive bibliography of publications dealing with nonparametric statistical methods has been presented by Savage (1953). All are listed in the References at the end of the chapter.

We have indicated that nonparametric statistical procedures are particularly useful when the experimental observations are susceptible to ordering but cannot be measured on a quantitative scale. Parametric statistical procedures usually cannot be applied to this type of data, hence all inferential procedures must be based on nonparametric methods.

A second application of nonparametric statistical methods is in testing hypotheses associated with populations of quantitative data when uncertainty exists concerning the satisfaction of assumptions about the form of the population distributions. Just how useful are nonparametric methods for this situation?

It is well known that many statistical tests and estimation procedures are only slightly affected by moderate departures from the assumed form of the population frequency distribution and that parametric test procedures are more efficient than their nonparametric equivalents when the assumptions underlying parametric tests are true. Furthermore, it is sometimes possible to transform statistical data and thereby make the population distributions of the transformed data satisfy the assumptions basic to a parametric procedure. In spite of these positive arguments in favor of parametric procedures, nonparametric statistical methods possess definite advantages in some experimental situations.

Nonparametric statistical methods are rapid and often lead to an immediate decision in testing hypotheses. When experimental conditions depart substantially from the basic assumptions underlying parametric tests, the response measurements can often be transformed to alleviate the condition, but an unfortunate consequence often develops. That is, the transformed response is no longer meaningful from a practical point of view, and analysis of the transformed data no longer answers the objectives of the experimenter. The use of nonparametric methods will often circumvent this difficulty. Finally, one should note that some nonparametric methods are nearly as efficient as their parametric counterparts even when the assumptions of the parametric tests are met. When the assumptions underlying the parametric procedures do not hold, the nonparametric tests may be nearly as efficient, or even more efficient, than corresponding parametric tests.

Exercises

1. Discuss the following concepts:
    (a) A nonparametric statistical method.
    (b) The relative efficiency of a pair of statistical tests.
    (c) Randomness of occurrence of events over time.
    (d) The relation between the Spearman rank correlation coefficient, r_s, and the correlation coefficient, r, from Chapter 12.

2. When would a statistician choose to employ a nonparametric statistical method instead of a parametric test like the t test or the z test?

3. The number of defective electrical fuses proceeding from each of two production lines, A and B, was recorded daily for a period of 10 days with the following results:

DAY	A	B
1	172	201
2	165	179
3	206	159
4	184	192
5	174	177
6	142	170
7	190	182
8	169	179
9	161	169
10	200	210

Assume that both production lines produced the same daily output. Compare the number of defectives produced by A and B each day and let y equal the number of days when B exceeded A. Do these data present sufficient evidence to indicate that production line B produces more defectives, on the average, than A? Use the sign test with a level of significance as near as possible to .01.

4.   Use the Wilcoxon signed ranks test to test the hypothesis of Exercise 3. (Let $\alpha = .01$.)

5.   An experiment was conducted by the advertising agent for a mail-order company to determine the effect of color versus black-and-white advertisements. To advertise a special sale, 1,000 households were selected in each of eight cities across the nation. In each city, the head of 500 households received a color advertising circular and another 500 received a black-and-white advertisement. Two months after all advertisements had been mailed, the number of mail orders placed by the recipients of each type of advertisement from each of the eight cities was found to be:

	TYPE OF ADVERTISEMENT	
CITY	COLOR	BLACK AND WHITE
Atlanta	113	87
Boston	126	101
Chicago	89	90
Denver	105	82
Los Angeles	135	80
San Francisco	117	79
Seattle	175	113
St. Louis	71	93

Test, using the sign test, the hypothesis that the two types of advertising are equally effective, as measured by the number of orders placed by the recipients of each type of advertisement, against the alternative that the two types of advertisements are not equally effective. Use a level of significance as near as possible to $\alpha = .05$.

6.   Two makes of automobile tires were tested on the rear wheels of 12 different automobiles. The number of miles before tire failure was recorded for each tire. The results are shown in the table.

	MAKE OF TIRE	
AUTOMOBILE	MAKE A	MAKE B
A	17,500	22,000
B	26,450	23,000
C	25,000	24,000
D	28,000	32,000
E	16,500	19,650
F	24,000	33,000
G	27,500	25,000
H	26,000	37,000
I	22,400	31,500
J	28,300	25,900
K	18,900	31,000
L	24,500	30,000

(a) Test, using the sign test, the hypothesis that the two makes of tires have the same usable life, as measured by the miles before failure, against the alternative that the usable lives are not equally effective. (Use $\alpha = .05$.)

(b) Suppose that make B is a fiberglass belted tire and make A a conventional, nylon cord tire, suggesting that make B has the capability of withstanding much more wear. Test the hypothesis of equal usable life against the alternative that make B is superior. (Use $\alpha = .05$.)

7. Refer to Exercise 6. Test the hypothesis of equal usable life against the alternative that make B is superior using the Wilcoxon test. Why might we consider the inferences drawn in this exercise more reliable than those drawn after using the sign test, Exercise 6?

8. An accounting firm is considering using a new format for their audit reports of their subscribing firms. The new format consists of numerous figures, graphs, and charts instead of simply numerical and verbal descriptions of the firm's financial records. A total of 12 subscribing firms were issued audit reports using the new format. Of this group, 8 indicated they prefer the new format while 4 said they prefer the old format. Do these results offer sufficient evidence to assume the new report format is preferred over the old report format? Use a significance level as near .10 as possible.

9. In a study to determine the acceptability of a new package design, a firm decided to issue the product only in its current package to one store (store B) and the product in its newly designed package to another store (store A). In the past when both stores sold the product in its current package, weekly sales were almost identical. Over a period of 15 weeks, sales of the product showed the following sales pattern:

Week	1	2	3	4	5	6	7	8	9	10	11	12	13	14	15
Store with greatest sales	B	0	A	A	B	A	B	B	A	A	A	A	0	A	A

(0 implies that the sales in store A and store B were equal for that week.) Do these results indicate a preference for the new package design? (Use a test with a significance level as near as possible to .10.)

10. The output from two filler machines in a food-processing plant was examined in order to compare their fill levels. The measurements below represent the fluid ounces of content from five filled containers selected from the output of each machine.

Machine A	30.5	30.2	30.0	31.2	30.7
Machine B	30.9	31.0	31.5	31.4	31.3

Do the data present sufficient evidence to indicate a difference in the population of fill levels for the two machines? (Use a level of significance of $\alpha = .10$.)
(a) Use the Mann–Whitney U test.
(b) Use Student's t test.

11.   The coded values for a measure of brightness in paper (light reflectivity), prepared by two different processes, A and B, are given for samples of size nine drawn randomly from each of the two processes:

A	B
6.1	9.1
9.2	8.2
8.7	8.6
8.9	6.9
7.6	7.5
7.1	7.9
9.5	8.3
8.3	7.8
9.0	8.9

Do the data present sufficient evidence ($\alpha = .10$) to indicate a difference in the populations of brightness measurements for the two processes?
(a) Use the Mann–Whitney U test.
(b) Use Student's t test.

12.   The life in months of service before failure of the color television picture tube in 8 television sets manufactured by firm A and 10 sets manufactured by firm B are as follows:

FIRM				LIFE OF PICTURE TUBE					
A	32	25	40	31	35	29	37	39	
B	41	39	36	47	45	34	48	44	43	33

Using the U test to analyze the data, test to see if the life in months of service before failure of the picture tube is the same for the picture tubes manufactured by each firm. (Use $\alpha = .10$.)

13.   Refer to Exercise 12. Test the hypothesis of equivalence of population frequency distributions using the runs test with $\alpha = .10$. Compare with the results of Exercise 12.

14.   Refer to Exercise 11. What answer is obtained if the runs test is used in analyzing the data? Compare with the answers to Exercise 11 and discuss reasons for any differences that may exist.

15.   Eight corporate advertising executives were asked to evaluate the comparative effectiveness to their firm for using television and radio advertisements versus advertisements in the printed media. Their responses were listed on a 10-point Likert scale:

EXECUTIVE	RADIO–TV	PRINTED MEDIA
A	5.0	4.0
B	6.2	3.0
C	7.5	5.0
D	8.0	4.0
E	4.5	6.0
F	6.6	5.0
G	6.0	6.0
H	5.0	5.5

Use the Wilcoxon signed ranks test to determine if the executives' opinions of advertising effectiveness differ significantly between the two advertising media. (Use $\alpha = .05$.)

16. Use the sign test to test the hypothesis implied in Exercise 15. Using a level of significance as near as possible to .05, is your conclusion consistent with the conclusion using the Wilcoxon test in Exercise 15? Discuss any differences that may exist.

17. An experiment was conducted to test the effectiveness of a sales training program. In order to remove the natural person-to-person variability in sales ability, the number of sales contracts signed during a month before the training program and the number of contracts signed during a month after the training program were recorded for each of 10 salesmen, thus permitting an analysis of the difference between sales ability *within* each salesman.

SALESMAN	BEFORE TRAINING	AFTER TRAINING
1	64	73
2	48	59
3	26	11
4	91	117
5	39	57
6	12	41
7	58	83
8	47	22
9	34	58
10	43	50

(a) Use the sign test to determine whether sufficient evidence exists to indicate a difference in average sales ability before and after the sales training program. Use a rejection region for which $\alpha \le .05$.

(b) Test the hypothesis of no difference in average sales ability using Student's t test.

18. Refer to Exercise 17. Test the hypothesis that no difference exists in the distributions of sales for the salesmen before and after the sales training program, using the Wilcoxon T test. Use a rejection region for which α is as near as possible to the α achieved in Exercise 17(a).

19. The home office of a corporation selects its executives from the staff personnel of its two subsidiary companies, Company A and Company B. During the past 3 years, nine executives have been selected by the parent company from the subsidiaries, the first selected from B, the second from A, and so on. The following sequence shows the order in which the executives have been selected and the subsidiary firms from which they came:

$$B, A, A, A, B, A, A, A, B.$$

Does this selection sequence provide sufficient evidence to imply nonrandomness in the selection of executives by the parent company from its subsidiaries?

20. Fifteen experimental batteries were selected at random from a pilot lot at plant A, and 15 standard batteries were selected at random from production at plant B. All 30 batteries were simultaneously placed under an electrical load of the same magnitude. The first battery to fail was an A, and second a B, the third a B, and so forth. The following sequence shows the order of failure for the 30 batteries:

$$A\,B\,B\,B\,A\,B\,A\,A\,B\,B\,B\,B\,A\,B\,A\,B\,B\,B\,B\,A\,A\,B\,A\,A\,A\,B\,A\,A\,A\,A.$$

(a) Using the large-sample theory for the U test, determine (use $\alpha = .05$) if there is sufficient evidence to conclude that the mean life for the experimental batteries is greater than the mean life for the standard batteries.

(b) If, indeed, the experimental batteries have the greater mean life, what would be the effect on the expected number of runs? Using the large-sample theory for the runs test, test (using $\alpha = .05$) whether there is a difference in the distributions of battery life for the two populations.

21.   The conditions (D for diseased, S for sound) of the individual trees in a row of 10 poplars were found to be from left to right; $S, S, D, D, S, D, D, D, S, S$. Is there sufficient evidence to indicate nonrandomness in the sequence and therefore the possibility of contagion?

22.   Items emerging from a continuous production process were classified as defective or nondefective. A sequence of items observed over time was as follows: $D, N, N, N, N, N,$ $N, D, D, N, N, N, N, N, N, D, D, D, N, N, N, D, N, N, N, D, D, N, N, N, D, D$.
(a) Give the appropriate probability that $R \leq 11$ where $n_1 = 11$ and $n_2 = 23$.
(b) Do these data suggest lack of randomness in the occurrence of defectives (D) and nondefectives (N)? Use the large-sample approximation for the runs test.

23.   A quality-control chart has been maintained for a certain measurable characteristic of items taken from a conveyor belt at a certain point in a production line. The measurements obtained today in order of time are

$$68.2, \; 71.6, \; 69.3, \; 71.6, \; 70.4, \; 65.0, \; 63.6, \; 64.7,$$
$$65.3, \; 64.2, \; 67.6, \; 68.6, \; 66.8, \; 68.9, \; 66.8, \; 70.1.$$

(a) Classify the measurements in this time series as above or below the sample mean and determine (use the runs test) whether consecutive observations suggest lack of stability in the production process.

(b) Divide the time period into two equal parts and compare the means, using Student's t test. Do the data provide evidence of a shift in the mean level of the quality characteristics?

24.   If (as in the case of measurements produced by two well-calibrated measuring instruments) the means of two populations are equal, it is possible to use the Mann–Whitney U statistic for testing hypotheses concerning the population variances as follows:
(i) Order the combined sample.
(ii) Rank the ordered observations "from the outside in"; that is, rank the smallest observation 1; the largest, 2; the next-to-smallest, 3; the next-to-largest, 4; and so forth. This final sequence of numbers induces an ordering on the symbols A (population A items) and B (population B items). If $\sigma_A^2 > \sigma_B^2$, one would expect to find a preponderance of A's near the first of the sequence, and thus a relatively small "sum of ranks" for the A observations.
(a) Given the following measurements produced by well-calibrated precision instruments A and B, test at near the $\alpha = .05$ level to determine whether the more expensive instrument, B, is more precise than A. (Note that this would imply a one-tailed test.) Use the Mann–Whitney U test.

A	B
1060.21	1060.24
1060.34	1060.28
1060.27	1060.32
1060.36	1060.30
1060.40	

(b) Test, using the F statistic of Section 9.7.

25. A large corporation selects college graduates for employment, using both interviews and a psychological-achievement test. Interviews conducted at the home office of the company were far more expensive than the tests which could be conducted on campus. Consequently, the personnel office was interested in determining whether the test scores were correlated with interview ratings and whether tests could be substituted for interviews. The idea was not to eliminate interviews but to reduce their number. To determine whether correlation was present, 10 prospects were ranked during interviews, and tested. The paired scores are as follows:

SUBJECT	INTERVIEW RANK	TEST SCORE
1	8	74
2	5	81
3	10	66
4	3	83
5	6	66
6	1	94
7	4	96
8	7	70
9	9	61
10	2	86

Calculate the Spearman rank correlation coefficient, r_s. Rank 1 is assigned to the candidate judged to be the best.

26. Refer to Exercise 25. Do the data present sufficient evidence to indicate that the correlation between interview rankings and test scores is less than zero? If this evidence does exist, can we say that tests could be used to reduce the number of interviews?

27. A political scientist wished to examine the relationship of the voter image of a conservative candidate and the distance between the residences of the voter and the candidate. Each of 12 voters rated the candidate on a scale of 1 to 20. The data are as follows:

VOTER	RATING	DISTANCE
1	12	75
2	7	165
3	5	300
4	19	15
5	17	180
6	12	240
7	9	120
8	18	60
9	3	230
10	8	200
11	15	130
12	4	130

Calculate the Spearman rank correlation coefficient, r_s.

28. Refer to Exercise 27. Do these data provide sufficient evidence to indicate a negative correlation between rating and distance?

References

Bradley, J. V., *Distribution-Free Statistical Tests*. Englewood Cliffs, N.J.: Prentice-Hall, Inc., 1968.

Conover, W. J., *Practical Nonparametric Statistics*. New York: John Wiley & Sons, Inc., 1971.

Kendall, M. G., and A. Stuart, *The Advanced Theory of Statistics*, Vol. 2. New York: Hafner Publishing Company, Inc., 1961.

Savage, I. R., "Bibliography of Nonparametric Statistics and Related Topics," *Journal of the American Statistical Association*, Vol. 48 (1953), pp. 844–906.

Siegel, S., *Nonparametric Statistics for the Behavioral Sciences*. New York: McGraw-Hill Book Company, 1956.

Wald, A., and J. Wolfowitz, "On a Test Whether Two Samples Are from the Same Population," *Annals of Mathematical Statistics*, Vol. 2 (1940), pp. 147–162.

Appendix

Tables

Table 1 *Binomial Probability Tables. Tabulated values are* $\sum_{y=0}^{a} p(y)$. *(Computations are rounded at the third decimal place.)*

(a) *n* = 5

P

a	0.01	0.05	0.10	0.20	0.30	0.40	0.50	0.60	0.70	0.80	0.90	0.95	0.99	a
0	.951	.774	.590	.328	.168	.078	.031	.010	.002	.000	.000	.000	.000	0
1	.999	.977	.919	.737	.528	.337	.188	.087	.031	.007	.000	.000	.000	1
2	1.000	.999	.991	.942	.837	.683	.500	.317	.163	.058	.009	.001	.000	2
3	1.000	1.000	1.000	.993	.969	.913	.812	.663	.472	.263	.081	.023	.001	3
4	1.000	1.000	1.000	1.000	.998	.990	.969	.922	.832	.672	.410	.226	.049	4

(b) *n* = 10

P

a	0.01	0.05	0.10	0.20	0.30	0.40	0.50	0.60	0.70	0.80	0.90	0.95	0.99	a
0	.904	.599	.349	.107	.028	.006	.001	.000	.000	.000	.000	.000	.000	0
1	.996	.914	.736	.376	.149	.046	.011	.002	.000	.000	.000	.000	.000	1
2	1.000	.988	.930	.678	.383	.167	.055	.012	.002	.000	.000	.000	.000	2
3	1.000	.999	.987	.879	.650	.382	.172	.055	.011	.001	.000	.000	.000	3
4	1.000	1.000	.998	.967	.850	.633	.377	.166	.047	.006	.000	.000	.000	4
5	1.000	1.000	1.000	.994	.953	.834	.623	.367	.150	.033	.002	.000	.000	5
6	1.000	1.000	1.000	.999	.989	.945	.828	.618	.350	.121	.013	.001	.000	6
7	1.000	1.000	1.000	1.000	.998	.988	.945	.833	.617	.322	.070	.012	.000	7
8	1.000	1.000	1.000	1.000	1.000	.998	.989	.954	.851	.624	.264	.086	.004	8
9	1.000	1.000	1.000	1.000	1.000	1.000	.999	.994	.972	.893	.651	.401	.096	9

Table 1 *Continued*

(c) $n = 15$

P

a	0.01	0.05	0.10	0.20	0.30	0.40	0.50	0.60	0.70	0.80	0.90	0.95	0.99	a
0	.860	.463	.206	.035	.005	.000	.000	.000	.000	.000	.000	.000	.000	0
1	.990	.829	.549	.167	.035	.005	.000	.000	.000	.000	.000	.000	.000	1
2	1.000	.964	.816	.398	.127	.027	.004	.000	.000	.000	.000	.000	.000	2
3	1.000	.995	.944	.648	.297	.091	.018	.002	.000	.000	.000	.000	.000	3
4	1.000	.999	.987	.836	.515	.217	.059	.009	.001	.000	.000	.000	.000	4
5	1.000	1.000	.998	.939	.722	.403	.151	.034	.004	.000	.000	.000	.000	5
6	1.000	1.000	1.000	.982	.869	.610	.304	.095	.015	.001	.000	.000	.000	6
7	1.000	1.000	1.000	.996	.950	.787	.500	.213	.050	.004	.000	.000	.000	7
8	1.000	1.000	1.000	.999	.985	.905	.696	.390	.131	.018	.000	.000	.000	8
9	1.000	1.000	1.000	1.000	.996	.966	.849	.597	.278	.061	.002	.000	.000	9
10	1.000	1.000	1.000	1.000	.999	.991	.941	.783	.485	.164	.013	.001	.000	10
11	1.000	1.000	1.000	1.000	1.000	.998	.982	.909	.703	.352	.056	.005	.000	11
12	1.000	1.000	1.000	1.000	1.000	1.000	.996	.973	.873	.602	.184	.036	.000	12
13	1.000	1.000	1.000	1.000	1.000	1.000	1.000	.995	.965	.833	.451	.171	.010	13
14	1.000	1.000	1.000	1.000	1.000	1.000	1.000	1.000	.995	.965	.794	.537	.140	14

Table 1 *Continued*

(d) $n = 20$

a	0.01	0.05	0.10	0.20	0.30	0.40	0.50	0.60	0.70	0.80	0.90	0.95	0.99	a
0	.818	.358	.122	.002	.001	.000	.000	.000	.000	.000	.000	.000	.000	0
1	.983	.736	.392	.069	.008	.001	.000	.000	.000	.000	.000	.000	.000	1
2	.999	.925	.677	.206	.035	.004	.000	.000	.000	.000	.000	.000	.000	2
3	1.000	.984	.867	.411	.107	.016	.001	.000	.000	.000	.000	.000	.000	3
4	1.000	.997	.957	.630	.238	.051	.006	.000	.000	.000	.000	.000	.000	4
5	1.000	1.000	.989	.804	.416	.126	.021	.002	.000	.000	.000	.000	.000	5
6	1.000	1.000	.998	.913	.608	.250	.058	.006	.000	.000	.000	.000	.000	6
7	1.000	1.000	1.000	.968	.772	.416	.132	.021	.001	.000	.000	.000	.000	7
8	1.000	1.000	1.000	.990	.887	.596	.252	.057	.005	.000	.000	.000	.000	8
9	1.000	1.000	1.000	.997	.952	.755	.412	.128	.017	.001	.000	.000	.000	9
10	1.000	1.000	1.000	.999	.983	.872	.588	.245	.048	.003	.000	.000	.000	10
11	1.000	1.000	1.000	1.000	.995	.943	.748	.404	.113	.010	.000	.000	.000	11
12	1.000	1.000	1.000	1.000	.999	.979	.868	.584	.228	.032	.000	.000	.000	12
13	1.000	1.000	1.000	1.000	1.000	.994	.942	.750	.392	.087	.002	.000	.000	13
14	1.000	1.000	1.000	1.000	1.000	.998	.979	.874	.584	.196	.011	.000	.000	14
15	1.000	1.000	1.000	1.000	1.000	1.000	.994	.949	.762	.370	.043	.003	.000	15
16	1.000	1.000	1.000	1.000	1.000	1.000	.999	.984	.893	.589	.133	.016	.000	16
17	1.000	1.000	1.000	1.000	1.000	1.000	1.000	.996	.965	.794	.323	.075	.001	17
18	1.000	1.000	1.000	1.000	1.000	1.000	1.000	.999	.992	.931	.608	.264	.017	18
19	1.000	1.000	1.000	1.000	1.000	1.000	1.000	1.000	.999	.988	.878	.642	.182	19

P

87.
10

Table 1   *Concluded*

(e) $n = 25$

a	0.01	0.05	0.10	0.20	0.30	0.40	0.50	0.60	0.70	0.80	0.90	0.95	0.99	a
0	.778	.277	.072	.004	.000	.000	.000	.000	.000	.000	.000	.000	.000	0
1	.974	.642	.271	.027	002	.000	.000	.000	.000	.000	.000	.000	.000	1
2	.998	.873	.537	.098	.009	.000	.000	.000	.000	.000	.000	.000	.000	2
3	1.000	.966	.764	.234	.033	.002	.000	.000	.000	.000	.000	.000	.000	3
4	1.000	.993	.902	.421	.090	.009	.000	.000	.000	.000	.000	.000	.000	4
5	1.000	.999	.967	.617	.193	.029	.002	.000	.000	.000	.000	.000	.000	5
6	1.000	1.000	.991	.780	.341	.074	.007	.000	.000	.000	.000	.000	.000	6
7	1.000	1.000	.998	.891	.512	.154	.022	.001	.000	.000	.000	.000	.000	7
8	1.000	1.000	1.000	.953	.677	.274	.054	.004	.000	.000	.000	.000	.000	8
9	1.000	1.000	1.000	.983	.811	.425	.115	.013	.000	.000	.000	.000	.000	9
10	1.000	1.000	1.000	.994	.902	.586	.212	.034	.002	.000	.000	.000	.000	10
11	1.000	1.000	1.000	.998	.956	.732	.345	.078	.006	.000	.000	.000	.000	11
12	1.000	1.000	1.000	1.000	.983	.846	.500	.154	.017	.000	.000	.000	.000	12
13	1.000	1.000	1.000	1.000	.994	.922	.655	.268	.044	.002	.000	.000	.000	13
14	1.000	1.000	1.000	1.000	.998	.966	.788	.414	.098	.006	.000	.000	.000	14
15	1.000	1.000	1.000	1.000	1.000	.987	.885	.575	.189	.017	.000	.000	.000	15
16	1.000	1.000	1.000	1.000	1.000	.996	.946	.726	.323	.047	.000	.000	.000	16
17	1.000	1.000	1.000	1.000	1.000	.999	.978	.846	.488	.109	.002	.000	.000	17
18	1.000	1.000	1.000	1.000	1.000	1.000	.993	.926	.659	.220	.009	.000	.000	18
19	1.000	1.000	1.000	1.000	1.000	1.000	.998	.971	.807	.383	.033	.001	.000	19
20	1.000	1.000	1.000	1.000	1.000	1.000	1.000	.991	.910	.579	.098	.007	.000	20
21	1.000	1.000	1.000	1.000	1.000	1.000	1.000	.998	.967	.766	.236	.034	.000	21
22	1.000	1.000	1.000	1.000	1.000	1.000	1.000	1.000	.991	.902	.463	.127	.002	22
23	1.000	1.000	1.000	1.000	1.000	1.000	1.000	1.000	.998	.973	.729	.358	.026	23
24	1.000	1.000	1.000	1.000	1.000	1.000	1.000	1.000	1.000	.996	.928	.723	.222	24

P

Table 2

X	e^{-x}	X	e^{-x}	X	e^{-x}	X	e^{-x}
0.00	1.000000	2.60	.074274	5.10	.006097	7.60	.000501
0.10	.904837	2.70	.067206	5.20	.005517	7.70	.000453
0.20	.818731	2.80	.060810	5.30	.004992	7.80	.000410
0.30	.740818	2.90	.055023	5.40	.004517	7.90	.000371
0.40	.670320	3.00	.049787	5.50	.004087	8.00	.000336
0.50	.606531	3.10	.045049	5.60	.003698	8.10	.000304
0.60	.548812	3.20	.040762	5.70	.003346	8.20	.000275
0.70	.496585	3.30	.036883	5.80	.003028	8.30	.000249
0.80	.449329	3.40	.033373	5.90	.002739	8.40	.000225
0.90	.406570	3.50	.030197	6.00	.002479	8.50	.000204
1.00	.357879	3.60	.027324	6.10	.002243	8.60	.000184
1.10	.332871	3.70	.024724	6.20	.002029	8.70	.000167
1.20	.301194	3.80	.022371	6.30	.001836	8.80	.000151
1.30	.272532	3.90	.020242	6.40	.001661	8.90	.000136
1.40	.246597	4.00	.018316	6.50	.001503	9.00	.000123
1.50	.223130	4.10	.016573	6.60	.001360	9.10	.000112
1.60	.201897	4.20	.014996	6.70	.001231	9.20	.000101
1.70	.182684	4.30	.013569	6.80	.001114	9.30	.000091
1.80	.165299	4.40	.012277	6.90	.001008	9.40	.000083
1.90	.149569	4.50	.011109	7.00	.000912	9.50	.000075
2.00	.135335	4.60	.010052	7.10	.000825	9.60	.000068
2.10	.122456	4.70	.009095	7.20	.000747	9.70	.000061
2.20	.110803	4.80	.008230	7.30	.000676	9.80	.000056
2.30	.100259	4.90	.007447	7.40	.000611	9.90	.000050
2.40	.090718	5.00	.006738	7.50	.000553	10.00	.000045
2.50	.082085						

Table 3 *Normal Curve Areas*

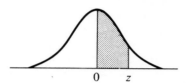

z	.00	.01	.02	.03	.04	.05	.06	.07	.08	.09
0.0	.0000	.0040	.0080	.0120	.0160	.0199	.0239	.0279	.0319	.0359
0.1	.0398	.0438	.0478	.0517	.0557	.0596	.0636	.0675	.0714	.0753
0.2	.0793	.0832	.0871	.0910	.0948	.0987	.1026	.1064	.1103	.1141
0.3	.1179	.1217	.1255	.1293	.1331	.1368	.1406	.1443	.1480	.1517
0.4	.1554	.1591	.1628	.1664	.1700	.1736	.1772	.1808	.1844	.1879
0.5	.1915	.1950	.1985	.2019	.2054	.2088	.2123	.2157	.2190	.2224
0.6	.2257	.2291	.2324	.2357	.2389	.2422	.2454	.2486	.2517	.2549
0.7	.2580	.2611	.2642	.2673	.2704	.2734	.2764	.2794	.2823	.2852
0.8	.2881	.2910	.2939	.2967	.2995	.3023	.3051	.3078	.3106	.3133
0.9	.3159	.3186	.3212	.3238	.3264	.3289	.3315	.3340	.3365	.3389
1.0	.3413	.3438	.3461	.3485	.3508	.3531	.3554	.3577	.3599	.3621
1.1	.3643	.3665	.3686	.3708	.3729	.3749	.3770	.3790	.3810	.3830
1.2	.3849	.3869	.3888	.3907	.3925	.3944	.3962	.3980	.3997	.4015
1.3	.4032	.4049	.4066	.4082	.4099	.4115	.4131	.4147	.4162	.4177
1.4	.4192	.4207	.4222	.4236	.4251	.4265	.4279	.4292	.4306	.4319
1.5	.4332	.4345	.4357	.4370	.4382	.4394	.4406	.4418	.4429	.4441
1.6	.4452	.4463	.4474	.4484	.4495	.4505	.4515	.4525	.4535	.4545
1.7	.4554	.4564	.4573	.4582	.4591	.4599	.4608	.4616	.4625	.4633
1.8	.4641	.4649	.4656	.4664	.4671	.4678	.4686	.4693	.4699	.4706
1.9	.4713	.4719	.4726	.4732	.4738	.4744	.4750	.4756	.4761	.4767
2.0	.4772	.4778	.4783	.4788	.4793	.4798	.4803	.4808	.4812	.4817
2.1	.4821	.4826	.4830	.4834	.4838	.4842	.4846	.4850	.4854	.4857
2.2	.4861	.4864	.4868	.4871	.4875	.4878	.4881	.4884	.4887	.4890
2.3	.4893	.4896	.4898	.4901	.4904	.4906	.4909	.4911	.4913	.4916
2.4	.4918	.4920	.4922	.4925	.4927	.4929	.4931	.4932	.4934	.4936
2.5	.4938	.4940	.4941	.4943	.4945	.4946	.4948	.4949	.4951	.4952
2.6	.4953	.4955	.4956	.4957	.4959	.4960	.4961	.4962	.4963	.4964
2.7	.4965	.4966	.4967	.4968	.4969	.4970	.4971	.4972	.4973	.4974
2.8	.4974	.4975	.4976	.4977	.4977	.4978	.4979	.4979	.4980	.4981
2.9	.4981	.4982	.4982	.4983	.4984	.4984	.4985	.4985	.4986	.4986
3.0	.4987	.4987	.4987	.4988	.4988	.4989	.4989	.4989	.4990	.4990

This table is abridged from Table I of *Statistical Tables and Formulas*, by A. Hald (New York: John Wiley & Sons, Inc., 1952). Reproduced by permission of A. Hald and the publishers, John Wiley & Sons, Inc.

…

Table 4   *Critical Values of t*

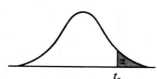

t_α

n	$t_{.100}$	$t_{.050}$	$t_{.025}$	$t_{.010}$	$t_{.005}$	d.f.
2	3,078	6.314	12.706	31.821	63.657	1
3	1.886	2.920	4.303	6.965	9.925	2
4	1.638	2.353	3.182	4.541	5.841	3
5	1.533	2.132	2.776	3.747	4.604	4
6	1.476	2.015	2.571	3.365	4.032	5
7	1.440	1.943	2.447	3.143	3.707	6
8	1.415	1.895	2.365	2.998	3.499	7
9	1.397	1.860	2.306	2.896	3.355	8
10	1.383	1.833	2.262	2.821	3.250	9
11	1.372	1.812	2.228	2.764	3.169	10
12	1.363	1.796	2.201	2.718	3.106	11
13	1.356	1.782	2.179	2.681	3.055	12
14	1.350	1.771	2.160	2.650	3.012	13
15	1.345	1.761	2.145	2.624	2.977	14
16	1.341	1.753	2.131	2.602	2.947	15
17	1.337	1.746	2.120	2.583	2.921	16
18	1.333	1.740	2.110	2.567	2.898	17
19	1.330	1.734	2.101	2.552	2.878	18
20	1.328	1.729	2.093	2.539	2.861	19
21	1.325	1.725	2.086	2.528	2.845	20
22	1.323	1.721	2.080	2.518	2.831	21
23	1.321	1.717	2.074	2.508	2.819	22
24	1.319	1.714	2.069	2.500	2.807	23
25	1.318	1.711	2.064	2.492	2.797	24
26	1.316	1.708	2.060	2.485	2.787	25
27	1.315	1.706	2.056	2.479	2.779	26
28	1.314	1.703	2.052	2.473	2.771	27
29	1.313	1.701	2.048	2.467	2.763	28
30	1.311	1.699	2.045	2.462	2.756	29
inf.	1.282	1.645	1.960	2.326	2.576	inf.

From "Table of Percentage Points of the *t*-Distribution." Computed by Maxine Merrington, *Biometrika*, Vol. 32 (1941), p. 300. Reproduced by permission of Professor E. S. Pearson.

Table 5   *Critical Values of Chi Square*

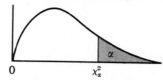

d.f.	$\chi^2 0.995$	$\chi^2 0.990$	$\chi^2 0.975$	$\chi^2 0.950$	$\chi^2 0.900$
1	0.0000393	0.0001571	0.0009821	0.0039321	0.0157908
2	0.0100251	0.0201007	0.0506356	0.102587	0.210720
3	0.0717212	0.114832	0.215795	0.351846	0.584375
4	0.206990	0.297110	0.484419	0.710721	1.063623
5	0.411740	0.554300	0.831211	1.145476	1.61031
6	0.675727	0.872085	1.237347	1.63539	2.20413
7	0.989265	1.239043	1.68987	2.16735	2.83311
8	1.344419	1.646482	2.17973	2.73264	3.48954
9	1.734926	2.087912	2.70039	3.32511	4.16816
10	2.15585	2.55821	3.24697	3.94030	4.86518
11	2.60321	3.05347	3.81575	4.57481	5.57779
12	3.07382	3.57056	4.40379	5.22603	6.30380
13	3.56503	4.10691	5.00874	5.89186	7.04150
14	4.07468	4.66043	5.62872	6.57063	7.78953
15	4.60094	5.22935	6.26214	7.26094	8.54675
16	5.14224	5.81221	6.90766	7.96164	9.31223
17	5.69724	6.40776	7.56418	8.67176	10.0852
18	6.26481	7.01491	8.23075	9.39046	10.8649
19	6.84398	7.63273	8.90655	10.1170	11.6509
20	7.43386	8.26040	9.59083	10.8508	12.4426
21	8.03366	8.89720	10.28293	11.5913	13.2396
22	8.64272	9.54249	10.9823	12.3380	14.0415
23	9.26042	10.19567	11.6885	13.0905	14.8479
24	9.88623	10.8564	12.4011	13.8484	15.6587
25	10.5197	11.5240	13.1197	14.6114	16.4734
26	11.1603	12.1981	13.8439	15.3791	17.2919
27	11.8076	12.8786	14.5733	16.1513	18.1138
28	12.4613	13.5648	15.3079	16.9279	18.9392
29	13.1211	14.2565	16.0471	17.7083	19.7677
30	13.7867	14.9535	16.7908	18.4926	20.5992
40	20.7065	22.1643	24.4331	26.5093	29.0505
50	27.9907	29.7067	32.3574	34.7642	37.6886
60	35.5346	37.4848	40.4817	43.1879	46.4589
70	43.2752	45.4418	48.7576	51.7393	55.3290
80	51.1720	53.5400	57.1532	60.3915	64.2778
90	59.1963	61.7541	65.6466	69.1260	73.2912
100	67.3276	70.0648	74.2219	77.9295	82.3581

Table 5 *Continued*

χ²0.100	χ²0.050	χ²0.025	χ²0.010	χ²0.005	d.f.
2.70554	3.84146	5.02389	6.63490	7.87944	1
4.60517	5.99147	7.37776	9.21034	10.5966	2
6.25139	7.81473	9.34840	11.3449	12.8381	3
7.77944	9.48773	11.1433	13.2767	14.8602	4
9.23635	11.0705	12.8325	15.0863	16.7496	5
10.6446	12.5916	14.4494	16.8119	18.5476	6
12.0170	14.0671	16.0128	18.4753	20.2777	7
13.3616	15.5073	17.5346	20.0902	21.9550	8
14.6837	16.9190	19.0228	21.6660	23.5893	9
15.9871	18.3070	20.4831	23.2093	25.1882	10
17.2750	19.6751	21.9200	24.7250	26.7569	11
18.5494	21.0261	23.3367	26.2170	28.2995	12
19.8119	22.3621	24.7356	27.6883	29.8194	13
21.0642	23.6848	26.1190	29.1413	31.3193	14
22.3072	24.9958	27.4884	30.5779	32.8013	15
23.5418	26.2962	28.8454	31.9999	34.2672	16
24.7690	27.5871	30.1910	33.4087	35.7185	17
25.9894	28.8693	31.5264	34.8053	37.1564	18
27.2036	30.1435	32.8523	36.1908	38.5822	19
28.4120	31.4104	34.1696	37.5662	39.9968	20
29.6151	32.6705	35.4789	38.9321	41.4010	21
30.8133	33.9244	36.7807	40.2894	42.7956	22
32.0069	35.1725	38.0757	41.6384	44.1813	23
33.1963	36.4151	39.3641	42.9798	45.5585	24
34.3816	37.6525	40.6465	44.3141	46.9278	25
35.5631	38.8852	41.9232	45.6417	48.2899	26
36.7412	40.1133	43.1944	46.9630	49.6449	27
37.9159	41.3372	44.4607	48.2782	50.9933	28
39.0875	42.5569	45.7222	49.5879	52.3356	29
40.2560	43.7729	46.9792	50.8922	53.6720	30
51.8050	55.7585	59.3417	63.6907	66.7659	40
63.1671	67.5048	71.4202	76.1539	79.4900	50
74.3970	79.0819	83.2976	88.3794	91.9517	60
85.5271	90.5312	95.0231	100.425	104.215	70
96.5782	101.879	106.629	112.329	116.321	80
107.565	113.145	118.136	124.116	128.299	90
118.498	124.342	129.561	135.807	140.169	100

From "Tables of the Percentage Points of the χ^2-Distribution." *Biometrika*, Vol. 32 (1941), pp. 188–189, by Catherine M. Thompson. Reproduced by permission of Professor E. S. Pearson.

Table 6 *Percentage Points of the F Distribution*

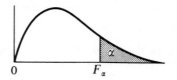

0 F_α

Degrees of Freedom $(\alpha = .05)$

d.f. v_2 \ d.f. v_1	1	2	3	4	5	6	7	8	9
1	161.4	199.5	215.7	224.6	230.2	234.0	236.8	238.9	240.5
2	18.51	19.00	19.16	19.25	19.30	19.33	19.35	19.37	19.38
3	10.13	9.55	9.28	9.12	9.01	8.94	8.89	8.85	8.81
4	7.71	6.94	6.59	6.39	6.26	6.16	6.09	6.04	6.00
5	6.61	5.79	5.41	5.19	5.05	4.95	4.88	4.82	4.77
6	5.99	5.14	4.76	4.53	4.39	4.28	4.21	4.15	4.10
7	5.59	4.74	4.35	4.12	3.97	3.87	3.79	3.73	3.68
8	5.32	4.46	4.07	3.84	3.69	3.58	3.50	3.44	3.39
9	5.12	4.26	3.86	3.63	3.48	3.37	3.29	3.23	3.18
10	4.96	4.10	3.71	3.48	3.33	3.22	3.14	3.07	3.02
11	4.84	3.98	3.59	3.36	3.20	3.09	3.01	2.95	2.90
12	4.75	3.89	3.49	3.26	3.11	3.00	2.91	2.85	2.80
13	4.67	3.81	3.41	3.18	3.03	2.92	2.83	2.77	2.71
14	4.60	3.74	3.34	3.11	2.96	2.85	2.76	2.70	2.65
15	4.54	3.68	3.29	3.06	2.90	2.79	2.71	2.64	2.59
16	4.49	3.63	3.24	3.01	2.85	2.74	2.66	2.59	2.54
17	4.45	3.59	3.20	2.96	2.81	2.70	2.61	2.55	2.49
18	4.41	3.55	3.16	2.93	2.77	2.66	2.58	2.51	2.46
19	4.38	3.52	3.13	2.90	2.74	2.63	2.54	2.48	2.42
20	4.35	3.49	3.10	2.87	2.71	2.60	2.51	2.45	2.39
21	4.32	3.47	3.07	2.84	2.68	2.57	2.49	2.42	2.37
22	4.30	3.44	3.05	2.82	2.66	2.55	2.46	2.40	2.34
23	4.28	3.42	3.03	2.80	2.64	2.53	2.44	2.37	2.32
24	4.26	3.40	3.01	2.78	2.62	2.51	2.42	2.36	2.30
25	4.24	3.39	2.99	2.76	2.60	2.49	2.40	2.34	2.28
26	4.23	3.37	2.98	2.74	2.59	2.47	2.39	2.32	2.27
27	4.21	3.35	2.96	2.73	2.57	2.46	2.37	2.31	2.25
28	4.20	3.34	2.95	2.71	2.56	2.45	2.36	2.29	2.24
29	4.18	3.33	2.93	2.70	2.55	2.43	2.35	2.28	2.22
30	4.17	3.32	2.92	2.69	2.53	2.42	2.33	2.27	2.21
40	4.08	3.23	2.84	2.61	2.45	2.34	2.25	2.18	2.12
60	4.00	3.15	2.76	2.53	2.37	2.25	2.17	2.10	2.04
120	3.92	3.07	2.68	2.45	2.29	2.17	2.09	2.02	1.96
∞	3.84	3.00	2.60	2.37	2.21	2.10	2.01	1.94	1.88

Table 6 *Continued*

10	12	15	20	24	30	40	60	120	∞	d.f./d.f.
241.9	243.9	245.9	248.0	249.1	250.1	251.1	252.2	253.3	254.3	1
19.40	19.41	19.43	19.45	19.45	19.46	19.47	19.48	19.49	19.50	2
8.79	8.74	8.70	8.66	8.64	8.62	8.59	8.57	8.55	8.53	3
5.96	5.91	5.86	5.80	5.77	5.75	5.72	5.69	5.66	5.63	4
4.74	4.68	4.62	4.56	4.53	4.50	4.46	4.43	4.40	4.36	5
4.06	4.00	3.94	3.87	3.84	3.81	3.77	3.74	3.70	3.67	6
3.64	3.57	3.51	3.44	3.41	3.38	3.34	3.30	3.27	3.23	7
3.35	3.28	3.22	3.15	3.12	3.08	3.04	3.01	2.97	2.93	8
3.14	3.07	3.01	2.94	2.90	2.86	2.83	2.79	2.75	2.71	9
2.98	2.91	2.85	2.77	2.74	2.70	2.66	2.62	2.58	2.54	10
2.85	2.79	2.72	2.65	2.61	2.57	2.53	2.49	2.45	2.40	11
2.75	2.69	2.62	2.54	2.51	2.47	2.43	2.38	2.34	2.30	12
2.67	2.60	2.53	2.46	2.42	2.38	2.34	2.30	2.25	2.21	13
2.60	2.53	2.46	2.39	2.35	2.31	2.27	2.22	2.18	2.13	14
2.54	2.48	2.40	2.33	2.29	2.25	2.20	2.16	2.11	2.07	15
2.49	2.42	2.35	2.28	2.24	2.19	2.15	2.11	2.06	2.01	16
2.45	2.38	2.31	2.23	2.19	2.15	2.10	2.06	2.01	1.96	17
2.41	2.34	2.27	2.19	2.15	2.11	2.06	2.02	1.97	1.92	18
2.38	2.31	2.23	2.16	2.11	2.07	2.03	1.98	1.93	1.88	19
2.35	2.28	2.20	2.12	2.08	2.04	1.99	1.95	1.90	1.84	20
2.32	2.25	2.18	2.10	2.05	2.01	1.96	1.92	1.87	1.81	21
2.30	2.23	2.15	2.07	2.03	1.98	1.94	1.89	1.84	1.78	22
2.27	2.20	2.13	2.05	2.01	1.96	1.91	1.86	1.81	1.76	23
2.25	2.18	2.11	2.03	1.98	1.94	1.89	1.84	1.79	1.73	24
2.24	2.16	2.09	2.01	1.96	1.92	1.87	1.82	1.77	1.71	25
2.22	2.15	2.07	1.99	1.95	1.90	1.85	1.80	1.75	1.69	26
2.20	2.13	2.06	1.97	1.93	1.88	1.84	1.79	1.73	1.67	27
2.19	2.12	2.04	1.96	1.91	1.87	1.82	1.77	1.71	1.65	28
2.18	2.10	2.03	1.94	1.90	1.85	1.81	1.75	1.70	1.64	29
2.16	2.09	2.01	1.93	1.89	1.84	1.79	1.74	1.68	1.62	30
2.08	2.00	1.92	1.84	1.79	1.74	1.69	1.64	1.58	1.51	40
1.99	1.92	1.84	1.75	1.70	1.65	1.59	1.53	1.47	1.39	60
1.91	1.83	1.75	1.66	1.61	1.55	1.50	1.43	1.35	1.25	120
1.83	1.75	1.67	1.57	1.52	1.46	1.39	1.32	1.22	1.00	∞

Table 7 *Percentage Points of the F Distribution*

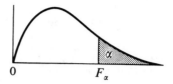

Degrees of Freedom $\qquad$ $(\alpha = .01)$

d.f. ν_1 / d.f. ν_2	1	2	3	4	5	6	7	8	9
1	4052	4999.5	5403	5625	5764	5859	5928	5982	6022
2	98.50	99.00	99.17	99.25	99.30	99.33	99.36	99.37	99.39
3	34.12	30.82	29.46	28.71	28.24	27.91	27.67	27.49	27.35
4	21.20	18.00	16.69	15.98	15.52	15.21	14.98	14.80	14.66
5	16.26	13.27	12.06	11.39	10.97	10.67	10.46	10.29	10.16
6	13.75	10.92	9.78	9.15	8.75	8.47	8.26	8.10	7.98
7	12.25	9.55	8.45	7.85	7.46	7.19	6.99	6.84	6.72
8	11.26	8.65	7.59	7.01	6.63	6.37	6.18	6.03	5.91
9	10.56	8.02	6.99	6.42	6.06	5.80	5.61	5.47	5.35
10	10.04	7.56	6.55	5.99	5.64	5.39	5.20	5.06	4.94
11	9.65	7.21	6.22	5.67	5.32	5.07	4.89	4.74	4.63
12	9.33	6.93	5.95	5.41	5.06	4.82	4.64	4.50	4.39
13	9.07	6.70	5.74	5.21	4.86	4.62	4.44	4.30	4.19
14	8.86	6.51	5.56	5.04	4.69	4.46	4.28	4.14	4.03
15	8.68	6.36	5.42	4.89	4.56	4.32	4.14	4.00	3.89
16	8.53	6.23	5.29	4.77	4.44	4.20	4.03	3.89	3.78
17	8.40	6.11	5.18	4.67	4.34	4.10	3.93	3.79	3.68
18	8.29	6.01	5.09	4.58	4.25	4.01	3.84	3.71	3.60
19	8.18	5.93	5.01	4.50	4.17	3.94	3.77	3.63	3.52
20	8.10	5.85	4.94	4.43	4.10	3.87	3.70	3.56	3.46
21	8.02	5.78	4.87	4.37	4.04	3.81	3.64	3.51	3.40
22	7.95	5.72	4.82	4.31	3.99	3.76	3.59	3.45	3.35
23	7.88	5.66	4.76	4.26	3.94	3.71	3.54	3.41	3.30
24	7.82	5.61	4.72	4.22	3.90	3.67	3.50	3.36	3.26
25	7.77	5.57	4.68	4.18	3.85	3.63	3.46	3.32	3.22
26	7.72	5.53	4.64	4.14	3.82	3.59	3.42	3.29	3.18
27	7.68	5.49	4.60	4.11	3.78	3.56	3.39	3.26	3.15
28	7.64	5.45	4.57	4.07	3.75	3.53	3.36	3.23	3.12
29	7.60	5.42	4.54	4.04	3.73	3.50	3.33	3.20	3.09
30	7.56	5.39	4.51	4.02	3.70	3.47	3.30	3.17	3.07
40	7.31	5.18	4.31	3.83	3.51	3.29	3.12	2.99	2.89
60	7.08	4.98	4.13	3.65	3.34	3.12	2.95	2.82	2.72
120	6.85	4.79	3.95	3.48	3.17	2.96	2.79	2.66	2.56
∞	6.63	4.61	3.78	3.32	3.02	2.80	2.64	2.51	2.41

Table 7 *Continued*

10	12	15	20	24	30	40	60	120	∞	d.f./d.f.
6056	6106	6157	6209	6235	6261	6287	6313	6339	6366	1
99.40	99.42	99.43	99.45	99.46	99.47	99.47	99.48	99.49	99.50	2
27.23	27.05	26.87	26.69	26.60	26.50	26.41	26.32	26.22	26.13	3
14.55	14.37	14.20	14.02	13.93	13.84	13.75	13.65	13.56	13.46	4
10.05	9.89	9.72	9.55	9.47	9.38	9.29	9.20	9.11	9.02	5
7.87	7.72	7.56	7.40	7.31	7.23	7.14	7.06	6.97	6.88	6
6.62	6.47	6.31	6.16	6.07	5.99	5.91	5.82	5.74	5.65	7
5.81	5.67	5.52	5.36	5.28	5.20	5.12	5.03	4.95	4.86	8
5.26	5.11	4.96	4.81	4.73	4.65	4.57	4.48	4.40	4.31	9
4.85	4.71	4.56	4.41	4.33	4.25	4.17	4.08	4.00	3.91	10
4.54	4.40	4.25	4.10	4.02	3.94	3.86	3.78	3.69	3.60	11
4.30	4.16	4.01	3.86	3.78	3.70	3.62	3.54	3.45	3.36	12
4.10	3.96	3.82	3.66	3.59	3.51	3.43	3.34	3.25	3.17	13
3.94	3.80	3.66	3.51	3.43	3.35	3.27	3.18	3.09	3.00	14
3.80	3.67	3.52	3.37	3.29	3.21	3.13	3.05	2.96	2.87	15
3.69	3.55	3.41	3.26	3.18	3.10	3.02	2.93	2.84	2.75	16
3.59	3.46	3.31	3.16	3.08	3.00	2.92	2.83	2.75	2.65	17
3.51	3.37	3.23	3.08	3.00	2.92	2.84	2.75	2.66	2.57	18
3.43	3.30	3.15	3.00	2.92	2.84	2.76	2.67	2.58	2.49	19
3.37	3.23	3.09	2.94	2.86	2.78	2.69	2.61	2.52	2.42	20
3.31	3.17	3.03	2.88	2.80	2.72	2.64	2.55	2.46	2.36	21
3.26	3.12	2.98	2.83	2.75	2.67	2.58	2.50	2.40	2.31	22
3.21	3.07	2.93	2.78	2.70	2.62	2.54	2.45	2.35	2.26	23
3.17	3.03	2.89	2.74	2.66	2.58	2.49	2.40	2.31	2.21	24
3.13	2.99	2.85	2.70	2.62	2.54	2.45	2.36	2.27	2.17	25
3.09	2.96	2.81	2.66	2.58	2.50	2.42	2.33	2.23	2.13	26
3.06	2.93	2.78	2.63	2.55	2.47	2.38	2.29	2.20	2.10	27
3.03	2.90	2.75	2.60	2.52	2.44	2.35	2.26	2.17	2.06	28
3.00	2.87	2.73	2.57	2.49	2.41	2.33	2.23	2.14	2.03	29
2.98	2.84	2.70	2.55	2.47	2.39	2.30	2.21	2.11	2.01	30
2.80	2.66	2.52	2.37	2.29	2.20	2.11	2.02	1.92	1.80	40
2.63	2.50	2.35	2.20	2.12	2.03	1.94	1.84	1.73	1.60	60
2.47	2.34	2.19	2.03	1.95	1.86	1.76	1.66	1.53	1.38	120
2.32	2.18	2.04	1.88	1.79	1.70	1.59	1.47	1.32	1.00	∞

Table 8   *Distribution Function of U.*
$P(U \leq U_0)$; U_0 is the argument $n_1 \leq n_2$; $3 \leq n_2 \leq 10$

$n_2 = 3$

n_1	1	2	3
0	.25	.10	.05
1	.50	.20	.10
U_0 2		.40	.20
3		.60	.35
4			.50

$n_2 = 4$

n_1	1	2	3	4
0	.2000	.0667	.0286	.0143
1	.4000	.1333	.0571	.0286
2	.6000	.2667	.1143	.0571
3		.4000	.2000	.1000
U_0 4		.6000	.3143	.1714
5			.4286	.2429
6			.5714	.3429
7				.4429
8				.5571

$n_2 = 5$

n_1	1	2	3	4	5
0	.1667	.0476	.0179	.0079	.0040
1	.3333	.0952	.0357	.0159	.0079
2	.5000	.1905	.0714	.0317	.0159
3		.2857	.1250	.0556	.0278
4		.4286	.1964	.0952	.0476
5		.5714	.2857	.1429	.0754
U_0 6			.3929	.2063	.1111
7			.5000	.2778	.1548
8				.3651	.2103
9				.4524	.2738
10				.5476	.3452
11					.4206
12					.5000

Table 8 *Continued*

$n_2 = 6$

n_1	1	2	3	4	5	6
0	.1429	.0357	.0119	.0048	.0022	.0011
1	.2857	.0714	.0238	.0095	.0043	.0022
2	.4286	.1429	.0476	.0190	.0087	.0043
3	.5714	.2143	.0833	.0333	.0152	.0076
4		.3214	.1310	.0571	.0260	.0130
5		.4286	.1905	.0857	.0411	.0206
6		.5714	.2738	.1286	.0628	.0325
7			.3571	.1762	.0887	.0465
8			.4524	.2381	.1234	.0660
U_0 9			.5476	.3048	.1645	.0898
10				.3810	.2143	.1201
11				.4571	.2684	.1548
12				.5429	.3312	.1970
13					.3961	.2424
14					.4654	.2944
15					.5346	.3496
16						.4091
17						.4686
18						.5314

$n_2 = 7$

n_1	1	2	3	4	5	6	7
0	.1250	.0278	.0083	.0030	.0013	.0006	.0003
1	.2500	.0556	.0167	.0061	.0025	.0012	.0006
2	.3750	.1111	.0333	.0121	.0051	.0023	.0012
3	.5000	.1667	.0583	.0212	.0088	.0041	.0020
4		.2500	.0917	.0364	.0152	.0070	.0035
5		.3333	.1333	.0545	.0240	.0111	.0055
6		.4444	.1917	.0818	.0366	.0175	.0087
7		.5556	.2583	.1152	.0530	.0256	.0131
8			.3333	.1576	.0745	.0367	.0189
9			.4167	.2061	.1010	.0507	.0265
10			.5000	.2636	.1338	.0688	.0364
11				.3242	.1717	.0903	.0487
U_0 12				.3939	.2159	.1171	.0641
13				.4636	.2652	.1474	.0825
14				.5364	.3194	.1830	.1043
15					.3775	.2226	.1297
16					.4381	.2669	.1588
17					.5000	.3141	.1914
18						.3654	.2279
19						.4178	.2675
20						.4726	.3100
21						.5274	.3552
22							.4024
23							.4508
24							.5000

Table 8 *Continued*

$n_2 = 8$

n_1	1	2	3	4	5	6	7	8
0	.1111	.0222	.0061	.0020	.0008	.0003	.0002	.0001
1	.2222	.0444	.0121	.0040	.0016	.0007	.0003	.0002
2	.3333	.0889	.0242	.0081	.0031	.0013	.0006	.0003
3	.4444	.1333	.0424	.0141	.0054	.0023	.0011	.0005
4	.5556	.2000	.0667	.0242	.0093	.0040	.0019	.0009
5		.2667	.0970	.0364	.0148	.0063	.0030	.0015
6		.3556	.1394	.0545	.0225	.0100	.0047	.0023
7		.4444	.1879	.0768	.0326	.0147	.0070	.0035
8		.5556	.2485	.1071	.0466	.0213	.0103	.0052
9			.3152	.1414	.0637	.0296	.0145	.0074
10			.3879	.1838	.0855	.0406	.0200	.0103
11			.4606	.2303	.1111	.0539	.0270	.0141
12			.5394	.2848	.1422	.0709	.0361	.0190
13				.3414	.1772	.0906	.0469	.0249
14				.4040	.2176	.1142	.0603	.0325
15				.4667	.2618	.1412	.0760	.0415
16				.5333	.3108	.1725	.0946	.0524
17					.3621	.2068	.1159	.0652
18					.4165	.2454	.1405	.0803
19					.4716	.2864	.1678	.0974
20					.5284	.3310	.1984	.1172
21						.3773	.2317	.1393
22						.4259	.2679	.1641
23						.4749	.3063	.1911
24						.5251	.3472	.2209
25							.3894	.2527
26							.4333	.2869
27							.4775	.3227
28							.5225	.3605
29								.3992
30								.4392
31								.4796
32								.5204

U_0

Table 8 *Continued*

$n_2 = 9$

n_1	1	2	3	4	5	6	7	8	9
0	.1000	.0182	.0045	.0014	.0005	.0002	.0001	.0000	.0000
1	.2000	.0364	.0091	.0028	.0010	.0004	.0002	.0001	.0000
2	.3000	.0727	.0182	.0056	.0020	.0008	.0003	.0002	.0001
3	.4000	.1091	.0318	.0098	.0035	.0014	.0006	.0003	.0001
4	.5000	.1636	.0500	.0168	.0060	.0024	.0010	.0005	.0002
5		.2182	.0727	.0252	.0095	.0038	.0017	.0008	.0004
6		.2909	.1045	.0378	.0145	.0060	.0026	.0012	.0006
7		.3636	.1409	.0531	.0210	.0088	.0039	.0019	.0009
8		.4545	.1864	.0741	.0300	.0128	.0058	.0028	.0014
9		.5455	.2409	.0993	.0415	.0180	.0082	.0039	.0020
10			.3000	.1301	.0559	.0248	.0115	.0056	.0028
11			.3636	.1650	.0734	.0332	.0156	.0076	.0039
12			.4318	.2070	.0949	.0440	.0209	.0103	.0053
13			.5000	.2517	.1199	.0567	.0274	.0137	.0071
14				.3021	.1489	.0723	.0356	.0180	.0094
15				.3552	.1818	.0905	.0454	.0232	.0122
16				.4126	.2188	.1119	.0571	.0296	.0157
17				.4699	.2592	.1361	.0708	.0372	.0200
18				.5301	.3032	.1638	.0869	.0464	.0252
19					.3497	.1942	.1052	.0570	.0313
U_0 20					.3986	.2280	.1261	.0694	.0385
21					.4491	.2643	.1496	.0836	.0470
22					.5000	.3035	.1755	.0998	.0567
23						.3445	.2039	.1179	.0680
24						.3878	.2349	.1383	.0807
25						.4320	.2680	.1606	.0951
26						.4773	.3032	.1852	.1112
27						.5227	.3403	.2117	.1290
28							.3788	.2404	.1487
29							.4185	.2707	.1701
30							.4591	.3029	.1933
31							.5000	.3365	.2181
32								.3715	.2447
33								.4074	.2729
34								.4442	.3024
35								.4813	.3332
36								.5187	.3652
37									.3981
38									.4317
39									.4657
40									.5000

Table 8 *Concluded*

$n_2 = 10$

n_1	1	2	3	4	5	6	7	8	9	10
0	.0909	.0152	.0035	.0010	.0003	.0001	.0001	.0000	.0000	.0000
1	.1818	.0303	.0070	.0020	.0007	.0002	.0001	.0000	.0000	.0000
2	.2727	.0606	.0140	.0040	.0013	.0005	.0002	.0001	.0000	.0000
3	.3636	.0909	.0245	.0070	.0023	.0009	.0004	.0002	.0001	.0000
4	.4545	.1364	.0385	.0120	.0040	.0015	.0006	.0003	.0001	.0001
5	.5455	.1818	.0559	.0180	.0063	.0024	.0010	.0004	.0002	.0001
6		.2424	.0804	.0270	.0097	.0037	.0015	.0007	.0003	.0002
7		.3030	.1084	.0380	.0140	.0055	.0023	.0010	.0005	.0002
8		.3788	.1434	.0529	.0200	.0080	.0034	.0015	.0007	.0004
9		.4545	.1853	.0709	.0276	.0112	.0048	.0022	.0011	.0005
10		.5455	.2343	.0939	.0376	.0156	.0068	.0031	.0015	.0008
11			.2867	.1199	.0496	.0210	.0093	.0043	.0021	.0010
12			.3462	.1518	.0646	.0280	.0125	.0058	.0028	.0014
13			.4056	.1868	.0823	.0363	.0165	.0078	.0038	.0019
14			.4685	.2268	.1032	.0467	.0215	.0103	.0051	.0026
15			.5315	.2697	.1272	.0589	.0277	.0133	.0066	.0034
16				.3177	.1548	.0736	.0351	.0171	.0086	.0045
17				.3666	.1855	.0903	.0439	.0217	.0110	.0057
18				.4196	.2198	.1099	.0544	.0273	.0140	.0073
19				.4725	.2567	.1317	.0665	.0338	.0175	.0093
20				.5275	.2970	.1566	.0806	.0416	.0217	.0116
21					.3393	.1838	.0966	.0506	.0267	.0144
22					.3839	.2139	.1148	.0610	.0326	.0177
23					.4296	.2461	.1349	.0729	.0394	.0216
24					.4765	.2811	.1574	.0864	.0474	.0262
U_0 25					.5235	.3177	.1819	.1015	.0564	.0315
26						.3564	.2087	.1185	.0667	.0376
27						.3962	.2374	.1371	.0782	.0446
28						.4374	.2681	.1577	.0912	.0526
29						.4789	.3004	.1800	.1055	.0615
30						.5211	.3345	.2041	.1214	.0716
31							.3698	.2299	.1388	.0827
32							.4063	.2574	.1577	.0952
33							.4434	.2863	.1781	.1088
34							.4811	.3167	.2001	.1237
35							.5189	.3482	.2235	.1399
36								.3809	.2483	.1575
37								.4143	.2745	.1763
38								.4484	.3019	.1965
39								.4827	.3304	.2179
40								.5173	.3598	.2406
41									.3901	.2644
42									.4211	.2894
43									.4524	.3153
44									.4841	.3421
45									.5159	.3697
46										.3980
47										.4267
48										.4559
49										.4853
50										.5147

Computed by M. Pagano, Department of Statistics, University of Florida.

Table 9 *Critical Values of T in the Wilcoxon Matched-Pairs Signed-Ranks Test*

$$n = 5(1)50$$

One sided	Two-sided	$n = 5$	$n = 6$	$n = 7$	$n = 8$	$n = 9$	$n = 10$
$P = .05$	$P = .10$	1	2	4	6	8	11
$P = .025$	$P = .05$		1	2	4	6	8
$P = .01$	$P = .02$			0	2	3	5
$P = .005$	$P = .01$				0	2	3

One-sided	Two-sided	$n = 11$	$n = 12$	$n = 13$	$n = 14$	$n = 15$	$n = 16$
$P = .05$	$P = .10$	14	17	21	26	30	36
$P = .025$	$P = .05$	11	14	17	21	25	30
$P = .01$	$P = .02$	7	10	13	16	20	24
$P = .005$	$P = .01$	5	7	10	13	16	19

One-sided	Two-sided	$n = 17$	$n = 18$	$n = 19$	$n = 20$	$n = 21$	$n = 22$
$P = .05$	$P = .10$	41	47	54	60	68	75
$P = .025$	$P = .05$	35	40	46	52	59	66
$P = .01$	$P = .02$	28	33	38	43	49	56
$P = .005$	$P = .01$	23	28	32	37	43	49

One-sided	Two-sided	$n = 23$	$n = 24$	$n = 25$	$n = 26$	$n = 27$	$n = 28$
$P = .05$	$P = .10$	83	92	101	110	120	130
$P = .025$	$P = .05$	73	81	90	98	107	117
$P = .01$	$P = .02$	62	69	77	85	93	102
$P = .005$	$P = .01$	55	68	68	76	84	92

One-sided	Two-sided	$n = 29$	$n = 30$	$n = 31$	$n = 32$	$n = 33$	$n = 34$
$P = .05$	$P = .10$	141	152	163	175	188	201
$P = .025$	$P = .05$	127	137	148	159	171	183
$P = .01$	$P = .02$	111	120	130	141	151	162
$P = .005$	$P = .01$	100	109	118	128	138	149

One-sided	Two-sided	$n = 35$	$n = 36$	$n = 37$	$n = 38$	$n = 39$	
$P = .05$	$P = .10$	214	228	242	256	271	
$P = .025$	$P = .05$	195	208	222	235	250	
$P = .01$	$P = .02$	174	186	198	211	224	
$P = .005$	$P = .01$	160	171	183	195	208	

One-sided	Two-sided	$n = 40$	$n = 41$	$n = 42$	$n = 43$	$n = 44$	$n = 45$
$P = .05$	$P = .10$	287	303	319	336	353	371
$P = .025$	$P = .05$	264	279	295	311	327	344
$P = .01$	$P = .02$	238	252	267	281	297	313
$P = .005$	$P = .01$	221	234	248	262	277	292

One-sided	Two-sided	$n = 46$	$n = 47$	$n = 48$	$n = 49$	$n = 50$	
$P = .05$	$P = .10$	389	408	427	446	466	
$P = .025$	$P = .05$	361	379	397	415	434	
$P = .01$	$P = .02$	329	345	362	380	398	
$P = .005$	$P = .01$	307	323	339	356	373	

From "Some Rapid Approximate Statistical Procedures" (1964), 28, F. Wilcoxon and R. A. Wilcox. Reproduced with the kind permission of R. A. Wilcox and the Lederle Laboratories.

Table 10 *Distribution of the Total Number of Runs R*
in Samples of Size (n_1, n_2); $P(R \leqslant a)$

					a					
(n_1, n_2)	2	3	4	5	6	7	8	9	10
(2,3)	.200	.500	.900	1.000					
(2,4)	.133	.400	.800	1.000					
(2,5)	.095	.333	.714	1.000					
(2,6)	.071	.286	.643	1.000					
(2,7)	.056	.250	.583	1.000					
(2,8)	.044	.222	.533	1.000					
(2,9)	.036	.200	.491	1.000					
(2,10)	.030	.182	.455	1.000					
(3,3)	.100	.300	.700	.900	1.000				
(3,4)	.057	.200	.543	.800	.971	1.000			
(3,5)	.036	.143	.429	.714	.929	1.000			
(3,6)	.024	.107	.345	.643	.881	1.000			
(3,7)	.017	.083	.283	.583	.833	1.000			
(3,8)	.012	.067	.236	.533	.788	1.000			
(3,9)	.009	.055	.200	.491	.745	1.000			
(3,10)	.007	.045	.171	.455	.706	1.000			
(4,4)	.029	.114	.371	.629	.886	.971	1.000		
(4,5)	.016	.071	.262	.500	.786	.929	.992	1.000	
(4,6)	.010	.048	.190	.405	.690	.881	.976	1.000	
(4,7)	.006	.033	.142	.333	.606	.833	.954	1.000	
(4,8)	.004	.024	.109	.279	.533	.788	.929	1.000	
(4,9)	.003	.018	.085	.236	.471	.745	.902	1.000	
(4,10)	.002	.014	.068	.203	.419	.706	.874	1.000	
(5,5)	.008	.040	.167	.357	.643	.833	.960	.992	1.000
(5,6)	.004	.024	.110	.262	.522	.738	.911	.976	.998
(5,7)	.003	.015	.076	.197	.424	.652	.854	.955	.992
(5,8)	.002	.010	.054	.152	.347	.576	.793	.929	.984
(5,9)	.001	.007	.039	.119	.287	.510	.734	.902	.972
(5,10)	.001	.005	.029	.095	.239	.455	.678	.874	.958
(6,6)	.002	.013	.067	.175	.392	.608	.825	.933	.987
(6,7)	.001	.008	.043	.121	.296	.500	.733	.879	.966
(6,8)	.001	.005	.028	.086	.226	.413	.646	.821	.937
(6,9)	.000	.003	.019	.063	.175	.343	.566	.762	.902
(6,10)	.000	.002	.013	.047	.137	.288	.497	.706	.864
(7,7)	.001	.004	.025	.078	.209	.383	.617	.791	.922
(7,8)	.000	.002	.015	.051	.149	.296	.514	.704	.867
(7,9)	.000	.001	.010	.035	.108	.231	.427	.622	.806
(7,10)	.000	.001	.006	.024	.080	.182	.355	.549	.743
(8,8)	.000	.001	.009	.032	.100	.214	.405	.595	.786
(8,9)	000	.001	.005	.020	.069	.157	.319	.500	.702
(8,10)	.000	.000	.003	.013	.048	.117	.251	.419	.621
(9,9)	.000	.000	.003	.012	.044	.109	.238	.399	.601
(9,10)	.000	.000	.002	.008	.029	.077	.179	.319	.510
(10,10)	.000	.000	.001	.004	.019	.051	.128	.242	.414

Table 10 *Continued*

a

(n_1, n_2)	11	12	13	14	15	16	17	18	19	20
(2,3)										
(2,4)										
(2,5)										
(2,6)										
(2,7)										
(2,8)										
(2,9)										
(2,10)										
(3,3)										
(3,4)										
(3,5)										
(3,6)										
(3,7)										
(3,8)										
(3,9)										
(3,10)										
(4,4)										
(4,5)										
(4,6)										
(4,7)										
(4,8)										
(4,9)										
(4,10)										
(5,5)										
(5,6)	1.000									
(5,7)	1.000									
(5,8)	1.000									
(5,9)	1.000									
(5,10)	1.000									
(6,6)	.998	1.000								
(6,7)	.992	.999	1.000							
(6,8)	.984	.998	1.000							
(6,9)	.972	.994	1.000							
(6,10)	.958	.990	1.000							
(7,7)	.975	.996	.999	1.000						
(7,8)	.949	.988	.998	1.000	1.000					
(7,9)	.916	.975	.994	.999	1.000					
(7,10)	.879	.957	.990	.998	1.000					
(8,8)	.900	.968	.991	.999	1.000	1.000				
(8,9)	.843	.939	.980	.996	.999	1.000	1.000			
(8,10)	.782	.903	.964	.990	.998	1.000	1.000			
(9,9)	.762	.891	.956	.988	.997	1.000	1.000	1.000		
(9,10)	.681	.834	.923	.974	.992	.999	1.000	1.000	1.000	
(10,10)	.586	.758	.872	.949	.981	.996	.999	1.000	1.000	1.000

From "Tables for Testing Randomness of Grouping in a Sequence of Alternatives," C. Eisenhart and F. Swed, *Annals of Mathematical Statistics*, Volume 14 (1943). Reproduced with the kind permission of the Editor, *Annals of Mathematical Statistics*.

Table 11 *Critical Values of Spearman's Rank Correlation Coefficient*

n	$\alpha = 0.05$	$\alpha = 0.025$	$\alpha = 0.01$	$\alpha = 0.005$
5	0.900	—	—	—
6	0.829	0.886	0.943	—
7	0.714	0.786	0.893	—
8	0.643	0.738	0.833	0.881
9	0.600	0.683	0.783	0.833
10	0.564	0.648	0.745	0.794
11	0.523	0.623	0.736	0.818
12	0.497	0.591	0.703	0.780
13	0.475	0.566	0.673	0.745
14	0.457	0.545	0.646	0.716
15	0.441	0.525	0.623	0.689
16	0.425	0.507	0.601	0.666
17	0.412	0.490	0.582	0.645
18	0.399	0.476	0.564	0.625
19	0.388	0.462	0.549	0.608
20	0.377	0.450	0.534	0.591
21	0.368	0.438	0.521	0.576
22	0.359	0.428	0.508	0.562
23	0.351	0.418	0.496	0.549
24	0.343	0.409	0.485	0.537
25	0.336	0.400	0.475	0.526
26	0.329	0.392	0.465	0.515
27	0.323	0.385	0.456	0.505
28	0.317	0.377	0.448	0.496
29	0.311	0.370	0.440	0.487
30	0.305	0.364	0.432	0.478

From "Distribution of Sums of Squares of Rank Differences for Small Samples," E. G. Olds, *Annals of Mathematical Statistics*, Volume 9 (1938). Reproduced with the kind permission of the Editor, *Annals of Mathematical Statistics*.

Table 12 *Sine and Cosine Values for the Functions,*

$$x = \sin\left(\frac{2\pi t}{L}\right) \text{ and } x = \cos\left(\frac{2\pi t}{L}\right), \text{ for } L = 4, 6, \text{ and } 12$$

t	$\sin\left(\frac{2\pi t}{4}\right)$	$\cos\left(\frac{2\pi t}{4}\right)$	$\sin\left(\frac{2\pi t}{6}\right)$	$\cos\left(\frac{2\pi t}{6}\right)$	$\sin\left(\frac{2\pi t}{12}\right)$	$\cos\left(\frac{2\pi t}{12}\right)$
1	1	0	.866	.500	.500	.866
2	0	−1	.866	−.500	.866	.500
3	1	0	.000	−1.000	1.000	.000
4	0	1	−.866	−.500	.866	−.500
5	1	0	−.866	.500	.500	−.866
6	0	−1	.000	1.000	.000	−1.000
7	−1	0	.866	.500	−.500	−.866
8	0	1	.866	−.500	−.866	−.500
9	1	0	.000	−1.000	−1.000	.000
10	0	−1	−.866	−.500	−.866	.500
11	−1	0	−.866	.500	−.500	.866
12	0	1	.000	1.000	.000	1.000

Table 13   *Squares, Cubes, and Roots*

Roots of numbers other than those given directly may be found by the following relations:

$$\sqrt{100n} = 10\sqrt{n}; \quad \sqrt{1000n} = 10\sqrt{10n}; \quad \sqrt{\tfrac{1}{10}n} = \tfrac{1}{10}\sqrt{10n};$$

$$\sqrt{\tfrac{1}{100}n} = \tfrac{1}{10}\sqrt{n}; \quad \sqrt{\tfrac{1}{1000}n} = \tfrac{1}{100}\sqrt{10n}; \quad \sqrt[3]{1000n} = 10\sqrt[3]{n};$$

$$\sqrt[3]{10{,}000n} = 10\sqrt[3]{10n}; \quad \sqrt[3]{100{,}000n} = 10\sqrt[3]{100n};$$

$$\sqrt[3]{\tfrac{1}{10}n} = \tfrac{1}{10}\sqrt[3]{100n}; \quad \sqrt[3]{\tfrac{1}{100}n} = \tfrac{1}{10}\sqrt[3]{10n}; \quad \sqrt[3]{\tfrac{1}{1000}n} = \tfrac{1}{10}\sqrt[3]{n}.$$

n	n^2	$\sqrt{n}$	$\sqrt{10n}$	n	n^2	$\sqrt{n}$	$\sqrt{10n}$
				30	900	5.477 226	17.32051
1	1	1.000 000	3.162 278	31	961	5.567 764	17.60682
2	4	1.414 214	4.472 136	32	1 024	5.656 854	17.88854
3	9	1.732 051	5.477 226	33	1 089	5.744 563	18.16590
4	16	2.000 000	6.324 555	34	1 156	5.830 952	18.43909
5	25	2.236 068	7.071 068	35	1 225	5.916 080	18.70829
6	36	2.449 490	7.745 967	36	1 296	6.000 000	18.97367
7	49	2.645 751	8.366 600	37	1 369.	6.082 763	19.23538
8	64	2.828 427	8.944 272	38	1 444	6.164 414	19.49359
9	81	3.000 000	9.486 833	39	1 521	6.244 998	19.74842
10	100	3.162 278	10.00000	40	1 600	6.324 555	20.00000
11	121	3.316 625	10.48809	41	1 681	6.403 124	20.24846
12	144	3.464 102	10.95445	42	1 764	6.480 741	20.49390
13	169	3.605 551	11.40175	43	1 849	6.557 439	20.73644
14	196	3.741 657	11.83216	44	1 936	6.633 250	20.97618
15	225	3.872 983	12.24745	45	2 025	6.708 204	21.21320
16	256	4.000 000	12.64911	46	2 116	6.782 330	21.44761
17	289	4.123 106	13.03840	47	2 209	6.855 655	21.67948
18	324	4.242 641	13.41641	48	2 304	6.928 203	21.90890
19	361	4.358 899	13.78405	49	2 401	7.000 000	22.13594
20	400	4.472 136	14.14214	50	2 500	7.071 068	22.36068
21	441	4.582 576	14.49138	51	2 601	7.141 428	22.58318
22	484	4.690 416	14.83240	52	2 704	7.211 103	22.80351
23	529	4.795 832	15.16575	53	2 809	7.280 110	23.02173
24	576	4.898 979	15.49193	54	2 916	7.348 469	23.23790
25	625	5.000 000	15.81139	55	3 025	7.416 198	23.45208
26	676	5.099 020	16.12452	56	3 136	7.483 315	23.66432
27	729	5.196 152	16.43168	57	3 249	7.549 834	23.87467
28	784	5.291 503	16.73320	58	3 364	7.615 773	24.08319
29	841	5.385 165	17.02939	59	3 481	7.618 146	24.28992

even # larger
odd # smaller

Table 13 *Continued*

n	n²	√n	√10n	n	n²	√n	√10n
60	3 600	7.745 967	24.49490	**100**	10 000	10.00000	31.62278
61	3 721	7.810 250	24.69818	101	10 201	10.04998	31.78050
62	3 844	7.874 008	24.89980	102	10 404	10.09950	31.93744
63	3 969	7.937 254	25.09980	103	10 609	10.14889	32.09361
64	4 096	8.000 000	25.29822	104	10 816	10.19804	32.24903
65	4 225	8.062 258	25.49510	105	11 025	10.24695	32.40370
66	4 356	8.124 038	25.69047	106	11 236	10.29563	32.55764
67	4 489	8.185 353	25.88436	107	11 449	10.34408	32.71085
68	4 624	8.246 211	26.07681	108	11 664	10.39230	32.86335
69	4 761	8.306 624	26.26785	109	11 881	10.44031	33.01515
70	4 900	8.366 600	26.45751	**110**	12 100	10.48809	33.16625
71	5 041	8.426 150	26.64583	111	12 321	10.53565	33.31666
72	5 184	8.485 281	26.83282	112	12 544	10.58301	33.46640
73	5 329	8.544 004	27.01851	113	12 769	10.63015	33.61547
74	5 476	8.602 325	27.20294	114	12 996	10.67708	33.76389
75	5 625	8.660 254	27.38613	115	13 225	10.72381	33.91165
76	5 776	8.717 798	27.56810	116	13 456	10.77033	34.05877
77	5 929	8.774 964	27.74887	117	13 689	10.81665	34.20526
78	6 084	8.831 761	27.92848	118	13 924	10.86278	34.35113
79	6 241	8.888 194	28.10694	119	14 161	10.90871	34.49638
80	6 400	8.944 272	28.28427	**120**	14 400	10.95445	34.64102
81	6 561	9.000 000	28.46050	121	14 641	11.00000	34.78505
82	6 724	9.055 385	28.63564	122	14 884	11.04536	34.92850
83	6 889	9.110 434	28.80972	123	15 129	11.09054	35 07136
84	7 056	9.165 151	28.98275	124	15 376	11.13553	35 21363
85	7 225	9.219 544	29.15476	125	15 625	11.18034	35.35534
86	7 396	9.273 618	29.32576	126	15 876	11.22497	35.49648
87	7 569	9.327 379	29.49576	127	16 129	11.26943	35.63706
88	7 744	9.380 832	29.66479	128	16 384	11.31371	35.77709
89	7 921	9.433 981	29.83287	129	16 641	11.35782	35.91657
90	8 100	9.486 833	30.00000	**130**	16 900	11.40175	36.05551
91	8 281	9.539 392	30.16621	131	17 161	11.44552	36.19392
92	8 464	9.591 663	30.33150	132	17 424	11.48913	36.33180
93	8 649	9.643 651	30.49590	133	17 689	11.53256	36.46917
94	8 836	9.695 360	30.65942	134	17 956	11.57584	36.60601
95	9 025	9.746 794	30.82207	135	18 225	11.61895	36.74235
96	9 216	9.797 959	30.98387	136	18 496	11.66190	36.87818
97	9 409	9.848 858	31.14482	137	18 769	11.70470	37.01351
98	9 604	9.899 495	31.30495	138	19 044	11.74734	37.14835
99	9 801	9.949 874	31.46427	139	19 321	11.78983	37.28270

Table 13 *Continued*

n	n²	√n	√10n	n	n²	√n	√10n
140	19 600	11.83216	37.41657	**180**	32 400	13.41641	42.42641
141	19 881	11.87434	37.54997	181	32 761	13.45362	42.54409
142	20 164	11.91638	37.68289	182	33 124	13.49074	42.66146
143	20 449	11.95826	37.81534	183	33 489	13.52775	42.77850
144	20 736	12.00000	37.94733	184	33 856	13.56466	42.89522
145	21 025	12.04159	38.07887	185	34 225	13.60147	43.01163
146	21 316	12.08305	38.20995	186	34 596	13.63818	43.12772
147	21 609	12.12436	38.34058	187	34 969	13.67479	43.24350
148	21 904	12.16553	38.47077	188	35 344	13.71131	43.35897
149	22 201	12.20656	38.60052	189	35 721	13.74773	43.47413
150	22 500	12.24745	38.72983	**190**	36 100	13.78405	43.58899
151	22 801	12.28821	38.85872	191	36 481	13.82027	43.70355
152	23 104	12.32883	38.98718	192	36 864	13.85641	43.81780
153	23 409	12.36932	39.11521	193	37 249	13.89244	43.93177
154	23 716	12.40967	39.24283	194	37 636	13.92839	44.04543
155	24 025	12.44990	39.37004	195	38 025	13.96424	44.15880
156	24 336	12.49000	39.49684	196	38 416	14.00000	44.27189
157	24 649	12.52996	39.62323	197	38 809	14.03567	44.38468
158	24 964	12.56981	39.74921	198	39 204	14.07125	44.49719
159	25 281	12.60952	39.87480	199	39 601	14.10674	44.60942
160	25 600	12.64911	40.00000	**200**	40 000	14.14214	44.72136
161	25 921	12.68858	40.12481	201	40 401	14.17745	44.83302
162	26 244	12.72792	40.24922	202	40 804	14.21267	44.94441
163	26 569	12.76715	40.37326	203	41 209	14.24781	45.05552
164	26 806	12.80625	40.49691	204	41 616	14.28286	45.16636
165	27 225	12.84523	40.62019	205	42 025	14.31782	45.27693
166	27 556	12.88410	40.74310	206	42 436	14.35270	45.38722
167	27 889	12.92285	40.86563	207	42 849	14.38749	45.49725
168	28 224	12.96148	40.98780	208	43 264	14.42221	45.60702
169	28 561	13.00000	41.10961	209	43 681	14.45683	45.71652
170	28 900	13.03840	41.23106	**210**	44 100	14.49138	45.82576
171	29 241	13.07670	41.35215	211	44 521	14.52584	45.93474
172	29 584	13.11488	41.47288	212	44 944	14.56022	46.04346
173	29 929	13.15295	41.59327	213	45 369	14.59452	46.15192
174	30 276	13.19091	41.71331	214	45 796	14.62874	46.26013
175	30 625	13.22876	41.83300	215	46 225	14.66288	46.36809
176	30 976	13.26650	41.95235	216	46 656	14.69694	46.47580
177	31 329	13.30413	42.07137	217	47 089	14.73092	46.58326
178	31 684	13.34166	42.19005	218	47 524	14.76482	46.69047
179	32 041	13.37909	42.30829	219	47 961	14.79865	46.79744

Table 13 *Continued*

n	n²	√n	√10n	n	n²	√n	√10n
220	48 400	14.83240	46.90416	**260**	67 600	16.12452	50.99020
221	48 841	14.86607	47.01064	261	68 121	16.15549	51.08816
222	49 284	14.89966	47.11688	262	68 644	16.18641	51.18594
223	49 729	14.93318	47.22288	263	69 169	16.21727	51.28353
224	50 176	14.96663	47.32864	264	69 696	16.24808	51.38093
225	50 625	15.00000	47.43416	**265**	70 225	16.27882	51.47815
226	51 076	15.03330	47.53946	266	70 756	16.30951	51.57519
227	51 529	15.06652	47.64452	267	71 289	16.34013	51.67204
228	51 984	15.09967	47.74935	268	71 824	16.37071	51.76872
229	52 441	15.13275	47.85394	269	72 361	16.40122	51.86521
230	52 900	15.16575	47.95832	**270**	72 900	16.43168	51.96152
231	53 361	15.19868	48.06246	271	73 441	16.46208	52.05766
232	53 824	15.23155	48.16638	272	73 984	16.49242	52.15362
233	54 289	15.26434	48.27007	273	74 529	16.52271	52.24940
234	54 756	15.29706	48.37355	274	75 076	16.55295	52.34501
235	55 225	15.32971	48.47680	**275**	75 625	16.58312	52.44044
236	55 696	15.36229	48.57983	276	76 176	16.61235	52.53570
237	56 169	15.39480	48.68265	277	76 729	16.64332	52.63079
238	56 644	15.42725	48.78524	278	77 284	16.67333	52.72571
239	57 121	15.45962	48.88763	279	77 841	16.70329	52.82045
240	57 600	15.49193	48.98979	**280**	78 400	16.73320	52.91503
241	58 081	15.52417	49.09175	281	78 961	16.76305	53.00943
242	58 564	15.55635	49.19350	282	79 524	16.79286	53.10367
243	59 049	15.58846	49.29503	283	80 089	16.82260	53.19774
244	59 536	15.62050	49.39636	284	80 656	16.85230	53.29165
245	60 025	15.65248	49.49747	**285**	81 225	16.88194	53.38539
246	60 516	15.68439	49.59839	286	81 796	16.91153	53.47897
247	61 009	15.71623	49.69909	287	82 369	16.94107	53.57238
248	61 504	15.74902	49.79960	288	82 944	16.97056	53.66563
249	62 001	15.77973	49.89990	289	83 521	17.00000	53.75872
250	62 500	15.81139	50.00000	**290**	84 100	17.02939	53.85165
251	63 001	15.84298	50.09990	291	84 681	17.05872	53.94442
252	63 504	15.87451	50.19960	292	85 264	17.08801	54.03702
253	64 009	15.90597	50.29911	293	85 849	17.11724	54.12947
254	64 516	15.93738	50.39841	294	86 436	17.14643	54.22177
255	65 025	15.96872	50.49752	**295**	87 025	17.17556	54.31390
256	65 536	16.00000	50.59644	296	87 616	17.20465	54.40588
257	66 049	16.03122	50.69517	297	88 209	17.23369	54.49771
258	66 564	16.06238	50.79370	298	88 804	17.26268	54.58938
259	67 081	16.09348	50.89204	299	89 401	17.29162	54.68089

Table 13 *Continued*

n	n^2	$\sqrt{n}$	$\sqrt{10n}$	n	n^2	$\sqrt{n}$	$\sqrt{10n}$
300	90 000	17.32051	54.77226	**340**	115 600	18.43909	58.30952
301	90 601	17.34935	54.86347	341	116 281	18.46619	58.39521
302	91 204	17.37815	54.95453	342	116 964	18.49324	58.48077
303	91 809	17.40690	55.04544	343	117 649	18.52026	58.56620
304	92 416	17.43560	55.13620	344	118 336	18.54724	58.65151
305	93 025	17.46425	55.22681	345	119 025	18.57418	58.73670
306	93 636	17.49286	55.31727	346	119 716	18.60108	58.82176
307	94 249	17.52142	55.40758	347	120 409	18.62794	58.90671
308	94 864	17.54993	55.49775	348	121 104	18.65476	58.99152
309	95 481	17.57840	55.58777	349	121 801	18.68154	59.07622
310	96 100	17.60682	55.67764	**350**	122 500	18.70829	59.16080
311	96 721	17.63519	55.76737	351	123 201	18.73499	59.24525
312	97 344	17.66352	55.85696	352	123 904	18.76166	59.32959
313	97 969	17.69181	55.94640	353	124 609	18.78829	59.41380
314	98 596	17.72005	56.03570	354	125 316	18.81489	59.49790
315	99 225	17.74824	56.12486	355	126 025	18.84144	59.58188
316	99 856	17.77639	56.21388	356	126 736	18.86796	59.66574
317	100 489	17.80449	56.30275	357	127 449	18.89444	59.74948
318	101 124	17.83255	56.39149	358	128 164	18.92089	59.83310
319	101 761	17.86057	56.48008	359	128 881	18.94730	59.91661
320	102 400	17.88854	56.56854	**360**	129 600	18.97367	60.00000
321	103 041	17.91647	56.65686	361	130 321	19.00000	60.08328
322	103 684	17.94436	56.74504	362	131 044	19.02630	60.16644
323	104 329	17.97220	56.83309	363	131 769	19.05256	60.24948
324	104 976	18.00000	56.92100	364	132 496	19.07878	60.33241
325	105 625	18.02776	57.00877	365	133 225	19.10497	60.41523
326	106 276	18.05547	57.09641	366	133 956	19.13113	60.49793
327	106 929	18.08314	57.18391	367	134 689	19.15724	60.58052
328	107 584	18.11077	57.27128	368	135 424	19.18333	60.66300
329	108 241	18.13836	57.35852	369	136 161	19.20937	60.74537
330	108 900	18.16590	57.44563	**370**	136 900	19.23538	60.82763
331	109 561	18.19341	57.53260	371	137 641	19.26136	60.90977
332	110 224	18.22087	57.61944	372	138 384	19.28730	60.99180
333	110 889	18.24829	57.70615	373	139 129	19.31321	61.07373
334	111 556	18.27567	57.79273	374	139 876	19.33908	61.15554
335	112 225	18.30301	57.87918	375	140 625	19.36492	61.23724
336	112 896	18.33030	57.96551	376	141 376	19.39072	61.31884
337	113 569	18.35756	58.05170	377	142 129	19.41649	61.40033
338	114 244	18.38478	58.13777	378	142 884	19.44222	61.48170
339	114 921	18.41195	58.22371	379	143 641	19.46792	61.56298

Table 13 *Continued*

n	n²	√n	√10n	n	n²	√n	√10n
380	144 400	19.49359	61.64414	**420**	176 400	20.49390	64.80741
381	145 161	19.51922	61.72520	421	177 241	20.51828	64.88451
382	145 924	19.54482	61.80615	422	178 084	20.54264	64.96153
383	146 689	19.57039	61.88699	423	178 929	20.56696	65.03845
384	147 456	19.59592	61.96773	424	179 776	20.59126	65.11528
385	148 225	19.62142	62.04837	425	180 625	20.61553	65.19202
386	148 996	19.64688	62.12890	426	181 476	20.63977	65.26868
387	149 769	19.67232	62.20932	427	182 329	20.66398	65.34524
388	150 544	19.69772	62.28965	428	183 184	20.68816	65.42171
389	151 321	19.72308	62.36986	429	184 041	20.71232	65.49809
390	152 100	19.74842	62.44998	**430**	184 900	20.73644	65.57439
391	152 881	19.77372	62.52999	431	185 761	20.76054	65.65059
392	153 664	19.79899	62.60990	432	186 624	20.78461	65.72671
393	154 449	19.82423	62.68971	433	187 489	20.80865	65.80274
394	155 236	19.84943	62.76942	434	188 356	20.83267	65.87868
395	156 025	19.87461	62.84903	435	189 225	20.85665	65.95453
396	156 816	19.89975	62.92853	436	190 096	20.88061	66.03030
397	157 609	19.92486	63.00794	437	190 969	20.90454	66.10598
398	158 404	19.94994	63.08724	438	191 844	20.92845	66.18157
399	159 201	19.97498	63.16645	439	192 721	20.95233	66.25708
400	160 000	20.00000	63.24555	**440**	193 600	20.97618	66.33250
401	160 801	20.02498	63.32456	441	194 481	21.00000	66.40783
402	161 604	20.04994	63.40347	442	195 364	21.02380	66.48308
403	162 409	20.07486	63.48228	443	196 249	21.04757	66.55825
404	163 216	20.09975	63.56099	444	197 136	21.07131	66.63332
405	164 025	20.12461	63.63961	445	198 025	21.09502	66.70832
406	164 836	20.14944	63.71813	446	198 916	21.11871	66.78323
407	165 649	20.17424	63.79655	447	199 809	21.14237	66.85806
408	166 464	20.19901	63.87488	448	200 704	21.16601	66.93280
409	167 281	20.22375	63.95311	449	201 601	21.18962	67.00746
410	168 100	20.24864	64.03124	**450**	202 500	21.21320	67.08204
411	168 921	20.27313	64.10928	451	203 401	21.23676	67.15653
412	169 744	20.29778	64.18723	452	204 304	21.26029	67.23095
413	170 569	20.32240	54.26508	453	205 209	21.28380	67.30527
414	171 396	20.34699	64.34283	454	206 116	21.30728	67.37952
415	172 225	20.37155	64.42049	455	207 025	21.33073	67.45369
416	173 056	20.39608	64.49806	456	207 936	21.35416	67.52777
417	173 889	20.42058	64.57554	457	208 849	21.37756	67.60178
418	174 724	20.44505	64.65292	458	209 764	21.40093	67.67570
419	175 561	20.46949	64.73021	459	210 681	21.42429	67.74954

Table 13 *Continued*

n	n²	√n	√10n	n	n²	√n	√10n
460	211 600	21.44761	67.82330	**500**	250 000	22.36068	70.71068
461	212 521	21.47091	67.89698	501	251 001	22.38303	70.78135
462	213 444	21.49419	67.97058	502	252 004	22.40536	70.85196
463	214 369	21.51743	68.04410	503	253 009	22.42766	70.92249
464	215 296	21.54066	68.11755	504	254 016	22.44994	70.99296
465	216 225	21.56386	68.19091	505	255 025	22.47221	71.06335
466	217 156	21.58703	68.26419	506	256 036	22.49444	71.13368
467	218 089	21.61018	68.33740	507	257 049	22.51666	71.20393
468	219 024	21.63331	68.41053	508	258 064	22.53886	71.27412
469	219 961	21.65641	68.48957	509	259 081	22.56103	71.34424
470	220 900	21.67948	68.55655	**510**	260 100	22.58318	71.41428
471	221 841	21.70253	68.62944	511	261 121	22.60531	71.48426
472	222 784	21.72556	68.70226	512	262 144	22.62742	71.55418
473	223 729	21.74856	68.77500	513	263 169	22.64950	71.62402
474	224 676	21.77154	68.84766	514	264 196	22.67157	71.69379
475	225 625	21.79449	68.92024	515	265 225	22.69361	71.76350
476	226 576	21.81742	68.99275	516	266 256	22.71563	71.83314
477	227 529	21.84033	69.06519	517	267 289	22.73763	71.90271
478	228 484	21.86321	69.13754	518	268 324	22.75961	71.97222
479	229 441	21.88607	69.20983	519	269 361	22.78157	72.04165
480	230 400	21.90890	69.28203	**520**	270 400	22.80351	72.11103
481	231 361	21.93171	69.35416	521	271 441	22.82542	72.18033
482	232 324	21.95450	69.42622	522	272 484	22.84732	72.24957
483	233 289	21.97726	69.49820	523	273 529	22.86919	72.31874
484	234 256	22.00000	69.57011	524	274 576	22.89105	72.38784
485	235 225	22.02272	69.64194	525	275 625	22.91288	72.45688
486	236 196	22.04541	69.71370	526	276 676	22.93469	72.52586
487	237 169	22.06808	69.78539	527	277 729	22.95648	72.59477
488	238 144	22.09072	69.85700	528	278 784	22.97825	72.66361
489	239 121	22.11334	69.92853	529	279 841	23.00000	72.73239
490	240 100	22.13594	70.00000	**530**	280 900	23.02173	72.80110
491	241 081	22.15852	70.07139	531	281 961	23.04344	72.86975
492	242 064	22.18107	70.14271	532	283 024	23.06513	72.93833
493	243 049	22.20360	70.21396	533	284 089	23.08679	73.00685
494	244 036	22.22611	70.28513	534	285 156	23.10844	73.07530
495	245 025	22.24860	70.35624	535	286 225	23.13007	73.14369
496	246 016	22.27106	70.42727	536	287 296	23.15167	73.21202
497	247 009	22.29350	70.49823	537	288 369	23.17326	73.28028
498	248 004	22.31591	70.56912	538	289 444	23.19483	73.34848
499	249 001	22.33831	70.63993	539	290 521	23.21637	73.41662

Table 13 *Continued*

n	n²	√n	√10n	n	n²	√n	√10n
540	291 600	23.23790	73.48469	**580**	336 400	24.08319	76.15773
541	292 681	23.25941	73.55270	581	337 561	24.10394	76.22336
542	293 764	23.28089	73.62065	582	338 724	24.12468	76.28892
543	294 849	23.30236	73.68853	583	339 889	24.14539	76.35444
544	295 936	23.32381	73.75636	584	341 056	24.16609	76.41989
545	297 025	23.34524	73.82412	585	342 225	24.18677	76.48529
546	298 116	23.36664	73.89181	586	343 396	24.20744	76.55064
547	299 209	23.38803	73.95945	587	344 569	24.22808	76.61593
548	300 304	23.40940	74.02702	588	345 744	24.24871	76.68116
549	301 401	23.43075	74.09453	589	346 921	24.26932	76.74634
550	302 500	23.45208	74.16198	**590**	348 100	24.28992	76.81146
551	303 601	23.47339	74.22937	591	349 281	24.31049	76.87652
552	304 704	23.49468	74.29670	592	350 464	24.33105	76.94154
553	305 809	23.51595	74.36397	593	351 649	24.35159	77.00649
554	306 916	23.53720	74.43118	594	352 836	24.37212	77.07140
555	308 025	23.55844	74.49832	595	354 025	24.39262	77.13624
556	309 136	23.57965	74.56541	596	355 216	24.41311	77.20104
557	310 249	23.60085	74.63243	597	356 409	24.43358	77.26578
558	311 364	23.62202	74.69940	598	357 604	24.45404	77.33046
559	312 481	23.64318	74.76630	599	358 801	24.47448	77.39509
560	313 600	23.66432	74.83315	**600**	360 000	24.49490	77.45967
561	314 721	23.68544	74.89993	601	361 201	24.51530	77.52419
562	315 844	23.70654	74.96666	602	362 404	24.53569	77.58866
563	316 969	23.72762	75.03333	603	363 609	24.55606	77.65307
564	318 096	23.74868	75.09993	604	364 816	24.57641	77.71744
565	319 225	23.76973	75.16648	605	366 025	24.59675	77.78175
566	320 356	23.79075	75.23297	606	367 236	24.61707	77.84600
567	321 489	23.81176	75.29940	607	368 449	24.63737	77.91020
568	322 624	23.83275	75.36577	608	369 664	24.65766	77.97435
569	323 761	23.85372	75.43209	609	370 881	24.67793	78.03845
570	324 900	23.87467	75.49834	**610**	372 100	24.69818	78.10250
571	326 041	23.89561	75.56454	611	373 321	24.71841	78.16649
572	327 184	23.91652	75.63068	612	374 544	24.73863	78.23043
573	328 329	23.93742	75.69676	613	375 769	24.75884	78.29432
574	329 476	23.95830	75.76279	614	376 996	24.77902	78.35815
575	330 625	23.97916	75.82875	615	378 225	24.79919	78.42194
576	331 776	24.00000	75.89466	616	379 456	24.81935	78.48567
577	332 929	24.02082	75.96052	617	380 689	24.83948	78.54935
578	334 084	24.04163	76.02631	618	381 924	24.85961	78.61298
579	335 241	24.06242	76.09205	619	383 161	24.87971	78.67655

Table 13 *Continued*

n	n²	√n	√10n	n	n²	√n	√10n
620	384 400	24.89980	78.74008	**660**	435 600	25.69047	81.24038
621	385 641	24.91987	78.80355	661	436 921	25.70992	81.30191
622	386 884	24.93993	78.86698	662	438 244	25.72936	81.36338
623	388 129	24.95997	78.93035	663	439 569	25.74879	81.42481
624	389 376	24.97999	78.99367	664	440 896	25.76820	81.48620
625	390 625	25.00000	79.05694	**665**	442 225	25.78759	81.54753
626	391 876	25.01999	79.12016	666	443 556	25.80698	81.60882
627	393 129	25.03997	79.18333	667	444 889	25.82634	81.67007
628	394 384	25.05993	79.24645	668	446 224	25.84570	81.73127
629	395 641	25.07987	79.30952	669	447 561	25.86503	81.79242
630	396 900	25.09980	79.37254	**670**	448 900	25.88436	81.85353
631	398 161	25.11971	79.43551	671	450 241	25.90367	81.91459
632	399 424	25.13961	79.49843	672	451 584	25.92296	81.97561
633	400 689	25.15949	79.56130	673	452 929	25.94224	82.03658
634	401 956	25.17936	79.62412	674	454 276	25.96151	82.09750
635	403 225	25.19921	79.68689	**675**	455 625	25.98076	82.15838
636	404 496	25.21904	79.74961	676	456 976	26.00000	82.21922
637	405 769	25.23886	79.81228	677	458 329	26.01922	82.28001
638	407 044	25.25866	79.87490	678	459 684	26.03843	82.34076
639	408 321	25.27845	79.93748	679	461 041	26.05763	82.40146
640	409 600	25.29822	80.00000	**680**	462 400	26.07681	82.46211
641	410 881	25.31798	80.06248	681	463 761	26.09598	82.52272
642	412 164	25.33772	80.12490	682	465 124	26.11513	82.58329
643	413 449	25.35744	80.18728	683	466 489	26.13427	82.64381
644	414 736	25.37716	80.24961	684	467 856	26.15339	82.70429
645	416 025	25.39685	80.31189	**685**	469 225	26.17250	82.76473
646	417 316	25.41653	80.37413	686	470 596	26.19160	82.82512
647	418 609	25.43619	80.43631	687	471 969	26.21068	82.88546
648	419 904	25.45584	80.49845	688	473 344	26.22975	82.94577
649	421 201	25.47548	80.56054	689	474 721	26.24881	83.00602
650	422 500	25.49510	80.62258	**690**	476 100	26.26785	83.06624
651	423 801	25.51470	80.68457	691	477 481	26.28688	83.12641
652	425 104	25.53429	80.74652	692	478 864	26.30589	83.18654
653	426 409	25.55386	80.80842	693	480 249	26.32489	83.24662
654	427 716	25.57342	80.87027	694	481 636	26.34388	83.30666
655	429 025	25.59297	80.93207	**695**	483 025	26.36285	83.36666
656	430 336	25.61250	80.99383	**696**	484 416	26.38181	83.42661
657	431 649	25.63201	81.05554	**697**	485 809	26.40076	83.48653
658	432 964	25.65151	81.11720	698	487 204	26.41969	83.54639
659	434 281	25.67100	81.17881	699	488 601	26.43861	83.60622

Table 13 *Continued*

n	n^2	$\sqrt{n}$	$\sqrt{10n}$	n	n^2	$\sqrt{n}$	$\sqrt{10n}$
700	490 000	26.45751	83.66600	**740**	547 600	27.20294	86.02325
701	491 401	26.47640	83.72574	741	549 081	27.22132	86.08136
702	492 804	26.49528	83.78544	742	550 564	27.23968	86.13942
703	494 209	26.51415	83.84510	743	552 049	27.25803	86.19745
704	495 616	26.53300	83.90471	744	553 536	27.27636	86.25543
705	497 025	26.55184	83.96428	745	555 025	27.29469	86.31338
706	498 436	26.57066	84.02381	746	556 516	27.31300	86.37129
707	499 849	26.58947	84.08329	747	558 009	27.33130	86.42916
708	501 264	26.60827	84.14274	748	559 504	27.34959	86.48699
709	502 681	26.62705	84.20214	749	561 001	27.36786	86.54479
710	504 100	26.64583	84.26150	**750**	562 500	27.38613	86.60254
711	505 521	26.66458	84.32082	751	564 001	27.40438	86.66026
712	506 944	26.68333	84.38009	752	565 504	27.42262	86.71793
713	508 369	26.70206	84.43933	753	567 009	27.44085	86.77557
714	509 796	26.72078	84.49852	754	568 516	27.45906	86.83317
715	511 225	26.73948	84.55767	755	570 025	27.47726	86.89074
716	512 656	26.75818	84.61678	756	571 536	27.49545	86.94826
717	514 089	26.77686	84.67585	757	573 049	27.51363	87.00575
718	515 524	26.79552	84.73488	758	574 564	27.53180	87.06320
719	516 961	26.81418	84.79387	759	576 081	27.54995	87.12061
720	518 400	26.83282	84.85281	**760**	577 600	27.56810	87.17798
721	519 841	26.85144	84.91172	761	579 121	27.58623	87.23531
722	521 284	26.87006	84.97058	762	580 644	27.60435	87.29261
723	522 729	26.88866	85.02941	763	582 169	27.62245	87.34987
724	524 176	26.90725	85.08819	764	583 696	27.64055	87.40709
725	525 625	26.92582	85.14693	765	585 225	27.65863	87.46428
726	527 076	26.94439	85.20563	766	586 756	27.67671	87.52143
727	528 529	26.96294	85.26429	767	588 289	27.69476	87.57854
728	529 984	26.98148	85.32292	768	589 824	27.71281	87.63561
729	531 441	27.00000	85.38150	769	591 361	27.73085	87.69265
730	532 900	27.01851	85.44004	**770**	592 900	27.74887	87.74964
731	534 361	27.03701	85.49854	771	594 441	27.76689	87.80661
732	535 824	27.05550	85.55700	772	595 984	27.78489	87.86353
733	537 289	27.07397	85.61542	773	597 529	27.80288	87.92042
734	538 756	27.09243	85.67380	774	599 076	27.82086	87.97727
735	540 225	27.11088	85.73214	775	600 625	27.83882	88.03408
736	541 696	27.12932	85.79044	776	602 176	27.85678	88.09086
737	543 169	27.14774	85.84870	777	603 729	27.87472	88.14760
738	544 644	27.16616	85.90693	778	605 284	27.89265	88.20431
739	546 121	27.18455	85.96511	779	606 841	27.91057	88.26098

Table 13 *Continued*

n	n^2	$\sqrt{n}$	$\sqrt{10n}$	n	n^2	$\sqrt{n}$	$\sqrt{10n}$
780	608 400	27.92848	88.31761	**820**	672 400	28.63564	90.55385
781	609 961	27.94638	88.37420	821	674 041	28.65310	90.60905
782	611 524	27.96426	88.43076	822	675 684	28.67054	90.66422
783	613 089	27.98214	88.48729	823	677 329	28.68798	90.71935
784	614 656	28.00000	88.54377	824	678 976	28.70540	90.77445
785	616 225	28.01785	88.60023	825	680 625	28.72281	90.82951
786	617 796	28.03569	88.65664	826	682 726	28.74022	90.88454
787	619 369	28.05352	88.71302	827	683 929	28.75761	90.93954
788	620 944	28.07134	88.76936	828	685 584	28.77499	90.99451
789	622 521	28.08914	88.82567	829	687 241	28.79236	91.04944
790	624 100	28.10694	88.88194	**830**	688 900	28.80972	91.10434
791	625 681	28.12472	88.93818	831	690 561	28.82707	91.15920
792	627 264	28.14249	88.99428	832	692 224	28.84441	91.21403
793	628 849	28.16026	89.05055	833	693 889	28.86174	91.26883
794	630 436	28.17801	89.10668	834	695 556	28.87906	91.32360
795	632 025	28.19574	89.16277	835	697 225	28.89637	91.37833
796	633 616	28.21347	89.21883	836	698 896	28.91366	91.43304
797	635 209	28.23119	89.27486	837	700 569	28.93095	91.48770
798	636 804	28.24889	89.33085	838	702 244	28.94823	91.54234
799	638 401	28.26659	89.38680	839	703 921	28.96550	91.59694
800	640 000	28.28472	89.44272	**840**	705 600	28.98275	91.65151
801	641 601	28.30194	89.49860	841	707 281	29.00000	91.70605
802	643 204	28.31960	89.55445	842	708 964	29.01724	91.76056
803	644 809	28.33725	89.61027	843	710 649	29.03446	91.81503
804	646 416	28.35489	89.66605	844	712 336	29.05168	91.86947
805	648 025	28.37252	89.72179	845	714 025	29.06888	91.92388
806	649 636	28.39014	89.77750	846	715 716	29.08608	91.97826
807	651 249	28.40775	89.83318	847	717 409	29.10326	92.03260
808	652 864	28.42534	89.88882	848	719 104	29.12044	92.08692
809	654 481	28.44293	89.94443	849	720 801	29.13760	92.14120
810	656 100	28.46050	90.00000	**850**	722 500	29.15476	92.19544
811	657 721	28.47806	90.05554	851	724 201	29.17190	92.24966
812	659 344	28.49561	90.11104	852	725 904	29.18904	92.30385
813	660 969	28.51315	90.16651	853	727 609	29.20616	92.35800
814	662 596	28.53069	90.22195	854	729 316	29.22328	92.41212
815	664 225	28.54820	90.27735	855	731 025	29.24038	92.46621
816	665 856	28.56571	90.33272	856	732 736	29.25748	92.52027
817	667 489	28.58321	90.38805	857	734 449	29.27456	92.57429
818	669 124	28.60070	90.44335	858	736 164	29.29164	92.62829
819	670 761	28.61818	90.49862	859	737 881	29.30870	92.68225

Table 13 *Continued*

n	n²	√n	√10n	n	n²	√n	√10n
860	739 600	29.32576	92.73618	**900**	810 000	30.00000	94.86833
861	741 321	29.34280	92.79009	901	811 801	30.01666	94.92102
862	743 044	29.35984	92.84396	902	813 604	30.03331	94.97368
863	744 769	29.37686	92.89779	903	815 409	30.04996	95.02631
864	746 496	29.39388	92.95160	904	817 216	30.06659	95.07891
865	748 225	29.41088	93.00538	905	819 025	30.08322	95.13149
866	749 956	29.42788	93.05912	906	820 836	30.09983	95.18403
867	751 689	29.44486	93.11283	907	822 649	30.11644	95.23655
868	753 424	29.46184	93.16652	908	824 464	30.13304	95.28903
869	755 161	29.47881	93.22017	909	826 281	30.14963	95.34149
870	756 900	29.49576	93.27379	**910**	828 100	30.16621	95.39392
871	758 641	29.51271	93.32738	911	829 921	30.18278	95.44632
872	760 384	29.52965	93.38094	912	831 744	30.19934	95.49869
873	762 129	29.54657	93.43447	913	833 569	30.21589	95.55103
874	763 876	29.56349	93.48797	914	835 396	30.23243	95.60335
875	765 625	29.58040	93.54143	915	837 225	30.24897	95.65563
876	767 376	29.59730	93.59487	916	839 056	30.26549	95.70789
877	769 129	29.61419	93.64828	917	840 889	30.28201	95.76012
878	770 884	29.63106	93.70165	918	842 724	30.29851	95.81232
879	772 641	29.64793	93.75500	919	844 561	30.31501	95.86449
880	774 400	29.66479	93.80832	**920**	846 400	30.33150	95.91663
881	776 161	29.68164	93.86160	921	848 241	30.34798	95.96874
882	777 924	29.69848	93.91486	922	850 084	30.36445	96.02083
883	779 689	29.71532	93.96808	923	851 929	30.38092	96.07289
884	781 456	29.73214	94.02127	924	853 776	30.39737	96.12492
885	783 225	29.74895	94.07444	925	855 625	30.41381	96.17692
886	784 996	29.76575	94.12757	926	857 476	30.43025	96.22889
887	786 769	29.78255	94.18068	927	859 329	30.44667	96.28084
888	788 544	29.79933	94.23375	928	861 184	30.46309	96.33276
889	790 321	29.81610	94.28680	929	863 041	30.47950	96.38465
890	792 100	29.83287	94.33981	**930**	864 900	30.49590	96.43651
891	793 881	29.84962	94.39280	931	866 761	30.51229	96.48834
892	795 664	29.86637	94.44575	932	868 624	30.52868	96.54015
893	797 449	29.88311	94.49868	933	870 489	30.54505	96.59193
894	799 236	29.89983	94.55157	934	872 356	30.56141	96.64368
895	801 025	29.91655	94.60444	935	874 225	30.57777	96.69540
896	802 816	29.93326	94.65728	936	876 096	30.59412	96.74709
897	804 609	29.94996	94.71008	937	877 969	30.61046	96.79876
898	806 404	29.96665	94.76286	938	879 844	30.62679	96.85040
899	808 201	29.98333	94.81561	939	881 721	30.64311	96.90201

Table 13 *Concluded*

n	n²	√n	√10n	n	n²	√n	√10n
940	883 600	30.65942	96.95360	**970**	940 900	31.14482	98.48858
941	885 481	30.67572	97.00515	971	942 841	31.16087	98.53933
942	887 364	30.69202	97.05668	972	944 784	31.17691	98.59006
943	889 249	30.70831	97.10819	973	946 729	31.19295	98.64076
944	891 136	30.72458	97.15966	974	948 676	31.20897	98.69144
945	893 025	30.74085	97.21111	975	950 625	31.22499	98.74209
946	894 916	30.75711	97.26253	976	952 576	31.24100	98.79271
947	896 809	30.77337	97.31393	977	954 529	31.25700	98.84331
948	898 704	30.78961	97.36529	978	956 484	31.27299	98.89388
949	900 601	30.80584	97.41663	979	958 441	31.28898	98.94443
950	902 500	30.82207	97.46794	**980**	960 400	31.30495	98.99495
951	904 401	30.83829	97.51923	981	962 361	31.32092	99.04544
952	906 304	30.85450	97.57049	982	964 324	31.33688	99.09591
953	908 209	30.87070	97.62172	983	966 289	31.35283	99.14636
954	910 116	30.88689	97.67292	984	968 256	31.36877	99.19677
955	912 025	30.90307	97.72410	985	970 225	31.38471	99.24717
956	913 936	30.91925	97.77525	986	972 196	31.40064	99.29753
957	915 849	30.93542	97.82638	987	974 169	31.41656	99.34787
958	917 764	30.95158	97.87747	988	976 144	31.43247	99.39819
959	919 681	30.96773	97.92855	989	978 121	31.44837	99.44848
960	921 600	30.98387	97.97959	**990**	980 100	31.46427	99.49874
961	923 521	31.00000	98.03061	991	982 081	31.48015	99.54898
962	925 444	31.01612	98.08160	992	984 064	31.49603	99.59920
963	927 369	31.03224	98.13256	993	986 049	31.51190	99.64939
964	929 296	31.04835	98.18350	994	988 036	31.52777	99.69955
965	931 225	31.06445	98.23441	995	990 025	31.54362	99.74969
966	933 156	31.08054	98.28530	996	992 016	31.55947	99.79980
967	935 089	31.09662	98.33616	997	994 009	31.57531	99.84989
968	937 024	31.11270	98.38699	998	996 004	31.59114	99.89995
969	938 961	31.12876	98.43780	999	998 001	31.60696	99.94999
				1000	1000 000	31.62278	100.00000

From *Handbook of Tables for Probability and Statistics*, 2nd ed. Edited by William H. Beyer (Cleveland: The Chemical Rubber Company, 1968). Reproduced by permission of the publishers.

Table 14 Random Numbers

Line/Col.	(1)	(2)	(3)	(4)	(5)	(6)	(7)	(8)	(9)	(10)	(11)	(12)	(13)	(14)
1	10480	15011	01536	02011	81647	91646	69179	14194	62590	36207	20969	99570	91291	90700
2	22368	46573	25595	85393	30995	89198	27982	53402	93965	34095	52666	19174	39615	99505
3	24130	48360	22527	97265	76393	64809	15179	24830	49340	32081	30680	19655	63348	58629
4	42167	93093	06243	61680	07856	16376	39440	53537	71341	57004	00849	74917	97758	16379
5	37570	39975	81837	16656	06121	91782	60468	81305	49684	60672	14110	06927	01263	54613
6	77921	06907	11008	42751	27756	53498	18602	70659	90655	15053	21916	81825	44394	42880
7	99562	72905	56420	69994	98872	31016	71194	18738	44013	48840	63213	21069	10634	12952
8	96301	91977	05463	07972	18876	20922	94595	56869	69014	60045	18425	84903	42508	32307
9	89579	14342	63661	10281	17453	18103	57740	84378	25331	12566	58678	44947	05585	56941
10	85475	36857	53342	53988	53060	59533	38867	62300	08158	17983	16439	11458	18593	64952
11	28918	69578	88231	33276	70997	79936	56865	05859	90106	31595	01547	85590	91610	78188
12	63553	40961	48235	03427	49626	69445	18663	72695	52180	20847	12234	90511	33703	90322
13	09429	93969	52636	92737	88974	33488	36320	17617	30015	08272	84115	27156	30613	74952
14	10365	61129	87529	85689	48237	52267	67689	93394	01511	26358	85104	20285	29975	89868
15	07119	97336	71048	08178	77233	13916	47564	81056	97735	85977	29372	74461	28551	90707
16	51085	12765	51821	51259	77452	16308	60756	92144	49442	53900	70960	63990	75601	40719
17	02368	21382	52404	60268	89368	19885	55322	44819	01188	65255	64835	44919	05944	55157
18	01011	54092	33362	94904	31273	04146	18594	29852	71585	85030	51132	01915	92747	64951
19	52162	53916	46369	58586	23216	14513	83149	98736	23495	64350	94738	17752	35156	35749
20	07056	97628	33787	09998	42698	06691	76988	13602	51851	46104	88916	19509	25625	58104
21	48663	91245	85828	14346	09172	30168	90229	04734	59193	22178	30421	61666	99904	32812
22	54164	58492	22421	74103	47070	25306	76468	26384	58151	06646	21524	15227	96909	44592
23	32639	32363	05597	24200	13363	38005	94342	28728	35806	06912	17012	64161	18296	22851
24	29334	27001	87637	87308	58731	00256	45834	15398	46557	41135	10367	07684	36188	18510
25	02488	33062	28834	07351	19731	92420	60952	61280	50001	67658	32586	86679	50720	94953

Abridged from *Handbook of Tables for Probability and Statistics*, Second Edition, edited by William H. Beyer (Cleveland: The Chemical Rubber Company, 1968). Reproduced by permission of the publishers, The Chemical Rubber Company.

Table 14 *Continued*

26	81525	72295	04839	96423	24878	82651	66566	14778	76797	14780	13300	87074	79666	95725
27	29676	20591	68086	26432	46901	20849	89768	81536	86645	12659	92259	57102	80428	25280
28	00742	57392	39064	66432	84673	40027	32832	61362	99947	96067	64760	64584	96096	98253
29	05366	04213	25669	26422	44407	44048	37937	63904	45766	66134	75470	66520	34693	90449
30	91921	26418	64117	94305	26766	25940	39972	22209	71500	64568	91402	42416	07844	09618
31	00582	04711	87917	77341	42206	35126	74087	99547	81817	42607	43808	76655	62028	76630
32	00725	69884	62797	56170	86324	88072	76222	36086	84637	93161	76038	65855	77919	88006
33	69011	65795	95876	55293	18998	27354	26575	08625	40801	59920	29841	80150	12777	48501
34	25976	57948	29888	88604	67917	48708	18912	82271	63424	69774	33611	54262	85963	03547
35	09763	83473	73577	12908	30883	18317	28290	35797	05998	41688	34952	37888	38917	88050
36	91567	42595	27958	30134	04024	86385	29880	99730	55536	84855	29080	09250	79656	73211
37	17955	56349	90999	49127	20044	59931	06115	20542	18059	02008	73708	83517	36103	42791
38	46503	18584	18845	49618	02304	51038	20655	58727	28168	15475	56942	53389	20562	87338
39	92157	89634	94824	78171	84610	82834	09922	25417	44137	48413	25555	21246	35509	20468
40	14577	62765	35605	81263	39667	47358	56873	56307	61607	49518	89656	20103	77490	18062
41	98427	07523	33362	64270	01638	92477	66969	98420	04880	45585	46565	04102	44880	45709
42	34914	63976	88720	82765	34476	17032	87589	40836	32427	70002	70663	84863	77775	69348
43	70060	28277	39475	46473	23219	53416	94970	25832	69975	94884	19661	72828	00102	66794
44	53976	54914	06990	67245	68350	82948	11398	42878	80287	88267	47363	46634	06541	97809
45	76072	29515	40980	07391	58745	25774	22987	80059	39911	96189	41151	14222	60697	59583
46	90725	52210	83974	29992	65831	38857	50490	83765	55657	14361	31720	57375	56228	41546
47	64364	67412	33339	31926	14883	24413	59744	92351	97473	89286	35931	04110	23726	51900
48	08962	00358	31662	25388	61642	34072	81249	35648	56891	69352	48373	45578	78547	81788
49	95012	68379	93526	70765	10592	04542	76463	54328	02349	17247	28865	14777	62730	92277
50	15664	10493	20492	38391	91132	21999	59516	81652	27195	48223	46751	22923	32261	85653
51	16408	81899	04153	53381	79401	21438	83035	92350	36693	31238	59649	91754	72772	02338
52	18629	81953	05520	91962	04739	13092	97662	24822	94730	06496	35090	04822	86774	98289
53	73115	35101	47498	87637	99016	71060	88824	71013	18735	20286	23153	72924	35165	43040
54	57491	16703	23167	49323	45021	33132	12544	41035	80780	45393	44812	12515	98931	91202
55	30405	83946	23792	14422	15059	45799	22716	19792	09983	74353	68868	30429	70735	25499
56	16631	35006	85900	98275	32388	52390	16815	69298	82732	38480	73817	32523	41961	44437
57	96773	20206	42559	78985	05300	22164	24369	54224	35083	19687	11052	91491	60383	19746
58	38935	64202	14349	82674	66523	44133	00097	35552	35970	19124	63318	29686	03387	59840
59	31624	76384	17403	53363	44167	64486	64758	75366	70654	31601	12614	33072	60332	92325
60	78919	19474	23632	27889	47914	02584	37680	20801	72152	39339	34806	08930	85001	87820
61	03931	33309	57047	74211	63445	17361	62825	39908	05607	91284	68833	25570	38818	46920
62	74426	33278	43972	10119	89917	15665	52872	73823	73144	88662	88970	74492	51805	99378
63	09066	00903	20795	95452	92648	45454	09552	88815	16553	51125	79375	97596	16296	66092
64	42238	12426	87025	14267	20979	04508	64535	31355	86064	29472	47689	05974	52468	16834
65	16153	08002	26504	41744	81959	65642	74240	56302	00033	67107	77510	70625	28725	34191

Table 14 *Concluded*

Line/Col.	(1)	(2)	(3)	(4)	(5)	(6)	(7)	(8)	(9)	(10)	(11)	(12)	(13)	(14)
66	21457	40742	29820	96783	29400	21840	15035	34537	33310	06116	95240	15957	16572	06004
67	21581	57802	02050	89728	17937	37621	47075	42080	97403	48626	68995	43805	33386	21597
68	55612	78095	83197	33732	05810	24813	86902	60397	16489	03264	88525	42786	05269	92532
69	44657	66999	99324	51281	84463	60563	79312	93454	68876	25471	93911	25650	12682	73572
70	91340	84979	46949	81973	37949	61023	43997	15263	80644	43942	89203	71795	99533	50501
71	91227	21199	31935	27022	84067	05462	35216	14486	29891	68607	41867	14951	91696	85065
72	50001	38140	66321	19924	72163	09538	12151	06878	91903	18749	34405	56087	82790	70925
73	65390	05224	72958	28609	81406	39147	25549	48542	42627	45233	57202	94617	23772	07896
74	27504	96131	83944	41575	10573	08619	64482	73923	36152	05184	94142	25299	84387	34925
75	37169	94851	39117	89632	00959	16487	65536	49071	39782	17095	02330	74301	00275	48280
76	11508	70225	51111	38351	19444	66499	71945	05422	13442	78675	84081	66938	93654	59894
77	37449	30362	06694	54690	04052	53115	62757	95348	78662	11163	81651	50245	34971	52924
78	46515	70331	85922	38329	57015	15765	97161	17869	45349	61796	66345	81073	49106	79860
79	30986	81223	42416	58353	21532	30502	32305	86482	05174	07901	54339	58861	74818	46942
80	63798	64995	46563	09785	44160	78128	83091	42865	92520	83531	80377	35909	81250	54238
81	82486	84846	99254	67632	43218	50076	21361	64816	51202	88124	41870	52699	51275	83556
82	21885	32906	92431	09060	64297	51674	64126	62570	26123	05155	59194	52799	28225	85762
83	60336	98782	07408	53458	13564	59089	26445	29789	85205	41001	12535	12133	14645	23541
84	43037	46891	24010	25560	86355	33941	25786	54990	71899	15475	95434	98227	21824	19585
85	97656	63175	89303	16275	07100	92063	21942	18611	47348	20203	18534	03862	78095	50136
86	03299	01221	05418	38982	55758	92237	26759	86367	21216	98442	08303	56613	91511	75928
87	79628	06486	03574	17668	07785	76020	79924	25651	83325	88428	85076	72811	22717	50585
88	85636	68335	47539	03129	65651	11977	02510	26113	99447	68645	34327	15152	55230	93448
89	18039	14367	61337	06177	12143	46609	32989	74014	64708	00533	35398	58408	13261	47908
90	08362	15656	60627	36478	65648	16764	53412	09013	07832	41574	17639	82163	60859	75567
91	79556	29068	04142	16268	15387	12856	66227	38358	22478	73373	88732	09443	82558	05250
92	92608	82674	27072	32534	17075	27698	98204	63863	11951	34648	88022	56148	34925	57031
93	23982	25835	40055	67006	12293	02753	14827	23235	35071	99704	37543	11601	35503	85171
94	09915	96306	05908	97901	28395	14186	00821	80703	70426	75647	76310	88717	37890	40129
95	59037	33300	26695	62247	69927	76123	50842	43834	86654	70959	79725	93872	28117	19233
96	42488	78077	69882	61657	34136	79180	97526	43092	04098	73571	80799	76636	71255	64239
97	46764	86273	63003	93017	31204	36692	40202	35275	57306	55543	53203	18098	47625	86684
98	03237	45430	55417	63282	90816	17349	88298	90183	36000	78406	06216	95787	42579	90730
99	86591	81482	52667	61582	14972	90053	89534	76036	49199	43716	97548	04379	46370	28672
100	38534	01715	94964	87288	65080	43772	39560	12918	86537	62738	19636	51132	25739	56947

Glossary

Acceptance region (Chapters 6, 8, and 9)
In the theory of hypothesis testing, the set of values of the test statistic such that if the test statistic assumes one of these values, the null hypothesis is accepted.

Arithmetic mean (throughout the text)
The arithmetic mean of a set of n measurements $y_1, y_2, y_3, \ldots, y_n$ is equal to the sum of the measurements divided by n.

Autocorrelation (Chapter 15)
The internal correlation between members of a time series separated by a constant interval of time.

Autoregression (Chapter 15)
The generation of a series of observations whereby the value of each observation is partly dependent upon the values of those which have immediately preceded it. A regression structure where lagged process values assume the role of the independent variables.

Bayes' law (Chapters 4 and 10)
If A is some event that occurs if and only if either B or $\bar{B}$ occurs, then

$$P(B|A) = \frac{P(A|B)P(B)}{P(A|B)P(B) + P(A|\bar{B})P(\bar{B})}$$

$$= \frac{P(AB)}{P(A)}.$$

Binomial experiment (Chapters 6 and 11)
An experiment consisting of n independent trials in which the outcome at each trial is a "success" with probability p or a "failure" with probability $1 - p$. We are interested in y, the number of successes observed during the n trials.

Binomial probability distribution (Chapter 6)
A probability distribution giving the probability of y, the number of successes observed during the n trials of a binomial experiment.

$$p(y) = C_y^n p^y (1 - p)^{n-y}, \qquad y = 0, 1, 2, \ldots, n.$$

Central limit theorem (Chapters 7, 8, 9, and 11)

If random samples of n observations are drawn from a population with finite mean, μ, and standard deviation, σ, then, when n is large, the sample mean $\bar{y}$, will be approximately normally distributed with mean equal to μ and standard deviation $\sigma/\sqrt{n}$. The approximation will become more and more accurate as n becomes large.

Coefficient of correlation (Chapter 12)

A number between -1 and $+1$ which measures the linear dependence between two random variables. The limiting values, -1 and $+1$, indicate perfect negative and positive correlation, respectively, while a correlation of zero suggests a complete lack of association between the two variables.

Combination (Chapter 4)

The number of combinations of n objects taken r at a time is denoted by the symbol C_r^n, where

$$C_r^n = \frac{n!}{r!(n-r)!}.$$

Complement of an event (Chapter 4)

The complement of an event A is the collection of all sample points in the sample space and not in A. The complement of A is denoted by the the symbol $\bar{A}$, and $P(\bar{A}) = 1 - P(A)$.

Compound event (Chapter 4)

An event composed of two or more simple events.

Conditional probability (Chapter 4)

The probability of occurrence of an event A given that another event, B, has occurred is called the conditional probability of A given B and is denoted as $P(A|B)$. Computationally, $P(A|B) = P(AB)/(P(B)$.

Confidence coefficient (Chapters 8 and 9)

A probability associated with a confidence interval expressing the probability that the interval will include the parameter value under study.

Confidence interval (Chapters 8 and 9)

An interval, computed from sample values. Intervals so constructed will straddle the estimated parameter $100(1 - \alpha)$ percent of the time in repeated sampling. The quantity, $(1 - \alpha)$, is called the *confidence coefficient*.

Contingency table (Chapter 16)

A two-way table for classifying the members of a group according to two or more identifying characteristics.

Continuous random variable (Chapter 5)

A random variable defined over, and assuming the infinitely large number of values associated with, the points on a line interval.

Correlogram (Chapter 15)

A graph illustrating the autocorrelations between members of a time series (vertical axis) for different separations in time k (horizontal axis).

Cost of uncertainty (Chapter 10)

The smallest expected opportunity loss in a decision-making problem involving uncertainty.

Critical value (Chapters 6, 8, and 9)

In a statistical test of an hypothesis, the critical value is the value of the test statistic that separates the rejection and acceptance regions.

Cyclic effect (Chapter 15)
A periodic movement in a time series that occurs as a result of stimuli from the economy and is generally not predictable.

Degrees of freedom (throughout the text)
The number of linearly independent observations in a set of n observations. The degrees of freedom is equal to n minus the number of restrictions placed upon the entire data set.

Dependent variable (Chapters 12 and 15)
The predictand in a regression equation. The variable of interest in a regression equation which is said to be functionally related to one or more independent or predictor variables.

Design of an experiment (throughout the text)
The sampling procedure which enables the gathering of a maximum amount of information for a given expenditure.

Discrete random variable (Chapter 5)
A random variable over a finite or a countably infinite number of points.

Empirical rule (throughout the text)
Given a distribution of measurements that is approximately bell-shaped, the interval

$\mu \pm \sigma$ will contain approximately 68 percent of the measurements,

$\mu \pm 2\sigma$ will contain approximately 95 percent of the measurements,

$\mu \pm 3\sigma$ will contain approximately 99.7 percent of the measurements.

Event (Chapter 4)
A collection of sample points.

Expected value (Chapters 5 and 10)
Let y be a discrete random variable with probability distribution $p(y)$ and let $E(y)$ represent the expected value of y. Then

$$E(y) = \sum_y yp(y),$$

where the elements are summed over all values of the random variable y.

Exponential smoothing (Chapters 14 and 15)
In time-series analysis, a computational method which averages the first t time-series process values by increasingly weighting out the contribution of remote process values. The exponentially smoothed process value at time t is

$$S_t = \alpha \sum_{i=0}^{t-2} (1 - \alpha)^i y_{t-i} + (1 - \alpha)^{t-1} y_1,$$

where $y_1, y_2, \ldots, y_t$ are the process values and α is the smoothing constant ($0 \le \alpha \le 1$).

Frequency distribution (Chapter 3)
A specification of the way in which, probabilistically, the relative frequencies of members of a population are distributed according to the values of the variates they exhibit.

Frequency histogram (Chapter 3)
A specification of the way in which the frequencies of members of a population are distributed according to the values of the variates they exhibit.

Independent variable (Chapter 12)
A nonrandom variable related to the response in a regression equation. One or more independent variables may be functionally related to the dependent variable. They are used in the regression equation to predict or estimate the value of the dependent variable.

Index number (Chapter 14)

A quantity that shows the changes over time from some base period to a reference period of a variable process that is not directly observable in practice.

Intersection (Chapter 4)

If A and B are two events in a sample space, S, the intersection of A and B is the event composed of all sample points that are in both A and B.

Laspeyres' Index (Chapter 14)

If the prices of a set of commodities in a base year are $p_{o1}, p_{o2}, p_{o3}, \ldots$ and $q_{o1}, q_{o2}, q_{o3}, \ldots$ are the quantities sold in the base period and $p_{n1}, p_{n2}, p_{n3}, \ldots$ are the prices of the same commodities in a given year, the Laspeyres Index is

$$L = \frac{\sum(p_n q_o)}{\sum(p_o q_o)}.$$

Linear correlation (Chapter 12)

A measure of the strength of the linear relationship between two variables, y and x, which is independent of their respective scales of measurement. Linear correlation is commonly measured by the coefficient of correlation.

Median (Chapter 3)

The median of a set of n measurements $y_1, y_2, y_3, \ldots, y_n$ is the value of y that falls in the middle when the measurements are arranged in order of magnitude.

Method of least squares (Chapters 12 and 15)

A technique for the estimation of the coefficients in a regression equation that chooses as the regression coefficients the values that minimize the sum of squares of the deviations of the observed values of y from those predicted.

Minimax decicion (Chapter 10)

In a decision analysis, the minimax decision is the decision to select the action whose maximum opportunity loss is the smallest.

Mode (Chapter 3)

The mode of a set of measurements $y_1, y_2, y_3, \ldots, y_n$ is the value of y that occurs with the greatest frequency. The mode is not necessarily unique.

Moving average (Chapter 14)

An average computed from a time series by selecting process values from k consecutive time periods, summing these values, and dividing by k. The moving average is then located at the middle of the span of the k values which contributed to it.

Mutually exclusive events (Chapter 4)

Two events, A and B, are said to be mutually exclusive if the event AB contains no sample points.

Nonparametric hypothesis (Chapter 17)

A statistical hypothesis that does not involve population parameters but is concerned with the form of the population frequency distribution.

Normal probability distribution (throughout the text)

A symmetric, bell-shaped probability distribution of infinite range represented by the equation

$$f(y) = \frac{1}{\sigma\sqrt{2\pi}}\, e^{-(y-\mu)^2/2\sigma^2} \qquad (-\infty < y < \infty),$$

where μ is the mean and σ^2 the variance of the distribution.

Null hypothesis (throughout the text)
In a statistical test of an hypothesis, the null hypothesis is a statement of the hypothesis to be tested.

One-tailed statistical test (Chapters 8 and 9)
A statistical test of an hypothesis in which the rejection region is wholly located at one end of the distribution of the test statistic.

Operating characteristic curve (Chapters 8, 9, and 11)
A plot of the probability of accepting the null hypothesis when some alternative is true (the probability of a type II error) against various possible values of the alternative hypothesis.

Opportunity loss (Chapter 10)
The opportunity loss L_{ij} for selecting action a_i given that the state of nature s_j is, in effect, the difference between the maximum profit that could be realized if s_j occurs and the profit obtained by selecting action a_i.

Optimal decision (Chapter 10)
In a decision analysis, the optimal decision is a decision to select the action that maximizes the decision maker's objective.

Paired-difference test (Chapter 9)
A test to compare two populations using pairs of elements, one from each population, that are matched and hence nearly alike. Thus the test involves two samples of equal size where the members of one sample can be paired off against members of the other. Comparisons are made within the relatively homogeneous pairs (blocks).

Parameter (throughout the text)
A numerical descriptive measure for the population.

Parametric hypothesis (throughout the text)
A statistical hypothesis about a population parameter.

Payoff table (Chapter 10)
In a decision analysis, the payoff table is a two-way table displaying the payoffs, either opportunity losses or profits, for selecting a particular action given that a specific state of nature is in effect.

Period of a cyclic or seasonal effect (Chapters 14 and 15)
The number of time points between identifiable points of recurrence—between peaks and valleys—in a time series. The number of time points for one complete cycle or for a complete seasonal pattern to be exhibited.

Permutation (Chapter 4)
An ordered arrangement of r distinct objects. The number of n objects selected in groups of size r is denoted by P_r^n, where

$$P_r^n = n(n-1)(n-2)\cdots(n-r+1).$$

Point estimator (Chapters 8 and 9)
A single number computed from a sample and used as an estimator of a population parameter.

Poisson probability distribution (Chapter 6)
A model for finding the probability of count data resulting from any experiment where the count, y, represents the number of rare events observed in a given unit of time or space.

Population (throughout the text)
A finite or infinite collection of measurements or individuals that comprises the totality of all possible measurements within the context of a particular statistical study.

Posterior probability (Chapters 4 and 10)

The probability of an event at the outset of an experiment, p_1, might be modified to p_2 in light of experimental evidence. The posterior probability, p_2, is usually determined by employing Bayes' theorem.

Power of a statistical test (Chapters 8, 9, and 17)

The probability that the statistical test rejects the null hypothesis when some particular alternative is true. Power equals $1 - \beta$. The power is greatest when the probability of a type II error is least.

Prior probability (Chapter 10)

The probability representing the likelihood of occurrence of an event before experimental evidence relevant to the event has been observed. The unconditional probabilities used in Bayes' theorem are prior probabilities.

Probability distribution (Chapter 5)

A formula, table, or graph providing the probability associated with each value of the random variable if the random variable is discrete or providing the fraction of measurements in the population falling in specific intervals if it is continuous.

Probability of an event (throughout the text)

The probability of an event A is equal to the sum of the probabilities of the sample points in A. (*See also* Subjective probability.)

Qualitative variables (Chapters 11, 13, and 16)

Variables concerning qualitative or attribute data. The data are not necessarily representable in numerical form.

Quantitative variables (Chapters 11, 13, and 16)

Variables concerning quantitative or measurement data. The data can be represented on a numerical scale.

Random sample (throughout the text)

Suppose that a sample of n measurements is drawn from a population consisting of N total measurements. If the sampling is conducted in such a way that each of the C_n^N samples has an equal probability of being selected, the sampling is said to be random and the result is said to be a random sample.

Random variable (throughout the text)

A numerical-valued function defined over a sample space.

Randomized block design (Chapter 13)

An experimental design whereby treatments are randomly assigned within a set of blocks to eliminate bias.

Range (Chapters 3 and 11)

The range of a set of n measurements $y_1, y_2, y_3, \ldots, y_n$ is the difference between the largest and smallest measurement.

Rank-sum test (Chapter 17)

A nonparametric statistical test proposed by F. Wilcoxon for comparing two population distributions by first ordering the combined observations from the samples selected from each population and then summing the ranks of the observations from one of the samples.

Regression equation (Chapter 12)

An equation expressing the dependence of the mean of a dependent variable, y, on one or more independent or predictor variables, $x_1, x_2, x_3, \ldots$.

Rejection region (Chapters 6, 8, and 9)

In the theory of hypothesis testing, the rejection region is the set of values such that if the test statistic assumes one of these values, the null hypothesis is rejected.

Relative efficiency (Chapter 17)
A method of comparing two test procedures by computing the ratio of the sample sizes for the two test procedures required to achieve the same α and β for a given alternative to the null hypothesis.

Run (Chapters 11 and 17)
In a series of observations of attributes, the occurrence of an uninterrupted series of the same attribute is called a run. A run can be of length 1.

Sample (throughout the text)
Any subset of a population.

Seasonal effect (Chapters 14 and 15)
The rises and falls in a time series which always occur at a particular time of year because of changes in the seasons.

Sign test (Chapter 17)
A nonparametric statistical test of significance depending on the signs of differences between matched or unmatched pairs and not on the magnitudes of the differences.

Sinusoidal forecasting model (Chapter 15)
A least-squares forecasting model using sine and cosine functions of time as the independent or predictor variables in order to pick up cyclic effects over time which may exist within the time series.

Skewed distribution (Chapter 3)
A frequency distribution that is not symmetric about its mean.

Smoothed statistic (Chapters 14 and 15)
In time-series analysis, the smoothed statistic is an average of a set of process values, usually a moving average or an exponentially smoothed statistic, used to represent a time series after eliminating random fluctuations.

Smoothing constant (Chapters 14 and 15)
The constant, α, $(0 \leqslant \alpha \leqslant 1)$, employed to weight out the contribution of remote process values in an exponential smoothing scheme.

Standard deviation (throughout the text)
The standard deviation of a set of n measurements $y_1, y_2, y_3, \ldots, y_n$ is equal to the positive square root of the variance of the measurements.

State of nature (Chapter 10)
In a decision analysis, the states of nature are the uncertain events over which the decision maker has no control.

Statistic (throughout the text)
A value computed from sample measurements, usually but not always as an estimator of some population parameter.

Student's t distribution (Chapters 9 and 12)
The distribution of $t = (\bar{y} - \mu)/s/\sqrt{n}$ for samples drawn from a normally distributed population and used for making inferences concerning population means when the population variance σ^2 is unknown and the sample size n is small.

Subjective probability (Chapters 4 and 10)
A probability based partially or totally on the personal judgment and intuition of the decision maker, with little or no base in empirical evidence.

Symmetric distribution (Chapter 3)
A frequency distribution for which the values of the distribution equidistant from the mean occur with equal frequency.

Systematic sampling (Chapter 13)
A method of selecting a sample by a systematic method as opposed to random sampling, such as selecting each tenth name from a list or by sampling every third resident in every other block in an area sample.

Tchebysheff's theorem (Chapter 3)
Given a number k greater than or equal to 1 and a set of n measurements $y_1, y_2, \ldots, y_n$, at least $(1 - 1/k^2)$ of the measurements will lie within k standard deviations of their mean.

Test statistic (Chapters 6 and 9)
A function of a sample of observations which provides a basis for testing a statistical hypothesis.

Time series (Chapters 14 and 15)
Any sequence of measurements taken on a variable process over time. Usually illustrated as a graph whose vertical coordinate gives the value of the random response plotted against time on the horizontal axis.

Treatment (Chapter 13)
A stimulus that is applied in order to observe its effect on the experimental situation. A treatment may refer to a physical substance, a procedure, or anything capable of controlled application according to the requirements of the experiment.

Two-tailed statistical test (Chapters 8 and 9)
A statistical test of an hypothesis in which the rejection region is separated by the acceptance region and is located in both ends of the distribution of the test statistic.

Type I error (throughout the text)
In the statistical test of an hypothesis, the error incurred by rejecting the null hypothesis when the null hypothesis is true.

Type II error (throughout the text)
In the statistical test of an hypothesis, the error incurred by accepting the null hypothesis when the null hypothesis is false and some alternative to the null hypothesis is true.

Unbiased estimator (Chapter 9)
An unbiased estimator $\hat{\theta}$ of a parameter θ is an estimator for which the expected value of $\hat{\theta}$ is equal to θ. That is, $E(\hat{\theta}) = \theta$.

Union (Chapter 4)
If A and B are two events in a sample space S, the union of A and B is the event containing all sample points in A or B or both.

Variance (throughout the text)
The variance of a set of n measurements $y_1, y_2, \ldots, y_n$ is the average of the square of the deviations of the measurements about their mean.

Venn diagram (Chapter 4)
A diagram portraying graphically each sample event as a sample point in a sample space S.

Reference

Kendall, M. G., and W. R. Buckland, *A Dictionary of Statistical Terms*. New York: Hafner Publishing Company, Inc., 1967.

Answers to Exercises

Chapter 2

1. (a) 3   (b) 7   (c) 11   (d) -1 (e) -5
   (f) $4a^2 + 3$ (g) $-4a + 3$ (h) $f(1-y) = 7 - 4y$

2. (a) 3/2   (b) $-8/3$ (c) 0   (d) $\dfrac{x^2-1}{x}$ (e) $\dfrac{a^2 - 2a}{a-1}$

3. (a) 7   (b) $a^2 + 2ab + b^2 - a - b + 1$

4. (a) 0   (b) undefined   (c) 3   (d) $-(a^2 + 1)$

5. $1, (1-a)$

6. (a) 1/4   (b) -6 (c) $3/x^2 - 3/x + 1$ (d) $3x^2 - 21x + 37$

7. (a) 2   (b) 2   (c) 2

8.ʾ 36

9. 18

10. 30

11. $5(x^2 + 6)$

12. $6x^2 + 55$

13. $3(3 + 2i)$

14. $10(y^2 + 1)$

15. $y_1 + y_2 - 3$

16. $\sum\limits_{i=1}^{n} y_i - na$

17. $\sum\limits_{i=}^{n} y_i^2 - 2a \sum\limits_{i=1}^{n} y_i + na^2$

18. 36

19. -29

20. 431

21. 610

22. 654

23. 649.077

Chapter 3

3. under \$5,000.00, 24%;   \$5,000.00 – \$9,999.00, 59%;
   \$10,000 – \$19,999.00, 10%;   \$20,000.00 or over, 7%

4. One possible set of class boundaries is 0–11.9, 12–23.9, 24–35.9, 36–47.9,
   48–59.9, 60–71.9, 72–83.9, 84–95.9, 96–107.9, 108–119.9.

7. One possible set of class boundaries is 0–3.999, 4–7.999, 8–11.999, 12–15,999, 16–19.999.

8. $\bar{y} = 5, s^2 = 6.8, s = 2.6$

9. $\bar{y} = -1, s^2 = 8.67, s = 2.94$

11. $\bar{y} = 36.32, s^2 = 51.14, s = 7.15$

14. 68% and 92%

15. $\bar{y} = 7.12, s^2 = .017, s = .13$

16. $\bar{y} \pm s = 7.12 \pm 13 = 6.99\text{–}7.25, 80\%; \bar{y} \pm 2s = 6.86\text{–}7.38, 100\%$

18. (a) $\bar{y} \pm 2s = 600 \pm 140$, at least 3/4; $\bar{y} \pm 3s = 600 \pm 210$, at least 8/9
    (b) $\bar{y} \pm s = 530\text{–}670, 68\%$　　　(c) 2½%

19 68%

20. 16%

22. (a) $\bar{y} = 69.57, s^2 = 239.56, s = 15.48$　　　(b) lower quartile = 60;
    upper quartile = 81; 90th percentile = 86

23. 70%, 96.67%

24. $70/15.48 = 4.52; 4$

25. $28/7.15 = 3.92$

26. (a) $28/s = 4, s = 7$　　　(b) $58/s = 4, s = 17.5$

27. 95%

28. 16.15%

29. $.5/4 = .125, .263; s = .132$

30. $\bar{y} \approx 1,705.05, s^2 \approx 1,779,548.30$

31. (a) $\bar{y} \approx 251.36, s \approx 95.47$　　　(b) 68%

32. $346.00

Supplementary Exercises

1. $\bar{y} = 19.3, S^2 = 8.127$

2. $10.20

3. $4,752.23 \text{ cm}^3$

4. 10 degrees centigrade

5. 16%

Chapter 4

1. Let W represent the woman, M_1 the older man, and M_2 the younger man.
   Let (M_1W) represent that M_1 is selected chairman, W is selected secretary.
   - (a) $S = [(WM_1), (WM_2), (M_1W), (M_1M_2), (M_2W), (M_2M_1)]$
   - (b) $A = [(M_1W), (M_1M_2)]$
   - (c) $B = [(M_1W), (M_1M_2), (M_2W), (M_2M_1)]$
   - (d) $C = [(M_1W), (M_2W)]$
   - (e) $D = [(M_1W)]$
   - (f) $E = [(M_1W), (M_1M_2), (M_2W), (M_2M_1)]$

2. $P(A) = 2/6, P(B) = 4/6, P(C) = 2/6, P(D) = 1/6, P(E) = 4/6$

3. Let (121) represent first patient selected first station, second patient second station, and third patient first station.
   - (a) $S = [(111), (112), (121), (211), (122), (212), (221), (222)]$
   - (b) $A = [(112), (121), (211), (122), (212), (221)]$
   - (c) $P(A) = 6/8$

4. $4/6$ 5. $6/10, 1/10$

6. (a) $3/9$ (b) $4/9$ (c) $2/9$

7. (a) $5/6$ (b) $1/6$

8. (a) $4/8$ (b) $1/8$

9. $P(A) = .28, P(B) = .38, P(E) = .12, P(F) = .64, P(AF) = .16, P(DG) = .02,$ $P(AB) = 0, P(A \text{ or } F) = .76, P(C \text{ or } F) = .70, P(F \text{ or } G) = .88,$ $P(A \text{ or } B \text{ or } C) = .84, P(A \text{ or } B \text{ or } F) = .86$

10. $P(A_1) = .475, P(B_3) = .25, P(A_1B_4) = .125, P(B_1|A_3) = .5, P(A_2 \text{ or } B_3) = .45,$ $P(B_1 \text{ or } B_4) = .625, P(B_2B_4) = 0$

11. (a) $.5$ (b) $.6$ (c) $.8$

12. $P(A|B) = 1/2, P(A|C) = 1/2, P(B|C) = 1, P(AB) = 1/3, P(AC) = 1/6,$ $P(BC) = 1/3, P(A \text{ or } B) = 2/3.$ A and B are neither independent nor mutually exclusive.

13. $P(A) = .4, P(B) = .5, P(AB) = .25, P(A \cup B) = .65, P(A|B) = .5$

14. (a) $.09$ (b) $.1$ (c) $.1$ (d) $.2$

15. (a) $2/5$ (b) $3/5$ (c) $2/25$ (d) $17/25$ (e) yes

16. $1/3$

17. (a) $5/6$ (b) $25/36$ (c) $11/36$

18. (a) $.81$ (b) $.01$ (c) $.99$

19. 1/4

20. 4/5

21. 27/64, 54/64

22. (a) .73   (b) .27

23. .05

24. 5/16

25. 9/23

26. (a) 1/10   (b) 4/10

27. 4/12

28. .7599

29. .68

30. 44/89

Chapter 5

1. $P(0) = .64, \quad P(1) = .32, \quad P(2) = .04$

2. $P(0) = 1/6, \quad P(1) = 4/6, \quad P(2) = 1/6$

3. $P(0) = .81, \quad P(1) = .18, \quad P(2) = .01$

6. $\mu = 1.4$

7. $\mu = 1.8$

8. $\mu = 23/12 = 1.92, \quad \sigma^2 = 131/144 = .91$

9. $\sigma = .95, P(\mu - 2\sigma < y < \mu + 2\sigma) = 11/12$

10. $\mu = 1, \quad \sigma^2 = 1/3 = .33$

11. $\sigma = .58, \quad P(\mu - 2\sigma < y < \mu + 2\sigma) = 1$

12. $P(1) = 3/10, \quad P(2) = 6/10, \quad P(3) = 1/10, \quad P(Y = 2 \text{ or } 3) = 7/10$

13. $1.75

14. $120

15. $P(0) = .064, \quad P(1) = .288, \quad P(2) = .432, P(3) = .216, \quad P(Y = 2 \text{ or } 3) = .648$

16. $140

17. $2,050

Chapter 6

2. (a) yes   (b) yes   (c) no   (d) yes   (e) no

3. (a) $p(0) = 1/8, \quad p(1) = 3/8, \quad p(2) = 3/8, \quad p(3) = 1/8$
    (c) $E(y) = 1.5, \quad \sigma = .866$

4. (a) $p(0) = .729$, $p(1) = .243$, $p(2) = .027$, $p(3) = .001$
    (c) $E(y) = .3$, $\sigma = .520$

5. .32805, .99999

6. $E(y) = 100$, $V(y) = 90$, $81 \leqslant y \leqslant 119$, $(\mu \pm 2\sigma)$

7. (a)   .9606   (b)   .9994

8. (a)   .01   (b)   .0523

9. Answers to Exercises 9–12 come from the binomial tables: (a)   1.000
    (b)   .590   (c)   .168   (d)   .031   (e)   .000

10. (a)   1.000   (b)   .919   (c)   .528   (d)   .188   (e)   .000

11. (a)   1.000   (b)   .736   (c)   .149   (d)   .011   (e)   .000

12. (a)   1.000   (b)   .764   (c)   .033   (d)   .000   (e)   .000

13. (a)   .575   (b)   1.000   (c)   .380

14. .608

15. $E(y) = 2$, $\sigma = 1.34$, $0–4.68$, $(\mu \pm 2\sigma)$

16. (a)   .002   (b)   .630

17. (a)   .387   (b)   .651   (c)   .264

18. (a)   .873   (b)   .027   (c)   .127

19. (a)   .178   (b)   .416

20. .3

21. (a)   1.25   (b)   .277   (c)   .127

22. (a)   .151   (b)   .302

23. (a)   .07   (b)   .383

24. No, the probability of this occurrence is .1536.

25. (b)   1/32   (c)   .7378

26. (a)   32/32,768   (b)   .833

27. (a)   242/32,768   (b)   .602

28. The probability of this occurrence is .044.

29. (b)   .343   (c)   .657

30. (a)   .919   (b)   .358

31. (a) n is large, p or $1 - p$ is small   (b)   model for count data when counts
                                                                 are rare events.

32. (a) no, $n = 10$ too small   (b) yes, Poisson approximation of the binomial
    appropriate   (c) yes   (d) no, $p = .4$ too large

33. .135

34. (a) .0067   (b) .1755   (c) .2650

35. .2149

36. (a) .3679   (b) .2642

37. .0067

38. .1991

39. .0025

40. (a) .0067   (b) .4405   (c) .9596

41. 5

Chapter 7

1. $n = 126$, $p = 1/126$

2. $\mu = 5.2$, $\sigma_y = 0.85$

3. (a) .3849   (b) .3159   6. (a) .4251   (b) .4778

4. (a) .4452   (b) .2734   7. (a) .3227   (b) .1586

5. (a) .4265   (b) .1628   8. (a) .0730   (b) .8623

9. .7734   11. 0   13. .2268   15. 1.645

10. .9115   12. 1.10   14. −1.645   16. 2.575

17. (a) .4332   (b) .4772   (c) .0401   (d) .5   (e) .8276
    (f) .1359

18. (a) .5   (b) .5   (c) .7653   (d) .2295   (e) .3218
    (f) .0548

19. (a) .50   (b) .3264   (c) .3472

20. (a) .1056   (b) .1056   (c) 44.72

21. .0668   23. .0401

22. .1056   24. 85.36 minutes

25. $32,800.00

26. (a) $116.60   (b) security B

27. (a) .578 (b) .5752

28. (a) .421 (b) .4013

29. (a) .444 (b) .4599

30. (a) .6129 (b) .9686

31. (a) .0287 (b) .4041

32. .9554

33. yes, $z = 3.26$

34. yes, $z = 1.88$

35. .9929

36. .8980

37. (a) .9977 (b) .0150

38. .9474

39. .1600

40. $\mu = 7.301$

41. (a) .0071 (b) .0571

42. 383.5

43. no, $z = -1.26$

44. .3307

45. 1072

46. (a) 20 (b) 4 (c) .9913

47. .3557

48. .1314

49. (a) .0228 (b) .00052

Chapter 8

3. (a) two-tailed (b) one-tailed (c) one-tailed (d) two-tailed
   (e) one-tailed

4. 1280 ± 28.4

5. .1587

6. .92 ± .0172

7. $1256.64 < \mu < 1303.36$

8. $.898 < p < .942$

9. $.075 < p < .125$

10. 34 ± .59

11. $6.50 ± $0.70

12. .12 ± .0889

13. .69 ± .08

14. −$42.00 ± $3.92

15. 5.4 ± .277

16. 1.7 ± .494

17. $1.294 < \mu_1 - \mu_2 < 2.106$

18. −.04 ± .104

19. $256, 4,751 < \mu < 4,849$

20. 40,000

21. 6,400

22. 21

23. (a) $H_0: \mu = 1,100$, $H_a: \mu < 1,100$ (b) $z < -1.645$
    (c) $z = -190$; yes, reject H_0

24. (a) .2 ± .08 (b) 400

25. 25   26. 72   27. 400

28. $z = 2.53$; yes, reject H_0

29. $z = 1.58$; do not reject H_0

30. $z = 4.71$; yes, reject H_0

31. .1342

32. $z = -1$; no, do not reject H_0

33. $z = -2.4$; reject H_0

34. $z = -2$; yes, reject H_0

35. $z = 5.24$; yes, reject H_0

36. $z = 4.0$; yes, reject H_0

37. $z = -3.1$; reject H_0

38. $z = 7.02$; reject H_0

39. $z = 3.12$; reject H_0

40. $z = -1.41$; do not reject H_0

41. $z = 6.88$; yes, reject H_0

42. $z = 1.68$; no, do not reject H_0

43. $z = -2.5$; reject H_0

44. $z = 4.0$; yes, reject H_0

45. (a) .06 ± .024 (b) 586

46. 22 ± 1.55

47. (a) $H_0: p = .2, H_a: p > .2$ (b) $\alpha = .0749$

48. .1151, .0228

49. $z = 1.5$; no, do not reject H_0

50. (a) 1.96 (c) 1.96 ± .11 (d) 1.96 ± .14 (e) use smaller
    z value, reduced confidence (g) reduce the width (h) 49,000 ± 3,511
    (i) $z = 2.94$; reject H_0

Chapter 9

3. $t = -1.34$; do not reject H_0

4. 795 ± 7.95

5. 31

6. $\$2.48 < \mu < \$2.82$

7. $-\$39.85 < \mu < -\$34.43$

8. (a) 24.7 ± 1.05

9. $t = 2.635$; reject H_0

10. $7.1 \pm .0696$

11. $t = 1.39$; no, do not reject H_0

12. $t = -1.44$; do not reject H_0

13. 3.68 ± 1.57

14. $t = 2.80$; reject H_0

15. $26.4 \pm .88$

16. (a) 11.3 ± 1.44

17. $t = -1.955$; do not reject H_0

18. $2.43 \pm .85$

19. 19

21. $t = 1.861$; reject H_0

22. $t = -1.8$; no, do not reject H_0

23. $t = 3.04$; yes, reject H_0

24. $t = 1.57$; do not reject H_0

25. $t = 5.28$; yes, reject H_0

26. (a) $t = -1.71$; do not reject H_0 (b) $-.75 \pm .771$

27. (a) $t = 2.50$; reject H_0 (b) $-.875 \pm .829$

28. $-.875 \pm .965$

29. $t = 9.57$; reject H_0

30. (a) 25.89 ± 4.99 (b) 25.9 ± 4.73 (c) wider with paired data

32. $t = 2.573$; reject H_0

33. $.01 \pm .0099$

34. (a) $t = 1.58$; do not reject H_0 (b) $n_1 = n_2 = 238$

35. $29.3 < \sigma^2 < 391.0$

36. (a) $X^2 = 12.6$; do not reject H_0 (b) $.00896 < \sigma^2 < .05814$

38. $F = 2.41 > 2.22$; yes, reject H_0

39. $X^2 = 22.45$; reject H_0

40. $F = 2.12$; do not reject H_0

41. $t = 2.42$; yes, reject H_0

42. (c) $t = 1.53$; do not reject H_0 (d) 600 ± 889
    (e) $24,000,000.00   (f) $24,000,000.00 \pm $35,558,208.00
    (g) $720,000.00   (h) $720,000.00 \pm $1,066,759.00

Chapter 10   .

3. See Section 10.6.

9. (c)   6   (d)   6   (e)   2.07

10. (a) A (b) $37,000.00

11. $0.59

12. (a)   .2, .5, .3   (c) $65,500.00   (d)   5,000.00

13. (b)   firm B

14. at least $1/6$

15. the Japanese supplier; $1,000.00 less expensive

16. (a)   tetra-essolan   (b) $128.00   (c) $22.00

17. 3

18. (a)   method B   (b) $60.00

19. (b)   Select the new machine.   (c) $17,500.00

20. Buy the $7,000.00 machine.

21. Internal production is $22,150.00 less expensive.

22. (a)   .013, .235, .573, .179   (b)   di-essolon
    (c) $22.00 - $6.39 = $15.61

23. (a)   .102, .392, .451, .055   (b)   di-essolan
    (c) $22.00 - $21.10 = $.90

24. Use di-essolan if 2 or more defectives in 25 are found.

25. method B; posterior probabilities are .121, .611, and .268

26. yes, publish

27. (a)   do not publish   (b)   publish

Chapter 11

1. See Section 11.1.

5. (a) $\bar{X}$ chart: UCL = 5.57, LCL = 4.83
        R chart: UCL = 1.2, LCL = 0
    (c) yes, days 1, 3, 4, and 5

6. (a) .7495   (b) 2505

7. (a) $\bar{X}$ chart: 2.44 ± .56;
        R chart: 1.68 ± 1.50
    (b) greater than 3.00

8. (a) .9082   (b) 908.2

9. (a) $\bar{p}$ = .032, UCL = .0848, LCL = 0   (b) .0848

10. .7806   (*Hint:* Use Poisson approximation.)

11. yes

12. (a) UCL = .081, LCL = 0   (b) .1894

13. .8212

14. (a) $c = 5$, UCL = 11.708, LCL = 0

15. (a) (25, 5)   (b) (25, 5)

16. (b) (25, 3)   (c) (25, 1)

18. (a) Increasing n decreases both the producer's risk and the consumer's risk.
    (b) Increasing a increases the consumer's risk and decreases the producer's risk.

19. $a = 1$

20. $n = 18$; reject lot if $\bar{y} < 92.44$

21. $n = 23$; reject lot if $\bar{y} < .94175$ or if $\bar{y} > 1.05825$

22. (a) .03210   (b) .04365   (c) .03680   (d) .04570

Chapter 12

3. All points lie on a straight line.

4. σ^2 ; the variance of the random error, ϵ

5. (a) y intercept = 6, slope = 3

6. y intercept = $-5/3$, slope = 2/3

7. (a) $\hat{y} = 1.0 + .7x$ (c)   .3666   (d) $t = 3.656$; yes, reject H_0

8. (a) $\hat{y} = 9.45 - 1.09x$ (c)   2.734   (d) $t = -3.844$; yes, reject H_0

9. $\hat{y} = 307.92 + 34.58x$

10. $t = 5.68$; yes, reject H_0; no

11. $21.02 < \beta_1 < 48.14$

12. $-1.66 < \beta_1 < -.52$

13. 5.09 ± 1.383

14. 515.417 ± 33.21

15. 411.667 ± 102.846

16. 7.27 ± 3.95

18. $r = -.8635$

19. $r = .8739$

20. (a) $\hat{y} = 1.732 \pm .445x$ (c) $S^2 = .066$

21. $t = 6.77$; yes, reject H_0

22. $r^2 = .9016$

23. $4.847 \pm .298$

24. (a) $\hat{y} = 4,600 - .317x$ (c) $S^2 = 19.03$

25. $-.419 < \beta_1 < -.215$

26. 30.165 ± 2.500

27. 30.165 ± 8.290

28. $r = -.8718$

29. (a) $\hat{y} = 4.3 + 1.5x$ (c) $S^2 = 1.5308$ (d) $t = 3.834$

30. (a) $\hat{y} = .8 + 1.4x$ (c) $S = .37$

31. 6.4 ± 1.34

32. $1.4 \pm .28$

33. no, $t = 2.06$

34. (a)   .99   (b)   98%

35. (a) $\hat{y} = 44.371 + 13.512x$ (c) $S^2 = 27.6233$ (d) $t = 4.554$

36. 67%

37. 79.5022 ± 2.819 38. 79.5022 ± 9.932

Supplementary Exercises

2. See Section 12.12.

3. $\hat{y} = 3.70 + 5.17x_1 + 5.48x_2$

4. (a)   .95   (b)   15.592

5. (a) $\hat{y} = -2.491 + .099x_1 + .029x_2 + .086x_3$
    (b)   78.38%
    (c) $F = 19.345$; reject H_0 and conclude that at least one useful predictor exists
    (d) $x_2 =$ elevation; largest F value
    (e) $x_1 =$ area; smallest F value

6. $.099 \pm .101$

7. \$3,469.00

8. (a) $\hat{y} = -1.51361 - .02879x_1 + 1.22394x^2 + .80526x^3$
    (b)   71.75%

Chapter 13

2. (a)   blocks out controllable variation   (b)   blocks are less homogeneous

3. SSE $= 18,864$, $F = 10.83$; reject H_0

4. SSE $= 200$, $F = 2.00$; do not reject H_0

5. (a) $219.63 < \mu_1 < 230.37$ (b) $-1.08 < \mu_1 - \mu_2 < 17.74$

6. SSE $= 4.98$; no, do not reject H_0

7. (a) $6.79 < \mu_A < 8.41$ (b) $5.58 < \mu_B < 17.74$
    (c) $-.36 < \mu_A - \mu_B < 2.30$ (d)   no, they are not independent

8. (a)   yes   (b)   randomized block design

9. no difference among sales areas (blocking ineffective); significant difference between promotional techniques

10. SSE $= 4.99$ (a)   no, do not reject H_0 (b)   no, do not reject H_0

11. $F = 7.33$; yes, reject H_0; blocking causes a loss of degrees of freedom for estimating σ^2. Blocking may produce a slight loss of information if the block-to-block variation is small.

12. (a)   randomized block design   (b)   SSE $= 58.91$ (c) $F = 23.57$; yes, reject H_0 (d)   minimize bias due to fatigue, etc.

13. 2.875 ± 2.35, $.505 < \mu_C - \mu_D < 5.245$

14.

SOURCE	d.f.	SS	MS	F
Dwellings	4	584.27	146.07	123.79
Models	2	18.90	9.45	8.01
Error	8	9.43	1.18	
Totals	14	612.60		

15. (a) randomized block design (b) SSE = 58.91 (c) $F = 23.57$; yes, reject H_0 (d) No, the judge's response may have been influenced by site location considerations not included within the study.

16. (a) SSE = .571, SST = 1.212, $F = 11.68$; yes, evidence exists to indicate a difference in mean recognition time.
   (b) $t = -2.73$ (7 degrees of freedom); evidence exists to indicate a difference in mean recognition times for layouts A and D.

17.

SOURCE	d.f.	SS	MS	F
Blocks	3	.140	.047	6.62
Treatments	4	.787	.197	27.70
Error	12	.085	.0071	
Totals	19	1.012		

$F = 27.70$; reject the hypothesis of no difference in treatment (layout) means

Chapter 14

2. (a) long-term trend, cyclic effect (b) long-term trend, seasonal effect (c) long-term trend, seasonal effect (d) long-term trend (e) long-term trend, seasonal effect.

3. (b) long-term trend, seasonal effect

6. no, not when random variation is excessive

9. The 12-month moving average model best eliminates the seasonal pattern. To remove the seasonal pattern using a moving average model, we must have $M = 12$, since, in this exercise, there are 12 time points in a complete seasonal period.

12. No, his income has risen only 31.2%. His "real" income in 1974 has actually dropped 11.8% since 1960.

13. (a) ground beef: 100, 114, 124, 136, 143; round steak: 100, 101, 106, 115, 121; rib roast: 100, 105, 110, 120, 129; ham: 100, 107, 102, 99, 91; frying chicken: 100, 109, 122, 138, 153; pork chops: 100, 86, 95, 102, 114
   (b) 100, 102, 107, 114, 120

14. 100, 102, 108, 116, 123

15. 126

16. 124

17. (a)   110, 118, 121   (b)   110, 118, 121

18. 110, 118, 121

19. electricity: 100, 113, 115; oil: 132, 136, 145; gas: 107, 109, 109; oil has increased in cost the greatest, natural gas, the least.

20. (a)   110, 120   (b)   110, 120

Chapter 15

2.   The underlying social and economic conditions may change over time. Latent variables may exist. See Section 15.3.

4.   long term: EWMA if a seasonal pattern exists; short term: regression models. In general, it depends on the type of time series we wish to forecast, the components inherent in the series, and the stability of social and economic conditions over time.

5.   (a)   sinusoidal model or EWMA   (b)   multiple linear regression model
     (c)   growth model, or multiple exponential smoothing model   (d)   EWMA
     (e)   multiple linear regression model, or multiple exponential smoothing model

6.   (a)   necessary to provide uniformity and consistency in analysis
     (b)   smoothing models

7.   (a)   multiple linear regression model or multiple exponential smoothing model
     (b)   EWMA or sinusoidal model

8.   The subjective information should be used to modify the forecast according to the nature of the information. The linear growth trend cannot be expected to continue in the light of legal restrictions against the use of nonreturnable containers.

9. $\hat{y} = 17.3458 + .332t$

10. yes

11. SSE = 25.4686 (Exercise 9)   SSE = 16.2941 (Exercise 10)

Supplementary Exercises

1. $\hat{y} = 2.1723 + .9149Y_{t-1}$

2. *Original Time Series with*
    Brown's Linear Model Superimposed

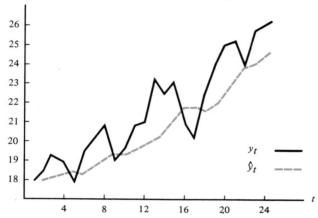

3. SSE (Exercise 7) = 25.4686   SSE (Exercise 8) = 16.2941
    SSE (Supplementary Exercise 1) = 32.2088
    SSE (Supplementary Exercise 2) = 54.65355

4. *Original Series with Brown's Multiple*
    Exponential Smoothing Model Superimposed

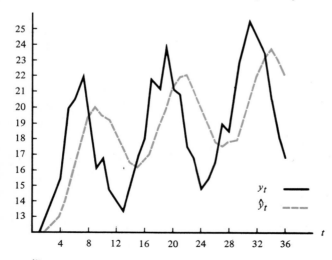

5. *True Values of the Series with EWMA
   1-Month Forecasts Superimposed*

   (Note that forecasts may vary with choice of initial values.)

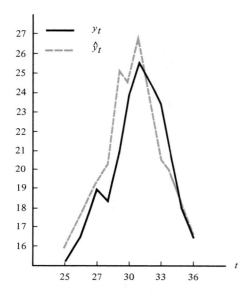

6. *True Values of the Series with EWMA
   3-Month Forecasts Superimposed*

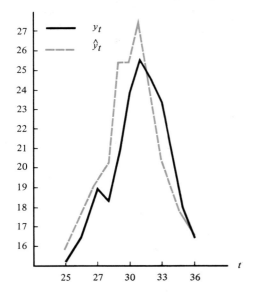

7. *True Values of the Series
with Forecasts Superimposed*

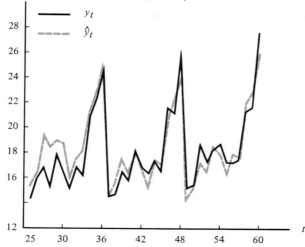

9. (a) $\hat{\beta_0} = .11526, \hat{\beta_1} = .01051, \hat{\beta_2} = -.08700, \hat{\beta_3} = -.05866$
   (b) $R^2 = .9153$

10. (a) $\hat{\beta_0} = .1151, \hat{\beta_1} = .01044, \hat{\beta_2} = .02953, \hat{\beta_3} = -.04049, \hat{\beta_4} = .00288,$
    $\hat{\beta_5} = -.00091$ (b)   .0272

11. *True Value of the Series
with Forecasts Superimposed*

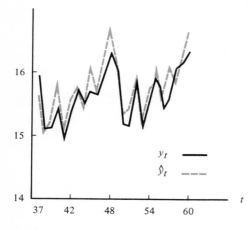

12. $\hat{g} = 12.58946e - .22312x$

Chapter 16

2. $X^2 = 24.48$; reject H_0 ($\chi^2_{.05} = 7.81$)

3. $X^2 = 95.06$; reject H_0 ($\chi^2_{.05} = 11.07$)

4. (a) $X^2 = .94$; do not reject H_0 ($\chi^2_{.05} = 3.84$)
   (b) $Z = -.97$; do not reject H_0

5. (a) $X^2 = 18.53$; reject H_0 ($\chi^2_{.05} = 3.84$)
   (b) $Z = 4.39$; reject H_0

6. $X^2 = 43.56$; reject H_0 ($\chi^2_{.01} = 6.63$)

7. $X^2 = 27.17$; reject H_0 ($\chi^2_{.10} = 6.25$)

8. $X^2 = 2.87$; do not reject H_0 ($\chi^2_{.05} = 5.99$)

9. $X^2 = 21.51$; reject H_0 ($\chi^2_{.05} = 7.81$)

10. $X^2 = 11.62$; reject H_0 ($\chi^2_{.05} = 9.49$)

11. $X^2 = 5.02$; do not reject H_0 ($\chi^2_{.05} = 5.99$)

12. $X^2 = 7.19$; reject H_0 ($\chi^2_{.05} = 5.99$)

13. $X^2 = 6.49$; reject H_0 ($\chi^2_{.05} = 5.99$)

14. $X^2 = 12.91$; do not reject H_0 ($\chi^2_{.05} = 15.5$)

15. $X^2 = 1.884$; do not reject H_0 ($\chi^2_{.05} = 5.99$)

16. $X^2 = 9.66$; reject H_0 ($\chi^2_{.05} = 5.99$)

17. $X^2 = 4.40$; do not reject H_0 ($\chi^2_{.05} = 9.49$)

18. $X^2 = 53.93$; reject H_0 ($\chi^2_{.05} = 15.5$)

Chapter 17

2. with data of nominal or ordinal scale of measurement; when concern exists about data satisfying the assumptions of the t test or z test

3. rejection region: $y > 9$, $\alpha = .011$; do not reject H_0

4. rejection region: $T < 5$; sample $T = 13$; do not reject H_0

5. rejection region: $y = 0, 1, 78$; $\alpha = .070$; do not reject H_0

6. (a) rejection region: $y < 2$ or $y > 10$, $\alpha = .0386$; do not reject H_0
   (b) rejection region: $y < 3$, $\alpha = .073$; do not reject H_0

7. reject region: $T < 17$; sample $T = 11$; reject H_0. Wilcoxon test is more powerful as it considers direction and magnitude of differences, whereas the sign test considers only the direction of differences.

8. rejection region: $y > 9$, $\alpha = .073$; do not reject H_0

9. rejection region: $y > 9$, $\alpha = .133$; reject H_0

10. (a) rejection region: $U < 4$, $\alpha = .0952$; sample $U = 2$; reject H_0
    (b) $t = -2.9$; reject H_0

11. (a) rejection region: $\alpha = .094$; sample $U = 32$; do not reject H_0
    (b) $t = .319$; do not reject H_0

12. rejection region: $U < 21$, $\alpha = .1012$; sample $U = 12.5$; reject H_0

13. $R = 8$; $P(R < 7) = .117$; do not reject H_0

14. $R = 13$; $P(R < 7) = .109$; do not reject H_0

15. rejection region: $T < 2$; sample $T = 4$; do not reject H_0

16. rejection region: $y = 0, 7$, $\alpha = .0156$; do not reject H_0. The sign test is less powerful and hence less likely to reject the hypothesis than the Wilcoxon signed ranks test.

17. (a) rejection region: $y < 1$ or $y > 9$, $\alpha = .022$; do not reject H_0
    (b) $t = -1.902$; do not reject H_0

18. rejection region: $T < 8$; sample $T = 11.5$; do not reject H_0

19. $R = 5$; $P(R < 2) = .024$, $P(R > 8) = 0$; do not reject H_0

20. (a) rejection region: $z = \dfrac{u - 112.5}{24.1} < -1.645$; $\alpha = .05$;

   sample $z = -1.805$; reject H_0
   (b) reduction of the expected number of runs; rejection region:
   $z = \dfrac{R - 16}{2.69} < -1.645$, $\alpha = .05$; sample $z = -.37$; do not reject H_0

21. rejection region: $R < 3$, $\alpha = .040$; sample $R = 5$; do not reject H_0

22. (a) .0256   (b) An unusually small number of runs (judged at $\alpha = .05$) would imply a clustering of defective items in time.

23. (a) rejection region: $R < 6$, $\alpha = .108$; sample $R = 7$; do not reject H_0
    (b) $t = .57$; do not reject H_0

24. (a) rejection region: $U < 3$, $\alpha = .056$; sample $U = 3$; reject H_0
    (b) rejection region: $F = S_A^2 / S_B^2 > 9.12$, $\alpha = .05$; sample $F = 4.91$; do not reject H_0

25. $-.845$

26. rejection region: $r_s < -.564, \alpha = .05$; reject H_0

27. $-.593$

28. rejection region: r_s

Index

Acceptable quality level (AQL), 313
Acceptance number, 119, 306
Acceptance region, 120, 191
Additive law of probability, 81
Alternative hypothesis, 121, 191
Analysis of variance, 369
  of a completely randomized design, 381, 384
  F test, 235, 376
  of a randomized block design, 388
  table, 384
Autocorrelation, 442
Autoregressive forecasting model, 438
Average outgoing quality (AOQ), 316

Bar chart, 32
Bayes' law, 83, 264
Biased estimator, 171
Binomial experiment, 109, 110
Binomial probability distribution, 113
  approximation to, 147
  formula for, 113
Binomial random variable:
  mean of, 116
  standard deviation of, 117
  variance of, 117

Central limit theorem, 136, 139
Chi square:
  distribution, 231
  test concerning a population variance, 230, 231
  use in analysis of enumerative data, 473
  variable, 231
Class boundaries, 26
Classes, 26
Class frequency, 26
Coding theorem, 57
Coefficient of linear correlation, 341
Complementary events, 75
Completely randomized design, 381, 384
  analysis-of-variance table, 384
  estimation for, 384
Compound events, 72
Conditional probability, 76
Confidence coefficient, 176
Confidence intervals:
  for binomial p, 185
  for difference between two binomial p's, 186
  for difference between two means, 183, 224
  for the $E(y|x)$, 339
  general, 175, 176
  large sample, 180
  for mean, 177, 179, 218

for slope of a regression line, 335
Confidence limits, 176
Consumer Price Index, 423
Consumer's risk, 307
Contingency table, 476
Continuous random variables, 95
Control chart, 286
  for attributes, 298
  c chart, 302
  p chart, 298
  R chart, 291
  for variables, 290
  $\bar{X}$ chart, 290
Control limits, 287, 290
Correlation, 341, 443
Correlation coefficient, linear, 341, 342
  of population, 345
Correlogram, 443
Critical value of a test statistic, 194
Cyclical effects, 403

Decision making, 4, 5, 118, 163, 247
Decision trees, 272
Degrees of freedom, 215
  chi-square, 231, 474, 479, 482
  F distribution, 235, 376, 381, 390
  Student's t, 215, 222, 334
Dependent events, 78
Design of an experiment, 4, 229, 386
Deterministic mathematical model, 326
Deviation from mean, 42
Deviation, standard, 45
Discrete distribution, 95
Discrete random variable, 94
Distribution, probability:
  binomial, 113
  chi-square, 231
  continuous, 99
  discrete, 95
  normal, 135, 136
  Student's t, 213
Dominant alternative, 249
Double smoothed statistic, 446
Dot diagram, 43

Empirical rule, 48, 286

Error:
  probability of type I, 121, 192
  probability of type II, 121, 192
  type I, 121, 192
  type II, 121, 192
Estimate, 165
Estimation:
  interval, 165, 180
  point, 165
Estimator, 165
  unbiased, 171
Events, 67
  complementary, 75
  compound, 72
  dependent, 78
  independent, 78
  intersection, 74
  mutually exclusive, 78
  simple, 67
  union, 73
Expectation, mathematical, 100
Expected monetary value, 257
Expected value:
  of a discrete random variable, 101
  of a function of a discrete random
    variable, 104
Experiment, 66
Exponentially weighted moving average
  forecasting model, 451
Exponential smoothing, 409
Extrapolation, 438

F distribution, 235
  analysis of variance, F-test, 381, 384, 390
  tabulation, 235
  testing equality of population variances,
    235, 236
Forecasting:
  autoregressive model, 438
  exponentially smoothing forecasting
    model, 445
  growth model, 458
  linear regression model, 323, 434
  multiple exponential smoothing model, 445
  sinusoidal model, 434
Frequency, 26
  relative, 26
Function, 10

Functional notation, 9

Goodness of fit test, 484
Gosset, W. S., 214
Growth model, 458

Histogram, 27
Hypothesis:
  alternative, 121, 191
  nonparametric, 491
  null, 121, 191
  parametric, 491
  test of, 120, 191

Independent events, 78
Index number, 417, 418
Index time series, 418
  Fisher's Ideal Index, 422
  Laspeyres Index, 421
  Paasche Index, 422
  simple aggregate index, 419
  weighted aggregate index, 420
Inference, 4, 65, 93, 119, 163, 213
Interval estimate, 165, 175
Interval estimator, 165, 175

Laws of probability:
  additive, 81
  multiplicative, 80
Least squares, method of, 329, 348
  equations, 330
Level of significance, 204
Limits, confidence, 176
Linear correlation, 341, 342
Linear equations, 330, 349
Long-term trend, 403
Lot acceptance sampling, 118, 305
Lot tolerance fraction defective (LTFD), 313
Lower confidence limit, 176

Mann–Whitney U statistic, 498

Mathematical expectation, 100
Mathematical model, 326
Mean:
  definition, 36
  inferences concerning, 173, 175, 217
  population, 36
  quality-control studies of, 29
  sample, 36
Median, 37
Method of least squares, 329, 348
Minimax decision, 271
Mode, 38
Model:
  mathematical, 326
  probabilistic, 327
Moving average, 408
Multinomial experiment, 472
Multiple exponential smoothing forecasting
    model, 445
Multiplicative law of probability, 80, 477
Multivariate predictor, 348
Mutually exclusive events, 78

Nonparametric methods, 491
Nonparametric tests:
  Mann–Whitney U test, 498
  runs test, 315, 507
  sign test, 494
  Spearman rank correlation, 511
  Wilcoxon rank sum (paired) test, 504
  Wilcoxon rank sum (unpaired) test, 498
Normal approximation to binomial, 147
Normal probability distribution, 135, 136
  standardization, 145
  tabulation of areas, 144
Null hypothesis, 120, 191
Numerical descriptive measures, 35
Numerical sequences, 13

Operating characteristic curve, 307-312
Opportunity loss, 253
Opportunity loss table, 253
Optimal decision, 253

Paired-difference test, 225

Parameters, population, 164
Payoff table, 250
Percentiles, 42
Pie chart, 34
Point estimate, 172
Poisson probability distribution, 122
Population, 3
Population correlation coefficient, 345
Population parameters, 164
Posterior probability, 84, 264
Power of a test, 493
Prediction (*see also* Estimation), 2, 323, 339
Prediction interval, 340
Prior probability, 84, 256
Probabilistic model, 84, 327
Probability, 65,
  additive law, 81
  conditional, 76
  event, 67
  multiplicative law, 80, 477
  posterior, 84, 264
  prior, 84, 256
  subjective, 85
Probability density, 99
Probability density function, 99
  normal, 136
Probability distributions (*see also* Distribution, probability)
  continuous, 98
  discrete, 95
Producer's risk, 307
Profit table, 251

Quality control, 285
Quartiles, 41

Randomized block design, 386
  analysis-of-variance table, 390
  estimation for, 393
Random sample, 142
Random variable, 86, 93
  continuous, 95
  discrete, 94
Random variation, 403
Range, 40

Range chart, 291
Rank correlation coefficient, 511
Regression line, 328
Rejection region, 120, 191
Relative frequency, 26
Runs test, 315, 507

Sample, 3, 66
  mean, 36
  random, 142
  standard deviation, 45
Sample size, determination of, 187
Sample space, 66
Sampling plan, 119, 306
Seasonal effects, 403
Seasonal factor, 452
Sequential sampling, 316
Significance level, 204
Sign test, 494
Simple event, 67
Sinusoidal forecasting model, 434
Smoothing constant, 409, 447, 453
Smoothing techniques, 408
Spearman's rank correlation coefficient, 511
Specification interval, 296
Standard deviation, 45
  significance of, 46
Standardized normal distribution, 145
State of nature, 248
Statistical inference (*see* Inference)
Student's t, 214
Student's t distribution, 213
  tabulated values, 215
Summation notation, 15

Taylor series expansion, 445
Tchebysheff's theorem, 47
Test of an hypothesis, 120, 191
  large-sample tests, 193
  power of a test, 493
  relative efficiency of tests, 493
  small-sample tests, 213
Test statistic, 120, 191
  critical value, 194
Time series, 401

Trend gain, 451
Triple-smoothed statistic, 446
Type I error, 121, 192
Type II error, 121, 192

Unbiased estimator, 171
Uncertainty, decision making under, 249
Upper confidence limit, 176

Variables:
  levels of, 369
  qualitative, 369
  quantitative, 369

Variance:
  calculation, short method, 50
  definition, 44
  estimation of population variance, 45, 234
  sample variance, s^2, 44
Venn diagram, 69

Wholesale Price Index (WPI), 423
Wilcoxon rank sum test:
  paired, 504
  unpaired, 498

z statistic, 145, 195